The Environmental Law Manual

Theodore L. Garrett, Editor

Section of Natural Resources, Energy, and Environmental Law
American Bar Association

Library of Congress Catalog Card Number 92-54384
ISBN: 0-89707-797-0

Discounts are available for books ordered in bulk. Special consideration is given to state bars, CLE programs, and other bar-related organizations. Inquire at Publications Planning & Marketing, American Bar Association, 750 North Lake Shore Drive, Chicago, Illinois 60611.

97 96 95 94 93   5 4 3 2 1

Part I
Administrative Procedure and Judicial Review

Dealing with government agencies can be baffling and difficult. However, it is vital to the practice of environmental law. Given the relatively narrow scope of judicial review of agency actions, the operative decision on a given problem is frequently made in an administrative forum. A successful practitioner needs to understand the organization, history, procedures, and peculiarities of administrative agencies dealing with environmental matters at the federal and state level.

The first four articles in this part deal with the administrative process. Andrea Bear Field and Kathy Robb offer practical suggestions for representing clients in EPA rule makings and other proceedings. The representation of nonprofit public interest organizations is discussed by James Tripp, who focuses on the Clean Water Act § 404 permit program.

The regulated community is affected by agency policies that do not constitute formal agency action subject to judicial review. Brian Tabler and Mark Shere address the use of informal documents, *de facto* regulations under the guise of memoranda or guidance documents, as a means for imposing duties on industry.

Is there a better alternative to the traditional, formal notice and comment administrative process? The relatively new concept of negotiated regulations is the subject of an article by David Pritzker, who presents the case for a consensus approach to rule making.

When parties are unsatisfied with the outcome of agency action, judicial review results. Karen Wardzinski discusses developments in the doctrine of standing that may present obstacles to judicial review.

In the final article in this part, Gregory Hobbs discusses the doctrines of ripeness and exhaustion, which play a role in ensuring that there is a requisite degree of hardship and that administrative avenues have not been bypassed. Additional aspects of litigation under particular statutes are discussed in subsequent parts of this book.

EPA Rule Makings: Views from Inside and Outside

Andrea Bear Field and Kathy E. B. Robb

An article by Alan Eckert in Volume 1, Number 1, of *Natural Resources & Environment* gave private practitioners a view of the intricacies of EPA rule makings from the perspective of an EPA "insider," namely, from someone who had been with the Agency virtually since its inception. Twenty years after the EPA's creation, we asked some EPA "outsiders"—lawyers now outside the Agency, representing private parties in EPA proceedings—to comment on Eckert's view of Agency proceedings and to offer their own practice-oriented tips on how best to represent clients in EPA rule makings and other proceedings.

Our interviewees include five lawyers who, though now in private practice, served as General Counsel of the EPA during its first twenty years: John Quarles, who was the EPA's first General Counsel, from 1970 to 1973; Bill Frick, 1976–77; Joan Z. Bernstein, 1977–79; Michele Corash, 1979–81; and Frank Blake, 1985–88. Other EPA graduates with whom we talked were Jeffrey Miller, Jim Rogers, Richard Stoll, and Peter Wyckoff.

Our final five commenters bring different perspectives to the private practice of environmental law. They include lawyers who have spent the vast majority of their careers in private practice (Joe Brecher and James Price); and those who, before entering private practice, had other experiences, e.g., working with a state environ-

Andrea Bear Field is a partner in the Washington, D.C., office of Hunton & Williams. Kathy Robb is a partner in the New York office of the same firm.

mental agency (Thomas McMahon), teaching at a major university (Neil Orloff), and working at the Department of Justice (Donald Stever). Most of our commenters primarily represent industrial clients. Joe Brecher, however, is well known for representing public interest groups like the Native American Rights Fund and the Sierra Club Legal Defense Fund. Our outsider advice follows a brief summary of Eckert's article.

Understanding the Basics

In that article, Eckert set out the "basics" of EPA rule-making actions, explaining that such proceedings follow the model for informal rule making set out in the Administrative Procedure Act, 5 U.S.C. § 553. Eckert explained that EPA rule makings can be divided into three phases: preproposal, postproposal, and postpromulgation. During the preproposal stage, the Agency gathers data to help it formulate a proposed rule. During the next stage of the process, the EPA publishes the proposed rule in the *Federal Register* and formally invites public comment. The public comments are part of the administrative record in the rule making; it is the practitioner's task to construct a record that will include all the information necessary to convince the Agency to develop the most favorable rule possible. In the final phase of the process, after considering the public comments, the EPA promulgates its final rule.

Members of the public who have problems with the final rule may seek judicial review of it. Since judicial review of the final rule will, in most cases, be limited in scope to the administrative record compiled by the Agency during the rule-making process, the practitioner must contribute to the record in the case and present it in a form that will convince a reviewing court that the Agency's failure to adopt the rule requested by the practitioner was arbitrary, capricious, or unlawful.

Against this background, Eckert then presented his precepts for effective representation of clients in EPA rule makings. Stripped down to the basics, they include:

- Get involved during the preproposal phase of an Agency rule making. That is when the regulation writers want reliable technical information that they can use in crafting their regulations and are thus most receptive to comments from interested persons. While Agency representatives may consider comments received after proposal and even after the close of the comment period, they will be less open to new ideas and new information as the proceeding develops.

- Be scrupulous in all dealings with Agency representatives. Make sure that all information submitted to them is accurate. If you treat Agency staff, counsel, and managers with respect, you will become part of an "elite bar" that has the respect of, and is presumably better able to get favorable results from, Agency personnel.
- Make sure that you submit to the Agency *all* relevant information supporting your concerns in the rule making. This is the best way to convince the Agency to respond favorably to your concerns. This is also the only way to get in a position to convince any reviewing court to overturn final Agency action unfavorable to you.
- Written comments are the single most effective technique for presenting views to the Agency. While such comments can and often must be lengthy and contain technical data and information, make sure that they are accurate and well organized.
- When you make an oral presentation to the Agency, whether in a meeting or at a hearing, be prepared, get to the point quickly, and do not be unduly technical. Follow up the oral presentation with a written submission.
- The arguments that have the greatest chance of being listened to by the Agency are those that address technical aspects of a proposed rule rather than the legal basis of that rule.
- If you challenge a final Agency action in court, you face formidable obstacles, including the skill of the Agency and Department of Justice in defending such suits and the fact that, following the *Chevron* line of cases, courts are inclined to defer to Agency discretion and expertise. *Chevron U.S.A. Inc. v. Natural Resources Defense Council, Inc.*, 467 U.S. 837 (1984). *See also K Mart Corp. v. Cartier, Inc.*, 486 U.S. 281, 292–93 (1988).

At the outset, we asked our fourteen commenters for their general responses to the issues raised by Alan Eckert. All agreed that Eckert had set out accurately the basic framework for participating in Agency proceedings, but many thought that Eckert presented too rosy a picture of EPA rule making, painting it as an elegant, stylized process where Agency personnel are all reasonable and open-minded and, as long as those presenting comments to the Agency are also reasonable and open-minded, the Agency will be able to develop first-class regulations that both effectuate congressional intent and take into account the concerns of the public.

Even when the EPA was in its infancy, our commenters say, the picture was not so rosy; interested parties could not count on playing nearly as influential a role as Eckert suggests. And the role to be played by private parties has decreased since Eckert wrote his article. One reason for this is the huge growth of the Agency, from three thousand employees in the mid-1970s to more than sixteen thousand current employees. And the increase in size, as Jody Bernstein explains, means that it is more difficult to know who is calling the shots. For example, during Jeff Miller's time at the Agency, he needed to obtain, at most, four sign-offs to settle a case, even a large case. Miller had heard of a recent case, though, where eighteen sign-offs within the EPA were needed to get a settlement approved.

Not only does the size of the Agency make it more difficult to make your voice heard in Agency proceedings; the political atmosphere in which the Agency now operates also contributes. In the early 1970s, Congress and the public assumed that the EPA would "do the right things" for the environment and gave the Agency a relatively free hand in conducting rule makings. Now, because of the legacy of distrust from the Gorsuch era and because the environmental problems currently facing the Agency are more intractable, the EPA does not have nearly as much freedom to run its own proceedings without fear of being second-guessed by Congress and the press.

Despite these identified problems with making your voice heard at the Agency, many of our commenters thought Eckert was unduly discouraging about the significance of the role outsiders played in shaping the legal and policy views of the Agency and in prevailing in litigation against the EPA. Based on their experience, for example, Bill Frick and Neil Orloff insist that the Agency can be persuaded to listen to well-thought-out, well-presented legal and policy arguments, as well as sound technical arguments. And, despite what Eckert says about the Agency's litigation advantages, John Quarles and Frank Blake remind us that the EPA still continues to lose its share of court cases and to settle others.

Whether or not you enter into an EPA proceeding convinced that you can have a large impact on a final Agency decision, though, all our outsiders agreed that there are commonsense steps that practitioners can take in EPA proceedings to improve their chances of persuading the Agency to accept their clients' views on specific issues. The remainder of this article focuses on some of those common-sense steps.

Our outsiders focused their comments, as Eckert did, on how to most effectively represent private clients in national Agency rule makings. Many of the tips offered here, however, also apply to other Agency proceedings—e.g., the permitting and enforcement action proceedings that, Jim Price and Don Stever point out, make up a large part of the environmental law practice outside Washington.

Getting Started

Eckert recommends getting involved in the earliest phase of Agency rule makings, i.e., *before* the regulation drafters' and other decision makers' ideas for regulations crystallize. Our outside experts agreed, noting that the get-there-early approach also applies to enforcement and permitting proceedings.

If your client wants to get involved early on, the best way to do so is to talk to the "right" people in the Agency. The right people, according to Richard Stoll, meet two criteria. First, they must be knowledgeable and have credibility within the Agency. They will be able to tell you what the Agency's current thinking is on various issues and, if they are convinced that you have sound ideas on those issues, they will be in a position to see that your ideas are taken seriously. Second, they must be accessible and will, when asked, answer your questions about the status of the proceeding and give you some guidance on the types of issues the Agency is most interested in. (If you encounter people who routinely force you to file FOIA requests before giving you copies of what should be publicly available documents, these are not, Stoll suggests, the right people.) In most Agency proceedings, there will be at least three or four knowledgeable people. And of those three or four, you should be able to ferret out one who will be willing and able to answer your questions.

If you have been involved in prior Agency proceedings, you may have a ready reference list of the right people to call. If you do not have such a handy list, though, other approaches often will work. If your client's interest in an EPA proceeding has been spurred by a *Federal Register* notice on a specific issue, that notice probably lists at least one Agency contact person who can give you basic information about the matter. Call that contact person first. Even if you cannot get the information you need in that initial telephone call, the person may well be able to recommend others with whom you can talk. Follow up on all such leads. In your quest for the right people, you can, notes Miller, get a wealth of information by talking to others along the way. Eventually, you should find someone who is both knowledgeable and willing to talk to you about your client's situation.

Another way of locating one of the right Agency people in a proceeding is to talk to the lawyers. Specifically, explain Jim Rogers and Don Stever, the lawyers in the EPA's Office of General Counsel are key players in many proceedings. They provide the EPA technical staff and senior management with legal and other guidance and thus can have a great deal of influence on the direction, scope, and content of EPA decisions. And, adds Joe Brecher, do not overlook lawyers in the Department of Justice, who often wield power not only on procedural issues but also on substantive matters.

If you are representing public interest groups, Brecher offers another tip. Deal first with the Agency's lower level staff people because the more junior Agency people—those right out of school—are more likely to be receptive to the approaches that the Sierra Club and other Brecher clients believe will offer the most environmental protection. If you can get to the EPA staff people early in a proceeding and convince them of the wisdom of your client's perspective, then, says Brecher, they will keep that perspective in mind as they draft rules and policies, thus putting your "spin" on those rules and policies.

If the environmental groups seek out more junior EPA staff, does that mean that those representing industry should make their initial contacts with those whom Brecher jokingly refers to as "right wing, high-level [political] appointees"? No, said our other commenters, who urged *all* practitioners to make initial contact with the Agency's lower level staff. Many clients do not appreciate the importance of working with junior staff, note Frick and Michele Corash. After a while, though, even the most skeptical clients appreciate why this approach works: the Agency's staff people are in the best position to help you during the early phases of Agency proceedings because they are the ones who are writing the rules and know the most about them.

Maintaining Good Working Relationships

Once you have located the right Agency people, Eckert and all of our outsiders believe it is important to achieve and maintain a good working relationship with them. If you have that good working relationship, and if you convince your Agency contacts that you are believable and trustworthy, your phone calls will be returned and your comments are likely to be considered. Everyone acknowledges that your goal must be to get a positive reputation for dealing with everyone at the Agency. Achieving that goal will involve patience and work.

Commonsense Rules for Building Good Relationships

All of our outside experts agree that, to get a reputation for trustworthiness, you must use common sense: maintain an open and honest track record with everyone you deal with (Bernstein); be a "straight shooter" (Stever); treat all Agency representatives as reasonable, well-intentioned people rather than mindless bureaucrats (McMahon); and be fair, firm, and persuasive rather than using strong-arm litigation tactics (Price).

Stoll offers more specific advice for developing good long-term relationships with Agency people. He recommends that you be understanding of just how busy and overworked the best Agency people are. Also, so that you do not overextend your welcome by calling your contacts too often, call only when you really need help and cannot figure out the answer yourself or readily get the answer elsewhere. Finally, be prepared when you call—know what the relevant rule or guidance says, why it presents a problem, and what your client would like to see done about it. "There is nothing worse," Stoll notes, "than calling up and asking someone at the EPA to do your homework for you. Don't sound like a dodo."

In this same vein, Tom McMahon notes that when you have started to develop a good working relationship with Agency people who ask you to provide information on a specific subject, give them the data they want, in a form that is easy for them to handle. You cannot simply dump documents on them. Also, Frick adds, be honest about any limitations of your data. For example, if areas of uncertainty exist in technical data you are providing, "acknowledge the uncertainties; don't be cute" about suggesting that your information says more than it does.

Even if you follow all these commonsense rules for dealing with people in the Agency, you may still occasionally encounter problems. In some cases, no matter how compelling you think your client's case and no matter how reasonable you may have been with your Agency contacts, those contacts may not give you the relief that you seek. One difficult decision is whether to appeal adverse decisions to more senior people inside or outside the Agency. As discussed below, perhaps you should.

Making Appeals within the EPA

Some people hesitate to make intra-Agency appeals of staff decisions because they fear appeals will irrevocably offend those whose decisions are being challenged. While acknowledging that some staff people will be offended if their decisions are appealed, Miller and other commenters note that most of the EPA people expect you to appeal their unfavorable decisions. In any case, all agreed, the fear of offending someone in the Agency should not inhibit you from making appeals that are in the best interests of your clients.

Whether making an appeal is in your client's best interests is not always clear. In general, it will be in your client's best interests to appeal where the matter is important to your client and there are sound arguments to support your client's views. This is not always the case, though. Stoll, for example, notes that clients will often claim that a certain EPA rule will devastate them when, in fact, its likely effect is not nearly that bad, and often the rule can be made acceptable (if not perfect) by some relatively straightforward refinements. In such cases, it may be better to work with the Agency staff to achieve the desired refinements than to take extreme approaches to try to prevent promulgation of the rule. If you follow the latter route and the extreme approaches fail, you will end up where you were before the appeal—trying to convince the staff to refine the rule—and your job of convincing the staff will be that much more difficult because of your prior actions.

In those cases where your client's best interests require you to appeal an unfavorable staff decision, our commenters all agree that there is a right way to appeal, a way in which you can reduce staff resentment. Quarles and Rogers explain that the right way to undertake an appeal within the Agency is to tell the subordinates that you understand their position but that your client disagrees with it. Ask if they would mind your appealing it. (Even if you do not want to appeal at the moment, Blake and Frick say that it is still useful to alert the staff early on that particular issues are important to your client and that, if not resolved satisfactorily, you plan to raise those concerns with more senior Agency people.)

Then, if possible, work with the affected staff as to the timing and mechanics of your appeal. If you file written documents making the appeal, make sure that the affected subordinates get a copy. If you call someone in senior management to set up a meeting to discuss the matter, make sure that the affected subordinates both know about your call and are invited to the meeting. In the meeting with senior EPA people, give credit to the staffers where appropriate. Then explain your client's problem, and give a specific proposal for fixing it.

Both Quarles and Blake note one downside to this open appeal procedure: if you tell the subordinates of your appeal plans, they will have the chance to tell their story to senior management before you can. Even if you do not tell the subordinates of your plans to appeal, though, it is unrealistic to expect that they will not get to tell their story to senior management at some point. When that happens, you just have to hope the senior people with whom you are meeting are savvy enough not to get locked into the position advocated by their subordinates without first hearing your views.

Orloff, Corash, and others advise not appealing too early in the process, i.e., do not appeal before you have talked the issue through with the staff. On the other hand, do not delay your appeal until the rule-making process is just about to be wrapped up, at which time you may find that the senior people already have been consulted and have signed off on the regulatory package. When, then, between these two extremes, should you make your appeal?

Our commenters suggest that the timing of an appeal may depend on when senior EPA people are likely to become involved in, and thus ready to pay attention to your views on, the issues arising in that proceeding. In some rule makings, senior level involvement may occur only late in the rule-making process. In such cases, early appeals are probably unnecessary, although you may want to notify the senior people, early on, of your concerns and your intent to meet with them later.

In other cases, though, continual communications will occur between the staff and senior management to resolve policy issues as they arise and to ensure that the proper focus of the rule making is maintained. When you have something valuable to say concerning issues arising throughout a proceeding, you may need to have repeated contact with the Agency's senior decision makers. In such cases, Quarles points out, there is no reason that you should be limited to just one appeal.

Making Appeals Outside the Agency

The rules of the appeal game may be different when you want to appeal a decision to those outside the EPA, i.e., to people on Capitol Hill, at the OMB, or elsewhere in the Administration. While some of our commenters suggest that such an appeal will so raise the hackles at the EPA that it will adversely affect all your future dealings with the Agency, others are not as hesitant to make appeals outside the Agency. The latter group point out that, in many proceedings, even though the EPA may be taking the lead in drafting a rule or policy statement, other parts of the government can be significantly affected by the Agency's actions. In such cases, the EPA expects these other entities to become involved on their own or because they are coaxed to do so by the various factions that are already involved in those proceedings. In high-profile EPA proceedings, for example, you will typically find those on one side of a hot issue seeking support for their views on the Hill or elsewhere in the Administration. This leads those on the other side of the issue to seek equally vocal and strong support from others on the Hill or in the executive branch. In such cases, the exercise becomes one that is aimed not so much at convincing the EPA as it is one designed to neutralize the political clout of the other side.

Thus, when it is clearly in your client's best interests to encourage the involvement of other governmental entities, the fear of EPA anger or retribution should not dissuade you from doing so. In making such appeals, however, you should do what you can to reduce the tensions that can be caused by them. Try to make the involvement by the other entities constructive rather than obstructive. For example, if you ask OMB to become involved in an EPA rule making, make sure that those OMB participants know enough to do more than merely criticize the Agency's proposed rules. It may make a client feel good to have someone from the Administration chide the EPA for its failure to embrace the client's position, but a mere chewing out is not likely to convince the EPA to change its mind. To make the OMB participation more fruitful, give the OMB participants enough background and other information so that they will understand *all* the issues and, based on that understanding, will make reasonable suggestions to improve the Agency's proposed rules.

The final word on intra- and interagency appeals is to use common sense. Although you should not be afraid to appeal unfavorable decisions, that does not mean that you should make an administrative appeal *every* time that you do not get what you want from the Agency. If the matter is important to your client, if your client has strong arguments that you can make to someone more senior in EPA management or elsewhere in the government, and if that more senior person is likely to respond favorably to your arguments, then appeal. An appeal, however, could be a waste of time and money if the issue is not that important to your client or if the people to whom you would appeal have already made it clear that they disagree with your client's position. Where there is not that much to be gained by an appeal, you should seriously consider living with the Agency's stated position or working with the staff to refine that position.

Choosing Your Arguments

Our commenters all emphasized that the main thing to remember in EPA rule makings is that your job is to build the best record that you can for your client. Having said that, though, they recognize that all comments are not treated with equal respect: the Agency is generally more receptive to comments on technical issues than to comments on legal or policy issues. "Technical comments," explains Corash, are those that "take the basic premise of the person drafting the regulations and show the drafter how to make that basic approach work" in the specific areas of concern to your client.

The reason that the Agency is generally receptive to well-reasoned technical comments, explains Rogers, is that if you point out specific problems with a regulatory program, those drafting the rules will generally try to solve those problems. They will do so not only because they want to appear to be reasonable and responsive to public comments, but also because their willingness to refine a regulatory program—to address identified flaws in the program—should help that program withstand judicial review. The heart of a regulatory program is thus more likely to survive over the long term if Agency people are willing to continue to refine that program as the need arises and is identified by the public.

Even though the Agency is more receptive to arguments on technical issues than to policy and legal arguments, that is no reason not to present the Agency with cogent policy and legal arguments when you have them. Quarles, Frick, Blake, and Orloff all urged practitioners not to be afraid to present strong legal and policy arguments to the Agency, particularly if you can pitch specific arguments to the Agency people most likely to be receptive to them, e.g., policy and economic arguments to EPA's Policy Office and legal comments to the Agency's lawyers.

"If you believe that the Agency is flat out wrong [on a legal or policy issue], then say so," Frick advises. But say so in the right way. It is not productive or convincing to argue that the legal approach that you prefer is the *only* one that the Agency can follow if the Agency has the legal authority to follow any of a range of options, which is usually the case. Where the Agency has a choice, you will get further if you acknowledge the existence of that choice and then give the technical, economic, and policy reasons why the EPA decision maker should follow your approach.

Keeping this in mind, Quarles says that one of the most useful ways in which to raise legal arguments is in situations where the Office of General Counsel has decided the Agency should adhere to one specific approach and that decision has led a program office to believe that the Office of General Counsel-preferred approach is the only one that is legal. In such cases, it is important to take on the Office of General Counsel and get the appropriate people there to acknowledge that their approach is *not* the only one available. If you can do that, you may be able to clear up confusion that the affected program office has concerning the range of options that it legally may consider. This, in turn, should make the program office more open to considering your alternative approaches.

Are Face-to-Face Meetings Valuable?

Even if you know generally what kinds of arguments the Agency is most inclined to listen to, you may need more help in focusing and fine-tuning those arguments. To get a handle on the most productive approach, you should consider whether to have face-to-face meetings with the Agency staff rather than telephone calls. In other words, it may be worth it to pack up yourself and your client and travel to EPA headquarters or an EPA regional office to meet with the people who are drafting the rule or policy affecting your client.

Virtually all our commenters agreed that, as long as you do not overdo meetings, it is worthwhile to meet with Agency representatives to have what Wyckoff refers to as "solar plexus to solar plexus contact."

Wyckoff offers several reasons why such meetings are important. First, once you have asked for a meeting on a discrete subject or group of subjects, that focuses the Agency's attention on those issues. Second, a meeting allows you to make a personal impression on decision makers, to convey to them how important an issue is to your client, and to convince them that your client is credible. Finally, by watching and listening to the reactions of the EPA staff as you present your arguments, you can get a better feeling for which of your arguments are most worth the effort to develop and which might better be dropped. If the EPA participants appear interested in specific arguments, i.e., by asking friendly questions and genuinely trying to draw out more information supporting those arguments, you have been given a clear signal that it is worthwhile to develop them. On the other hand, if you notice the EPA participants drifting off as you raise an argument (or smirking to each other as you bring up a specific concern), you have received a clear signal that, at best, you have an uphill battle in convincing your EPA audience to focus on or accept that particular argument. In short, Miller sums up, a meeting can be an excellent place both to learn what the Agency is thinking and to advocate your client's position.

Preparing for a Meeting with the Staff

Once you have decided to meet with the EPA staff, you and your clients can take several steps to help make that meeting a success. The most important thing is to be prepared. Rogers, Wyckoff, and other Agency graduates expressed amazement at the lack of sophistication and preparation of many lawyers and their clients. They frequently saw people with no understanding of the relevant facts, science, Agency policies, or proposed rules on which they were meeting.

One important way to prepare for the meeting is to talk to an Agency representative and ascertain in advance what the Agency people want to discuss. Outline the specific matters that you want to cover and the specific relief that you hope to get as a result of the meeting. Then go over all the information that you have on those subjects and any relevant data that the Agency has previously made available to you.

At the meeting, particularly a meeting with the technical staff, you should let a client with technical expertise do the talking. As Stoll succinctly puts it, the lawyers should "keep their damn mouths shut." Wyckoff explains why this is so, stating that although he is embarrassed to say so, his prejudice and that of others at the EPA "was that private counsel tended to be sleek, overdressed fat cats who would tell me anything they believed necessary to win the day for their clients. On the other hand, if a down-to-earth line manager talked about the problems from his perspective, even if he was inarticulate and vague, there was an emotional charge that came when the information went directly from that manager to the bureaucrat making the decision."

Price agrees that this holds true at the EPA regional level. He says that he often places the client up front at meetings and negotiations because it is the client that is going to have a long-term relationship with—and therefore must have credibility with—the program people at the regional level.

This does not mean that the lawyer plays no role before or during such meetings. Before the meetings, McMahon points out, lawyers should help their clients put together competent credible cases that the technical personnel can present. And Rogers suggests that at meetings, lawyers should take the pulse of events and keep things on track, i.e., keep participants focused on the three or four issues that are supposed to be covered. Also, at the end, lawyers may be in the best position to distill the main points raised, state the relief requested, and offer to provide specific additional information that the Agency may have requested.

And if the Agency people suggest at a meeting or at any other time that it might be helpful for them to see something in writing, then lawyers should offer to do the drafting. Brecher, in particular, notes the value of offering to draft language that the Agency might later want to use. If you draft it, Brecher points out, then whatever the Agency doesn't take out reflects your thinking and has your perspective.

Preparing for Meetings with Senior Management

The rules for meeting with more senior Agency people are basically the same as for meetings with the staff, but the need for preparation is heightened. Recognizing that the senior personnel with whom you are meeting are busy and preoccupied with numerous other issues, you must choose carefully the issues that you want to present, and present them clearly and simply.

You will probably also want to realistically prepare your clients for their encounter with senior management. For example, you should disabuse your clients of the notion that they are likely to have a cozy, one-on-one meeting with the EPA Administrator or any of the Assistant Administrators. More often than not, such meetings will include hordes of other Agency people. Also make sure your clients understand that rarely, if ever, will their meetings with senior EPA people produce any definitive, on-the-spot positive or negative response. Generally, no response occurs until there have been many post-meeting discussions between the senior decision makers and their staffs.

Recognizing all this, you may question the value of meetings with senior EPA people. Your clients, though, will not doubt their value for a minute. There is an intangible here, Jody Bernstein reminds us: regardless of the likelihood that the senior people will be able to give your clients the relief they seek, your clients will inevitably say that they feel better just having had the chance to meet with and present their cases directly to someone more senior in the Agency.

Assessing Litigation Prospects

If the Agency makes a final decision and your client is not satisfied with it, you must decide whether to seek judicial review. Eckert summarizes the obstacles you will face if you seek judicial review of final EPA action: the ability of skilled Agency and Justice Department lawyers to defend the EPA in litigation and the tendency of courts to defer to the expertise of administrative agencies.

Eckert is correct that you will face some major obstacles if you challenge final Agency action in cases where (1) the EPA has seriously engaged and resolved all relevant technical and policy issues, (2) the

EPA has developed a solid record supporting and explaining the decisions it has made, and (3) the Agency and Justice Department lawyers do a good job of defending the Agency's decision. But these obstacles do not mean that you should not seek judicial review of final EPA action. Even when the EPA does everything right and has the *Chevron* line of cases to rely on, it still loses its share of cases.

In addition, in many cases the Agency does *not* do everything right. This happens for several reasons. There might, for example, be tight court-imposed deadlines that limit the ability of the Agency to fully address all relevant issues. In other instances, Stever notes that the Agency may decide for any of a variety of reasons that it simply does not yet want to grapple with a tricky legal or policy issue, thus creating a record that is vulnerable to judicial challenge. Or, in a given case, you might find that substantial Agency and Justice Department employee turnover has created a situation where the people who are developing the record and those who are defending the Agency's decision do not have the experience necessary to put the Agency's case in the best possible light. If, for any of these or other reasons, the Agency does not present the best possible record to a court, that increases the chances that it will not prevail despite its getting every ounce of deference that *Chevron* provides. In short, where you have a good case and have built a good record, pointing out specific, understandable problems with an Agency decision—and especially when the stakes are high—you should litigate.

In fact, several commenters pointed out that there are dangers of not litigating in cases where your record is good and your client is severely affected by Agency action. As Stoll explains, if your client's activities make it subject to numerous Agency rules and continuing Agency scrutiny, you want the Agency to take that client's views seriously. In the real world, that means challenging the Agency when it makes unjustifiable decisions adverse to your client.

Once you have decided to litigate, there are strategies to help you get the most out of litigation. Several commenters recommended doing everything possible to narrow the issues that you litigate. Where your client is the only one challenging a final Agency action, you should review the record and choose to pursue only those procedural and technical issues where the Agency's conduct is most egregious. This process becomes much more difficult in multiparty cases.

Corash notes that if you can pick out a few key issues on which the Agency looks vulnerable, even before you brief the case, the Agency may feel uncomfortable enough and try to settle voluntarily.

And, once settlement negotiations start on a few issues, that may open the door to resolving others. Recognizing that there is frequently a chance to settle cases with the EPA instead of litigating them to the death, many people may file suit just to "get a seat at the negotiating table." Knowing this, the Agency frequently is willing to settle cases that it might be able to litigate successfully. Rogers explains that is because the Agency understands that all litigants take a risk in litigating. In these cases, you are essentially plunking down a huge administrative record before a judge and from there you are just "spinning the wheel. The Agency might win, those challenging the Agency might win, or you might get a result that no one is satisfied with."

The Agency will thus consider settlements in many cases where it is primarily concerned about preserving the essence of a regulatory program. If the EPA can reach a settlement that does not substantially impinge on the underlying goals of its regulations, then it is advantageous for it to make that settlement and not risk having a rogue judge throw out those parts of the program the Agency most cares about.

All litigants, though, should note the wisdom of the EPA's approach toward settlements. The goal in such talks is not necessarily to get *everything* your client wants. A settlement is worthwhile if, without the expense of briefing the case, you are able to get clear victories on several key issues of primary concern to your client, issues where your client's case is strongest. If you are able to reach agreement on those key issues, it generally makes sense to accept the settlement agreement and to not risk litigation to try to get the few remaining issues resolved in your favor.

Just because it makes sense to settle a case, that does not mean that your client or the other parties will agree to do so. Our commenters cited numerous cases in which they were able, through negotiation with the Agency, to resolve all but one issue in a case only to find that one stubborn party insisted on litigating everything in order to prevail on that one remaining issue. Not surprisingly, these tales generally ended sadly for those suing the EPA, with the courts giving them much less than they could have obtained through settlement.

In summary, the general principles for litigating against the Agency are like the principles cited for other dealings with the EPA. Use common sense about when to litigate. Do so only when you have a good case and the issues are important ones. And use common sense about when to settle. If you are able through settlement negotiations to convince the EPA to give you most of what you want, settle rather than litigate. Your clients will almost always be better off when you do so. Also by working with the EPA to settle a case instead of litigating the matter to the death, you and the Agency negotiators will complete the case on good terms. And, as discussed above, staying on good terms with the EPA is what it is all about when you have an active environmental law practice.

Public Input in the Permitting Process: The Section 404 Example

James T. B. Tripp

The effectiveness of federal programs in protecting the quality of the environment depends to a great extent on active participation in administrative decision-making processes by members of the public concerned with environmental protection. Nonprofit conservation groups and other public interest organizations have several opportunities to influence the outcome of the permitting process under federal regulatory programs. This article focuses on section 404 of the Clean Water Act, 33 U.S.C. § 1344, because it offers a prime example of the potential effectiveness of public input in the permitting process.

Ninety-five million acres of wetlands, of which most are freshwater inlands, remain in this country. A very large portion of the public strongly supports federal and state efforts to protect these wetlands. The primary federal regulatory program for wetland protection is section 404 of the Clean Water Act. Section 404 empowers the U.S. Army Corps of Engineers to regulate discharges of dredged and fill material into waters of the United States. In reviewing permit applications under section 404(b), the Corps is authorized to apply guidelines of the EPA, known as the 404(b) guidelines, 40 C.F.R. § 230. The EPA has the authority to veto Corps's permits or otherwise prohibit disposal in designated waters under section 404(c).

The section 404 program, strictly applied, should contribute to a sharp reduction in wetland loss. It should be immediately apparent,

James Tripp is a legal counsel for the Environmental Defense Fund in New York.

however, that the federal administrative agency in charge of that program is an agency that has had wetland destruction, not wetland protection, as its traditional mission. Through construction of billions of dollars worth of agricultural drainage projects, particularly in the South, the Corps has contributed directly to the clearing and drainage of millions of acres of wetlands. The Corps's navigation, water supply, and urban flood control projects have caused the loss of vast amounts of additional wetland acreage.

At least three well-tested opportunities are available to the public to influence the implementation of the section 404 program at various stages of the permitting process. First, public participation in formulating agency regulations that implement the Clean Water Act is an appropriate way to predetermine the application of statutory provisions by influencing the use of certain definitional terms. Second, the organized public may force the assertion of regulatory jurisdiction over activities that affect the environment, demanding permit review and approval where it might otherwise not be required. Third, the public may participate in the permit review process by suggesting alternatives to a proposed action or by seeking to affect substantive analysis of the permit application in the implementation of statutory terms of art. Further, conservation groups may rely to some extent on the EPA to advocate the public interest in jurisdictional disputes with the Corps regarding accomplishment of the section 404 program.

Public Involvement in Formulating Agency Regulations

Since regulations are the flesh on Congress's statutory bones, conservation groups must review proposed regulations in detail and make sure they further the statutory mandates, particularly as they relate to the agency's jurisdiction. Absent agency jurisdiction, environmental permitting programs are not applied to particular resources and the public has no administrative process in which to make its views known.

As an example, conservation groups have twice sued the Corps over the section 404 regulations when that agency failed to comply with basic statutory mandates. In 1974, the NRDC and the NWF sued the Corps over its regulatory definition of "navigable waters," the jurisdictional term used in section 404. In that case, *NRDC v. Callaway*, 392 F. Supp. 685 (D.D.C. 1975), the court held that Congress intended this term to include a broader area than the traditional navigable waters subject to the Corps's jurisdiction under the 1899

Rivers and Harbors Act. In 1977, in response to this lawsuit, the Corps promulgated regulations that greatly expanded the meaning of this term, defined in the Clean Water Act to cover "all waters of the United States." Among other things, navigable waters were defined to include tributaries of traditional navigable waters, lakes, and wetlands.

The NWF, the EDF, the National Audubon Society, and several other conservation organizations also challenged several provisions of the Corps's July 22, 1982, regulations in federal court, most notably the so-called general permits for categories of waters. These regulations excluded about one-half of the nation's wetlands from effective section 404 regulatory jurisdiction. Section 404(e) of the Clean Water Act authorizes the Corps to issue general permits for categories of activities similar in nature that individually and cumulatively have only minimal impact on the environment. Dredge and fill activities subject to general permits do not require individual permits, i.e., the Corps does not exercise effective regulatory jurisdiction, and a discharger may conduct the activity covered by the general permit without any agency review and public scrutiny. In the July 1982 regulations, the Corps included general permits for all dredge and fill activities occurring in headwaters and isolated waters. Headwaters were defined as those waters, including wetlands, above the point in headwater streams where the mean annual flow is less than five cubic feet per second. Isolated waters were defined as those waters, including wetlands, that have no surface hydrologic connection to other navigable waters. In a settlement between the Corps, the EPA, and conservation plaintiffs, the Corps agreed to restrict the regulatory exemption to activities in headwaters and isolated waters that affected less than ten acres of water, including wetlands. In addition, any activities affecting more than one acre were subject to agency notification. These jurisdictional components were incorporated in the Corps's October 5, 1984, regulations and in its November 13, 1986, section 404 regulations.

As a result of these citizen group actions, the Corps's section 404 regulations do not restrict the scope of federal Clean Water Act jurisdiction over wetlands nearly as much as they would have without effective citizen input. As shown below, however, the Corps has developed other techniques for limiting its jurisdiction and in the process has restricted opportunities for meaningful public participation.

The Public's Role in Delineating Federal Jurisdiction

In addition to challenging regulations that limit the Corps's jurisdiction over wetlands in a manner inconsistent with section 404 statutory mandates, nonprofit conservation groups have played an important role in compelling exercise of section 404 jurisdiction in several resource-specific cases. In *Avoyelles Sportsmen's League v. Marsh,* 715 F.2d 897 (5th Cir. 1983), conservation groups successfully argued that bottom land hardwood forests in the Red River backwater area of Louisiana were section 404 wetlands and that mechanized clearing operations involved redeposits or discharges of fill material so that the Corps should require permits for agricultural conversion activities in such wetlands. Since the issuance of the Fifth Circuit Court of Appeals opinion in *Avoyelles,* however, the Corps has continued to make wetland determinations in bottom land hardwood forest according to its previous policy and in general has not regulated most conversion operations.

In *NWF v. Hanson,* 623 F. Supp. 1539 (D.N.C. 1985), conservation group plaintiffs contended that North Carolina pocosins fit the definition of wetlands in the Corps's regulations. The court remanded the case to the Corps to conduct a revised wetland delineation and to support this delineation with substantial scientific evidence. In another case, the NWF is challenging the Corps's exemption of isolated wetlands in west Texas on the ground that they lack substantial connection to interstate commerce, as 3 C.F.R. § 328.3(a) requires. The NWF challenge is based on evidence of widespread use of the area by migratory waterfowl, which should be sufficient to meet the regulatory test for the assertion of jurisdiction by the Corps.

The Public's Role in the Permit Review Process

Once the Corps has asserted its section 404 authority over a proposed dredge or fill operation in waters of the United States, the public has an opportunity to participate by responding to a public notice. The public may comment on the proposed action, request a hearing, or seek preparation of a full-scale EIS in the event that the proposed action might have a significant impact on the environment.

The advantage the public gains in getting the permit applicant to prepare an EIS is the chance to evaluate alternatives to the applicant's proposed action. Those alternatives may reveal measures to accomplish the applicant's "basic purpose" that are less damaging to the environment and thus more acceptable to the public.

A critical issue for the Corps, other agencies responding to the public notice, the applicant, and the public is whether the proposed action complies with the EPA section 404(b) guidelines. A key provision of the guidelines is 40 C.F.R. § 230.10(a), which requires permit denial if practicable alternatives are available that would have less impact on the environment. A practicable alternative is one that accomplishes the basic purpose of the proposed action. 40 C.F.R. § 230.10(a)(3) sets forth a presumption that practicable alternatives are available for non–water dependent activities that avoid wetland use or destruction.

Unfortunately, Corps district offices, under guidance from the Corps's Office of the Chief of Engineers in Washington, D.C., have been defining the basic purpose of a proposed action subject to section 404 review very narrowly in terms of the applicant's financial and project specifications. As a consequence, the districts have been describing alternatives that fulfill the basic purpose so specifically that often no practicable alternatives are available. The result is that the conservation-oriented public, rather than the permit applicant, is faced with the burden of finding alternatives that could satisfy the applicant, turning the presumption of practicable alternatives for non–water dependent activities in the section 404(b) guidelines upside down.

How does the public provide meaningful information about alternatives to a proposed action? Proposed actions affecting wetlands and other sensitive aquatic areas may include highways, other public facilities, residential and commercial real estate developments, or agricultural operations. Recent guidance to Corps district offices indicates that the Corps intends to look to the permit applicant to define what the basic purpose of its proposed action is.

This guidance in effect says to the public that it must become expert on matters pertaining to all financial and technical aspects of the project in order to be able to define alternatives to the specific proposal. In other words, the public and resource agencies, to be effective participants in the section 404 review process, must be able to assess alternatives on the applicant's terms. This puts the public at an enormous disadvantage in rebutting an applicant's assertion that no practicable alternatives are available. A clever applicant can describe its proposed activity with such technical and financial specificity that the public could not possibly define an alternative, much less provide information that such an alternative is practicable.

It is instructive to compare the Corps's analysis of alternatives in two well-known section 404 permit decisions, separated in time by almost a decade, and to analyze what the difference in those decisions means for the public's ability to present useful evidence of alternatives.

The earlier decision concerned a large-scale, finger-fill canal residential development that the Deltona Corporation proposed to situate in thousands of acres of mangrove swamp wetlands at Marco Island, Florida. Deltona contended that the basic purpose of its development was to provide waterfront housing in a master-planned community. According to Deltona, its project was "water dependent" in that it had to be proximate to or in waters of the United States and no alternatives were available to accomplish this purpose.

In denying two of three requested permits, the Chief of Engineers in his April 1976 decision rejected the applicant's description of the project's basic purpose and instead described that purpose to be the provision of shelter. With the basic purpose of the project so described, the Corps readily found that housing or shelter in general could be located anywhere, that is, it was not water dependent. Further, the Corps found that alternatives were available in the form of housing lots located elsewhere in Collier County, Florida, as well as on undeveloped lots in other Marco Island permitted tracts and small pieces of uplands on the two mangrove swamp islands. During the Corps's administrative process, conservation groups—including the EDF, the National and Florida Audubon Societies, and the Collier County Conservancy—offered evidence prepared by professional planners on radically different development configurations that consumed only a small fraction of the acreage that Deltona intended to use, preserving virtually all mangrove swamp wetlands. They were able to offer this evidence because they were addressing alternatives to a basic concept, namely, the provision of housing in a large area. By describing the development in terms of a general function, the public interest groups were able to overcome the Deltona's effort to define its proposal so specifically that the Corps could find there was no available practicable alternative. In *Deltona Corporation v. United States,* 657 F.2d 1184 (Ct. Cl. 1981), *cert. denied,* 455 U.S. 1017 (1982), furthermore, the Court of Claims found that the Corps's permit denials did not result in a taking.

The later Corps's permit decision concerned a proposal to construct a shopping mall in a fifty-acre red maple swamp in Attleboro, Massachusetts, known as Sweedens Swamp. Overruling the District Engineer's recommendation that the requested section 404 permits be denied, the Office of the Chief of Engineers defined the basic purpose of the project largely in terms of the applicant's characterization relating to the type of shopping mall, size, layout, proximity to major highways, zoning approvals, and likelihood of financial success. Where an alternative must satisfy the applicant's financial and technical specifications, few practicable alternatives are likely to be identifiable and the public is effectively shut out of the process of assessing alternatives. The public may be in a position to provide fairly detailed information about the availability of sites in the general region for the type of activity proposed or alternative designs or patterns of development, perhaps on a smaller scale, than proposed. Instances are rare, however, when the public will be in a position to prepare specific designs for a development of comparable size at an alternative location supported by detailed financial and engineering studies to buttress a claim that a practicable alternative is available.

The Corps's permit review process has become further obfuscated because of the evolving role of mitigation in assessing impacts of a project and alternatives. To some degree, Corps policy seems to suggest that every impact is mitigatable. Thus the pertinent consideration is not so much the inherent value of natural wetland ecosystems as the exchange value of different man-made and natural upland and wetland areas. Thus applicants may propose to convert uplands to man-made wetlands and to enhance or improve natural wetlands as mitigation measures.

This Corps mitigation policy was clearly evident in its decision granting a section 404 permit to a shopping mall developer to fill in Sweedens Swamp. There, the Corps found that the applicant's proposal, which entailed filling in much of the swamp, converting most of the remainder of the swamp to a marsh and open water, and transforming an old gravel mine miles away into a man-made wetland, represented an overall environmental improvement. Thus, the Corps concluded no alternative would have fewer adverse impacts on the environment.

The public interested in protecting critical water resources, including wetlands, should insist that the standard of measure in a mitigation analysis should be the natural aquatic system. This approach is consistent with the Clean Water Act's concept of pollution as alteration of a natural ecosystem. Fortunately, in developing information about the magnitude of project impacts and evaluating mitigation schemes, the public is able to rely extensively on the federal resource agencies, in particular the U.S. Fish and Wildlife Service and the National Marine Fisheries Service, as well as EPA scientists.

The EPA's Role in the Permitting Process

It should be evident from this discussion that citizen groups have increasingly felt themselves to be excluded from meaningful participation in the Corps's section 404 review process. As a remedy, these groups have looked to the EPA to play a more aggressive role in that process than in the past. The source of the EPA's legal authority to play that role is fourfold.

First, an opinion of the U.S. Attorney General in September 1979 designated the EPA as the lead agency for making section 404 wetland determinations as part of its overall responsibility for administration of the Clean Water Act. The EPA also plays a role in defining what activities are subject to section 404 regulatory authority since any discharge into wetlands that does not involve dredge or fill material may involve pollutants in other forms subject to the EPA's section 402 jurisdiction. In addition, under the Clean Water Act, the EPA has the express authority to issue administrative orders to enforce the Act, including orders to halt actions in wetlands not authorized under section 404.

Second, the EPA is the agency primarily responsible for developing the section 404(b) guidelines. It therefore has a central role to perform in interpreting those guidelines.

Third, under section 404(c), the EPA may designate waters, including wetlands, the loss of which would have an unacceptable adverse effect on ecological functions, as prohibited disposal sites for dredge and fill material. Under this authority, the EPA may veto the Corps's permits.

Fourth, the EPA has the express authority to take enforcement action against violations of section 404 as part of its overall Clean Water Act enforcement authority by issuing administrative orders to halt illegal activities. EPA Region II, for example, has initiated a program of seeking out perpetrators of activities not authorized under section 404 and requiring restoration of illegally degraded wetlands. This initiative reflects in part an active interest on the part of New York and New Jersey conservation groups, as well as the U.S. Fish and Wildlife Service, in aggressive enforcement of the section 404 program.

The assertion of section 404 authority inevitably brings the EPA into conflict with the Corps. In terms of the scope of jurisdictional authority, this conflict became apparent during the course of *Avoyelles*, discussed above.

Most recently, agency differences over the interpretation of the section 404(b) guidelines have been revealed in the context of the Sweedens Swamp controversy in Attleboro, Massachusetts, where numerous state and national environmental groups sought active EPA involvement. After the Corps decided to grant a permit to the shopping mall developer, EPA Region I initiated the section 404(c) review process. The developer then challenged the EPA's authority to interpret section 404(b) guidelines and make findings about alternatives and mitigation that differed from those of the Corps. Ten state and national conservation groups intervened in that case in support of the EPA. In *Newport Galleria Group v. Deland,* 618 F. Supp. 1179 (D.D.C. 1985), the court upheld the EPA's authority to proceed with the section 404(c) review. Citizens' groups then participated actively in that review.

On May 13, 1986, the EPA rendered its section 404(c) final determination, in which it effectively vetoed the Corps's permit. In this determination, the EPA clarified the relationship between the alternatives analysis and mitigation evaluation by holding that mitigation in the form of compensation for adverse impacts to wetlands is not a factor in the section 404(b) guidelines water dependency test as long as impacts on wetlands are avoidable, that is, alternatives are available. In addition, the EPA held that an alternative that was available to the developer or its predecessor in interest at the time that developer made its real estate investment decision remains available for purposes of the water dependency test. While the EPA in this final determination did not deal with many questions about what the term "practicable alternatives" means, its interpretations make effective public input far more feasible than the Corps's posture does. The shopping mall developer is now challenging this agency action in *Bersani v. EPA,* No. 86-CIV-772 (N.D.N.Y.), and twelve state and national conservation groups have intervened.

In addition to asserting its section 404 authority in the Sweedens Swamp case, the EPA has recently announced the establishment of an Office of Wetlands. These EPA actions are a positive response to a strong desire on the part of citizen groups for much more active EPA involvement in wetland protection initiatives.

The EPA has begun recently using a forward-looking wetland resource planning tool that provides significant opportunities for the public to participate in agency decision making affecting wetlands and other sensitive aquatic systems in large areas. Known as "advanced identification," 40 C.F.R. § 230.80, this process can allow for an assessment of a large, integrated wetland system and the contribution of a large number of recent and proposed actions to its degradation.

From the public's perspective, it makes more sense to address the unacceptability of impacts of proposed projects added to past projects in terms of a definable ecosystem or basin. In addition, there is an advantage in considering alternative sites, patterns of development, or designs for projects in advance of receipt by the Corps of individual permit applications. Once a permit applicant has made investment commitments that entail wetland losses and foreclose other opportunities, the effective burden that the public or resource agencies have of demonstrating that alternatives are available can be huge.

Under the advanced identification concept, the EPA, with assistance from the Corps and other federal and state resource agencies, evaluates all of the wetlands in a particular ecosystem to determine which are viable and which are badly degraded, perhaps irreversibly, while the EPA can still assert its section 404(c) authority to protect wetlands slated for preservation. The involvement of local units of government with zoning powers can assist in effectuating the recommendations of this process.

Experience with this planning technique is limited. Since public groups always have limited resources, it does allow them to marshal their energies toward resource conservation on a large scale. How other agencies—in particular the Corps—will use the results of this process is still something of an unknown. At the same time, private investors and public agencies can know in advance which actions that lead to resource degradation or restoration, if any, are most likely to be permittable. Because that advance knowledge is valuable, the public may be able to achieve levels of resource protection in this advanced identification process that the individual permit review process does not allow. While the time commitment to making the advanced identification process work is considerable, it does allow the public to focus on the kinds of issues on which it has the most expertise: what resources should be preserved with what priority of commitment; what institutional arrangements must be in place to attain that conservation objective; and what alternatives are available in general.

Ultimately, public participation in the environmental permitting process is the mechanism by which the public in a democratic society expresses its value preferences. In a society that respects private property, this process of weighing values is unending. Thus effective public participation in the permitting process requires the presence of federal agencies ready and willing to act to uphold statutorily mandated jurisdictional and enforcement authority, as well as a willingness and ability on the part of conservation groups to cajole, urge, persuade, and, on occasion through legal maneuvering, coerce those agencies into action.

The EPA's Practice of Regulation by Memorandum

Bryan G. Tabler and Mark E. Shere

In 1780, the Massachusetts Bill of Rights stated the goal of establishing a "government of laws and not of men." Today, in the environmental area at least, we increasingly have a government of memoranda and not of laws. For important programs, the EPA's primary method of imposing requirements on industry is to use memoranda and other informal documents, which is a serious problem. Regulation by memo is unlawful, undemocratic, and in many cases all but unstoppable.

Regulation by memorandum is one of the EPA's primary methods of implementing important programs. Perhaps the leading example of such a program is the cleanup of hazardous wastes under RCRA. RCRA authorizes the EPA to require companies that transport, store, or dispose of hazardous waste to clean up previous contamination at their facilities as a condition of staying in business. 42 U.S.C. § 9004(u), (v). This RCRA "corrective action" authority is currently the basis for extensive cleanup work. In the future, RCRA corrective action is expected to dwarf the scope of the Superfund program.

The Corrective Action Plan Memorandum

The EPA implements RCRA corrective action through an internal memorandum called the "Corrective Action Plan—Interim Final," which was promulgated in November 1986. This interim final plan consists of sixty single-spaced pages detailing the studies and reports a company must undertake in the course of a cleanup. The EPA routinely

Bryan Tabler is a partner and Mark Shere is an associate in the Indianapolis, Indiana, office of Barnes & Thornburg.

incorporates these sixty pages verbatim into hazardous waste permits. Yet no statutory or regulatory authority supports the EPA's practice in this regard. Indeed, the EPA's verbatim use of the document ignores the statutory requirement that corrective action plans must be developed on a *"case-by-case* basis." 42 U.S.C. 6924(v) (emphasis added).

Following the lead of EPA headquarters, EPA's Region V office, which is the most active regional office in the corrective action area, has crafted a regional regulation by memorandum for corrective action. In a memorandum dated June 16, 1987, the region decided that corrective action must clean groundwater to drinking water standards. It stated, "These standards should be used for all groundwater . . . [and] *should not be waived* . . . [even if] there are no current or projected plans or intentions to use the aquifer as a source of drinking water." (Emphasis added.) By this memorandum, then, Region V imposed standards that should not be waived by its administrators. The memorandum makes no reference to the statutory requirement that corrective action standards be developed on a case-by-case basis.

These examples of regulation by memorandum are unlawful under the APA. The APA requires that "substantive rules of general applicability" must be published in the *Federal Register* and subject to public comment before promulgation. 5 U.S.C. §§ 552(a)(1), 553(b). The region's statement that its groundwater standards "should not be waived" and EPA's verbatim use of its interim final plan show that these memoranda are being used as "substantive rules of general applicability" in violation of the APA.

The EPA's use of regulation by memorandum in the corrective action area has not, to our knowledge, been challenged in court. But, in other areas, courts have clearly articulated that the APA means just what it says—i.e., substantive administrative rules that have not been promulgated in accordance with the APA's procedures have no binding effect. The leading case is *McLouth Steel Products Corporation v. Thomas*, 838 F.2d 1317 (D.C. Cir. 1988). In *McLouth*, the EPA's "vertical and horizontal spread" (VHS) model was at issue. This VHS model simulates, under certain worst-case assumptions, the potential for a release of hazardous constituents from wastes placed in a landfill. The EPA used the VHS model to decide requests from companies to have their wastes "delisted," i.e., declared nonhazardous.

The EPA's unpromulgated *de facto* rule was that it would delist wastes that passed the model and reject those that failed. The court in *McLouth* held this *de facto* rule unlawful. According to the court, the APA's procedural requirements for promulgating regulations ap-

ply wherever a rule "constrains the . . . [administrator's] discretion."
Id. at 1320. The court held that the VHS model constrained discretion
and so the EPA had to promulgate the model to give it binding effect.

Similarly in *United States v. Zimmer Paper Products*, 20 Envtl.
L. Rep. 20,556 (S.D. Ind. 1989), the court held that air emission
standards that the EPA sought to impose on a paper coating company
through an internal memorandum were invalid. Where the published
regulations required the company to reduce its prior emissions by
approximately 60 percent, the standards contained in the memorandum would have required a 95-percent reduction. Relying on *Mc-
Louth*, the court held that the EPA could not impose "new and more
stringent duties" on a company through a memorandum. *Id.* at
20,558. Accordingly, the coating company was not bound by the
memorandum's requirements. *Zimmer* and *McLouth* show that the
judicial rule is the same as the statutory rule—agency memoranda
and other unpublished "rules" have no legal effect.

Short-Circuiting the Democratic Process

Besides being unlawful, regulation by memorandum leads to poor
decisions and short-circuits the political process. In general, administrators acting alone will not make decisions as sound as those refined
through public comment and participation. In the corrective action
area, for example, the studies and reports required in the EPA's interim final corrective action plan have in many cases prevented the
prompt start of cleanup work. In some situations in which companies
have already conducted thorough, voluntary investigations of their
sites, the Agency has prevented cleanup work from beginning until
the companies have redone all of their reports in the format contained
in the interim final plan.

Region V's rule concerning groundwater standards can similarly
lead to perverse results. In a perfect world, all water would of course
be cleaned to drinking water standards or even better, as the region
envisions. Given limited resources, however, cleanup dollars need
to be targeted to the most pressing environmental concerns. For relatively clean, deep groundwater that no one is using or planning to
use, treatment to make the water drinkable without further purifi-
cation is often an ineffective use of cleanup dollars. Indeed, the EPA's
own reports suggest that the region's standards will often be unattainable because of limitations in the current pump-and-treat technology for groundwater cleanup. *See* "Considerations in Ground
Water Remediation at Superfund Sites," at 2, 4–7 (Oct. 18, 1989).

More important than the deficiencies in these particular examples is the short-circuiting of the democratic process that occurs when administrative memoranda take the place of law. Arguably, at least, the *regulatory* notice and comment system of the APA does not meet democratic standards in situations where Congress has failed to provide a policy framework to structure those regulations. *See, e.g.,* Carl McGowan, "Congress, Court, and Control of Delegated Power," 77 *Colum. L. Rev.* 1119, 1127–30 (1977); J. Skelly Wright, "Beyond Discretionary Justice," 81 *Yale L.J.* 575, 580–87 (1972). Congressional delegation of hard policy choices to unelected administrators is "undemocratic, in the quite obvious sense that by refusing to legislate, our legislators are escaping the sort of accountability that is crucial to the intelligible functioning of a democratic republic." J. Ely, *Democracy and Distrust* (1980).

Because Congress evaded the hard issues in drafting RCRA's corrective action provisions, that program would still raise significant democratic concerns *even if* the EPA used the notice and comment procedures of the APA. RCRA provides only that corrective action must clean up contamination to a level that will "protect human health and the environment." 42 U.S.C. § 6924(v). This cleanup standard provides the reassurance characteristic of any statement devoid of meaning. Everyone wants to protect "human health and the environment." Congress left the hard policy questions—what risks are acceptable, how much money should be spent to eliminate marginal risks, and what are the cleanup priorities—to the Agency, with no statutory guidance. Science and administrative expertise do not provide answers to these policy questions. Rather, the answers depend on the values and politics of the decision maker. Congress's transfer of these decisions to unelected administrators, with no more instruction than that they should protect "human health and the environment," undermines democratic accountability even if the Agency were to hold itself to the most scrupulous procedural standards.

The Agency's substitution of administrative memoranda for the notice and commment procedures required by the APA makes this bad situation even worse. The regulatory process at least maintains some of the public character of law making—hearings are held, interested groups may participate, and the reasons for decisions are a matter of public record. *See, e.g., Community Nutrition Institute v. Young,* 818 F.2d 943, 951 (D.C. Cir. 1987) (Starr, J., concurring in part and dissenting in part). In other words, the public character of the APA's regulatory process serves as a partial surrogate for the public deliberations and committee meetings that Congress would have conducted had it acted on the matter in question through legislation. Regulation by memorandum lacks any of this public legislative character. Instead, a lone administrator imposes binding requirements by typing a memorandum. In short, where Congress fails to provide specific policy guidance, the regulatory notice and comment process is an uneasy part of our democratic system. In turn, the regulation-by-memorandum "process" should not be part of our system at all.

Enforcement Difficulties and the Role of the Courts

Despite the clear provisions of the APA, the holdings in cases such as *McLouth* and *Zimmer*, and the democratic interests at stake, the EPA's practice of regulation by memorandum persists. The main reason for this is the difficulty of enforcing the law. *McLouth* illustrates this difficulty. Again, in *McLouth* the court squarely held that the EPA could not use the VHS model as the basis for deciding delisting petitions. But in effect *the EPA has simply ignored that decision*. By our count, in every post-*McLouth* delisting decision, the EPA has denied the delisting if the wastes fail the VHS and has approved the delisting if the wastes pass (leaving aside only those petitions that were incomplete or which raised dioxin issues). In other words, the VHS model continues to be the *de facto* rule of delistings.

The *McLouth* court sowed the EPA's subsequent conduct in its opinion. Because the VHS model has never been promulgated, the court should have held that any decision on a delisting petition that relies on the model is *per se* invalid. And, indeed, the court edged toward such a *per se* holding in stating that, when any particular decision follows a policy contained in a memorandum or other policy statement, the Agency " 'must be prepared to support the policy *just as if the policy statement had never been issued.*' " *McLouth*, 838 F.2d at 1324 (emphasis added) (quoting *Pacific Gas & Elec. Co. v. Federal Power Comm'n*, 506 F.2d 33, 38 (D.C. Cir. 1974). But instead of following through on this statement by requiring the EPA to justify its position in each case without any regard to the VHS model, the court stated that the Agency needs only show "open-mindedness" in its decision making. 838 F.2d at 1325.

This requirement of open-mindedness means that the Agency "must truly exercise discretion in individual delisting cases, remaining open to all challenges to the use of the VHS model as well as its application in each delisting petition." *Id.* at 1324. A company that wants to challenge a denial of a delisting petition, then, must show that the Agency did not maintain an open mind and exercise true discretion. As long as the Agency couches its decision in the appropriate "after considering all of the factors" language, a showing that the Agency did not have an open mind in any particular case will be difficult or impossible to make. Further, the most that a company can achieve under *McLouth* is a remand to the Agency for open-minded reconsideration. Indeed, now more than two and a half years after the court's remand, the Agency has still failed to take final action on McLouth Steel Products' delisting petition.

Along these lines, the interim final memorandum that the EPA copies into its RCRA corrective action plans is innocuous on its face. The memorandum says that its provisions must not be used as "boilerplate" and that "it is necessary to stress the importance of site-specific technical detail in the development of . . . corrective action [plans]." The practice, however, is quite different, as our experience and our collection of corrective action plans from across the country attests. It is easier for administrators to incorporate the interim final plan verbatim into corrective action orders than to invest the time to figure out what work actually needs to be done at a site. It is also bureaucratically safer for administrators to incorporate the document verbatim than to take responsibility for deviations. As long as companies are forced to prove the Agency's state of open-mindedness and can expect no more relief than a remand, administrators have every incentive to continue their practice of making the interim final plan a *de facto* rule.

Zimmer provided a practical case for challenging the Agency's conduct because the requirements that the Agency sought to impose by memorandum were numeric *and they differed from the numeric standards contained in the published regulation*. Because of the objective nature of these numeric restrictions, the Agency's state of mind was not an issue. Further, because the context was an enforcement proceeding against the company, the court simply stated the governing standards and did not issue any sort of remand to the Agency.

If the courts are to enforce the law—that the Agency cannot impose requirements on industry by memorandum—they will need to issue decisions that, like *Zimmer*, are effective. This means providing remedies that take account of practical considerations. A *de facto* rule taints the administrative decision-making process, regardless of whether the Agency explicitly relies on the rule in a particular case.

Accordingly, remand to an agency that has shown its adherance to a *de facto* rule will rarely be an effective remedy. Until the Agency presents evidence that it has reformed its decision making, the courts should use their declaratory powers to substitute for the defective administrative procedure. And instead of warning the Agency to maintain an open mind in the future, the courts should enjoin *per se* the Agency's use of memoranda and other informal guidance that the court has found violate the procedural requirements of the APA. Judicial authority to use these remedies is clear. *See generally* K. Davis, *Administrative Law Treatise* § 23:6 (1983). Only by putting these remedies into practice will courts be able to make the law stick.

Further examples of regulation by memorandum abound. In the area of air standards, the EPA has forced firms to spend considerable sums defending against alleged violations based on test methods issued only by memorandum. *See, e.g., Donner Hanna Coke Corp. v. Costle*, 464 F. Supp. 1295 (W.D.N.Y. 1979). On a national scale, the EPA and the U.S. Army Corps of Engineers have recently sought to implement (and have been forced to withdraw and reissue under political pressure) a "no net loss" wetlands policy through an administrative MOA. Also, as this article goes to press, the timber industry has stated plans to sue the Department of the Interior regarding its plan to protect the spotted owl, a plan that the Department developed without any public comment.

Indeed, absent counterpressure from the courts, regulation by memorandum is arguably endemic to any administrative structure. Administrative agencies are tiered, bureaucratic organizations. The upper tiers can direct the organization only by issuing rules to restrict the discretion of the lower tiers. Over time, the network of these rules becomes ever greater. *See, e.g.,* Max Weber, *The Theory of Social and Economic Organization*, at 339-41 (trans. A. Henderson & T. Parsons 1947). Administrators will naturally be tempted to use a quick, relatively effortless means of issuing these rules—i.e., a memorandum—rather than going through the delay and effort of public notice and comment procedures.

Zimmer and *McLouth* hopefully will provide a starting point for courts to start taking regulation by memorandum seriously. This will require courts to use *per se* rules against administrative use of memoranda-based tests and restrictions. And, in appropriate cases, it will require judicial willingness to provide remedies beyond a mere remand. Courts, of course, cannot enforce the law unless litigants present cases to them. Industry must be willing to tell administrators that their memoranda have no legal effect and to reject the inevitable "that's the way we've always done it before" responses. No one is going to vindicate a company's rights if the company itself is unwilling to fight for them.

Working Together for Better Regulations

David M. Pritzker

An idea is evolving that has the potential to reduce the delay, expense, and contentiousness of resolving many regulatory disputes. The procedure—generally known as "negotiated rule making," "regulatory negotiation," or simply "reg-neg"—has been used successfully for several years by a growing number of federal regulatory agencies and by some states. While the principal aim is to produce better rules, additional benefits include avoiding protracted litigation and reducing the cost of agency enforcement efforts.

The basic idea is for a regulatory agency considering drafting rules to bring together representatives of the various affected interests for face-to-face negotiations, open to the public, with the goal of reaching consensus on a proposed text. The agency would commit itself in advance to publishing the proposal and seeking public comment in accordance with the APA and other applicable statutory requirements. The agency's active participation in the negotiations would assure its support for any resulting consensus rule and ensure that the rule is within the scope of the agency's statutory authority.

In essence, the agency's internal drafting efforts are replaced by an open process in which potential or actual antagonists can be motivated to work cooperatively to find a solution to the regulatory problem before the agency. Participants are first encouraged to set priorities among their own goals. As in traditional labor-management negotiations, they may be willing to engage in trade-offs and accept

David Pritzker is a senior attorney in the Office of the Chairman of the Administrative Conference of the United States, in Washington, D.C.

a package that addresses their most significant needs while giving up relatively minor concerns.

The give-and-take of the negotiation process fosters creative and acceptable solutions to difficult problems. If, in fact, all viewpoints have been considered in the negotiations, and if truly representative parties have come to an agreement on how to balance their differences, then subsequent challenges to the resulting rule should be minimal. Ultimately, however, it is the effective participation of representatives of all of the diverse interests that assures the essential fairness of the process.

The Movement Toward Reg-Neg

In the early 1980s, widespread concern about the excessive cost and delay in regulation—concern among industry groups, public interest organizations, and government at all levels—led to a major study of the potential for negotiating regulations. In 1982, the Administrative Conference of the United States, a federal agency created to study ways to improve administrative procedures, recommended that agencies consider using negotiated rule making. The Conference listed criteria for identifying when the process would be likely to be beneficial. It also suggested procedures for assembling an appropriate negotiating committee, providing adequate public notice, and encouraging consensus. *See* 1 C.F.R. § 305.82-4. These procedures have been followed successfully by the EPA, the FAA, and several other agencies. On the basis of the early agency experiences, the Conference amplified its original advice in a 1985 recommendation. *See id.* at § 305.85-5.

Negotiated rule making affords agencies an alternate approach to the formulation of policy, which is ordinarily governed by the APA's basic framework for rule making. 5 U.S.C. § 553. Customarily, the agency's staff would study the problem by using agency resources and reach a tentative solution. During this period, the agency might choose to consult with interested parties or to hold a public hearing on the subject. The agency typically would publish its tentative solution in the *Federal Register* and offer the public an opportunity to submit comments. It must then consider any comments it received and ultimately issue its final rule.

Since the APA was enacted in 1946, the complexity of government regulation has increased greatly. In numerous regulatory programs, Congress has given administrative agencies the responsibility of filling in the details of regulatory policy, with the expectation that the rule-making process will give the public a role in creating that policy. Unfortunately, agencies attempting to implement environmental, health, and occupational safety legislation too frequently find that their proceedings have become a battleground for special interest groups and other affected parties—in effect, little more than the first round in the expected litigation. For example, the EPA has been reporting for years that over 80 percent of its proposed rules are challenged in court.

In these circumstances, the need to prepare a record as a basis for litigation tends to harden the divisions between parties and may foreclose any willingness to recognize the legitimate viewpoints of others. Parties often take extreme positions and may withhold information that they view as damaging. Moreover, the agency may have little understanding of the relative importance the parties place on the various issues. What is lacking is an opportunity for the parties to exchange views and to focus on finding constructive, creative solutions to problems.

The observation that many lawsuits challenging regulations are eventually settled—but often only after protracted litigation–suggested the possibility, under some circumstances, of moving the settlement negotiations forward to the early part of the rule-making process. A suitable model was found in the experiences of private sector organizations that write voluntary consensus standards such as the National Electric Code or the standards listed by the American National Standards Institute. Many such standards are widely adopted as regulations by local and state governments and by federal agencies. They are usually the product of negotiations conducted by a committee representing the different affected interests, followed by publication and an opportunity for interested persons to comment.

Negotiated rule making incorporates a similar negotiating committee structure into the rule-making process at the rule-drafting stage, often before the agency has formulated its own position. Participants are given the opportunity to discuss their mutual problems and their differing views in a setting that encourages cooperative problem solving. They may find it useful to exchange technical data and information about their own experiences and their respective needs. Negotiation and consensus techniques are used, ordinarily with the assistance of a skilled mediator, to channel the resources and efforts of the parties toward resolving the issues presented.

An agency embarking on negotiated rule making is not abdicating its responsibility. The agency is saying, in effect, that a range of regulatory options is available and that it is willing to share its authority to choose among them with those who will have to live with the rules. Of course, the agency is ultimately responsible for ensuring that its rules are consistent with statutory requirements.

The development of negotiated rule making over the last decade has been part of a more general movement toward alternative dispute resolution or ADR. This term refers to a range of procedural options— including mediation, arbitration, minitrials, or neutral evaluation— available to disputing parties and settlement judges, options that may be used as alternatives to traditional hearings or litigation. These techniques are characterized by informality and an element of consensus-building. The success of this approach, particularly in environmental disputes, has led administrative agencies and courts across the United States increasingly to make these options available to disputants.

Has Reg-Neg Worked?

The FAA was the first federal agency to use negotiated rule making following the procedures recommended by the Administrative Conference. Reg-neg succeeded after three failed attempts by the FAA to revise outdated flight and rest-time requirements for domestic airline pilots. The prior rules had been in effect for thirty years, a period of substantial change in the airline industry, during which the FAA had issued more than one thousand pages of interpretations. In 1983, the Agency formed a negotiating committee consisting of representatives of airlines, pilot organizations, public interest groups, and other interested parties. The FAA's final rule, adopted in 1985, was based on the committee's negotiations and was not challenged in court.

The Department of Transportation has convened three subsequent negotiating committees to draft proposed rules. A committee working on a rule concerning nondiscrimination on the basis of handicap in air travel did not reach consensus, but the negotiations led to adoption of a final rule covering many of the issues. Another committee negotiated a proposal for a uniform system for parking by disabled persons. And early in 1992 a committee was convened by the U.S. Coast Guard to negotiate a rule concerning tank vessel oil spill response plans, in accordance with requirements of the Oil Pollution Act of 1990.

The EPA has had the most vigorous program for using reg-neg. Final rules based on negotiations include penalties for manufacturers of vehicles not meeting Clean Air Act standards, emergency exemptions from pesticide regulations, performance standards for wood-burning stoves, inspection and abatement of asbestos-containing materials in school buildings, underground injection of hazardous wastes, and modifications of permits issued under RCRA. The first three rules listed were based on a committee consensus. In the other proceedings, the EPA based its rule on substantial agreements reached in the negotiations even though the committees were unable to agree completely on the proposals. During 1991, the EPA's negotiated rule making on reformulated gasoline requirements under the Clean Air Act Amendments of 1990 received substantial national publicity when the negotiators reached consensus on an outline of the underlying principles for the proposed rule.

The wood-burning stove experience is especially interesting because the early resolution of the standard met key concerns of manufacturers, environmentalists, and consumers. Manufacturers could plan production under the new standard with a certainty that would have been nonexistent if the rule were litigated. Under the new standard, environmentalists and consumers benefited from the inclusion of many stoves that otherwise would have produced more pollution.

The EPA's rule on removal of asbestos from schools was the first reg-neg rule to come before a court. The rule, based on negotiations that fell short of consensus, was upheld by the Court of Appeals for the D.C. Circuit in May 1988. The court determined that the EPA's regulation embodied a reasonable interpretation of the governing statute. Neither the appellants nor the court raised questions about the negotiation procedure. *See Safe Buildings Alliance v. EPA*, 846 F.2d 79 (D.C. Cir.), *cert. denied*, 109 S. Ct. 366 (1988). The EPA's underground injection rule, based in part on negotiated rule making, was also challenged and essentially upheld by the same court. *See NRDC v. EPA*, 907 F.2d 1146 (D.C. Cir. 1990).

OSHA has convened committees to negotiate proposed standards for worker exposure to benzene and to a chemical known as MDA, an animal carcinogen used in the manufacture of plastics. Although the benzene effort did not result in a negotiated rule, the MDA committee reached consensus on a set of recommendations to OSHA, which served as the basis for a proposed rule. Other federal agencies that have used negotiation procedures in rule making include the NRC, the FTC, and the Departments of the Interior, Agriculture, and Education.

Although the procedures described above are primarily federal government initiatives, the general principles can be applied on the state and local levels. In the tradition of serving as "laboratories of democracy," several states have been developing consensus-building approaches to regulation, particularly in the area of the environment. For example, "policy dialogues" bring representatives of different interests together, not to draft a proposed rule as in negotiated rule making, but to identify issues and work cooperatively to resolve them. The degree of formality can vary with the particular circumstances, and state agencies have adapted the concept to their own needs. Examples of reg-neg and its variants among the states include groundwater standards in Arizona and Virginia, resource planning in Colorado, underground petroleum storage tank rules in New Mexico, and regulation of timber, fish, and wildlife in Washington.

Negotiated rule making clearly is not a universally applicable approach to resolving concerns, but many people who have studied the situation believe that reg-neg can be highly beneficial in appropriate circumstances. The acceptance of the process in controversial policy areas like environmental and occupational safety regulation is an encouraging development. Negotiated rule making can be resource-intensive in the short term for both the agency and the other participants. For the agency, extra expenses include the costs of determining who should participate in negotiations and the cost of hiring one or more skilled mediators. Long-term savings from reduced litigation and enforcement activities are likely to be significant but documenting them with any precision is difficult.

Public interest groups and others with very limited budgets may find the necessary staff time and resources for effective participation to be an excessive burden. Sometimes, it has been possible for the regulatory agency or others supporting the reg-neg process to arrange for a "resource pool" to support travel, training, or other appropriate expenses incurred by participants or expended on behalf of the negotiating group.

Regulated businesses also will have greater expenses in the early stages of negotiated rule making. However, beyond the direct savings from avoiding litigation, there may be substantial savings from knowing the content and effect of new rules much earlier than otherwise anticipated, as exemplified by the wood-burning stove experience. Participation in drafting also can prevent misunderstandings about the meaning of rules and can lead to more cooperative future relationships among the affected parties and the agency.

Congressional interest in negotiated rule making has grown as agency experience demonstrates the usefulness of the procedure. Passage of the Negotiated Rulemaking Act of 1990, Pub. L. No. 101–648, established a statutory framework for agency use of reg-neg, codifying important procedural protections for openness and accountability and clarifying some provisions of prior law. The Act incorporates the basic principles of the Administrative Conference's recommendations on reg-neg, as well as some practical lessons from the experience of the agencies that have used the process, but it does not require its use. Agencies are encouraged to use negotiated rule making when it will enhance the ordinary informal rule-making procedure, and the statutory language is not to be construed to limit innovation or experimentation with the technique. The Act also authorizes a small fund to support development of the procedure and participation by essential parties who could not otherwise afford the cost, though funds have not yet been appropriated for this purpose. Finally, the terms of the Act provide for repeal in 1996, after six years, though this provision was intended to ensure appropriate congressional oversight rather than termination of use of the process.

On three occasions, Congress has inserted mandatory reg-neg provisions in substantive bills. These include the Hawkins-Stafford Elementary and Secondary School Improvement Amendments of 1988 (Pub. L. No. 100–297), in connection with the federal program of aid for education of disadvantaged children; the Carl D. Perkins Vocational and Applied Technology Education Act Amendments of 1990 (Pub. L. No. 101–392); and the Price-Anderson Amendments Act of 1988 (Pub. L. No. 100–408), in connection with indemnification of radiopharmaceutical licensees. The specified procedures in these acts differ from each other and from the reg-neg procedures used by other agencies. If Congress were to employ reg-neg in any future legislation, the Negotiated Rulemaking Act could serve as a standard procedural reference so as to avoid a confusing proliferation of varying procedures.

Deciding to Use Negotiated Rule Making

The idea of using negotiated rule making may originate with the regulatory agency or may be proposed by anyone interested in the content of a proposed rule. The request may be submitted formally, as in a petition for rule making, or may be suggested in informal contacts with agency officials. The agency then must determine the appropriateness of the procedure for the regulatory problem at hand.

Certain characteristics of rule-making proceedings favor trying to negotiate a proposed rule. First, the number of distinct interests concerned with the proposed rule, including any relevant government agencies, must be small enough so that they can be fairly represented by not more than twenty to twenty-five negotiators. A number of diverse issues should be identified so that participants can rank them according to their priorities and so that room for compromise will exist on some of the issues as an agreement is sought. However, the issues to be negotiated should not require compromise of principles so fundamental to the parties that there is no hope of achieving a consensus.

Parties must indicate a willingness to negotiate in good faith, and no single interest should be able to dominate the negotiations. *Parties will engage in meaningful negotiations only when they believe they have something to gain from the exercise.* A deadline for completion of negotiations, whether imposed by statute, the agency, or other circumstances, may lend a degree of urgency that can spur the negotiators to reach a consensus on a proposed rule.

Agencies usually approach the decision whether to use reg-neg by asking a "convenor" to assess how well the particular circumstances fit these criteria. Convenors have generally been private contractors with experience in dispute resolution procedures, but they have sometimes been government employees not otherwise involved in the proceeding. The convenor would recommend to the agency whether to establish a committee to negotiate a draft rule. He or she might also submit a proposal for the composition of the committee and identify a preliminary set of issues to be negotiated.

It is essential for the success of reg-neg that all concerned interests be represented in the negotiations. Therefore the agency and the convenor must make reasonable efforts to ensure that all relevant interest groups and others who may be affected by the rule are aware of the proceeding. Public notices in the *Federal Register* and in appropriate trade journals are required by the Negotiated Rulemaking Act, and they must explain the agency's plans for the proceeding and allow for a thirty-day period for applications for committee membership from affected persons who believe they are not adequately represented. These notices, as well as adherence to general requirements for establishing advisory committees (e.g., the Federal Advisory Committee Act, where applicable), can be very useful as a check against an inadvertent omission of an essential party. Keeping the public informed also helps to avoid the perception that a private deal is being arranged behind closed doors.

The convenor normally proceeds by contacting relevant agency officials and known interest groups and interviewing them in an effort to identify all other interests, to define the issues that need to be addressed in the rule making, and to explore whether it is possible to obtain commitments to negotiate from representative parties and agency personnel. The convenor attempts to assemble a balanced committee willing and able to work toward the goal of consensus on a rule that is within the agency's statutory authority and that addresses the issues that cause the agency to consider adopting a rule.

Negotiating the Rule

The central feature of the reg-neg process is the negotiation itself. The negotiations are not merely a substitute for public hearings or a public comment period. Rather, the negotiations present all participants with an extraordinary opportunity to have their views and needs heard and understood by persons actually engaged in crafting the regulation. Opposing views also will be discussed, and the negotiating group will attempt to find a balanced resolution.

Most federal agencies using reg-neg have found it worthwhile to begin with a four- to six-hour training and orientation session for participants. These informal meetings introduce participants to the overall process and expose them to consensus-building techniques and a common vocabulary. At the same time, parties have an opportunity to become acquainted with each other in a neutral setting and to begin building a constructive relationship.

Regulatory negotiations tend to be more successful when the committee has the assistance of one or more experienced mediators. Mediators may be the same persons who acted as convenors. For both convenors and mediators, careful selection is crucial to success. Each member of the negotiation committee must have confidence in the mediator's skills in managing the process, the mediator's neutrality on the issues, and the mediator's lack of bias with respect to the parties.

The agency must participate fully in the negotiations, making sure at all times that the participants are aware of what action the agency is likely to take if the committee does not reach a consensus. The knowledge that the agency will write its own rule if the negotiators cannot agree often provides a strong incentive to the parties to find a common ground for achieving those points that are most important to them, while compromising on those matters of less importance.

Early in the negotiations, the committee will need to agree on the issues to be negotiated and set the committee's agenda. Subcommittees or working groups may be formed to assemble data or examine issues and prepare proposals for consideration by the full committee. Allied interests may want to caucus privately to explore joint negotiating positions.

Participants in reg-neg often represent large constituencies that must be kept informed continually throughout the proceeding. Before a final commitment is made, the participants must be assured that they really are speaking for their constituencies. Especially if consensus is reached, it will be important for the negotiators to explain to their constituents the nature of the proposal and the value of supporting the agreement.

The goal of the committee is to reach consensus on a draft rule. This term is usually understood to mean that each interest represented concurs in the result, unless all members of the committee agree at the outset to a different meaning. In practice, consensus has meant that no interest represented on the committee opposes the decision. Achieving consensus does not necessarily require a formal "yes" or "no" vote. Nor is it necessary that each interest represented affirmatively endorse the decision as long as each agrees *not to oppose* the decision. In effect, requiring unanimity gives every interest group a potential veto power. This can be important in obtaining participation by all of the affected interests, particularly those believing that they will be at a disadvantage in numbers or resources.

Negotiations that do not result in consensus on a draft rule can still be very useful to the agency by helping it to understand the concerns and viewpoints of all parties, narrowing the issues in dispute, identifying information necessary to resolve issues, ranking regulatory priorities, and finding potentially acceptable solutions.

A growing body of experience shows that the negotiated rulemaking process can be valuable to regulatory agencies, regulated entities, and other affected interests. Generally, the participants in the more successful negotiations have expressed satisfaction with the process and only limited litigation has occurred to date.

The search for alternative procedures is not really new. For example, administrative agencies were created and given rule-making authority in part to obviate the need for ongoing congressional legislation. Similarly, administrative adjudication is, in effect, a substitute for court litigation. The current effort to expand the use of alternative procedures in administrative practice is motivated by a desire to ameliorate the factors that tend to formalize these agency processes and encourage contentious behavior among parties to regulatory disputes.

The Doctrine of Standing: Barriers to Judicial Review in the D.C. Circuit

Karen M. Wardzinski

The standing doctrine imposes important jurisdictional limitations on a court's ability to review government actions. Standing is a uniquely case-specific determination, even in the face of generalized principles of application. The doctrine has been referred to as "among the most amorphous [concepts] in the entire domain of public law," *Marshall & Ilsley Corp. v. Heimann,* 652 F.2d 685, 690 (7th Cir. 1981), *cert. denied,* 455 U.S. 981 (1981), generalizations about which are "largely worthless," *Association of Data Processing Service Organizations, Inc. v. Camp,* 397 U.S. 150, 151 (1970). Such admonitions, pervasive in the opinions of nearly all courts addressing the issue, reflect the difficulty that courts have in determining whether a particular plaintiff is appropriately before them.

Current standing decisions by the U. S. Court of Appeals for the District of Columbia play a significant, if not preeminent, role in the implementation of federal environmental statutes. This is because Congress has given the D.C. Circuit exclusive jurisdiction over EPA rule-making decisions under most of the major environmental statutes. For example, the court has review authority under RCRA, 42 U.S.C. § 6976(a)(1), for any regulations promulgated under RCRA; the Clean Air Act, 42 U.S.C. § 7607(b)(1), for, among other things, national primary or secondary ambient air quality standards, emissions standards, or standards of performance for new sources; CERCLA, 42 U.S.C. § 9613(a), for any regulation promulgated under

Karen Wardzinski is a partner with the Washington, D.C., firm of Freedman, Levy, Kroll & Simonds.

CERCLA; and the Safe Drinking Water Act, 42 U.S.C. § 300j-7(a)(1),for national primary drinking water regulations, including maximum contaminant level goals.

Standing involves both constitutional limitations on federal court jurisdiction and judge-made "prudential" limitations on the exercise of that jurisdiction. *Warth v. Seldin*, 422 U.S. 490, 498 (1975). With respect to the elements of constitutional standing, the D.C. Circuit had traditionally taken a fairly expansive approach, particularly where the facts involved environmental organizations challenging governmental action. That approach, however, has been put into some question by the Supreme Court's reversal of the D.C. Circuit's most recent standing decisions and the Circuit's most recent application of this Supreme Court precedent. In addition, in several very recent decisions, the D.C. Circuit has set forth a highly restrictive interpretation of the prudential requirements of standing, more restrictive arguably than mandated by Supreme Court directives on the issue.

Constitutional Requirements

To appreciate the significance of D.C. Circuit decisions on standing, one must consider them in the context of rulings on the subject by the Supreme Court. The Supreme Court has construed the constitutional requirements, which emanate from the "cases or controversies" language of article III of the U.S. Constitution, as containing three distinct yet interrelated requirements. First, the party seeking court review must have suffered some real or threatened injury as a result of the challenged action (injury-in-fact). Second, the injury must be caused by the challenged action (causation or traceability). Third, the injury must be capable of redress by a court decision (redressability). *Valley Forge Christian College v. Americans United for Separation of Church and State, Inc.*, 454 U.S. 464, 472 (1982).

The Case Law of Standing and Injury-in-Fact

When evaluating injury-in-fact, traditional standing decisions required that a litigant demonstrate a direct and personal harm arising from the action being challenged. Most often the injury took the form of economic harm, such as injury to one's property or injury arising from a breach of a contract or a tort committed upon the plaintiff. The Supreme Court paved the way for liberal interpretation of standing to challenge environmental laws, however, in the landmark decision of *Sierra Club v. Morton*, 405 U.S. 727, 734 (1972). In that case, the Court expressly recognized that aesthetic, recreational, or environmental interests will support a claim of standing to the same extent as more traditional economic interests.

In *Morton*, the Sierra Club alleged that the government's plans to authorize extensive recreational development of public lands in the Mineral King Valley would impair the organization's recreational use and aesthetic appreciation of the valley. While recognizing that such noneconomic injury was sufficient to justify standing, the Supreme Court nonetheless denied standing because the Sierra Club failed to allege that any one of its members directly used the valley and thus would be directly harmed. The Court made it clear that generalized concerns about protection of the environment were insufficient without a direct injury to the interests of the particular plaintiff.

In a later case, *United States v. Students Challenging Regulatory Agency Procedures (SCRAP)*, 412 U.S. 669 (1973), the Supreme Court took the sufficiency of noneconomic injury one step further, stating that the injury complained of need not be great and even "an identifiable trifle" would be sufficient to substantiate standing. Under this premise, the Court found that standing existed where the alleged injury derived from a surcharge on railroad freight rates that would discourage the use of recyclable goods, resulting in greater use of virgin materials that, in turn, would result in injury to local forests, streams, and mountains used by members of the plaintiff organization. The plaintiff in *U.S. v. SCRAP* avoided the pitfalls of *Morton* by specifically alleging that certain of its members used lands affected by the government's actions.

The D.C. Circuit adopted the teachings of *Morton* and *SCRAP* in its own liberalized approach to the standing doctrine in several recent decisions. In *Wilderness Society v. Griles*, 824 F.2d 4 (D.C. Cir. 1987), the D.C. Circuit acknowledged that threatened harm, in addition to actual harm, could be sufficient to demonstrate an injury-in-fact. In that case, the threatened harm claimed by the Wilderness Society resulted from the Secretary of the Interior's decisions affecting the method by which Alaskan land claimed for ownership by the state and native Alaskan organizations would be surveyed. The Wilderness Society alleged that its members used various wilderness areas and other public lands throughout Alaska for recreational activities that could now be withdrawn under the DOI's new surveying policy. Although recognizing the adequacy of threatened harm, the court nonetheless held that the alleged harm was insufficient for standing because the plaintiffs did not pinpoint any specific lands used by its members that would be affected by the land claims.

In *Griles,* the D.C. Circuit relied on procedural distinctions to justify its failure to rely on *SCRAP,* in which the Supreme Court found standing on even more attenuated factual allegations of harm. The D.C. Circuit noted that *SCRAP* was decided in the context of the defendant's motion to dismiss in which the pleadings must be construed liberally in favor of the nonmoving party. In contrast, *Griles,* decided on a motion for summary judgment, demanded a greater showing by the plaintiff because it was required to substantiate its allegations with factual support.

In a more recent decision, the D.C. Circuit cautioned against an overly technical reading of the specificity requirement for injury-in-fact. The case, *NWF v. Hodel,* 839 F.2d 694 (D.C. Cir. 1988), involved a challenge to DOI issuance of relaxed surface mining regulations where the NWF relied on affidavits from members that lived in communities affected by past and ongoing mining operations to establish standing. The court rejected the mining industry's allegation that NWF was required to point to specific mines that would operate in a different manner under the revised regulations and thus affect its members.

The D.C. Circuit further addressed the degree of specificity needed in alleging harm in a series of decisions that relied heavily on *SCRAP.* In each, the court repeatedly held that the NWF and its members had suffered injury-in-fact sufficient to support standing to challenge DOI's decision to reclassify and withdraw from protection against development and mineral exploration millions of acres of public land. *See NWF v. Burford,* 835 F.2d 305 (D.C. Cir. 1987), 844 F.2d 889 (D.C. Cir. 1988), 878 F.2d 422 (D.C. Cir. 1989), *rev'd, Lujan v. NWF,* 110 S. Ct. 3177 (1990). Pointing to the minimal standards employed in *SCRAP,* the court held that an affidavit filed by an NWF member to support the allegation of use of lands "in the vicinity" of certain reclassified lands was sufficient to show harm. The court further stated that even if the original affidavits were not specific enough as to which of the affected millions of acres were used by NWF's members, this flaw was cured by affidavits filed later from members alleging use of specific affected lands. The court also found that a showing of concrete injury to any covered land was sufficient to satisfy a challenge to DOI's entire reclassification.

Recently, in *Lujan,* the Supreme Court reversed the D.C. Circuit on each of these points. Justice Scalia, writing for a five-to-four majority, stated that the original NWF member affidavits did not allege harm specific enough to satisfy standing requirements. In its opinion, the Court discussed at length the difference in standards and burdens of proof between a motion to dismiss and a motion for summary judgment. Just as the D.C. Circuit itself had done in its decision in *Griles*, the Supreme Court rejected the relevance of *SCRAP* because it had evaluated the specificity of the alleged harm in the context of a motion to dismiss, not a motion for summary judgment as was then before the Court. In an interesting editorial note, Justice Scalia pointed out that the *SCRAP* opinion's expansive expression of what would suffice for standing "has never since been emulated by this Court."

The Supreme Court also rejected NWF's supplemental affidavits as insufficient to satisfy standing. Unlike the D.C. Circuit, the Supreme Court found that DOI's actions did not represent one final agency rule or order, but rather more than one thousand individual agency determinations. Given this fundamental difference in the characterization of DOI's actions, the Supreme Court held that allegations of harm as to a couple of specific areas could not justify standing to challenge all of the thousands of individual DOI actions. Moreover, with respect to even the areas for which specific allegations of harm were made in supplemental affidavits, the Court questioned whether DOI's actions here were ripe for judicial review without the need for additional agency actions. In any event, the Supreme Court held that the D.C. Circuit had erred in requiring the district court to accept supplemental affidavits filed so late in the case.

More recently, in *Foundation on Economic Trends v. Lyng*, 943 F.2d 79 (1991), the D.C. Circuit applied the Supreme Court's decision in *Lujan* to significantly limit the basis for standing, at least in cases alleging failure to prepare an EIS under NEPA, 42 U.S.C. § 4331 *et seq.* The substantive dispute in *Foundation on Economic Trends* related to the USDA's program to preserve the genetic diversity of plants through a germplasm program. The USDA's "program" involved various steps undertaken to collect, store, label, and distribute plant germplasm. The plaintiffs alleged that the USDA's failure to prepare an EIS on its germplasm activities injured the plaintiffs' ability to educate the public on the issue. The D.C. Circuit reasoned that in light of the Supreme Court's decision in *Lujan*, this "informational injury" alone would not constitute a constitutionally sufficient injury on which to base standing. The court equated informational injury to the "mere interest in a problem" that was found insufficient to justify standing by the Supreme Court in *Morton. Id.* at 84.

Despite its lengthy discussion of informational injury, the D.C. Circuit went on to state that it was unnecessary to decide this issue because an alternative basis to deny standing existed under *Lujan*. Even assuming that informational injury was sufficient to demonstrate an injury-in-fact, the court held that the plaintiffs had failed to identify any particular agency action that was the cause of the harm. The court determined that the failure to prepare an EIS could not be considered the cause. Rather, in the NEPA context, the "identifiable action" that demonstrates an injury-in-fact is the agency action giving rise to potential NEPA review, which under substantive NEPA requirements must be a "major federal action significantly affecting the quality of the human environment." *Id.* at 85.

The court found that the USDA's germplasm program consisted of a wide array of activities involving day-to-day decision making. As such, it was no more an "identifiable action" than was DOI's land withdrawal review program in *Lujan*. The court acknowledged that the result of its opinion is to "merge standing under the APA with the merits of a plaintiffs' NEPA claim." *Id.* at 85.

The court's decision in *Foundation on Economic Trends* reverses substantial precedent in the D.C. Circuit upholding informational injury as a basis for standing. *See City of Los Angeles v. National Highway Traffic Safety Administration,* 912 F.2d 478, 492 (D.C. Cir. 1990) ("The procedural and informational thrust of NEPA gives rise to a cognizable injury from denial of its explanatory process, so long as there is a reasonable risk that environmental harm may occur.").

Quite recently, the U.S. District Court for the District of Columbia relied on the D.C Circuit's decision in *Foundation on Economic Trends* in dismissing, for lack of standing, an action brought by a group named Public Citizen to require the U.S. Trade Representative to prepare an EIS on certain international trade agreements being negotiated under the General Agreement on Tariffs and Trade. The plaintiff claimed that lack of information about the proposed agreements impedes its efforts to educate the public and Congress about the possible environmental and health consequences of the agreements. Stating, seemingly reluctantly, that it was bound to rely on *Foundation for Economic Trends* (and its interpretation of *Lujan*) as the law of the circuit, the district court reasoned that this informational injury was no longer sufficient to justify standing. The court noted, however, that the standing issue has not been uniformly decided by the circuit courts and that further guidance may come from the Supreme Court in the recently argued *Defenders of Wildlife v.*

Lujan, 911 F.2d 117 (8th Cir. 1990), *cert. granted,* 111 S. Ct. 2008 (1991) (argued Dec. 3, 1991).

Causation and the Issues of Traceability and Redressability

The two remaining requirements of constitutional standing, traceability and redressability, are most often evaluated as combined elements of causation. The plaintiff must demonstrate that the injury it has suffered is "traceable" to the action being challenged, and that the relief it seeks from the court will "redress" the injury. Where the harm complained of is direct regulation of the plaintiff, causation is generally not an issue. The D.C. Circuit had also previously held that even indirect causation resulting from the intermediary actions of a third party could be sufficient to satisfy standing requirements, as long as the links connecting the challenged conduct and the asserted injury were not "multiple [and] tenuous." *CAS v. National Highway Traffic Safety Administration (NHTSA) (CAS I),* 793 F.2d 1322, 1335 (D.C. Cir. 1986). Moreover, a party seeking judicial relief need not show to an absolute certainty that a favorable decision will redress the injury; a mere likelihood of redressability is sufficient. *NWF v. Hodel,* 839 F.2d 694 (D.C. Cir. 1988).

Although these standards are useful, they do not provide an automatic answer to the question of causation. Like other requirements of standing, causation depends on the facts of the particular case. Even then the issue can be confusing, as illustrated in the series of cases concerning the Center for Auto Safety's (CAS) challenges to government rule-making under EPCA.

In *CAS I,* CAS, a consumer organization established to promote energy conservation, challenged mandatory fuel economy standards set by the NHTSA under EPCA. The court had little difficulty finding that CAS satisfied constitutional standing requirements, including causation. It held that the petitioner's injury—less fuel-efficient vehicles leading to increased gasoline consumption—was directly linked or traceable to the NHTSA's standards lowering fuel economy requirements and, in turn, would be remedied by a favorable court decision.

In *CAS v. Thomas (CAS II),* 806 F.2d 1071 (D.C. Cir. 1986), *reh'g en banc,* 847 F.2d 843 (D.C. Cir. 1988), *vacated,* 856 F.2d 1557 (D.C. Cir. 1988), CAS again challenged regulations promulgated under EPCA, this time by the EPA. Whereas NHTSA sets fuel economy standards under EPCA, the EPA establishes the testing and calculation procedures for measuring fuel economy. Relying on its decision in *CAS I,* the D.C. Circuit panel in this case unanimously held that the petitioners had standing to challenge the EPA's regulations.

On rehearing *en banc,* however, the D.C. Circuit reconsidered the issue of standing and was unable to get a majority to agree on any issue related to standing. The most significant disagreement was on the issue of causation. Five of the ten judges on the panel would have upheld the original finding of standing, including its finding of causation. They reasoned that the petitioners' injury, that is, diminished availability of fuel-efficient cars, was directly traceable to the EPA's regulatory action that, by granting massive fuel credits to automobile makers, removed financial incentives to produce fuel-efficient cars. The redressability issue was equally clear: remove the credits and the incentives are restored. The five judges relied heavily on a congressional determination, found in the statutory scheme and legislative history, that financial incentives would ensure fuel economy.

In sharp contrast, the remaining five judges found that the petitioners' injury was neither fairly traceable to the EPA's actions nor likely to be redressed by a favorable court decision. They also strongly disagreed that congressional fact finding should be relied on in evaluating causation. Accurately describing the D.C. Circuit's decision making on this issue, Judge Williams ended his concurring opinion by noting that the doctrine of standing "suffers from 'inconsistency, unreliability, and inordinate complexity.' " 847 F.2d at 887.

A more recent decision raises further questions concerning the requirements of traceability and redressability, particularly where intervening causal factors exist. *See Fulani v. Brady,* 935 F.2d 1324 (D.C. Cir. 1991). In *Fulani,* Leonora Fulani, an independent candidate for U.S. President, sought to invalidate the tax-exempt status of the sponsor of the 1988 presidential debates, which denied her participation in these televised debates. The D.C. Circuit denied her challenge for want of standing, finding that the IRS's action caused her harm only in connection with other intervening causal factors, such as the Federal Election Commission's rules limiting sponsorship of these debates to tax-exempt entities and the actions of the sponsoring organization in conducting the debates.

This opinion appears to reflect a more constricted reading of causation than certain past cases dealing with indirect causation. Arguably, however, its holding should be limited to cases challenging the tax liability of another, which cases the court stressed raise unique problems relating to standing. The court noted: "[I]f we were to find that a case does exist in which one party can litigate properly the tax exemption of another, it would have to be something far removed from the norm." *Id.* at 1327.

Prudential Considerations

In addition to the constitutional requirements of standing, the Supreme Court has established "prudential requirements" or practical considerations that militate against a court taking an action, even where a plaintiff may have demonstrated an injury-in-fact. These considerations include general prohibitions against such things as a litigant asserting the legal rights of another person and the adjudication of abstract questions or generalized grievances that would be addressed more appropriately in the representative branches of government. In addition, a litigant's complaint must fall within the "zone of interest" protected or regulated by the statutory provision at issue.

This latter requirement is more often the subject of debate than the first two prudential considerations because the court must identify the underlying harm that Congress intended to remedy under the statute and determine whether the petitioner's injury falls within the zone of interests Congress intended to protect. In its evaluation of this particular concern, the D.C. Circuit has employed a very restrictive interpretation of the law.

The zone of interest test as first articulated by the Supreme Court in *Association of Data Processing Service Organizations, Inc. v. Camp*, 397 U.S. 150, 153 (1970), requires that if the interest the plaintiff seeks to protect is "arguably within the zone of interest" that Congress intended to protect or regulate by the relevant statute, then the plaintiff is an appropriate person to complain of the injury, and standing exists.

The Supreme Court attempted to clarify this test in *Clarke v. Securities Industry Association*, 479 U.S. 388 (1987). The Court noted that the test was to be applied in light of a trend toward enlarging the class of plaintiffs seeking review of agency action. The Court stressed that the test was not intended to be especially demanding and did not require an express indication of congressional purpose to benefit the plaintiff. Indeed, in *Clarke* the Supreme Court expressly disapproved of a prior line of D.C. Circuit opinions that had set forth more substantial prudential barriers to review of agency actions, specifically the "intent to benefit" requirement applied in *Control Data Corp. v. Baldrige*, 655 F.2d 283, 293–94 (D.C. Cir. 1981), *cert. denied*, 454 U.S. 881 (1981). The Court held that as long as Congress has not manifested an intent to preclude review, the zone of interest test is satisfied if the plaintiff's interests bear a "plausible relationship" to the policies underlying the relevant statute.

The D.C. Circuit has recently issued several decisions that continue to impose significant prudential barriers that appear to conflict with the standards the Supreme Court set forth in *Clarke v. SIA*. For example, in *Hazardous Waste Treatment Council v. EPA (HWTC II)*, 861 F.2d 277 (D.C. Cir. 1988), *cert. denied*, 109 S. Ct. 3157 (1989), the court found that the injury asserted by the petitioner was to its competitive interest in ensuring that companies engaging in various waste treatment practices were subject to the same level of regulatory stringency. The court ruled that such competitive or commercial interests were merely incidental benefits of RCRA. Although the court acknowledged that the petitioner had sought a tightening of regulations that could benefit the environment, nonetheless it found that the HWTC did not meet prudential requirements of standing because "in the absence of either some explicit evidence of an intent to benefit such firms, or some reason to believe that such firms would be unusually suitable champions of Congress's ultimate goals, no one would suppose them to have standing to attack regulatory laxity." 861 F.2d at 283. This new test thus imposes limitations explicitly repudiated in *Clarke v. SIA*.

The D.C. Circuit made a similar finding in the more recent case of *Petro-Chem Processing, Inc. v. EPA*, 866 F.2d 433 (D.C. Cir. 1989), where the petitioners again challenged EPA regulations as being too lax, thereby providing an economic advantage to the petitioners' competitors. Considering itself bound by its earlier decision in *HWTC II*, the court held that the prudential requirements for standing under RCRA were not met by the commercial injury alleged by the petitioners. These cases appear to impose substantial new barriers on the ability of a private company to challenge environmental decision making.

Both the Supreme Court and the D.C. Circuit have recognized that Congress can eliminate prudential limitations by granting an express right of action to persons who would otherwise be barred by prudential rules. As an example, in *CAS I,* the D.C. Circuit held that the provision in EPCA entitling "any person who may be adversely affected" by an agency rule to seek review clearly demonstrated congressional intent to eliminate prudential barriers. Similarly, in *NWF v. Hodel*, 839 F.2d 694, 704 n.7 (D.C. Cir. 1988), the D.C. Circuit interpreted a statutory provision authorizing suit by any "adversely affected" person to eliminate prudential limitations.

Getting Past the Hurdles

Certain guidelines emerge from the rules of standing as constituted now. First, on a cautionary note, despite the fact that the parties or the courts below have not raised the issue of standing, as a jurisdictional limitation a court can raise the issue on its own at any time during the proceedings. *See FW/PBS, Inc. v. City of Dallas*, 493 U.S. 215 (1990). Second, the manner in which a complaint is pleaded and supported by affidavits will influence significantly a determination of standing. Whether asserting economic or environmental injury, the plaintiff must identify a specific, personal harm to itself or, in the case of an organization, at least to one of its members. While prior D.C. Circuit opinions appeared to adopt a very liberal standard on the degree of specificity needed in asserting harm, the Supreme Court's recent decision in *Lujan* certainly argues for a return to the stringency required in *Griles*.

Third, the procedural setting in which the standing issue is raised is also extremely significant. A court will evaluate an insufficiently specific allegation of harm less stringently in the case of a motion to dismiss than in a motion for summary judgment. Moreover, while past D.C. Circuit opinions had liberally allowed plaintiffs to supplement the record to cure alleged defects in standing, the Supreme Court's reversal of its decision in *NWF v. Hodel* could indicate an opposite trend.

Overall, recent decisions indicate a disturbing trend toward imposing substantial new barriers on the ability of parties to challenge environmental regulations. Where economic injury was traditionally the norm in demonstrating an injury sufficient to satisfy standing requirements, economic harm now appears suspect as a basis for private parties to challenge governmental action under environmental legislation. Unless a private party is directly regulated by the precise statutory or regulatory provision being challenged, that party may be hard pressed to get the D.C. Circuit to review its challenge in the face of indirect, though equally concrete, injury. Such parties apparently are not deemed to be appropriate champions of the environmental issues at stake.

In addition, while the D.C. Circuit seemed quite liberal in its past evaluation of the standing of environmental groups, the Supreme Court's decision in *Lujan*, and the Circuit's application of this decision in *Foundation for Economic Trends,* appears to indicate a move in the direction of imposing more difficult barriers. While the full development of such changes has not yet been seen, it is clear that the D.C. Circuit's and the Supreme Court's recent decisions have and will encourage the government to challenge the standing of all litigants who attempt to review agency actions.

Ripeness, Exhaustion, and Administrative Practice

Gregory J. Hobbs, Jr.

Clients often assume that a lawsuit is the cure for every perceived threat or unwelcome circumstance visited upon them by a federal, state, or local administrative agency. For example, citizen and neighborhood groups, in their anxiety to halt a proposed road project, the siting of a landfill, or a rezoning action, believe on the basis of newspaper articles that courts often block construction activities when environmental problems are perceived. Business client reaction to an agency notice of violation, cease and desist order, or penalty assessment may involve an immediate call to counsel regarding how to sue the agency for harassment, unfounded allegations, or to block an agency investigation.

But practitioners of administrative law know the basic truth of their practice—that courts are the last resort. Executive, and even legislative, remedies are often surer, less expensive, and more effective than litigation. Litigants arrive in court with little realistic chance of success unless the agency has completely failed to discharge a legal duty when requested to do so, ignored basic procedural or substantive requirements applicable to it by statute, violated its duly promulgated rules, or proceeded clearly in excess of—or without—statutory authority.

Courts utilize three "doctrines" by which to open or shut the courthouse door to decisions on the merits: ripeness, standing, and exhaustion of administrative remedies. These principles, which are

Greg Hobbs is group leader for the water and environmental practice of Davis, Graham & Stubbs, based in Denver, Colorado.

often blended into one another by courts and counsel, are used to determine whether litigation should proceed or be terminated.

Ripeness focuses on whether the matter is fit for judicial review. *Abbott Laboratories v. Gardner*, 387 U.S. 136, 148–49 (1967). Standing addresses whether a case or controversy exists for the purpose of conferring jurisdiction upon the judicial branch to perform its governmental function of case-by-case decision making under the U.S. Constitution. *Sierra Club v. Morton*, 405 U.S. 727, 732 (1972); *NWF v. Hodel*, 839 F.2d 694, 704 (D.C. Cir. 1988). Exhaustion tests whether an administrative agency has been given a fair opportunity to resolve a dispute short of litigation. *See Toilet Goods Ass'n v. Gardner*, 387 U.S. 158, 165–66 (1967). Each is a facet of the judiciary's effort to define its role as distinct from the other two branches of government.

During the 1970s and 1980s, regulatory reform through litigation became a significant tool for building the national environmental agenda. Under *United States v. SCRAP*, 412 U.S. 669, 686–88 (1973), standing was fairly easy to maintain, and the courts seemed to invite broad programmatic review of regulatory activities. Judicial decisions had the effect of turning general statutory statements of purpose into far-reaching regulatory programs.

Although the EPA was a defendant in many cases, it became the beneficiary of expanded powers under directives issued from the bench. Congress was called upon to ratify or reverse decisions that broke new ground. For example, the EPA's prevention of significant deterioration program for air quality derived from a federal district court decision, *Sierra Club v. Ruckelshaus*, 344 F. Supp. 253 (D.D.C. 1972), which was upheld *per curiam* by the D.C. Circuit Court, 4 E.R.C. 1815 (D.C. Cir. 1972), and then by a four-to-four vote of the U.S. Supreme Court, affirmed by an equally divided court, *sub nom. Fri v. Sierra Club*, 412 U.S. 541 (1973). From the statutory purpose section of the 1970 Clean Air Act, 42 U.S.C § 7401(b)(1), to "protect and enhance" air quality, an increment rationing program was formulated for apportioning growth in areas better than the national ambient standards. Upon reauthorizing the Act in 1977, Congress embodied in statute the litigation's outcome. *See Alabama Power Co. v. Costle*, 636 F.2d 323 (D.C. Cir. 1979).

The amazing growth of wetlands regulation under section 404 of the Clean Water Act, 33 U.S.C. § 1251 *et seq.,* has run a similar course of litigation and subsequent congressional ratification regarding the applicable scope of "waters of the United States." *NRDC v. Callaway*, 392 F. Supp. 685 (D.D.C. 1975). *See* Hobbs & Raley, "Water Rights Protection in Water Quality Law," 60 *U. Colo. L. Rev.*

841, 848–52 (1989). Yet, in 1990, when the Sierra Club sought to require the Forest Service to embark on a nationwide program of claiming federal reserved water rights for wilderness areas, the U.S. Court of Appeals for the Tenth Circuit, relying on *Lujan v. NWF*, 110 S. Ct. 3177 (1990), vacated a federal district court decision that had declared the existence of implied federal reserved water rights for wilderness areas. *Sierra Club v. Yeutter*, 911 F.2d 1405 (10th Cir. 1990).

In the *Lujan* decision, the Supreme Court emphasized that it would not make policy decisions that resided with the legislative and executive branches. As a result, the three threshold doctrines—ripeness, standing, and exhaustion—are crucial to maintaining an environmental lawsuit, particularly one for judicial review under the APA, 5 U.S.C. § 701 *et seq.*

Ripeness and Standing

Ripeness has been described as the "fitness for judicial review" doctrine whereby courts consider and give weight to the institutional relationship between themselves and administrative agencies in determining whether to entertain a complaint for relief. Standing is a jurisdictional prerequisite for a court to exercise its governmental function. Exhaustion, by way of contrast, focuses on whether the person seeking a judicial remedy is attempting to short-circuit the administrative process and has not been reasonably diligent in protecting his or her interests. *See Ticor Title Ins. Co. v. FTC*, 814 F.2d 731, 735 (D.C. Cir. 1987). Courts and counsel often have difficulty distinguishing the theoretical difference between the three, although the effect thereof—whether a case will or will not proceed to a decision on the merits—becomes quite practical.

The ripeness doctrine was once viewed as jurisdictional in nature within the Article III case or controversy requirement. As a result, a complainant could not obtain review of a rule making or adjudicatory action of an agency without risking civil or criminal penalties. Usually, illegality of an agency's policy or course of conduct could be challenged only in the context of an enforcement action. 4 K. Davis, *Administrative Law Treatise, Second*, at 349–56 (1983).

No longer must citizens or businesses become enforcement targets to invoke judicial scrutiny of administrative action. Courts will conduct review when the agency has failed to take required action, has taken a concrete action, or has articulated a policy from which legal consequences to the complainant will likely flow, even if the anticipated injury has not yet occurred. The matter presented for judicial consideration, however, must be "real and present" rather than "hypothetical and imaginary."

Forging New Directions Regarding Ripeness

In the leading case, which forged a sharp redirection in ripeness law, the Supreme Court stated that the ripeness doctrine is meant to "prevent the courts . . . from entangling themselves in abstract disagreements over administrative policies, and also to protect the agencies from judicial interference until an administrative decision has been formalized and its effects felt in a concrete way by the challenging parties." The reviewing court must make two basic inquiries: (1) whether the question presented is fit for judicial decision, and (2) what the hardship to the parties would be if judicial resolution were withheld. *Abbott Laboratories v. Gardner*, 387 U.S. 136, 148–49 (1967).

In accordance with *Abbott Laboratories*, a number of factors should be examined and weighed by a court in making the ripeness analysis. Will development of a factual record before the agency help to further define the issues and assist in resolving them? Might further administrative proceedings terminate the controversy without the necessity of judicial decision? Will the expertise of the administrative agency be helpful, or is the question solely one of statutory construction or legal interpretation? Is the agency position tentative, or has it become "final"? Are the impacts of the agency's position sufficiently direct and immediate? Does the agency action or policy require the complainant to change his or her conduct?

The above areas of inquiry underscore the observation that the " 'law of ripeness is now very much a matter of common sense.' " *Seafarers Int'l Union v. U.S. Coast Guard*, 736 F.2d 19, 26 (2d Cir. 1984). For example, agency rules or policies that have widespread impact upon a regulated industry or the public interest, such as licensing standards, are ripe for review when adopted, regardless of whether an individual license application is at issue. *See NRDC v. U.S. Nuclear Regulatory Comm'n*, 539 F.2d 824, 837 (2d Cir. 1976). On the other hand, a proposed highway alignment that may never be built because the agency has not finally committed to building it is not properly subject to judicial review even though design work is proceeding. *See NWF v. Goldschmidt*, 677 F.2d 259, 264 (2d Cir. 1982).

Narrowing the Scope of Judicial Review

Ripeness, standing, and exhaustion continue to merge into one another in opinions dealing with judicial review of agency action. In

Lujan, the NWF challenged the BLM's program for making land withdrawal and classification review decisions. The process eventually led to determining allowable uses of specific tracts of federal property, whether for oil, gas, mineral development, timbering, grazing, recreation, fish, wildlife, or aesthetic purposes. Instead of waiting for BLM permit-by-permit disposition under the FLPMA, 43 U.S.C. § 1701 *et seq.*, Sierra Club filed a generic complaint alleging membership interest in the vicinity of broad geographical reaches to protect wildlife, aesthetics, and recreational use. Through this device, the NWF sought to reform the agency review process and avoid tract-by-tract litigation.

But the Supreme Court refused to engage in programmatic policy making, which it viewed as more appropriate for the administrative agency or Congress. Standing to bring judicial review litigation under the APA, said the Court, must be predicated on a complaint brought: (1) by a named plaintiff, (2) who has been injured or is threatened with injury, (3) by a concrete agency action, (4) in violation of a statute, (5) whose zone of interests is protective of the plaintiff's interest, (6) and the agency action is focused and final. *See Lujan v. NWF*, 110 S. Ct. at 3186, 3190. To withstand a summary judgment motion, the Court required an affidavit setting forth a detailed description of plaintiff's interest and the alleged or threatened harm with respect to a specific geographical site. Judicial review would not be allowed absent a permit decision or other specific regulatory disposition.

The *Lujan* opinion had immediate effect. Two months later, in August 1990, the Tenth Circuit Court of Appeals in *Sierra Club v. Yeutter*, 911 F.2d at 1415–20, vacated a Colorado federal district court declaration that federal reserved water rights exist by reason of wilderness designation under the 1964 National Wilderness Preservation Act. The circuit court's order was based to a significant degree on a Forest Service report that outlined the means by which the agency could protect wilderness water resources other than by a federal reserved water right. For example, the agency could deny access needed for the construction of new water facilities across federal lands. The Tenth Circuit labeled the lawsuit "speculative" and "hypothetical" because Sierra Club failed to demonstrate that any of the existing twenty-four wilderness areas in Colorado would be harmed or threatened with harm in the absence of federal reserved water rights.

Other recent decisions have applied *Lujan* to allow or disallow judicial review. An animal rights group alleging that its enjoyment of the San Francisco Bay area was being harmed by federally funded research involving animals was unsuccessful. *People for the Ethical Treatment of Animals v. Department of Health & Human Servs.*, 917 F.2d 15 (9th Cir. 1990). But the D.C. Circuit allowed the City of Los Angeles and others to maintain a "global warming" suit under NEPA against the National Highway Traffic Safety Administration. The court ultimately disagreed with petitioners respecting agency duties with regard to the corporate average fuel economy program but recognized standing and ripeness in *City of Los Angeles v. National Highway Traffic Safety Administration*, 912 F.2d 478, 483, 493 (D.C. Cir. 1990). And citizens who swore by affidavit that they would boat on New Jersey's Kill Van Kull if it were not so polluted demonstrated sufficient injury to maintain a PSD suit against the defendant corporation in *Public Interest Research Group of New Jersey v. Powell Duffryn Terminals*, 913 F.2d 64, 71 (3d Cir. 1990).

Agency decisions not to bring an enforcement action generally are not reviewable. The Supreme Court has long recognized that

> [A]n agency's decision not to prosecute or enforce, whether through civil or criminal process, is a decision generally committed to an agency's absolute discretion. . . . The agency is far better equipped than the courts to deal with the many variables involved in the proper ordering of its priorities.

Heckler v. Chaney, 470 U.S. 821, 831–32, 105 S. Ct. 1649, 1655–56 (1985). However, citizen suit provisions that are contained in many environmental statutes can counteract an agency's decision not to enforce by providing a private cause of action for members of the public.

The underlying premise of the ripeness doctrine is that only final agency action, when no other adequate remedy exists, is judicially reviewable. Critical to the analysis is the appropriate timing of administrative and judicial proceedings and the proper relationship between the judicial function and the administrative function. Abstract questions of agency practice or policy will not be considered. Hence, although the ripeness concept resembles case and controversy analysis in that the court will not issue advisory opinions, a flexible approach applies. Such flexibility works either as an invitation to careful work and innovation by counsel in framing a complaint for judicial review of administrative action or inaction or as a costly trap for litigants who can waste their time in court proceedings only to find that administrative recourse was the best or only hope for resolving the problem.

Exhaustion

Whereas ripeness analysis tests whether an issue is fit for judicial determination and the degree of hardship that will be visited on the parties from withholding judicial resolution and standing determines whether the court has jurisdiction, exhaustion of administrative remedies focuses on whether an avenue for relief exists at the agency level and has been bypassed or short-circuited. The presumption is that a judicial remedy cannot be granted if an available administrative remedy has not been sought or is in the process of being duly considered by the agency.

Assessing Jurisdiction

As with ripeness, the exhaustion principle is not jurisdictional in nature *unless* a statute sets forth and prescribes administrative remedies as a prerequisite for invoking the jurisdiction of the court. Here is a trap for clients and counsel. Adherence to provisions of agency law or statutes granting general subject matter authority or setting forth time periods or other procedural steps to be taken by those affected may be viewed as jurisdictional prerequisites unless prior judicial interpretation has held that they are not jurisdictional in nature. *See Evans v. Simpson*, 190 Colo. 426, 547 P.2d 931 (1976). Therefore "exhaust, exhaust, exhaust" is a byword of administrative practice. Counsel should always assume that when an agency has jurisdiction over the matter (1) issues of fact must be presented first to the agency and, further (2) issues of law will not be decided by a court unless the agency has been presented with the first opportunity to construe and apply the statute or regulation at issue. *See Toilet Goods Ass'n v. Gardner*, 387 U.S. 158, 165–66 (1967). Whether an agency has jurisdiction in the first instance is not exempt from initial administrative purview. Administrative agencies, like courts, are entitled to determine whether they have jurisdiction over the controversy. Sometimes a statutory scheme may involve proceedings by two different administrative agencies before the court may assume jurisdiction. Exhaustion in such circumstances tests the perseverance, knowledge, and legal research of counsel.

Counsel has a much better chance of proceeding by way of complaint when the issue to be decided is purely a legal question. While courts give great deference to agency actions and policies involving their assigned expertise, whether a particular statute confers the scope of jurisdiction that the agency asserts is primarily a matter of law and is within the essential function of the judicial branch. *See*

Gardner v. Toilet Goods Ass'n, 387 U.S. 167, 171 (1967). Nevertheless, if an agency has not been presented with an opportunity to consider the legal issue, particularly when factual and policy questions are also implicated, counsel who files a complaint will likely return to the client with only a dismissal in hand.

Exceptions to Exhaustion

There are situations in which the exhaustion principle will not be applied. For example, exhaustion of administrative remedies will not be required when the agency has attempted to exercise powers that it does not have by statute; the agency's position has been so firmly announced or fixed that it would be futile to seek a change; an effective opportunity to seek a judicial remedy will be lost; the complainant's rights would be severely affected during the time it would take for administrative consideration; or the determinative policy of the agency is internal, secretive, or otherwise not available to those affected. *See, e.g., Bowen v. City of New York*, 476 U.S. 467, 483–87 (1986).

The primary exceptions to the exhaustion principle are when (1) exhaustion, if required, will result in irreparable injury to the complainant; (2) agency jurisdiction over the matter is plainly lacking; and (3) special agency expertise will be of no help in resolving the question. *See Rogers v. Bennett*, 873 F.2d 1387, 1393 (11th Cir. 1989) (where a state board of education sought and was refused relief enjoining a U.S. agency investigation of parental complaints involving the education of handicapped children). Since the exhaustion principle is not jurisdictional in nature and does not affect the power of the court, an agency may waive exhaustion of remedies and the court may ignore it in appropriate circumstances. For example, when an agency's policy of delay in making rules and its long-standing practice in not enforcing certain provisions of a statute is the issue, that administrative body cannot rightfully insist that the plaintiffs should have brought their grievance to it first. *Cutler v. Hayes*, 818 F.2d 879, 890–92 (D.C. Cir. 1987).

Although administrative processes may be bypassed when exhaustion of remedies would be futile or inadequate, the judicial branch should be expected to avoid premature or piecemeal interruption of the administrative process. *See Honig v. Doe*, 108 S. Ct. 592, 605–06 (1988). The executive branch is entitled to utilize agency expertise and to develop facts that may resolve the matter and obviate the need for judicial recourse. Thus, the court will ask: Could the complainant's rights be vindicated or alleged injury be rectified by the agency? If so, the court will not proceed. In the administrative adjudicatory context, the litigant before the agency must raise all available factual or legal issues or be precluded thereafter. *See Umberfield v. School Dist. No. 11*, 185 Colo. 165, 169, 522 P.2d 730, 734 (1974). The primary objective of the exhaustion doctrine is to promote administrative and judicial efficiency by avoiding premature disruption of the administrative process, but exhaustion will not be required, for example, when an agency asserts powers, such as adjudicatory and discovery authority, that has not been granted by statute. *See Atlantic Richfield Co. v. U.S. Dep't of Energy*, 769 F.2d 771, 781–82 (D.C. Cir. 1984).

When the matter sought to be reviewed is a mixed question of fact and law, or when a constitutional question is accompanied by nonconstitutional legal issues, and an opportunity for agency decision is capable of terminating the controversy, the court will normally dismiss the complaint or stay the action during the pendency of additional administrative proceedings. Dismissal of the complaint is not appropriate, however, when a statute of limitations may be involved and the litigant may be precluded from returning to court for effective judicial review. In such instances, a stay of judicial proceedings is appropriate while the agency takes another look. *Morrison-Knudsen Co. v. CHG Int'l, Inc.*, 811 F.2d 1209, 1223–24 (9th Cir. 1987).

Exhaustion of administrative remedies is definitely required when a statute contains or necessarily implies an exhaustion requirement by its terms. When such a statutory requirement does not exist, however, the courts are to determine whether application of the exhaustion requirement is consistent with the statutory scheme. When exhaustion of administrative remedies is not in conflict with a statute and agency proceedings can be helpful to resolution of the issue or the court's consideration of it, exhaustion of administrative remedies will be required. *See Coit Indep. Joint Venture v. Federal Sav. & Loan Ins. Corp.*, 109 S. Ct. 1361, 1372 (1989).

Using Citizen Suit Provisions

Counsel for environmental groups have creatively used the citizen suit provisions of such major national environmental laws as the Clean Water Act and the Clean Air Act to require agencies to follow provisions of statutes and regulations, obtain facts, and make decisions in circumstances that indicate that the agency has not been diligent in carrying out its statutory mission or has been more favorable to a permit applicant or to a potential enforcement defendant than appears to be justified. Such statutes employ an exhaustion-type provision that requires notice to the agency of intent to file suit and a waiting period for filing suit (normally sixty days) while an agency considers taking action. A particularly good example of a court retaining jurisdiction over a complaint in order to prod the agency into fulfilling its statutory role is a section 404 Clean Water Act wetlands case involving three reported decisions. *Avoyelles Sportsmen's League v. Alexander*, 473 F. Supp. 525 (W.D. La. 1979); 511 F. Supp. 278 (W.D. La. 1981); *aff'd in part, rev'd in part, Avoyelles Sportsmen's League v. Marsh*, 715 F.2d 897 (5th Cir. 1983).

Applying These Concepts to Administrative Practice

The Agency/Judicial Dichotomy

The ripeness, standing, and exhaustion doctrines often force environmental counsel back to the fundamental truth of administrative practice—that there is no substitute for a convincing presentation to the agency decision maker. Courts serve primarily to ensure that administrators follow procedural requirements in making substantive determinations required by law or assigned to the agency's sound discretion. The judicial branch does not properly decide matters of policy or undertake the agency's mission for it. But courts will require administrative agencies to do their job in the manner the legislative branch directs. Whether or not there are sufficient statutory and administrative standards and safeguards to protect against unnecessary and uncontrolled exercise of discretionary authority is a key area of judicial inquiry. *Cottrell v. City & County of Denver*, 636 P.2d 703, 709 (Colo. 1981).

Administrative agencies exist to resolve issues quickly, simply, in the public interest, and with a minimum of expense. At least, this is the view of the courts, and the administrative process can sometimes approach this ideal. On the other hand, getting an agency's attention and surviving the bureaucratic maze can be difficult. The challenge of counsel in administrative law practice is to frame the issue to an agency in a manner that elucidates public policy implications, entices the agency to consider the matter, evaluates the strengths and weaknesses of the agency's case, invents procedures for getting the agency to resolve the issue, makes a record favorable to the client, exposes to the agency its misinterpretation of statute or regulation, allows the agency to correct its past or current mistakes, appeals to the agency's sense of fairness, stresses the equities of the client's case, and proposes a solution that serves the agency's public purpose while advancing the client's cause.

The successful practitioner understands and gauges the particular agency forum and develops the facts and law for his or her client in such a way that the decision on the merits, or a settlement, will be in the client's favor or at least less damaging to the client's interest than other alternatives. There are five basic steps in preparing a defense to administrative enforcement: avoidance, evaluation, discovery, settlement, and resistance. Hopefully, the necessity to defend an enforcement case never arises because violations are avoided through self-monitoring for compliance with all applicable law, including regulations and permit requirements. When a case is received by counsel, there is no substitute for immediately reading and carefully analyzing the applicable statutes and regulations and inspecting the facility or location involved. Fact finding by counsel, usually with the aid of the client and frequently with the active assistance of technical experts, followed by the development of a strategy, are the next steps. Settlement must always be considered. Avoidance of future occurrences is paramount to the client's long-term interests. In analyzing and structuring any settlement, counsel should expend reasonable efforts to help the client eliminate possible recurrence of the same or similar problems. Settlement terms that have no assurance of being kept should be eliminated from consideration. The next round of proceedings may be criminal in nature, rather than civil, under the more stringent enforcement provisions of new laws such as the 1990 Clean Air Act amendments. *See, e.g.,* 42 U.S.C. § 7413(c).

Counsel should always advise a client to proceed first to the administrative agency, if there is time to do so, and irreparable injury will not immediately occur. Even then, when irreparable injury is imminent, counsel should simultaneously ask the agency to immediately issue the appropriate order preventing or rectifying the injury. Counsel's role in the administrative context is to understand the interests of the client, determine if and how those interests can be forwarded in the agency process, recommend accommodation and/ or behavior modification where appropriate, and pursue a resolution favorable to the client through negotiation with agency personnel or presentation to the assigned decision maker in adjudicatory or rule-making proceedings or in whatever informal process may be available or invented to match the circumstances.

Knowing the Law and Arguing Effectively

A persuasive argument before an administrative agency is one that appeals to the policy of the agency's law, the equities of the client's cause, the decision maker's interest in the matter, and his or her sense of rightness and importance regarding the decision to be made. Of primary significance is the manner in which the agency views both the substance of the presentation and the manner in which it is presented. Often the agency's perception of the client's and counsel's good faith in dealing with administrative personnel will be influential, and even sometimes determinative, to the ultimate resolution. Counsel must educate the decision maker about the legal and policy parameters of the matter at issue, whether an enforcement action, permit decision, proposed rule, or other pending administrative action. The tools for accomplishing this objective are contained in the substantive statutes governing the agency, in the federal and state administrative procedure acts, in the procedural rules and practices of the particular agency, in the federal and state freedom-of-information and public records acts, in the inventiveness of counsel in framing issues and suggesting procedural steps, and in counsel's ability to command the agency's attention and respect. Generally, effective administrative practice depends on well-conceived steps designed to focus the agency on a resolution favorable or least damaging to the client.

The manner of presenting witnesses before formal agency tribunals should be carefully considered. Citizen decision makers normally do not appreciate combative trial-type tactics. When conducting cross-examination, for example, counsel should not appear to browbeat or belittle a witness. Even worse is a perceived misrepresentation or lie. Particularly when counsel may again appear before the agency on behalf of the same or another client, an lawyer's foremost tool is his or her credibility with the forum. If a lawyer believes that he or she cannot maintain credibility in light of what the client would like to do or argue, even despite internal efforts to agree upon the appropriate tone and content of the presentation to be made to the agency, withdrawal from the representation in a manner that will not compromise the client's case should be considered.

In sum, clients, whatever their interest, need to hear, *before* complaints are drafted and filed, that courts are very reluctant to second-guess administrators acting within the scope of their authority. Ripeness, standing, and exhaustion play a concrete role in directing clients and counsel away from the courthouse and back to the administrative agencies where they usually belong.

PART II

Solid and Hazardous Waste

Part II
Solid and
Hazardous Waste

Τhe United States has a unique legal regime in which hazardous wastes are controlled from cradle to grave and companies are subject to strict, retroactive liability for remediation and natural resources damages for the disposal of hazardous substances. These two related programs have resulted in the identification of more than one thousand priority sites for remediation and have enmeshed thousands of manufacturing companies and other responsible parties in lawsuits and administrative proceedings.

The Comprehensive Environmental Response, Compensation and Liability Act, 42 U.S.C. § 9601 *et seq.*, is concerned with remediation of past waste disposal. The EPA has two enforcement options. It may arrange to have the necessary remedial work performed by the government or an outside contractor, using money in a federal trust fund, and seek reimbursement from responsible parties. Alternatively, the government may order responsible parties to undertake remedial action under section 106 CERCLA or negotiate a voluntary private cleanup.

We begin our discussion with an overview of Superfund liability under section 107 of CERCLA, 42 U.S.C. § 9607. Theodore Garrett discusses how liability is triggered, what defenses are available, and the right to contribution.

CERCLA contains unique provisions designed to encourage settlements and avoid unnecessary litigation. 42 U.S.C. § 9622. The article by Robert Frantz analyzes the EPA's settlement policy and Model Consent Decree and suggests key areas to address in negotiations.

The issue of "how clean is clean" remains a subject of lively debate. Elizabeth Temkin's article maintains that one can be in favor of hazardous waste cleanup and still reject many of the program's unnecessarily stringent elements. Raul Deju and Dean Calland present a practical description of the procedure by which sites are cleaned up, highlighting technical and legal issues that are key to a cost-effective remedy.

CERCLA has spawned a great volume of litigation. James Price discusses the judiciary's changing role in Superfund cases, its impact on parties facing Superfund claims, and several areas in which the courts remain very involved in resolving disputes. The restoration aspects of Superfund are another potentially controversial aspect of the law. Thomas Campbell explores the evolution of the methods used to determine natural resource damages under Superfund.

Companies must also deal with their present generation, treatment, storage, and disposal of hazardous wastes. First enacted in 1976, the Resource Conservation and Recovery Act is one of the most pervasive features of U.S. environmental law. 42 U.S.C. § 6901 *et seq.* Donna Kolar summarizes the history of RCRA and offers practical advice for permitting a waste disposal facility. Generators wishing to export hazardous waste, whether for treatment and disposal or for recycling, must comply with additional requirements, which are described in the final article by Mark Semenoff.

Superfund Liability and Defenses: A 1992 Primer

Theodore L. Garrett

An understanding of the reach of CERCLA is important for companies to consider in their compliance programs and in transactions involving the purchase or sale of property. For those unlucky parties involved in CERCLA suits or administrative actions, evaluating CERCLA liabilities and defenses is of paramount interest. This article reviews the basic features of CERCLA liability, including general elements of liability, the liability of particular parties, contribution and indemnification, defenses, and recoverable costs. Each of these areas is complex and, despite the burgeoning case law, many aspects of CERCLA liability remain controversial and unsettled. Only the general outlines can be presented here.

Section 107(a) of CERCLA sets forth the basic elements of liability. 42 U.S.C. § 9607(a) (1988). The statute provides that where there is a release or threatened release of a hazardous substance from a facility that causes the incurrence of response costs, responsible parties are liable *inter alia* for "(A) all costs of removal or remedial action incurred by the United States Government or a State . . . not inconsistent with the national contingency plan; (B) any other necessary costs of response incurred by any other person consistent with the national contingency plan; [and] (C) damages for injury to, destruction of, or loss of natural resources. . . ." *Id.* The Act establishes four categories of responsible parties:

1. the current owner and operator of a vessel or a facility;

Ted Garrett is a partner in the firm of Covington & Burling in Washington, D.C.

2. any person who at the time of disposal of any hazardous substance owned or operated the facility;
3. any person who by contract, agreement, or otherwise arranged for disposal or arranged with a transporter for disposal of hazardous substances owned or possessed by such person; and
4. any person who accepts hazardous substances for transport to disposal facilities or sites selected by such person. *Id.*

These categories of parties are commonly referred to as "present and past owners" and "operators, generators, and transporters."

The statute as enacted in 1980 was silent on the issue of whether liability was joint and several or whether a defendant was liable only for costs and damages caused by its conduct. Relying on general tort law principles, the first court to address the issue held that if two or more defendants cause an indivisible harm, "each is subject to liability for the entire harm." *United States v. Chem-Dyne Corp.*, 572 F. Supp. 802, 810 (S.D. Ohio 1983). The court suggested, however, that response costs might be apportioned among the defendants. Subsequent judicial decisions have adopted the approach in *Chem-Dyne* and have held that the statute imposes strict, joint and several liability to the government. *See, e.g., United States v. Monsanto*, 858 F.2d 160 (4th Cir. 1988).

The Elements of Liability

Liability under section 107(a) arises from the "release or threatened release" of a hazardous substance from a facility that causes the incurrence of response costs. These provisions are discussed below.

The requirement of a release or a threatened release has not proved difficult for the government to satisfy. CERCLA defines the term "release" to mean "any spilling, leaking, pumping, pouring, emitting, emptying, discharging, injecting, escaping, leaching, dumping, or disposing into the environment," including the abandonment or discarding of barrels or containers of hazardous substances. 42 U.S.C. § 9601(22). The statute exempts the following categories of releases:

1. any release which results in exposure to persons solely within a workplace;
2. emissions from the engine exhaust of motor vehicles, rolling stock, aircraft, vessels, or pipeline pumping stations;
3. release of source, byproduct or special nuclear material from a nuclear incident or from any processing site pursuant to the Atomic Energy Act; and

4. the normal application of fertilizer. *Id.*

CERCLA requires that the release be from a "facility," which is defined as "any building . . . equipment . . . pit, pond . . . landfill, storage container, or any site or area where a hazardous substance has been deposited. . . ." 42 U.S.C. § 9601(9). The courts have held that a facility includes "every conceivable area where hazardous substances come to be located." *New York v. General Electric Co.*, 592 F. Supp. 291, 296 (N.D.N.Y. 1984). This provision of the statute specifically exempts "any consumer product in consumer use or any vessel" or water craft, however. Moreover, CERCLA does not authorize the cleanup of contamination that is confined solely to the interior of a building, with no possibility of release into the "environment." *See, e.g., 3550 Stevens Creek Assocs. v. Barclay's Bank of Cal.*, 915 F.2d 1354, 1360–61 (9th Cir. 1990).

CERCLA requires that there be a release of a "hazardous substance." CERCLA defines a hazardous substance as a substance falling within six categories of substances regulated under other environmental statutes. 42 U.S.C. § 9601(14). The EPA has codified the list of CERCLA hazardous substances in 40 C.F.R. Part 302.

Should parties be liable for the disposal of substances that are naturally occurring or that are present in only trace amounts? In *United States v. Carolawn Co.*, 21 E.R.C. 2124 (D.S.C. 1984), the court stated that CERCLA "does not distinguish hazardous substances on the basis of quantity or concentration." *Id.* at 2126. *See also United States v. Western Processing*, 734 F. Supp. 930, 942 (W.D. Wash. 1990); *B.F. Goodrich Co. v. Murtha*, 754 F. Supp. 960 (D. Conn. 1991) (municipal waste). In *United States v. Ottati & Goss*, 900 F.2d 429, 437–38 (1st Cir. 1990), however, the court emphasized that the metals disposed of at the site were not above background levels, stating: "nature, not man, is likely responsible for high metal concentrations throughout the site." *Id.* at 438. Similarly, in *Amoco Oil Co. v. Borden*, 889 F.2d 664, 670–71 (5th Cir. 1989), the court indicated that a release must exceed a cleanup standard or ARAR for the defendant to be liable for response costs. Moreover, CERCLA provides that the government may not take response action with respect to the release of a "naturally occurring substance" in its natural form from a location where it is naturally found, absent emergency conditions. 42 U.S.C. § 9604(a)(3).

CERCLA imposes liability for a release "which causes the incurrence of response costs. . . ." 42 U.S.C. § 9607(a). Several decisions have given the causation requirement short shrift. *See New York v. Shore Realty Corp.*, 759 F.2d 1032, 1044–45 (2d Cir. 1985). Other decisions, however, have held that there must be a "causal connection between a release and the incurrence of costs." *Artesian Water Co. v. New Castle County*, 659 F. Supp. 1269, 1282 (D. Del. 1987). In *Amoco Oil Co. v. Borden*, the court stated that "holding parties liable who have not posed any threat to the public or the environment" would be contrary to the statute's purposes. 889 F.2d at 670. *See also Colorado v. Idarado Mining Co.*, 707 F. Supp. 1227, 1247 (D. Colo. 1989) ("there is inadequate proof of causation of harm to justify imposition of the state's proposed remedy and expenditure plan"); *United States v. Ottati & Goss*, 900 F.2d at 438 (levels of metals in defendant's waste were not higher than those in natural metal deposits).

Liable Parties

As noted above, four classes of persons are liable under CERCLA, namely, present and former owners and operators, generators, and transporters. Suits by the government and private parties have tested the boundaries of these classes of parties.

Past owners and operators are liable if they owned or operated the facility "at the time of disposal" of hazardous substances. 42 U.S.C. § 9607(a)(2). A current owner is liable even if it did not own the site at the time of disposal. *New York v. Shore Realty Corp.*, 759 F.2d at 1043–44. Congress amended CERCLA in 1986 to exclude innocent landowners from the definition of "contractual relationship." 42 U.S.C. § 9601(35)(A). This provision allows a defendant to avail itself of the third-party defense in section 107(b) if it can show that the property was acquired after the disposal took place and the defendant "did not know and had no reason to know" that hazardous substances had been disposed of on the property. *Id.*

The courts have focused on the degree of control exercised by a party for purposes of deciding operator liability. For example in *Edwards Hines Lumber Co. v. Vulcan Materials Co.*, 861 F.2d 155 (7th Cir. 1988), the court did not hold liable a company that designed a manufacturing facility and trained its workers, concluding that the company did not exercise sufficient control over the manufacturing facility's operations.

In *FMC Corp. v. Department of Commerce*, 31 E.R.C. 1959 (E.D. Pa. 1990), the court held that the federal government may be liable as an operator because of its pervasive regulatory control over the production activities of a private contractor during World War II. With respect to state liability, the court in *United States v. Stringfellow*,

31 E.R.C. 1315 (C.D. Cal. 1990), held that California was liable as the operator of a site where the state selected the site and controlled the dumping at the site. Not all state involvement triggers liability. CERCLA excludes from the definition of owner or operator a unit of state or local government that acquires ownership or control involuntarily by virtue of its function as a sovereign, such as by escheat or through eminent domain authority. *See* 42 U.S.C. §§ 9601(2)(D) and (35)(A)(ii); *In re Bergsoe Metal Corp.*, 910 F.2d 668 (9th Cir. 1990).

CERCLA exempts from owner or operator "a person, who, without participating in the management of a vessel or facility, holds indicia of ownership primarily to protect his security interest. . . ." 42 U.S.C. § 9601(20)(A). Decisions interpreting this provision have caused concern in the financial community. A bank that forecloses on property has been held liable as an owner. *United States v. Maryland Bank & Trust Co.*, 632 F. Supp. 573 (D. Md. 1986). In *United States v. Fleet Factors Corp.*, 901 F.2d 1550 (11th Cir. 1990), *cert. denied*, No. 90–504 (Jan. 14, 1991), the court indicated that where there is no foreclosure, a secured creditor may be liable if its involvement with the management of the facility is sufficiently broad to support the inference that it could affect hazardous waste disposal decisions if it so chose. In contrast, another court has stated that there is no liability absent some active participation in management. *In re Bergsoe Metal Corp.*, 910 F.2d 668, 672 (9th Cir. 1990). The uncertainty in this area has prompted various legislative proposals and a proposed EPA interpretative rule to clarify the activities that may be undertaken by lending institutions. *See* 56 Fed. Reg. 28,798 (1991).

"Persons who by contract, agreement or otherwise arranged for disposal" of hazardous substances owned or possessed by them are liable under CERCLA. 42 U.S.C. § 9607(a)(3). This "generator" liability has been most frequently applied to manufacturing companies. The government has argued that a generator is liable if (1) it disposed or arranged for the disposal of hazardous substances, (2) hazardous substances were disposed of at a facility, and (3) the facility contains wastes of the kind the generator disposed of. *See United States v. Mottolo*, 695 F. Supp. 615, 625 (D.N.H. 1988); *Violet v. Picillo*, 648 F. Supp. 1283, 1289 (D.R.I. 1986), *affirmed*, 883 F.2d 176 (1st Cir. 1989).

To be liable, a generator must have owned or possessed a waste, and the waste must have been shipped to the site in question. *See United States v. Consolidated Rail Corp.*, 729 F. Supp. 1461 (D. Del.

1990); *United States v. Wade*, 21 E.R.C. 1346, 1348 (E.D. Pa. 1984). Courts have held that a generator of waste need not have affirmatively selected the site where the hazardous wastes were disposed, however, as shown in *United States v. Parsons*, 723 F. Supp. 757, 762 (N.D. Ga. 1989), and may be liable even if it intended to have its wastes deposited elsewhere. *Missouri v. Independent Petrochemical Corp.*, 610 F. Supp. 4, 5 (E.D. Mo. 1985); *O'Neill v. Picillo*, 441 F. Supp. 706 (D.R.I. 1988).

CERCLA does not impose liability on a party that sold finished primary product or raw material. *See United States v. A&F Materials Co.*, 582 F. Supp. 842, 845 (S.D. Ill. 1984); *United States v. Westinghouse Elec. Corp.*, 22 E.R.C. 1230 (S.D. Ind. 1983). In *New York v. General Elec. Co.*, 592 F. Supp. 291 (N.D.N.Y. 1984), however, a company that sold waste oil to a drag strip to be used for dust control was held liable. A below market sale of property was considered an arrangement for disposal in one case. *Sanford Street Corp. v. Textron, Inc.*, 768 F. Supp. 1218 (W.D. Mich. 1991). Moreover, in *United States v. Aceto Agric. Chems. Corp.*, 872 F.2d 1373 (8th Cir. 1989), the court affirmed the denial of a motion to dismiss a suit against eight companies that had supplied raw materials to a bankrupt pesticide formulator where the government alleged that the companies owned the pesticides throughout the formulation process and that the generation of wastes was an inherent part of the process. *Id.* at 1380–84.

Transporters who accept hazardous substances for shipment are liable if they select the disposal site. *See United States v. Hardage*, 32 E.R.C. 1073, 1081 (W.D. Okla. 1990); *Alcatel Info. Sys. v. Arizona*, 33 E.R.C. 1278 (D. Ariz. 1991).

Under traditional common-law principles, parent corporations are held liable for the torts of their subsidiaries only in the limited circumstances in which it is appropriate to pierce the corporate veil. Under CERCLA, however, some courts have based liability on the extent to which the parent has had the capacity to control or actually has controlled its subsidiary's activities, including waste disposal activities. *See, e.g., United States v. Kayser-Roth, Inc.*, 910 F.2d 24 (1st Cir. 1990), *cert. denied*, 111 S. Ct. 957 (1991). *But see Joslyn Mfg. Co. v. T.L. James & Co., Inc.*, 893 F.2d 80 (5th Cir. 1990), *cert. denied*, 111 S. Ct. 1017 (1991).

Similarly, under the traditional concept of limited liability, corporate officers and shareholders are usually shielded from personal liability resulting from the unlawful acts of the corporate entity. Under CERCLA, however, some courts have found such persons personally liable as operators or owners if they exercised or had the capacity to exercise control over the day-to-day operations of the corporation. *See, e.g., Shore Realty Corp.*, 759 F.2d at 1052; *United States v. NEPACCO*, 579 F. Supp. at 848–49.

Contribution

Although the issue of whether the statute imposed joint and several liability was vigorously debated following the enactment of CERCLA, there was widespread agreement that a right to contribution exists if such liability may be imposed. In several early decisions, federal courts held that such a right of contribution exists as a matter of federal common law. *United States v. Ward*, 22 E.R.C. 1235 (E.D.N.Y. 1984). CERCLA itself provides a direct right of contribution, stating that covered parties are liable for costs and damages "incurred by any other person." 42 U.S.C. § 9607(a)(4)(A). *See City of Philadelphia v. Stepan Chem. Co.*, 544 F. Supp. 1135, 1141–43 (E.D. Pa. 1982). In addition, that Act was amended in 1986 to expressly provide that "[a]ny person may seek contribution from any other person who is liable or potentially liable under section 9607(a)." 42 U.S.C. § 9613(f)(1). The amendment also provides contribution protection for parties that have settled their CERCLA liability with the United States or a state. *Id.* § 9613(f)(2).

The factors to be considered in allocating liability are not specified in the statute, which instructs the courts to employ "such equitable factors as the court determines are appropriate" *Id.* § 9613(f)(1). Courts and commentators have focused on factors set forth in the legislative history, which include the amount of the hazardous waste involved, the degree of toxicity of the hazardous waste, the degree of involvement by the parties, the degree of care exercised, and the degree of cooperation by the parties with federal, state, or local officials. H. Rep. No. 153, 99th Cong., 1st Sess. 18–19 (1985). *See, e.g., United States v. A&F Materials Co.*, 578 F. Supp. at 1256; *Amoco Oil Co. v. Borden*, 889 F.2d at 672–73; *United States v. Monsanto*, 858 F.2d 160, 168 n.13.

Defenses

CERCLA liability is subject to limited defenses set forth in the Act: (1) an act of God, (2) an act of war, and (3) an act or omission of a third party. 42 U.S.C. § 9607(b). Defendants have rarely relied upon the first two defenses. In one reported decision, the court held that heavy rainfall was not an act of God. *United States v. Stringfellow*, 661 F. Supp. 1053, 1061 (C.D. Cal. 1987).

The third-party defense applies to an act or omission of a third party "other than an employee or agent of the defendant, or than one whose act or omission occurs in connection with a contractual relationship, existing directly or indirectly with the defendant." 42 U.S.C. § 9607(b). To qualify for the defense, the defendant must show (1) that it exercised due care with respect to the hazardous substance concerned and (2) took precautions against foreseeable acts or omissions of third persons. *Id.* Judicial decisions have tended to construe this provision narrowly. *See United States v. Monsanto*, 858 F.2d at 168–69 (owners "presented no evidence that they took precautionary action against the foreseeable conduct" of their lessees); *O'Neill v. Picillo*, 682 F. Supp. 706 (D.R.I. 1988), *affirmed,* 883 F.2d 176 (1st Cir. 1990). As noted above, the 1986 amendments to CERCLA define the term contractual relationship to create a so called "innocent purchaser" defense. 42 U.S.C. § 9601(35).

Defendants have also raised equitable defenses such as waiver, estoppel, and unclean hands. In *United States v. Conservation Chem. Co.*, 619 F. Supp. 162, 204–05 (D. Mo. 1985), the court stated that equitable defenses are proper under CERCLA in suits under section 107, which seek the "equitable remedy of restitution." *See United States v. Mottolo*, 695 F. Supp. at 626–27; *Violet v. Picillo*, 648 F. Supp. at 1294–95. In *United States v. Ottati & Goss*, the court discounted certain costs and fees claimed by the government as a result of "untoward conduct" of the government in handling its lawsuit. 694 F. Supp. 997, 995. Other decisions have indicated that the defenses in CERCLA are exclusive, however, and that equitable defenses are not available. *Versatile Metals v. Union Corp.*, 693 F. Supp. 1563, 1572 (E.D. Pa. 1988); *Allied Corp. v. Acme Solvents Reclaiming*, 691 F. Supp. 1100, 1119 (N.D. Ill. 1988).

Recoverable Costs

Section 107(a) of CERCLA provides that the government may recover "all costs of removal or remedial action . . . not inconsistent with the national contingency plan." 42 U.S.C. § 9607(a).

The NCP is required to include "means of assuring that remedial action measures are cost-effective." 42 U.S.C. § 9605(a)(7). *United States v. NEPACCO*, 810 F.2d 726, 748 (8th Cir. 1986), *cert. denied,* 484 U.S. 848 (1987); *J.V. Peters & Co. v. EPA*, 767 F.2d 263, 266 (6th Cir. 1985). Parties facing demands for response costs should evaluate the NCP requirements in detail, including the limitations on response, appropriateness of removal action, selection of the remedy, opportunity for public comment, and documentation of the remedial decision and costs. *See e.g.*, 40 C.F.R. §§ 300.160, 300.430.

With respect to the kinds of costs recoverable, the terms "removal action" and "remedial action" are defined broadly in the Act. 42 U.S.C. §§ 9601(23) and (24). The following response costs have been held to be recoverable:

- security fencing or other measures to limit access—*see Amoco Oil Co. v. Borden*, 889 F.2d at 672
- investigation, monitoring, testing and evaluation costs—*see United States v. Wade*, 577 F. Supp. 1326, 1333 n.4 (E.D. Pa. 1983)
- alternative water supplies—*Artesian Water Co. v. New Castle County*, 659 F. Supp. 1269, 1287–88 (D. Del. 1987)
- medical testing and screening for purposes of assessing the effect of a release upon public health—*Brewer v. Ravan*, 680 F. Supp. 1176, 1179 (M.D. Tenn. 1988); this category does not include monitoring for personal health reasons or to allow private parties to recover tort damages—*Hopkins v. Elano Corp.*, 30 E.R.C. 1782, 1786 (S.D. Ohio 1989)
- remedial actions, including storage, confinement, clay cover, neutralization, recycling or reuse, destruction, dredging or excavation, collection of leachate or runoff, and on-site treatment or incineration—42 U.S.C. § 9601(24)
- prejudgment interest—*United States v. Mexico Feed & Seed Co.*, 729 F. Supp. 1250, 1253–54 (E.D. Mo. 1990)
- enforcement costs—42 U.S.C. § 9601(25); *see United States v. NEPACCO*, 579 F.2d at 85.

CERCLA also imposes liability for damages to natural resources. The statute bars recovery, however, where the damages and the release causing the damages occurred wholly before December 11, 1980, the date CERCLA was enacted. 42 U.S.C. § 9607(f)(1). This provision also bars damages specifically identified as irreversible and irretrievable in an EIS or similar analysis. *Id.*

CERCLA defines natural resources to mean "land, fish, wildlife, biota, air, water, ground water, drinking water supplies, and other such resources" belonging to the United States or a state. 42 U.S.C. § 9601(16). In 1986 and 1987, the DOI promulgated regulations for the assessment of natural resource damages, which are codified at 43 C.F.R. § 11.10 *et seq.* These regulations were challenged in

Ohio v. U.S. Dep't of the Interior, 880 F.2d 432 (D.C. Cir. 1989), which remanded the rules. Natural resources damages are discussed later in this Part.

In conclusion, although the broad contours of CERCLA liability are set forth in the statute, numerous and difficult issues not specifically addressed in the Act are being resolved though developing case law. These issues are complex and controversial due to the perception that the government is stretching the boundaries of liability, is wasteful and ineffective in its remediation efforts, and is not fostering settlements. Lawyers can make a contribution by developing fair and effective approaches to resolve CERCLA disputes and to minimize future liabilities.

Superfund Settlements: A Vanishing Breed

Robert W. Frantz

The EPA's current approach to Superfund settlements flies in the face of traditional settlement principles. The traditional reasons for a defendant to settle are to resolve a matter expeditiously and to achieve a complete and final resolution of the matter, thereby avoiding litigation or transaction costs. To achieve these goals, the defendant pays money or performs designated tasks. In the resulting compromise, the defendant gives something but gets something in return: finality. While this may be a statement of the obvious, it is currently ignored by the EPA, and the settlement of a Superfund case no longer achieves any of these goals. Because the EPA imposes terms and conditions in settlement documents requiring open-ended commitments by the PRPs, the settlement does not achieve finality. In essence, the PRPs give much and get virtually nothing in return. Settlements under the EPA's current approach even fail to resolve the matters expeditiously or fail to avoid transaction costs because experience has shown that disputes continue throughout the implementation of EPA consent decrees.

On July 8, 1991, the EPA issued the Model Consent Decree for Remedial Design and Remedial Action (Model Consent Decree). 56 Fed. Reg. 30,996. The publication of this document completes the set of model documents for the resolution of Superfund cases. On January 30, 1990, the EPA had issued the Model Administrative Order on Consent., OSWER Directive No. 9835.3-1A (Model Order), and

Robert Frantz is manager and counsel of the Environmental Remediation Program, General Electric Company.

on March 30, 1990, it had issued the Model Unilateral Administrative Order for Remedial Design and Remedial Action under Section 106 of CERCLA, OSWER Directive No. 9833.0-2(b) (Model UAO).

The PRPs perceive the common theme in these documents to be unreasonableness—from their viewpoint, they see a one-sided document offered with an unwillingness to compromise. To be sure, Congress did not consider fairness to be an overriding concern when it created the Superfund statute. As one district court judge has characterized it:, "CERCLA, as we read it, is not a legislative scheme which places a high priority on fairness to generators of hazardous waste." *United States v. Rohm & Haas,* 721 F. Supp. 666, 686 (D.N.J. 1989). Congress's overriding concerns were the expeditious cleanup of hazardous waste sites, the restoration of our natural resources, and the use of private funds to clean up sites. Nevertheless, the inflexible adherence to these theoretical principles without appropriate consideration of fairness is having an unexpected adverse effect on achieving those goals: Superfund settlements are likely to become the next endangered species.

This chapter discusses briefly how the Superfund process works and how the new Model Consent Decree is being applied. It evaluates settlement under the decree versus the various alternative approaches that may be available under Agency guidance and regulations and provides some practical advice on which provisions are most important and which modifications should be sought. Finally, it offers an assessment of the implications to the EPA's approach to settlement.

The Superfund Process

As most Superfund practitioners know, the Superfund process begins with notification of some involvement at a site, either through a request for information or a general notice letter under CERCLA. If the PRP is lucky, the Agency has not yet begun to assess the site regarding the nature and extent of contamination, nor has it completed the study of alternative remedies, a process called the RI/FS. Under these circumstances, the initial contact may be to provide a PRP with an opportunity to perform the RI/FS. At this stage, the EPA would introduce the use of the Model Order. Once the RI/FS is completed and submitted to the Agency, the EPA issues a proposed remedial action plan for public comment, after which it issues its ROD, in which it specifies the remedy for the site. The Model Consent Decree now comes into play. When Congress amended CERCLA in 1986, new section 122 imposed the requirement that all remedial action settlements be embodied in a consent decree. 42 U.S.C. § 9622.

As the Superfund program has matured, the EPA's approach to settlement has become more and more one-sided. Early agreements often provided clear benefits to settling parties and disincentives to nonsettling parties. Noteworthy in this regard was the *Seymour* settlement, which provided a fairly full release to settling parties. *See U.S. v. Seymour Recycling*, 554 F. Supp. 1334, 1336 (S.D. Ind. 1982). Following this and other similar agreements, however, Congress charged the EPA with granting PRPs "sweetheart deals" and demanded that it use the strong enforcement tools Congress had provided in the statute. Even as late as 1988, however, the EPA recognized the need for incentives to settlers. *See* Letter from Lee M. Thomas, EPA Administrator, to Regional Administrators, dated August 4, 1988.

In the 1986 amendments to CERCLA, Congress recognized the benefits of settlements and provided mechanisms to encourage them. Congress recognized that the PRPs would have to do a substantial portion of the work to clean up sites quickly because the EPA simply does not have the resources to perform all the work. Even if the EPA could perform all the remedial work, the courts and the EPA would be rapidly buried in an avalanche of cost recovery suits. Further, the EPA has had difficulty maintaining the necessary records for cost recovery suits; having them as the standard mode of operation would probably only tax agency resources further.

As a result of the amendments, CERCLA's settlement-inducing mechanisms now include mixed funding, allowing the Superfund to be used for orphan or nonparticipating PRP shares; nonbinding preliminary allocation of responsibility, allowing the Agency to estimate the PRP's share of responsibility; and *de minimis* settlements, establishing a mechanism for allowing small-share PRPs to settle early in the process. Yet the EPA has very seldom used these mechanisms.

Of course, the EPA's position is not without some justification. In light of the strong congressional scrutiny over the Agency's earlier attempts at flexibility, and combined with courts' abdication of any substantive scrutiny of the reasonableness of settlements, no matter how unfair (*see, e.g., U.S. v. Acton*, 733 F. Supp. 666 (D.N.J. 1990)), the EPA simply took the easiest course by imposing onerous, one-sided provisions. In reacting to these pressures, however, it has taken a course that is ultimately counter to its own interest.

The Model Consent Decree

Before reviewing the specific terms and conditions of the Model Consent Decree, I provide an overview of the nature of the basic deal.

Under the new decree, the PRPs have an obligation to finance and perform the cleanup; pay for past and future oversight costs; perform additional work "consistent with the Record of Decision" if the EPA determines it necessary; perform any additional work arising out of five-year reviews; provide financial assurance; pay stipulated penalties if any specified work is not completed on time; and indemnify the government for any damages that may arise out of activities performed pursuant to the Model Consent Decree. In return, the PRPs get from the government a covenant not to sue relating only to the work performed and, if the government is willing to grant it in the particular case, contribution protection, that is, protection from suits by other parties who believe they have paid more than their fair share of responsibility.

The government reserves its right to assess not only stipulated penalties, but statutory penalties of up to $25,000 per day. The government also reserves its right to impose criminal sanctions, seek natural resource damages, and seek additional work not specifically required under the decree—even beyond the "additional work" clause. The government also reserves its right to require the PRPs to perform work identified in the statutory five-year review process under CERCLA if this is not already specifically required in the decree.

To virtually every objective reviewer, this is a bad deal. There is no finality and transaction costs often continue to be incurred regarding disagreements concerning implementation of the decree. Whether this speeds cleanups is subject to debate. Let us discuss in detail a few of the more interesting provisions.

The mere name of one provision—additional work—raises concern. Under the terms of this provision, if the EPA determines that additional work is necessary to meet the performance standards specified in the Model Consent Decree or to carry out the remedy selected in the ROD, the EPA may require the PRPs to perform such work. Therefore the fundamental "deal" that was struck is really no deal at all. Rather, it is virtually open-ended, leaving the EPA to request any additional work it desires "to carry out the remedy selected in the ROD." If the PRPs disagree with the EPA's position, they may invoke the dispute resolution provisions of the decree.

Those dispute resolution provisions set forth a two-tier approach depending upon whether the dispute pertains to the selection or adequacy of any response action. For those disputes pertaining to the selection or adequacy of any response action, review is limited to the administrative record under an arbitrary and capricious standard of review. Thus, in the scenario identified above concerning additional work, since that pertains to the adequacy of any response action, review would be limited to the record under this arbitrary and capricious standard. Under it, Agency actions are almost uniformly upheld. *See, e.g., Marsh v. Oregon Natural Resources Council*, 490 U.S. 360 (1989). It should be noted that virtually all disputes arising during implementation of the remedy would likely be argued by the EPA to relate to the adequacy of the remedy.

For disputes not involving selection or adequacy of any response action, judicial review of any dispute shall be governed by "applicable provisions of law." In any such review, the EPA would undoubtedly argue for—and be accorded—substantial deference by the courts.

The EPA adds insult to injury by requiring that stipulated penalties continue to accrue during the pendency of the dispute. Thus, for those parties that do not prevail in any such dispute, stipulated penalties will have run during the entire period. This threat is likely to have a substantial chilling effect upon the parties' willingness to invoke the dispute resolution provisions. Not only, then, do the substantive terms of the dispute resolution provision favor the EPA, the EPA discourages parties from seeking relief by making stipulated penalties run during the pendency of the dispute, even where a PRP has a reasonable basis for its position.

The indemnification provision requires that the PRPs indemnify and hold harmless the government for all damages arising from activities undertaken pursuant to the decree. This means that regarding work performed pursuant to a decree, even where the EPA directs the remedy design or the means and methods for implementing the remedy, the PRPs will be liable for all damages arising out of the implementation. The PRPs would be well advised to ensure that their technical experts agree that the EPA's technical directions are sound from an engineering standpoint because the PRPs will not be able to argue that the EPA directed a particular approach and that the EPA should therefore be liable. If the technical experts do not agree, the PRPs should invoke dispute resolution.

Lastly, there is another infirmity of the stipulated penalties provision. Aside from the running of stipulated penalties during the pendency of any dispute, the EPA's use of the term "stipulated" is indeed improper. Although the PRPs are certainly stipulating that these penalties will be binding upon them, the government is not. Instead, the government retains its right to impose statutory penalties up to and including $25,000 per day. It might thus be more accurate to describe them as "stipulated minimum" penalties.

Why then would any right-minded manager voluntarily enter into such an agreement? Typically, when a party enters an agreement to settle a case, it is generally done on the grounds that some benefits will be derived. It is hard to find any benefits here for the PRPs. Counsel presenting such deals to corporate managers unfamiliar with the relative bargaining strengths of the parties in Superfund cases may find themselves ushered quickly out of the manager's office, if not out of a job.

Another way to look at settlement is to evaluate the alternatives to not signing a decree. First, the government might perform the work itself and seek to recover its costs. In these circumstances, the PRP would not waive any rights. All defenses would be retained, no indemnities would be granted, and stipulated penalties would not be specified. Moreover, the government would run all the risks associated with implementing the remedy. (Recognize, however, that the EPA could seek to recover such costs from the PRPs.) Parties would also retain use of the funds during the interim period and, assuming that those funds could be invested at a rate of return in excess of the government's interest charge, would receive a benefit associated with using those funds during the interim period.

The conventional reason for signing such an agreement and avoiding a government cleanup is that the PRPs can do the work much more cost-effectively. It is commonly believed that with government contracting procedures and inefficiencies associated with government review, costs will be much higher when the government performs the work. It must be recognized, however, that no oversight costs are incurred under these circumstances. Where the PRPs perform the work, they are required to pay government oversight costs, which range upwards from 15 percent of remedy costs. These costs are not incurred where the government performs the work.

If a decree is not signed, parties will also retain the ability to challenge the government's choice of remedy as inconsistent with the NCP. Although this would be a difficult task, the government will be required to demonstrate that its costs are justifiable from an accounting perspective. This standard may not be particularly burdensome for the government, but it requires some reasonable record keeping and accounting, which are not prevalent at Superfund sites to date.

Unilateral Orders

The second alternative is that the government might issue a Model UAO, referred to earlier. It should be noted that this is the more likely scenario, given that the government will be seeking to lay the foundation for seeking statutorily authorized treble damages where the PRPs do not comply. But, in a situation where the government issues a UAO, the PRPs waive nothing and agree to nothing. Parties also retain all rights to refuse to comply and interpose defenses. Judicial decisions have confirmed that parties are not obligated to comply if they have "sufficient cause" to believe that they have a defense. *Solid State Circuits v. EPA,* 812 F.2d 383, 390 (8th Cir. 1987). In general, however, unless they have been named improperly, parties will find it best to perform the work if a UAO is issued to them. Because they have signed no waiver of their rights to make claims against the Superfund under sections 106(b)(2) and 111, they may choose to make a claim against the fund for any amount they expend in response costs in excess of their liability.

Although there are a number of intangibles associated with performing work pursuant to a UAO versus performing work pursuant to a decree, my view is that it is generally better to accept the UAO and perform the work than it is to sign the decree. First, a thorough comparison of each of the provisions of the Model Consent Decree versus the Model UAO indicates that the Model UAO provisions are more favorable in general. Although it may be argued that a few specific provisions of the Model Consent Decree are more favorable than those of the Model UAO, on balance, the latter is better. *See* Practical Analysis of EPA's Model Consent Decree for Superfund Cleanups, Information Network for Superfund Settlements (1991). Second, and most significantly, the PRPs do not sign UAOs and therefore retain all rights to challenge them during implementation.

Practical Advice on Responding to the Model Consent Decree

Assuming that these one-sided provisions have not completely discouraged you from beginning negotiations with the EPA, you should at a minimum address the issues discussed below. Note, however, that the items discussed are by no means exhaustive.

First, three provisions are critical to the basic deal: the performance standards, additional work, and the certificate of completion. The Model Consent Decree specifies that the performance standards in the ROD will be incorporated into it. 56 Fed. Reg. at 30,999 (1991). This may not be adequate to specify what must be done. For example, numerical cleanup standards may not have been specified. If not, you must insist that adequate specificity regarding target cleanup levels be added to the statement of work, which is included as an appendix to the decree.

Second, you should seek to eliminate any obligation to perform additional work. The EPA reserves its rights to order you to do additional work, and thus there is no need for it to be in the decree. Short of that, you should at least limit the additional work provision to a circumstance where significant new information is discovered and it is necessary to meet the performance standards in the ROD. Third, the certification clause should be modified so that the EPA will certify completion when a remedy has been constructed in accordance with EPA-approved designs. In other words, if the remedy design specified by the EPA does not work, the EPA should be required to issue an order or negotiate a new consent decree before it can require that another remedy be implemented.

Turning to provisions relating to implementing the decree, the indemnity provision should be modified to make clear that where the EPA directs that particular actions or approaches be undertaken, the PRPs are not required to indemnify the EPA for claims arising from such actions or approaches.

The dispute resolution provision should be revised so that the language on the standard of review conforms with the statute. Only disputes over the selection of the remedy should be subject to the arbitrary and capricious standard of review. *See* 42 U.S.C. § 9613 (j)(2). Second, stipulated penalties should not accumulate during a dispute. Otherwise, parties will be loath to invoke the provision in all but egregious cases. To avoid frivolous disputes, the provision could provide that penalties will run during any dispute in which a court determines that a party did not have a reasonable basis for its position. Furthermore, the stipulated penalties provision should allow parties to "catch up" and thereby avoid penalties. That is, if a party can bring the entire project in on time, stipulated penalties for missing interim deadlines should be forgiven. It is, after all, only the completion of the remedy that really matters.

What is the likelihood that the EPA will be willing to negotiate these provisions? Unfortunately, it is not high. In its *Federal Register* notice, the EPA states that certain provisions are deemed to have "national significance" and that any deviation from the model will require approval of both the DOJ and EPA headquarters. Such provisions include those for access, contribution protection, covenants, dispute resolution, *force majeure*, additional response actions (additional work), certification of completion, stipulated penalties, and indemnification. The EPA has displayed only a limited willingness to even discuss—much less negotiate—these provisions.

Assuming, then, that you have been unable to persuade the EPA and the DOJ that they should modify these provisions, should you sign the decree or live with a unilateral order? My clear preference is to take the UAO and then perform the work.

If most of the PRPs agree that it is less beneficial to sign an agreement than not, it seems a mere tautology to state that there will be a decline in the number of decrees. Concomitantly, an increase in the number of UAOs issued or work performed by the government can be expected. As a collateral matter, this will mean that the DOJ will be less involved because, as a matter of practice, the EPA does not significantly involve DOJ in decision making concerning issuing UAOs.

Some may argue that a decline in the number of decrees is not significant. They will argue that the work will still get done pursuant to UAOs or to government direction. However, Congress directed and supported a settlement-oriented approach. This was not without good reason. A reasonable settlement-oriented approach, by its very nature, should be more expeditious. It would result in quicker, more cost-effective cleanups. Moreover, if the EPA is put in the position where it is forced to perform significantly more of the cleanups, the program will likely stall. Ultimately, then, this approach will be detrimental to the Superfund program.

Cleaning Up ARARs: Reflections from the Field

Elizabeth H. Temkin

The issue of appropriate cleanup standards for Superfund sites has been hotly contested since approximately 1983 as a matter of practice and, after the 1986 amendments to CERCLA, as a matter of law. At this point, the cleanup standard issue is denominated as the "ARARs question." That is, as to any given Superfund site, what are the applicable or relevant and appropriate cleanup standards and criteria as defined by and arguably explicated in CERCLA section 121?

The ARAR Debate

The ARARs debate has been framed and constrained primarily by three basic points of view. First, what might be called the environmentalist stance focuses on the perceived need for consistency in the application of ARARs in the belief that consistent application will ensure the protection of public health and the environment. Second is the congressional penchant, largely at the goading of the OTA, for permanent site remedies. The belief here is that a permanent technology, itself a difficult concept to grasp (for example, is a treatment plant with a thirty-year operational horizon a permanent remedy?), will protect the public health and the environment. Third is the regulated community's perspective, which decries Superfund's costs and associated allocation inequities without offering a responsive alternate cleanup philosophy or approach.

Elizabeth Temkin is a partner in Ballard Spahr Andrews & Ingersoll's Denver, Colorado, office.

Confronted with this debate, the position almost uniformly staked out at sites across the country by the agencies charged with implementing CERCLA—namely, the EPA and the DOJ—is to extract a commitment from PRPs to immediately install the maximum possible amount of technology to demonstrate the government's commitment to remediation. This technology-laden approach has the added advantage of maximizing the total number of dollars targeted for cleanup, which in turn helps to ensure that investigatory costs, however exorbitant, remain less than cleanup costs and also provides ammunition against congressional oversight charges of lackluster enforcement efforts.

The justification for the technological arsenal typically is two-fold. As a preliminary matter, the agencies more often than not seem to succumb to the environmentalists' cries for consistency by assuming that most Superfund sites eventually will be a housing development or a nursery school. Additionally, the agencies seem convinced that the majority of significant corporate PRPs will be bankrupt five years from now. Therefore the agencies perceive an obligation to protect the public weal by loading up the remedy and the cash payments on the front end.

This attitude seems driven partly by EPA headquarters' practice in reviewing and often rejecting regional office judgment calls. How many times as a regional office staffer do you risk being overruled by headquarters, even if official Agency policy arguably supports the regional position or is just plain silly? And understandable concern exists about backing off the extreme and generating precedent that will plague future enforcement efforts under both Superfund and the regulatory programs from which ARARs are borrowed. Meanwhile, industry's concerns remain unaddressed, presumably on the theory that industry prefers profits over toddlers and has as a death wish to be out of business five years hence.

When viewed from this extreme, the problems with this mindset are evident. The source of these problems lies at least in part with the underlying assumptions.

Turning first to "consistency," consistency in application of ARARs can only be a virtue if in fact all sites are alike, or at least can be grouped into categories, in terms of the environmental problems to be addressed and the uses to which a site and its environs might be put. While certain patterns are emerging with time and experience on types of sites and appropriate response activities (e.g., railroad tie dipping operations, mill tailing impounds, etc.), the environmental impacts or threats driving cleanup as a factual, scientific matter vary widely with geography and demographics.

As to "permanence," the concept itself reflects a faith in technology that, in light of the environmental havoc technology has wrought in the last one hundred years, seems to reflect an incredible naiveté about what technology can and cannot achieve. Given mankind's track record in this regard, will any technical expert seriously guarantee that enhanced microbial biodegradation may not create equally noxious problems (witness the natural degradation of TCE to vinyl chloride) or, given our varied experience with "impermeable bedrock," that solidified source material will truly *never* leach?

The practical effect of the government's position is tragic, not just for the PRPs footing the bill but for anyone who believes that there is a finite amount of money in this country that can be devoted to environmental cleanup and that we dare not waste any of it.

Two Hypothetical Cleanups

Two examples from the trenches may well illustrate the point that money is often unwisely spent in cleanup activities.

The first example is a gas plant, one of several older industrial facilities, each with its own distinct and separate plume, that together comprise the sources of primary concern to the EPA within this Superfund site. Downgradient from the site lies a relatively new subdivision. Each home has its own water supply well. Absent the Superfund-related impacts, groundwater arguably is drinkable, although the quality is not very good. When groundwater contamination at the site was first documented, the EPA installed a public water supply system, which has since been completed. The gas plant initiated a removal action (groundwater pump-and-treat and soil vapor extraction) and took other steps early in the Superfund process to limit the prospective impact of its operations, particularly off-site. As a result of these steps, combined with natural biodegradation, groundwater just downgradient of the site met the key selected ARAR, the relevant drinking water standard—i.e., MCL—before the remedy for the site was even selected.

In light of industry's prior experience, the PRP did not even try to argue that compliance with MCLs should be measured at the water tap, where the MCL actually applies, rather than at the site boundary. Nor did the PRP argue the fairly obvious point that with installation of a public water supply, groundwater cleanup to achieve drinking water standards was rather redundant. Instead, the PRP took the much less extreme and simple position that as long as the groundwater exiting the site met MCLs, and the land use at the PRP's facility remained industrial, no additional cleanup of either on-site groundwater or soil should be required.

The PRP's argument was premised on practicalities, the PRP's corporate stability, and the positing of various sureties and regulatory constraints and precedents. The very practical consideration was that digging up soil amidst the labyrinth of above ground and underground piping at the seventy-year-old facility was likely to be a nightmare—and a potentially dangerous one at that. Additionally, as a regulated utility and the only gas provider in the area, the chances of a significant change in land use at the site were quite small, particularly given the facility's industrial neighbors. The PRP, while not a Fortune 500 company, also had a substantial, long-standing regional presence, was willing to commit (and provide the necessary financial sureties) that if MCLs were exceeded in the future off-site or if the facility was ever abandoned, the necessary on-site remediation would then be performed. The PRP also suggested deed restrictions and possible county regulation to ensure that no wells were drilled on-site in the future. These commitments were in addition to the standard consent decree language mandating a five-year review of the selected remedy (because waste would be left on-site) and PRP performance of any additional cleanup activities identified in that review as being necessary. The PRP also emphasized that this approach was consistent with the soon-to-be-proposed regulations for corrective action under RCRA, which, while not technically an ARAR because the regulations had not yet been promulgated, clearly were "relevant and appropriate" in the true sense of the words. Finally, the cost of undertaking an on-site soil and groundwater cleanup was prohibitive and the ultimate effectiveness less than clear. Given the lack of risk on-site or off-site, particularly with the public water supply up and operating, it just did not make any sense to require more on-site cleanup.

Nevertheless, the EPA insisted that on-site groundwater meet MCLs that, quite likely, will require extensive groundwater treatment and additional soil remediation. The EPA's objections were fairly predictable. First, the existing removal technology was not a permanent remedy. Second, and by extension, the NCP does not allow institutional controls such as deed restrictions and the like. (In fact, the NCP specifically *does* allow institutional controls to supplement engineering controls for short- and long-term hazardous substance management.) Third, someday someone might rip out the tons of piping and other gas plant hardware and build a housing subdivision on the property. As a result, hundreds of thousands of dollars likely will be spent studying the on-site remediation issues and, if the federal government prevails, presumably much more on cleanup for an elusive environmental benefit.

The second site involves radium contamination largely attributable to the U.S. Bureau of Mines and smelter-related contamination that predated the Bureau of Mines's activities. The current owner, who bought the property in the late 1940s, sued the federal government for a declaration of the government's responsibility for the radium cleanup and related past response costs. The government stipulated to a judgment against it as to the radium contamination on the eve of the trial. The government also has basically conceded that the same innocent purchaser defense that protects the current owner vis-a-vis radium-related liability immunizes it from metals-related liability. In other words, there can be no serious concern about PRP stability here—the federal government is paying for the radium cleanup and the Superfund is addressing the metals cleanup because the smelting operations disappeared without a corporate trace.

There is some metals contamination above relevant MCLs in the groundwater under the site and the state insisted that the groundwater had to meet MCLs. As a technical matter, this would have required construction of a RCRA-type cell on this innocent landowner's property with the consolidation of the metals-contaminated soil in the cell, plus possibly groundwater treatment. The site owner took the position—with some support from the EPA—that groundwater cleanup was unnecessary because the metals were not mobile and were not moving toward a nearby surface watercourse. The site also was located in a decidedly commercial/industrial neighborhood with easy and cheap access to a public water supply. In contrast, utilization of the groundwater would have required the preparation, approval, and implementation of an expensive water augmentation plan. Finally, the cost of this "goldplated" cleanup was likely to be in the neighborhood of $10 million. An equally protective cap, albeit permeable, was estimated to cost $825,000. Plus, if this capping strategy failed, there would always be a PRP (i.e., the federal government or the Superfund) to look to for additional work.

The outcome of this dispute is not yet known, although there is some hope of the state moderating its stridency. But months have passed and thousands of dollars have been spent arguing about consistency, permanence, and the like. This site has been in the cleanup process for twelve years!

The Need to Assess Land Use

Not all the blame for this state of affairs should be heaped on the EPA and the DOJ. As the second example illustrates, the states need to bear their share as well. Congress also deserves a good dressing down for allowing hazardous waste cleanup to attain the status of mom and apple pie—something that cannot be voted against or even questioned, except possibly as to the liability of lenders and municipalities. And then there is industry's Greek chorus, which pretty clearly is not getting anywhere on the ARARs issue or any of the other real world problems CERCLA presents, probably because industry has offered few practical solutions to replace the current system that industry so routinely disparages.

The likely answer here carries with it the variability, uncertainty, and judgment calls that the environmentalists and the OTA invariably equate with industry's purported dominance of the administrative process and outgunning a flaccid EPA. Nonetheless, it is time to topple the gods of consistency and permanence and recognize the potentially dynamic role that land use considerations and institutional controls can play at many sites in devising innovative and effective remedial strategies. Particularly given the dearth of realistic, yet satisfying, remedial technologies for so many sites, a pragmatic approach that recognizes the value of nontechnical solutions seems to be one of the more sensible alternatives.

This proposal is not that original, nor will it necessarily benefit industry across the board. It will not provide the finality that industry—as much as Congress and the OTA—craves in addressing Superfund issues. To the contrary, the risk of remedy failure and consequent additional costs will often remain with industry much longer. This approach also puts more discretionary authority in the very agencies that, from industry's perspective, are already causing too much pain. And from the agency perspective, exercising that discretion necessarily carries enormous responsibility that many regulatory officials want to avoid, if only because of the array of vociferous critics lying in wait in the wings.

But an approach that recognizes significant roles for land use considerations and land use controls just might help stem the overspending that has plagued the Superfund program. This would, of course, benefit everyone. Maybe we could use one-half of the money saved for a much needed, heavily capitalized research and development initiative on realistic remedial technologies. Any such R&D effort also must consider the almost inevitable attendant impacts

associated with favored technologies that will become the next generation's dilemma.

Dethroning consistency and permanence alone will not be
enough to improve the quality of the ARARs debate. As the gas plant
example suggests, resolution at each site of the geographic point at
which ARAR compliance must occur and associated monitoring questions will be critical to the successful incorporation of realistic land
use objectives and institutional controls into ARAR development and
implementation. Equally important is the time frame within which
ARARs must be achieved, particularly if there is uncertainty about a
future funding mechanism should more or different remedial hardware be required. This problem could be ameliorated by a more
realistic view of industry's own permanence.

Also critical to increased reliance on land use constraints and
institutional controls is better understanding and coordination among
the federal and state agencies implementing CERCLA, agencies that
typically have no land use authority, and the local officials who have
land use jurisdiction and the concomitant enforcement power. These
local leaders are often reluctant to shoulder the costs and potential
controversy attendant on exercising their authority in a Superfund
context. Remedial strategies need to respond to these concerns.

Finally, the ARARs debate deserves better science and better risk
analysis than it currently receives. The heart of the problem is that
there is no credible process under the current NCP for correlating
the actual risks at the site with ARARs that address those risks. This
is so because the only risk assessment required or arguably allowed
by the NCP is a "baseline risk assessment" of actual and potential
risk—a function of actual and potential exposure and toxicity—that
assumes that no cleanup activity has occurred or will ever occur at
the site. Thus, as in the gas plant example, the fact that a public water
supply had been installed (at a cost in excess of $6 million) was
deemed irrelevant in delineating the risks that the ARARs were to
address. It also is in this risk assessment process that the EPA seems
almost uniformly compelled to a posit a nursery school or a housing
development as the likely future land use to address the specter of
potential risk. This is so notwithstanding the EPA's ostensible policy
that a *"reasonable* maximum exposure scenario" is to control.

The Need for Site-Specific Data

A related issue is that site-specific analytical data on actual impacts
are generally ignored or severely discounted in developing the ex-

posure scenario, with a disproportionate emphasis on the potential exposures and risks. Thus, for example, at several mining sites, the EPA has refused to consider blood-lead data as evidence of health-related impact on the ground that blood-lead data merely give you a very limited snapshot of impacts instead of an average body loading over time, and conditions could worsen. This position ignores the fact that many of these sites have not seen mining activity in several decades and, as a rule, environmental conditions are either constant or improving with time, such that an epidemiological snapshot of blood lead levels does have considerable value. Instead, the EPA wants to rely on theoretical "cookbook" values of intake, toxicity, and impact. Alternatively, the current vogue is to feed prodigious quantities of lead-laden soil to pigs (albeit, partially in response to industry demands for consideration of contaminant bioavailability) on the theory that a pig's digestive system is like ours and to ignore the epidemiological data altogether.

Neither approach determines whether the actual source of any elevated blood lead is the mining-related material the Agency seeks to clean up at a cost of hundreds of millions of dollars or whether it is existing background levels of metals and/or lead-based paint. There is no room in the reasonable maximum exposure scenario for details such as metals speciation, although the EPA, at least in Region VIII, is relenting a bit on this point.

This inattention to site-specific detail goes further. For example, when there is no applicable regulatory standard for a perceived risk at a site, the EPA develops its own cleanup standard. This most often occurs with soil cleanup levels. Here again, rarely will the EPA consider site-specific data on porosity, leachability, or actual impact (as often is reflected by groundwater data), preferring instead the posited values of the various manuals and models available to address potential exposures and risk over field data and bench-scale analysis. Meanwhile, the fact that oftentimes both the soil and the groundwater underneath are inaccessible as a practical matter, as was shown in the gas plant example, is ignored.

The EPA and the DOJ are under enormous congressional pressure to keep the Superfund program moving and make industry pay—and pay a lot—for it. Introducing additional variability and discretion into site-specific decision making may not always expedite this result. But is this a race to spend money or a hazardous waste cleanup program? One can very much be an advocate for hazardous waste cleanup and still reject many of the existing program's unnecessary components. Cleaning up ARARs is a good place to start.

The Cleanup of Inactive Hazardous Waste

Raul A. Deju and Dean A. Calland

During the past decade, the safe management of toxic and hazardous materials has become a societal issue of tremendous proportions. Although certain members of the environmental bar deal with these issues on a daily basis, many in-house lawyers and outside counsel who have a myriad of other responsibilities increasingly are being asked to advise corporate management on these issues. The cleanup of abandoned hazardous waste sites is one such issue that has already affected virtually every sector of American business.

Our purpose in writing this article is to provide corporate attorneys and management potentially confronted with Superfund liability with a practical and general description of the procedure by which abandoned sites are investigated, characterized, and eventually cleaned up. Because this process involves complex technical and legal decision making, we highlight important technical and legal considerations crucial to implementing a successful, cost-effective remedy. Finally, we draw upon actual experience gained in handling numerous site cleanups in suggesting certain key elements of a proactive corporate strategy for responding to Superfund actions.

Many states have enacted their own legislation addressing the remediation of abandoned hazardous waste sites. However, because of space restrictions and the fact that many state programs are patterned after the federal Superfund program, we focus only on the federal program.

Raul Deju is a vice-president and general manager of Chemical Waste Management, Inc., in Fremont, California. Dean Calland is a partner in Babst, Calland, Clements & Zomnir, P.C., in Pittsburgh, Pennsylvania.

Since the passage of CERCLA in 1980, the EPA has identified many inactive (and active) hazardous waste sites that require immediate attention. These sites are included on the NPL. They all require some form of response to prevent or remedy the release of hazardous substances into the environment. It should be noted that a site need not be listed on the NPL for the EPA to have authority to implement or direct response activities.

Under CERCLA, a Hazardous Substance Response Trust Fund has been established by raising money from taxes on petroleum imports and the production of certain feedstock chemicals, as well as general revenue appropriations. Using this fund, the EPA administers a broad program commonly referred to as Superfund. The Superfund program entails two essential functions carried out by or under the supervision of the EPA. Those functions are removal response and remedial response. Normally, removal response deals primarily with the short-term control measures designed to stabilize an existing or threatened hazard, such as limiting public access to a site or providing alternative drinking water supplies. Remedial response, on the other hand, normally involves the planned long-term correction of existing or potential hazards. It may include the cleanup of existing contamination, as well as long-term monitoring of the environment and institution of procedures to prevent or contain future contamination.

At present, the majority of NPL sites are under some type of investigation by federal, state, local, and/or private parties in an effort to define the actions required to effect a successful remedial response. This process is commonly referred to as a RI/FS.

Investigation of Inactive Hazardous Waste Sites

Inactive hazardous waste sites can be discovered in a variety of ways. Perhaps the two most common ways are through required reporting of the existence of such sites to the EPA and the contamination of water supplies by subsurface contaminants. Under CERCLA, once an inactive hazardous waste site is discovered, the EPA or state personnel investigate the potential threat and assess the extent of any needed emergency response. Upon completion of this preliminary assessment, sites are ranked using a standardized hazard ranking system. This system scores the site based upon direct on-site exposure as well as the ability of contaminants to release from the site via air, surface water, and groundwater exposure pathways. Sites posing serious problems according to the system's scoring methodology are then placed on the NPL and become eligible for subsequent removal action and remedial planning studies. If removal action is deemed necessary, it can be taken before the site is proposed or listed on the NPL and normally will be implemented relatively quickly. Either the EPA or the state may undertake lead regulatory responsibility. The federal government and many state regulatory agencies often contract with private consulting firms to assist them in this responsibility. The actual investigation is generally conducted by private consultants through a contract with the lead agency. However, as discussed later, the PRPs at the site will often develop the remedial action studies for the lead agency in an effort to retain some degree of control over the work performed, the response adopted, and the cost of the investigation.

The Superfund law was reauthorized in 1986 by the enactment of SARA, and a number of changes were made:

1. SARA expresses a preference for permanent and definitive remedial action over a simple transfer of waste from one location to another;
2. SARA addresses and encourages settlements with PRPs, and among these settlement provisions are protections from contribution actions by nonsettlers and the establishment of "cash out" settlements for small or *de minimis* contributors;
3. federal agencies are subject to CERCLA just as nongovernment organizations are (with some administrative and national security exemptions); and
4. public participation in cleanup actions is encouraged by technical assistance grants to citizen groups and by comment opportunities on proposed and final actions.

How a Typical Superfund Case Unfolds

Superfund provides that the following entities are liable for the cost of the removal and remedial actions described above: (1) the owner and operator of the facility, (2) the owner and operator of the site at the time of disposal, (3) any person who arranged for disposal or treatment at the site (i.e., a generator), and (4) any transporter who also selected the site for disposal or treatment. Although there are countless variations on the theme, typically these entities are informed of their potential involvement in the case through receipt of an information request letter from the EPA or the state agency asking them for all documentation in their possession relating to the site under investigation. If a large number of entities are involved, the

PRPs generally meet shortly thereafter to form a steering committee. The steering committee's purpose is to represent the PRPs as a whole, negotiate for the group with the EPA or the state, organize the group effort, and make recommendations for group strategies.

In many cases, responses by the PRPs to the information request letters and the documents already in the government's possession through site records or state records prompt the EPA to issue notice letters to the PRPs. Notice letters typically state that the EPA has determined that removal, remedial action, or both must be taken at the site and offer the PRPs an opportunity to perform the work with EPA oversight. SARA includes a special notice procedure that, if deemed appropriate by the Agency, establishes a sixty-day moratorium so that the PRPs can develop a good faith proposal to undertake the requested work voluntarily. Should no good faith proposal be made, or in other situations where the Agency determines that conditions present an imminent and substantial endangerment to human health, welfare, or the environment, the EPA may use its UAO authority to require specified parties to undertake the work.

Regardless of who undertakes the responsibility for cleanup action, a remedial plan must be developed. The elements of this plan are delineated in the NCP, which is considered to be the blueprint of the Superfund process. As will be discussed in greater detail below, for a private party to recover its costs of response from others, it must substantially comply with the requirements of the plan outlined in the NCP.

Remedial planning generally involves three basic activities: initial planning, the RI, and the FS. The initial planning stage involves preparing a work plan, defining community issues, acquiring needed permits for work conducted off-site, and compiling existing data. After planning has been completed, an RI is conducted. This phase involves a complete technical assessment of the site, including characterizing local geology and hydrology, defining the extent of contamination, assessing the type of contamination, defining contaminant types, and assessing the extent of public health and environmental risk. The investigation of specific site characteristics such as depths to groundwater and bedrock, permeability or water-bearing strata, direction of groundwater flow, precipitation and temperature ranges, soil moisture content, slope characteristics, vegetation, receptor characteristics, and existing land use is an important aspect of this phase in the response process.

Once an RI is completed, the data is used to assess the risk the site poses to the environment and public. Risk assessments historically have been hotly contested because of the many assumptions that must be made in generating "risk numbers." Partly because of disagreements between PRPs and the Agency, since mid-1990, the EPA has taken the position that even when the PRPs have agreed to do the RI/FS, the Agency will do the risk assessment. However, as a result of recent litigation on this policy, the EPA is reconsidering this approach. Even when the EPA does the risk assessment, PRPs usually do their own to double-check the Agency's findings.

Information generated during the RI also is used to define the cost-effective alternative that best suits the site characteristics as defined during the RI. The feasibility study process for identifying the cost-effective remedial alternative goes through a screening step of possible alternatives and technologies followed by a more detailed analysis of the most promising alternatives. The result of the detailed analysis is to identify the cost-effective alternative, i.e., the option that is technologically feasible and reliable and that effectively mitigates and minimizes damage to and provides adequate protection of public health, welfare, or the environment.

If the PRPs come forward to perform the studies and implement the removal or remedial action recommended, their commitment typically is embodied in a consent agreement with the EPA and the relevant state agency. In most large multiparty cases, the cleanup is conducted in phases known as operable units. That is, surface cleanup is negotiated, assessed, and remedied in a separate proceeding evidenced by a separate agreement from matters concerning subsurface and groundwater cleanup.

In light of the general description above, a number of technical and legal considerations should be considered by companies faced with a Superfund action.

Technical Suggestions for an RI/FS

Perhaps the most critical technical issue is the appropriateness of an RI/FS. Because the end result of the RI/FS evaluation is a decision regarding the level of response that is appropriate, this work in large part will determine how much money the PRPs will pay. A review of RI/FS evaluations completed to date reveals that the majority of the problems encountered in defining the appropriate remedial response are the result of inadequate data bases—or, at least, the EPA's opinion that the data bases are inadequate. Often the data are not adequate to determine the extent of soil and groundwater contamination; support a cost estimate; identify possible surrogates of contamination; assess actual threat, potential threat, and impact on future land uses; or develop realistic designs and select viable alternatives. Discussed below are several technical suggestions for improving the quality of RI/FS investigations.

First, in planning an RI, one must keep in mind that the data will be necessary to assess the level of risk posed by the site. To accomplish this, it is useful to assess in a preliminary fashion at the work preparation stage the site conditions, waste characteristics, and likely dominant pathway for contaminant migration. It is also essential to properly define the sampling program requirements, including needed chemical indicators. Data necessary for risk assessment and definition of a cost-effective remedial action must also be included. After a brief review of the site by a qualified engineer, it is advisable to review the likely options for remedial action using an experienced remedial construction contractor. One can then develop a checklist to ensure that a proper decision can be made between those likely options upon completion of the RI/FS.

Second, emphasis should be placed on health and safety before commencing field operations. A comprehensive site safety plan must be put in place and personnel trained before operations begin. Any sampling must be carefully conceived not only to ensure that the samples are representative but to ensure that they are taken in a safe manner. At hazardous waste sites there could be a latent fire, explosion, toxic gas, or chemical spill hazard. Field personnel must be aware of not only the possible hazards but the actions they need to take if these hazards are encountered.

Third, emphasis should be placed on data validation. The sampling and analysis program must be carefully conceived and executed to ensure that the results of the analyses are valid and representative. Statistical techniques should be used to design the sampling program and the program of data validation. Careful analyses by competent chemists are essential to ensure data representativeness.

Fourth, continuing engineering innovation and practicality are needed. Selecting the cost-effective remedial option requires a careful and practical understanding of treatment processes and civil engineering principles. Textbook answers cannot be easily applied in many cases. Many of the remedial options require the combination of a number of technologies. Emphasis must be given to the workability of the technology in the environment where it is to be applied.

Fifth, in developing a work plan for gathering the data needed to characterize a site, the waste source, and the extent of migration, a phased program that minimizes the need for drilled borings and extensive analytical studies on well samples by maximizing the use of geophysical surveys and field chemical screening techniques should be used. Extensive use of field screening is especially appropriate when a limited number of hazardous compounds are found at the site, the components are well defined, and these compounds are measurable by field screening techniques. When boreholes are constructed, care must be exercised during the drilling and testing program so as not to increase the potential for contaminant migration by enhancing the possibility of aquifer cross-contamination.

Finally, in assessing the risk posed by a site, proper consideration must be given to defining the dominant pathways for contaminant migration, the likely contaminants, their concentrations, and the likely contaminant receptors. The greatest risk at most sites is posed by a small universe of chemicals. It is essential to realistically model the migration of the high-risk substances rather than trying to model just the migration of groundwater or the migration of numerous constituents that may not pose the major risk at the site. Site characteristics that enhance or retard the migration of the major contaminants must be properly considered. The threshold levels above which a given chemical constituent is expected to constitute a hazard at a given site must be defined.

Nevertheless, no matter how extensive an RI is, residual uncertainty about site conditions exists. This uncertainty must be accepted, communicated, and dealt with when developing a plan for the site. For example, at one site, some leachate had reached a fractured aquifer system underlying the site. It was clear from the investigation that modeling contaminant flow in this aquifer would be nearly impossible and extremely costly; however, it was also clear early in the planning process that the source of leachate had to be removed from the site. The uncertainty in the feasibility of modeling was accepted, and detailed modeling was not attempted. Instead, a simplified model was used to assess the effect of removing the source on loading contaminants into the aquifer.

Basic Legal Considerations

Superfund actions have a number of unique legal characteristics. Many Superfund cleanups are essentially reluctant voluntary actions in which PRPs decide for the reasons discussed above to conduct the work themselves rather than to allow the government to do so. Consequently, counsel for a PRP must juggle a complex set of interests and strategies, including those of the client or clients, the EPA, the state, local governments, the owner/operator of the site, the other PRPs, unidentified PRPs, the PRP steering committee, environmental groups, and the general public. In the midst of this confusion, counsel must remember that the goal is to extricate your client from liability—or minimize that liability—at the lowest possible cost and to preserve any claims you may have against other PRPs. Included below are a few basic considerations in setting up and implementing a workable strategy.

First, remember that you are faced with an extremely stringent standard of liability. The courts generally agree that Superfund liability is strict, joint, and several where the harm is indivisible, that is, incapable of apportionment. Thus a possibility exists that a PRP could be forced to pay substantially more for cleanup than its volumetric share would otherwise suggest. This possibility is greatly increased at sites where one or more of the major contributors are insolvent or otherwise absent. This potential inequity is even further exacerbated if some parties have already settled with the government and obtained contribution protection.

Second, remember that CERCLA provides a mechanism for a private party to recover the response costs it has incurred, but only as long as those costs were necessary and in substantial compliance with the NCP. In famous cases such as *Amland* and *Channelmaster*, claims for literally millions of dollars in response costs were disallowed by the courts because the plaintiffs did not follow the strict and complicated standards in the NCP. If you were to voluntarily undertake a response action, it is critical to obtain advice from technical and legal experts to guide you through these requirements so that you can maximize your ability to recoup funds expended from other responsible parties.

Third, pay particular attention to the transaction costs associated with Superfund actions. Due to the tremendous costs associated with cleanup of these sites and the potential exposure of even the smallest contributor, these sites often become the focus of a swirl of litigation between and among the EPA, the state, the PRPs, and other intervenors. In a celebrated cleanup case in Ohio, counsel for a PRP has informed the court that the attorney fees in the case alone are likely to far outstrip the possible cost of cleanup at the site. As a result, the use of cost-controlling mechanisms are being employed at many sites. Common counsel, liaison counsel, special masters, nonjudicial dispute resolution mechanisms, PRP agreements, mediators, and outside cost allocation services are being tried with some favorable results.

Fourth, obtain a clear understanding of the facts surrounding the site and your client's alleged involvement. In fact, the explicit directive of Superfund's liability sections has made these cases more like factual contests than legal battles. Command of the facts is critical in establishing the limited defenses available. For example, a complete review of records may indicate that your waste materials were only shipped through the site in question or perhaps the materials were incinerated at the site prior to the dates of concern.

Fifth, realistically assess your status as a contributor to the site. Large contributors to the site should focus on broadening the base of liability. In some cases, the EPA can be persuaded to add new companies to the list of PRPs. However, in light of joint and several liability, the EPA will often pursue only the largest contributors to the site, leaving it to them to initiate contribution actions, third-party actions, and discovery against nonparties. To add insult to injury, the United States will routinely move to stay these third-party claims until its case against the selected few is completed.

Small contributors to the site find Superfund cases particularly troublesome because the transaction costs often seriously outweigh their *pro rata* share. One of the settlement provisions in SARA was designed to address this problem by giving small-volume contributors—known as *de minimis* parties—the opportunity to quickly "cash out" of the site by paying its proportionate share plus a premium. This provision has not been used extensively by the EPA, although there are currently plans to renew this effort. Normally, to the extent that a *de minimis* settlement is available, small generators should make every effort to avail themselves of its advantages.

The proper allocation formula will be a critical issue for both large and small contributors in considering settlement proposals. The major physical factors influencing this determination are the volume, toxicity, fate (e.g., incinerated or neutralized), and the unique properties of the hazardous substances in question.

Finally, carefully consider the nature of the protection provided by the EPA, the state, and the other PRPs in any consent agreement in return for a paid share of liability. As mentioned previously, SARA creates several settlement incentives, such as covenants not to sue from the government, contribution protection from nonsettlers, "mixed funding," etc., that are designed to encourage PRPs to voluntarily clean up sites. Although covenants not to sue are available under the statute, recognize that except for *de minimis* settlements, the EPA and the DOJ are not likely to grant a full release from liability at the site. Any such covenant will only cover liability for the actual work performed and will undoubtedly contain reopener provisions enabling the government to reinstitute legal action in the event of future harm to human health and the environment.

It is also imperative that the government agency or PRP group responsible for undertaking the investigation set up proper lines of communication with interested parties in a manner that allows for information to be credibly disseminated and ideas to be calmly exchanged. Public meetings, information repositories at local libraries, and frequent newsletters have been effectively used at sites where community interest is very high. Communication programs must be set up in a fashion that is responsive to community interests. Again, the NCP sets forth the framework within which community relations should be designed.

The overall goal for a PRP in responding to a Superfund action is to eliminate or minimize liability at the site while successfully restoring the site to an acceptable environmental condition. This goal requires a team effort by trained and experienced individuals who understand the critical issues to be addressed and the proper legal and technical procedures for doing so. In this way, a PRP may be able to minimize liability and at the same time further the ability of the group or the government to restore the site to an acceptable environmental condition.

A Proactive Corporate Strategy for RIs

We have now reviewed the process by which inactive hazardous waste sites are investigated and remedial responses defined. These actions are part of a necessary proactive strategy that a company identified as a PRP or a steering committee representing the PRPs at a Superfund site should develop to deal with the RI and ultimate actions taken at the site. The following ten points constitute the core of the strategy.

1. *Know the site in question.* Every abandoned waste site is unique. The PRP or steering committee must make a diligent effort to gather the pertinent facts available regarding the site. The owner or operator, as well as federal, state and local agencies, may have considerable information available regarding the site. FOIA requests may be helpful in obtaining such information from the government. The RI will provide critical information about the site and develop the data base needed to select and implement the proper response option. For example, cleanup options may be severely limited if the RI shows that the site sits above a specially protected drinking water aquifer. The technical team should ensure that the data gathered will

be both necessary and sufficient to assess the risk currently posed by the site and to select the appropriate remedy.

2. *Recognize the authority of the government.* In dealing with federal and state officials responsible for Superfund actions, one should recognize that CERCLA gives the responsible agencies very broad authority. Negotiations with the government should be conducted with a realistic appreciation of the strength of a PRP's bargaining position. Given the broad scope of liability under Superfund, the minimal causation requirements, the very limited defenses available, the EPA's unilateral order authority, and the high transaction costs, parties should move toward settlement and away from litigation. SARA and more recent EPA policy continue the trend in favor of negotiated—although sometimes still unbalanced—settlements. To position yourself in this regard, those site-specific considerations that serve as incentives for the government to settle should be identified. The EPA has shown a desire to settle when overriding health concerns exist (e.g., when private parties could effect a cleanup much more rapidly than the government), when the government itself is a PRP, or when court action is likely to be protracted and possibly unsuccessful.

3. *Take the initiative.* Every PRP or group of PRPs should assess the risks and benefits of conducting the necessary cleanup steps instead of having the government do so. The EPA readily admits that private parties can study a site and institute cleanup measures much more quickly and cost-effectively than the government. In addition, if the EPA does the work, they will be establishing the record by which you will be judged in court. If the PRPs decide to control the work, they should develop a work plan for the RI with proper technical advice and get agency approval prior to implementation. As the investigations are carried out, keep the agencies informed of major findings. Upon completion of the RI/FS, be ready to recommend a complete remedial program to the responsible agency. If the work is done pursuant to a consent agreement with the government, these various steps will be prescribed in advance. During each step, keep the requirements of the NCP firmly in mind.

4. *Retain control of critical decisions.* Perhaps the most critical issue in Superfund cleanups is the appropriate level of cleanup that will ensure the protection of human health and the environment, commonly referred to as the "how clean is clean" issue. The difference between whether a certain area will be cleaned to 50 ppm or 1 ppm of a particular pollutant can be a multimillion dollar issue. Negotiators must reach agreement with the government as to how

clean is clean at the particular site. The level of cleanliness to be achieved at a site is a function of, *inter alia*, relevant federal public health or environmental standards, technical feasibility, adverse consequences of alternative remedial actions, pertinent public concerns, and cost. In an effort to resolve the "how clean is clean" question, SARA requires that the cleanup achieve ARARs or applicable or relevant and appropriate federal and state standards. At a given site, it may be impossible to select a remedy that totally prevents migration or restores the site to its original uncontaminated condition. Remember that your knowledge is as good as the EPA's in this area of scientific uncertainty. Highly qualified consultants may be retained who have as much or more experience in these areas than anyone in the government. However, it should be recognized that in the battle of the experts in court, the EPA will normally receive a presumption of correctness on technical matters.

   5. *Do not lose sight of your client's interests amidst the confusion.* Celebrated Superfund cases such as *Seymour, ChemDyne,* and *Ludlow,* in which hundreds of parties with diverse interests are involved, illustrate that cleanup actions at large sites can become procedural nightmares. More and more often, courts are issuing case management orders that can significantly affect the parties' ability to prepare their cases. It is imperative that your specific goals are kept in mind in the midst of this confusion. For example, representation on steering committees, technical groups, and allocation committees should be determined in proportion to involvement at the site. If actual representation is not warranted, maintain close contact with at least one member of the committee so that information can be relayed quickly and accurately. Take advantage of the use of common or liaison counsel where warranted to cut transaction costs. Carefully monitor court rulings on the rights of individual counsel to safeguard your client's rights to make its own case.

   6. *Carefully plan your technical strategy.* To convince the EPA or the state that a private party's plan should be accepted, one must use technical expertise that is respected by the government. Technical resources must be capable of identifying the appropriate and cost-effective response, as well as the unique site characteristics that affect the final decision. For example, at a very isolated site considerably above the water table, an on-site alternative may be acceptable, while at a populated area in the flood plain removal may be necessary. Given those considerations, your technical support personnel can in the former case orient their efforts toward on-site containment and in the latter toward defining the necessary level of removal.

7. *Know your negotiators*. In dealing with Superfund regulators you should attempt to understand their priorities. Understand that these agencies have special concerns, desires, and timetables because of political pressures, consistency restrictions, and public concerns. Appreciate the intangibles associated with negotiating an agreement from the government's perspective. Obtain sufficient advice in the negotiations, and try to keep your side of the negotiating team stable through what can be a long and protracted process.

8. *Understand applicable requirements*. The Superfund statutory and regulatory framework is quite complex and rapidly changing. Many of the government's positions appear only in guidance form and are subject to change. Furthermore, large numbers of cases are moving through the district courts to the courts of appeals and continually set new precedents for the program. A myriad of environmental laws at the federal and state level can alter your strategy at a site. A PRP or steering committee must keep abreast of the technical and legal impacts of applicable regulatory and legislative changes.

9. *Assess short-term financial commitments versus long-term liabilities*. As a result of an RI/FS, the cost-effective remedial solution will be defined. In selecting an option for implementation, each PRP should consider long-term liability for the proposed response, e.g., if you remove the waste to another site, what guarantee do you have that the new site will not be a Superfund site five years from now? Long-term operations and maintenance costs associated with the remedial response should be carefully defined. The waste management hierarchy needs to be factored into the solution. The reputation and balance sheet of any remedial contractor and any disposal site used in remediation constitute an important consideration for any PRPs.

10. *Be credible with the EPA and the public*. Superfund cleanups cannot be conducted in a vacuum. The RI/FS process, for example, involves not only a technical decision but also a societal decision. The PRPs are interested and involved because they will likely be paying for the remedial action. Neighboring residents and businesses in the area are generally interested because they perceive an abandoned hazardous waste site as a major health threat and as something that negatively affects their property values. State and federal government officials are involved as representatives of the public interest. Members of the media are interested in the work insofar as they are responsible for keeping their readership informed. In such a fishbowl, it is imperative that PRPs and their technical and legal personnel be extremely competent, conscientious, and innovative in their approaches to these difficult issues.

The Role of the Courts in Superfund Cases

James T. Price

On August 9, 1990, Judge Layne Phillips issued a dramatic ruling in *United States v. Royal N. Hardage*, 750 F. Supp. 1460 (W.D. Okla. 1990). After a lengthy trial, which itself had followed years of civil discovery on remedy-related issues, Judge Phillips rejected the government's remedy in favor of one proposed by a group of PRPs liable to remedy the contamination at the Hardage toxic waste site near Criner, Oklahoma.

The government, which had the most to lose from this ruling, yawned. At public meetings and seminars, government lawyers downplayed its significance. *Hardage*, the government argued, was a dinosaur, a relic from the days when the Superfund program was in its infancy and the government routinely filed actions for injunctions under CERCLA section 106 asking courts to enjoin PRPs to clean up waste sites. The government filed those cases without having selected a remedy. Most courts viewed their own role as one of selecting the appropriate remedy after a *de novo* factual hearing.

No longer, the government asserted, was it routinely filing actions in court except to enforce its orders and collect reimbursement of its expenses. In both types of cases, court filings would occur well after the government had selected the site remedy. In *Hardage*, the government did not even appeal Judge Phillips's decision.

The lengthy remedy trial in *Hardage*—and the PRPs' success there—provides a contrast to the government's and the courts' current

James Price is a partner in the firm of Spencer Fane Britt & Browne in Kansas City, Missouri.

methods of handling Superfund cases and illustrates the changing roles of courts in such matters. Instead of filing lawsuits under section 106 before the government selects a preferred remedy, as had been the case in *Hardage*, the government now routinely follows one of two approaches. First, the government can use the special notice procedures of CERCLA section 122(e), giving the PRPs a limited time (typically sixty days) in which to sign a consent agreement to undertake the work the EPA wants at a site. If the PRPs refuse, the EPA retains its own contractors to do the work and charges the PRPs for the costs pursuant to CERCLA section 107. Second, the government can determine the work to be done and, pursuant to CERCLA section 106, issue an administrative order to the PRPs to perform that work. As a result of these procedures, for more than five years courts have been cutting back on their roles of finding facts and determining appropriate remedies, especially in disputes between the government and PRPs.

This article discusses these changing roles for courts in Superfund cases and the effect these changes have on PRPs facing Superfund claims. It also identifies several areas in which courts remain very involved in resolving Superfund disputes.

Defining Liability

Despite these changes, hundreds of cases are brought annually before courts under CERCLA. When they are, courts perform the critical function of defining the parameters of CERCLA liability. Commonly, these are cost recovery actions brought by the government or by private parties. In such cases, it is not unusual for the plaintiffs to push the envelope of CERCLA liability to the bounds of decided cases and beyond. This gives courts plenty of opportunities to define the outer limits of CERCLA liability by deciding who is liable to whom and for how much.

Some examples illustrate the types of issues courts now are addressing and will continue to address during the 1990s. In *Pennsylvania v. Union Gas Co.*, 491 U.S. 1 (1989), the court held that states are not immune from claims by private parties for CERCLA liability. This decision undoubtedly will lead to more CERCLA claims against states and cities and their agents asserting a variety of theories. In *United States v. Fleet Factors Corp.*, 901 F.2d 1550 (11th Cir. 1990), the court created an uproar in the lending community when it held that a secured lender could be held liable under section 107, even if it was not an actual operator, if it had the ability to influence the borrower's hazardous waste disposal decisions. In *3550 Stevens Creek Associates v. Barclays Bank of California*, 915 F.2d 1355 (9th Cir. 1990), the court held that the removal of asbestos from a commercial office building did not pose the type of problem that CERCLA was designed to address, and the court held that the owner of the building did not have a claim under CERCLA to recover the costs of its removal.

Other debates rage about liability for what has come to be called "municipal waste"; whether chemical manufacturers can be held liable for contamination caused by a product into which their chemical is incorporated during manufacture by an unrelated entity; when an "innocent purchaser" of property has conducted sufficient inquiry to escape CERCLA's landowner liability scheme; when, where, and under what circumstances one targeted PRP can bring a claim against another PRP and for what costs; when parent corporations can be held liable for the waste disposal practices of their subsidiaries; when one corporation will be deemed to have succeeded to the CERCLA liabilities of an earlier corporation; when a shareholder or a corporate officer will be held individually liable for the corporation's hazardous waste disposal acts; etc. There even are debates about whether state or federal law determine the outcomes of some of these questions.

These decisions and others like them make clear that despite the wide range of Superfund litigation in recent years, many issues remain unsettled. Even for the issues that seemingly are settled, many of the rulings of this type are destined to create in subsequent cases factual issues that will have to be resolved following trials. In *United States v. Kayser-Roth Corp., Inc.*, 910 F.2d 24 (1st Cir. 1990), the court held a parent corporation liable for cleanup costs caused by the operations of a dissolved subsidiary. The court based its ruling on the parent's involvement in and control over the activities of the subsidiary. Similarly, in *Fleet Factors,* the court held that a lender would be liable if the lender participated in the financial management of the borrower and had the ability to influence the borrower's handling of hazardous waste. Thus, under the analyses of *Kayser-Roth* and *Fleet Factors*, a separate company's control or ability to control the waste disposal activities of another would be one of the linchpins upon which liability would rest. These would require factual reviews by courts called upon to apply these principles in later cases.

Courts during the next decade will continue ruling upon questions such as these, questions that will help establish the outer bounds of liability. In the process, they will define for PRPs circumstances in which litigation is appropriate or, conversely, settlements are prudent.

A Review of Response Actions

The courts' exit from the roles of finding facts and selecting remedies largely is the result of CERCLA section 113(j), passed as part of the 1986 SARA amendments. Under this section, judicial review of the government's response measures is limited to the administrative record. The objecting party must demonstrate that on that record the government's decision was arbitrary and capricious. Moreover, under CERCLA section 113(h), challenges to the government's response action may not be heard until the government files suit to enforce an administrative order or to recover its costs. These provisions, courts have held, in most instances bar a *de novo* trial of the appropriate remedy and preclude any review of the government's selected remedy until the government seeks to enforce a claim.

PRPs complain bitterly about these restrictions. The limitation on the scope of review appears to encourage courts to grant extraordinary deference to the Agency's selected remedy, resulting in scarcely a second look at those remedies. PRPs worry that courts will be led to overlook remedy selection errors such as those that caused Judge Phillips to reject the government's remedy in *Hardage*. Moreover, the limitations on the timing of judicial review means that very, very few cases receive even that reduced amount of remedy review. The pressures to settle that exist in most of these cases usually lead PRPs to agree to perform the government's selected remedy. Thus even a flawed remedy gets implemented with scarcely any review by the court.

Significantly, decisions such as *United States v. Ottati and Goss, Inc.*, 900 F.2d 429 (1st Cir. 1990), and *United States v. Hardage*, 663 F. Supp. 1280 (W.D. Okla. 1987), have held that the limitation of judicial review to the administrative record does not apply in a judicial proceeding for injunctive relief under section 106. Each of those cases involved extensive trials concerning the appropriate remedy, and substantial portions of the government's remedies were rejected. While the government no longer routinely files actions for injunctive relief under section 106 where it has not already selected a remedy, the possibility remains in certain circumstances that courts will conduct *de novo* reviews of the government's remedy selection.

Procedural Reviews

With the limitations on the courts' review of remedies and costs, courts increasingly will be involved in disputes about whether procedural requirements, including those of the NCP, were followed and what evidence may be allowed to establish consistency with the NCP. In *United States v. Wastecontrol of Florida, Inc.*, 730 F. Supp. 401 (M.D. Fla. 1990), the court denied the defendant's motion to supplement the EPA's administrative record. In *United States v. Charles George Trucking Co.*, 31 Env't Rep. Cas. (BNA) 1512 (D. Mass. 1990), the court remanded the matter to the EPA for further development of the administrative record in light of remedy alternatives submitted by the defendants and others. In *General Electric Co. v. Litton Industrial Automation Systems, Inc.*, 920 F.2d 1415 (8th Cir. 1990), the court held that the plaintiff's cleanup of property previously owned by the defendant was a removal action rather than a remedial action and that, as such, was consistent with the NCP.

In *County Line Investment Co. v. Tinney*, 33 Env't Rep. Cas. (BNA) 1081 (10th Cir. 1991), the court held the site owners could not recover their site cleanup costs because they had failed to allow public comment on the cleanup plan. The court held they had failed to comply with the NCP.

While the EPA has attempted to minimize the obstacles imposed by the NCP consistency requirement by requiring "substantial compliance" and a "CERCLA-quality cleanup," courts likely will have to address these issues in several cases to delineate for PRPs how those general, abstract standards will be applied in specific and often complex factual situations.

Cost Recovery Cases

Many decisions defining the contours of Superfund liability are issued in cost recovery cases under CERCLA section 107(a). Such claims may be brought by either the government or private parties seeking to recover their costs.

Under CERCLA section 113(g), cost recovery claims must be brought within three years after the conclusion of a removal action at a site. A longer period applies to remedial actions. The three-year limitations period has run or is close to running at many sites. Given the government's commitment to seek full reimbursement of its costs from viable PRPs at all sites, filings of government cost recovery claims are expected to escalate.

As a group, cost recovery cases have gone well for the government. A number of cases have applied CERCLA to limit review of the government's remedy selection and costs in such cases. If this trend continues, it does not appear that even the filing of these cases will restore to prominence the courts' role as arbiters of factual disputes.

Given the government's successes in cost recovery litigation, the issues have tended to be narrow and legal rather than factual. Citing the limitations imposed by section 113(j), most courts have held that the review of the government's selected remedy is limited to the administrative record, and the remedy may be rejected only if the selected remedy is arbitrary and capricious. Indeed, in *Hardage,* the court held that the government's costs for developing a remedy the court ultimately *rejected* were chargeable to the PRPs as response costs recoverable under CERCLA section 107. This ruling is one of several in that proceeding being appealed by the PRPs.

Because of the long odds against success, many PRPs attempt to settle quickly such government cost recovery claims. When they do not, typically it is because they believe they are not liable as a matter of law. Thus, in *United States v. Aceto Agricultural Chemical Co.,* 872 F.2d 1173 (8th Cir. 1989), the PRPs litigated in a government cost recovery claim the question whether pesticide manufacturers could be held liable for the costs of cleaning up the processing facility of a separate corporation to which the manufacturers had sent their products for final refining and formulation. In *O'Neil v. Picillo,* 883 F.2d 176 (1st Cir. 1989), a group of *de minimis* PRPs litigated the question of whether they could be held jointly and severally liable for the entire unfunded share of response costs at a site to which they contended their contributions were minimal and divisible. In each of these cases, the courts held the PRPs liable, further expanding the bounds of CERCLA liability.

Private Cost Recovery Cases

Private cost recovery claims also continue to provide fertile ground for litigation. These lawsuits often require courts to allocate liability between two or more PRPs when they are unable to come to agreement among themselves. This trend will continue as more liable PRPs bring contribution claims against nonparticipating PRPs to help spread the response costs.

This is one area of Superfund litigation in which courts continue to play a pivotal role in making factual findings. CERCLA section 113(f) provides that contribution allocations shall be determined by the court on the basis of "such equitable factors as the court determines are appropriate." In rulings such as *Amoco Oil Co. v. Borden, Inc.,* 889 F.2d 664 (5th Cir. 1989), courts have held that various factors may be considered in determining each party's equitable share, including the amounts of hazardous substances contributed by the parties, the toxicity of the materials contributed by each party, and the degrees of involvement, care, and cooperation by each party. These factors will require factual review and, in some cases, prolonged trials in private cost recovery cases.

Private cost recovery cases also often present issues concerning the types of costs that one PRP can recover from another under CERCLA. In *General Electric v. Litton*, 920 F.2d 1415, the court held that a private party's reasonable attorney fees are recoverable as response costs against another PRP. Several courts have been called upon to address whether medical monitoring costs are recoverable as CERCLA response costs, reaching varying conclusions.

Private cost recovery cases appear more likely than government cost recovery cases to present significant disputes about whether the response costs have been incurred consistently with the NCP, a prerequisite for cost recovery under section 107(a). In the private cost recovery arena, when such disputes are substantial, they may lead to a trial. In *General Electric v. Litton,* the district court had held a trial to determine that the plaintiff's cleanup of property previously owned by the defendant was a removal action rather than a remedial action and that, accordingly, the response actions were consistent with the NCP.

Private cost litigation also frequently involves difficult factual and legal questions of contracting intent as increasing numbers of cost recovery cases are brought as a result of property transactions. As more contracts address cleanup issues, courts will be called upon to address the role of Superfund versus contractual intent in allocating liability among the contracting parties.

The Use of Summary Judgment

Although there are many types of Superfund cases that might lend themselves to detailed factual inquiries, courts regularly use summary judgment to rule without trial in those cases in which the facts are not truly in dispute and the principal issue is the application of law to the facts. In *Amoco v. Borden*, 889 F.2d 664, 667–68, the court stated that summary judgment provides an appropriate approach to CERCLA cases. CERCLA cases can be bifurcated so that summary judgment can be entered on certain issues, such as liability, while other issues remain for trial. This approach of bifurcating Superfund cases and issuing summary judgment on certain issues—especially liability—has been adopted in a number of cases, including *Borden*.

This willingness of courts to issue summary judgment on certain issues in CERCLA cases represents both an opportunity and a potential disadvantage for the private Superfund litigant. For the private cost recovery plaintiff, summary judgment in the liability phase of a case issued relatively early can be a powerful weapon that promotes settlement of other issues such as allocation. For cost recovery defendants, however, it increases the pressure to quickly conduct any discovery they believe is necessary to absolve them of liability. In *United States v. Consolidated Rail Corp.*, 729 F. Supp. 1461 (D. Del. 1990), the court held that an affidavit made on information and belief is not sufficient to rebut a summary judgment motion. This is consistent with recent U.S. Supreme Court pronouncements on the subject.

In government cost recovery cases, courts have been willing to go so far as to allow the government to present its entire response cost claim by affidavits and summary statements and thereby preclude lengthy trials over the government's costs. This procedure was employed in *United States v. Bell Petroleum Services, Inc.*, 734 F. Supp. 771 (W.D. Tex. 1990), and in *Hardage*, 733 F. Supp. 1424 (W.D. Okla. 1989). While this type of procedure may promote judicial efficiency, it appears likely to invite abuse when carried to the extremes the government has been willing to go—with the blessing of some courts. The cost recovery plaintiff, after all, is the one that controls its own damages information. It is not unfair to require such a plaintiff, whether private or governmental, to present appropriate documentation of its costs and foundation information so that an impartial fact finder can assess whether the costs claimed are appropriate for recovery. Judges unwilling to hear detailed accounting and cost information themselves have the authority to refer the matter to a magistrate or, under Federal Rule of Civil Procedure 53, to a special master. Special masters often are used to hear such detailed accounting and damages evidence outside the environmental context, and their use for such purposes specifically is mentioned in Rule 53(b). Such a procedure would seem preferable to the short shrift most PRPs fear they receive when the government's cost claim is presented in severely redacted and summarized form in a summary judgment motion alone.

Enforcing Administrative Orders and Rights of Access

The EPA increasingly is relying upon its administrative order authority under CERCLA section 106 to require PRPs to clean up sites. When PRPs do not comply with those orders, the EPA can file an action in court under CERCLA section 106 to enforce them with substantial penalties. As the EPA relies more heavily upon administrative orders to require cleanups, courts increasingly will be called upon to address situations in which the respondents fail to comply. Among other issues, courts will define "sufficient cause" for noncompliance under section 106.

Moreover, as the EPA attempts to collect stipulated penalties in some cases pursuant to consent decrees with PRPs, contentious litigation may ensue to determine whether penalties are appropriate in given cases. Many of those disputes will be determined in the administrative arena pursuant to dispute resolution provisions in such decrees.

Courts also are being called upon to enforce EPA orders for access under CERCLA section 104(e). Courts have granted access for a number of activities, including investigation, sampling, and remediation. Courts have held that once the government establishes there is a release or a threat of release of a hazardous substance upon property, the court must uphold the EPA's demand unless it is arbitrary and capricious. Landowners who believe their property rights are infringed by the EPA's access can pursue a claim in the claims court.

Courts have not, however, given the government unlimited access to private property. In *In re Bunker Hill Mining & Smelter Complex*, 728 F. Supp. 626 (D. Idaho 1990), the court quashed a portion of an administrative warrant granted to the EPA. The court held that the warrant was overly broad and sought documents beyond those the facility was required to keep by regulation. The court held that the facility—not the EPA—would search for the responsive documents.

The Review of Consent Decrees and Settlements

CERCLA consent decrees are entered in U.S. district courts, where they must be approved. The test generally applied by courts in reviewing these consent decrees is whether the settlement was fair, reasonable, and lawful. Courts rarely have disapproved proposed settlements, although they regularly conduct hearings before approval. During these reviews, courts have considered the volumetric contributions of the settling parties as well as the toxicity of the wastes they contributed to a site, the estimated total response costs, the proportion of those total costs being paid by the settling parties, the premiums, if any, being charged to settlers, and other similar factors.

In several cases, including *United States v. Cannons Engineering Corp.*, 899 F.2d 79 (1st Cir. 1990), courts have approved the government's decision to use a series of escalating settlement proposals that reward PRPs that settle sooner rather than later. Courts such as *Cannons* also have reviewed the negotiating process and have rejected nonsettling PRPs' objections to the process.

In some instances, courts have refused to enter consent decrees, generally where the court found the consent decree failed to meet the requirements of CERCLA sections 121 and 122. In *In re Storage Technology Corp.*, No. 89–2–1322 (D. Colo.), the court allowed discovery into the proposed settlement and its alleged deficiencies in comparison to CERCLA's requirements.

Thus we can see that in the past five years the courts' role in Superfund cases has moved from one of factual adjudication and remedy selection to one more closely associated with administrative review and judicial oversight. This trend will continue as the government proceeds with its practice of selecting site remedies in an administrative procedure that is subject to judicial review under administrative law restrictions.

Despite this trend, courts will perform a critical function in deciding the parameters of CERCLA liability and in conducting full factual reviews in at least certain types of cases. In the other cases, a danger exists that courts, under the guise of deference to administrative and perceived technical expertise, essentially will abdicate their role as the final arbiters of the appropriateness of the government's site activities and remedies. Courts that have carefully considered such matters in several instances have found the government's actions lacking. PRPs must advocate forcefully the notion that even where judicial review is restricted by administrative law principles, courts must take a close look to ensure that the government does not exceed its authority and implement a flawed remedy.

The Economic Valuation of Injury to Natural Resources

Thomas A. Campbell

CERCLA, 42 U.S.C. §§ 9601–75, also known as Superfund, has often been hailed as a milestone in legislative environmental protection. Its passage in 1980, along with the 1986 amendments codified in SARA, represent a commitment to both cleanup of contaminated natural resources, 42 U.S.C. 9604(1980), and restoration of injured natural resources where warranted. 42 U.S.C. 9607(f)(1980). The concept of cleanup has become well understood while the concept of environmental restoration has proven elusive.

In the past two years, however, the executive branch has begun to give effect to the restoration aspects of the Superfund legislation and related statutes such as the Clean Water Act, 33 U.S.C. §§ 1251–1387, and the Marine Protection, Research, and Sanctuaries Act, 16 U.S.C. §§ 1431–45. This has occurred through a steady progression of litigation and negotiation. In the past two years, restoration settlements have been reached for injury to natural resources that total approximately $50 million.[1]

The implementation of the restoration provisions of the three acts mentioned above also establishes a demarcation line in the development of how our society values natural resources. The intent of Congress to provide for the restoration of natural resources evidences a realization of the potential for their diminution. This realization developed slowly in this country, which has always been blessed with an abundance of natural resources.

Thomas Campbell is general counsel of the National Oceanic and Atmospheric Administration of the Department of Commerce.

The Evolution of Resources Law:
A Historical Background

Just as man learned to crawl before he walked, society first had to decide to protect natural resources before it began to value the cost associated with their loss. The evolution into this environmentally sensitive phase has resulted in the development of a body of complex law, lengthy litigation, and the controversial valuation of the environment.

Since the beginning of our nation's jurisprudence, or at least from the beginning of Property Law 101, natural resources have been mainly characterized as *ferae naturae*—a thing of wild or natural disposition that only became owned when reduced to possession. As generations of law students can attest, the pursuit of the eighteenth-century fox was not enough to gain ownership. However, neither was it necessary to have actual manual possession of the "wild and noxious beast." It was sufficient to mortally wound such a beast, so that possession became inevitable. *Pierson v. Post*, 3 Caines 175 (Supreme Court of N.Y. 1805). In addition, the fox was referred to as "a pirate," "ruthless," and "cunning," and its death was seen as a benefit to society.

From the fox's point of view, ownership was immaterial because the result was the same. However, as owned property, the fox fell into a legal and economic framework through which value could be assigned. The message sent to Lodowick Post and to the rest of the population was that there was a wild continent there for the taking. The message also said that, in its natural state, the continent's resources were without value and that a growing nation would give its rewards to those strong and bold enough to take possession and hold them. This simple concept fueled Manifest Destiny and motivated the pioneers to endure great hardship in settling the nation. In today's more enlightened society, this attitude toward natural resources may seem wasteful, but it is likely that *Pierson v. Post* is an accurate representation of our frontier fathers' frame of reference. This attitude also is evidenced by the passage of many statutes, including the Homestead Act, ch. 75, 12 Stat. 392 (1862), the Mining Act of 1866, ch. 262, 14 Stat. 265 (1866), and the Mining Law of 1872, ch. 152, 17 Stat. 91 (1872), which are based upon the *pedis possessio* tenet—a foothold or an actual possession.

But the principles that tamed a continent, if continued, could now destroy it. The traditional rules of law and economics that failed to adequately value unpossessed resources are flawed today. As natural resources became more scarce, the extent of the flaw became more apparent. A developing nation needed industrial capacity. It needed pulp mills, tanneries, chemical plants, and refineries. But these types of activities had negative impacts on our natural resource base that can be exemplified by Mr. Post's fox. If the fox is not possessed, it cannot be owned. If the fox is not owned, there can be no recovery for its destruction. Finally, if a claim cannot be pursued, there can be no recovery, and the wild fox can be destroyed indiscriminately. The fox in the wild had to be owned to provide a claim and valued to reflect the importance that society now placed on what had previously been considered a noxious beast.

The Modern Approach

Governments thus evolved into caretakers, or trustees, of natural resources to ensure their continued existence. This evolution has continued and led to the passage of environmental protection laws such as those mentioned above. This family of statutes clearly reflects society's developing cognizance that the destruction of natural resources results in a cost to society, a cost that society is no longer willing to absorb. Implementing these statutes results in what economists refer to as the internalization of externalities. In other words, *the polluter pays* for the degradation of the environment that results from its activities. Previously, we failed to value natural resources that were not possessed. In essence, society subsidized our industrial development by not requiring companies to pay for the destructive environmental consequences resulting from their activities. This subsidy occurred as a natural response to law, and the law developed as a response to the priorities of the times.

CERCLA and SARA represent far more than Congress's desire to provide for a strict liability scheme to assure the cleanup of actual or threatened releases of hazardous substances. 42 U.S.C. § 9607(a)(1980). Language of the act provides for the recovery of "damages for injury to, destruction of, or loss of natural resources, including the reasonable costs of assessing such injury . . .," *id.* § 9607(a)(4)(c)(1980), and specifically authorizes representatives of the federal government, states, and Indian tribes to pursue damages for injuries to natural resources, *id.* § 9607(f)(1980). Had Congress been solely concerned with the safety and welfare of the human population, it could have stopped with the creation of the response and enforcement authority of the federal and state agencies. But Congress went further and authorized the use of these agencies to act as trustees for the environment. As trustees, these agencies are responsible to see that PRPs are held accountable for the injury, destruction, or loss of natural resources due to releases of hazardous substances. Society must be fully compensated for injury or loss of natural resources. It is not enough merely to remove or stabilize the hazardous substances. Efforts must be undertaken to restore, replace, or acquire equivalent resources. *Id.* § 9607(f)(1)(1980). Removal or stabilization alone may not suffice because this may leave a sterile environment that may never regain its ecological niche through natural recovery.

The fallout and subsequent litigation from CERCLA and SARA has produced two cousin concepts, namely, that the protection and restoration of the environment are now costs of doing business, and resources must be valued to ensure their complete protection and restoration. As lawyers and litigators, many in our profession had a basic understanding of what was needed to demonstrate the actual injury and/or the loss of a natural resource. However, the need to value that injury has resulted in the shotgun wedding between lawyers and economists. In its simplest terms, if the trustees cannot establish a value for the resource, there is likely to be no recovery of damages for the injury to that resource. Those who cry that the beauty of a beach or marshland is priceless and cannot be valued in crass economic terms may very will be left holding the proverbial bag, since judges and juries are not likely to award damages based upon an undefined or unsubstantiated claim.

With apologies to my natural resource economist colleagues who may read this article, in its simplest form, valuation of damages for injuries to natural resources is based upon a two-part scheme: (1) the costs of restoration, replacement, or acquiring the equivalent of the affected resource; and (2) the determination of lost use and nonuse values of the natural resource from the time of injury until restoration. For the purposes of this article, lost use and nonuse values include such values as existence and intrinsic values.

Such values are established through a variety of methodologies, including (1) restoration and replacement costs, where restoration and/or replacement costs of injured or destroyed resources are determined; (2) market valuation, where the market price, if available, of the affected resource is determined; (3) behavioral use valuation, using methodologies including travel cost and hedonic valuation; and (4) contingent valuation, using a survey technique to derive the value humans place upon a natural resource. For a detailed description and explanation of damages and economic methodologies, see Cross, "Natural Resource Damage Valuation," 42 *Vand. L. Rev.* 269 (Mar. 1989).

The Evolution in Case Law

While it is not the purpose of this article to pontificate upon the evolution of the natural resource trustees since CERCLA, a brief history might prove valuable. The trustees were authorized by CERCLA to pursue recoveries from PRPs, yet efforts were sluggish due to a dearth of knowledge, experience, and financial resources to prepare an assessment claim. To assist in this effort, Congress required the promulgation of regulations to provide guidance to natural resource trustees on how to determine the adverse effect of hazardous substances and oil upon natural resources—and on how to attach a monetary value as compensation for that adverse effect. Through Executive Order 12,316, 48 Fed. Reg. 42,237 (Aug. 14, 1983), as superseded by Executive Order 12,580, 52 Fed. Reg. 2923 (Jan. 29, 1987), the DOI was delegated the task of drafting regulations and promulgated two types of procedures in 1986 and 1987. *See* 43 C.F.R. Part 11.

In addition to a significant amount of scientific and biological information on how to determine the extent of injury to an organism or species, the DOI procedures provide the most comprehensive standard guidance to the trustees on placing a value in relation to that injury. Not surprisingly, the valuation of natural resources was, and continues to be, a "hot" topic of controversy. This valuation process became a target of litigation in *Ohio v. U.S. Department of the Interior*, 880 F.2d 432 (D.C. Cir. 1989), and *Colorado v. U.S. Department of the Interior*, 880 F.2d 481 (D.C. Cir. 1989). Based largely upon a common-law argument, DOI promoted the concept that the measure of damages should be the lesser of the diminution of market value or the cost of restoration or replacement. *See* 51 Fed. Reg. 27,690 (Aug. 1, 1986).

The court ruled otherwise, on a practical and statutory interpretation basis:

> Although our resolution of the dispute [use of "lesser of" rule] submerges us in the minutiae of CERCLA text and legislative materials, we initially stress the enormous practical significance of the "lesser of" rule. A hypothetical example will illustrate the point: imagine a hazardous substance spill that *kills a rookery of fur seals* and destroys a habitat for seabirds at a sea life reserve. The lost use value of the seals and seabird habitat would be measured by the market value of the fur seals' pelts (which would be approximately $15 each) plus the selling

price per acre of land comparable in value to that on which the spoiled bird habitat was located. Even if, as likely, that use value turns out to be far less than the cost of restoring the rookery and seabird habitat, it would nonetheless be the only measure of damages eligible for the presumption of recoverability under the Interior rule. After examining the language and purpose of CERCLA, as well as its legislative history, we conclude that Interior's "lesser of" rule is directly contrary to the expressed intent of Congress.

Ohio v. Interior, 880 F.2d at 442. In addition, the court indicated that trustees should be able to sum up all reliably calculated use and nonuse values and not be limited to a hierarchy of use values hinging upon market value. *Id.* at 464.

The DOI rules had failed to make the transition from the traditional concept that the fox could only be valued when reduced to possession, as in the court's example, in the form of a pelt. The court, however, made the transition and required that the value of the fox to the public be measured with regard to the existence of the fox in the wild. In its court-required revisions to the rule, the DOI has proposed that trustees are able to recover the costs of restoration, rehabilitation, replacement, and/or acquisition of equivalent resources and the value of the services lost to the public during the recovery period. *See* 56 Fed. Reg. 19,756 (Apr. 29, 1991). The DOI also introduced the term "compensable value" to "encompass all of the public economic values associated with an injured resource, including use values and nonuse values such as option, existence, and bequest values." *Id.* at 19,760. In explanation, DOI stated:

> The concept of compensable value allows for many different reasons why the public may value natural resources—including reasons not represented by market prices. For example, some individuals might be willing to pay to avoid an injury to a favorite recreation area. Others may be willing to pay to avoid the loss associated with knowing wildlife were injured, even thought they will never visit the injured area. . . . The term compensable value incorporates a wide spectrum of values, and is intended to address the court's ruling that option and existence values may be included as a part of damages.

Id.

After *Ohio*, conditions were ripe for an increased focus on natural resources and the development of methods to value injury and destruction of these resources to society. However, the catalyst that focused attention on natural resources was the discharge of approximately eleven million gallons of oil from the *Exxon Valdez* into Alaska's Prince William Sound. This environmental disaster demanded tremendous public, governmental, and legal resources. Worldwide attention was focused on the effect of a pollutant upon the ecosystem and the subsequent injury to natural resources. Never before had so much attention been focused on the destruction of natural resources that no one of us possesses but that we all jointly hold. After three field sessions, the costs for the state and federal trustees conducting the natural resource damages assessment, including federal economic studies, are approximately $108 million.

Further evidence of the recognition of society of the importance of recouping the full value of natural resources is the passage of the Oil Pollution Act of 1990, 33 U.S.C. §§ 2701–61. Even though Congress authorized trustees to recover for injuries due to a discharge of oil under the Clean Water Act, through the 1990 Act Congress clearly established an independent scheme establishing liability for injuries to natural resources to include damages for injury to, destruction of, loss of, or loss of use of natural resources, including the reasonable costs of assessing the damage, which shall be recoverable by a U.S. trustee, a state trustee, an Indian tribe trustee, or a foreign trustee. *Id.* § 1002(b)(2)(A). In addition, that Act provides that the measure of damages for natural resources is the cost of restoring, rehabilitating, replacing, or acquiring the equivalent of the damaged natural resources, plus the diminution in value of those natural resources pending restoration, plus the reasonable cost of assessing those damages. *Id.* § 1006(d). To assist the trustees in conducting assessments, Congress authorized a portion of the Oil Spill Liability Trust Fund to be available to the trustees to initiate natural resource damages assessments. *Id.* § 6002(b).

We are in the midst of a period of transition that has and will continue to have significant impact on the business, legal, and economic communities. Natural resources that once seemed inexhaustible now are clearly finite and, in some cases, scarce. These resources that once were only valued when reduced to possession now have an existence value in the wild. Through the passage of CERCLA, the decision in *Ohio v. U.S. Department of Interior*, and the prosecution of restoration claims, the legislative, judicial, and executive branches have each respectively shown their commitment to this change. The business community must recognize the change and live in harmony with a new set of priorities that society has mandated. The legal community must lend definition and clarity to this emerging area of law. Finally, the economic community must provide a better and more reliable means of measuring the value of our nation's natural resources.

Looking forward, as trustees and PRPs gain experience in the area of natural resources, I hope that the trend will be away from litigating at any cost to an atmosphere of cooperation and rational concern for restoring the environment. Speaking to economic valuation of natural resources, time and experience will fine-tune the economic studies and methodologies necessary for accurately placing a value on injury to natural resources. Economic evaluations will not only measure a market price but societal value as well. Reaching agreement on these values will require continued effort, but it is clear that the economics of restoration are here to stay.

Notes

1. This figure may be somewhat misleading because these settlements may be partial, have a consent decree pending before a court, or be on appeal. However, the relevant dollar amounts and cases are: $24.25 million, *United States v. City of Seattle and Municipality of Metro. Seattle*, Civil Action No. C90–395 (W.D. Wash.); $10 million or more, *United States et al. v. AVX, Inc., et al.*, Civil Action No. 83–3882–Y (D. Mass.); $500,000, *United States et al. v. Simpson Tacoma Kraft Co., et al.*, Civil Action No. C91–5260T (W.D. Wash.); $10 million, *United States, et al. v. Exxon Corp., et al.*, Civil Action No. 91–1003 (E.D.N.Y.); $570,000, *In re Ballard Shipping Co. for Exoneration from or Limitation of Liability*, Civil Action No. 89–0685 (D.R.I.); $800,000, *United States v. BP America, Inc., et al.*, Civil Action No. 91–409 (D. Del.); $1.45 million, *United States v. M/V Alec Owen Maitland, et al.*, Civil Action No. 90–10081(K) (S.D. Fla.); $2 million, *United States v. M/V Elpis, et al.*, Civil Action No. 90–10011–CIV–JLK (S.D. Fla.).

Practical Advice for Permitting a Waste Disposal Facility

Donna L. Kolar

The permitting of hazardous and solid waste disposal facilities in this country is a long and arduous process. It is also extremely complex because one must work through the federal, state, and local requirements and regulations that are as interwoven as they are separate. These regulations change constantly, and one must be ever vigilant and aware of regulatory changes at the draft proposal level, both so that one can plan what will need to be done if a proposed regulation passes and also so that one can provide meaningful comments to the regulatory agency. Another problem area in the permitting process revolves around the tension and rivalry between the federal and state programs and also between different states. Each state wants its program to be up-to-date and stringent, which further explains why the regulations are constantly changing.

Obviously, permitting a waste disposal facility is a highly political matter. This is partly due to the fact that many local permits are granted by city or county commissioners or city councils. Permittees have been told many times that a member of a board would like to vote for the disposal facility because it would be good for the community; however, it would destroy his or her political career. This is very often the result of what is commonly referred to as the NIMBY (not in my back yard) syndrome among the constituents. The NIMBY

Donna Kolar is a senior counsel for Browning-Ferris Industries in Houston, Texas.

syndrome is very much responsible for the waste disposal crisis in this country. The NIMBY proponents are against anything—land disposal, incineration, transfer facilities, recycling facilities, treatment and processing facilities, and the like. Ultimately, however, every community needs *something* to deal with its waste disposal needs. Perhaps the answer is more community involvement *up front*, before a location is even selected.

Certainly one cause of the NIMBY position is fear of environmental harm. The federal government recognized the need to ensure environmental protection while still recognizing the realities of waste generation, storage, and disposal when it passed RCRA in 1976, 42 U.S.C. § 6901 *et seq.* RCRA developed a "cradle to grave" waste regulation scheme administered by the EPA or, in states that have received delegation of authority to administer the program, by the state environmental agency. The regulations promulgated pursuant to RCRA cover the generation, treatment, storage, transportation, and disposal of waste. Actually, most of the focus to date has been on what is referred to as subtitle C waste—hazardous waste regulated under subtitle C of RCRA. However, with the recent promulgation of the subtitle D regulations covering municipal solid waste landfills, one would expect the focus to shift. Although the federal regulations have been issued, the EPA has not yet issued regulations relating to how states are to deal with these regulations.

This article concentrates on hazardous waste facility permitting, both because it is so complex and also because, with the passage of subtitle D regulations, the nonhazardous solid waste facilities will virtually parallel the hazardous waste facilities in many ways. This article explores the permitting of hazardous waste facilities both in states that have authorized RCRA programs and in nonauthorized states. It also examines local requirements that are found in virtually all states. And, finally, it identifies some problem areas that exist in these systems as a result of complex intergovernmental relations. Because of the strong historical influences affecting intergovernmental relations in waste regulation, this article begins with an overview of that history.

RCRA's History

When the federal government passed RCRA, the intent was always that the states eventually would take over the program because environmental protection is definitely a state issue as well. Congress thus set up, as part of the regulatory scheme, a way in which a state

could become "authorized" to administer the "program." It was relatively easy in the early days of RCRA for a state to become authorized—it had to adopt regulations that were equal to or more stringent
than the federal requirements. Initially, most states chose to adopt
RCRA and the underlying regulations verbatim. The state then would
enter into a MOA, a contract between the state and federal government
establishing the state adoption and federal delegation of the RCRA
program.

For those entities and facilities that were in existence at the time
RCRA was passed and the regulations first promulgated, it was a confusing and worrisome time. Much of the concern was caused by the
new cumbersome permitting regulations. It was obvious that it would
take a while to get a permit (little did we know then *how* long), so
what would one do in the meantime? RCRA dealt with this through
a concept known as "interim status," which was a quasi-permitted
status granted to "existing facilities" as long as certain requirements
were met. To be granted interim status, a facility needed to be in
"existence" and file a Notification of Hazardous Waste Activity and
a Part A (the first part of a bifurcated permit application) by August
19, 1980, and November 19, 1980, respectively. As long as a facility
met those requirements, it could continue to operate while going
through the formal permitting process. Since the government had to
set priorities in the permitting process, priority was given to these
existing facilities. To ensure interim status and some priority treatment in the permitting process, many filings were made for not only
the open and operating facilities and those under construction, but
also for gleams in the developers' eyes. Notifications for sanitary landfills were even filed because one never knew if in a few years one
might wish to develop the nonhazardous facility into a hazardous
waste site instead. Most of those notifications were later withdrawn
when the Agency requested Part B permit applications, which were
much more complex and represented the "meat" of the permits.

The Part As and Notifications of Hazardous Waste Activity that
were filed were very simple and consisted only of the applicant's
name, facility address, type of activity (e.g., generator, storer, treater,
transporter, or disposer), type of facilities (e.g., tanks), and the types
of waste to be handled. The Part As had to be amended a number of
times because the government did not start requesting Part Bs to be
filed until a number of years later. To maintain interim status, the
Part A had to remain current and the facility must have continued to
meet all requirements and file any certifications then or subsequently
required. For instance, HSWA required groundwater monitoring cer-

tifications by November 8, 1985, or loss of interim status would result. In the meantime, everyone was working on their Part Bs because one did not want to wait until the Agency requested it. As it turned out, the Part Bs were often gargantuan, and some filled as many as twenty-seven volumes.

There were numerous problems in the early days before states had obtained RCRA authorization in trying to deal with the permitting process. At the very least, dual filings were required; one had to file copies with the state and with the federal EPA, and both the state and the EPA had to sign off on anything that the facility wished to do or anything having to do with the permit. As the states began obtaining authorization to operate their own programs, everyone breathed a little easier, thinking that the system would become easier to handle. Unfortunately, that has not happened, not because the authorized program concept is not working, but rather because HSWA was passed. HSWA affected every authorized program, at least for what is referred to as the "HSWA portions" of the program, which involve corrective action.

Before HSWA, section 3006(b) of RCRA provided that an authorized state is "authorized to carry out such program in lieu of the Federal program under this subchapter in such State and to issue and enforce permits for the storage, treatment, or disposal of hazardous waste. . . ." 42 U.S.C. § 6926(b). The EPA promulgated a corresponding regulatory provision. 40 C.F.R. § 271.3(b). It took the position prior to HSWA that the federal RCRA requirements no longer applied in a state with final authorization. *See, e.g.,* 52 Fed. Reg. 45,796 (1987). While an authorized program was required to be modified to reflect changes in the federal program, the new provision did not become effective until incorporated into the state program. The state program had a period of time to conform to the new federal requirement, and even if the state did not comply, the EPA's remedy was not enforcement of the new provision but rather withdrawal of the state's authorization. 40 C.F.R. § § 271.21–23. This is still the procedure for non-HSWA portions of the RCRA program.

HSWA changed the state-federal relationship. Section 3006(g), which was added by HSWA, provides that "any requirement or prohibition . . . which is imposed . . . pursuant to the amendments made by the Hazardous and Solid Waste Amendments of 1984 shall take effect in each State having an interim or finally authorized State program on the same date as such requirement takes effect in other States." This language was adopted verbatim by the EPA in the Codification Rule. 40 C.F.R § 271.3(b)(1). This aspect of HSWA has fundamentally altered intergovernmental relations and thus has raised uncertainties for regulated facilities. For example, a major issue looming on the horizon that both applicants and the federal government are dancing around is the extent of authority, if any, that the EPA has to impose corrective action requirements pursuant to HSWA at a facility that is fully permitted in an authorized state. 42 U.S.C. § 3008(h). It is an interesting issue because corrective action, at least when issued under an order, may not be relevant at a state-permitted facility. Until the states obtain authorization of the HSWA portion of RCRA, issues like this will flourish.

Thus the history of RCRA has come full circle—from dual federal-state regulation to state regulation through fully authorized programs to the return of dual federal-state regulation after HSWA. That history has left the intergovernmental relations of waste facility permitting quite complex. Facilities now face two scenarios, dependent on the authorized status of the state, for dealing with those complexities.

RCRA Permitting in Authorized States

Obviously, in an authorized state, a facility will receive its "RCRA" permit from that state. However, the state program permit may also include permits to construct, permits to operate, air permits, etc. A state may include these as part of an overall RCRA package for a facility or may simply require separate permits from the applicable state agencies. Moreover, it is important that an interim status facility applying for a permit look at the MOA between the federal government and the particular state regarding how existing permits will be handled and the effect on existing permits. The EPA regulations provide that "[a]ll permits issued under State law prior to the date of approval of final authorization shall be reviewed by the State Director and modified or revoked and reissued to require compliance with the requirements of this part." 40 C.F.R § 271.13(d).

In addition to the state RCRA permit, a facility also needs the federal HSWA review or HSWA portion of the permit, which is referred to as the corrective action component. Section 3004(u), enacted by HSWA, provides that "a permit issued after the date of enactment of [HSWA] by the *Administrator or a State* shall require corrective action for all releases. . . ." (Emphasis added.) There are two potential problem areas involved in the federal HSWA portion of a permit. First, many states have their own correction action authority written into their programs, which may cause some overlapping in the corrective actions and some conflicts in terms and conditions. It is not uncommon to find that a state agency may provide for a corrective action that involves a "final" remedy for the state, while that same action and area of the facility may entail an entirely new federal remedy a year or two later. Obviously, this is of great concern to the facility because it potentially involves a tremendous expenditure of money that may go to waste in another year or two. This is a tough situation, since the facility is caught between two authorities whose only concern, and rightfully so, is environmental protection. One will have the greatest likelihood of success if one can present a cost-effective alternative that provides the needed environmental protection and also meets the regulatory requirements of each program simultaneously. Thus, in authorized states, the principal concern for the facility is coordinating the state RCRA program with the federal HSWA program, and then taking into account any additional state permits.

RCRA Permitting in Nonauthorized States

Permitting in nonauthorized states is probably the worst of all worlds. If the facility applicant thinks *it* is confused, so are the state and federal regions that are trying to deal with the situation. Obviously, in nonauthorized states, you will need a federal RCRA permit that will include the HSWA portion. However, just because a state does not have a RCRA-authorized program, that does not mean that the state does not have its own separate facility permitting program that may add to or conflict with the federal requirements. The facility will be required to obtain the state program permits, which may duplicate the very RCRA-type permit it is obtaining from the federal government (i.e., a permit to operate a hazardous waste disposal facility), as well as construction permits, air permits, and water permits.

Although the state and federal permits may conflict, if the state has its own permit requirements the facility *must* have *both* the federal and state permits to operate. Further, in a nonauthorized state, a facility will still need to receive a federal wastewater discharge permit and, if the state has its own water program, a state water permit if the facility intends to discharge. Terms or conditions in such permits may differ. In fact, there are facilities that have higher and lower limits on one of the permits, making it confusing when one is compiling a discharge monitoring report each month. The facility may have an excursion in regard to one permit and not the other. Clearly, then, hazardous waste permitting in nonauthorized states requires heightened sensitivity to the politics and practicalities of intergovernmental relations.

The Pitfalls of Complex Intergovernmental Relations

The reason the permitting system is so complex is not just because one must deal with all of the federal, state, and local requirements under RCRA and similar programs, but one must also deal with other acts as well, including the Clean Water Act, 33 U.S.C, § 1251 *et seq.*, the Clean Air Act, 42 U.S.C. § 7401 *et seq.*, and CERCLA, 42 U.S.C § 9601 *et seq.* Most states have also adopted state equivalents of these statutes. These overlapping statutes and jurisdictions raise a host of pitfalls.

Facilities should assess the effect of overlapping statutes before developing permit proposals. For example, a facility almost always will need a NPDES permit and/or the state equivalent under an authorized federal wastewater discharge program or the state's own program. This is not only an essential permit from the standpoint of being able to operate, it is essential for economical operation of a facility as well. In a state with an authorized NPDES program, you will only be dealing with the particular state requirements for the NPDES permit. It is important that one determine the need for an NPDES permit early in the process. The facility will be required to deal with water management in its Part B, so one should be able to determine the need for NPDES permitting well before the time for filing the Part B. The permitting agency will want to be sure the facility can handle its water effectively and safely. While one need not have an NPDES permit to obtain a RCRA permit, to not have an NPDES permit can be very costly. Without a way to discharge treated runoff, the facility would have to arrange to have millions of gallons of water transported to a treatment facility for treatment and discharge or disposal.

Companies operating facilities in several states face special problems. A definite pride of program exists in each state, which often results in a state trying to "one up" another state. For companies with multiple facilities, this can be a major problem. A state in which the company is seeking a permit often will ask about the requirements requested in other states and then may make their requirement more strict or cumbersome. The most common example of this syndrome involves the amount of financial assurance and insurance required by each state. It is important for one to try to focus the individual state's attention on its own needs, concerns, and regulatory framework while stressing the uniqueness of each facility. The one-upmanship of the states has become increasingly fierce given the current interstate waste flow issues. In addition to each state's desire for greater environmental protection, one is now also faced with each state's desire to protect its own waste disposal capacity. The goals are valid ones, but the states need to work together for the benefit of their citizens.

Above and beyond these problems, a relatively new requirement is emerging across the United States—a licensing disclosure requirement. New Jersey was the innovator of this trend with its New Jersey Act A–901, and a number of states are following in its footsteps. Basically, this part of the licensing procedure requires disclosure of the applicant's compliance history as well as personal information on officers, directors, and key employees of the applicant. Several problem areas are involved in these disclosure requirements. First, they take a great deal of time to prepare, at least for a major corporation, and they also take a lot of time in the review process and thus could hold up a facility's permit. The delay can be major, sometimes a year or more. Obviously, a start-up company would not want to risk constructing a facility that may cost many millions of dollars before receiving a positive recommendation from the licensing board. Second, there are quirks in each one of these disclosure requirements. For example, if an applicant or a key employee of the applicant is indicted, a temporary permit may be issued, but the permanent permit will be held in abeyance pending the outcome of the trial on the indictment. Interestingly enough, however, if one is convicted of a misdemeanor or felony, one is allowed the chance to rehabilitate oneself and obtain a permanent license. In essence, an indicted company or person is treated worse than a convicted felon or misdemeanant. The definitions are very broad and vague, which creates other problems. For example, in some states, a company can be denied a permit based on the record of a key employee, which can even include a dispatcher.

The licensing disclosure rules have disparate effects. For a large company with hundreds of facilities, its compliance history may be rather lengthy, while a start-up company or a ''mom and pop'' operation will have fewer requirements, although relatively speaking the large company may have a better overall record. The problem for large companies is that the sheer number of compliance items—even though spread out over many facilities—can trigger a number of issues. Hence, if your state is considering such a requirement, review it carefully and get involved in trying to shape the legislation. Certainly there is a need for what a state is trying to accomplish, and it is a goal that any responsible company should at least support. However, we need to develop an appropriate means to achieve the lofty end.

Of course, permitting problems do not begin and end with the RCRA and NPDES permits. Whether a state is authorized or not, one must obtain *all* necessary permits to operate. In addition to a state/federal RCRA permit and an NPDES permit for any discharges, one may need a sewer/wastewater permit, a transportation permit if any waste transport is performed by the facility, licenses for any on-site labs, and an air permit, if required. The major problem in obtaining these permits is that neither the federal EPA regions nor the states have easily accessible procedures for how to deal with one another. Often one observes greater *de facto* "delegation" in a nonauthorized state than in any authorized state—in both the RCRA permit area and the Superfund off-site policy area. The permittee is often unsure with whom it should deal and thus has to act as it did early on in the RCRA program, by offering dual submissions and obtaining consensus from everyone. It is critical when this is the case that one deal consistently with both the state and federal agencies. It will sometimes be necessary to meet with both agencies at once to clear up any misunderstandings or, better yet, to ensure that there will be no misunderstandings. If there are conflicts between the agencies, one must let them work it out; getting involved can result in the permittee getting "whipsawed" without knowing what hit it. Where the federal agency appears to defer to the state or vice versa, one should defer similarly. Remember that the paramount concern of the agency personnel is environmental protection, which must be the permittee's concern as well.

One must also be aware of how the agencies review permit applications in order to prepare one that can be easily reviewed. Clients will want to write an operationally oriented permit application. That is, the client will want an application that outlines what happens at the facility from the time it opens its gates in the morning to when it closes them at night. From the standpoint of everything but the review process, this makes the most sense. However, taking this approach could cause the applicant the most problems with the agencies and will result in very long review times and extensive NOD. The reason is simple—the agencies normally use a regulatory checklist in reviewing the application, so if the application does not follow the order of the checklist, the reviewer may not be able to locate the required information, and the result may be the issuance of an NOD. This is understandable given the work load of the agency and the length and complexity of Part B applications. After having been through this process several times, I heartily recommend a regulatory permit application approach.

Local Permitting

Regardless of the state and whether it is authorized or not, a number of local permits are required. Examples of these types of permits include business permits, solid waste permits, drainage and flood control permits, and sewage/wastewater permits. Further, in many states, siting permits must be obtained or siting requirements in addition to those present in RCRA must be satisfied for the facility to operate. These requirements include certificates of designation, site assignments, siting board recommendations, and zoning designations. In some states, the siting issue alone can take years to resolve.

Overall, the local permitting process is by far the most political and most contentious. Local, state, and even federal politicians will get involved when their constituents are upset. The constituents are often driven by the NIMBY syndrome. Supporting a waste disposal facility can cost a politician his or her career. For these reasons, the facility must involve the community early in the permitting process. If it is a new facility, one might consider involving the community even before a location is sited to avoid the NIMBY problem. If it is an existing facility, one must establish and maintain good community relations. The permittee must understand the potential fear and anger of the surrounding community. Information, knowledge, and an open line of communication, coupled with trust built up over time, are the best ways to diffuse these feelings.

The importance of good relations does not end with the local community. The importance of good working regulatory relationships cannot be stressed enough. The agencies are not your enemies! The permittee and the regulatory agencies are on the same side–ensuring safe disposal of waste. Because a company wants to make a profit does not make it evil or prove a lack of concern for the environment, and because an agency is not concerned with the company's profit does not make it an adversary. The common goal is environmental protection. Finally, when dealing with agencies, one must recognize that agency personnel are extremely overworked; as busy as the private sector is, the public sector is more so. One must not take one's anger at the system out on some very dedicated people serving the public sector.

To prevail in the waste permitting process, one needs patience, perseverance, constant communication, and the trust of the agencies and communities that one will operate the facility in a way that maximizes environmental protection. And a little luck never hurts.

Foreign Trade in Trash? Exporting Hazardous Waste

Mark N. Semenoff

National media attention has repeatedly focused on the diminishing hazardous waste disposal capability in the United States. Existing hazardous waste disposal facilities have reached or are reaching capacity. Proposals for new hazardous waste disposal facilities are vigorously opposed by communities identified as sites for new facilities. The federal land disposal restrictions specified in 40 C.F.R. Part 268 impose strict treatment standards for certain hazardous wastes intended for land disposal. As a result, hazardous waste generators have started considering alternative disposal methods and locations. One alternative that some hazardous waste generators have considered and used is hazardous waste export.

The Progression toward Increased Controls

Attitudes toward importing and exporting hazardous waste differ widely among countries. Most of the developed nations—the United States, Canada, and the European Community—seem to accept hazardous waste export and import as an unavoidable result of industrialization. As a result, the majority of transboundary waste shipments occur between these countries. Hundreds of waste shipments occur annually between the United States and Canada and the members of the European Community. For example, in 1987, approximately four hundred U.S. firms shipped hazardous waste to Canada and a similar number of Canadian companies exported hazardous waste to TSD

Mark Semenoff practices environmental law with Parcel, Mauro, Hultin & Spaanstra, P.C., in Denver, Colorado.

facilities in the United States. The United Kingdom imported 250,000 tons of hazardous waste from Europe and New Zealand in 1987.

Europe and the United States have also exported varying amounts of hazardous waste to developing countries such as Nigeria, Jamaica, Haiti, and Guinea. The EPA estimates that less than 5 percent of U.S. waste shipments are sent to developing countries. Recently, however, developing countries have objected to Western nations "dumping" hazardous waste in the Third World. These countries have criticized Western nations for exploiting the developing countries' lack of technical expertise in hazardous waste management, thereby placing their citizens at risk. For example, Jamaica has supported a worldwide ban for countries that "lack the technical sophistication to measure the degree of toxicity in wastes and are at great risk when receiving such wastes." Other countries have required removal of hazardous waste from their territory. In July 1988, a ship carrying 15,000 tons of Philadelphia incinerator ash was forced to return to the United States after Guinea ordered the shipment removed from its territory.

These countries, supported by environmental organizations such as Greenpeace, have urged strict worldwide controls on international trade in toxic and hazardous wastes. Responding to such calls for action, the Basel Convention on the Transboundary Movements of Hazardous Waste and Their Disposal was negotiated. The Basel Convention, which opened for signature in March 1989, prohibits the transboundary transport and management of hazardous and "other" wastes without the written consent of the nations involved and obligates the waste-exporting nation to verify that the importing nation will manage wastes in an "environmentally sound" manner. As of January 1992, seventeen countries had ratified the Convention.

Hazardous waste export has also been a subject of continuing congressional concern. Hearings following the adoption of the Basel Convention led to the introduction of legislation, the Waste Export Control Act, to conform existing U.S. waste export controls with the Basel Convention's requirements. WECA received consideration during congressional committee hearings on the reauthorization of RCRA, but the 101st Congress failed to reauthorize RCRA. While legislation similar to WECA should be a component of the RCRA reauthorization package considered by the 102nd Congress, until WECA or an equivalent statute is signed into law, the U.S. waste export controls will continue to differ from those specified in the Basel Convention.

This article intends to familiarize practitioners with RCRA's current requirements for hazardous waste export. HSWA added a new section to RCRA that specifically addresses hazardous waste export.

Section 3017 prohibits hazardous waste export unless the person exporting the hazardous waste has notified the EPA of its intent to export, the government of the receiving country has consented to accept the waste, a copy of the receiving country's written consent is attached to the manifest accompanying the waste shipment, and the shipment conforms to the terms of the consent. Section 3017 also provides that a person may export hazardous waste if the United States and the government of the receiving country have entered into a bilateral agreement establishing notice, export, and enforcement procedures for the transportation, treatment, storage, and disposal of hazardous waste and the shipment conforms to the terms of such an agreement. Currently, the United States has entered into bilateral agreements with Canada and Mexico.

Pursuant to Section 3017, the EPA proposed and promulgated hazardous waste export regulations at 51 Fed. Reg. 28,664 (Aug. 8, 1986). These requirements, identified at 40 C.F.R. Part 262, Subpart E, impose notification, manifest, and shipment requirements on generators and transporters engaged in hazardous waste export. This article focuses on the mechanics of export notification. As described below, hazardous waste export requires prior written consent from the foreign country receiving the waste shipment and notification of any country through which the waste shipment will pass. As a result, practitioners with clients seeking to export hazardous waste should expect to interact with the State Department and the receiving country's government. Finally, this article suggests sources of information about export options and foreign attitudes toward receiving hazardous waste and assesses the future of hazardous waste export.

Primary Exporter and Hazardous Waste Identification

Who must notify the EPA about the export of a hazardous waste shipment? The hazardous waste export regulations impose notification obligations on "primary exporters" of hazardous waste. Primary exporters is a somewhat broader regulatory class than the class of generators normally obligated under RCRA to submit notification of hazardous waste activity. Primary exporters are defined as (1) persons required to originate the manifest for a shipment of hazardous waste that specifies a TSD facility in a receiving country as the facility to which the hazardous waste will be sent, and (2) any intermediary arranging for the export.

An intermediary is a party who arranges hazardous waste export by acting as a middleman between the party originating the manifest and another party involved in the export, such as the transporter or foreign waste management facility. A transporter can be an intermediary if it takes on intermediary responsibilities, such as arranging for the management of the waste with the foreign management facility. As noted below, the export regulations hold intermediaries directly responsible for accurate notification and compliance with the consent of the receiving country.

The RCRA export regulations only apply to hazardous (as opposed to nonhazardous) wastes destined for export. Thus the export regulations apply to shipments of hazardous waste for which manifests would be required if the shipments were sent to domestic waste management facilities. If a domestic hazardous waste shipment falls within a regulatorily defined hazardous waste exemption and is not subject to RCRA domestic manifest requirements, the shipment is also not subject to the export regulations. For example, if a waste shipment was exempted from RCRA hazardous waste regulations because it contained reclaimable discarded commercial chemical products, the shipment would not be subject to the export requirements. Exporters of materials exempted from regulation based on how the materials are managed must remember that they bear the burden of proving that such materials are being managed in the receiving country in a manner exempting the materials from hazardous waste regulation. For this reason, exporters should keep records or other methods of substantiating their claims that their shipments are exempt from hazardous waste regulation because of the way the materials are being managed. Exporters should prepare or retain descriptions of the foreign facility, collect evidence that the foreign facility is licensed or otherwise approved by the receiving country to conduct exempted activities, and document the terms of the contract with the foreign facility. Documentation of this type will allow exporters to respond effectively to allegations of sham recycling or other claims of illegal or improper waste management.

Notification and Consent

The Requirements Affecting Primary Exporters
The export regulations impose several notification and consent requirements on primary exporters of hazardous waste. A primary exporter must notify the EPA of an intended export before the shipment is scheduled to leave the United States. Single notifications can cover export activities extending up to one year. The EPA recommends that a complete notification be submitted to it sixty days before the initial

shipment is intended to be shipped off-site. Exporters can submit a notification of intent to export less than sixty days before the intended shipment date, but they run the risk of delayed consent from the receiving country and therefore delayed shipment.

Primary exporters are required to provide enough information to allow the designated receiving country to make an informed decision about whether to accept the waste. An NOI to export must be in writing, signed by the primary exporter, and include information identifying the primary exporter, the exported waste, the method of transportation, and the route the shipment will take.

For example, to export waste solvents to Japan, the primary exporter would submit an NOI to export containing its name, address, and EPA identification number. The NOI would describe the shipment using the EPA and DOT identifiers—e.g., waste trichloroethylene, FOO1 (the EPA hazardous waste number), Class 6.1 (DOT hazard class), UN1710 (DOT hazardous material identification number)—and identify the shipment's quantity. The primary exporter must describe the method of transport and the points of departure and entry of the shipment, e.g., the shipment will be transported by cargo ship from Seattle to Osaka. In addition, the primary exporter must identify the consignee of the shipment and describe how the waste will be treated, stored, or disposed of in the receiving country. In this example, a microchip manufacturer in Osaka will recycle the waste solvent for use in its manufacturing process.

Once the EPA has received a complete NOI, it, in conjunction with the State Department, provides a complete notification to the receiving country and any transit countries. RCRA section 3017(d) requires that the EPA notify the receiving country within thirty days of receipt by the EPA of a complete notification from the primary exporter.

The Role of the State Department

Translation and information transmission are the State Department's main roles in hazardous waste export. The EPA and the State Department normally transmit the notification and the receiving country's response telegraphically to expedite the notification and consent process. Notifications are sent from the EPA to the State Department for telegraphic transmission to the U.S. embassy in the receiving country. The embassy then forwards the information to the appropriate authorities in the receiving country in translation, if necessary, with a request for an expedited written response. In addition to receiving the primary exporter's notification, the receiving country is also advised that U.S. law prohibits the export of hazardous waste unless the receiving country consents to accept the waste. The receiving country is requested to provide the State Department with a response to the notification that either consents to its full terms, consents to it with specified modifications, or rejects receipt of the hazardous waste. The receiving country is also provided with a description of the federal regulations that would apply to the TSD of the hazardous waste in the United States.

Once the embassy obtains the receiving country's response, it translates the response, if necessary, and cables the response to the State Department for transmission to the EPA. If the receiving country consents to the hazardous waste shipment, the EPA forwards an EPA acknowledgment of consent to the primary exporter. A receiving country's consent can take several forms. The consent may only reference the export notification without reiterating its terms. Consents can impose specific modifications or conditions on the waste shipment's management. In that case, the cabled modifications constitute the EPA's acknowledgment of consent and are provided to the primary exporter for attachment to the shipment's manifest. If the receiving country rejects the shipment, the EPA notifies the primary exporter in writing of the rejection. In addition to providing a telegraphically transmitted response, the original written communication from the receiving country is sent to the State Department in Washington in the diplomatic mail pouch. The written communication is then forwarded to the EPA and a copy provided to the primary exporter. The EPA also notifies the primary exporter of any transit country's responses, e.g., if a transit country will not allow the shipment to pass through its territory. The EPA urges exporters to reroute waste shipments objected to by transit countries, since they may take action to prohibit entry.

An exact translation of the exporter's notification and the receiving country's response is critical to the success of hazardous waste export. While U.S. embassy personnel in the receiving country are certainly well trained in translation and the EPA has indicated that it will work closely with embassy personnel, the possibility of erroneous translation remains. For this reason, the EPA has indicated that it will not take enforcement action against an exporter who relies in good faith on an embassy translation. Furthermore, the EPA has stated that difficulties created in the receiving country by an erroneous State Department translation are matters of foreign relations best left to the State Department.

The Need for Record Keeping

Assuming consent is received, the primary exporter must prepare a manifest for the shipment. Manifests are generally obtained from the state in which the primary exporter is located. If the primary exporter's state does not supply manifest forms, the exporter may obtain manifest forms from EPA regional or headquarters offices. Manifests for hazardous waste exports differ somewhat from domestic hazardous waste manifests. These differences result primarily from the foreign destination of the hazardous waste shipments. For example, in lieu of the name, site address, and EPA identification number of the designated permitted facility, the primary exporter is required to identify the name and site address of the consignee or alternate consignee in the receiving country. The primary exporter must identify the departure point from the United States of the hazardous waste shipment. The exporter must also certify that the shipment conforms with the terms of the the EPA acknowledgment of consent attached to the manifest.

The export regulations prescribe that a primary exporter must require the consignee to confirm in writing the delivery of the hazardous waste and describe any significant discrepancies between the manifest and the shipment. A copy of the manifest signed by the consignee may be used to confirm delivery. Exporters should keep this requirement in mind when drafting contracts with foreign TSD facilities. Export contracts should stress the importance of delivery confirmation by consignees and provide breach of contract damages for failure of consignees to notify exporters of shipment delivery.

If the shipment cannot be delivered for any reason to the designated or alternate consignee, the exporter must renotify the EPA of a change in the conditions of the original notification to allow shipment to a new consignee. Prior to delivery to the new consignee, the exporter must obtain a new EPA acknowledgment of consent. Alternatively, the exporter can instruct the transporter to return the waste to the primary exporter or designate another facility within the United States to receive the waste.

When the conditions specified in the original notification change, especially if the estimated quantity of hazardous waste specified in the original notification is exceeded, the primary exporter must provide the EPA with written notification of the change. Exporters should promptly notify the EPA of any changes in the notification because shipments cannot take place until the receiving country consents to the changes and the primary exporter receives an EPA acknowledgment of consent reflecting the receiving country's consent to the changes.

The export regulations require that hazardous waste transporters comply with applicable RCRA requirements, e.g., manifesting and record-keeping requirements. These requirements are set out in 40 C.F.R. Part 263.20. A transporter may not accept a hazardous waste shipment from a primary exporter unless the shipment is accompanied by a manifest and an EPA acknowledgment of consent. Furthermore, a transporter may not accept a waste export shipment if it knows that the shipment does not conform to the EPA acknowledgment of consent. Transporters must ensure that manifests and the EPA acknowledgments of consent accompany hazardous waste shipments. Finally, transporters are required to provide a copy of the manifest to the U.S. Customs official at the point of departure from the United States.

Other Miscellaneous Concerns

The export regulations impose several reporting and record-keeping obligations on primary exporters. A primary exporter is required to prepare exception reports if it has not received a copy of the manifest, signed by the transporter, stating the date and place of departure from the United States, within forty-five days of the shipment. The primary exporter must also file an exception report if it has not received written confirmation that the waste shipment was received within ninety days of shipment. Finally, the primary exporter must file an exception report if the waste is returned to the United States.

Primary exporters are also required to prepare annual reports summarizing the types, quantities, frequency, and ultimate destination of all hazardous wastes exported during the previous calendar year. These reports identify the types of wastes exported, the identities and location of consignees, the total amount of waste shipped to each consignee, the number of shipments to a consignee and, in even numbered years, a description of the exporter's efforts to reduce the volume and toxicity of waste generated by the exporter.

Primary exporters are required to retain copies of each NOI to export for at least three years from the date the hazardous waste shipment was accepted by the transporter. Exporters must also retain copies of each EPA acknowledgment of consent for the same time period, as well as copies of each confirmation of delivery of the waste shipment. Annual reports must also be retained for at least three years from the due date of the report.

One issue that practitioners should keep in mind when advising clients about hazardous waste export is confidentiality. An apparent conflict exists between RCRA sections 3007(b) and 3017. Section 3007(b) can be read as prohibiting all disclosure of any confidential business information contained in an NOI to export; however, this reading seems to contradict section 3017. The EPA's stated interpretation of section 3017 requires transmission of notification information to a receiving country despite the information's confidentiality. The EPA's stated reason for this is that the purpose of section 3017 is to allow receiving countries to make informed decisions as to whether to accept waste shipments, and, if accepted, how to manage the shipments. Because the regulations prohibit hazardous waste exports absent receiving country consent, sufficient information must be divulged to the State Department and receiving countries for the receiving countries to grant informed consent. The EPA resolves the apparent conflict between these sections by prohibiting disclosure of confidential business information to persons other than receiving countries.

The EPA has indicated that it will exercise discretion in assessing claims of confidentiality. If the information claimed confidential is deemed to be information that a foreign country should know, the thirty-day limit for submitting a complete notification to a receiving country will not begin to run until the EPA determines the validity of the confidentiality claim. Once the EPA has completed processing the confidentiality claim, the notification information is provided to the receiving country. Since export cannot occur without informed consent by the receiving country, practitioners and exporters should be aware that confidentiality claims can significantly delay shipment.

Noncompliance with the hazardous waste export rules may subject violators to civil and criminal enforcement under RCRA section 3008. Section 3008(d) authorizes criminal sanctions to be imposed against any person who exports hazardous waste without the consent of the receiving country or not in conformance with a bilateral agreement between the United States and the receiving country. Penalties for violation of the hazardous waste export rules include imprisonment for up to two years and/or fines up to $50,000 per day for knowingly exporting hazardous waste without consent or in violation of a bilateral agreement. Knowing exportation includes exportation without notification or renotification, exportation after notification but without consent, or exportation with consent based upon false representations in the notification. Penalties and prison terms can be doubled for second offenses. The EPA has indicated that it will prosecute violators to the fullest extent possible. EPA's Office of International Activities reports that, to date, most enforcement actions have focused on paper violations such as inaccurate manifests. In May 1991, the United States secured its first conviction for a section 3017 violation when a California man pleaded guilty to two felony counts of illegally exporting hazardous waste to Mexico.

Assessing export options entails determining the existence and availability of TSD facilities as well as understanding receiving country regulations. Several sources of this information exist. Domestic TSD facility owners and operators, especially national waste disposal companies, may operate or have some relationship with foreign TSD facilities. Industry associations are likely to have information about foreign TSD options. Embassy or consulate staff will often know of TSD options in their country or at least know who the practitioner or generator can contact. Finally, the United Nations Environment Program can identify which countries have adopted the Basel Convention's requirements.

Practitioners should identify and assess foreign hazardous waste regulations concurrently with foreign TSD facility evaluation. Foreign government environmental authorities are the chief source of information about regulations. Foreign TSD facility owners and operators are also a good source of information about the regulations under which their facilities operate. Either of these sources may be able to provide some insight as to whether a particular shipment will be consented to by the receiving country. Finally, practitioners should determine if a bilateral agreement between the United States and the receiving country exists that may impose different or additional requirements on exports. As noted above, the United States currently has bilateral agreements with Canada and Mexico.

The future of domestic and international hazardous waste export controls is likely to be guided by the Basel Convention. As more nations ratify the Convention and conform their national hazardous waste management requirements to its standards, export options may become more limited. The number of potential receiving countries may diminish. Potential receiving countries may also require their domestic TSD facilities to utilize waste management techniques that are more stringent than those currently in place. Congress could go beyond the Basel Convention and ban hazardous waste exports from the United States. Initiatives by Greenpeace or others may result in a post-Convention agreement banning hazardous waste exports similar to the agreement banning chlorofluorocarbons. However, until additional limitations are placed on hazardous waste export, export remains a viable waste management alternative that generators should consider.

PART III

Water Quality

Clean Water Act Permitting: The NPDES
Program at Twenty

New Clean Water Act Toxics Control
Initiatives

What Water Quality Lawyers Should Know
about Water Law

The Regulation of Toxic Pollutants under
the Clean Water Act: EPA's
Technology-Based Limits

A Primer on Wetlands Permitting and
Section 404 Decision Making

Discharges of Hazardous Substances under
the Clean Water Act

State and Federal Roles under the Clean
Water Act

Local Government Control
of Water Quality—
Is This a Good Idea?

Part III
Water Quality

Water quality, originally the province of the states, has been subject to extensive federal control since the 1972 enactment of the Federal Water Pollution Control Act, better known as the Clean Water Act. 33 U.S.C. § 1251 *et seq.* The cornerstone of the federal program is the NPDES permit program under section 402 of the Act, 33 U.S.C. § 1342. Kristy Niehaus Bulleit and Diane Montgomery discuss the major features of the permit program as well as areas where important issues remain.

The Clean Water Act contains two basic types of controls, water quality standards and technology-based controls. Dischargers must comply with the more restrictive of these requirements. Water quality standards are established by the states, with EPA oversight, based on scientific information as to the concentrations of pollutants that are consistent with various uses of water bodies. 33 U.S.C. §1313. David Heineck's article discusses the EPA's new initiatives in this area, which have focused on toxic pollutants. The relationship between water quality and state water law, which governs water use, is analyzed by Arne Rovick and Lee Decker.

Technology-based effluent limitations are established by the EPA and apply to all direct and indirect discharges in an industrial category unless an individual company can show that it is entitled to a variance. 33 U.S.C. §§ 1311, 1314. The EPA's regulations establish "best practicable" and "best available" technology limitations for a number of industry categories as well as pretreatment standards for discharges to municipal treatment works. 40 C.F.R. Part 400. EPA efforts in establishing these regulations are discussed in an article by Bradford Wyche.

Long before the Clean Water Act was enacted, federal law governed the discharge of dredged or fill material into waters of the United States. Section 404 of the Clean Water Act currently gives the Army Corps of Engineers the authority to issue dredge and fill permits. 33 U.S.C. § 1344. This program has been criticized as arcane and complex, particularly as it regulates wetlands, as explained by Bruce Ray.

Section 311 of the Clean Water Act deals with spills of hazardous substances. 33 U.S.C. § 1321. A forerunner of the federal Superfund statute, this provision imposes liability to the federal government for cleanup costs as well as penalties for discharges. Theodore Garrett's article discusses the EPA's development of regulations in this area, which led to the federally permitted release concept.

The Clean Water Act's programs involve a partnership between the EPA and the states. Mr. Cherney and Ms. Wardzinski discuss federal and state roles and issues that have arisen in connection with state implementation of federal programs. From a somewhat different perspective, Sara Burgin considers issues that arise when local governments effectuate significant land use controls for the purpose of protecting water quality.

Clean Water Act Permitting: The NPDES Program at Twenty

Kristy A. Niehaus Bulleit and Diane U. Montgomery

One of the central features of the Clean Water Act is the NPDES, a permitting program that transforms the general regulatory standards established under the Act into enforceable requirements for individual dischargers. Under the EPA's direction, the NPDES program has been up and running for nearly twenty years. Under it, the EPA and a number of states that have assumed responsibility for NPDES permitting have issued tens of thousands of NPDES permits. Yet, even after so many years of experience, difficult new issues continue to arise and old issues remain unresolved. This article discusses three major aspects of the current NPDES permitting program—the scope of the program, substantive permit application requirements, and permit terms and conditions—and examines several areas where important issues remain.

The Scope of the NPDES Permit Program

The Debate over Definitions

The Act requires an NPDES permit only for the "discharge of pollutants" from a "point source" to "navigable waters." Section 502 of the Act defines each of these terms expansively, and over the years both the EPA and the courts have interpreted the statutory definitions liberally. As a result, an NPDES permit is required for virtually any

Kristy Niehaus Bulleit is a partner in the Washington, D.C., office of Hunton & Williams. Diane Montgomery is an associate in the Richmond, Virginia, office of the same firm.

discernible, confined, and discrete conveyance through which virtually any sort of waste flows to virtually any sort of surface water body, including certain types of wetlands.

The Act's rather vague definition of "waters of the United States" has raised a number of issues over the years, and the debate continues even today. In particular, determining which wetlands qualify as "waters of the United States" has been the subject of much controversy over the past five years. For example, the term "navigable waters" includes "wetlands," a term whose interpretation has changed repeatedly and still is being debated. Although the basic definition of a wetland has remained unchanged for some time, the criteria used to determine whether that definition is met in any given case have been evolving. *See* 40 C.F.R. § 122.2 (1991); 33 C.F.R. § 328.3(b) (1991). In 1989, the EPA, the Army Corps of Engineers, the Fish and Wildlife Service, and the Soil Conservation Service issued an interagency manual for identifying and delineating wetlands. The Bush Administration recently proposed a new draft version of that manual, but that draft document has been roundly criticized for being unscientific, too difficult to implement, and not protective enough of areas currently defined as wetlands under prior versions of the manual. The debate is likely to continue long after the final manual is published, although the Administration reportedly is considering major revisions.

Distinguishing between Point and Nonpoint Sources

Although the scope of the NPDES program undeniably is broad, it does not cover all sources of pollution. Nonpoint sources of pollution, a class of sources that to this day remains amorphous, are excluded from the program. A classic example of nonpoint source pollution is unchannelled runoff that flows over land and into navigable waters. Other types of discharges may also be classified as nonpoint sources. Indeed, courts have acknowledged that the Act gives the EPA broad authority to define point and nonpoint sources. *NRDC, Inc. v. Costle,* 568 F.2d 1369, 1382 (D.C. Cir. 1977).

The EPA's attempts to distinguish point source discharges of pollutants from nonpoint sources of pollution have been fraught with controversy, most notably with respect to discharges of stormwater runoff. Stormwater discharges present peculiar regulatory problems because they are often difficult or impossible to monitor or control. The fact that there are hundreds of thousands of such discharges, many of which are believed to be *de minimis* in terms of their environmental effects, compounds the regulatory dilemma.

After years of battling among the EPA, environmentalists, and industry groups over the proper scope of regulation for stormwater discharges, Congress attempted to resolve the issue, at least in part. In the Water Quality Act of 1987, Congress amended the Act to provide statutory mandates for the regulation of stormwater discharges. The amendments require the EPA to promulgate two sets of regulations, the first to govern the stormwater discharges most likely to be problematic (i.e., discharges from large and medium-sized municipal storm sewer systems and stormwater discharges associated with industrial activities, or "larger discharges") and the second to govern other problem discharges ("smaller discharges") that are to be identified in studies conducted by the EPA and the states.

Although the amendments require the EPA to regulate the larger stormwater discharges sooner, they established what seemed to be a reasonable schedule by which that permitting process would proceed. Unfortunately, the process has not proceeded as smoothly as Congress intended. The amendments required the EPA to promulgate regulations establishing permit application requirements for larger discharges by late 1989. Applications required under those regulations were to be filed by 1990, and permits were to be issued within one year of application. Thus the EPA theoretically should have issued permits for all larger discharges by late 1991.

In fact, the EPA failed to publish the regulations governing larger discharges until November 16, 1990. 55 Fed. Reg. 47,990. To make matters worse, those regulations have been fraught with problems. Most notably, many industries and municipalities had a difficult time establishing whether they were required to file an application because they could not determine with certainty whether their facility generated any "stormwater discharges associated with industrial activity." Accordingly, deadlines for filing individual permit applications have been extended until as late as October 1, 1992. 56 Fed. Reg. 56,548 (Nov. 5, 1991). The NRDC has challenged that extension, as well as other aspects of the EPA's permit rules.

Moreover, the EPA has barely begun to determine which smaller discharges will require stormwater discharge permits after October 1992. Accordingly, even Congress's intervention has not eliminated the issues associated with determining those stormwater discharges that will require an NPDES permit.

Other Exclusions
In addition to nonpoint sources, certain kinds of discharges that otherwise would fall within the NPDES program are specifically excluded

and instead are subjected to regulation under other provisions of the Act. For instance, discharges to "publicly owned treatment works" by "indirect dischargers" do not require NPDES permits. Instead, indirect dischargers are required to comply with any applicable pretreatment standards or other pretreatment program requirements developed by the EPA under section 307 of the Act.

Also, discharges of "dredged" or "fill" materials must be permitted by the Corps under section 404 of the Act but generally do not require NPDES permits. The relationship between the NPDES program under section 402 of the Act and the dredge and fill permit program under section 404, nevertheless, historically has engendered some confusion. While the EPA has recognized that discharges of dredged or fill material regulated by the Corps under section 404 do not require NPDES permits, the EPA maintains that different aspects of a single operation may indeed require both NPDES and section 404 permits. For example, a federal district court in the Ninth Circuit granted a preliminary injunction enjoining a log transfer operation without an NPDES permit, even though a section 404 permit had been issued. *City of Angoon v. Marsh*, 19 Env't Rep. Cas. (BNA) 1743 (D. Alaska 1983). The EPA, however, has pledged to work with the Corps to develop a means of expediting permit issuance in such cases.

Confusion also arises because the EPA and the Corps have adopted somewhat conflicting definitions of the term "fill." The EPA's NPDES permit regulations define fill using an "effects" test, which provides that the discharge of any material, including waste, that has the effect of converting waters into dry land or changing the bottom elevation of a water body is considered a discharge of fill regulable under section 404, regardless of the purpose of the discharge. 40 C.F.R. § 232.2(i) (1991). By contrast, the Corp's regulations employ a "primary purpose" test, under which any pollutant discharged primarily for the purpose of disposing of waste is not considered fill, even if its effect is to change the bottom elevation. 33 C.F.R. § 323.2(e) (1991).

The EPA and the Corps, at some point, are expected to propose a uniform definition of fill. In the interim, the two agencies have entered into a MOA that provides criteria and procedures for resolving questions regarding the appropriate permitting requirements for discharges of solid and semisolid wastes. 51 Fed. Reg. 8,871 (Mar. 14, 1986). The MOA provides that a discharge may be considered fill if its primary purpose is to replace waters with dry land or to raise the bottom elevation, or if its principal effect is the physical loss or modification of the water body. The MOA also indicates that the discharge of material identified with construction-type activities or associated with sanitary landfill discharges normally will be considered discharge of fill. Despite these criteria, the MOA specifies that discharges in a liquid, semiliquid, or suspended form that are of a homogeneous nature and that are normally associated with single industry wastes will not be considered fill, even if one or more of the above criteria otherwise would be met.

Substantive Permit Application Requirements

Over the years, the EPA also has grappled with the question of what information the Agency reasonably may require a discharger to supply to obtain a permit. The EPA has developed specialized application requirements for existing sources, new sources and new dischargers, dischargers of nonprocess wastewater, and stormwater discharges, as well as for discharges associated with specific operations, such as concentrated animal feeding operations and aquatic animal production facilities. Those application requirements vary widely due to a number of factors, including the types of operations performed by the discharging facility and the types of pollutants that the EPA determines are likely to be contained in the discharge. The information required ranges from the very general (such as the name and location of the facility) to the very specific (such as representative data on specific pollutants in the discharge). The application requirements for three types of sources—stormwater point sources, nonprocess dischargers, and new sources and new dischargers—provide a good illustration of the differences among various application requirements. The requirements for stormwater point source discharges are particularly topical because industrial sources presently are in the process of filing those applications.

Individual Stormwater Discharge Applications

The EPA has revised NPDES Form 2F for individual stormwater discharge applications. 55 Fed. Reg. 47,990, 48,076 (Nov. 16, 1990). Applicants must identify all stormwater discharge outfalls, all areas of their facilities that drain to those outfalls, and the types of "significant materials" that are exposed to stormwater in those areas. Applicants must take samples of the effluent discharge from identified outfalls during a qualifying storm event and report the results with the application.

The individual stormwater application is complicated and time consuming. In an effort to reduce the regulatory burden, the EPA has provided two alternatives to that process. First, the EPA adopted a group application approach, under which similarly situated dischargers (i.e., an industry or trade group) may opt to submit a single application. The group application process minimizes the number of facilities that must submit quantitative sampling data. The application process consists of two parts. Part I of the group application consists only of (1) a list that identifies those members who wish to participate in the group, (2) a narrative description summarizing the industrial activities of participants, (3) a list of significant materials stored outdoors, and (4) identification of those group members who will submit quantitative data on behalf of the group (10 percent of group members for groups consisting of greater than ten facilities; 50 percent of group members for groups consisting of ten or fewer facilities). After the EPA approves the group, those facilities identified in Part I as supplying quantitative data must prepare and submit the information required in Form 2F. The EPA will use the information collected to develop general permits covering all facilities in the group.

General Permitting

For many dischargers, even the group approach is unnecessarily burdensome. To help many smaller facilities covered under the stormwater regulations, the EPA recently proposed a draft general permit to cover many "storm water discharges associated with industrial activity." 56 Fed. Reg. 40,993 (Aug. 16, 1991). Dischargers who qualify to use the general permit approach would only need to file a NOI that the facility wishes to be covered under the general permit to satisfy their application requirements.

Coverage under a general permit, however, is limited. The EPA's general permit would only apply in those states where the EPA is the NPDES permitting authority. Nevertheless, many states that have assumed the responsibility for administering the NPDES permit program have the authority to adopt general permits, and the EPA is working with several other states to obtain that authority. A number of those states with existing authority to issue general permits either have proposed to adopt the EPA's proposed general permit or have developed their own.

The EPA has developed a separate Form 2E for use by sources of nonprocess discharges such as sanitary wastes, restaurant wastes, and noncontact cooling water, which do not come into contact with industrial processes, products, or raw materials. 51 Fed. Reg. 26,982, 25,994 (Jul. 28, 1986). This form may be used only by facilities that discharge solely nonprocess wastewaters and that do not discharge wastewaters regulated by categorical technology-based effluent limitations guidelines or standards. Form 2E requires only minimal testing for a list of eleven parameters (mostly conventional pollutants) as well as some general information about the type of wastes discharged, the frequency and duration of wastewater flows, and the treatment system used. Where stormwater is combined with nonprocess wastewater, the applicant must file both form 2E and 2F.

The EPA designed a special Form 2D for use by new sources and new dischargers. 51 Fed. Reg. 26,982, 26,999 (Jul. 28, 1986). Briefly, new sources are those sources of pollutant discharges that begin construction after the EPA proposes applicable NSPS under section 306 of the Act (if those NSPS are thereafter promulgated within 120 days of the proposal). New dischargers are sources that do not qualify as new sources but which began discharging pollutants at a particular site after August 13, 1979, and which have never received a final, effective NPDES permit. While this form requires fairly extensive information on toxic pollutants present in the discharge, it allows applicants to estimate pollutant levels. Within two years after commencement of the discharge, applicants must submit follow-up data on the actual levels of toxic pollutants discharged. As with form 2E, where a new source discharge will be combined with a stormwater discharge, dischargers must submit both Form 2D and 2F.

Permit Terms and Conditions

No description of the NPDES permit program would be complete without at least a brief discussion of the types of permit terms and conditions normally included in permits. While permit terms and conditions vary depending upon the characteristics of the individual discharge and upon whether the EPA or the state is the permit issuer, the EPA has established certain minimum requirements against which all permits are to be measured.

The Minimum Requirements

Many permit conditions are standardized, boilerplate terms applicable to all NPDES permittees. For example, permit terms established by the EPA require the permittee to mitigate violations that would adversely affect human health or the environment, to properly operate and maintain the treatment system, to allow the EPA or its authorized representative to enter and inspect the facilities, to conduct monitoring representative of the regulated activity and keep complete records of the monitoring activities for three years, and to comply with the permit. Other standard terms limit the circumstances under which the permit may be modified, revoked and reissued, or terminated; prohibit bypassing (i.e., diverting waste streams from any portion of the treatment facility) except under limited circumstances; and limit the conditions under which a permittee may claim that violations of the Act or the permit are excused by an upset in the process or treatment system. The permit also will include standard reporting requirements that compel the permittee to submit monthly discharge monitoring reports and to notify the permitting authority of certain changes in the facility or its discharges.

The More Specialized Requirements

In addition to these boilerplate terms, in most cases the permit must contain specialized requirements applicable to the particular discharger. For instance, permits for dischargers belonging to a major industrial category must contain limits based upon nationally uniform technology-based effluent limitations guidelines or NSPS developed by the EPA under sections 304 and 306 of the Act. These guidelines or standards, which reflect the levels of pollutant reduction that a given technology can achieve, limit the amount of pollutants a facility may discharge. The guidelines and standards in turn become the basis for NPDES permit limitations.

Where the EPA has not established categorical effluent limitations guidelines applicable to the discharger, section 402(a)(1) of the Act allows the permit issuer to develop technology-based limits on a case-by-case basis, based upon his or her best professional judgment (BPJ). These so-called BPJ limits must reflect consideration of the same factors that the EPA must take into account in establishing national guidelines. It is particularly important for permittees to carefully evaluate BPJ limits when the permit issuer first seeks to impose them, because the EPA's anti-backsliding rule severely restricts the circumstances under which BPJ limits may later be relaxed.

Besides technology-based limits, the permits also must include any more stringent water quality–based limits necessary to meet state water quality standards. State water quality standards consist of designated uses of the waters and numerical and narrative water quality criteria adequate to protect those uses. Once water quality standards have been established, it is the responsibility of each state under section 303(d) of the Act to establish the total maximum daily load (TMDL) of particular pollutants necessary to implement the water quality standards. These TMDLs are allocated among the various dischargers to a water body and eventually are incorporated into NPDES permits as water quality–based permit limitations.

The Debate over Water Quality–Based Standards

As part of the Water Quality Act of 1987, Congress enacted Clean Water Act section 304(l), which requires states to submit to the EPA lists of those water bodies within the state that do not meet water quality standards, even after the imposition of all technology-based requirements. For those water bodies, the states were required to identify any specific point source discharges of toxic pollutants that contributed to the impairment of the water body and to develop for each listed water body an "individual control strategy" to bring it into compliance with water quality standards. This process is largely complete, except to finish the process of implementing the individual control strategies. Accordingly, many facilities discharging into listed water bodies have been, or will be, subject to significant permit modifications as a result of the section 304(l) process.

Even for discharges not regulated under section 304(l), water quality–based permit limitations are becoming increasingly widespread. Now that the EPA has largely completed the first layer of technology-based controls, it has begun to shift its attention to the Act's backup water quality–based regulatory system. At the same time, the enormous difficulties inherent in setting single-number water quality standards and water quality–based permit limitations has prompted the EPA and many states to begin using whole effluent toxicity tests to identify areas where water quality standards are likely to be violated and to measure and regulate the toxicity of effluents from individual discharges. Effluent toxicity tests involve exposing selected species to an undiluted effluent sample to determine its short- or long-term biological effect. While laboratory toxicity tests have existed for many years, their increasing use in the regulatory context has engendered a good deal of controversy.

Dischargers have expressed concern over the use of toxicity testing to establish permit limits and to conduct related compliance monitoring for several reasons. First, they argue that there is evidence suggesting that the existing test methods may produce widely variable results; thus, there may be an unacceptably high possibility that the tests will not accurately measure the toxicity of a given effluent. Second, they point out that the methods for correlating the results of effluent toxicity tests conducted in the laboratory with actual instream environmental effects are not well established. Third, they protest the fact that the EPA has developed these procedures and related guidance on their use without publishing them in the *Federal Register* and providing an opportunity for public comment. (The EPA has proposed to remedy this omission by proposing to incorporate toxicity test methods into the analytical procedures regulations codified at 40 C.F.R. Part 136. *See* 54 Fed. Reg. 50,216 Dec. 4, 1989). Finally, dischargers have argued that the use of such methods in cases where state water quality standards are not expressed in terms of toxicity illegally circumvents the water quality standards-setting process.

Despite these objections, the EPA adopted a rule that specifically allows the use of such tests to establish both technology-based and water quality–based permit limitations. 40 C.F.R. § 125.3(c)(4) (1991). Industry groups challenged that rule, raising many of these arguments. In *NRDC v. EPA*, 859 F.2d 156, 189–91 (D.C. Cir. 1988), the U.S. Court of Appeals upheld the rule but cautioned that permit writers who chose to propose limits would be required to justify such limits on technical and scientific grounds at the time the limits are proposed. The court found that the industry petitioners' many challenges to the scientific and technical underpinnings for the general rule were unripe. *Id.* at 190.

Best Management Practices Requirements

Finally, permits also may contain best management practices (BMPs), which section 304(e) of the Act authorizes the EPA to establish. BMPs are procedures designed to prevent or minimize the release of toxic pollutants or hazardous substances. They are supplemental to other requirements (such as effluent limitations guidelines) and can include such relatively simple measures as cleaning up spilled chemicals promptly or storing containers and drums out of traffic areas where a forklift truck might collide with them and cause a spill. Whether BMPs also may include more structural and expensive measures, such as building dikes around storage tanks, is still a controversial matter. The final BMP regulations that the EPA promulgated in 1979 contemplated the use of such measures in some cases; however, those regulations have been suspended indefinitely. Nevertheless, the EPA asserts that BMPs may be placed in permits on a case-by-case basis under the authority of section 402(a)(1) of the Act. It seems likely that BMPs will appear in permits more frequently in the future, especially as the process for issuing permits for stormwater discharges gets underway.

Although the NPDES program at age twenty is in many respects mature, the EPA still has before it a number of questions for which there are no easy answers. Indeed, issues such as how to regulate stormwater and how to set water quality–based limits have been left for last precisely because they are so difficult. But the EPA must continue its efforts to resolve these questions in a balanced, reasonable fashion if the goals of the Act are to be met.

New Clean Water Act Toxics Control Initiatives

David M. Heineck

The most recent National Water Quality Inventory has indicated that one-third of all monitored river miles, lake acres, and coastal waters have elevated levels of toxics. Most of the 586 fishing advisories and 135 bans that the states have issued to date can be attributed to discharges of pollutants, in particular toxic pollutants, from industrial facilities and land disposal operations. Toxics-related water quality impairment often has occurred even where industrial dischargers have been in full compliance with BAT and all other technology-based effluent limits. These factors have prompted Congress, the EPA, and the states to place renewed emphasis on developing and enforcing water quality standards, in particular those for toxic pollutants.

Much of this emphasis is the result of two key provisions that the Water Quality Act of 1987, Pub. L. No. 100–4, added to the federal Clean Water Act. These are codified as sections 304(1) and 303(c)(2)(B) of the Act, 33 U.S.C. §§ 1314(1) and 1313(c)(2)(B). These sections respectively set an accelerated timetable for dealing with toxic "hot spots" and require states to incorporate numerical criteria for toxics in their water quality standards. They reflect a somewhat paradoxical attitude on the part of Congress—on the one hand impatience with the pace of state efforts in these areas and, on the other, continued recognition that the states rather than the EPA have the primary responsibility for implementing water quality con-

David Heineck is special counsel in Heller, Ehrman, White & McAuliffe in Seattle, Washington.

trols. The requirements and implications of these two sections are the principal focus of this article.

Early Clean Water Act Approaches

Some background on the history and structure of the Clean Water Act is necessary to place these new provisions in context. Prior to 1972, federal regulation of water pollution focused almost exclusively on achieving state water quality standards. This approach proved unsuccessful. Enforcement was difficult because it required the government to disentangle the myriad sources of the water quality impairment to establish that any particular discharger was responsible. Also, by focusing on the impacts of discharges rather than on their causes, it did little to reduce the actual amount of pollutants that were discharged.

The Clean Water Act of 1972 sharply departed from this approach. Pollution prevention became the basic regulatory goal, to be approached through progressively more stringent technology-based effluent limits developed for each industry category. Section 301(b)(1)(A) required use of "best practicable technology" by 1977, with the more demanding "best available technology" to be achieved by 1987. These technological standards represented a minimum degree of effluent reduction that applied to all industry without regard to the quality of the receiving waters. Section 402 of the Act established the NPDES permit system to implement these requirements. The Act prohibited any point source discharge that was not authorized under an NPDES permit.

Although the primary focus of the Clean Water Act is industry-wide technology rather than site-specific water quality, Congress recognized that in some situations technological standards alone cannot achieve state water quality standards. Sections 301(b)(1)(C) and 402(a)(1) of the Act thus require NPDES permits to contain more stringent limits as necessary to meet these standards.

In practice, however, water quality standards often have not been integrated into NPDES permit limits. To some extent this has been due to the fact that these standards have been met by BAT or other technological controls alone. To a large extent, however, it reflects the absence of definite standards. This has been particularly true in the case of toxic pollutants. Although section 307 of the Act required the EPA to develop technology-based effluent limits for toxics, the unwieldy section 307 process and other factors have resulted in EPA issuance of effluent limits for only six toxic pollutants. *See* 40 C.F.R.

Part 129. Toxics regulation under the Clean Water Act thus is based almost exclusively on state-promulgated water quality standards. The perception in Congress that the states were not doing an adequate job in issuing or enforcing these standards was the major factor leading to enactment of new sections 304(l) and 303(c)(2)(B).

The basic problem that has plagued the states can be seen from examining the steps that are involved in establishing water quality standards. The first step is to designate the uses for the water body in question. This may be contact recreation that meets the Clean Water Act target of fishable and swimmable water or, assuming that certain conditions are met, a more restricted use that does not require this highest degree of water quality. See 40 C.F.R. Part 131. The second step is to set "criteria," meaning the maximum pollutant concentrations the water body can contain without jeopardizing its designated uses. The problems connected with toxic pollutants have arisen in this second step. States typically established only descriptive criteria for toxic pollutants—often expressed as "no toxics in toxic amounts"—rather than numerical criteria expressed in units such as μg/l. States for a variety of reasons chose not to adopt the numerical criteria that the EPA had developed under section 304(a) of the Act and did not develop numerical criteria of their own. This imprecision made it difficult to determine whether the designated uses were being impaired. How much of what forms of heavy metals in the ambient conditions of a given stream segment, for example, would harm fish? It also was technically difficult, and legally contentious, to translate these often vague narrative criteria into more stringent NPDES permit limits applicable to specific pollutants and dischargers.

The Water Quality Act of 1987 attempted to fix many of these problems by adding sections 304(l) and 303(c)(2)(B) to the Clean Water Act. These sections are the foundation of the "beyond BAT" program for controlling toxic pollutants.

Section 304(l)

Section 304(l) required states to develop lists of impaired waters, to identify the point sources discharging toxic pollutants to those waters, and to prepare "individual control strategies" for these point sources. Section 304(l) does not represent a change in direction for the Clean Water Act, since the statute always has required states to identify impaired waters and develop wasteload allocations or other controls to restore water quality where needed. See section 303(d). The significance of section 304(l) is that it sets an accelerated schedule for achieving water quality standards where toxics-related standards are not being met. The deadlines are ambitious: June 1992 in states that prepare their own lists of impaired waters and ICSs and June 1993 where the EPA issues the lists and ICSs itself after disapproving a state's proposal. Meeting these deadlines will require more stringent NPDES permit limits on many point sources, industrial and municipal alike, that discharge to impaired waters. As discussed below, the section 304(l) process also could result in added controls on nonpoint sources.

The first requirement under section 304(l) related to preparation of lists of impaired waters in each state. States were required by February 4, 1989, to prepare and submit to the EPA three separate but overlapping lists. Their common denominator is that they identified waters where technological controls alone would not achieve water quality goals. The lists identified:

- waters that after implementation of technology-based controls could not be expected to meet the broad water quality goals of the Act (which may be higher than the promulgated state water quality standards) due to *discharges of any pollutant by any point or nonpoint source*, referred to as the "(A)(ii) list" or "long list," this is the broadest of the three lists;
- waters that after implementation of technological controls could not be expected to meet water quality standards due to *discharges of toxics by point or nonpoint sources*, referred to as the "(A)(i) list"; and
- waters that after technological controls could not be expected to meet water quality standards due *"entirely or substantially" to discharges of toxics from point sources*, referred to as the "(B) list" or "short list," this is the narrowest of the three.

These lists set the stage for two follow-up actions by the states or, if the states failed to act, the EPA. First, section 304(l)(1)(C) required the states to identify the point sources that were discharging toxics in amounts believed to be impairing the listed waters. Second, and more importantly, section 304(l)(1)(D) required the states to develop individual control strategies (interpreted by the EPA to mean modified NPDES permits) for these waters so that "in combination with existing controls on point and nonpoint sources" they would achieve compliance with water quality standards.

The EPA issued regulations in 1989 that interpreted the two follow-up requirements of subsections (C) and (D) as applying only to waters on the short list, i.e., waters impaired substantially or entirely due to point source discharges of toxic pollutants. One regulation, codified at 40 C.F.R. § 130.10(d)(3), indicated that the only point sources that had to be identified were those discharging to waters on the short list. A second regulation at 40 C.F.R. § 123.46(a) similarly provided that states had to develop ICSs only for point sources that discharged to the short list of waters. The first of these regulations was invalidated and the second remanded, in *NRDC v. EPA*, 31 E.R.C. 2089 (9th Cir. 1990). The effect of this ruling is unclear since the statutory deadlines for identifying the relevant point sources and developing the ICSs have passed. The states and the EPA may have to develop a more comprehensive list of point sources and develop ICSs for each of them. This may be a somewhat hollow victory for the environmentalists, however. The waters that appear only on the longer lists by definition are not substantially affected by point source discharges of toxics. Identifying the point sources discharging to those waters and developing ICSs for them thus will result in little added environmental benefit.

With the exception of the additional listings and ICSs that may be required by *NRDC v. EPA*, the actions required by section 304(l) have been completed. The EPA made section 304(l) a high priority and completed its review of state listings and proposed ICSs by the June 1989 deadline. These reviews resulted in EPA designation of 595 water bodies on the short list and 869 point source dischargers of toxic pollutants to those waters, including 240 POTWs. Revised NPDES permits incorporating ICSs have been issued to these sources. These permits were designed to achieve the ambitious compliance deadline of June 1992 (or June 1993 for EPA-issued permits) that was set by section 304(l). Most of these permits now are in various stages of administrative appeals.

Since most of the actions required by section 304(l) now have been completed, it is fair to ask how the exercise has added to the body of knowledge concerning toxics-related water quality problems and how it has affected dischargers. There is no doubt that the scrutiny involved in developing the section 304(l) lists has resulted in a more complete water quality inventory. The lists themselves, however, should not be viewed as the definitive indication of where there are (or are not) water quality problems. The lists have two basic shortcomings. First, they were generated by reference to often imprecise water quality standards. As described above, at the time they prepared the section 304(l) lists, most states had only a narrative toxics criterion of "no toxics in toxic amounts." The difficulties of applying these narrative criteria to complex ambient conditions make them an unreliable gauge of water quality. Second, the lists were prepared on the basis of existing water quality information that often was incomplete. The tight deadlines imposed by section 304(l) did not allow the states or the EPA to develop more complete information before developing the lists. In the absence of such information, the states in many cases presumably had to rely on simple dilution calculations to determine whether water quality was impaired. These calculations usually assume that pollutants are being discharged in the amounts authorized by permit, and they also assume complete mixing of the discharges. The lists generated on this basis may be either too broad or too narrow. They can be too broad by ignoring important factors that may reduce toxicity, such as sorption and biological transformation. The lists at the same time may be too narrow, since actual discharges of toxics may exceed permit limits, some toxics are non-soluble and tend to accumulate in sediments rather than be dispersed by dilution, and nonpoint source impacts may be unknown and disregarded.

The impact of section 304(l) on dischargers will depend on the ICSs that ultimately are incorporated into their NPDES permits. Whether the states or the EPA were justified in designating particular water bodies on the section 304(l) lists and in imposing particular ICSs on sources discharging to those waters are issues that apparently will be litigated only in the permit modification process. The courts have held that EPA approval of the section 304(l) lists developed by a state, and EPA action in issuing the section 304(l) lists itself, do not constitute "promulgation" of ICSs and thus are not reviewable. *Municipal Authority of Borough of St. Mary's v. U.S. EPA*, 945 F.2d 67 (9th Cir. 1991); *P.H. Glatfelter Co. v. EPA*, 32 E.R.C. 1595 (4th Cir. 1990). Similarly, the courts have held that EPA approval of draft or final NPDES permits issued by a state that have been modified to contain ICS requirements is not a reviewable EPA "promulgation." *Boise Cascade Corp. v. U.S. EPA*, 942 F.2d 1427 (9th Cir. 1991); *Roll Coater, Inc. v. Reilly*, 932 F.2d 668 (7th Cir. 1991). The result of these decisions is that judicial review can be obtained only if the ICS has been embodied in a final NPDES permit and other prerequisites have been met, such as exhaustion of administrative remedies. Review will be in state court for state-issued NPDES permits; permits issued by the EPA will be reviewable, pursuant to Clean Water Act section 509, in federal circuit court.

Although the actions required by section 304(l) largely have been completed, they are likely to have continuing effects. One of the more interesting possibilities is that section 304(l) may engender greater efforts on the part of states to control nonpoint source discharges. This possibility arises from the requirement in section 304(l)(1)(D) that ICSs must be designed to achieve compliance with state standards "in combination with existing controls . . . on nonpoint sources." The EPA has issued guidance under section 304(l) that interprets the term "existing" to refer to those controls that will be effective by the compliance deadline of June 4, 1992. States are free under section 304(l) to allocate the necessary pollutant reductions among point sources and nonpoint sources as they see fit. Few states so far have effective enforcement programs relating to nonpoint sources. In these circumstances, it is not difficult to make the prediction that where listed waters are receiving toxic pollutants from nonpoint sources—which may be the case from mining and agricultural operations, for example—point source dischargers will attempt to persuade the states to place some of the burden of compliance where it rarely has been: on the nonpoint sources. This section 304(l)-induced conflict between point sources and nonpoint sources will be even more likely to occur if the EPA, in response to the Ninth Circuit's remand in *NRDC v. EPA*, ultimately requires ICSs even for point sources discharging to waters on the two longer section 304(l) lists that are impaired largely due to nonpoint discharges.

If section 304(l) in fact provokes a conflict between point source and nonpoint source dischargers, this may breathe unexpected life into the nonpoint source provisions of section 319. Clean Water Act section 319, like section 304(l), was added by the 1987 amendments. It requires the states to identify waters that are being impaired due to nonpoint source impacts. Since it has no enforcement provisions and the states have a great deal of discretion in carrying out the program, section 319 has been regarded as something of a lame duck provision that would result in few if any actual controls on nonpoint sources. That may change as point source dischargers whose permits are being tightened under section 304(l) demand that the states exercise their discretion under section 319 to tighten controls on nonpoint sources as well.

A second issue in modifying NPDES permits to incorporate ICSs is that a new and unfamiliar permit condition may be added, one requiring biological monitoring to limit the "whole effluent toxicity" of the discharge. The EPA issued guidance in December 1989 identifying five species, three for fresh water and two for salt water, to be used in such biomonitoring. While there appears to be legal authority under section 301(b)(1)(C) of the Act for establishing such a permit condition, issues such as the appropriate species to be used in estuarine conditions and the point within or outside any mixing zone where the biomonitoring should be conducted will make this requirement a controversial one.

Additional issues will be raised in incorporating ICSs in the permits for the 240 municipal POTWs that the EPA determined were discharging toxics to waters on the short list, and in listing waters and developing ICSs for sources on Indian lands. Municipalities whose NPDES permits are made more stringent to incorporate ICSs are likely to place more stringent pretreatment requirements on industrial dischargers. This could be in the form of additional requirements or stricter enforcement of existing limits. The issue with regard to Indian lands is that, with few exceptions, Indian tribes have not developed water quality standards that are enforceable under the Clean Water Act. This means that, as a general rule, there are no water quality standards to serve as the reference for the section 304(1) lists, or as the target for any needed ICSs, for waters on Indian lands. It is not clear what impact these shortcomings may have with respect to making any needed improvements to water quality on Indian lands.

A final issue relating to section 304(1) concerns the effect of new section 302(b)(2)(B). This section appears to allow the EPA, but not the states, to grant a five-year suspension of NPDES permit limits that the EPA tightens under section 304(1) if the discharger is making "reasonable progress" to the extent of its economic ability in reducing toxic pollutant discharges. No EPA guidance has been issued on this section, and its usefulness as a basis for modifying EPA-imposed ICSs is not yet clear.

Section 303(c)(2)(B)

The second major toxics-related provision added by the Water Quality Act of 1987 was section 303(c)(2)(B). This section required states to adopt EPA-promulgated numerical criteria for toxic pollutants "the discharge or presence of which in the affected waters could reasonably be expected to interfere with those designated uses adopted by the State, as necessary to support such designated uses." These numerical criteria would replace narrative standards such as "no toxics in toxic amounts." The EPA guidance encouraged the states to use the information they developed in compiling the section 304(1) lists to identify the toxic pollutants that needed these numerical controls.

In contrast to section 304(1), which merely accelerates compliance with existing standards, section 303(c)(2)(B) requires structural changes to the standards themselves. This makes it a much more significant provision. The EPA has issued aquatic and human health criteria for 126 different toxic pollutants. These pollutants are listed in Appendix A to 40 C.F.R. Part 423. Adoption of these criteria into state water quality standards, and later into revised limits for NPDES permits, will permanently change the "beyond BAT" regulation of toxics.

The states were required to adopt the EPA numerical criteria as necessary during the first triennial review of their water quality standards after enactment of the Water Quality Act of 1987. Since this review was required at some point during fiscal years 1988–90, EPA guidance concluded that the deadline for such adoption was September 30, 1990.

The thirty-five states that the EPA determined had fully complied with section 303(c)(2)(B) as of late 1991 took a variety of approaches in adopting the numerical criteria. While the states generally adopted the aquatic life and noncarcinogenic human health criteria with few changes, they took widely different approaches with respect to the human health criteria for carcinogens. This divergence to some extent reflects disagreement with the basic assumptions underlying these criteria, including the belief that carcinogenicity is a "no-threshold" phenomenon, the use of a linear extrapolation model to determine the cancer potency of low doses based on experimental results from high dosages, and assumptions regarding the extent to which carcinogens tend to accumulate in fish tissues.

State efforts to adopt numerical criteria for the toxic pollutant 2,3,7,8-TCDD (dioxin) illustrate this divergence. The EPA classifies dioxin as a human carcinogen that, in order to achieve a cancer risk level of one in one million (i.e., 10^{-6}), must not exceed an ambient water concentration of 0.013 picograms per liter (equivalent to 0.013 parts per quadrillion). Some states have disagreed with the cancer slope factor and fish bioconcentration ratios that the EPA has derived for dioxin and have expressed their disagreement by exercising their discretion under EPA policy to adopt more lenient standards based on a 10^{-5} or 10^{-4} risk level. Use of different potency factors and risk levels has resulted in up to a hundredfold difference in the numerical criteria the states have adopted for dioxin. The criteria for dioxin are likely to evolve and create added controversy as the EPA identifies human health effects other than cancer for this compound.

Approximately twenty-two states had not adopted the EPA numerical toxics criteria as of late 1991. In the EPA's view, this violated the congressional directive of section 303(c)(2)(B) and made it necessary under section 304(c)(4) for the Agency to itself amend the water quality standards for those states. *See* 56 Fed. Reg. 58,420 (Nov. 19, 1991). The EPA accomplished this through revisions to 40 C.F.R. Part 131 that were issued in early 1992. The EPA incorporated in the state standards virtually all the numerical toxics criteria that these states had not adopted and, with regard to carcinogens, adopted human health criteria corresponding to a risk level of 10^{-6}. States remain free to adopt less stringent criteria, up to a risk level of 10^{-4}, if they develop a record showing that such action is in the public interest.

Adoption of these numerical toxics criteria will accomplish a number of useful purposes. For example, it will make it easier to determine whether water quality standards are being violated, simplify the translation of water quality criteria into NPDES permit limits, and introduce a measure of uniformity, at least in the near term, in the water quality standards of the affected states.

This added administrative efficiency may come at an unacceptable cost, however. The numerical criteria are the product of conservative assumptions that probably restrict toxics to levels far below those needed for environmental and human health protection. The EPA itself acknowledges in its 1991 Technical Support Document for Water Quality–Based Toxics Control that the criteria can be overly stringent. The criteria for heavy metals, for example, are based on total concentrations that ignore their chemical form and other factors that affect their bioavailability. Also, the criteria for maximum short-term exposures, referred to as "criterion maximum concentrations" (CMCs), require the use of a one-hour averaging period that is based on the action time of ammonia, one of the fastest-acting toxicants. Similarly, the criteria for chronic exposures, known as "criterion continuous concentrations" (CCCs), require the use of a four-day average that reflects the fastest time any organism experiences toxicity at those levels. Very conservative criteria are the result when it is assumed that all toxics act, and all organisms respond, as rapidly as the fastest do. More generally, the criteria by their very nature are uniform standards that ignore site-specific factors such as chemical sorption and precipitation, acid/base reactions, and biochemical transformation. Such factors can greatly affect chemical bioavailability.

These and other shortcomings in the EPA criteria are likely to lead to greater efforts by industry, municipalities, and the states to develop more site-specific criteria that are a better measure of actual toxic effects. Stormwater regulation—given its financial impacts and the technical issues it presents—is the context in which these site-specific adjustments are most likely to be sought. For example, the episodic nature of stormwater discharges will challenge the EPA's rationale in using short averaging periods for its CMC and CCC limits. Also, the fact that stormwater discharges often contain substantial amounts of metals will call into question the EPA's approach in applying the toxics criteria to total metals, rather than the fraction that is biologically available.

As the foundation of the "beyond BAT" program, Clean Water Act sections 304(l) and 303(c)(2)(B) mark the transition to an era in which technological standards will be more closely integrated with water quality–based controls. One of the results of this transition will be greater variation in permit conditions. NPDES permits that up to this point have been based almost exclusively on nationally uniform BAT and secondary treatment requirements increasingly will reflect state-specific, and potentially site-specific, water quality criteria. This divergence already has been seen in the case of numerical criteria for dioxin. NPDES permit limits also may vary from state to state to the extent that section 304(l) prompts particular states to place more controls on nonpoint sources.

Although these new effluent limits certainly will reduce levels of toxic pollutants, this kind of geographical variation could undo much of the progress the Clean Water Act has made in establishing nationally uniform standards and eliminating pollution havens. One wonders whether the next set of Clean Water Act amendments might introduce new technological standards, perhaps known as "beyond beyond BAT," to restore order in the realm of water pollution control.

What Water Quality Lawyers Should Know about Water Law

Arne M. Rovick and D. Lee Decker

American water law is a compilation of common law and state statutes. Early water law in the United States evolved from English common law, especially because the topography and climate of the East Coast were similar to England's. Therefore English common law was easily adapted to early American water needs. As the nation expanded, new theories developed to deal with the limited water supplies of the arid and semi-arid West. Now, most western states have developed extensive statutory programs to regulate water use. The federal government has to a large extent left water law matters to the states; Congress has not enacted comprehensive water use laws but generally has limited its laws to water quality issues.

Surface Water

An analysis of American water law must start with a discussion of surface water. Rivers and streams were the early primary sources of water. Common-law rules on water rights evolved out of controversies concerning the allocation and use of flowing surface water. The fundamental principle of surface water rights—the riparian doctrine—is that landowners bordering a river have some rights or privileges in maintaining the natural flow past their property. The riparian landowners do not have a right in or title to the flowing waters. They only have a right to *use* the water. Two distinct theories have devel-

Arne Rovick is senior vice-president and general counsel for Edina Realty, Inc., in Minneapolis, Minnesota. Lee Decker is an associate in the Phoenix, Arizona, law firm of Kimball & Curry, P.C.

oped relating to the manner in which the riparian right may be exercised. They are the English rule of natural flow and the American rule of reasonable use.

Under the English rule of natural flow, landowners adjacent to a stream or river have the right to have the water flow past their property undiminished in quantity and unimpaired in quality. Strictly applied, this rule is unworkable. No one could withdraw any water or discharge any substance into the river without diminishing the quantity or impairing the quality. The American rule of reasonable use looks to balancing the uses by the riparian landowners. The test of reasonableness is whether the use causes injury to other riparians. In contrast to the English rule, which ties water use to adjacent land, the American rule does not. The American reasonable use rule may allow a use unconnected with the riparian land or even on nonriparian land.

The early eastern courts dealt with uses of stream flow for domestic purposes, stock watering, and water power. Consumption from such uses was not large. The growth of irrigated agriculture and mining in the West, however, made significant consumptive demands on streams that had relatively small undependable flows. With significant investment required for large farms or mines, the demand for a more absolute right to water became necessary.

The concept of prior appropriation, which developed in the arid and semi-arid states of the West, is based on the principle of first in time, first in right. Priority is fixed at the time of the first substantial act that leads to the diversion and beneficial use of the water. In states having statutory administration, the date of priority is usually determined by the date a permit is filed to divert water. Appropriative rights are fixed and certain as to time and amounts of water that can be taken. The senior appropriator is allowed to take his or her full share before the junior appropriator is allowed to take any water. The appropriation right is tied to use, and unlike the riparian right, an appropriation right can be lost by nonuse or abandonment. The uses that can be made of the water are not as limited as under the riparian theories. The use need not be connected to the land and can even be on nonriparian lands. However, the use must be beneficial in the sense of not being wasteful.

A relatively new issue facing western appropriation water rights is the concept of minimum instream flows. Traditionally, water has been appropriated and diverted from a stream for use in agricultural, mining, municipal, and, more recently, in energy development settings. These beneficial uses are all consumptive. The appropriation theory contemplates, indeed expects, that there will be consumptive uses that will affect the natural flows and may even dry up the streams. Advocates of the minimum instream flow concept argue that the maintenance of instream flows for fish and wildlife preservation and for recreation and aesthetic purposes is a beneficial use. But maintenance of natural flows is the cornerstone of the riparian theory. The appropriation theory emerged in the West to do away with the riparian theory and allow a stream to be fully used and diverted to consumptive uses. Thus placing a minimum instream flow concept within the prior appropriation theory is inconsistent with its purpose and history.

The basic arguments against minimum instream flows are threefold. First, the use is not beneficial in the traditional sense because it is not a consumptive use. Second, no diversion occurs whereas appropriation requires a taking of water from the stream. Third, the water is not in the exclusive control of the appropriator. Appropriation contemplates the conversion of a public resource to private property by taking exclusive control of the water.

The arguments for minimum instream flows were discussed at length in *State Department of Parks v. Idaho Department of Water Administration*, 96 Idaho 440, 530 P.2d 924 (1974). The court reasoned that beneficial use is an evolving concept that changes with society's development. While traditional beneficial uses involved mining, agricultural, and municipal uses, there was no common-law or statutory prohibition against environmental or aesthetic concerns becoming beneficial uses. The court reasoned that, to the extent society's values change, new uses become recognized and, as long as society benefits from those uses, they can be recognized as beneficial uses. *See also Nebraska Game and Parks Comm'n v. The 25 Corporation, Inc.*, 236 Neb. 671, 463 N.W.2d. 591 (1990) (as corrected); *State v. Morros*, 766 P.2d 263 (Nev. 1988); *Colorado River Water Conservation Dist. v. Colorado Water Conservation Bd.*, 594 P.2d 570 (Colo. 1979); *McClellan v. Jantzen*, 26 Ariz. App. 223, 547 P.2d 494 (1976).

Another relatively new development concerning western appropriation water rights, and one which is closely related to instream flows, is the movement to establish riparian area protection. For example, riparian area protection legislation has been proposed in Arizona, which would make extensive changes to state water law. The legislation would establish certain protective standards that would have to be met before new appropriations or changes to existing appropriation rights would be authorized. Additionally, the legislation would evaluate the effect of groundwater pumping on riparian areas and, depending on the results of the evaluation, would impose restrictions on groundwater use to the extent that it adversely affects riparian areas. Other western states have adopted or are in the process of adopting similar legislation.

Evidencing society's growing environmental concerns is the establishment in California of the public trust doctrine as an independent water preservation consideration on equal footing with prior appropriation rights. *See National Audubon Soc'y v. Superior Court of Alpine County*, 33 Cal. 3d 419, 658 P.2d 709, 189 Cal. Rptr. 346 (1983). The basic principle of the public trust doctrine is that a state has the sovereign authority to supervise and control the navigable waters and the lands underlying those waters. Just as the appropriation theory has expanded to encompass aesthetic considerations for minimum instream flows, the public trust doctrine has expanded from navigation to protection of recreational and ecological values.

In *National Audubon Society*, the City of Los Angeles had been diverting water from four tributaries of Mono Lake for more than forty years. During this time, the lake's surface elevation had fallen forty-three feet and its area had diminished from eighty-five to sixty square miles. Salinity had risen due to the reduction of fresh water inflow. The National Audubon Society and others alleged that this was causing severe environmental damage and filed suit to enjoin future diversions.

The court determined that the public trust doctrine in California had expanded to protect ecological as well as navigational values. The court went on to hold that the doctrine protects navigable waters from harm caused by diversion from nonnavigable tributaries. More importantly, the court held that the state's power as administrator of the public trust extends to the revocation of previously granted appropriation rights. The court further reasoned that the state, as sovereign, retains continuing supervisory control, and no party may acquire a vested right to appropriate water in a manner harmful to the public trust. The case was remanded to the trial court to balance the interests of the state under the public trust doctrine against the interests of Los Angeles under its appropriation rights.

What is significant is that well-established appropriation rights, in existence for forty years, could be challenged by a long-dormant but evolving ecological claim. The city had constructed dams, aqueducts, and hydroelectric power plants to develop its appropriation water rights. Nonetheless, the city's long-established appropriation rights based on priority, quantification, and use could be challenged and modified by a claim to protect environmental concerns, a claim that had no established priority date, no quantification, and no record of use.

The federal government has generally left the application of water law to the states. Federal mining statutes have specifically recognized state water rights. No national legislation has been enacted to establish a comprehensive national water law. However, federal common law and federal legislation can affect state water rights.

The most significant federal law principle affecting water rights is the federal reserved water rights doctrine first enunciated in *Winters v. United States*, 207 U.S. 564 (1908). The *Winters* doctrine provides that when the federal government reserved federal lands for a specific purpose—such as an Indian reservation, national forest, or military reservation—the federal government also implicitly reserved a quantity of water sufficient to carry out the primary purpose of the reserved land. The federal reserved rights exist independently of the beneficial use concepts of prior appropriation and therefore are quite different from water rights established by prior appropriation. Federal reserved water rights and prior appropriation water rights differ in three significant factors, namely, use, quantification, and notice.

Appropriation rights arise out of the taking and using of water. The right can be lost if the water is no longer put to a beneficial use. Appropriative rights therefore demand open and continuous diversion of the stream. *Winters* rights, however, exist without any use. These rights can spring into use after many years of inactivity, just as the public trust doctrine rights did in the California case regarding Mono Lake.

Federal reserved water rights are not quantified; indeed, they are generally no more than implied rights. The federal legislation creating the federal enclave may not even address water per se. The *Winters* doctrine merely holds that Congress, in setting aside the land, certainly contemplated that a certain minimum amount of water must be reserved to carry out the legislated purposes. The date of priority is the date of the creation of the federal reservation. It is left for a later time to determine and quantify that need.

Appropriation rights are now recorded in statutory schemes that have been established in all the appropriation rights states. The claims on a stream can be determined by reference to a public record. *Winters* rights, on the other hand, need not be recorded or filed. They quietly exist by virtue of federal legislation passed many years ago, and the water right is not indexed along with other state water rights.

Harmonizing well-established prior appropriation rights with long-dormant federal reserved rights will result in confrontations that will necessitate considerable effort to resolve. For example, Arizona is currently facing perhaps decades of litigation over the priority, quantification, and scope of federal reserved rights. Two major water rights adjudications are pending in Arizona: the Gila River adjudication, covering river basins in the central and southern portions of the state, and the Little Colorado River adjudication, covering river basins in the northern portion of the state. In each adjudication, the claims of federal reserved rights holders and prior appropriation rights holders have been joined. Most basins within the areas covered by the two adjudications are fully subscribed by the recorded prior appropriation rights. The unquantified federal reserved rights claims, mostly by the Indian tribes, necessarily result in a confrontation over water being used by another. It will be difficult to allocate the scarce water resources among parties now claiming several times more than proven reliable under supplies.

The federal Clean Water Act, 33 U.S.C. § 1251 *et seq.*, has as its primary purpose the protection of the quality of the nation's surface water. Section 101(g) of the Clean Water Act states that one of Congress's policies is that "the authority of each State to allocate quantities of water within its jurisdiction shall not be superseded, abrogated or otherwise impaired by this [Act]." This is yet another expression of the congressional policy to stay out of state water rights issues. However, the Clean Water Act and other federal environmental statutes, as enforced, can have an effect on water rights. In *Riverside Irrigation District v. Andrews*, 758 F.2d 508 (10th Cir. 1985), the court upheld the Army Corps of Engineers's denial of a nationwide permit under section 404 of the Clean Water Act to construct a dam because the reservoir would deplete the downstream flow and thereby adversely affect the habitat of an endangered species, the whooping crane. The irrigation district argued that the Corps could not deny a nationwide permit for the dam because the denial of the permit would prevent the district from using its state water rights in contravention of section 101(g) of the Clean Water Act. The court rejected this argument and held that the irrigation district would have to seek permission to construct the dam under the Clean Water Act's individual permit procedure even if such procedure incidentally affected the district's water rights. *See also United States v. Akers*, 785 F.2d 814 (9th Cir.), *cert. denied*, 479 U.S. 828 (1986) (incidental effect on state water law rights is justified if requirements of Clean Water Act achieve legitimate purposes of the Act). Federal environmental statutes, including the Clean Water Act, the Federal Power Act, and the Endangered Species Act, therefore can affect state water rights.

Groundwater

Groundwater is water percolating through the soil and rock beneath the surface of the earth. As with surface water, common law and statutory law developed to regulate the use of groundwater. The English rule, American rule, correlative rights, and prior appropriation doctrines have evolved. Many western states apply the doctrine of prior appropriation to groundwater. However, a few western states apply either the American rule, the correlative rule, or a combination of the two.

The English common-law rule was one of absolute ownership. Percolating waters were part and parcel of the land in which they were found. The groundwater belonged absolutely to the owner of the land. The owner could without liability withdraw any quantity of water for any purpose. This was true even though the withdrawal might drain all the water from beneath adjacent lands. The English groundwater rule contrasted remarkably with the English riparian surface rights doctrine. Groundwater was governed by absolute ownership, indifferent to the effects of the use on others. The English riparian rights doctrine for surface water was guided by the concept of balancing the effects of the use on all other riparian owners. Thus, England had two contrasting rules, one for surface water and one for groundwater.

The American rule or reasonable use doctrine softens the English rule somewhat by limiting the rights of absolute ownership. The overlying property owner owns the water beneath the surface of the land, but the groundwater may be used only on the land from beneath which it is withdrawn. The water must be used for purposes incidental to the beneficial enjoyment of the land such as agricultural, mining, or municipal uses. As long as the groundwater is withdrawn for reasonable use in connection with the land from which it is withdrawn, there is no liability to an adjoining landowner for whatever damage may occur from the withdrawal. If the landowner uses the water off the premises, an adjoining landowner may recover damages or an injunction if he or she can show actual damage resulting from the withdrawal.

The correlative rights doctrine is another modification of the English rule, and it is similar to riparian rights in surface water. Again, the landowner has a proprietary right to the water beneath his or her land. However, the rights are limited not by beneficial use but by the concept of sharing *pro rata* among all owners overlying the aquifer when there is a scarcity of supply. A landowner may not use more than his or her fair share if other landowners would be injured by a greater use. The largest landowner of a region has the largest water right.

The same economic considerations that led to the development of the doctrine of prior appropriation for surface water led to the development of prior appropriation of groundwater. Large investments in irrigated agriculture and mining required a reliable right to water. The right should not be eroded away by the correlative rights of others who later came to the area.

Following a pure appropriation system can lead to unreasonable water allocations, especially as arid western states are further developed. The trend has been to modify the prior appropriation systems by statute and to establish priorities by classification. Domestic uses are generally deemed to have the highest preference and commercial uses the least. During periods of scarcity, uses of a higher preference will be allocated water before a lower preference, regardless of any priority of time.

The federal reserve rights doctrine has been applied to surface water since it was first enunciated in the *Winters* case in 1908. The U.S. Supreme Court had an opportunity to apply the doctrine to groundwater but declined to do so in *Cappaert v. United States*, 426 U.S. 128 (1976).

In *Cappaert*, the United States sued to enjoin a Nevada rancher from withdrawing water from the ground to protect the water level in caverns in Devil's Hole National Monument. Residing in these caverns were pupfish, an endangered species. In 1952, Devil's Hole was added to the Death Valley National Monument to preserve the unique subsurface pools in which the pupfish resided. The Court had a clear opportunity to extend federal reserved right to groundwater but declined to do so. Instead, the Court classified the pool as surface water. The case therefore can be narrowly interpreted to restrict withdrawal that lowers water levels in interconnected pools of surface water on federal reservations to the extent that such withdrawal jeopardizes the purposes of the federal reservation. However, broadly interpreted, *Cappaert* has been cited for the principle that federal reserved water rights are applicable to groundwater.

Lower courts have differed when deciding whether to extend federal reserved rights to groundwater. For instance, in *In re General*

Adjudication of All Rights to Use Water in the Big Horn River System, 753 P.2d 76, 99–100 (Wyo. 1988), *aff'd on other grounds by an equally divided court sub nom. Wyoming v. United States*, 492 U.S. 406, *reh'g denied*, 492 U.S. 938 (1989), the court held that federal reserved rights do not extend to groundwater. In contrast, however, an Arizona water rights adjudication court has held that federal reserved rights apply to groundwater that is unappropriable under state law as long as the groundwater's diversion causes the federal reservation to have an insufficient supply of water to satisfy the reservation's purpose. The Arizona Supreme Court recently granted interlocutory review of the adjudication court's holding. A definitive ruling is needed.

Water scarce western states in regulating their groundwater have commonly enacted statutes to prohibit the transport of groundwater from the state of origin. These statutes came under attack in *Sporhase v. Nebraska*, 458 U.S. 941 (1982). The Court held that groundwater is an item of interstate commerce and therefore the embargo statute imposed an impermissible burden on interstate commerce. However, the Court recognized that limitations on transport of groundwater could be imposed in a reasonable manner for water conservation and protection of the public welfare. The case is significant because it is the first decision holding that water is an article of interstate commerce. But, more importantly, the decision could portend a significant shift in regulation of groundwater from the states to the federal government. Congress has traditionally deferred to state water law; however, the authority to regulate was always believed to exist. The *Sporhase* decision clearly establishes the legal basis for federal regulation. The growing concern over groundwater quality and the depletion of interstate aquifers could lead to congressional action to regulate water rights as well as water quality.

In sum, American water law has changed with the changing demands of our society. The relatively recent environmental movement is yet another societal change that will alter the principles of water law. Already principles of prior appropriation have been limited by emerging concepts of minimum instream flows, public trust, riparian area protection, and habitat protection. Additionally, the growing concern over groundwater quality will no doubt result in modification of existing groundwater law, either on a state or federal level, to accommodate these new concerns.

Toxic Pollutant Regulation under the Clean Water Act: EPA's Technology-Based Limits

Bradford W. Wyche

One notable, if not dubious, distinction of the EPA is its inability to issue regulations in accordance with statutory deadlines. The EPA maintains that compliance with the timetables is usually impossible, while environmental groups charge that the Agency is engaged in deliberate foot-dragging and delay. Whatever the reason, there is no doubt that the EPA has failed to meet most of its deadlines for issuing regulations, affording environmental lawyers the happy prospect of first litigating the question of when the EPA must issue the regulations and later challenging the rules themselves after they are promulgated.

This article focuses on the best known of the EPA's struggles with statutory deadlines—its monumental effort to establish regulatory controls on toxic pollutants under the federal Clean Water Act. 33 U.S.C. §§ 1251–1387. It will review the basic elements of the statutory scheme, examine how a 1976 consent decree determined the scope and pace of the EPA's program for the last fifteen years, and explain the terms of a new decree that will direct the program into the next century.

The Statutory Framework

Although enacted in 1948, the Clean Water Act did not become an effective piece of environmental legislation until 1972. In that year, Congress passed sweeping amendments to the Act that merged the traditional but unsuccessful "ambient" approach of controlling water

Bradford Wyche is an attorney with Wyche, Burgess, Freeman & Parham, P.A., in Greenville, South Carolina.

pollution with direct "end-of-the-pipe" controls on the discharge itself. Pub. L. No. 92–500, 86 Stat. 816. *See generally* Fogarty, "A Short History of Federal Water Pollution Control Law," *in Clean Water Deskbook* (Envt'l. L. Inst. 1991).

The 1972 amendments directed the EPA to issue regulations establishing uniform, technology-based "effluent limitations" for existing dischargers and "standards of performance" for new sources. 33 U.S.C. §§ 1311, 1314, 1316; *E. I. duPont de Nemours & Co. v. Train*, 430 U.S. 112, 97 S. Ct. 965 (1977). Effluent limitations would be incorporated in individual discharge permits issued under the NPDES permit program. 33 U.S.C. § 1342. Henceforth it would be unlawful to discharge any pollutant into the nation's waters without such a permit. 33 U.S.C. § 1311(a).

Effluent limitations, simply put, were to specify the quality of wastewater that could be discharged from a particular point source. All dischargers within a given category of industrial facilities generally would have to meet the same "bottom line" level of control as defined by the effluent limitations, regardless of the quality of the particular watercourse into which the waste was discharged.

At the same time, Congress retained and strengthened the role of water quality standards in controlling pollution. Subject to the EPA's review, the states were directed to continue in force and periodically revise their existing water quality standards and establish new ones for intrastate waters. 33 U.S.C. § 1313. Dischargers remained subject to the traditional rule that their wastes must not cause a violation of these standards. Thus, despite complying with the effluent limitations, a discharger might have to perform additional treatment to ensure that applicable water quality standards were not contravened. 33 U.S.C. § 1311 (b)(1)(C).

Congress directed the EPA to establish effluent limitations on the basis of the degree of pollution control achievable through the installation and operation of certain technologies—"best practicable control technology currently available" and "best available control technology economically achievable" for existing sources, 33 U.S.C. § 1311(b), and "best available demonstrated control technology" for new sources. 33 U.S.C. § 1316. For each industrial category, the EPA was to identify BPT, BAT, and BADT after considering several factors specified in the Act, determine the amount of pollution reduction achievable by the installation and proper operation of those technologies, and translate that reduction into numerical effluent limitations. 33 U.S.C. §§ 1314 (b)(1)(B), 1314(b)(2)(B) and 1316 (b)(1)(B). Existing dischargers were required to meet BPT and BAT effluent limitations by July 1, 1977, and July 1, 1983, respectively; on the other hand, new source performance standards take effect upon promulgation. Congress gave the EPA one year to issue the effluent limitations and new source performance standards. 33 U.S.C. §§ 1314(b) and 1316(b).

Because the industry-wide regulations issued by the EPA may not establish controls on each pollutant of concern in a particular discharger's waste stream, permits writers were given authority under the Act to set discharge limits based on the exercise of his or her "best professional judgment" (BPJ) 33 U.S.C. § 1342(a)(1).

Congress also directed the EPA to establish in six months regulations controlling "indirect dischargers," i.e., persons discharging wastes into a POTW. 33 U.S.C. § 1317(b)-(c). Such dischargers would be required to "pretreat" those pollutants that might interfere with, or escape treatment by, the POTW. 33 U.S.C. § 1317(b)(1).

In 1972, Congress recognized that industrial wastewater often contains not only the well-known conventional pollutants—such as suspended solids and oxygen-demanding wastes—but also many toxic pollutants. 33 U.S.C. § 1362(13). With respect to these pollutants, Congress adopted a strategy based on the issuance of "toxic pollutant effluent standards." 33 U.S.C. § 1317(a)(2). The key features of this approach were short deadlines and stringent controls. The EPA was directed to publish in ninety days pollutants for which toxic effluent standards would be established and to issue the standards six months thereafter. 86 Stat. 856. Compliance was required within one year from the date the standards were issued. *Id.*

The overriding factor in setting such standards was the protection of human health and the environment. In contrast to its mandate in issuing effluent limitations, the EPA was not required to give any consideration to technological feasibility or economic factors in establishing toxic pollutant effluent standards. *Hercules, Inc. v. EPA*, 598 F.2d 91 (D.C. Cir. 1978).

The 1976 Consent Decree

Congress's vision of a swiftly established and effective toxic pollutant control program proved illusory. Faced with large gaps in scientific information on toxic pollutants, the EPA failed to meet the ninety-day deadline for publishing its list of toxic pollutants. The Agency then missed the six-month deadline for issuing pretreatment standards and the one-year deadline for promulgating effluent limitations and new source performance standards. *See generally* Hall, "The Evolution and Implementation of EPA's Regulatory Program to Control the Discharge of Toxic Pollutants to the Nation's Waters," 10 *Nat. Resources Law.* 507 (1977).

As a result, between 1973 and 1975 environmental organizations brought five suits against the EPA. One action involved issuance of the effluent limitations and resulted in the entry of a court order requiring the EPA to promulgate its regulations by no later than December 31, 1974. *NRDC v. Train,* 510 F.2d 692 (D.C. Cir. 1975). Acting under this order, by 1976 the EPA had established regulations for 418 industrial subcategories.

The other four suits focused on toxic pollutants. One action sought an order requiring the Agency to expand its list of toxic pollutants. Two others asked that the EPA be ordered to promulgate toxic effluent standards for the toxic pollutants already listed. The final action demanded that the Agency promulgate pretreatment standards for indirect dischargers.

All four suits were consolidated before Judge Thomas A. Flannery of the U.S. District Court for the District of Columbia. Several industries were permitted to intervene in the suit. While the case was pending, the EPA and the environmental groups, led by the NRDC, settled their differences and presented a proposed agreement to the court. Before considering the settlement, the court allowed the intervenors and other interested persons to submit comments. Over the objections of the intervenors and several of the commenters, the court approved the settlement agreement with certain modifications. *NRDC v. Train,* 8 E.R.C. 2120 (D.D.C. 1976).

This agreement, now known as the 1976 Consent Decree, established a comprehensive program for controlling the discharge of toxic pollutants into the nation's waters. Most important, it authorized the EPA to regulate toxic pollutants on an industry-by-industry basis through the establishment and enforcement of technology-based controls, an approach that the Agency found far superior to regulation on a pollutant-by-pollutant basis through the issuance of toxic effluent standards. As the D.C. Circuit Court of Appeals later explained:

> Adoption of the industry-by-industry, technology-based approach, using statutory authority conferred by various sections of the FWPCA [Clean Water Act], marked a change in EPA's regulatory strategy. Its previous efforts to control discharge of toxic pollutants had relied on authority conferred by Section 307 of the FWPCA in developing health-based standards on a pollutant-by-pollutant basis. The new strategy offered substantial advantages over the old. First, it allowed EPA to cover far more substances and emission sources than could have been handled under

the old approach. Second, it allowed the Agency to develop a single regulatory package which would apply to all of the problem pollutants in the discharge of a particular industry, enabling the industry to predict the entire cost of pollution control. Third, the Agency could allow consideration of cost and technology to enter into its decisionmaking and industry was allowed a longer compliance period. Finally, EPA also expected that the new program would be easier to administer.

EDF v. Costle, 636 F.2d 1229, 1235–36 (D.C. Cir. 1980).

The 1976 decree thus required the EPA to promulgate, by no later than December 31, 1979, effluent limitations, new source performance standards, and pretreatment standards for sixty-five toxic pollutants, known as the "priority pollutants," for each of twenty-one major industrial categories, the so-called "primary industries." Because the "priority pollutants" consisted of compounds or classes of compounds, the EPA concentrated on 126 specific toxic pollutants; the primary industries were later subdivided to include thirty-four specific industrial categories.

The decree included more than simply a schedule for issuing regulations. The EPA also agreed to identify point sources discharging toxic pollutants not included on the priority pollutant list, to regulate at least 95 percent of all point sources within each industrial category for which national regulations would be issued, to publish water quality criteria for each priority pollutant, to establish a "specific and substantial program" to determine whether additional measures would be necessary to control toxic pollutants, and to include "reopener" clauses in NPDES permits providing that upon promulgation of the toxic pollutant regulations, the permit would be revised or modified to require compliance with any limitation or standard more stringent than the conditions of the permit. An important provision of the consent decree, paragraph 8, afforded the EPA the opportunity to exclude from national regulation specific toxic pollutants under certain circumstances, such as where a pollutant is present in wastewater "only in trace amounts and is neither causing, nor likely to cause, toxic effects."

The Clean Water Act of 1977

At the time the 1972 amendments were enacted, Congress created the National Commission on Water Quality to assess the effectiveness of the new statutory scheme in improving water quality and to suggest any changes in the Act that may be necessary. Based on the Commission's final report in 1976 and following a number of legislative hearings, Congress passed certain amendments to the Act in 1977. This bill, known as the Clean Water Act of 1977, did not alter the basic philosophy and approach of the 1972 amendments but did make what have been described as certain "mid-course corrections" to the law. Pub. L. No. 95–217, 91 Stat. 1566.

Among the significant amendments was the creation of a new category of pollutants known as "conventional pollutants"—biological oxygen demand, total suspended solids, fecal coliform, and pH. 33 U.S.C. § 1314(a)(4). (The EPA later added oil and grease to the list of conventional pollutants.) The EPA was directed to establish effluent limitations for these pollutants on the basis of applying "best conventional pollutant control technology," and dischargers were given until July 1, 1984, to comply with such limitations. 33 U.S.C. § 1311(b)(2)(E). Three statutory classes of pollutants now existed: toxic, conventional, and nonconventional.

With respect to toxic pollutants, Congress endorsed the 1976 Consent Decree's approach. In fact, several parts of the decree were written into law. The list of the sixty-five priority pollutants was codified, 33 U.S.C. § 1317(a)(1), and the EPA was given clear authority to regulate toxic pollutants on the basis of technology-based effluent limitations. 33 U.S.C. § 1311(b)(2)(C). Congress established July 1, 1980, as the new deadline for promulgating such limitations and at the same time extended the BAT compliance deadline for the priority pollutants by one year to July 1, 1984. 91 Stat. 1582, 1590.

Modifications of the 1976 Consent Decree

In late 1978, frustrated by the EPA's failure to comply with the decree's schedule, NRDC instituted a contempt action against the EPA Administrator. At the same time, the intervenors moved to vacate the decree, contending that it has been superseded by the 1977 amendments and that the four original suits had become moot.

The NRDC and the EPA again settled their differences and tendered a modified consent decree to the court. On March 9, 1979, Judge Flannery approved the modified settlement and denied the intervenors' motion to vacate the decree. *NRDC v. Costle*, 12 E.R.C. 1833 (D.D.C. 1979). The most significant change under the modified decree was the extension of time given to the EPA to issue the effluent limitations, new source performance standards, and pretreatment standards. The new schedule required the promulgation of all regulations by mid-1981.

The intervenors appealed Judge Flannery's denial of their motion to vacate to the D.C. Circuit Court of Appeals. Reviewing the language of the 1977 amendments and the legislative history, the appellate court agreed with Judge Flannery that "Congress intended for the [Consent Decree] to remain in effect to supply the missing details of a cohesive strategy for controlling toxic water pollution." *EDF v. Costle*, 636 F.2d 1229, 1242 (D.C. Cir. 1980). On the question of mootness, the court determined that the toxic criteria and pretreatment cases remained live controversies that gave the district court jurisdiction to enter its order approving the modified decree.

The court of appeals, however, raised *sua sponte*, and remanded to Judge Flannery, the question "whether the modified settlement agreement impermissibly infringes on the discretion Congress committed to the Administrator to make certain decisions under the Clean Water Act by binding the EPA to follow certain procedures and use certain decision making criteria not mandated by the statute." 636 F.2d at 1258.

On February 5, 1982, Judge Flannery answered the question:

> [The agreement] does not seek to control any of the EPA's final results, which are lawfully within the province of the agency alone to determine, but instead merely seeks to compel the EPA to implement the process that Congress intended to provide to protect both this nation's waters and the users of those waters. As a process-oriented decree, the instant settlement agreement does not impermissibly infringe on the EPA's discretion.

NRDC v. Gorsuch, 16 E.R.C. 2084, 2088 (D.D.C. 1982).

Judge Flannery relied on three factors to support his conclusion. First, the parties were the architects of the decree; the court merely approved what the EPA had agreed voluntarily to undertake to settle the litigation. Second, the decree was flexible and could be modified upon showing a change in circumstances. Finally, in 1977 Congress was aware of the consent decree and approved of its approach to the control of toxic water pollution. While having "no doubt that the instant settlement agreement infringes to some degree on the EPA Administrator's discretion," the court did not believe that the infringement was "impermissible." *Id.* at 2087.

The beleaguered intervenors appealed again, challenging Judge Flannery's refusal to delete the so-called "non-statutory provisions" of the decree. The D.C. Circuit affirmed. *Citizens for a Better Environment v. Gorsuch*, 718 F.2d 1117 (D.C. Cir. 1983), *cert. denied*, 467 U.S. 1219 (1984). The court rejected the contention that only those provisions of the consent decree that were specifically mandated by the Clean Water Act could be approved. Rather, a consent decree, to pass judicial muster, need only be consistent with the purposes of the underlying statute, and the modified decree in question was clearly consistent with the Clean Water Act. The court also held that no "impermissible infringement" existed since the decree neither dictated the content of any regulation nor directed the EPA in how to enforce the rules. Judge Wilkey lodged a strong dissent in which he objected to "government by consent decree." 718 F.2d at 1135.

By 1987, the EPA had succeeded in issuing final standards for all of the industries subject to the 1976 Consent Decree. Appendix A is a category-by-category summary of when the limitations were originally promulgated and where they appear in the *Code of Federal Regulations*. Most of the limitations were amended at later dates pursuant to settlement agreements between the EPA and various parties challenging the regulations. *See* Appendix A.

One major challenge that was not entirely settled involved the effluent limitations for the organic chemicals, plastics, and synthetic fibers industry that were generally upheld by the Fifth Circuit in 1989. *Chemical Manufacturers Ass'n v EPA*, 870 F.2d 177 (5th Cir. 1989), *modified*, 885 F.2d 253 (5th Cir. 1989), *cert. denied*, 110 S. Ct. 1936 (1990). Four aspects of the rule were remanded to the EPA for reconsideration, but the Agency has proposed not to change its mind. 56 Fed. Reg. 63,897 (Dec. 6, 1991). Another judicial challenge resulted in the complete withdrawal of the effluent limitations for the pesticide chemicals category in 1986. 51 Fed. Reg. 44,911 (Dec. 15, 1986).

When the EPA issues standards for the pesticide chemicals industry, which are now due in 1993, the Agency's duties under the 1976 Consent Decree will have been satisfied and presumably the case, at long last, will be dismissed.

The 1992 Consent Decree

As the EPA's work under the 1976 decree was winding down, Congress turned its attention to the Clean Water Act and in 1987 succeeded in enacting, over President Reagan's veto, the first major set of amendments to the law since 1977. Water Quality Act of 1987, Pub. L. No. 100–4, 101 Stat. 7 (1987). *See* Lieberman & Laws, "The Water Quality Act of 1987: A Major Step in Assuring the Quality of the Nation's Waters," *in Clean Water Deskbook* (Envtl. L. Inst. 1991). In these amendments, Congress expressed its dissatisfaction with both the pace and scope of the EPA's regulatory program for controlling toxic pollutants. It required the EPA not only to issue immediately final standards for the organic chemicals and pesticide categories, 101 Stat. 30 (1987), but also to develop and implement a plan for reviewing and revising existing effluent limitations and for promulgating new ones.

The planning requirement is set forth in section 304(m), 33 U.S.C. § 1314(m), which directs the EPA to publish by February 4, 1988, and biennially thereafter, a plan that shall:

> (A) establish a schedule for the annual review and revision of promulgated effluent limitations in accordance with Section 304(b);
> (B) identify categories of sources discharging toxic or non-conventional pollutants for which limitations under Section 304(b)(2) and Section 306 have not been previously published; and
> (C) establish a schedule for the promulgation of effluent limitations for categories identified in subparagraph (B), under which such limitations shall be promulgated by no later than February 4, 1991 for categories identified in the first published plan or three years after the publication of the plan for categories identified in later published plans.

The EPA continued its near-perfect record of noncompliance with Clean Water Act deadlines by publishing the proposed plan on August 25, 1988, 53 Fed. Reg. 32,589, and the final plan on January 2, 1990, 55 Fed. Reg. 80, nearly two years late.

The ever-vigilant NRDC, along with Public Citizen, Inc., filed suit in October 1989 to compel the EPA to promulgate its section 304(m) plan. *NRDC v. Reilly*, Civ. Action No. 89-2980 (D.D.C.). The EPA did so a few months later, but the plaintiffs were hardly placated by what the plan provided.

The plan announced the EPA's intention to promulgate new effluent limitations for five categories, to revise existing limitations for three categories, to review existing limitations for three categories, and to study eight categories to determine whether rule makings should be initiated. The EPA's "best estimate" of when existing limitations would be revised and new limitations issued ranged from 1992 to 1995. No dates were given for completing either the review of the existing regulations or the studies of the eight additional categories. While the EPA acknowledged that the plan did not address "many industry categories discharging toxic or nonconventional pollutants for which limitations have not been published," 55 Fed. Reg. 81, it did not believe that section 304(m) required the first plan to apply to each and every source.

The plaintiffs were not sympathetic, finding it "difficult to imagine a more blatant flaunting of legislative intent." And that intent, the plaintiffs argued, was crystal clear in section 304(m), which required an identification of all "unregulated sources" (i.e., sources of toxic or nonconventional pollutants that are not subject to effluent limitations) and a schedule for promulgating effluent limitations for those sources by no later than February 4, 1991. Moreover, the plaintiffs contended that "EPA's section 304(m) plan contains nothing even remotely resembling a systematic 'schedule for the annual review and revision' of effluent limitations already passed."

The plaintiffs found the EPA's approach particularly egregious in view of prior Agency memoranda and studies that indicated that 80 percent of all facilities discharging toxic pollutants are not subject to national BAT standards, that "unregulated categories are major sources of pollution and creators of environmental and human harm," that even as to the "regulated categories," standards for many toxic pollutants do not exist, and that "BPJ-based limitations require an excessive amount of time in order to become familiar with treatment technologies and to gather the information necessary to set limits that are defensible; consequently, many of the states deliberately avoid doing BPJ-based limitations and wait for ELG [effluent limitations guidelines] to be promulgated."

The last point was underscored in an *amicus* brief submitted by several states in support of the plaintiffs' position. These states maintained that they face "extreme difficulties in establishing water pollution controls in the absence of federal effluent limitations." Not only does it take more time, effort, and money to issue defensible BPJ-based permits, but "States face economic pressures not to develop their own stringent limitations for fear of losing industry to States with more lax limitations."

Undaunted, the EPA opposed the plaintiffs' motion and filed its own motion for summary judgment. The Agency argued that section 304(m)(1)(C)'s February 4, 1991, deadline is only a "target date." It explained to the court, as it did in its plan, the painstaking process by which an industry is studied and effluent limitations are drafted, reviewed, proposed, revised, promulgated, and defended in court. Thus, "it strains credulity to maintain, as NRDC does, that Congress expected the EPA to schedule all industry categories identifiable under section 304(m)(1)(B) in the first plan, and promulgate limitations for them all within four years, without dramatically increasing funding for the program." The EPA essentially said it was doing the best it could and should not be required to do the impossible.

The court rejected the EPA's position and held that Congress meant what it said:

For regardless of EPA's assertions of good faith, the undisputed fact is that Congress has spoken unqualifiedly and EPA has failed to comply. Indeed, were the court to accept EPA's excuses and recharacterization of the statutory deadline as a mere "target date," Congressional timetables would serve no purpose: statutory deadlines would have meaning only to the extent that agency action happens to occur within the stated "deadline." Since a court should not fail to give import to the explicit dates set by Congress, the court finds that February 4, 1991, is an unambiguous deadline and that EPA is in default of this statutory mandate.

NRDC v. Reilly, 22 Envtl. L. Rep. 20,108, 20,110–11 (D.D.C. 1991). The court had more difficulty in resolving the obligations imposed by sections 304(m)(1)(A) and (B). With respect to subparagraph (A), which requires "a schedule for the annual review and revision of promulgated effluent limitations, in accordance with [section 304(b)]," the EPA contended that the reference to section 304(b), which requires revision of limitations only "if appropriate," signified congressional intent to allow the Agency wide discretion in setting its own schedule for the review and revision of its regulations. But "appropriate" does not appear in section 304(m), and the court declined to construe the provision to be merely duplicative of section 304(b). Henceforth the EPA was required to review and revise its regulations every year.

With respect to section 304(m)(1)(B)'s requirement to identify unregulated categories, the EPA argued that construing section 304(m) to require the identification of each and every unregulated source in the first plan would render meaningless the legislative directive to issue new plans every two years.

Judge Lamberth disagreed. He pointed out that "advances in pollution detection technology may allow the EPA to uncover industries not currently known to be dischargers of dangerous chemicals," *Id.* at 20,111, and these dischargers would be the subject of future section 304(m) plans. The biennial plan requirement "furthers the Clean Water Act's goal of creating and maintaining up-to-date water standards." *Id.*

The court thus granted the plaintiffs' motion, held that the EPA had violated section 304(m), and ordered a status conference to be held "for the establishment of a timetable for the proper implementation of 33 U.S.C. § 1314(m)." *Id.* at 20,112.

The status conference never took place as the EPA and the plaintiffs were able to agree to a timetable. In what is probably the most important development in the EPA's effluent limitations program since the 1976 decree, Judge Lamberth approved this schedule in a consent decree entered on January 31, 1992. This schedule will set the rule-making agenda for effluent limitations controlling toxic pollutants well into the next century.

Three schedules are contained in the decree:

A. Effluent Limitations Currently under Development

Point Source Category	Proposal	Final Action
1. Pesticide Manufacturing	1992	July 1993
2. Pesticide Formulating and Packaging	1994	August 1995
3. Centralized Waste Treatment (Phase I)	1994	January 1996
4. Machinery Manufacturing and Rebuilding (Phase I)	1994	May 1996
5. Pharmaceutical Manufacturing	1994	February 1996
6. Organic Chemicals, Plastics & Synthetic Fibers	(published 1991)	May 1993
7. Coastal Oil and Gas	1995	July 1996

B. Development of Additional Effluent Limitations

Point Source Category	Start	Proposal	Final Action
1. Centralized Waste Treatment (Phase II)	1993	1995	1997
2. Industrial Laundries	1993	1996	1998
3. Transportation Equipment Cleaning	1993	1996	1998
4. Machinery Manufacturing and Rebuilding (Phase II)	1995	1997	1999
5. New or Revised Rule #5	1996	1998	2000
6. New or Revised Rule #6	1996	1998	2000
7. New or Revised Rule #7	1997	1999	2001
8. New or Revised Rule #8	1997	1999	2001
9. New or Revised Rule #9	1998	2000	2002
10. New or Revised Rule #10	1998	2000	2002
11. New or Revised Rule #11	1999	2001	2003
12. New or Revised Rule #12	1999	2001	2003

C. Studies

Point Source Category	Proposal	Final Action
1. Petroleum Refining	1992	1993
2. Metal Finishing	1992	1993

C. Studies (continued)

Point Source Category	Proposal	Final Action
3. Iron and Steel	1993	1994
4. Inorganic Chemicals	1993	1994
5. Leather Tanning	1994	1995
6. Coal Mining	1994	1995
7. Onshore/Stripper Oil & Gas	1995	1996
8. Textiles	1995	1996
9. Study Category #9	1996	1997
10. Study Category #10	1996	1997
11. Study Category #11	1996	1997

Unlike the 1976 decree, the 1992 decree affords wide discretion and flexibility to the EPA. Not only is the Agency able to announce at later dates the industrial categories to be studied and reviewed, but those that are identified may be replaced by the EPA upon giving the plaintiffs thirty days' notice.

The parties, however, agreed to disagree as "to what discretion, if any, the EPA has under applicable law to decide not to proceed with an effluent guideline." The consent decree thus establishes a procedure where the EPA must notify the plaintiffs of its decision not to develop a regulation, after which the plaintiffs have 180 days to challenge that decision.

The consent decree contains several other significant provisions:

- the EPA's next section 304(m) plan must be proposed by no later than April 30, 1992, and promulgated by no later than August 28, 1992;
- by August 1, 1992, a special task force must be established to assist the EPA on such issues as expediting the promulgation of effluent limitations, deciding when additional point source categories should be regulated, establishing zero discharge technologies, and addressing cross-media transfers of pollution;
- any provision in the consent decree, including any deadline, may be modified for "good cause shown"; and
- the court retains jurisdiction to determine and effectuate compliance with the decree.

Dischargers who become subject to effluent limitations established under the new decree will face their own deadline dilemma. The Clean Water Act plainly provides that compliance with any effluent limitation promulgated for a toxic or nonconventional pollutant must be achieved "in no case later than March 31, 1989." 33 U.S.C. §§ 1311(b)(2)(C), (D), and (F). Read literally, this provision would require immediate compliance with limitations established after March 31, 1989. The legislative history of the 1987 amendments, however, reveals that Congress was not so callously minded. The conferees recognized that an effluent limitation based on technology that is the best available necessarily means that many dischargers will not be in immediate compliance. Therefore they specifically endorsed the policy that the EPA was using for handling violations of the original July 1, 1984, BAT deadline. H.R. CONF. REP. NO.1004, 99th Cong., 2d Sess. 115 (1986). Under this policy, dischargers can be given up to three years from the date of permit issuance to achieve compliance with the new standards. *Id.* Presumably the EPA will continue to use this policy as effluent limitations are established under the new consent decree.

Beyond BAT: Renewed Emphasis on Water Quality Standards

The effluent limitations issued under the 1976 decree have achieved significant reductions in the discharge of toxic pollutants into the nation's waters and no doubt more progress will be made as the EPA performs its obligations under the 1992 decree. Yet effluent limitations are no panacea. They do not, and will not, apply to every source of pollution or to every specific pollutant. Moreover, even where the source and the pollutant are regulated, compliance with effluent limitations does not necessarily mean achievement of the water quality standards established for the receiving stream.

Indeed, when it amended the Clean Water Act in 1987, Congress was painfully aware of the fact that numerous water bodies would remain plagued by toxic contamination despite full compliance with the BAT standards. For these so-called "toxic hot spots," Congress launched a "beyond BAT program" that is founded on comprehensive water quality standard requirements and tight deadlines for action by the EPA and the states.

First, the 1987 amendments required the states to adopt numeric criteria for specific toxic pollutants. 33 U.S.C. § 1313(c)(2)(B). Henceforth the vague narrative standards that many states had adopted, such as "no unreasonable impact" or "no adverse effect," would no longer, in and of themselves, be acceptable.

Second, by February 1989, the states had to submit three lists of their "hot spot" waters to the EPA: (1) a "short list" of waters that do not meet water quality standards due entirely or substantially to point source discharges of toxic pollutants, (2) a "medium list" of waters that do not meet water quality standards due to any source of toxic pollutants, and (3) a "long list" of waters that do not meet the goals of the Act due to the presence of any pollutant. 33 U.S.C. § 1314(l)(1). The states then must identify the specific point source dischargers of toxic pollutants responsible for the impairment and propose, in an "individual control strategy" for each point source, the NPDES permit modifications necessary to achieve compliance with water quality standards within three years following establishment of the ICS. 33 U.S.C. § 1314(l)(D). The EPA, in turn, must approve or disapprove the lists and the ICSs submitted by the states; if disagreements with a state cannot be resolved, the EPA itself will issue the lists and the ICSs. 40 C.F.R. §§ 123.46(f), 130.10(d)(10) (1991).

Not all the statutory deadlines, of course, were met, but the EPA and the states moved ahead at a remarkable pace. As of March 2, 1992, the EPA had approved the water quality standards for priority pollutants submitted by thirty-eight of the fifty-seven states and territories. More approvals are expected and even in the unapproved jurisdictions, acceptable criteria for some of the priority toxic pollutants have been adopted. The EPA itself will promulgate criteria for the recalcitrant jurisdictions. 56 Fed. Reg. 58,420 (Nov. 19, 1991) (EPA proposal to establish water quality criteria for toxic pollutants in states lacking such standards).

By the end of 1989, virtually all the lists had been submitted by the states to the EPA. There are presently 529 water bodies and 686 contributing facilities on the short list. Pursuant to a Ninth Circuit decision, *NRDC v. EPA*, 915 F.2d 1314 (9th Cir. 1990), the EPA is requiring the states to identify facilities and sources contributing to contamination of waters on the medium and long lists. Meanwhile, the Agency is considering whether to require ICSs for these sources. As for facilities on the short list, 497 ICSs have now been approved or issued by the EPA.

The success of the "beyond BAT program" will depend, in the final analysis, on the bottom line changes made in the NPDES permits of the offending dischargers. Professor Houck has presented a sobering account of how discharge limitations are often the result of shaky assumptions, manipulated data, and political influences. Houck, "The Regulation of Toxic Pollutants Under the Clean Water Act," 21 Envtl. L. Rep. 10,528 (Sept. 1991). Moreover, the inevitable litigation will affect the enforceability, if not the substance, of many

ICSs. It remains to be seen how much shorter the short list will become in the years ahead.

Courts and the Issue of Setting Deadlines

In the "deadline suit" involving issuance of the hazardous waste landfill regulations, U.S. District Judge Gerhard Gesell expressed a frustration no doubt shared by most judges faced with an agency's failure to comply with statutory deadlines:

> My role has been a very limited one. It is to set target dates, which will not be met, and then set other target dates, which will not be met. . . . I sit here still at the same bench and I don't accomplish anything.

Citizens for a Better Environment v. Gorsuch, Civ. Action No. 82–1035 and consolidated cases, Record at 19–20 (D.D.C. 1982).

The basic problem is that the "deadline" suit interjects a court in the middle of what is essentially a political dispute between the legislative and executive branches of government. Moreover, any order issued in such a case, as a practical matter, is unenforceable because a court cannot write the regulation in question or appropriate additional funds for the agency to do so. *See* Frug, "The Judicial Power of the Purse," 126 *U. Pa. L. Rev.* 715, 792 (1978). There is little a court can (or should) do except to ensure that the agency is proceeding diligently and in good faith and "to heighten the response and to stimulate the fullest use of resources." *NRDC v. Train*, 510 F.2d at 712. But this is an important role that tends not to be fully appreciated even by the courts themselves. The involvement of a federal court in the rule-making process, even if confined to shouts of encouragement or shots of adrenaline, has enormous practical consequences for the simple reason that court orders usually make things happen. A task that may have been impossible to accomplish before litigation begins somehow finds more funding and additional personnel after a court order is signed. It may well be that without the litigation, the EPA's toxic pollutant control program would never have become a reality.

Appendix A

Promulgation History of Effluent Limitations
Under 1976 Consent Decree

Industrial Category	Original Promulgation Date	40 C.F.R. Part No.
Aluminum Forming	Oct. 1983*	467
Battery Manufacturing	Mar. 1984*	461
Coal Mining	Oct. 1982*	434
Coil Coating (Phases I & II)	Dec. 1982 and Nov. 1983*	465
Copper Forming	Aug. 1983*	468
Electrical & Electronic Components (Phases I & II)	Apr. 1983 and Nov. 1983*	469
Inorganic Chemicals (Phases I & II)	June 1982 and Aug. 1984	415
Iron & Steel	May 1982*	420
Leather Tanning	Nov. 1982*	425
Metal Finishing	July 1983*	433
Metal Molding & Casting (formerly known as Foundries)	Oct. 1985	464
Nonferrous Metals Forming	Aug. 1985*	471
Nonferrous Metals Manufacturing	Mar. 1984 and Sept. 1985*	421
Ore Mining & Dressing	Dec. 1982	440
Organic Chemicals, Plastics & Synthetic Fibers	Nov. 1987	414
Pesticide Chemicals	Dec. 1986 but withdrawn	455
Petroleum Refining	Oct. 1982*	419
Pharmaceuticals	Oct. 1983	439
Plastics Molding & Forming	Dec. 1984	463
Porcelain Enameling	Nov. 1982*	466
Pulp & Paper	Nov. 1982*	430
Steam Electric	Nov. 1982*	423
Textile Mills	Sept. 1982*	410
Timber Products	Jan. 1981*	429

* Relatively minor amendments were made at later dates, primarily as the result of agreements settling litigation challenging the regulations.

A Primer on Wetlands Permitting and Section 404 Decision Making

Bruce D. Ray

Since its enactment in 1972, the permit program established by section 404 of the Clean Water Act, 33 U.S.C. § 1344, has been criticized by both the regulated community and environmental groups. The Army Corps of Engineers and the EPA, which share principal responsibility for implementing section 404, have over the years criticized each other for either not doing enough or doing too much. The purpose of this article is not to resolve this seemingly inevitable dialectic; rather, its purpose is to acquaint the reader with section 404 and its requirements from the viewpoint of a lawyer who has experienced section 404 issues from both the public and private perspectives. These perspectives are derived not from national policy making or appellate advocacy but from the daily problems facing a staff level EPA lawyer in a regional office and a lawyer in the legal department of a large manufacturing company. Special emphasis is given to mitigation and the alternatives analysis in the individual permit process because they are potential pitfalls for many applicants.

Few would dispute the contention that section 404 is the most arcane regulatory program established by the Clean Water Act. Because of the program's complex and time-consuming requirements, a developer (applicant) is well advised to take one of two courses: use a specific decision-making process to determine which section 404 requirements apply and make this determination *before* any major economic or investment decision *or* avoid section 404 jurisdiction

Bruce Ray is a counsel with Manville Corporation in Denver, Colorado.

altogether by choosing nonwetland (i.e., upland) areas for project sites and activities.

The section 404 permit program regulates the discharge of dredged or fill material into waters of the United States. Generally, this permit program regulates nonwaste material discharges, such as those associated with construction and development activities. The principal focus of section 404 has become the protection of wetlands and other special aquatic sites from unnecessary destruction or impairment. Congress wisely has chosen to afford substantial protection to wetlands since they serve several important and often unnoticed functions. They act as filters purifying the water that flows through them. Wetlands, as a transition zone between water and land, often perform flood protection functions. The habitat function of wetlands is perhaps the most widely known. Indeed, wetlands are not only critical habitat for waterfowl but also provide habitat for small mammals, reptiles, and wetland plant species. Moreover, most wetlands serve aesthetic functions, especially when their other functions are recognized.

Defining the Agency Responsibility

Wetlands protection is effected through a permit program administered by the Corps. Any discharge (placement) of pollutants (fill material) from a point source (bulldozer, etc.) into any waters of the United States (jurisdictional wetlands) is prohibited by section 301 of the Act unless carried out under a permit issued by the Corps pursuant to section 404. Any unpermitted discharges are violations of the Act against which the Corps may invoke its enforcement authority.

Although the Corps directly administers the permit program, Congress intended that the Corps seek and rely upon the expertise of two resource agencies, namely, the EPA and the USFWS. The USFWS provides critical expertise concerning habitat evaluation and other biological issues. The EPA supplements this input with water quality and general environmental expertise.

Congress was not so naive as to plan on the three agencies working in harmony to provide comprehensive but balanced wetlands protection. The agencies, especially the Corps and the EPA, sometimes disagree as to section 404 requirements. To resolve these disputes, the Corps has executed section 404(q) MOAs with the EPA and USFWS. The MOAs are intended to expedite resolution of any such disputes, first through informal means at the local level and then through elevation to higher levels in each agency.

The role of states in implementing section 404 cannot be over-looked. Under section 401 of the Act, states must essentially certify that activities regulated under section 404 do not violate state-promulgated water quality standards, including uses, numeric criteria, and antidegradation requirements. Conditions attached to state certifications are usually made enforceable conditions of the section 404 permit. In addition, many states now have their own wetland protection laws and several even administer the section 404 in lieu of the Corps.

The EPA has three principal roles under section 404: determining Clean Water Act jurisdiction, promulgating and policing implementation of the section 404(b)(1) guidelines, and enforcement. Since the EPA is responsible for overall implementation of the Act, it also has the final word on section 404 jurisdiction. This means that the EPA, not the Corps, is the final administrative arbiter of which wetlands are waters of the United States and hence subject to the permit requirements. This principle, as put forward in a 1979 U.S. Attorney General's Opinion, also means that the EPA makes the initial decision as to the applicability of the few exemptions set forth in section 404(f).

Section 404(b)(1) requires the EPA to promulgate guidelines for use by the Corps in selecting disposal sites, i.e., in issuing permits to fill wetlands. The guidelines, found at 40 C.F.R. Part 230, were promulgated by the EPA in essentially their present form in 1980. Despite their name, both the guidelines and the Corps regulations reflect that the Corps's application of the guidelines in permitting decisions is mandatory. The guidelines contain two principal features: the substantive criteria, which must be satisfied before a permit may be issued, and restrictions placed on all proposed discharges.

The EPA polices compliance with the requirements of the guidelines by making informal and formal comments on permits and permit applications. If a dispute arises, the EPA may seek to elevate the issue through the section 404(q) MOA. In certain instances, the EPA may even choose to exercise its power under section 404(c) to remove the area in question from consideration as a disposal site. Although not explicitly described as such in the Act, this section essentially constitutes an EPA veto authority with respect to individual permits.

Similar to the NPDES established in section 402 of the Act, the EPA has a significant enforcement role in the section 404 program. Any discharge of fill material to a jurisdictional wetland without a permit or any violation of a Corps permit is a violation of section 301. Any such violation of section 301 gives rise to the EPA's civil and criminal enforcement powers under section 309. Given the increased federal focus on criminal enforcement and individual criminal liability, the applicant or developer must assess the potentially great risk in making any unauthorized discharges.

Threshold Determinations by the Applicant

When an individual section 404 permit is required, the regulatory process can be costly and time consuming. In determining whether an individual permit will be required, an applicant should address a series of threshold questions. The first question is whether section 404—i.e., Clean Water Act—jurisdiction exists. This entails determining whether the wetland in question is a "water of the United States" and whether the contemplated activities are regulated under the Act. If jurisdiction exists, the second question is whether the proposed activity is exempted from the section 404 requirements by section 404(f). Section 404(f) exempts from regulation certain activities determined by Congress not to have unacceptable environmental effects. If jurisdiction exists and the activity is not exempted, the third question is whether the activity is covered by a nationwide or general permit. Such permits may essentially preauthorize various activities with only minor impacts. If no such nationwide or general permit applies, the applicant must plan early for application for an individual permit.

Determining Jurisdiction

Clean Water Act jurisdiction triggering section 404 requirements is determined by the interplay among sections 301, 404, and 506 of the Act. The principal jurisdictional elements are (1) a discharge of pollutants, (2) from a point source, (3) to waters of the United States. The courts have interpreted each of these terms very expansively to effect the congressional intent to regulate as many activities and as many waters as permissible under the commerce clause of the U.S. Constitution. Thus, virtually any material used to fill a wetland is a pollutant, and virtually any equipment or method used to place or discharge the fill material is a point source.

Much attention has been directed to the issue of which wetlands are in fact waters of the United States. To qualify, a wetland must have both the requisite physical characteristics and a nexus to interstate commerce. Both the Corps and the EPA regulations set forth the necessary physical characteristics: the area must be inundated or saturated by surface water or groundwater at a frequency and duration sufficient to support—and that under normal circumstances does support—a prevalence of vegetation typically adapted for life in saturated soils. Not surprisingly, most methods used to identify these characteristics focus on vegetation, soils, and hydrology.

This issue has been complicated recently by controversial changes proposed for the federal manual used by the agencies to determine whether a given area possesses the requisite physical characteristics. Any developer or potential applicant is advised to carefully evaluate under the manual currently in use such characteristics as duration of inundation or saturation and presence of facultative wetland vegetation. In addition, the applicant may want to evaluate the area in question by alternative methods under consideration by the agencies to avoid unwelcome surprises if and when final agency action is taken on amendments.

The required nexus to interstate commerce is usually readily apparent. If the wetland is adjacent (or tributary) to other waters of the United States, the EPA considers the wetland itself to be a water of the United States. According to the EPA, virtually all nonadjacent or isolated wetlands will also have a nexus to interstate commerce since virtually all such wetlands either are or could be used by migratory waterfowl or interstate travelers.

Statutory Exemptions

If jurisdiction exists, it is then necessary to determine whether the proposed activity is exempt from section 404 requirements under section 404(f). Section 404(f)(1) exempts a variety of specific activities, including normal farming, silvicultural, and ranching activities; maintenance activities relating to dams, riprap, and other similar structures; and construction or maintenance of irrigation ditches and certain farm, forest, and mining roads.

The section 404(f) exemptions are no panacea, however. First, several cases have verified the EPA and Corps views that the exemptions are to be very narrowly interpreted so as to have little or no adverse impact, either individually or cumulatively. In addition, any section 404(f)(1) exemption is subject to the "recapture" provisions of section 404(f)(2). Where the purpose of the otherwise exempt activity is to convert an area of waters of the United States to a use to which it was not previously subject, and where the flow or circulation of the waters of the United States is impeded or the reach of such waters is reduced, then section 404(f)(2) requires a permit.

Nationwide and General Permits

If the statutory exemptions do not apply, a thorough analysis should be performed to determine whether the proposed activity is sanctioned by a nationwide or general permit. Nationwide permits were in effect issued for categories of activities through the promulgation of Corps regulations at 33 C.F.R. Part 330. As with the statutory exemptions, nationwide permits are generally to cover only those activities that would have minimal impact both individually and cumulatively.

It is vitally important for the applicant to follow any procedural requirements for nationwide permits such as the predischarge notification requirement applicable to specified categories of discharges. Moreover, in addition to certain enforceable requirements applicable to all nationwide permits, many have their own permit-specific conditions. Finally, the applicant must comply with additional conditions or limitations imposed by the state under state law or as part of the section 401 certification process.

The developer or applicant is advised to consult the recent major revision to the nationwide permit regulations published at 56 Fed. Reg. 59,110 (Nov. 22, 1991). Several changes are worthy of special note. First, the district engineer now has significantly increased discretionary authority to consider all aspects of the public interest in deciding whether to allow a proposed activity to proceed under a nationwide permit. This new authority will no doubt entail decisions to impose extra conditions to nationwide permits on a project-specific or districtwide basis as well as decisions to require individual permits for proposed activities. Second, the Corps will now require mitigation for activities that will have more than minimal adverse effects. Such mitigation may be subject to interagency review similar to individual permits.

Individual Section 404 Permits

If there is not a nationwide or general permit that covers the proposed activity, the applicant must plan early for application for an individual permit. The individual permit process requires that the applicant comply with four interrelated requirements.

First, the applicant must satisfy all substantive and procedural requirements of the Corps permitting regulations. Thus the applicant must fulfill the application content and signatory requirements, taking into account the public interest review and other criteria the Corps uses in making a permit decision.

Second, any Corps permit decision must comply with NEPA. The larger the project, the greater the impacts and the more likely that an EIS will be required. Early planning is essential here as this is an area of potentially major delay. The applicant must analyze the Corp's NEPA regulations and consult with the Corps to determine what will be required for NEPA compliance.

The third requirement, compliance with the section 404(b)(1) guidelines, is generally what concerns the EPA and the Corps the most and is often the most troublesome aspect of the process to the applicant. As mentioned earlier, the guidelines contain several important limitations on discharges of fill material. The guidelines establish certain specific prohibitions in 40 C.F.R. § 230.10(b). Thus no discharge is allowed if it will cause or contribute to a violation of either any applicable state water quality standard or toxic effluent standard, or if it violates any Department of Commerce requirement imposed to protect marine sanctuaries. The guidelines in 40 C.F.R. § 230.10(c) also establish a general prohibition disallowing any discharge that will cause or contribute to significant degradation of waters of the United States. In making any determination under this general prohibition, the EPA and the Corps will give special consideration to the persistence and permanence of discharge impacts. To minimize discharges and discharge impacts, 40 C.F.R. § 230.10(d) prohibits discharges unless appropriate and practical mitigation is provided. Finally, if there are alternatives to discharge that would have less adverse impact, the discharge is prohibited. This limitation is discussed more fully below.

The fourth requirement is section 401 certification by the state. Any condition to such certification, e.g., an additional management practice, will be made an enforceable condition of the permit. Further, denial of certification will result in denial of the permit.

The relationship among section 401, state water quality standards, and the guidelines is both evident and important. If the proposed activity will cause or contribute to a state water quality standards violation, the activity likely will be barred both by denial of section 401 certification and by the specific prohibition in 40 C.F.R. § 230.10(b). Even in the absence of a standards violation, the activity may be barred by the general prohibition in 40 C.F.R. § 230.10(c). A related issue is the antidegradation policy that 40 C.F.R. § 131.12 requires each state to establish as part of its water quality standards regulations. That policy's prohibition against impairing existing uses and the water quality necessary to fully protect those uses, as well as the policy's limitations on degrading high-quality waters, are similar to the discharge prohibitions in the guidelines.

Alternatives Analysis

The alternatives analysis required by 40 C.F.R. § 230.10(a) is perhaps the most important component of the section 404(b)(1) guidelines. This requirement directly fulfills the wetlands protection function of section 404 by steering applicants away from wetlands and toward upland sites. The alternatives analysis is also the most controversial aspect of the guidelines. It has been criticized as a usurpation of local land use control and as an unacceptable infringement on private property rights. Not only does the analysis often take considerable time to complete, it may be a source of tremendous delay when the Corps and the EPA disagree as to the sufficiency of the analysis. Such disagreements may entail elevations under the section 404(q) MOAs or even an EPA permit "veto" under section 404(c).

The basic rule is established by 40 C.F.R. § 230.10(a) reads:

> no discharge of dredged or fill material shall be permitted if there is a practicable alternative to the proposed discharge which would have less adverse impact on the aquatic ecosystem so long as the alternative does not have other significant adverse environmental impacts.

40 C.F.R. § 230.10(a)(1) elaborates on this basic rule by stating that practicable alternatives include, but are not limited to, activities that do not involve a discharge into waters of the United States and discharges in other locations in waters of the United States. Further, 40 C.F.R. §§ 230.3(q) and 230.10(a)(2) define "practicable" as available and capable of being done after taking into consideration cost, existing technology, and logistics in light of overall project purposes. If it is otherwise a practicable alternative, an area not presently owned by the applicant that could reasonably be obtained, used, expanded, or managed to fulfill the basic purpose of the proposed activity may be considered.

The basic rule is strengthened by two presumptions when the discharge is proposed for special aquatic sites. Special aquatic sites are defined in 40 C.F.R. §§ 230.3(q-1) and 230.40–45 and include all wetland and other areas possessing special ecological characteristics. Other types of special aquatic sites include riffle and pool complexes, sanctuaries and refuges, and coral reefs. Under the first presumption, practicable alternatives are presumed to be available for an activity that does not require proximity to or sitting in the special aquatic site in question to fulfill its basic purpose, i.e., for a nonwater-dependent activity. Under the second presumption, all practicable alternatives to the proposed discharge into a special aquatic site are presumed to have less adverse impact on the aquatic ecosystem. These presumptions are rebuttable but are applicable unless clearly demonstrated otherwise. The result is that any applicant must overcome one, and often two, strong presumptions before being allowed to fill a wetland.

Since the first presumption will apply only to nonwater-dependent activities, the type of project is of critical importance to the burden of proof in the alternatives analysis. Naturally, the agencies tend to take a restrictive view of which types of activities are water dependent. Usually, only the traditional water dependent activities will qualify, e.g., flood control dams or bridges. Attempts by applicants to bootstrap their proposed activities into water dependency by, e.g., making the project purpose more specific, are usually met with great skepticism by the agencies.

As with NEPA, the starting point in determining the availability of alternatives under the guidelines is to define the project purposes. According to the EPA, this must be done on two levels. First, the most basic and fundamental purpose of the applicant's project must be ascertained. Then, through searching scrutiny, the applicant and the agencies must identify all the other possible ways of meeting this basic project purpose as well as all other locations where the purpose could be met. More often than not, an alternative to the applicant's proposal can be identified by the EPA or the Corps that either does not entail a discharge or that has a less adverse effect on the aquatic ecosystem.

Second, the applicant and the agencies must consider the applicant's specific project criteria and purposes. The agencies generally guard against letting the applicant bootstrap the project into a very narrow or specific purpose. Otherwise, so argue the agencies, the alternatives analysis becomes merely a well-documented rationalization of why the wetland should be filled.

Mitigation

Another area where early planning is critical for the individual section 404 permit is in measuring impacts to wetlands and designing potential mitigation. To the extent adverse impacts and discharges are unavoidable, the guidelines at 40 C.F.R. § 230.10(d) require some form of mitigation.

To properly design potential mitigation for project impacts, the applicant must have both a quantitative and qualitative method for measuring impacts. The first essential step in such measurements is to complete a thorough baseline study of the wetland. Such a study should focus on both the wetland's physical features (i.e., its size, vegetation, soils, and hydrology) and its functions. Usually the wetland's location and physical features will determine its function. The applicant should document this relationship.

Under the terms of the mitigation MOA between the EPA and the Corps, the agencies will be issuing additional federal guidance on particular mitigation goals and techniques. Until such guidance is issued, the applicant should try to satisfy the requirements of the draft EPA mitigation policy in designing and proposing mitigation. This policy is not published but is available from the regional and headquarters offices of the EPA. Although the policy is only in draft form, it contains useful ideas and recommendations that are followed by many regional EPA offices. The principal requirement of the policy is functional equivalency to achieve no net loss of wetlands. Thus, to the extent impacts on wetlands are unavoidable, the EPA generally will require filled wetlands to be replaced acre for acre and type for type. Preservation of nonaffected wetlands generally is not considered adequate mitigation.

Despite recent advancements, wetlands science is still nascent. Scientific certainty and unanimity simply do not exist as to how or why wetlands are formed or carry out their functions. Consequently, grandiose plans to re-create large wetland areas—even those intended to be qualitatively superior to the filled wetland—will often be met with skepticism by the agencies. Usually the agencies consider the best mitigation plans to be those that are simple, modest in scope, and based on a proven methodology. If those plans feature new wetlands, the wetlands should be self-sustaining and require minimal maintenance.

Both the EPA and the Corps look to the Council on Environmental Quality NEPA regulations at 40 C.F.R. § 1508.20(a)–(e) to determine what constitutes mitigation. In addition, under the mitigation MOA, the agencies also consider those regulations to establish the proper sequence of steps in the mitigation decision process. This means that any applicant's mitigation approach should adhere to the following priorities in this order: impact avoidance, impact minimization, on-site compensation, and off-site compensation. The highest level of mitigation appropriate and practicable should be achieved at a given step prior to applying techniques in subsequent steps. Accordingly, a satisfactory alternatives analysis is key and must always be conducted regardless of any proposed mitigation plan.

To avoid delay, it is critical to consider mitigation, including impact avoidance and minimization, when designing the project. The more project design preserves on-site wetlands, the fewer disagreements the applicant will have with the agencies. Further, it is often a good idea to consult with the agencies to determine the acceptability of any mitigation plan before a permit application is filed. Agency experts should be able to suggest improvements and will appreciate the opportunity to review the plan prior to commenting formally on the permit application. Usually, the EPA and the Corps will require any mitigation plan to be made an enforceable condition of the permit.

True Value and True Costs

At least some of the misunderstandings, frustrations, and delays applicants experience in the section 404 process are attributable to a failure to ascertain the true value of wetlands and other special aquatic sites before an economic or investment decision is made. We all have heard the cliché about the sucker buying swampland in Florida. Because they are less valuable and less desirable as real estate, wetlands usually fetch a lower market price. With the passage of the Clean Water Act, Congress and the public began to recognize the vital water quality, habitat, flood protection, and other functions of wetlands. Clearly, wetlands have certain environmental values that are not present in other real estate. These values, however, are more social or public than private. As such, these values generally are not reflected in the marketplace. Even when the functions of a wetland are known, the wetland will still not elicit a high market price because of these functions.

The restrictions on filling wetlands established by the section 404 program tend to bridge the price gap between wetlands and other real estate. Of course, section 404 will not drive up market prices. To the contrary, section 404 may drive down market prices of wetlands. However, section 404 bridges the gap by imposing additional and potentially large development costs. These costs take the form of project redesign and reconfiguration to minimize impacts, and in some instances, project—i.e., permit—denial for a proposed location to avoid impacts.

Since the tendency of the section 404 process is to push the true cost of developing in wetlands up to the level of the true value of the wetlands, early planning is critical. Ideally, the applicant should determine the true cost of development before the site is purchased or before some other large economic or investment decision is made. This, however, presupposes that the applicant knows with some precision exactly what is necessary to satisfy section 404 requirements. As discussed above, the section 404 program can be quite arcane. The best the applicant can do is to undertake an analysis to predict the extent of section 404 requirements in advance by addressing the threshold issues to determine whether an individual permit will be required, and, it if will be, considering the likely outcome of the alternatives analysis and the determination of appropriate mitigation requirements. Alternatively, if the applicant has not purchased any real estate and wishes to avoid the frustrations, delays, and complications of the section 404 process, an upland site sometimes can be selected.

Discharges of Hazardous Substances under the Clean Water Act

Theodore L. Garrett

In 1979, the EPA adopted final regulations, published at 44 Fed. Reg. 50,766, governing the discharge of hazardous substances under section 311 of the Clean Water Act, 33 U.S.C. § 1321. A key issue in controversy was the application of section 311 to discharges regulated by the NPDES permit program. The ensuing litigation and a legislative amendment gave rise to an exemption for these discharges, as discussed below, which was later incorporated into the concept of federally permitted releases under CERCLA. 42 U.S.C. §§ 9601(10), 9607(j). This article also examines the EPA's determination of "reportable quantities," which bear no relation to actual environmental harm, and issues raised by this reporting scheme.

Developing the Statutory Scheme

Liability for the discharge of oil or hazardous substances prior to 1970 was based on a welter of common law and admiralty principles, international treaties, and state and federal statutes. In 1970, Congress added new sections 11 and 12 of the Federal Water Pollution Control Act to establish liability for spills of oil. Pub. L. No. 91–224, 84 Stat. 91 (1970). In the 1972 amendments to the Act, Congress revised and extended these provisions to hazardous substances in what is now section 311 of the Clean Water Act. 33 U.S.C. § 1321. This provision gave the EPA the responsibility for fashioning a scheme that would

Ted Garrett is a partner in the law firm of Covington & Burling in Washington, D.C.

regulate the discharge of a wide range of chemical elements and compounds by vessels and onshore and offshore facilities.

The basic thrust of section 311 of the Clean Water Act may be summarized as follows. Section 311(b)(4) authorizes the EPA to determine by regulation "those quantities of oil and any hazardous substances the discharge of which may be harmful to the public health or welfare," known as the "reportable quantities." 33 U.S.C. § 1321(b)(4). The reportable quantities trigger the reporting and liability provisions of the Act. The responsible person is required to notify the appropriate federal agency as soon as he or she has knowledge of any discharge of oil or a hazardous substance in a reportable quantity. *Id.* § 1321(b)(5). Discharges of a reportable quantity of oil or a hazardous substance are subject to civil penalties. *Id.* § 1321(b)(6). In addition, the federal government is authorized under section 311(c) of the Act to remove or arrange for the removal of oil or a hazardous substance and to assess the costs of removal to the owner or operator of any facility from which the discharge in a reportable quantity occurs. *Id.* § 1321(c), (f).

As noted above, the statutory scheme for discharges of hazardous substances was enacted in 1972. The EPA published regulations to implement section 311 on March 13, 1978 (43 Fed. Reg. 10,474). Prior to their effective date, however, these regulations were challenged by a group of industry plaintiffs. *Manufacturing Chemists Ass'n et al. v. Costle et al.*, 445 F. Supp. 968 (W.D. La. 1978). This litigation resulted in an order declaring invalid the EPA's determinations of harmful quantities and the application of these regulations to facilities with NPDES permits.

After the district court's decision on August 4, 1978, the EPA was faced with the alternatives of either prosecuting an appeal, attempting to rewrite the regulations to conform to the court's order, or seeking an amendment of section 311 of the Act by Congress. Believing that the basic core of section 311 was sound, the EPA developed proposed legislative amendments to address the specific problems raised by the industry parties and the court. *See* 124 Cong. Rec. H. 13,600 (daily ed. Oct. 14, 1978).

On November 2, 1978, section 311 of the Clean Water Act was amended by Pub. L. No. 95–576, 92 Stat. 2467. Grafted onto a research and development authorization bill, the amendments changed the basis for determining "reportable quantities" (formerly "harmful quantities") and clarified the application of section 311 of the Act to facilities subject to the NPDES permit program. In 1979, the EPA promulgated revised regulations implementing section 311 of the Act as amended. 44 Fed. Reg. 50,766 (1979).

The Applicability to Discharges from NPDES Facilities

A fundamental issue that the EPA had to address was the relationship between prohibited spills and routine industrial process wastewater discharges. The term "discharge" in section 311 is defined broadly to include "any spilling, leaking, pumping, pouring, emitting, emptying or dumping." 33 U.S.C. § 1321(a)(2). On the other hand, as discussed below, the NPDES permit provisions of the Clean Water Act were apparently drafted on the assumption that section 311 was not applicable to industrial dischargers subject to this permit program.

The EPA's initial regulations contained an exemption for discharges "in compliance with a . . . NPDES permit which has been issued pursuant to section 402 of the Act." Section 118.1, 43 Fed. Reg. 10,493 (1978). The regulations defined such compliance as follows:

> A discharge during a 24 hour period of a designated hazardous substance . . . when such discharge is equal to or less than the maximum daily amount expressly allowed in such permit, or is equal or less than the average daily discharge for a hazardous substance not limited expressly in the permit, but as disclosed in the permit application.

Id.

This rather simple-looking exemption was fraught with numerous difficulties, as pointed out in some detail by the industry plaintiffs in *Manufacturing Chemists Association*. In the first place, continuous industrial discharges are regulated under the NPDES program established by section 402 of the Act, 33 U.S.C. § 1342. Under this NPDES permit program, industrial discharges were required by July 1, 1977, to meet effluent limitations requiring the application of the "best practicable control technology currently available." 33 U.S.C. § 1311(b)(1)(A). The Act also required the attainment by that date of "any more stringent limitation . . . necessary to meet water quality standards . . . established pursuant to any State law or regulations" or under the Act. 33 U.S.C. § 1311(b)(1)(C). To meet the requirements of the NPDES permit program, industrial facilities had spent millions of dollars to install and operate pollution control equipment.

In the 1978 regulations, the EPA had established its so-called harmful quantities without considering actual harm to the environment. As a result, the prohibited discharge quantities were set at levels well below those routinely discharged by many industrial facilities. Industrial dischargers were thus faced with the Hobson's choice of either closing numerous plants that were discharging in excess of the allowed quantities or running the risk of severe penalties—even though continued operation of the plants would be consistent with existing NPDES permits and would not cause harm to the environment.

Under the EPA's 1978 regulations, an NPDES-permitted discharge would be exempt under two circumstances, namely, where the discharge is not greater than the maximum daily amount expressly allowed in the permit or the average daily discharge for a substance mentioned in the permit application. The difficulty with the first exemption was that, as of 1978, the hazardous substances had not been limited in permits. As to the second, the EPA seldom asked for identification of the hazardous substances. Even where such identification was made (without setting any fixed limitation in the permit), the EPA had effectively removed the intended exemption from 50 percent of these discharges, since half of the time the amount being discharged would be above the daily average.

Finally, the industry plaintiffs argued that the EPA's position that every permit violation is also a violation of the section 311 regulations is arbitrary and contrary to the statute. Plaintiffs emphasized that a permit violation has no relationship to environmental harm. Assume, for example, that a particular plant has a water quality– or technology-based effluent limitation for chlorine of 100 pounds. In the usual case, this means that the plant can discharge 101 pounds without causing harm to the environment. This is because the technology-based limits have no relation to environmental harm, and water quality–based limits are typically based on low flow and other conditions providing a margin of safety. In other words, the mere fact that a permit limitation has been violated does not necessarily indicate that actual environmental harm is going to result. Quite apart from section 311, moreover, a violation of an NPDES permit is subject to severe penalties under section 309 of the Act, 33 U.S.C. § 1319, and there is no basis for concluding that Congress would have intended to impose multiple penalties under the two statutory provisions for the same discharge.

In its decision in *Manufacturing Chemists Association*, the district court was troubled by the relationship between permit violations and section 311 of the Act. Significantly, the court held that Congress did not intend to apply section 311 penalties to NPDES discharges, stating that the "rational underpinnings for the limitations to be found in NPDES permits are completely different from those which form the basis" of the section 311 regulations. 455 F. Supp. at 980. Concluding that the reporting provisions and financial penalties found in section 402 of the Clean Water Act "act as sufficient deterrent" to discharges of hazardous substances, the court concluded that "the only rational course would be to require applications for amended permits to be filed (through a more reasonable and ordered process) and then to penalize permit violations solely under the provisions of section 402." *Id.*

After the decision of the district court, Congress responded to the EPA's request for legislation to clarify the applicability of section 311 of the Act to discharges of hazardous substances from facilities holding NPDES permits. In the language and legislative history of the amendments, Congress expressed its intent broadly to exempt such discharges from liability under section 311 of the Act and instead to regulate these discharges under sections 402 and 309. As Senator Muskie stated during the Senate discussion of the 1978 amendments: "Chronic discharges from a point source permitted under section 402 which are associated with manufacturing and treatment technology are to be regulated under Sections 402 and 309." 124 CONG. REC. S. 18,995 (daily ed. Oct. 14, 1978). Accordingly, the 1978 amendments to section 311(a)(2) of the Act exclude from section 311 three categories of discharges related to industrial facilities:

> (A) discharges in compliance with a permit under Section 1342 of this Title, (B) discharges resulting from circumstances identified and reviewed and made a part of the public record with respect to a permit issued or modified under Section 1342 of this Title, and subject to a condition in such permit, and (C) continuous or anticipated intermittent discharges from a point source, identified in a permit or permit application under Section 1342 of this Title, which are caused by events occurring within the scope of relevant operating or treatment systems.

33 U.S.C. § 1321(a)(2).

This amendment contemplated that manufacturing plants would deal with their process waste and associated manufacturing discharges under the NPDES program rather than section 311. Further, as EPA Assistant Administrator Jorling testified before the Senate on October 5, 1978, the reportable quantities established under section 311(b)(4) would not be the basis for effluent limitations in permits under section 402.

After issuing proposed regulations and considering public comments, the EPA on August 29, 1979, announced its final regulations defining the three exemptions.

The first exclusion covers discharges in compliance with an effluent limit in an NPDES permit where "the permit contains an effluent limitation specifically applicable to the substance discharged or an effluent limitation applicable to another waste parameter which has been specifically identified in the permit as intended to limit such substance." 40 C.F.R. § 117.12(b). The latter provision is intended to allow the control of one or more hazardous substances by placing limits on other "indicator" pollutants. *See* 44 Fed. Reg. 50,768 (1979).

The second exclusion deals with cases where the discharge results from circumstances reviewed and made part of the NPDES permit record and is subject to a condition in the permit. To qualify for this exclusion, a discharge does not have to be in compliance with an NPDES permit. Congressman Breaux testified on this score as follows:

> It is recognized that, during the course of an industrial process, equipment malfunctions and human error can occur such that there will be some discharge of a hazardous substance outside the permitted effluent stream. Such circumstances are to be identified by the dischargers as part of their application for a section 402 permit. In addition, procedures must be developed for controlling and mitigating the impacts of such events. These procedures are to be incorporated as conditions in the section 402 permit.

124 CONG. REC. H. 13,599 (daily ed. Oct. 14, 1978).

The EPA's 1979 regulations placed three conditions upon the availability of the second exclusion. First, the permit application, the permit, or another portion of the public record must specifically identify (1) the substance and amount of the substance, (2) the origin and source of the substance, and (3) the treatment that is to be provided for the discharge. 40 C.F.R. § 117.12(c)(1), 44 Fed. Reg. 50,778 (1979). The treatment may be provided by a system designed to treat the permittee's normal process wastewater, by a separate system, or by a combination of these. Second, the permit must contain a requirement that the substance and the amounts of the substance identified in the public record be treated in the event of an on-site release. *Id.* § 117.12 (c)(2). Finally, the treatment to be provided must be in place. *Id.* § 117.12(c)(3).

In the preamble to the final regulations, the EPA states that the second exclusion principally will cover discharges resulting from on-site spills to permitted treatment systems. 44 Fed. Reg. 50,769 (1979). This is because continuous and anticipated intermittent discharges that are exempt under the second exclusion are also exempt under the third exclusion regardless of the existence of a permit condition. For example, a discharge from a ruptured hose could be exempt under the second exclusion if the discharger has a drainage system that would route the spilled material to holding tank or basin for subsequent treatment. The level of treatment is not specified in the section 311 regulations, and instead would be a section 402 NPDES permit matter. 44 Fed. Reg. 50,773 (1979).

The third exclusion deals with situations where, as to the discharges in question, the NPDES permits contain neither effluent limitations nor conditions. This provision thus exempts discharges that are not covered by the first and second exclusions. The third exclusion broadly exempts all continuous or anticipated intermittent discharges from a permitted point source where they are caused by events occurring within the scope of relevant operating or treatment systems. Examples of the discharges that would be regulated under sections 309 and 402 of the Act, rather than section 311, were stated by Representative Breaux as follows:

> System upsets caused by control problems or operator error, system failures or malfunctions, equipment or system startups or shutdowns, equipment washes, production schedule changes, noncontact cooling water contamination, storm water contamination, or treatment system upsets or failures.

124 CONG. REC. H. 13,599 (daily ed. Oct. 14, 1978).

The EPA's regulations set forth three categories of discharges exempt under the third exclusion, provided that a permit exists (or a permit application has been submitted) covering the source in question:

> (A) A continuous or anticipated intermittent discharge of process waste water, and the discharge originates within the manufacturing or treatment systems; or

> (B) The contamination of noncontact cooling water or storm water, provided that such cooling water or storm water is not contaminated by an on-site spill of a hazardous substance; or

> (C) An upset or failure of a treatment system or of a process producing a continuous or anticipated intermittent discharge where the upset or failure results from a control problem, an operator error, a system failure or malfunction, an equipment or system startup or shutdown, an equipment wash, or a production schedule change, provided that such upset or failure is not caused by an on-site spill of a hazardous substance.

40 C.F.R. § 117.12(d)(2), 44 Fed. Reg. 50,779 (1979). Note that this exclusion focuses on continuous or anticipated intermittent industrial discharges. On-site spills are covered under the second ex-

clusion if they are processed through a treatment system capable of eliminating or abating such spills and the permit record contains the appropriate information. 124 CONG. REC. H. 13,599. Otherwise, such spills are subject to penalties and removal costs under section 311.

The Applicability to POTWs

The EPA's February 16, 1979, proposal sought public comments on the applicability of section 311 to discharges from industrial sources into POTWs (44 Fed. Reg. 10,274). In announcing the final section 311 regulations, the EPA reserved the possibility of future regulation of such discharges from industrial facilities due to the complexity of the issues and "the potential impact of any decision on the thousands of facilities which regularly discharge hazardous substances to POTWs." 44 Fed. Reg. 50,769 (1979).

There are substantial reasons to question the EPA's authority to regulate industrial users of POTWs under section 311 of the Act. Section 311(b)(3) of the Act is carefully limited to discharges of reportable quantities of oil or hazardous substances "into or upon the navigable waters of the United States" or adjoining shorelines. Public sewer systems are not "navigable waters of the United States" within the meaning of the Act, and nothing else in section 311 of the Act purports to establish liability for discharges into such systems.

The practical reason for imposing section 311 liability upon industrial users of POTWs may also be questioned. The POTW itself is subject to comprehensive regulation as a direct discharger, including technology-based standards and water quality standards. 33 U.S.C. §§ 1311(b)(1)(B), (b)(2)(B). Under the EPA's general pretreatment regulations, 40 C.F.R. Part 403, and local and state law, POTWs have ample authority to regulate incoming discharges by industrial users. In addition, the EPA categorical pretreatment standards under section 307(b) of the Act require that technology-based standards be achieved by industrial users, focusing on toxic pollutants. 40 C.F.R. Part 400.

Determining Reportable Quantities

After hazardous substances are designated by the EPA, the next step in the regulatory process consists of determining the particular quantity of a given substance that will trigger the reporting, cleanup, and liability provisions of the Act. Under the statute as passed in 1972, the basis for determining this quantity turned on a showing of actual harm to the environment in the particular circumstances. This congressional mandate proved unworkable for the EPA, and eventually the statute was amended in 1978 to allow the EPA simply to establish "reportable" quantities in units that are convenient for reporting purposes, with actual harm to the environment to be considered in enforcement proceedings.

The key statutory language that defined harmful quantities appeared in section 311(b)(4) of the 1972 Act. This provision directed the EPA to determine "those quantities of . . . any hazardous substance the discharge of which, at such times, locations, circumstances and conditions, will be harmful to public health or welfare." 33 U.S.C. § 1321(b)(4). In enacting this provision, it appeared clear that Congress intended the EPA to take into account the "circumstances" surrounding particular discharges and in that context determine what amounts would cause actual environmental harm.

When the EPA announced its first section 311 regulations in March 1978, it attempted to implement this provision by dividing the list of designated substances into five categories based upon their relative toxicity. 43 Fed. Reg. 10,492 (1978). At that point, however, instead of examining the actual harm that certain quantities of these substances would cause in the environment, the EPA simply defined the smallest common commercial container size—one pound—as the harmful quantity for all substances in the most toxic category. For the remaining categories, the agency simply established larger multiples of one pound as the harmful quantities. *Id.*

The difficulty with the EPA's approach is that the harm produced by the introduction of any pollutant to water is dependent on the resulting concentration of that material in the water and upon receiving water characteristics. *See* 40 Fed. Reg. 59,985 (1975). The EPA had not attempted to conduct such an analysis. An "action memorandum" prepared in 1975 by the EPA Assistant Administrator who developed the proposed regulations stated that:

> Rather than the definition of harm, this regulation should be viewed as the definition of a quantity, the discharge of which is significant enough to warrant reporting, clean-up, damage mitigation, civil penalty assessment, preventative measures, and possible Federal response.

In the *Manufacturing Chemists Association* litigation that ensued after the 1978 regulations were promulgated, the question whether EPA's one-pound system for establishing harmful quantities complied with the statute was one of the principal issues. The plaintiffs argued that Congress obviously intended to base the harmful quantities on actual environmental effects. The district court had little difficulty in concluding that EPA's one-pound system did not comport with the 1972 statutory language. Noting that "even the EPA itself does not contend that the values chosen for enforcement of the regulations represent discharges which are harmful in fact," the court held the harmful quantities invalid:

> In order for a statutory system intended to control pollution to have any reliability in legitimacy, the tests which formed the underpinnings of that system must have some rational relationship to the harm sought to be prevented.

455 F. Supp. at 977.

In its briefs, the EPA had attempted to defend its one-pound approach on grounds of administrative convenience, urging that any more complicated system would be difficult to administer and enforce. In the course of its decision, the court pointed out that "EPA could accomplish its avowed purpose of requiring compliance with the notification provisions for all substantial discharges by developing a two stage process. Stage one could require notification after any discharges of hazardous substances in amounts exceeding the 'hazardous quantities' now proposed as part of the 'one-pound' regulations. The second stage would trigger the penalty provisions based on an in-depth consideration of 'times, locations, circumstances and conditions' . . ." 455 F. Supp. at 977–78. This judicial statement foreshadowed subsequent developments.

As part of the legislative "quick fix" to section 311 in 1978, Congress expressly deleted the statutory language that required the EPA to consider the "times, locations, circumstances and conditions" of a discharge. Instead, new section 311(b)(4) of the Act simply requires the EPA to "determine . . . those quantities of oil and any hazardous substances the discharge of which may be harmful to the public health or welfare." 33 U.S.C. § 1321(b)(4). Congress intended that the EPA go forward with the list of substances and quantities that had been previously established, without the need for an extensive program for gathering additional data and lengthy rule making:

> The amendments we are proposing would allow us to build on the rulemaking effort conducted for the last few years and enable EPA to get a basic program into operation within a few months after enactment.

124 Cong. Rec. S. 19,259 (daily ed. Oct. 14, 1978) (Senator Stafford).

In the amended regulations promulgated on August 29, 1979, the EPA changed the term "harmful quantity" to "reportable quantity." 40 C.F.R. § 117.3, 44 Fed. Reg. 50,777 (1979). This change was intended to reflect the fact that under the amendment the determination of the quantities that triggered the provisions of section 311 no longer require an assessment of actual harm in the variety of circumstances in which hazardous substances might be discharged. The EPA accordingly reissued regulations designating as reportable quantities the same quantities for the 271 hazardous substances that were promulgated on March 13, 1978, and an additional 28 hazardous substances that had been proposed earlier. 44 Fed. Reg. 50,766 (1979).

The section 311 reportable quantities were subsequently incorporated into the Superfund statute. Section 103 of CERCLA requires a person in charge of a facility to notify the National Response Center of any release (other than a federally permitted release) of a hazardous substance in quantities equal to or greater than the reportable quantities. 42 U.S.C. § 9603(a). Section 102 of CERCLA designates quantities established under section 311 of the Clean Water Act as quantities requiring notification under section 103 of CERCLA, unless superseded by regulations under CERCLA. 42 U.S.C. § 9602(b).

Evolving Issues

The program reflected in the 1978 amendments resulted in a major step forward in the implementation of the hazardous spill program. First of all, it clarified the applicability of section 311 to industrial sources otherwise regulated by the NPDES permit program. Although it seems quite clear from the structure of the 1972 Act that Congress intended that industrial discharges would be regulated separately, the relationship between section 311 and the NPDES permit program has been expressly addressed by Congress and defined by the EPA in the new regulations.

Second, the EPA was relieved of the responsibility for determining the extent to which actual harm will be caused by the discharge of certain quantities of hazardous substances under various times, locations, conditions, and circumstances. The intended result of the legislative "quick fix" is that the EPA's prior harmful quantities, which concededly bore scant relationship to actual harm to the environment, have now been established as the reportable quantities under section 311. The EPA promptly was able to put into effect the reporting and penalty scheme under section 311.

A troublesome side effect, however, is that vessels and onshore and offshore facilities are now charged with the duty to report discharges of quantities of hazardous substances that will in many cases not result in any harm to the environment. To the extent that this occurs, there will be an unwarranted drain on the resources of the government in responding to reports of such discharges. In addition, both enforcement agencies and the federal courts should recognize the need to examine carefully the circumstances surrounding discharges of reportable quantities in any proceedings for the imposition of penalties.

As the EPA implements its section 311 regulations and the related reporting requirements under section 103 of CERCLA, the Agency should be mindful of the foregoing problems and consider whether it is appropriate to develop criteria that would distinguish between reportable quantities that pose a substantial threat to the environment and those that may safely be regarded as *de minimis*. Such criteria would enable the government more selectively to utilize its response and cleanup resources and to deal more equitably with discharges of hazardous substances.

State and Federal Roles under the Clean Water Act

Colburn T. Cherney and Karen M. Wardzinski

The federal Clean Water Act is intended to "restore and maintain the chemical, physical and biological integrity of the nation's waters." To this end, the Act creates a comprehensive program to control water pollution. That program, established in 1972 under section 402 of the Act, is known as the NPDES program. The primary mechanism for control is a prohibition of any point source discharge to surface waters without an NPDES permit.

The administration of the permit program was initially the sole responsibility of the federal government. However, Congress provided that states desiring to administer their own permit programs could do so if the EPA approved their programs as meeting the minimum standards of federal law and implementing regulations. In approving state NPDES programs, the EPA does not delegate its own authority to the state but rather authorizes the state to administer its program in lieu of the federal program and pursuant to the state's own legal authorities. In doing so, the Act requires the EPA to carefully review the state's authority to ensure that it is at least as stringent as the federal program. This requirement is intended to ensure that the transition from federal to state programs will not slow progress toward achievement of the goals of the Act. It is also designed to allow states to retain or adopt standards more stringent than federal requirements while ensuring a consistent minimum level of protection among the fifty states and federal territories. Congress felt

Colburn Cherney is a partner in the Washington, D.C., office of Ropes & Gray. Karen Wardzinski is a partner in Freedman, Levy, Kroll & Simonds.

233

strongly that such national consistency was essential to protect against the unfair competition that could result if states were allowed to establish weaker pollution controls to lure industries from those states having more stringent pollution controls.

The minimum federal requirements for state program approval therefore dictate that the program created by a state be more than just similar to the federal program. This is not to say, however, that approved state programs must be in absolute uniformity with the federal program. States retain flexibility, both in the implementation and the administration of the program, to account for particular problems experienced by individual states.

The EPA's policy has been to transfer the administration of the NPDES program to state governments to the fullest extent possible, consistent with statutory intent and good management practice. Since 1972, thirty-nine jurisdictions have been approved to administer their own NPDES programs. The EPA recognizes, as did Congress, the wisdom of state and local management of day-to-day operations as long as federal requirements are met.

State Program Requirements

Section 402(b) of the Act authorizes the approval of state programs in lieu of federal administration and sets forth most of the underlying authorities the state must possess. These include the authority to issue permits in conformance with federal requirements (e.g., technology-based and water quality–based controls), to provide adequate public input into the permit issuance process, to develop a pretreatment program to regulate indirect discharges of pollutants into municipal treatment works, and to inspect, monitor, and enforce, both civilly and criminally, violations of the Act. Sections 303(e), 318, and 405 contain additional state program requirements with respect to continuing planning processes, aquaculture, and disposal of sewage sludge.

In addition, sections 101(e) and 304(i) direct the EPA to develop, through regulations, minimum procedural and other elements of any state program under section 402, including uniform application forms, as well as monitoring, reporting, enforcement, personnel, funding, and public participation requirements. These minimum requirements must include a prohibition against persons with conflicts of interest serving on state permit issuance boards.

The elements of a formal state program submission are set forth in published regulations. In addition to the statutory and regulatory authorities that form the legal basis for the state program, a formal state program submission includes (1) an attorney general's statement, (2) a MOA between the state and the EPA region overseeing the state program, and (3) a program description. It is through these documents that issues concerning the state's authority and ability to administer an adequate NPDES program generally are resolved. Whereas the state attorney general explains and certifies to the state's legal authority to implement a program, it is in the program description that the state agency explains how it intends to administer the program and the state's resource and manpower capabilities to do so. Through the MOA, the state and the EPA enter into agreements governing their respective roles in the day-to-day operation of the program.

Oversight Responsibility

The Act mandates extensive oversight responsibility on the part of the EPA after state programs have been approved. The EPA remains responsible and accountable for continued progress toward meeting national environmental goals of the Act and thus for ensuring that federal requirements are adequately implemented and enforced. Section 402(c) of the Act requires that approved state programs continue at all times to be consistent with federal requirements. Thus, the law contemplates an ongoing reexamination of state programs to ensure continued compliance with federal law.

The EPA accomplishes this oversight in several ways. On a case-by-case basis, the EPA has the ability to remedy individual problems. Pursuant to section 402(d), EPA regions review the most significant state permits and can object to those permits that do not comply with federal requirements. If the state does not remedy the objection, the EPA may veto the state permit and issue an appropriate permit under federal law. In addition, section 309 provides the EPA independent authority to enforce a state-issued permit or a violation of the prohibition against discharging without a permit if the state has failed to take enforcement action or has taken inadequate action.

Where more serious problems with the state's administration of the NPDES program develop, the EPA has additional remedies. Under section 309(a)(2), whenever the EPA finds that violations of the permit program are so widespread that they appear to result from a failure of the state to effectively enforce the Act, the EPA may assume primary enforcement responsibility for the program. The EPA also may use monetary incentives to encourage states to remedy outstanding program problems. Under section 106, grants made to a state for pollution control programs may be withheld in certain circumstances where the state program is not being administered in accordance with the purposes of the Act and the grant agreement. Finally, under section 402(c)(3), the EPA must withdraw approval of a state NPDES program in its entirety if it is determined that the state is not administering its program in conformance with the requirements of the Act.

With thirty-nine states approved to administer the NPDES program, state performance now largely determines the success of the program. Thus it is imperative to ensure that these states continue to implement the program in the manner directed by the Act. The EPA and the states must work cooperatively to ensure this result. For the EPA's part, it must periodically review the state's controlling legal authorities and program performance to ensure continued consistency. For the state's part, it must see that its legal authorities keep pace with the requirements of the Act and that its program performance is maintained at a high quality. Historically, both the EPA and the states have been less than diligent in ensuring that these goals are attained.

In the early years of the program, the EPA focused its attention primarily on the approval of new state programs. Less attention was given to following the progress of approved state programs to ensure the continued adequacy of legal authorities, notwithstanding the fact that during this time significant changes were made to federal NPDES requirements. Key among these changes were amendments to the Act in 1977 and 1987, which in part focused new attention on the control of toxic pollutant discharges. In addition, comprehensive revisions to the federal NPDES regulations were made in 1979, 1980, and in 1984, and numerous other specific requirements were changed over the years. Given the degree of the EPA oversight at the time, there was insufficient incentive for states to modify their programs to keep pace with new requirements. In addition, a number of states have been hampered by budget or personnel cuts or reprogramming of resources as new responsibilities in other environmental areas are transferred to the states. These losses may have left inadequate resources or personnel too inexperienced to implement effectively the NPDES program. Moreover, decreases in EPA resources in the early 1980s and new emphasis on federal/state relations may have led states to believe that the EPA lacked the ability or will to consider seriously withdrawal of existing state programs that showed evidence of substantial deficiencies.

In recent years, the EPA has begun to focus greater attention on the reevaluation of existing state programs, many of which have not been reassessed since their initial approval in the 1970s or early 1980s. These reevaluations often reveal problems. The types of problems discovered can be divided into four general categories, each of which is discussed below. It is important to keep in mind that problems in any one of these areas can result in deficiencies in the others since each is an integral part of the functioning of an adequate state program.

Adequate and Complete Legal Authority
The EPA's approval of a state program focuses first on the state's statutes and regulations to ensure that the state has the underlying authority to issue permits that comply with the substantive requirements of the federal Act and to enforce violations of those requirements. Legal deficiencies may be caused by a number of factors. As noted, several important changes have been made to the NPDES program since its creation in 1972, and in many cases, states have failed to make conforming changes to their statutes and regulations. Several of these changes have required an expansion of the scope of coverage of the state program. For example, in the 1977 amendments to the Act, states were authorized (and, in the case of already approved programs, required) to regulate federal facilities and the discharge of pollutants from industrial dischargers into municipal treatment works. Although the 1987 amendments to the Act for the first time authorized partial or phased state program approval, such approvals are only authorized for states that were not approved prior to 1987. Currently, of the thirty-nine existing state NPDES programs, five are still not approved to issue permits to federal facilities and, more importantly, twelve do not have approved pretreatment authority.

Even greater are the number of states that have failed to revise their state regulations to conform to new federal regulations. In many cases, this deficiency initially arose from the long-standing uncertainty surrounding these regulations (which challenges took years to resolve). In other cases, there is a reluctance to implement what is viewed by some states as an excessively complex regulatory scheme. The EPA is now conducting comprehensive reviews of the approved states to seek corrective action from states found to have inadequate legal authorities.

In addition to failure to revise state authorities to keep pace with new federal requirements, some states have made changes to their existing authorities that are inconsistent with federal requirements.

In some cases, the changes evidence an unwillingness to impose the requirements of the Act in the face of growing costs for pollution control; in others the changes indicate a fundamental disagreement with or a misunderstanding of the mandates of the Act.

Two significant issues that have been raised as a result of changes are the role of economics in imposing substantive requirements of the Act and the interrelationship of the NPDES program with the states' development of water quality standards under section 303 of the Act. These issues have been the basis of many debates in the EPA's ongoing review of NPDES programs.

Issues concerning funding of municipal treatment plants and the application of state water quality standards also have been raised in the context of the NPDES program reviews. In several cases, the EPA has initiated state permit program reviews in response to notices of intent to file suit against the EPA for failure to withdraw the state's program.

The EPA has been criticized for putting too much emphasis on the legal requirements of a state program without looking at the impact of these paper requirements on the state's performance or on the quality of the state's program. (On the other hand, some have accused the EPA of being satisfied with a state's paper program and ignoring the state's inability or unwillingness to implement an effective program.) In considering the importance of complete and adequate legal authorities, several factors must be kept in mind. The Act mandates that state programs be approved only if they meet and continue to maintain minimum requirements. The EPA cannot ignore its legal obligations because a requirement is felt to be unnecessary or has not been demonstrated to cause a specific benefit. In many cases, the minimum federal requirements were established by Congress after protracted, heated debate among regional interests, public interest groups, industries, and state and local governments. The EPA lacks the authority to substitute its views for the will of Congress even if it were so inclined. Equally important, a state's legal authorities provide the basis for ensuring that necessary substantive requirements can be imposed in permits. Lack of adequate authority can create the potential for problems at a later date. The law does not allow the EPA to wait until an environmental problem occurs to take action; prevention is also the better practical response. For example, the claim is sometimes made that where no degradation to the state's water quality had been demonstrated, the EPA should not be concerned about the state's legal requirements. Such comments fail to recognize that water quality effects often cannot be observed for some time.

The EPA simply does not have the resources to review thirty-nine state programs each time legal requirements are changed by Congress or new regulations. An alternative under consideration by the EPA is to require state attorneys general to recertify every five years that their state program still meets all legal requirements, including any new or revised provisions.

Permit Issuance Performance

In reviewing a state's permit issuance record, the EPA looks at both the number and quality of permits issued. A program is ineffective if the state is not issuing technically sound or legally sufficient permits, or is issuing them at a rate that creates an unacceptable backlog of expired permits, thereby delaying the imposition of necessary, often more stringent pollution controls. Although the EPA has the ability to object to a permit that is not consistent with the requirements of the Act, case-specific veto authority is not an appropriate remedy where widespread inefficiencies are seen in the state's performance. Use of veto authority as the sole oversight tool would require the EPA involvement in the day-to-day operation of a state program to an extent far greater than envisioned by the Act or than is consistent with a healthy relationship between the EPA and the states.

The EPA will evaluate states with large numbers of backlogged or inadequate permits. In the past, the most common complaint was that permits incorporating limitations based on the BAT economically achievable were not being issued where the EPA had not yet issued national BAT effluent limitations guidelines. In more recent years, this problem has been significantly alleviated as the EPA has issued more of the guidelines. Currently, the most significant complaints concern whether additional pollution controls beyond the BAT effluent limitations are being required where needed to address site-specific water quality concerns. This is particularly true with respect to municipally owned treatment works, where the costs of funding such controls may be locally unpopular and where federal subsidies for such projects are becoming increasingly difficult to obtain.

Enforcement

Timely and effective enforcement also is a key component of an effective NPDES program. In reviewing the adequacy of a state's enforcement record, the EPA will look at the number and type of enforcement responses taken. For example, in approval of the Kentucky program, concern over the state's performance record led to the requirement for a mandatory reevaluation, with public comment, one year after initial program approval. Although this was an unusual step in the approval of a state program, it appears to have been a productive one since the EPA's later audits of the state program indicated satisfactory performance. Some have suggested that all state programs be subjected to a similar formal evaluation process with public input.

Funding and Personnel

In addition to reviewing a state's authority to administer and enforce an NPDES program, the EPA is concerned with a state's practical ability to do so. This element encompasses both adequate resources and properly trained personnel to run the program. In the mid-1980s, the EPA was sued for its approval of Michigan's pretreatment program. The petitioner alleged that the staff responsible for administering the pretreatment program did not have the appropriate expertise to effectively carry out its job. In response to this action, the state revised its program to specify minimum personnel qualifications and to provide a role in the pretreatment program for personnel elsewhere within the Department of Natural Resources.

In conclusion, Congress has entrusted to the EPA and the states the joint responsibility of implementing the NPDES permit program under the Clean Water Act. Neither party can shirk this responsibility. Only through a cooperative, rather than adversarial, relationship between the EPA and the states can this obligation be carried out effectively. Where deficiencies are identified in state-administered programs, the EPA must continue to work with states to resolve the problems, and all available options to this end should be pursued. However, it must be kept in mind that the Act requires state-administered programs to meet minimum federal requirements and further requires the EPA to ensure such compliance. Recent attention to this area by Congress and interested citizens groups makes clear that neither will allow the EPA and the states to ignore these legal duties.

Local Governmental Control of Water Quality — Is This a Good Idea?

Sara Burgin

A town in New York enacts an ordinance prohibiting the construction or maintenance of sewage disposal systems within the town. As a result, a mobile home park is unable to expand even though state environmental requirements are satisfied.

A town in Maine enacts an ordinance requiring duplicate permitting for discharges previously permitted pursuant to state law. As a result, permittees must go through the time and expense of duplicate permitting and run the risk that political pressure on the local government could result in permit denial.

A city in Texas enacts a comprehensive watershed ordinance that establishes water quality, erosion, and sedimentation standards for development within and around the city. The ordinance imposes citywide limitations on effluent discharges and effluent irrigation disposal that are more stringent than required by state statute or regulation. As a result, merely because a development is within the city or its extraterritorial jurisdiction, the landowner must provide more acreage for irrigation disposal of sewage effluent than required elsewhere in the state.

A city in Alabama considers enacting public water supply protection regulations that would have significantly restricted use of the watershed area. The draft ordinance would have prohibited (1)

Sara Burgin is a partner in Brown, Maroney & Oaks Hartline in Austin, Texas.

the placement of treated utility poles within the normal right-of-way easement of most roadways within the watershed, (2) the location of vehicle service or repair facilities within one-half mile of the one-hundred-year-old floodplain of the river and related reservoir, and (3) the location of manufacturing operations within the district if they used or stored toxic substances.

New York City distributes a discussion draft of new water supply protection regulations that will dictate land use in the Catskill Mountains up to 125 miles from the city. The draft regulations are more stringent than existing regulations and would significantly affect some current landowners directly, including local dairy farmers and service station owners. The regulations would require more stringent sewage treatment, restrict spreading of road salt, and require city approval for the use of pesticides or herbicides on land near the reservoirs. The driving force for the regulations are the 1986 amendments to the federal Safe Drinking Water Act that will require the city to filter its water unless it can ensure that the watershed is protected from pollution. With estimates that it would cost the city at least $4 billion to filter the water used from the reservoir system, local Catskill residents argue that the city is attempting to assure its residents clean water at the Catskill residents' expense.

What all of these local entities have in common are attempts, sometimes consummated and sometimes not, to effectuate significant land use controls for the stated purpose of protecting water quality. Each of the controls is more stringent than or duplicates state and federal environmental laws and regulations, yet each restricts an individual's use of his or her property.

Arguments certainly exist for local enactment of environmental control regulations. For example, the local entity is most familiar with the sensitivity of the local terrain, the city is in the best position to develop a master plan for development, and the local entity is most familiar with local growth patterns. However, the drawbacks are many. Local regulations are often initiated by groups whose real goal is something other than reasonable environmental protection, such as no growth or restrictions on the location and availability of multifamily housing or low-income housing. Local governments often lack the expertise necessary to develop or implement effective regulations tailored to actual water quality concerns, leading to inefficient, unnecessarily intrusive regulations. Thus when water quality regulations are implemented at the local level, affected landowners often legitimately question whether their property use is being restricted to protect real water quality problems or whether they are merely being unjustly penalized by a lobby with no-growth or other goals in mind.

The issues discussed herein address the legitimate justifications for water quality–based land use controls, the source of power to implement such controls, and the restrictions on that power. Finally, the article discusses whether other methods exist that would accomplish the water quality protection goal while providing better protection for individual property rights.

Why Has Local Government Control Occurred?

Federal water pollution control legislation and most state programs have focused on point source forms of pollution. The discharge of a pollutant, as prohibited by section 402 of the Clean Water Act, is any addition of any pollutant to navigable waters from any point source. Implementation of the section 402 NPDES permit program has resulted in effective control of point source discharges of industrial and domestic waste. Further, significant advances are made each year in the additional control of toxic pollutant discharges through development of new or revised categorical effluent limitation guidelines and implementation of more stringent state water quality standards. Control of point and nonpoint discharges of stormwater and agricultural runoff has, however, lagged far behind.

Highly technological methods for the control of stormwater discharges and agricultural runoff do not really exist. Controls must be implemented through developing and implementing individualized stormwater management practices, behavioral changes in the general population, and modified farming practices. Costs are significant. For example, concern regarding the impact of stormwater controls on farming practices was such that the definition of point source in the Clean Water Act specifically excludes from regulation agricultural stormwater discharges and irrigated agriculture return flows. However, it is now generally acknowledged that stormwater runoff in both urban and agricultural environments is a large source of water pollution and that such runoff has a significant impact on water quality.

Even though federal or state governments have not generally regulated these discharges of pollutants, local governments have long known that stormwater and agricultural drainage constituted a threat to the purity of their drinking water sources. Because of the immediate health implications and the potential economic impacts of treating a contaminated water source, local governments have often taken the lead in attempting to regulate urban and agricultural runoff that affects their cities. Due to the complex nature of the issues involved, those efforts have sometimes been misdirected, overzealous, and not well-tailored to achieve their actual goals.

What Is the Source of Power and What Are the Limitations?

A local government, when authorized, may restrict an individual's use of private property to promote the health, safety, and general welfare of its people. This power is traditionally referred to as the police power and it is entitled to great deference by the reviewing courts, as noted in *Mugler v. Kansas*, 123 U.S. 623 (1887). However, the Fifth and Fourteenth Amendments to the U.S. Constitution impose two limits on the power of government to restrict property rights. The Fifth Amendment provides that no person shall "be deprived of . . . property, without due process of law; nor shall private property be taken for public use, without just compensation." The Fourteenth Amendment incorporates these due process protections to state action. In addition, political subdivisions of state government such as counties and municipalities are generally considered creatures of the state with powers limited to those authorized by statute. An exercise of such power may be subject to challenge as beyond the entity's authority, depending upon applicable state law.

Substantive Due Process

The due process clause of the Fifth Amendment prohibits the arbitrary exercise of government power. Due process requires that government regulation both pursue a legitimate end and that the legitimate end be advanced by application of the regulation. With respect to the issue of pursuit of a legitimate end, it should be noted that the government's power to enact regulations to promote the health, safety, and welfare of its people is broadly interpreted. *See* Wiseman, "When the End Justifies the Means: Understanding Taking Jurisprudence in a Legal System with Integrity," 63 *St. John's L. Rev.* 433, 437 (1988). Further, it is generally accepted that the regulation of environmental matters, such as the prevention of water pollution, is an appropriate application of such power. Therefore little question exists that a court would conclude that regulations to protect water quality have a legitimate end. As a result, the important substantive due process issue is whether the ordinance or regulation is reasonably drafted to achieve the stated goal.

Several tests have been loosely set out by the U.S. Supreme Court to describe the necessary relationship between the limitations imposed by the regulation and the end to be achieved. Previous language has indicated that a regulation would be sustained if it were rationally related to legitimate state interests. *Schad v. Borough of Mount Ephraim*, 452 U.S. 61, 68 (1981). The Court has also considered whether the relationship between the means and the end was fairly debatable. *Zahn v. Board of Public Works of City of Los Angeles*, 274 U.S. 325, 328 (1927). Obviously, applying either of these tests would provide great deference to a legislative body in its attempt to effectuate an end. The Court recently addressed the issue in *Nollan v. California Coastal Commission*, 483 U.S. 825 (1987), and indicated that it may have a new willingness to review seriously the relationship between regulatory action and a legitimate goal.

In *Nollan*, the Court struck down a condition that the California Coastal Commission had attached to a coastal development permit. The majority opinion concluded that the condition failed adequately to further the interests the state had advanced as a justification for imposing it. The majority could find no relationship between the means adopted by the state and the ends asserted to be the purpose of the regulation. Although the Court's language is not clear, the Court intimates that it would consider whether the regulation "substantially" advanced a legitimate governmental purpose.

Although the Court's use of the word "substantial" indicates that a resurgence of substantive due process review may be on the horizon, it is likely that the degree of nexus between the means and the end will depend upon the legitimacy of, and degree of public interest in achieving, the end. In analyzing regulations directed at protecting water quality, it is likely that courts will continue to grant local governments great deference in the means they select to achieve those ends and will only find a failure of substantive due process in egregious situations. Therefore it will be the unusual case where a court will find that a statute or regulation does not bear the necessary relationship to the goal of protecting water quality.

Takings of Property

Even though a regulation is found to substantially advance a legitimate goal such as the protection of water quality, if it completely destroys the economic viability of a landowner's property rights, compensation must typically be made. Justice Holmes, in *Pennsylvania Coal Co. v. Mahon*, 260 U.S. 393, 415 (1922), introduced the idea that regulation of property may constitute a taking under the Fifth Amendment. However, under Supreme Court cases, the issue of what degree of regulation constitutes a taking is not at all clear. The Court in *Ruckelshaus v. Monsanto Co.*, 467 U.S. 986, 1005 (1984), identified several factors that should be taken into account in determining when a governmental action effects a taking including the character of the governmental action and its economic impact, including its interference with reasonable investment-backed expectations.

The Court also analyzed the character of the governmental action complained of in *Keystone Bituminous Coal Association v. DeBenedictis*, 480 U.S. 470 (1987). In that case, several Pennsylvania coal companies challenged a Pennsylvania statute that prohibited coal mining that causes subsidence damages to preexisting buildings, dwellings, cemeteries, or water courses. The coal companies challenged, contending that the act constituted a taking of their private property without compensation, which was in violation of the Fifth and Fourteenth Amendments. While reaching a five-to-four decision that the particular statute in question did not constitute a taking, the Court unanimously approved a "public nuisance" exception to the just compensation clause. In other words, the Court held that the nature of the governmental action is critical in the takings analysis. The majority noted that "the determination that governmental action constitutes a taking is, in essence, a determination that the public at large, rather than a single owner, must bear the burden of an exercise of state power in the public interest." In situations where the action being taken restrains uses of property that are tantamount to public nuisances, courts have consistently held that the action does not constitute a taking but is merely treated as a "burden of common citizenship."

The dissent in *Keystone* notes a limitation on the nuisance exception to the takings analysis overlooked by the majority—i.e., that a regulation has not been allowed to destroy essential uses of private property without compensation. The dissent notes that "[t]hough nuisance regulations have been sustained despite substantial reduction in value, we have not accepted the proposition that the State may completely extinguish a property interest or prohibit all use without providing compensation."

The scope of the limitation noted by the dissent, however, is not broad. The Court has repeatedly made it clear that an ordinance does not constitute a taking merely because it deprives a landowner of the most beneficial use of the property. *Goldblatt v. Town of Hempstead*, 369 U.S. 590, 592 (1962). In fact, a taking will not likely be found if any economically viable use of the property remains. *Agins v. City of Tiburon*, 447 U.S. 255, 267 (1980).

Returning to the question of the limitations on water quality protection ordinances, it should be noted that the constitutional bases for challenges are few. A challenge exists when the ordinance is not rationally related to a water quality goal. An example of this limitation may be the ordinance where a town merely establishes a duplicative permitting requirement. As long as the objectives for the local permit are exactly the same as those set out for a state or federal permit, it is difficult to perceive how a requirement for a duplicate permit would advance a water quality goal. Further, challenges exist where the ordinance substantially destroys any economically viable use of the property. However, where protection of water quality is the goal, the courts will look hard at such an argument. Finally, a Fourteenth Amendment equal protection argument may be applicable, particularly where the regulation imposes more restrictive conditions on development of some areas than others.

It should be noted that other state-specific arguments exist. In some instances, the subject ordinance may be preempted by state law. In other instances, the regulation may otherwise be beyond the statutory authority of the governmental body attempting to enact it. Nevertheless, any attempt to challenge a water quality protection ordinance is extremely difficult and costly for the landowner. The question then becomes, Is there a better, more objective method to accomplish the goal?

What Options Will Ensure Environmental Integrity While Protecting Landowners?

It is evident that a need exists for local governments that are experiencing an unprecedented state of growth to expand and tailor environmental programs to meet the localities' specific needs. The state and federal governments, also pressured by growth and budgetary constraints, have in the past not focused enough on the types of pollution most significantly affecting cities. As a result, local governments have been compelled to act on their own with little guidance from the federal or state agencies typically responsible for water quality protection.

The lack of central guidance has often resulted in very inconsistent approaches to local water quality and other land use problems across the nation. The lack of consistency has caused significant problems for businesses involved in state- or nationwide activities. It has often caused intergovernmental tensions, particularly when a downstream community is more concerned about clean water than an upstream community. Further, the lack of consistency has caused inadvertent relocation of low-income housing and general mistrust of local governing boards. The lack of central guidance and oversight has also left local landowners very vulnerable to groups whose real agenda is no growth.

These problems can be reduced in several ways. As discussed above, one reason for a lack of consistency from one city to another has been lack of guidance. Due to important recent federal developments relating to nonpoint and point source discharges of stormwater, federal guidance for controlling these discharges at the local level should soon greatly improve.

Recognizing that stormwater and agricultural runoff are significant uncontrolled sources of pollutants, Congress incorporated two important sections into the Water Quality Act of 1987. Section 319 was added to address control of nonpoint sources of water pollution. It directs the governor of each state to complete two major reports on nonpoint source pollution by August 4, 1988. The first report was an assessment describing each state's nonpoint source problems. The second report was a management report explaining what each state plans to do by 1992 to address the problems.

Texas provides an example of what can be accomplished as a follow-up to the federal reporting requirements. Subsequent to developing the reports, Texas established a Nonpoint Source Advisory Committee charged with the task of developing means, both financially and substantively, to implement the plan outlined by the state's management report by 1992. The committee outlined educational programs, local pilot nonpoint source control programs, monitoring and data base programs, and funding sources. Assuming that Texas and the other states implement the goals that they have described in response to this federal initiative, progress can be made in developing widely applicable and effective nonpoint source pollution control measures.

The second important section included in the Water Quality Act of 1987 was section 402(p), which contains a timetable for promulgation by the EPA of regulations containing application and permit requirements for point source discharges of stormwater. Section 402(p)(3)(iii) mandates specifically that permits for discharges from municipal separate storm sewers require controls to reduce the discharge of pollutants to the maximum extent possible, including management practices, control techniques and systems, design and engineering methods, and other appropriate controls. Regulations containing application requirements for point source discharges of stormwater from areas associated with industrial activity and for stormwater discharges from medium and large cities were finally promulgated on November 16, 1990. 55 Fed. Reg. 47,990 *et seq.*

The regulations indicate that municipalities must develop stormwater management practices and incorporate those practices into a written plan as part of their stormwater permit application. Hopefully, in developing such plans, local governments can draw upon federal guidance and the information and data developed by those cities that already have successful stormwater programs in place. The program provides a basis for development of systemwide or basinwide permits that are an important incentive for developing consistent, comprehensive stormwater management programs. Once the federal stormwater permit program is implemented, it should enable cities to control much more effectively point source discharges of pollutants in stormwater from industrial and construction sources within the local stormwater system, assuming they are prepared and able to commit the significant moneys that will be required for this massive undertaking.

Some cities perceive a strong need to be involved in nonstormwater discharges of pollutants within their jurisdiction or watershed. This may involve state or federally permitted industrial discharges or irrigation disposal and nonmunicipal discharges of domestic wastewater. Two options are available to a city to participate in these permitting situations. It can, subject to any limits on its authority, establish system- or areawide limitations applicable to such discharges that are more stringent than otherwise applicable minimum standards established by state or federal law. This is the route often taken by cities, and it is based upon a perception that what is good enough statewide is not good enough for its unique circumstances. Unfortunately, these programs often select a set of treatment standards that, for the sake of systemwide uniformity, are more stringent than would be required on a case-by-case basis. The previous hypotheticals involving a city in Texas and a town in New York fall within this category. The town in New York enacted an outright prohibition on any discharges, while the city in Texas established more stringent system-wide limitations.

Alternatively, a city can work with the state or federal agency charged with protecting water quality and propose appropriate restrictions above the minimum standard on a case-by-case basis. This approach is typically not favored by cities because it leaves the ultimate decision to another governmental entity. However, the state-wide perspective that is necessarily incorporated into this approach is much more likely to result in consistent decision making that is not as easily driven by restrictions urged by local pressure groups.

Where adequate state or federal laws and regulations do not exist, particularly for nonpoint source runoff, individual local regulation may be necessary. However, such regulation should be enacted within the context of some form of a state-wide consistency requirement. New York City is interesting in this context. Although it is enacting both point and nonpoint source controls on landowners up to 125 miles away, the city's regulations are at least subject to state approval.

Several states, including Oregon, Florida, Vermont, and California, have adopted statutory consistency programs characterized by the requirement that all subsequent local government acts be consistent with a comprehensive plan. These plans typically address traditional land use concerns such as subdivisions, flooding and traffic flow as well as the quality of local air, water, and land resources. In states having consistency programs, local ordinances relating to covered subjects must obtain consistency approval by the state agency responsible for the program. Although this type of program ensures that all local programs have consistent minimum standards, cities are typically free to implement more stringent restrictions as long as they are not inconsistent with the enumerated state goals. Therefore, although this plan lends some consistency to the process, it provides little protection to landowners from local political pressure of no growth groups.

Another alternative under consideration in some states is the development of statewide land use and nonpoint source regulations drawing upon a statewide set of minimum standards. At the local level, an opportunity would be provided for the expression of local environmental values by the development of programs custom-fitted to local conditions based upon the principle of meeting or exceeding the minimum statewide standards. The difference between this and other programs is that the local program would be required to be submitted to the state department for authority to establish more stringent requirements than those of the state. The local program would need to show good reason why additional requirements are necessary in the local area. This option, while providing local governments an opportunity to tailor their program to specific needs, would provide better control, oversight, and protection of local landowners than the other alternatives described.

The tools are available to enable local governments to implement objectively and consistently nonpoint and point source runoff controls within their jurisdictions, either through development of well-thought-out local programs or through regional or state oversight. The recent promulgation of federal regulations applicable to point source discharges of stormwater provides a unique opportunity for local entities to work cooperatively to develop regional programs. Limited tools exist, however, to enable individual landowners to protect their property from overzealous local government. Because of the potential for political pressures on local government, courts should look closely at local ordinances. Scrutiny of such ordinances under a due process test to ensure that the ordinance substantially advances a legitimate environmental purpose could significantly increase the protection of landowner rights. To a large extent, however, because of the deferential treatment given such regulations by courts, the quality of a local program depends almost exclusively upon the extent that objectivity and consistency are demanded by the landowners subjected to regulation. If local demands for quality regulations fail, often the only practical approach is to seek a change in the state legislative system.

PART IV

Air Quality

Air Quality Standards: A New Round of
Implementation Plans

Air Toxics: Congress Mandates
Technology-Based Limits for
189 Substances

Acid Rain Control: A Market-Based
Approach to Pollution

Permits for Existing and New Sources:
Clearer Requirements or a New
Controversy?

Motor Vehicles and Fuels: New Approaches
to an Old Problem

Stratospheric Ozone: Addressing Global
Environmental Issues

Enforcement and Citizen Suits: Upping
the Ante for Violations

New Growth in the PSD Forest:
A Trail Map

Part IV
Air Quality

The Clean Air Act of 1970 was the first modern federal environmental control statute. 42 U.S.C. § 7401 *et seq.* It established a then-unique federal and state partnership for developing and implementing air quality regulations. Today the Act has significantly changed as a result of amendments in 1977 and again in 1990.

The EPA has adopted national ambient air quality standards pursuant to section 109 of the Act. 42 U.S.C. § 7409. These standards are designed to protect the public health and welfare. To date, standards have been established for six pollutants, namely, sulfur dioxide, particulate matter, nitrogen dioxide, carbon monoxide, ozone, and lead. 40 C.F.R. Part 50.

These NAAQS are implemented through state implementation plans. 42 U.S.C. § 7410. The SIPs are regulations setting forth specific emission limitations designed to attain and maintain the NAAQS. The plans are developed by the states and submitted to EPA for approval. Once approved, they are enforceable by both the states and the federal government.

The Act was amended in 1977 to address problems of continuing nonattainment of the NAAQS. It required attainment by 1982, with certain extensions to 1987. A new Part D was added to deal with nonattainment, which required the "reasonably available control technology" for all existing major sources. 42 U.S.C. § 7502. The 1977 amendments also required preconstruction permits for major new sources in nonattainment areas, which were to require the attainment of the "lowest achievable emission rate."

The 1977 amendments also adopted a new program to prevent significant deterioration of air quality in clean air areas. Part C required preconstruction review and permits for major new sources in attainment areas, which are to achieve limits based on the "best available control technology." 42 U.S.C. § 7475. In addition, SIPs in attainment areas must assure that maximum allowable "increments" or increases in the concentration of pollutants not be exceeded. 42 U.S.C. § 7473. The article by Amy R. Porter, Eric Groten, and Steven Burr discusses this nearly impenetrable forest of PSD regulation.

A separate subchapter of the Act deals with moving sources. The 1970 Act authorized the EPA to establish tailpipe standards for emissions from motor vehicles. 42 U.S.C. § 7521. The EPA is also authorized to establish standards for fuels and fuel additives to protect emission control devices used in motor vehicles and to protect public health. 42 U.S.C. § 7545.

Finally, the 1970 Act adopted provisions for enforcement and judicial review. Violations of the Act are subject to civil and criminal penalties as well as citizen suits. 42 U.S.C. §§ 7413 and 7604. EPA actions in promulgating regulations or taking other final action are subject to direct judicial review in the courts of appeals. 42 U.S.C. § 7607.

A number of concerns over the structure and implementation of many of the major programs under the 1977 amendments to the Act had led to a conclusion that the Act required significant revision. The three most cited areas of concern for legislative attention were the nonattainment program for air quality standards, the hazardous air pollutant program, and the perceived need to significantly reduce emissions of pollutants thought to contribute to acid rain.

On November 15, 1990, President Bush signed into law sweeping amendments to the Clean Air Act that revamp its prior versions. Clean Air Act Amendments of 1990, Pub. L. No. 101–549, 104 Stat. 2399 (1990), to be codified at 42 U.S.C. §§ 7401–7642. The 1990 amendments culminated a process begun ten years earlier, as well as a relatively intense fifteen-month period of legislative activity in the 101st Congress marked by committee hearings, floor action, and late night negotiating sessions. The result is a set of amendments that dwarfs the prior Act in size and complexity. The costs of implementation have been estimated from a conservative figure of $20 billion to perhaps $100 billion or more per year. The number of sources that will be included in many of the regulatory programs will increase greatly. The amendments will require significant changes in the manner in which American business conducts its operations and meets its environmental obligations.

Unlike other portions of this book, the majority of the following chapters were not printed as articles in *Natural Resources and Environment*. Instead, the materials are generated from reports prepared by the Section of Natural Resources, Energy, and Environmental Law's Air Quality Committee, which is chaired by Michael R. Barr. Persons responsible for the preparation of these chapters include Theodore L. Garrett of Covington & Burling in Washington, D.C.; Charles S. Carter of McGuire, Woods, Battle and Boothe in Washington, D.C.; Norman W. Fichthorn and Lauren E. Freeman of Hunton & Williams in Washington, D.C.; Margaret Gilhooley, Robert J. Martineau, Jr., Kevin McLean, and Sara Schneeberg of the Office of General Counsel of the EPA in Washington, D.C.; Juan Carlos Molina of Merichem Company in Houston, Texas; Neil Orloff and Susan Sakai of Irell & Manella in Los Angeles, California; David R. Wooley of Pace University School of Law in White Plains, New York; Kathy D. Bailey of the Chemical Manufacturers Association in Washington, D.C.; and R. Dean Cooper and Jean A. Crites of the Dow Chemical Company in Midland, Michigan.

Air Quality Standards: A New Round of Implementation Plans

Title I of the Clean Air Act Amendments of 1990 addresses the attainment and maintenance of NAAQS. Under the amendments, the Clean Air Act continues to give each state primary responsibility for assuring attainment of air quality standards within its borders through a SIP. The amendments, however, make revisions and additions to Clean Air Act provisions that require states to identify noncomplying areas and submit content-specific SIPs for federal approval. More important, the legislation adds several new subparts to the Act requiring that states implement specific measures in areas that have failed to attain the NAAQSs for ozone, carbon monoxide (CO), and fine particulate matter (PM_{10}). The amendments also add new provisions for interstate pollution, NAAQS maintenance plans, and sanctions against noncomplying states.

NAAQSs

The NAAQS are the keystone to the Clean Air Act's scheme to control air pollution. Under section 109 of the Act, the EPA has promulgated standards for six pollutants designed to protect the public health and welfare. 42 U.S.C. § 7409; 40 C.F.R. Part 50. These standards are subject to judicial review, and in general the courts have tended to defer to the EPA.

In *NRDC v. Administrator, EPA*, 902 F.2d 962 (D.C. Cir. 1990), the District of Columbia Circuit addressed and rejected several claims by industry groups that the EPA's primary NAAQS under section 109 of the Clean Air Act for PM_{10}—that is, particulates with an aerodynamic diameter of 10 microns or less—were arbitrary and capricious. First, the court rejected an argument that the EPA must identify the risk to public health that it considers acceptable when setting primary standards under section 109. The court held that its 1987 decision in *NRDC v. EPA*, 824 F.2d 1146 (D.C. Cir. 1987), was inapposite because section 109, unlike section 112 of the Act, which was the provision at issue in the 1987 decision, focused exclusively on public health.

Second, the court dismissed an argument that the EPA must consider the indirect health effects of regulation, i.e., the effects on the public health associated with unemployment and other costs of complying with emission regulations, in setting section 109 standards. According to the court, only the health effects of a pollutant as it is present in the ambient air are relevant in setting a standard for that pollutant.

The court also rejected industry arguments that the levels that the EPA set for the standards were unsupported by the record, the EPA improperly failed to issue up-to-date control techniques information for PM_{10}, and the EPA acted improperly in retaining the TSP indicator (rather than adopting a PM_{10} indicator) for purposes of the PSD program.

Finally, the court addressed a claim by an environmental group and others that the court should compel the EPA to revise the PM standards to address acid deposition and visibility impairment. In an order issued on January 2, 1991, however, the court vacated the part of its opinion (and separate opinions by the three panel judges) that addressed this claim at the request of the environmental group and its fellow petitioners in light of the Clean Air Act Amendments of 1990.

Nonattainment Area Designations

The first step in the nonattainment program is identifying and designating nonattainment areas by states. The amendments make several important revisions to section 107(d) under which states must designate regions as attainment, nonattainment, or unclassifiable with respect to NAAQSs. Regarding initial designations, the amendments require that states make new designations for ozone, carbon monoxide, and fine particulate matter. The amendments also authorize the EPA Administrator to require new designations for lead. States must redesignate all areas within their borders after promulgating any new or revised NAAQS.

After the EPA has promulgated the state's designations, either the EPA or the state may seek a redesignation. While preserving a state's right to request a redesignation, the amendments require that states submit an approvable maintenance plan showing maintenance of the NAAQS for at least ten years as a condition to redesignation of a nonattainment area. Section 175A. The amendments also provide a new procedure whereby the EPA Administrator is able to redesignate an area based on air quality–related considerations with or without the state's cooperation. Section 107(d)(3). The Administrator's authority to redesignate a nonattainment area to attainment, however, is subject to limitations under section 107(d)(3)(E).

Submission and Approval of SIPs

The next step in the nonattainment program is the submission and approval of SIPs by the states for attainment and nonattainment areas. In addition to providing new schedules for state submissions of SIPs following the EPA's promulgation of an NAAQS, section 110(a)(1), or nonattainment designation, section 172(b), the amendments establish some new procedures and requirements for EPA action on SIP submissions. Under a new section 110(k), the EPA must promulgate minimum completeness criteria that the Agency will use to determine whether a SIP submission complies with the Act. The EPA Administrator, however, has authority to give partial or conditional approval of a SIP or SIP revision. Sections 100(k)(3) and (4).

The EPA Administrator must comply with deadlines for determining completeness and for approving or disapproving a completed SIP. Sections 110(k)(1)(B) and (k)(2). In the event that the Administrator determines that a previously approved SIP is "substantially inadequate" to comply with the requirements of the Act and calls for a SIP revision, the noncomplying state is not relieved of any requirements or deadlines under the Act unless the Administrator provides otherwise. Section 110(k)(5). Although the Administrator has some discretion to adjust deadlines after a SIP call, attainment deadlines for nonattainment areas can be adjusted only if the deadline has elapsed.

The EPA proposed and made final the section 110(k) SIP completeness criteria. 56 Fed. Reg. 23,826 (May 24, 1991); 56 Fed. Reg. 42,216 (Aug. 26, 1991). The revised completeness criteria made only minor amendments to the existing completeness criteria promulgated by the EPA in February 1990. 55 Fed. Reg. 5824 (Feb. 16, 1990). The criteria require the EPA to make a completeness determination within sixty days after submission of a SIP or SIP revision but no later than six months after the date by which the state was required to make the submission. If the EPA fails to act within six months after receiving the submission, the submission is deemed complete by operation of law. If the EPA deems a submission inadequate, the Agency will identify absent or insufficient components.

More recently, the EPA published a notice of finding of failure to submit required SIP revisions for several ozone nonattainment areas. 56 Fed. Reg. 54,554 (Oct. 22, 1991). Revisions making corrections to the SIPs for these areas to address RACT requirements were due by May 15, 1991, pursuant to section 182(a)(2)(A) of the Act. The EPA's notice triggered the eighteen-month time clock for mandatory imposition of sanctions under section 179(a), the Administrator's discretionary authority to impose sanctions under section 110(m), and the two-year time clock for promulgation of federal regulations governing volatile organic compound emissions for the nonattainment areas, as required by section 110(c)(1).

In a recent decision, in *Delaware Valley Citizens Council for Clean Air v. Davis*, 932 F.2d 256 (3d Cir. 1991), the Third Circuit affirmed the district court's holding that it lacked jurisdiction under section 304 over three counts in a citizen suit that in effect challenged the ozone provisions of Pennsylvania's SIP on the ground that it failed to meet the Act's requirements. The court held that those claims should have been brought under section 307(b)(1) in the court of appeals because they are challenges to the SIP itself. The court made clear, however, that claims seeking to enforce state implementation of plan provisions once they are in effect may be brought in district courts under section 304. The court of appeals therefore vacated the district court's dismissal of a fourth count containing such a claim, which alleged that the state had failed to take the measures it had committed to take. Although it made no holding on the proper interpretation of the plan's provisions, the court of appeals held the district court was wrong to decide that the state's interpretation was the only permissible one as a matter of law and remanded the claim to the district court.

General SIP Requirements

While retaining all of the minimum SIP requirements under section 110, the amendments add two new general SIP provisions. All SIPs (whether initial, maintenance, or nonattainment) must provide for air quality modeling and submission of related data as prescribed by the Administrator. Section 110(a)(2)(K). In addition, a new provision under title V requires that states adopt and submit with their SIPs a program to provide technical assistance to small business sources. Section 507. Those programs must meet minimum requirements, including mechanisms for providing information on compliance technologies, permit applications, and procedures for modifying compliance methods. The EPA is required to establish guidelines to assist states in developing their programs.

In addition to preserving the minimum SIP requirements for nonattainment SIPs under section 172, the amendments require that all nonattainment SIPs include specific contingency measures that will be automatically implemented if the area fails to make reasonable further progress or to attain the NAAQS by the attainment deadline. Section 172(c)(9).

New or modified sources seeking permits for construction and operation under section 173 are also subject to some new provisions. While retaining the requirement that sources obtain offsets for their emissions before commencing operation, the amendments clarify that, in most cases, permit offset requirements can be satisfied only by emission reductions from the same source or from other sources in the same nonattainment region. Section 173(c)(1). In addition, state permit programs are required to provide for an analysis of alternative sites, processes, and control techniques before issuing a permit. Section 173(a)(5). The amendments also address use of allowances and the creditability of reductions.

Classification of Ozone, CO, and PM Nonattainment Areas

To address ozone, CO, and PM_{10} nonattainment, the amendments add new subparts requiring classification of nonattainment areas for those pollutants and setting out specific additional SIP requirements for each class. Nonattainment areas for ozone, CO, and PM_{10} are classified by operation of law based on design values or other criteria set out in the amendments. Section 172(a)(1)(C). Ozone nonattainment areas are classified progressively as either "marginal," "moderate," "serious," "severe," or "extreme." Section 181(a)(1). Carbon monoxide and PM_{10} nonattainment areas are classified as either "moderate" or "serious." Section 186(a)(1), 188(a) and (b). To provide for increasingly strict control, each class of nonattainment area for those pollutants must meet the requirements of the class below as well as the requirements of its own class. The EPA also has discretion to classify other nonattainment areas in order to apply attainment dates and other relevant requirements. Section 172(a)(1)(A).

Although nonattainment designations and classifications are usually based solely on air quality within the region, several provisions under the amendments could require different results. When making designations, states must designate as nonattainment not only those areas that have failed to meet the NAAQS but also those that contribute to ambient air quality in a nearby nonattainment area. Section 107(d)(1)(A)(i). In addition, special provisions regarding ozone nonattainment could require designation of entire metropolitan areas as nonattainment for ozone. Section 107(d)(4)(A)(iv). On the other hand, provisions regarding "rural transport areas" may allow less stringent requirements in some marginal ozone nonattainment regions if the emissions in the region do not contribute significantly to the area's nonattainment problem. Section 182(h).

The EPA, in November 1991, published a final rule announcing designations, classifications, and boundaries of areas of the country attaining and not attaining the NAAQSs for ozone, carbon monoxide, PM_{10}, and lead. 56 Fed. Reg. 56,694 (Nov. 6, 1991). Also, in November 1991, the EPA proposed to reclassify fourteen of the areas initially classified as "moderate" PM_{10} nonattainment areas as "serious" PM_{10} nonattainment areas, 56 Fed. Reg. 58,656 (Nov. 21, 1991).

New Requirements for Ozone, CO, and PM Nonattainment Areas

The amendments add a number of new control and data-gathering requirements in ozone, CO, and PM_{10} nonattainment areas. Among the provisions added for ozone nonattainment areas is a requirement that states update their emission inventories on a regular basis, section 182(a)(3)(A), and require sources of VOCs and nitrogen oxides (NO_x) to submit annual emissions statements to the EPA. Section 182(a)(3)(B)(i). SIPs for areas classified as "serious" or higher for ozone must also provide for improved monitoring and ambient concentrations of VOCs and NO_x. Section 182(c)(1).

Sources of VOCs, NO_x, and PM_{10}, are subject to the following control requirements, with the additional complication that the definition of "major source" under the amendments may vary according to the area's classification, to provide regulation of increasingly smaller sources in more polluted areas. Sections 182(c), (d), and (e), 187(c), 189(b)(3). In ozone nonattainment areas, major sources of VOCs and NO_x are required to apply all reasonably available control technologies. Sections 182(a)(2)(A) and (b)(2). There are several exceptions for NO_x sources if the Administrator determines that NO_x reductions would not benefit air quality. Section 182(f). Sources of PM_{10} and PM_{10} precursors in "moderate" PM_{10} nonattainment areas are also required to apply RACT. Sections 189(a)(1)(C), (e). Sources in "serious" PM_{10} areas must apply BACT. Section 189(b)(1)(B).

Major sources of VOCs and NO_x in ozone nonattainment areas are also affected by new provisions relating to permits for new or modified sources. Emission offsets required for issuance of a permit under section 173 vary between 1.1 and 1.5 to 1, according to the area's classification. Sections 182(a)(4), (b)(5), (c)(10), (d)(2), and (e)(1). In addition, special rules apply in "serious," "severe," and "extreme" ozone nonattainment areas regarding the definition of "modification" and the possibility for exceptions to pollution control and offset requirements. Sections 182(c)(6)–(8) and (e)(2).

The amendments also include a special provision addressing the regulation of electric utilities and commercial boilers in "extreme" ozone nonattainment areas. Section 182(e)(3). Under that provision, the state must provide certain "advanced control technology" (e.g., catalytic control) for NO_x emissions within eight years. As yet, only the Los Angeles basin is classified as "extreme" for ozone.

A number of provisions added by the amendments affect the use and servicing of motor vehicles. In ozone nonattainment areas, SIPs must include motor vehicle emissions control inspection and maintenance programs of varying stringency, depending upon the area's classification. Sections 182(a)(2)(B)(i), (b)(4) and (c)(3). In addition, SIPs for ozone nonattainment areas classified as "moderate" or higher must provide for the regulation of vehicle refueling at gasoline stations of certain sizes. Section 182(b)(3). SIPs for ozone nonattainment areas classified as "serious" or higher must also provide for a clean-fuel program under section 212. Section 182(c)(4). In carbon dioxide nonattainment areas classified as "serious," SIPs must require oxygenated gasoline in certain areas if necessary to attain the NAAQS by the attainment deadline. Section 187(b)(3).

In some cases, states may be required to institute transportation control measures to offset growth or bring emissions within projected levels. Sections 182(c)(5) and (d)(1)(A). In ozone nonattainment areas classified as "severe" or higher, states must require that employers reduce employee work-related travel according to the EPA guidelines. Section 182(d)(1)(B). In "extreme" ozone nonattainment areas, states may establish traffic control measures during heavy traffic hours to reduce the use of high-polluting vehicles. Section

182(e)(4). In certain carbon monoxide nonattainment areas, SIPs must include an annual forecast of vehicle miles traveled as well as contingency measures to be implemented if a forecast is exceeded later. Sections 187(a)(2) and (3).

Consumer and commercial products will be regulated for the first time under the amendments. The amendments establish new federal ozone measures under section 183 to achieve reductions from sources that Congress felt could be controlled more effectively on a national level. Under that section, the EPA is required to conduct a study of VOC emissions from consumer and commercial products and to establish criteria for regulation. Section 183(e)(2). The EPA must then categorize and prioritize the products and begin a phased system of regulation according to the schedules set out in that section. Section 183(e)(3)(A). States submitting adequate plans for implementation and enforcement under state law will be allowed to regulate at the state level. Section 182(e)(7).

The new federal ozone measures also address emissions that may occur in several other discrete industries. Section 183 adds a provision requiring that the EPA promulgate standards to control emissions from the loading and unloading of marine tank vessels under certain circumstances. That section also requires that the EPA issue control technique guidelines for eleven new categories of stationary sources as well as for the use of paints and solvents in the shipbuilding and aerospace industries.

Attainment Deadlines and Percent Reduction Milestones

Deadlines for attainment of the NAAQSs under the amendments vary depending on the severity of the pollution problem. For ozone nonattainment areas, deadlines range from the year 1993 in "marginal" areas to 2010 in "extreme" areas. Section 181(a)(1). Special deadlines also apply in CO and PM_{10} nonattainment areas. Sections 186(a) and 188(c). All other nonattainment areas must achieve the NAAQSs no later than five years after designation with the possibility of extension by the EPA Administrator to ten years. Section 172(a)(2). The Administrator is also authorized to allow other limited extensions under certain circumstances. Sections 172(a)(2)(C), 181(a)(5), 186(a)(4), and 188(e).

In addition to attaining the NAAQSs by the applicable deadline, SIPs for ozone, CO, and PM_{10} nonattainment areas must provide for percent reduction milestones and demonstrate that those milestones have been reached. In "moderate" ozone nonattainment areas, SIPs must provide for a 15 percent reduction of VOC emissions over six years, section 182(b)(1), with an additional 9 percent every three years thereafter in "serious" areas. Section 182(c)(2). Specific reductions in NO_x emissions may also be required in some cases or may be chosen by a state as an alternative to providing for VOC reductions alone. Sections 182(b)(1)(A)(i) and (c)(2)(C).

Similar reductions are required in CO and PM_{10} nonattainment areas to assure reasonable further progress toward attainment. Sections 187(d) and 189(c). Specific remedies and requirements apply in the event that a state fails to meet a required milestone or submit a demonstration.

For areas designated nonattainment for sulfur oxides, nitrogen oxides, and lead, the amendments add a new subpart requiring that areas submit SIPs and provide for attainment no later than five years after designation. Sections 191 and 192.

Alternate Compliance Plans

In *United States v. Ford Motor Co.*, 736 F. Supp. 1539 (W.D. Mo. 1990), the court held that when a state had approved in good faith a source's alternate compliance plan (ACP) for controlling emissions of volatile organic compounds, and such a plan was allowed under the terms of a federally approved SIP, the source's compliance with air quality standards would be measured against the ACP and not against specific emission standards in the SIP. Although the court refused to hold that the state's finding that the course complied with the ACP was enough to establish compliance as a matter of law, the court granted summary judgment for Ford because the EPA's notice charged violations of the SIP's specific emission standards, not violations of the ACP. The court further held that although the EPA could proceed against the source by serving a notice of violation of the ACP, the EPA could not use an enforcement action to attack the adequacy of the ACP itself. The EPA's sole recourse upon determining that the ACP was substantially inadequate to attain the NAAQSs was to call for a SIP revision through proper administrative procedures.

The court dismissed Ford's claim that the EPA had violated the APA by failing to use proper procedures in adopting an alleged policy of ignoring valid ACPs in enforcement actions. The court held that the claim, if true, was a challenge to final Agency action and that such challenges could be brought only in the court of appeals under section 307(b)(1) of the Clean Air Act.

Sanctions and the Consequences of a Failure to Attain

The amendments add a new section authorizing sanctions in the event that a state fails to submit or implement an approved SIP. Under section 179, the EPA Administrator is allowed to choose between cutting off federal highway funds and imposing additional emission offset requirements for new source permits as initial punishment for a noncomplying state. Both sanctions apply after six months or if the state shows a "lack of good faith." Section 179(a). The Administrator may also withhold support grants for air pollution planning and control programs under section 105. The EPA has two years to promulgate a FIP for the area unless the state corrects the deficiency. Section 179(h). Construction bans currently in place in nonattainment areas remain in place until the Administrator approves a plan correcting the deficiencies. Section 110(n)(3).

Nonattainment areas for ozone, CO, or PM_{10} that fail to reach attainment by the deadline are automatically reclassified to the next higher classification and must meet all SIP requirements for that class. Sections 181(b)(2), 186(b)(2)(A), and 188(b)(2). Additional remedies are provided for those areas in the highest classifications. Sections 181(b)(4), 187(g), and 189(d). Ozone nonattainment areas classified as "severe" or "extreme" are also subject to stringent fee provisions under section 185. Other nonattainment areas that fail to reach attainment must execute all measures that can be feasibly implemented in light of certain statutory considerations. Section 179(d).

Two relatively recent cases deserve mention. In *Delaney v. EPA*, 898 F.2d 687 (9th Cir. 1990), *cert. denied*, 59 U.S.L.W. 3405 (1990), the Ninth Circuit held that the 1982 deadline for attainment of the NAAQS for carbon monoxide was absolute (in the absence of an approved extension until 1987, which did not exist in the case before the court). The court held that where that deadline was missed, the standards must be attained as soon as possible with every available emission control measure and that it was arbitrary and capricious for the EPA to approve plans for two Arizona counties that did not contain all such measures.

In *Coalition for Clean Air v. EPA*, 762 F. Supp. 1399 (C.D. Cal. 1991), the court held that the EPA need not prepare a FIP for California under the 1990 amendments, even though the EPA had disapproved the SIP submitted under the pre-amendment Act. Because the EPA in 1988 disapproved the proposed SIP submitted by the state under the pre-1990 criteria, the plaintiffs argued the EPA must issue a FIP under the amendments' criteria without waiting for the state's submission of a new SIP proposal under the amendments. A FIP would not be required, the court held, unless the EPA disapproved a revised SIP that the amended Act required the state to prepare and submit to the EPA pursuant to the schedules and substantive criteria of the amended Act.

The court also held that section 193 of the amended Act—the "savings clause"—was inapposite. A reference in that clause preserving "control requirements," the court held, was not intended to apply to any requirement that the EPA promulgate a FIP or to any requirements that might be included in any FIP possibly promulgated by the EPA.

Interstate Pollution

The amendments establish a new provision to address the interstate transport of air pollutants. Under section 176A, whenever the EPA Administrator determines that the interstate transport of pollutants from one or more states is contributing significantly to a violation of an NAAQS in another state or states, the Administrator may establish a "transport region" including those states. After designating a transport region, the EPA must establish a transport commission that will consider strategies for mitigating interstate pollution and recommend measures to assure that all SIP requirements regarding interstate pollution are met. A majority vote of all non-Agency members of the Commission may request that the EPA issue a SIP call to one or more states. The amendments also establish an ozone transport region (encompassing the Northeast and Middle Atlantic states) that is subject to additional control measures and monitoring and modeling requirements. Section 184(a).

OCS

On December 5, 1991, the EPA proposed regulations to implement section 328 of the Clean Air Act, which requires air pollution control measures for OCS sources. 56 Fed. Reg. 63,774 (Dec. 5, 1991) (to be codified at 40 C.F.R. Part 55). The purpose of the section 128 requirements is to attain and maintain federal and state ambient air quality standards, to comply with the PSD program, and to provide for equity between onshore sources and OCS sources. The proposed requirements would apply to all OCS sources except those in the

Gulf of Mexico west of 87.5 degrees longitude, which is near the border of Florida and Alabama.

For sources located within twenty-five miles of a state boundary, the requirements would be the same as the requirements applying if the source were in the corresponding onshore area. Boundaries of states affected by the proposal extend three miles from the coastline except on the Gulf Coast of Florida, where the state's boundary extends three leagues (about nine miles) from the coastline.

Sources located farther than twenty-five miles from state boundaries would be subject to federal requirements for PSD, NSPSs, and section 112 hazardous air pollutant standards to the extent that those requirements are rationally related to protection of ambient air quality standards. For these sources, OCS program requirements would be implemented and enforced solely by the EPA. The proposal also would establish procedures to allow the EPA to exempt any OCS source from a specific onshore control requirement if the requirement is technically infeasible or poses an unreasonable threat to health or safety.

EPA Studies and Technical Guidelines

The amendments include a number of additional provisions requiring the EPA to conduct studies or to issue technical guidance to the states. For instance, the EPA is required under section 185B to undertake a study to explore the effect of NO_x reductions on ozone levels. That study will be used by the EPA and the states to make determinations regarding the appropriateness of NO_x reductions in ozone nonattainment areas. Sections 182(b)(1)(A)(i) and (c)(2)(C). To aid in decisions regarding transportation control measures in ozone nonattainment areas, the EPA is required to update prior planning guidelines and publish information regarding the emission reduction potential of specific measures. Sections 108(e) and (f). The EPA is also required to issue technical guidance on control measures for VOCs, NO_x, and PM_{10}, sections 183(c), (d), and 190, and to establish a clearinghouse for the dissemination of information about emission control technology (i.e., RACT, BACT, and LAER). Section 108(h).

Recent Judicial Decisions

The Sixth Circuit, in *Navistar International Transportation Corp. v. EPA*, 941 F.2d 1339 (6th Cir. 1991), held that the EPA acted properly in disapproving a proposed site-specific revision to Ohio's SIP to provide variances for surface coating at Navistar's truck manufacturing and assembly plant in an ozone nonattainment area. The proposed revision sought a compliance date extension for three coating lines and either an extension of an emission limit (in Navistar's view) or a relaxation of the emission limit (in the EPA's view) of seven other lines. The court first addressed whether a 1979 attainment demonstration for the area remained valid and upheld the EPA's decision that, because ozone standard exceedances and violations had occurred during the five-year extension period, a new demonstration was required. The court also held even if a new demonstration were not required, the EPA was justified in finding the state and Navistar had failed to comply with the requirement in section 172(b)(2) of the Act that nonattainment area SIPs must provide for "implementation of all reasonably available control measures as expeditiously as practicable." The court rejected Navistar's argument that this requirement did not apply to proposed site-specific SIP revisions and held that it was reasonable for the EPA to decide that Ohio and Navistar had made an inadequate factual showing that this requirement had been met.

In addition, the court agreed that the EPA standard for the EPA review of proposed SIP relaxations, which requires a demonstration both that the existing SIP imposes a level of emission control more stringent than RACT and that the proposed SIP revision represents RACT, was applicable to the proposed SIP changes for seven coating lines. The court held that the EPA acted properly in concluding Navistar had failed to show that compliance with the existing SIP limits was not technically feasible (i.e., that the existing SIP was more stringent than RACT).

Finally, the court found meritless an argument that the EPA had failed to respond adequately to Ohio and Navistar's comments and held Navistar had presented no evidence that the pendency of EPA enforcement actions against the company for alleged violations of the existing SIP caused the EPA to be biased against the proposed SIP revisions.

In *NRDC, Inc. v. EPA*, 941 F.2d 1207 (4th Cir. 1991), the Fourth Circuit affirmed the EPA's approval of a Maryland SIP revision that allowed the averaging, or "bubbling," of volatile organic compound emissions from four coating lines at a facility in determining compliance with a 2.9 pounds per gallon limit in an ozone nonattainment area. The court rejected the petitioner's argument that the SIP revision was contrary to the EPA's control techniques guidelines covering volatile organic compound emissions. The court upheld the EPA's interpretation of the statute's RACT requirement as allowing grouping of individual sources into what is, in effect, a single source. The court refused to overturn use of "bubbling" under the Maryland SIP revision merely because the EPA had disapproved such proposals in other contexts; the court noted the permissibility or impermissibility of "bubbling" in particular cases is highly fact-specific.

In conclusion, it becomes obvious that the Clean Air Act Amendments of 1990 have had a significant impact on the attainment and implementation of NAAQSs and SIPs. It is perhaps too early to ascertain just what the outcome of this new round of implementation plans will accomplish, but we can all be sure that it will have a profound impact on the states that are empowered to implement them and the industries that are regulated thereunder.

Air Toxics: Congress Mandates Technology-Based Limits for 189 Substances

The Clean Air Act of 1970 authorized the EPA to set health-based standards for hazardous air pollutants. 42 U.S.C. § 7412. These so-called NESHAP standards were to protect the public health with an ample margin of safety. However, the section 112 program met with only limited success. The EPA established standards for only seven pollutants. 40 C.F.R. Part 61. In addition, its efforts were mired in litigation and confusion as to the appropriate level of control. *See NRDC v. EPA*, 824 F.2d 1146 (D.C. Cir. 1987). These perceived defects in the program were addressed in the Clean Air Act Amendments of 1990, which established a list of 189 hazardous pollutants and directed the EPA to establish standards based on the use of MACT. The amendments also contained a new health-based approach for dealing with any residual risk remaining after implementing MACT.

The Substances Covered

The 1990 amendments established a list of hazardous air pollutants in section 112(b)(1) that must be addressed by the new air toxics program. The list includes organic chemicals and metals common to many industrial processes. Notably, the provisions for PSD will not apply to pollutants on this list. Section 112(b)(6).

Under section 112(b), the EPA may add to or delete from the list based on its review of each substance's health or environmental effects. Any person may petition the EPA Administrator to modify the list. The petitioner must make a showing that "there is adequate data on the health or environmental effects of the pollutant or other evidence adequate to support the petition." Section 112(b)(3)(A). The Administrator must grant or deny the petition within eighteen months and publish his or her reasons for doing so.

On December 4, 1991, President Bush signed into law a joint resolution of Congress that strikes "hydrogen sulfide" from the list of hazardous air pollutants in section 112(b)(1) of the Clean Air Act as amended by the 1990 amendments S. J. Res. 187, 102d Cong., 1st Sess. (1991); Pub. L. No. 102–187. The text of the Clean Air Act Amendments approved by both houses in 1990 did not include hydrogen sulfide on the list. While the final bill was being prepared for the President's signature in 1990, however, hydrogen sulfide was inadvertently added to the list. If Congress had not corrected the mistake, it could have required controls for many sources that would not otherwise be subject to them.

The Sources Covered

Within twelve months of enactment, the EPA must develop and publish a list of source categories and subcategories of major sources and area sources of hazardous air pollutants that will be regulated under the Act. Section 112(c)(1). The EPA may add categories and subcategories to the list. Section 112(c)(5). If the EPA adds a category after it publishes the initial list, the Agency must promulgate emission standards for that category within ten years after enactment or within two years after adding the category, whichever is later.

On June 21, 1991, the EPA published a preliminary draft list of source categories and subcategories to provide an opportunity for members of the public to comment on the draft list. 56 Fed. Reg. 28,548 (June 21, 1991). Once it promulgates a final list, the Agency will use the list to develop the schedule for promulgating emission standards.

In general, a "major source" is any stationary source (or group of stationary sources located within a contiguous area and under common control) that emits or could emit, considering controls, ten tons per year or more of any listed hazardous air pollutant or twenty-five tons per year or more of any combination of hazardous air pollutants. Section 112(a)(1). The EPA Administrator may establish a lesser quantity (or, in the case of radionuclides, different criteria) for defining a major source based on "the potency of the air pollutant, persistence, potential for bioaccumulation, other characteristics of the air pollutant, or other relevant factors."

An "area source" is any stationary source that is not a major source, but the category does not include motor vehicles or nonroad vehicles that are subject to regulation under title II. Section 112(a)(2). The Administrator must list each category and subcategory of area sources that he or she determines "presents a threat of adverse effects to human health or the environment (by such sources individually or in the aggregate) warranting regulation under this section." Section 112(c)(3). Within five years of enactment and pursuant to section 112(k)(3)(B), the EPA must list "sufficient categories or subcategories of area sources to ensure that area sources representing 90 percent of the area source emissions of the 30 hazardous air pollutants that present the greatest threat to public health in the largest number of urban areas are subject to regulation under this section." The EPA must promulgate these regulations within ten years of enactment.

The Administrator may delete any source category from the list upon petition or upon his or her own motion if (1) in the case of a carcinogen, no source in the category emits pollutants that may cause a lifetime risk of cancer greater than one in one million (10^{-6}) to the most exposed individual, or (2) for pollutants that may cause adverse health effects other than cancer to adverse environmental effects, public health will be protected with an ample margin of safety and no adverse environmental effects will occur as a result of emissions of the pollutant. Section 112(c)(9)(B). The Administrator must grant or deny a petition within one year.

The EPA must conduct a study of the "hazards to public health reasonably anticipated to occur as a result of emissions" by fossil fuel–fired electric utility power plants "after imposition of the requirements of this Act." Section 112(n)(1)(A). The EPA must complete the study and report to Congress within three years of enactment and must regulate these plants under section 112 if it finds that regulation is "appropriate and necessary after considering the results of the study."

The EPA must also establish a monitoring network to examine deposition of hazardous air pollutants in the Great Lakes and coastal waters and must complete a study, within three years of enactment, of the effects of hazardous air pollutants on these waters. Section 112(m). It must promulgate regulations based on the results of the study to the extent that it determines is "necessary and appropriate." Section 112(m)(6).

Technology-Based Standards

The EPA must establish control technology-based emission standards for new and existing sources for all categories and subcategories of major and area sources. Section 112(d). The Agency may distinguish among classes, types, and sizes of sources within categories and sub-categories in setting these standards.

The standards must require "the maximum degree of reduction in emissions of the hazardous air pollutants subject to this section" that the Administrator determines is achievable, "taking into consideration the cost of achieving such emission reduction, and any non-air quality health and environmental impacts and energy requirements." Section 112(d)(2). Standards for new sources must require a degree of reduction that is not "less stringent than the emission control that is achieved in practice by the best controlled similar source." Section 112(d)(3). Standards for existing sources may be less stringent than new source standards, but they may not be less stringent than the average emission limitation achieved by the best performing 12 percent of existing sources in the same category or the best performing five sources where the source category has fewer than thirty sources.

For area sources, in lieu of setting standards under generally applicable provisions, the EPA may promulgate standards or requirements that "provide for the use of generally available control technologies or management practices . . . to reduce emissions of hazardous air pollutants." Section 112(d)(5).

Existing sources can avoid, for six years, otherwise applicable control technology-based standards through "early reductions." Section 112(i)(5). If an existing source demonstrates "a reduction of 90 per centum or more in emissions of hazardous air pollutants (95 per centum in the case of hazardous air pollutants which are particulate)" before proposal of the technology-based standard, the EPA or a state with an approved permit program must issue a permit allowing the source to meet an alternative limitation reflecting the reduction. Section 112(i)(5)(A). A state may require a larger reduction, if it so chooses.

The EPA recently proposed regulations to implement the early reductions program under section 112(i)(5) of the Act. 56 Fed. Reg. 27,338 (June 13, 1991). Section 112(i)(5) allows a source to obtain a six-year extension of compliance with control technology-based standards under section 112 if the source achieves a 90 percent reduction in hazardous air emissions either (1) before the date of proposal of the relevant standard or (2) after proposal but before January 1, 1994, in cases where, before the date of proposal, the source makes an enforceable commitment to achieve the reduction. The EPA's proposal was designed to give source owners and operators flexibility in defining what constitutes a "source" for purposes of the early reductions program. Reductions generally are to be measured from a 1987 baseline, and the proposed rule provides a mechanism to account for reductions of pollutants deemed to pose particularly high risks.

The EPA must promulgate the control technology-based standards on a ten-year phased schedule. It must set standards for at least forty source categories (not counting coke oven batteries, for which the deadline is December 31, 1992) within two years of enactment, for 25 percent of the source categories within four years of enactment, for an additional 25 percent within seven years of enactment, and for all categories within ten years of enactment. Section 112(e)(1).

In late 1991, the EPA proposed the first emission standards under the amended section 112. 56 Fed. Reg. 64,382 (Dec. 9, 1991). The proposal would require control of perchloroethylene emissions from new and existing dry cleaning facilities. Further, it would establish MACT standards for major sources and GACT requirements for smaller area sources. Because it proposed the section 112 standards, the EPA withdrew a 1980 proposal to establish NSPSs governing perchloro-ethylene emissions from these sources under section 111 of the Act. 45 Fed. Reg. 78,174 (Nov. 25, 1980).

Also in 1991, the EPA published a final order staying the effec-tiveness of the section 112 radionuclide emission standard, which was promulgated in 1989, for facilities licensed by the NRC (except nuclear power reactors) until November 15, 1992, or until an earlier date when the EPA is prepared to make an initial determination under section 112(d)(9) of the amended Act as to whether the NRC reg-ulatory program provides an ample margin of safety to protect public health. 56 Fed. Reg. 18,735 (Apr. 24, 1991). Shortly thereafter, the EPA published a rule staying the effectiveness of the radionuclide standard as applied to nuclear power reactors. 56 Fed. Reg. 37,158 (Aug. 5, 1991). The stay is effective until the EPA takes final action on a proposal to rescind the standard as applied to nuclear power reactors pursuant to the criterion in section 112(d)(9). 56 Fed. Reg. 37,196 (Aug. 5, 1991).

The EPA also proposed to stay the effectiveness of the section 112 emission standard governing emissions of benzene from waste operations. 56 Fed. Reg. 64,217 (Dec. 9, 1991). The stay affects chemical manufacturing plants, coke by-product recovery plants, pe-troleum refineries, and facilities at which waste management units are used to treat, store, or dispose of waste generated by those facil-ities. The EPA proposed the stay to allow the Agency to take final action clarifying various provisions of the standard. If made final, the proposal would lift the March 7, 1992, compliance date for affected facilities.

In 1989, the EPA promulgated section 112 standards for benzene emissions from coke by-product recovery plants. 54 Fed. Reg. 38,044 (Sept. 14, 1989). The EPA proposed in April 1991 and made final in September 1991 revisions to those standards. 56 Fed. Reg. 13,368 (Apr. 1, 1991); 56 Fed. Reg. 47,404 (Sept. 19, 1991). The revisions add provisions for the use of certain add-on control devices as alternative means of complying with the standards for process vessels, storage tanks, and tar-intercepting sumps. The rule changes were designed to implement a settlement of a judicial challenge to the originally promulgated standards.

Risk-Based Standards

The Administrator must report to Congress within six years of enactment on the risks to public health that remain or are likely to remain after application of control technology-based standards and must recommend legislation that addresses those risks. Section 112(f)(1). If Congress does not act on the Administrator's legislative recommendations, the Administrator must adopt additional standards for each source category (within eight years of promulgation of the control technology-based standards for a source category or within nine years in the case of those source categories that the EPA must regulate within two years of enactment) if necessary to protect the public health with an ample margin of safety or to prevent adverse environmental effects. A risk-based standard is required if the maximum individual lifetime cancer risk from a source category is 10^{-6} or more.

Other Issues

Compliance schedules. Emission standards are effective on the date of promulgation, and new sources generally must comply any time after the effective date. Sections 112(d)(10), (f)(3), and (i)(1). Existing sources, however, are to be subject to a compliance date to be set by the EPA, which may not be later than three years after the standard's effective date (with a possible one-year extension). Section 112(i)(3). If an existing source has installed BACT or technology to meet a LAER before promulgation of a section 112 standard, that source need not meet the section 112 standard until five years after installation of the technology. Section 112(i)(6).

The area source program. The EPA must conduct research on hazardous air pollutant sources in urban areas and report preliminary results within three years of enactment. Section 112(k)(2). Within five years of enactment, it must provide Congress with a comprehensive area source control strategy that identifies at least thirty hazardous air pollutants that, as the result of area source emissions, present the greatest health threat in the largest number of cities. The strategy must contain a schedule of specific actions to reduce health risks from area source emissions, and the EPA must implement the strategy by requiring that all sources are in compliance with all requirements within nine months of enactment. Section 112(k)(3).

Equivalent emission limitations by permit. Permitting for sources of hazardous air pollutants is covered by the general permitting provisions of title V. Section 112(j) of the Act, however, provides for "equivalent emission limitations by permit" where the EPA fails to promulgate a control technology-based standard by an applicable deadline. Within forty-two months after enactment, if (1) the Administrator misses a promulgation deadline, (2) eighteen months have passed since that deadline, and (3) the state's permit program has become effective, the owner or operator of a major source must submit a permit application. Section 112(j)(2). A permit must be issued pursuant to title V and must contain emission limitations that the Administrator or the state "determines, on a case-by-case basis, to be equivalent to the limitation that would apply . . . if an emission standard had been promulgated in a timely manner." Section 112(j)(5).

State programs. Each state may develop and submit to the EPA for approval a program for implementing and enforcing section 112 emission standards or requirements for preventing and mitigating accidental releases under section 112(r). Section 112(l)(1). The EPA must, within twelve months of enactment, publish guidance to the states for developing programs. Section 112(l)(2). Pursuant to statutorily specified criteria, the EPA must approve or disapprove state-submitted programs within 180 days of receipt. Section 112(l)(5). The EPA may withdraw approval after ninety days' notice to the state of program deficiencies and the state's failure to correct the problem. Section 112(l)(6).

The EPA retains full enforcement authority even in a state with an EPA-approved implementation and enforcement program. Section 112(l)(7).

Preventing accidental releases. Section 112(r) of the Act imposes on the "owners and operators of stationary sources producing, processing, handling or storing" hazardous substances the obligation "to identify hazards which may result from such releases using appropriate hazard assessment techniques, to design and maintain a safe facility taking such steps as are necessary to prevent releases, and to minimize the consequences of accidental releases which do occur." Section 112(r)(1). The EPA must, within twenty-four months of enactment, promulgate a list of one hundred substances that in the case of an accidental release are known to cause or may reasonably be anticipated to cause death, injury, or serious adverse effects on human health or the environment, section 112(r)(3), and must set a "threshold quantity" for each listed substance, section 112(r)(5).

The President must appoint an "independent safety board" called the Chemical Safety and Hazard Investigation Board, which is to investigate serious accidental releases, issue recommendations to reduce the likelihood or consequences of accidental releases, propose corrective measures, and establish binding accidental release reporting requirements. Section 112(r)(6).

The EPA must promulgate regulations within three years of enactment on accidental release prevention, detection, and response. Section 112(r)(7)(B). The regulations must require covered source owners and operators to prepare and implement risk management plans that include hazard assessment.

Finally, as to chemical process safety management, the Secretary of Labor, in coordination with the EPA Administrator, must promulgate under the Occupational Safety and Health Act a chemical process safety standard to protect employees from hazards caused by accidental workplace releases of highly hazardous chemicals. Section 304(a).

Acid Rain Control: A Market-Based Approach to Pollution

Title IV of the Clean Air Act, enacted as part of the Clean Air Act Amendments of 1990, directs the EPA to establish an acid rain program designed to reduce the adverse effects of acidic deposition. The Act mandates a national emissions cap of 8.95 million tons per year on emissions of sulfur dioxide (SO_2) from electric utility power plants, to be achieved in two phases. In Phase I, which begins in 1995, the 110 utility plants with the highest emission rates must meet an intermediate SO_2 emission limitation requirement. By 2000, the first year of Phase II, most existing utility units (i.e., fossil fuel–fired boilers) with output capacity greater than twenty-five megawatts, as well as new utility units, will be required to meet emission limitations that in many cases are far more stringent than existing limitations under SIPs or other Clean Air Act rules. As a result of these stringent new limitations, total annual SO_2 emissions will be reduced by 10 million tons below 1980 levels. In addition, sources not subject to the mandatory requirements of title IV (e.g., industrial facilities and small existing utility units) may elect to participate in the program by "opting in."

Title IV also requires that certain coal-fired electric utility boilers reduce their emissions of nitrogen oxides (NO_x) by installing "low NO_x" burner technologies or their equivalent.

The EPA plans to codify the acid rain program requirements in six different regulations: permits (40 C.F.R. Part 72); the allowance system (Part 73); opt-in provisions (Part 74); continuous emission monitoring (Part 75); NO_x controls (Part 76); and excess emissions (Part 77).

Recently, the EPA proposed four parts of the acid rain rules, namely, permits, allowances, continuous emission monitoring, and excess emissions. 56 Fed. Reg. 63,002 (Dec. 3, 1991). The EPA plans to adopt rules to implement the opt-in provisions and the NO_x provisions in later rule making.

The Allowance Program

The centerpiece of the acid rain program is the SO_2 control program and, more specifically, an innovative trading system with a fixed number of fully marketable allowances. An allowance authorizes the emission of one ton of SO_2 in a given year or any subsequent year. Existing utility sources are to be allocated allowances based on their historic fuel use and the emission limitations applicable in 1985. Utility units must not emit SO_2 in quantities exceeding the number of allowances they hold for a given year.

The EPA must issue SO_2 emission allowances to "affected units" or elective affected units according to the formulas specified under the legislation. An allowance is a limited authorization to emit one ton of SO_2 in a specific calendar year. The allowance is not a property right. Allowance holders may carry allowances forward to future years but could not use an allowance before the year for which the EPA has issued it. The EPA must promulgate regulations within eighteen months of enactment outlining the requirements for tracking, recording, and transferring allowances.

Under the legislation, allowance holders may trade allowances. Allowance holders who trade allowances must record allowance transfers with the EPA. Allowance holders may transfer allowances before the year in which they become effective, but the allowances may not actually be used before that year.

The Agency must publish a list of Phase II allowances to be allocated, with the initial list no later than December 31, 1991, and the final list by December 31, 1992.

The legislation includes provisions to require that EPA regulations ensure electric reliability; temporary increases and decreases in emissions during the year would not be considered as long as the unit had enough allowances as of the end of the year to accommodate its total emissions during that year. Affected units in a utility system, power pool, or an allowance pool arrangement could pool their allowances for greater flexibility.

The proposed allowance system regulation includes several components, some of which the EPA is developing on different schedules.

The EPA proposed the provisions addressing the allowance tracking and trading system and allowance incentives for energy conservation and renewable energy on December 3, 1991. The EPA proposed rules implementing provisions governing EPA-sponsored allowance auctions and sales on May 23, 1991, and published final rules on December 17, 1991. 56 Fed. Reg. 65,592 (1991). The EPA will propose allowance allocations for utilities and a special allowance program for small diesel refineries in the future.

Since allowances are fully transferable and may be bought and sold, utilities may meet their SO_2 emission control requirements in the most cost-effective way possible. Each affected source must apply for a permit that, among other things, certifies that the source will hold a sufficient number of allowances to cover its emissions in a given year. Affected sources also may specify one or more optional compliance methods. The proposed regulations governing permit requirements are included in the December 3 proposal, as are the requirements for monitoring (i.e., measurement) of emissions and for imposing penalties in cases of excess emissions.

SO₂ Emissions: Phase I

For Phase I (1991 to 1999), section 404 establishes an effective annual emission limit of 2.5 lbs/mmBtu for affected units. Units could emit at higher levels only if they acquire additional allowances. The limit applies to 107 utility power plants listed in the legislation, and the measure specifies the annual emission allowances that the EPA will allocate to each unit. (Of these allowances, 2.8 percent will be withheld by the EPA to create a special reserve for auctions and direct sales under section 416.) The legislation defines an allowance as an authorization to emit one ton of SO_2 in a calendar year. By December 31, 1991, the EPA must calculate the total tonnage reduction of SO_2 emissions anticipated in Phase I and must establish a reserve of allowances equal to that amount, not to exceed 3.5 million tons. The Agency would allocate Phase I allowances from this reserve.

The EPA must maintain a reserve of 300,000 bonus allowances for Phase I affected units that employ renewable energy technology (solar, geothermal, biomass, or wind sources). The allowances for this reserve would be derived by reducing on a *pro rata* basis the allowances to which Phase II affected units would otherwise be eligible.

Plants that use flue gas desulfurization or "scrubber" control technologies to meet their Phase I reduction requirements may postpone compliance until 1997 and receive early reduction bonus allowances.

Section 404 of the Act allows the owners or operators of affected Phase I units to apply to the EPA to reassign their SO_2 emission reduction requirements to other units that they own or operate. In addition, retirement of an affected unit after enactment does not affect the allowances that the unit would be eligible to receive under either Phase I or Phase II. Thus the unit may continue to receive allowances for the retired unit and could bank, trade, or use those allowances for other purposes.

Section 408(c)(1)(B) provides that if the owner or operator of an affected unit proposes to meet the Phase I emission requirements by either reducing use of or shutting down the unit, the owner or operator must specify in its compliance plan submitted to the EPA the unit or units that will be used to compensate for the reduced output. Units to be used for compensating generation would be deemed Phase I affected units and would receive allowances equal to the lesser of the unit's actual or allowable 1985 emissions rate, divided by two thousand.

SO₂ Emissions: Phase II

The legislation establishes more stringent and far-reaching SO_2 emissions limits for Phase II, effective January 1, 2000, and thereafter. Section 405 sets out detailed emission allowance formulas for various kinds of units. Generally, existing coal-fired electric utility units— i.e., those that began commercial operation before enactment—with a 1985 emission rate of 1.2 lbs/mmBtu or greater could not exceed an annual emission rate of 1.2 lbs/mmBtu in Phase II. These units would be eligible for allowances equal to the product of 1.2 lbs/ mmBtu and the unit's "baseline" (i.e., its 1985–87 average annual heat input in mmBtu), divided by two thousand. Section 405 also sets out allowance allocation formulas for units with 1985 emission rates below 1.2 lbs/mmBtu. In addition, the legislation contains a series of special allowance provisions for oil- and gas-fired units, units that began operation after 1985, and various special categories of units.

Any new unit, generally defined as a unit that commences operation on or after the date of enactment, may not emit any SO_2 after December 31, 1999 (in the absence of allowances), and would not be eligible to receive any allowances from the EPA. Thus the owners or operators of new units will have to purchase allowances for any

SO_2 emitted in 2000 and thereafter. Title IV contains certain limited provisions authorizing allowance allocations to units under construction but not yet in operation at the time of enactment.

Section 403(a), with limited exceptions, caps Phase II allowances at 8.9 million tons per year and directs the EPA to reduce the number of allowances to affected units on a *pro rata* basis should the allowances calculated under the detailed formulas in the legislation exceed that amount. The EPA must further reduce allowances by 2.8 percent to create a special reserve of allowances to be offered by the Agency for direct sale or auction.

Section 409 provides for a four-year extension (until December 31, 2003) of the Phase II compliance date for affected units repowered with a qualifying clean coal technology. To qualify for the extension, the unit's coal-fired boiler would have to be replaced with clean coal technology, e.g., atmospheric or pressurized fluidized bed combustion, integrated gasification combined cycle, magnetohydrodynamics, direct and indirect coal-fired turbines, or integrated gasification fuel cells.

NO_x Emissions

Section 407 sets NO_x emission limits for coal-fired utility units. Although it sets different emission limits for different kinds of boilers, it contemplates that the limits would not be more stringent than "low-No_x" burner technology or technology comparable in cost.

Section 407 also calls for NO_x emission limitations on both Phase I and Phase II affected units. The bill sets specific annual emission limits in Phase I for tangentially fired boilers (0.45 lbs/mmBtu) and dry-bottom wall-fired boilers (0.5 lbs/mmBtu), effective January 1, 1995. The EPA may set higher limits if it finds that these limits cannot be met using low-NO_x burner technology. By January 1, 1997, the EPA would have to promulgate emission limits on a lb/mmBtu basis for wet-bottom wall-fired boilers, cyclones, cell burners, and all other types of utility boilers, basing such limits on technology comparable in cost to low-NO_x burners. Section 407 allows the EPA to set more stringent limits for tangentially fired and dry-bottom wall-fired boilers if the Agency determines that more effective low-NO_x burner technology is available. However, any of these stringent limits could not apply to Phase I affected units that are subject to the 0.45 or 0.5 lbs/mmBtu limit.

In addition, section 407 allows the acid deposition control permitting authority to set a less stringent emission standard for an individual unit upon a showing that the unit could not meet the generally applicable standard using low-NO_x burner technology. To be eligible for an alternative emission limit, the owner or operator must demonstrate to the permitting authority that the appropriate control equipment has been installed and operated for fifteen months (or some other appropriate period established by rule by the EPA) and that the unit cannot meet the generally applicable limit. If the owner or operator meets these requirements, the permitting authority would issue a permit that allows the unit to emit NO_x in excess of the statutory limit during the demonstration period for the control equipment. At the end of this demonstration period, the permitting authority would revise the operating permit to reflect the alternative emission rate the unit is deemed capable of meeting.

Election for Additional Sources

The SO_2 and NO_x emission restrictions apply only to electric utility steam generating units. Thus industrial and other nonutility sources are not subject to Phase I or Phase II emission limits. Under section 410, however, industrial sources may elect to have their facilities that emit SO_2 considered affected sources for purposes of the SO_2 program and to receive SO_2 emission allowances. These sources would receive allowances equal to baseline, multiplied by the lesser of the 1985 actual or allowable emissions rate, divided by two thousand. The EPA would select another representative year if the unit was not in operation in 1985. Unlike other affected sources, elective sources could trade or bank surplus allowances resulting from reduced use or shutdown only under certain limited circumstances. Allowances could be transferred or carried forward for use in subsequent years only to the extent that the reduced use or shutdown resulted from the replacement of thermal energy from the elective unit with thermal energy from any other unit subject to acid deposition control requirements and the allowances were used for those units. The EPA may not allocate allowances to an elective source in an amount greater than the emissions resulting from operation of the source in full compliance with all requirements of the Clean Air Act.

Although the Act does not require industrial source emission reductions, section 406 of the amendments directs the EPA to conduct a study of industrial emissions of SO_2 and to report its findings to Congress in 1995 and every five years thereafter. If the EPA estimates that industrial emissions could reasonably be expected to exceed 5.6 million tons per year, the Agency must "take such actions under the

Clean Air Act as may be appropriate to ensure that such emissions do not exceed" that amount.

Other Issues

EPA sale of allowances. Section 416 requires the EPA to withhold 2.8 percent of the allowances affected units would otherwise receive to be held in a special allowance reserve for the direct sale and auction of allowances by the Agency. The price, adjusted for inflation, would be $1,500 per allowance.

The excess emission penalty. In another monetary matter, the legislation imposes a penalty of $2,000 per ton for emissions that exceed a unit's SO_2 allowances of NO_x limitation. This penalty will also be adjusted annually for inflation. Section 411. The owner or operator of a unit exceeding its annual emission limit also must reduce emissions in the following year to offset the exceedance. In the case of SO_2 exceedances, the EPA also must reduce the allowances to which the unit otherwise would be entitled by a corresponding amount.

Permits and compliance plans. Section 408 of the Act imposes permitting and compliance plan requirements in addition to the general permitting requirements of title V of the Clean Air Act. The owners and operators of affected units must prepare permit applications and compliance plans to implement applicable SO_2 and NO_x requirements. Section 408 stipulates that, except in certain limited circumstances, a simple statement that the owner or operator of the affected unit will comply with the title IV emission limitation requirements in a timely manner or will hold the necessary allowances for SO_2 emissions will satisfy the compliance plan requirements. An acid deposition control permit will apply for a period of five years.

The EPA will issue Phase I permits. Applications and compliance plans are due within twenty-seven months of enactment. The EPA must act on the applications within six months of receipt. For Phase II units, designated state permitting authorities will issue the permits. Applications and compliance plans are due by January 1, 1996, and permits are scheduled to be issued by the end of 1997.

The owners or operators of new electric utility units must submit applications and compliance plans no later than twenty-four months before the later of January 1, 2000, or the commencement of commercial operation.

Monitoring, record keeping, and reporting. The owner or operator of an affected unit must install and operate a continuous emission monitoring system (or an alternative monitoring system designated by the EPA by rule) and quality assure the data for SO_2, NO_x, opacity, and volumetric flow. Section 412. The owners or operators of Phase I affected units must install and operate monitoring equipment within thirty-six months of enactment. The owners or operators of Phase II affected units must install and operate monitoring equipment by January 1, 1995. New units must install and operate monitoring equipment upon commencing operation.

Owners or operators of affected units must comply with record-keeping and reporting regulations to be promulgated by the EPA.

Permits for Existing and New Sources: Clearer Requirements or a New Controversy?

Unlike the Clean Water Act, the Clean Air Act did not have a general permit program until enactment of the Clean Air Act Amendments of 1990. In 1977, the Clean Air Act was amended to require permits for major new sources in attainment and nonattainment areas. *See* 42 U.S.C. §§ 7475 and 7503. In addition, many states adopted permit programs as part of their implementation plans. However, there was no general federal requirement that existing sources have operating permits. The 1990 amendments add a new chapter V to establish a permit program modeled after the Clean Water Act. 42 U.S.C. § 7661 *et al.* In theory, the permit program should render the obligations of sources more definite and thereby facilitate compliance and enforcement.

The permit program established by title V is designed to be run by the states but only after the EPA gives the states extensive guidance on how they should establish the program and only with considerable oversight by the EPA. Under the scheme set out by Congress, it is the EPA's responsibility to develop in a rule making detailed guidelines that the states must then follow in setting up their individual operating permit programs. The EPA also judges the adequacy of each state program and may actually write and administer permit programs in states that do not develop such programs in a timely manner. After a state permit program is in effect, the EPA still plays a large role in the review of individual permits being reviewed and issued by the states. In fact, the EPA may veto any permit that it believes does not comply with the applicable Act requirements. And, after a permit is issued, the EPA may terminate, modify, or revoke any permit upon determining that cause exists to do so.

The new statutory operating permit program covers all major stationary sources and many other sources as well. Once the program is in effect, each covered source will have to apply for and operate in compliance with the terms of an operating permit that contains (1) enforceable emission limitations; (2) a schedule for complying with any statutory requirements not yet being met; (3) inspection, monitoring, and reporting requirements to assure compliance with Clean Air Act requirements; and (4) other conditions and measures necessary to assure compliance with Clean Air Act requirements.

On May 10, 1991, the EPA issued its proposed state permit regulations pursuant to title V of the 1990 amendments. 56 Fed. Reg. 21,712 (May 10, 1991). The EPA's proposal generated extensive debate among industry, states, environmental groups, the Administration, and members of Congress. The proposed provisions relating to operational flexibility and the public participation requirements for certain permit amendments were particularly controversial.

Sources subject to the permit provisions would be required to obtain an operating permit addressing all applicable pollution control obligations under the SIP (or, if applicable, the FIP), the title IV acid rain program, the hazardous air pollutant program under section 112 of the Act, and other applicable provisions of the Act (e.g., the NSPSs). Sources also must submit periodic reports to the state and the EPA as appropriate concerning the extent of their compliance with permit obligations. The permit and compliance reports will be available to the public, subject to any applicable confidentiality protection procedure.

The regulations that the EPA proposed on May 10, 1991, covered all aspects of the title V permit requirements, including permit application requirements; provisions for permit reopening, revisions, and renewal and operational flexibility; permit review by the EPA; permit fees; and federal oversight, sanctions, and enforcement authority.

Deadlines for Implementing the Operating Permit Program

The 1990 amendments require that, within one year of enactment, the EPA must promulgate regulations establishing the "minimum elements" of the permit program. Section 502(b). States have three years from the date of enactment to develop and submit to the EPA for approval a permit program under state law (or under an interstate compact). Section 502(d)(1). Within one year of receiving a state's proposed permit program, and after notice and opportunity for public comment, the EPA must either approve or disapprove the program, in whole or in part. If the EPA disapproves the program, in whole or in part, the EPA will notify the state, which will then be required to revise and resubmit the program within 180 days of receiving notification of the EPA's disapproval. If, within two years of the date required for state submission of a permit program, no such program has been approved, the EPA shall promulgate, administer, and enforce a permit program for the state. Section 502(d)(3).

Once their program is approved, states must act upon each permit application within eighteen months of receipt of the completed application. Recognizing, however, that the states will be inundated with applications at the beginning of the program, the Act directs each state to establish a "phased schedule" for acting on applications that are submitted during the first year after a state's permit program becomes effective. This phased schedule shall assure that at least one-third of these permits will be acted on annually, for a period not to exceed three years. Section 503(c). A course will not be considered to be out of compliance if it has applied for the permit and has submitted all required information by the deadline. Section 503(d).

The Minimum Criteria for State Permitting Programs

The "minimum elements" of a permit program to be established by the states include:

1. requirements for permit applications, including a standard application form and a method for determining in a timely fashion when applications are complete—Section 502 (b)(1);
2. monitoring and reporting requirements—section 502 (b)(2);
3. a requirement under state law that each permit applicant pay an annual fee that is "sufficient to cover all reasonable (direct and indirect) costs" of developing and administering the permit program, in an amount not less than $25 per ton of each regulated pollutant (or such other amount as the EPA may determine adequately reflects the permit program's reasonable costs) up to four thousand tons (or such higher

amount that the state determines is appropriate)—section 502(b)(3)(B);

4. requirements for adequate personnel and funding to administer the program—section 502(b)(4);

5. a requirement that the state has adequate authority to issue permits and assure compliance by all sources required to have a permit; issue permits for a fixed term, not to exceed five years; assure that, upon issuance or renewal, permits incorporate emission limitations and other requirements in an applicable implementation plan; terminate, modify, or revoke and reissue permits for cause; and enforce permits, permit fee requirements, and the requirement to obtain a permit—section 502(b)(5);

6. a requirement that the state has adequate procedures for processing permit applications expeditiously—sections 502(b)(6)-(7);

7. a requirement that permit applications, compliance plans, permits, and monitoring or compliance reports be made available to the public, subject to the trade secrecy protection requirements of section 114 of the Act—section 502(b)(8);

8. a requirement that the state, in the case of permits with a term of three or more years for major sources, mandate permit revisions to incorporate applicable standards and regulations promulgated after the permit is issued—section 502(b)(9);

9. provisions to allow the owner of a permitted facility to make some limited changes at the facility without undergoing a permit revision—section 502(b)(10);

10. a requirement that a permit applicant submit with an application a compliance plan describing how the source will "comply with all applicable requirements" under the Act—section 503(b)(1); and

11. a requirement that each permittee is to certify at least annually that the permitted facility "is in compliance with any applicable requirements of the permit, and to promptly report any deviations from permit requirements to the permitting authority"—section 503(b)(2).

The Sources Required to Obtain a Permit and the Contents Thereof

Under section 502(a) of the Act, the following sources are subject to the new permitting requirements:

1. any source covered by the acid deposition control requirements of title IV;
2. any "major source," defined as any "stationary source" that is either a "major source" as defined in section 112 or a "major stationary source" as defined in section 302 or part D of title I;
3. any source subject to standards or regulations under sections 111 or 112;
4. any source required to have a permit under part C or part D of title I; or
5. any source in a source category or subcategory designated by regulations promulgated by the EPA.

The EPA may, by regulation, exempt from the new permitting requirements one or more source categories or subcategories if the Agency finds that compliance is "impracticable, infeasible, or unnecessarily burdensome." The EPA may not, however, exempt any major source. Section 502(a).

Each permit must contain:

1. enforceable emission limitations, a compliance schedule, and a requirement that the permittee submit the results of any required monitoring—section 504(a);
2. inspection, entry, monitoring, compliance certification, and reporting requirements—section 504(c); and
3. any other conditions "as are necessary" to assure compliance with applicable requirements of the Act—section 504(a).

Under section 504(b), the EPA may adopt rules requiring procedures and methods for determining compliance and for monitoring and analysis of pollutants. Continuous emission monitoring need not be required if alternative and sufficiently reliable methods are available. Permittees must submit the results of any required monitoring at least every six months.

The Permit Shield

Section 504(f) of the Act provides that, except as otherwise provided by the EPA by rule, the permit may also provide that compliance with the permit shall be deemed compliance with other applicable provisions of the Act if (1) the permit includes the applicable requirements or (2) the permitting authority, in acting on the permit application, makes a determination that the other requirements are not applicable to the permit holder and the permit includes the determination or a "concise summary thereof." This shield provision is much narrower than the comparable provision of the Clean Water Act, 33 U.S.C. § 1341(k), which basically provides that compliance with a permit is compliance with the Act.

The importance of the qualifications to the permit shield is illustrated by the decision in *United States v. General Dynamics Corp.*, 755 F. Supp. 720 (N.D. Tex. 1991). In that section 113 suit, the court held that even though an aircraft manufacturer was complying with an order of the Texas Air Control Board concerning emissions of volatile organic compounds, the company was not in compliance with the Texas SIP. The Texas board had issued a compliance order that allowed plant-wide averaging of volatile organic compound emissions to meet the limit of 3.5 pounds per gallon of coating applied. The court agreed with the EPA that the state board's interpretation of the SIP as allowing plant-wide averaging was invalid because it contradicted specific language of the SIP, which required each distinct surface coating operation to comply with the 3.5-pound-per-gallon limit. The court therefore concluded that the order required the EPA approval to be effective because the effect of the order was to raise the emission limits set by the SIP. In the absence of that approval, the court held, compliance with the order was not compliance with the SIP. Permittees will need to be on the alert for similar issues as to possible discrepancies between SIPs and permits.

The Consequences of Failure to Obtain a Permit

A source that is subject to the title V permit program must have a permit on the later of the date on which it becomes subject to the permitting requirements or the effective date of the applicable permit program. Section 503(a). A source will not be subject to penalty for failure to have a permit if the source has submitted a timely and complete application for a permit and the delay in issuing a permit is not due to the applicant's failure to submit information required or requested to process the application. Section 503(d).

Failure to obtain a permit after the effective date of a permit program is subject to civil penalties "in a maximum amount of not less than $10,000 per day for each violation." There may also be criminal sanctions. Section 502(b)(5)(E).

Other Issues

The EPA's role in issuing and enforcing permits. The state must provide the EPA with a copy of each permit application and each permit that the state proposes to issue. Section 505(a)(1). The EPA then has forty-five days to object in writing to issuance of the permit. Objections by the EPA are to be predicted on a determination by the EPA that the proposed permit is not in compliance with the applicable implementation plan or other applicable requirements of the Act. Section 505(b). If the state does not revise the proposed permit to meet the EPA's objections within ninety days, the EPA will either issue or deny the permit in accordance with the requirements of title V. Section 505(c).

Once a permit is issued, the EPA has the authority, after giving notice to the affected state and source and following applicable procedures, to terminate, modify, or revoke any permit, upon determining that cause exists to do so. The permit-issuing state must be given at least ninety days to correct the problem itself. Section 505(e).

The role of other states in the permitting process. The Act requires the permit-issuing state to provide notice of any permit application or proposed permit to all states (1) whose air quality may be affected and that are contiguous to the state in which the emission originates or (2) that are within fifty miles of the source. These states may submit written recommendations on the proposed permit. If any of these recommendations are not accepted by the permitting state, the permitting state must provide the other state and the EPA with its reasons for not accepting the recommendations. Section 505(a)(2).

The role of the public in the permitting process. Under section 502(b)(6) of the Act, each state permit program must provide for public notice of, and an opportunity for public comment and hearing on, all permit applications. Section 505(b)(2) provides that members of the public may petition the EPA to prevent issuance of a permit if the petition is based only on objections that were raised "with reasonable specificity" during the public comment period. Section 505(b)(2) provides that denial of such a petition is subject to judicial review.

The effect on the existing permit program. Under title I of the Act, major new sources (and, under certain conditions, modified sources) are subject to preconstruction review and permitting requirements. Section 502(a), which contains the basic permitting requirements, provides that "[n]othing in this subsection shall be construed to alter the applicable requirements of this Act that a permit be obtained before construction or modification."

In addition, section 506(a) provides that "[n]othing in this title shall prevent a State, or interstate permitting authority, from establishing additional permitting requirements not inconsistent with this Act."

The Standards and Permits for New Sources

Section 111 of the Clean Air Act authorizes the EPA to promulgate standards of performance for new stationary sources. 42 U.S.C. § 7411. These standards are to require the degree of emission limitation achievable by "the best system of emission reduction which (taking into account the cost of achieving such reduction and any non-air quality health and environmental impact and energy requirements) the Administrator determines has been adequately demonstrated." 42 U.S.C. § 7411(a)(1). These standards apply to sources whose construction commences after publication of proposed standards. 42 U.S.C. § 7411(a)(2).

The EPA has established standards of performance for a number of industry categories, including:

- steam generating units
- incinerators
- petroleum refineries
- steel plants
- sulfuric and nitric acid plants
- kraft pulp mills
- automotive surface coating
- synthetic organic chemicals plants
- natural gas processing plants

The EPA regulations for these and other industry categories are set forth at 40 C.F.R. Part 60. For a discussion of the EPA's approach to promulgating standards under section 111, *see National Lime Ass'n v. EPA*, 627 F.2d 416 (D.C. Cir. 1980).

On June 29, 1990, the EPA issued two final rules and one proposal for control of VOC emissions from parts of the synthetic organic chemical manufacturing industry (SOCMI). The first rule sets standards for air oxidation facilities within the SOCMI. 55 Fed. Reg. 26,912 (June 29, 1990). The standards cover any reactors that use air as an oxidizing agent to produce various chemicals. The second rule applies to SOCMI facilities distillation operations operating as part of a process unit to produce certain chemicals as listed in the regulation. 55 Fed. Reg. 26,931 (June 29, 1990). The proposed rule would establish VOC emission limits for SOCMI reactor process facilities. 55 Fed. Reg. 26,931 (June 29, 1990). A reactor process is the means by which one or more synthetic chemicals are produced by the reaction of feedstocks or chemical intermediaries other than air. The proposed standards would cover the production of 173 high production volume chemicals and are estimated to account for the majority of the emissions from reactor processes.

On September 12, 1990, the EPA issued an NSPS for small industrial-commercial-institutional industrial boilers. 55 Fed. Reg. 37,674 (Sept. 12, 1990). This source category covers boilers with a capacity from 10 million Btu/hour to 100 million Btu/hour. The EPA previously established standards for units above 100 million Btu/hour, *see* 40 C.F.R. Part. 60, subpart Db. This action completes the EPA's obligations to set an NSPS for industrial boilers as established by the court order in 1985. These standards limit emissions of sulphur dioxide and PM from these sources.

The EPA also issued an NSPS to limit VOC emissions from the polymer manufacturing industry. 55 Fed. Reg. 51,010 (Dec. 11, 1990). These standards apply to process vents in these plants. The standards cover emissions from polypropylene, polyethylene, polystyrene, and polyethylene terephthalate plants and certain copolymer plants. In addition, the standards also cover equipment leaks in all polymer manufacturing plants except those producing polyethylene terephthalate or polyethylene terephthalate copolymers.

It should be noted that major new sources are subject to additional permit and technology-based requirements. Major new sources in nonattainment areas must achieve LAER. 42 U.S.C. § 7503(a)(2). Major new sources in attainment areas are subject to BACT. 42 U.S.C. § 7475(a)(4). These LAER and BACT emission limits are determined on a case-by-case basis in permit proceedings and may in any event not exceed the emissions allowed by the section 111 NSPSs. 42 U.S.C. §§ 7501(3) and 7479(3). Finally, state plans contain additional provisions for review of new sources to assure that air quality standards are attained and maintained.

Motor Vehicles and Fuels: New Approaches to an Old Problem

Section 202 of the Clean Air Act authorizes the EPA to establish motor vehicle emission standards. 42 U.S.C. § 7521. The 1970 Act generally required a 90 percent reduction of hydrocarbons and carbon monoxide (CO) from a 1970 baseline. The Act also authorized the EPA to test vehicles for compliance or require that manufacturers perform such testing. 42 U.S.C.§ 7525.

The 1970 Act also authorized the EPA to regulate fuels. Pursuant to section 211 of the Act, the EPA has promulgated two sets of standards that limit the lead content of fuels. These standards are designed to prevent interference with catalytic emission control devices and to protect public health. 42 U.S.C. § 7545; 40 C.F.R. Part 80.

The Clean Air Act Amendments of 1990 require more stringent tailpipe standards to control exhaust pollutants from cars and trucks, improvements in the controls of evaporative emissions from vehicles, and the installation of equipment on vehicles to control refueling emissions. The amendments contain a new standard to control CO emissions at cold temperatures and require the installation of self-diagnostic equipment on vehicles to monitor the functions of critical emission control equipment and alert the driver to the need for repairs when a problem occurs.

These amendments place great emphasis on emission reductions that can be achieved through the use of cleaner fuels—emission reductions that can be achieved from the existing fleet of vehicles, not only from new ones. Title II of the amendments establishes a new program requiring the sale of "reformulated gasoline" in the nine worst ozone nonattainment areas to reduce emission of VOCs and toxic air pollutants. Furthermore, the amendments require (1) further reductions in the volatility (rate of evaporation) of gasoline nationwide, (2) oxygenated fuel programs requiring the use of gasoline blended with clean-burning additives such as ethanol and methanol to reduce CO emissions in all CO nonattainment areas during the winter months, and (3) reductions in the amount of sulfur in diesel fuel.

Title II of the amendments establishes a clean fuels program to encourage the use of even cleaner fuels in new motor vehicles. The program contains a pilot program that is scheduled to begin in California in 1996, and a fleet program that could begin as early as 1998 in more than twenty-five of the nation's worst ozone and CO nonattainment areas.

Finally, the amendments seek to achieve emission reductions in other ways, such as requiring periodic emission inspections of on-road vehicles by requiring certain states to begin new or enhance existing inspection/maintenance programs and providing the EPA new authority to regulate emissions from nonroad engines and fuels.

The Tailpipe Standards

Title II tightens the current standards for tailpipe emissions from both gasoline- and diesel-powered vehicles. Perhaps the most significant of these standards concerns light-duty vehicles, which are tightened initially in model year 1994. The new standards establish more stringent levels for emissions of nitrogen oxides, CO, and PM and establish a new standard for nonmethane hydrocarbons, the type of hydrocarbons that are ozone precursors. A second phase of tailpipe standards that are 50 percent more stringent than the 1994 standards could go into effect in model year 2003 if (1) the EPA determines that the emissions reductions they would bring about are necessary, (2) the necessary technology is available, and (3) the emission reductions would be cost-effective.

The EPA recently published a notice proposing PM standards for urban buses, for heavy-duty diesel engines used in urban buses, and for all heavy-duty engines. 56 Fed. Reg. 48,350 (Sept. 24, 1991). In addition, the notice proposed a separate standard for nitrogen oxides for heavy-duty engines beginning with the 1998 model year. The EPA said that it expected the proposed standard to reduce nationwide emissions of nitrogen oxides by 2 percent when fully implemented.

Also significant are the new cold CO standards that require reductions in emissions of CO at cold temperatures. These new standards also begin in model year 1994 and may have a second phase beginning in model year 2001 if more than a specified number of cities are still CO nonattainment areas as of 1996.

On September 24, 1991, the EPA proposed a rule requiring on-board diagnostic systems for light-duty vehicles and light-duty trucks beginning with the 1994 model year. 56 Fed. Reg. 48,272 (Sept. 24, 1991). The proposal requires manufacturers to install systems that monitor the functioning of emission control components and warn the vehicle operator of the need for repairs. In addition, when a malfunction occurs, diagnostic information must be stored in the vehicle's computer to assist the mechanic in diagnosis and repair. The EPA also proposed requirements to make available to the service and repair industry information necessary to perform repair and maintenance service of on-board diagnostic systems and other emission-related vehicle components.

On July 26, 1990, the EPA announced new programs for banking and trading of PM and nitrogen oxide emission credits for gasoline-, diesel-, and methanol-powered heavy-duty engines. These trading and banking programs are voluntary programs to allow manufacturers of heavy-duty engines who reduce emissions below regulatory requirements for a particular model year for a particular engine to offset these reductions against emissions in a later model year or to trade credit for these reductions to other manufacturers of similar engines. 55 Fed. Reg. 30,584 (July 26, 1990).

In *United States v. Economy Muffler & Tire Center, Inc.*, 762 F. Supp. 1242 (E.D. Va. 1991), the United States brought a civil action against an automobile repair shop for violations of the Clean Air Act's "tampering provision," section 203(a)(3)(B). The government charged the shop had replaced three-way catalytic converters, which control nitrogen oxide emissions, with two-way catalytic converters, which do not control them. The court rejected the defendant's argument that the EPA's tampering enforcement policy imposed legal obligations not imposed by the Act itself and therefore should have been promulgated as substantive rules using notice and comment procedures under the APA. The court held the enforcement policy simply clarified congressional intent and added no substantive content of its own.

The Fifth Circuit in *United States v. Gardner*, 894 F.2d 708 (5th Cir. 1990), affirmed a denial of a motion to dismiss an indictment charging that, to avoid the cost of modifying nonconforming German automobiles to meet the EPA emission standards, the defendant had submitted forms listing "straw" importer-owners to unlawfully take advantage of the EPA's personal use waiver. The defendant argued that the listed individuals were properly listed because an importer need not be the owner of imported goods. The court, however, held that the defendant's scheme was unlawful because he knew that the EPA would not have granted the waivers had the government known that the automobiles were not being imported for the personal use of the named importers.

The Regulation of Fuels

Reformulated Gasoline

The new amendments establish a program to require the sale of gasoline that is reformulated to be cleaner than gasoline that is currently used. This program will apply to the nine worst ozone nonattainment areas and will require the sale of reformulated gasoline with significantly reduced emission of VOCs and toxic air pollutants beginning in 1995. A second, tighter set of standards goes into effect in the year 2000. A significant benefit of this program is that, unlike emission controls required on new vehicles, all vehicles, old or new, will be achieving reduced levels of emissions by being operated on the cleaner fuels.

Related to the reformulated gasoline program is the oxygenated fuels program, which requires the use of gasoline blended with clean-burning additives to achieve a specified oxygen content in forty-one CO nonattainment areas during the winter months when most CO problems occur. This problem will reduce emissions of CO from all vehicles in those areas, not just new ones.

Section 211(m) of the Act requires certain states with CO nonattainment areas to submit SIP revisions to implement an oxygenated gasoline program. Section 211(m)(4) directs the EPA to promulgate regulations requiring the labeling of retail fuel pumps for dispensing oxygenated gasoline pursuant to the revised SIP requirements. On July 9, 1991, the EPA published proposed labeling regulations. 56 Fed. Reg. 31,148 (July 9, 1991). The oxygenated gasoline program—and therefore the proposed labeling rules—apply to all states with CO nonattainment areas with design values of 9.5 parts per million or more based on data for 1988 and 1989. The proposed rules apply to retail gasoline pumps in the control area of the state's oxygenated gasoline program and apply during the period of the year covered by that program.

On the same date, the EPA published a proposed guidance pursuant to section 211(m)(2) that requires the Agency to specify the part of the year during which a CO nonattainment area is prone to high ambient concentrations of CO. 56 Fed. Reg. 31,151 (July 9, 1991). That part of the year, called the "control period," generally is not to be shorter than four months. The proposed guidance discusses both the control period and the geographic scope of the control area. The proposed guidance identifies the forty-one geographic areas covered.

Also on July 9, the EPA issued proposed guidelines for state credit programs allowing the use of marketable oxygen credits for gasolines with higher oxygen than required to offset the sale or use of gasoline with a lower oxygen content than required. 56 Fed. Reg. 31,154 (July 9, 1991).

The Clean Fuels Program

The clean fuels program in the 1990 amendments establishes a means to develop the technology and infrastructure to make available new fuels and vehicles that can use them that are significantly cleaner burning than today's gasoline. The program has two elements, a California pilot program and a fleet program. The California pilot program begins in model year 1996 and requires vehicles that will be substantially cleaner than those required by the general emission standards that will be in effect at that time. A second, tighter set of clean-fuel vehicle standards is slated to go into effect in model year 2001. Furthermore, California has the ability to adopt standards tighter than those spelled out in the new amendments. California is also required to adopt measures designed to ensure the availability of the fuels necessary for the clean-fuel vehicles to operate. Other states may choose to adopt the clean-fuel vehicle standards adopted by California.

The fleet program will begin in model year 2001 and will have the same emission standards as the second phase of the California pilot program. If vehicles meeting those standards are being sold in California in 1998, however, the fleet program could start in that year. The fleet program applies to fleet operators (including governmental entities) with centrally fueled fleets above a certain size in more than twenty-five of the worst ozone and CO nonattainment areas across the country. It requires that covered fleet operators make clean-fuel vehicles a certain percentage of the new fleet vehicles that they purchase.

State fleet programs must meet several statutory requirements, including one requiring a credit program and one exempting clean-fuel fleet vehicles from certain transportation control measures

(TCMs). The EPA recently proposed regulations for the credit program, certain federal fleet requirements, and the TCM exemptions. 56 Fed. Reg. 50,196 (Oct. 3, 1991) (to be codified at 40 C.F.R. Part 88). The EPA said it would propose emission standards applicable to clean-fuel fleet vehicles later. The EPA said the intended effect of its proposed credit program is to permit the fleet industry to collectively meet the fleet program requirements in the most cost-effective way, and the proposed TCM exemptions provide a business incentive to those fleets that participate in the program.

The use of cleaner burning fuels will also be encouraged by the new urban bus program contained in Title II. That program establishes far more stringent standards for emissions of diesel PM from urban buses in cities across the country. Those standards require emissions to be reduced by more than 50 percent from 1991 levels in 1993, with a further substantial reduction (either 30 or 50 percent) in 1994. The EPA, however, is required to establish a testing program beginning in 1994. If the EPA finds that the new buses are not meeting the 1994 standards throughout their useful lives in actual use, it is to begin requiring the use of buses that operate on low-polluting fuels in the nation's larger cities. Such fuels could include natural gas, methanol, ethanol or other comparably low-polluting fuels. Buses operating on these fuels could be on the road in significant numbers shortly after the year 2000.

Fuel Volatility

The EPA proposed to revise the fuel volatility requirements for summertime gasoline in the areas designated as unclassifiable or in attainment with the NAAQSs for ozone. 56 Fed. Reg. 24,242 (May 29, 1991). The proposal would amend existing regulations scheduled to take effect in the summer of 1992 by providing Reid vapor pressure limits below 9.0 pounds per square inch will go into effect for nonattainment areas only. The proposal was designed to conform the existing regulations with the requirements of the 1990 Clean Air Act.

Recent Judicial Decisions

In *National Tank Truck Carriers, Inc. v. EPA*, 907 F.2d 177 (D.C. Cir. 1990), the D.C. Circuit reviewed the EPA rules promulgated under section 211(c)(1) that impose presumptive liability on a tank truck carrier for violations of fuel volatility standards if the EPA finds noncomplying gasoline in the carrier's tank. The carriers argued that the rules unlawfully established a engine of vicarious liability and that the affirmative defense provided by the rules was arbitrary and capricious.

The court held that because a carrier could be held liable only for the fuel in its own trucks, the rules did not unlawfully impose vicarious liability. Nor did the possible existence of "less punitive" regulatory alternatives make the rules unlawful. The court held, however, that it was arbitrary and capricious for the EPA to require carriers, as part of their affirmative defense, to produce documents from shippers showing lawful volatility levels since the EPA had not required shippers to provide those documents to carriers. The court remanded to the Agency for a reasoned explanation or for amendment. Finally, the court dismissed as unripe the carriers' challenges to the affirmative defense requirement that they perform "periodic sampling and testing." The carriers had argued that the requirement was unlawfully vague, that such testing was unsafe, and that the carriers were without contractual authority to take samples for testing.

In *United States v. Coastal Refining & Marketing, Inc.*, 911 F.2d 1036 (5th Cir. 1990), the Fifth Circuit vacated a district court's judgment in a case in which the United States claimed that Coastal had invalidly created "lead usage rights" by importing petroleum products that Coastal classified as gasoline but that did not meet the EPA's regulatory definition of gasoline. The EPA's rules defined gasoline as a product that is "commonly or commercially known or sold as gasoline" and "sold in any state for use in motor vehicles and motor vehicle engines." The EPA argued that the octane level of Coastal's petroleum was too low to qualify as gasoline. The Fifth Circuit disagreed, holding that the record established that Coastal's petroleum met the first part of the EPA's definition of gasoline because it satisfied a commonly accepted industry specification and met the second part of the definition because Coastal had presented an unrebutted *prima facie* case that fuel with even lower octane levels was sold as gasoline.

The Fifth Circuit also disagreed with the district court's determination that section 211(d), which established a mandatory $10,000-per-day penalty that could be remitted or mitigated only by the EPA and not by any court, was unconstitutional. The Fifth Circuit said that section 211(d) violated neither the separation of powers principles nor due process.

Stratospheric Ozone: Addressing Global Environmental Issues

During the last several years, there has been increasing concern that chlorofluorocarbons (CFCs) and certain other chemicals are depleting the stratospheric ozone layer. Unlike ground-level ozone, which is subject to emission standards, stratospheric ozone is considered to be a valuable shield against harmful radiation from the sun.

In 1987, a number of countries established a protocol to limit CFC consumption and production in a document called the Montreal Protocol. The EPA regulations implementing the protocol are codified at 40 C.F.R. Part 82.

In the 1990 amendments to the Clean Air Act, Congress took further steps to phase out consumption and production of ozone-depleting substances. 42 U.S.C. § 7671 *et al*. The amendments also regulate the use and disposal of these substances, authorize the EPA to ban nonessential products, require labeling, and regulate substitute products.

Listing of Class I and Class II Substances

Within sixty days of enactment of the amendments, the Administrator is to publish an initial list of Class I substances that includes five groups specified in the amendments, including a number of CFC and halon compounds, carbon tetrachloride, methyl chloroform, and isomers of the listed compounds. Section 602. Additions to this list are to be based on a finding that a substance "causes or contributes significantly to harmful effects on the stratospheric ozone layer," including all substances that have an ozone depletion potential of 0.2 or greater.

304

At the same time that the EPA must publish the Class I list, the Agency must also publish an initial list of Class II substances specified in the amendments, including thirty-three hydrochlorofluorocarbons and their isomers. Additions to this list are to include any substance that the EPA finds "is known or may reasonably be anticipated to cause or contribute to harmful effects on the stratospheric ozone layer."

The EPA is authorized to add substances to the lists that meet the specifications for each list. When adding a substance to Class I, the Agency is to classify it within one of the five groups consistent with the Montreal Protocol or place it in a new group. The EPA is to consider additions to the lists not less than every three years. Any person may petition the EPA to add a substance to either list. A proposed decision required on a petition is to be made within 180 days of receipt, with a final decision within one year.

Only a Class II substance that has been added by the EPA may be removed from the list, and no substance listed in the amendments may be removed from the Class I list. For any substance added to either list after the initially proposed list, the EPA may extend any schedule or compliance deadline under sections 604 or 605.

The EPA is to assign a numerical value representing each listed substance's ozone-depleting potential and its chlorine- and bromine-loading potential and atmospheric lifetime. The depletion potential of twenty-five of the substances listed in the amendments is specified.

Monitoring and Reporting Requirements

Within 270 days of enactment, the EPA is to amend existing regulations on monitoring and reporting of Class I and II substances. Section 603.

On a quarterly basis or other basis set by the EPA, each person producing, importing, or exporting any Class I or II substance must file a report with the EPA regarding the amounts.

The EPA is to monitor and report to Congress every three years on the production, use, and consumption of Class I and II substances. The Administrators of National Aeronautics and Space Administration and NOAA are also to monitor and report every three years on the current average tropospheric concentrations of chlorine and bromine, as well as on the level of stratospheric ozone depletion. A technology status report on progress in the development of alternative systems or products necessary to manufacture and operate appliances without Class II substances is due from the EPA in 2015. If the EPA determines that global production, consumption, and use of Class II substances are projected to contribute to an atmospheric chlorine loading in excess of the base case, the EPA is to inform Congress immediately.

Phasing Out the Production and Consumption of Class I Substances

Effective on January 1 of each year from 1991 through 2001, it is unlawful for any person to produce any Class I substance in an annual quantity greater than a declining percentage, specified in Table 2, of the quantity produced during the baseline year. Section 604. Production of any Class I substance is prohibited after January 1, 2000, except for methyl chloroform, which may be produced until January 1, 2002. The EPA is to publish regulations within ten months to implement the production phase-out and to assure a consumption phase-out at the same time.

There are a number of exceptions, however. For methyl chloroform, the EPA may, by rule, extend the phase-out deadline to January 1, 2005, solely for use of limited quantities in essential applications, e.g., nondestructive testing for metal fatigue and corrosion of existing airplane engines. The Agency may also, in consultation with the FDA, authorize production of Class I substances necessary for use in medical devices. Correspondingly, the EPA may, in consultation with the FAA, authorize production of limited quantities of specified halons solely for aviation safety purposes if no safe and effective substitute has been developed and may extend the deadline on methyl chloroform beyond January 1, 2005, if necessary for prescribed testing uses. The EPA may authorize production of limited quantities of Class I substances in excess of the amounts specified above solely for export to, and domestic use in, developing countries that are parties to the Montreal Protocol. Even the President has an exception. He may issue an order authorizing production and use of certain halons and CFCs as necessary to protect the national security interests, for a period not to exceed one year, which may be renewed. Finally, notwithstanding the production phase-out, the EPA may authorize production of limited quantities of specified halons solely for purposes of fire suppression and explosion prevention if no effective substitute has been developed.

Phasing Out the Production and Consumption of Class II Substances

After January 1, 2015, it is unlawful for any person to introduce into interstate commerce or use any Class II substance unless it (1) has been used, recovered, and recycled; (2) is used and entirely consumed in the production of other chemicals; or (3) is used as a refrigerant in appliances manufactured before January 1, 2020. Section 605.

On January 1, 2015, it is unlawful for any person to produce any Class II substance in an annual quantity greater than the quantity produced during the baseline year. After January 1, 2030, production of any Class I substance is unlawful.

By December 31, 1999, the EPA is to promulgate regulations phasing out production and restricting use of Class II substances under this section. Regulations to phase-out consumption of Class II substances in the United States on the same schedule are also required.

The EPA may authorize limited production and use of Class II substances for use in medical devices, and in developing countries that are parties to the Montreal Protocol.

On March 6, 1991, the EPA published a temporary rule to implement the 1991 limits on the production and consumption of ozone-depleting chemicals required by section 604 of the Act. 56 Fed. Reg. 9518 (Mar. 6, 1991) (to be codified at 40 C.F.R. Part 82). The rule took effect as of January 1, 1991, and was to remain in effect only during 1991. The temporary rule revised the EPA's regulations under the Montreal Protocol as necessary to implement the section 604 production and consumption limits for 1991 in a manner consistent with U.S. obligations under the protocol.

On September 30, 1991, the EPA proposed to revise its stratospheric ozone protection regulations to conform them to the requirements of section 604 and related provisions of title VI for 1992 and later years. 56 Fed. Reg. 49,548 (Sept. 30, 1991). Like the March 6 temporary rule for 1991, the September 30 proposal seeks to implement the title VI requirements in a manner consistent with U.S. obligations under the Montreal Protocol.

Other Issues

The accelerated schedule. The EPA shall promulgate regulations phasing out Class I and II substances on a more stringent schedule than specified under sections 604 and 605 if the EPA determines that (1) the more stringent schedule "may be necessary" to protect human health and the environment; (2) the schedule is practicable, considering technological achievability, safety, and other relevant factors; or (3) the Montreal Protocol is modified to include a more stringent schedule. Section 606. Data developed during 1991-92 has led to discussions at the EPA and in Congress as to the need for a more rapid phase-out.

Exchange authority. The EPA is to issue rules within ten months providing for issuance and transfer of allowances for production of Class I and II substances. Section 607. The rules are to ensure that transactions will result in greater total reductions in production in each year than would occur without transactions. A production allowance for any year may be transferred for an allowance for another substance for the same year on an ozone depletion-weighted basis. For Class I substances, allowances may only be transferred for another substance in the same group. For Class II substances, the EPA shall establish groups of substances for trading purposes and trading will be limited within each group.

The rules may also provide for issuance of consumption allowances.

The national recycling and emission reduction program. By January 1, 1992, the EPA is to promulgate regulations setting standards for use and disposal of Class I substances during service, repair, or disposal of appliances and industrial process refrigeration. Section 608. Within four years, the EPA must promulgate regulations on use and disposal of other Class I and II substances. Regulations are to reduce use and emission of such substances to the lowest achievable level and maximize recapture and recycling, including requirements for use of alternatives.

After January 1, 1992, it is unlawful for any person to knowingly vent or otherwise release or dispose of any Class I or II substance in the course of maintaining, servicing, repairing, or disposing of an appliance or industrial process refrigeration. *De minimis* releases associated with good faith attempts to recapture and recycle or safely dispose of such substances are not subject to the prohibition. Five years after enactment, the prohibition shall also apply to venting, release, or disposal of any substitute substance.

Servicing motor vehicle air conditioners. Within one year, the EPA must promulgate regulations setting standards for the servicing of motor vehicle air conditioners. Section 609.

Effective January 1, 1992, no person repairing or servicing motor vehicles "for consideration" may perform any service on a motor vehicle air conditioner involving the refrigerant without properly using approved recycling equipment and unless such person has been properly trained and certified. For entities servicing fewer than one hundred air conditioners during calendar year 1990, these requirements do not apply until January 1, 1993.

Effective two years after enactment, each person servicing motor vehicle air conditioners for consideration must certify to the EPA the proper use of approved refrigerant recycling equipment and training for personnel.

Nonessential products containing CFC. The EPA is to promulgate regulations within one year to identify nonessential products that release Class I substances and to prohibit sale or distribution of any such product, including (1) plastic party streamers and noise horns, (2) cleaning fluids for noncommercial electronic and photographic equipment, and (3) other nonessential consumer products determined by the EPA to release Class I substances into the environment. Sale or distribution is unlawful twenty-four months after enactment. Section 610.

Effective January 1, 1994, it is unlawful for any person to sell or distribute (1) any aerosol product containing a Class II substance or (2) any plastic foam product containing or manufactured with a Class II substance. The EPA may grant specified exceptions to these prohibitions. This section does not apply to any medical device.

Labeling. Within eighteen months the EPA is to promulgate regulations requiring labeling of containers used to store or transport a Class I or II substance with a specified warning. Section 611. The labeling requirement also applies to products manufactured with Class I or II substances if the EPA finds that substitutes are available.

The labeling requirements shall not constitute a defense to liability or a cause for reduction in damages in any suit brought under any other law.

The safe alternatives policy. To the maximum extent practicable, Class I and II substances shall be replaced by chemicals, product substitutes, or alternative manufactured processes that reduce overall risks to human health and the environment. Section 612.

The EPA shall (1) recommend federal research programs and other activities to assist in identifying alternatives to the use of Class I and II substances as refrigerants, solvents, fire retardants, foam-blowing agents, and other commercial applications, and in achieving a transition to such alternatives; (2) examine federal procurement practices for Class I and II substances and recommend measures to promote the transition to safe substitutes; (3) specify initiatives to promote development and use of safe substitutes; and (4) maintain a public clearinghouse of available alternative chemicals, product substitutes, and alternative manufacturing processes.

Within two years, the EPA is to promulgate rules providing that it is unlawful to replace any Class I or II substance with any substitute substance that may present adverse effects to human health or the environment if the EPA has identified an alternative to that substitute.

The EPA is to require any person who produces a substitute for a Class I substance to provide the EPA with that person's unpublished health and safety studies and require producers to notify the EPA not less than ninety days before new or existing chemicals are introduced into interstate commerce for significant new uses as substitutes for a Class I substance.

Federal procurement. The EPA is to promulgate regulations requiring each federal department or agency to conform its procurement regulations to the policies and requirements of this title. Section 613.

The relationship to other laws. During the two-year period after enactment, no state or local government may enforce any requirement for design of any new or recalled appliance for the purpose of protecting the stratospheric ozone layer. Section 614.

This title is to be applied as a supplement to the terms and conditions of the Montreal Protocol but not abrogate the obligations of the United States to fully implement the provisions of the protocol. In the case of any conflict, the more stringent provision will govern.

The authority of the administrator. For any other substance, practice, process, or activity reasonably anticipated to affect the stratosphere, and especially ozone, and to endanger the public health or welfare, the EPA is to promptly promulgate control regulations and submit notice of them to Congress. Section 615.

Transfers among parties to the Montreal Protocol. Section 616 of the Act specifies the conditions under which the United States may engage in transfers with other parties to the protocol.

International Air Pollution

Section 617 of the Act directs the President to enter into international agreements to foster cooperative research, to develop standards to protect the stratosphere, and to provide technical and financial assistance to developing countries that are parties to the Montreal Protocol.

In *Her Majesty the Queen in Right of Ontario v. EPA*, 912 F.2d 1525 (D.C. Cir. 1990), the D.C. Circuit rejected an argument that the EPA acted arbitrarily by denying the requests of Ontario and the state of New York that the EPA make "findings" under section 115 of the Clean Air Act. Ontario and New York had asked the EPA to conduct a proceeding to make two findings: (1) that air pollutants emitted from sources in the United States cause acid deposition that endangers public health or welfare in Canada (the "endangerment" finding); and (2) that Canada gives the United States essentially the same rights with respect to air pollution control that section 115 gives Canada (the "reciprocity" finding). Ontario and New York did not ask the EPA to order states to revise their SIPs to abate pollution. In letters from EPA's Acting Assistant Administrator for Air and Radiation, the Agency denied the Ontario and New York requests because the EPA interpreted section 115 as contemplating a "unitary proceeding," not bifurcated proceedings (one on the endangerment and reciprocity "findings" and a later one on the issuance of EPA notices to the states to mandate SIP revisions).

The court first rejected the EPA's argument that the Agency had taken no final action in rejecting the requests for a separate proceeding on the endangerment and reciprocity findings. The court held that the EPA had taken final action on the issue presented by those requests whether section 115 contemplated bifurcated proceedings rather than a unitary one. The court also found the challenge to the EPA's action to be ripe because it presented a purely legal question, would not be more sharply focused by the development of additional information, did not interfere with any pending Agency proceeding, and because Congress in section 307(b)(1) of the Act had expressed a preference for prompt judicial review.

On the merits, the court upheld the EPA's action. The court concluded, based on the statute, that unless the EPA was prepared to identify specific sources in specific states as contributors to air pollution endangering the public health or welfare in Canada and to call for SIP revisions to impose additional controls on those sources, there would be no point to issuing the endangerment and reciprocity findings. The court also rejected an argument that the EPA had delayed unreasonably on those findings; any delay was reasonable given the permissibility of the EPA's unitary proceeding interpretation and the complexity of the scientific and technical questions that would have to be answered before section 115 would be triggered.

Enforcement and Citizen Suits: Upping the Ante for Violations

The Clean Air Act is enforceable by the United States, and most of the Act's regulatory programs are also enforceable by the states under state law. At the federal level, the EPA has the authority to issue compliance orders and to seek administrative penalties. The government may also seek injunctive relief and civil and criminal penalties in federal district courts. 42 U.S.C. §§ 7413 and 7420. In addition, citizens are also given authority to bring suits seeking compliance and penalties. 42 U.S.C. § 7604.

Civil Enforcement

Section 113(a)(1) of the Clean Air Act, as amended, allows the EPA to take enforcement action for an alleged violation of a SIP any time at least thirty days after giving a notice of violation to an alleged violator, even if the violation is not continuing on the thirtieth day. Section 113(a)(1).

Administrative compliance orders issued by the EPA must require compliance "as expeditiously as practicable," but in no case more than one year after the date on which the EPA issued the order. Compliance orders are nonrenewable. The Act provides that the issuance of compliance orders affects neither the right of the enforcement authority to assess penalties nor the obligations of the violator to comply with the Act or any applicable SIP or permit. Section 113(a)(4).

Section 113(a)(5) of the Act provides that the EPA Administrator may issue an enforcement order prohibiting construction or modification of a major stationary source, issue an administrative penalty order, or file a civil suit whenever he or she finds that "a State is not acting in compliance with any requirement or prohibition of the Act relating to the construction of new sources or the modification of existing sources."

The Clean Air Act Amendments of 1990 allow actions to be brought for violations of more sections of the Act, not just for violations of the few sections enumerated under the old law. For example, section 113(b)(2) allows the Administrator to commence a civil action whenever an owner or operator of a covered source has violated or is in violation of any requirement or prohibition of title I, section 303 of title III, title IV, title V or title VI. Section 113(b)(2) applies where the Agency alleges that the defendant "has violated" the Act, not merely where he "is violating" the Act. Moreover, the maximum civil penalty is $25,000 "per day for each violation" rather than "per day of violation." Section 113(b)(2).

In *General Motors Corp. v. United States*, 110 S. Ct. 2528 (1990), the Supreme Court addressed the question of whether the EPA may enforce provisions of a SIP where the state had proposed to the EPA a revision to the SIP that would allow emissions that would not be allowed under the original SIP but the EPA had taken no action to approve or disapprove the revision within the four-month period that section 110(a)(2) specifies for the EPA action on SIP submittals. The court held that the four-month deadline under section 110(a)(2) applies only to original SIPs, not to revisions to SIPs. Moreover, although the court noted that the EPA is subject to the general APA requirement that it act within a reasonable time, it refused to bar enforcement even if the EPA unreasonably delays action. The court suggested, however, that a district court could reduce or eliminate penalties in the case of unreasonable Agency delay and that separate litigation might be brought to force the EPA to act.

The pre-1990 Act allowed the EPA to issue emergency orders only when there was imminent and substantial endangerment to the health of persons, and the orders were effective for twenty-four hours in the absence of court action. The 1990 Amendments allow emergency orders when there is "imminent and substantial endangerment to the public health or welfare, or the environment." The EPA is not required to allow state and local authorities to address the emergency, and the orders are effective for up to sixty days and may be extended by court order. Section 303.

Under the old section 114(1), the Administrator had the authority to order any owner or operator of an emission source (or those subject to other requirements of the Act) to establish and maintain records; make reports; install, use, and maintain monitoring equipment or methods; sample emissions; and provide other information. Under the amended section 114(a), the Administrator may require the use of audit procedures; record keeping on control equipment parameters, production variables, or other indirect emission monitoring when direct monitoring is impractical; and compliance certifications. Section 114(a) authorizes the EPA to require submittal of information not only by owners and operators of sources but also by any manufacturer of emission control equipment or process equipment or by any person who the Administrator believes "may have information necessary for the purposes set forth in this subsection."

In *In re Bunker Hill Mining and Smelter Complex*, 728 F. Supp. 626 (D. Idaho 1990), the court held that the grant of authority to the EPA in section 114 was not limited to inspection of records that the source owner or operator is required to maintain. The court concluded, based on its review of the case law and the legislative history, that the EPA's right of access extends to all records that are directly related to the purpose of the inspection. The court held that the warrant was overbroad because it called for documents "of any type" maintained or filed at the source. The court also held that the EPA's administrative warrant was analogous to an administrative subpoena and therefore that the mining company had the right to search its documents and to provide those that it found to be responsive to the warrant.

Criminal Enforcement

Section 113(c)(1) of the Act provides for the assessment of fines for knowing violations of the Act. The amount of a fine is to be set pursuant to title 18 of the United States Code. Section 113(c)(1) also allows the imposition of a prison term of up to five years and provides that both the fine and the imprisonment shall be doubled for repeat offenders.

As amended, section 113(c)(2) of the Act imposes a penalty of a fine set pursuant to title 18 of the United States Code or imprisonment for up to two years, or both in cases of violation of reporting and record-keeping requirements. Penalties are to be doubled for repeat offenders. The provision also expands the list of violations to include omissions of material information from required reports and failure to file or maintain any document required to be filed or maintained. Under section 113(c)(3), penalties may be imposed for failure to pay fees.

Section 113(c)(5)(A) of the Act imposes criminal penalties for knowing ambient air releases (except releases in compliance with a permit or an the EPA emission standard) of hazardous air pollutants listed under section 112 or "extremely hazardous substances" listed under SARA where the releaser "knows at the time that he thereby places another person in imminent danger of death or serious bodily injury." The penalty is a title 18 fine or up to fifteen years' imprisonment, or both. The penalty for a corporate violation is a fine of up to $1 million.

In *United States v. Buckley*, 934 F.2d 84 (6th Cir. 1991), the court affirmed a defendant's criminal conviction for knowingly emitting asbestos during a demolition project in violation of the national emission standards for hazardous air pollutants under section 112. The court held the jury had to find only that he knew that asbestos was emitted to convict the defendant, not necessarily that he knew that the emissions violated the Act. The court cited cases stating the principle that where a statute does not otherwise specify, general intent is presumed to be the required element. The court also established the principle that when dealing with dangerous materials such as asbestos, the probability of regulation is so great that anyone dealing with them should be presumed to be aware of the regulation.

Negligent ambient air releases of hazardous air pollutants or extremely hazardous substances are also subject to criminal penalties where the releaser at the time negligently places another person in imminent danger of death or serious bodily injury. Section 113(c)(4).

The Administrative Penalty Scheme

Section 113(d)(1) authorizes the EPA Administrator to assess administrative penalties for (1) past or present violations of SIPs; (2) past or present violations of other requirements imposed by or under the Act; or (3) violations of new source requirements. The EPA may impose administrative penalties in "matters where the total penalty sought does not exceed $200,000," and the administrative proceeding must be initiated within one year of the first alleged date of violation. The $200,000 cap and the requirement that the action be brought within one year of the first alleged date of violation, however, do not apply where the Administrator and the Attorney General decide that they are not "appropriate." That decision is not subject to judicial review. Section 113(d)(1). The fine is assessed by an EPA order after a hearing on the record pursuant to the APA. Discovery rules and hearing procedures shall be issued by the Administrator. Section 113(d)(2)(A).

By regulation, the Administrator may implement a field citation program under which designated employees may assess civil penalties not to exceed $5,000 per day of violation for "appropriate minor violations." Assessees may request a hearing or simply pay the fine. The hearing is not subject to the APA, but it must "provide a reasonable opportunity to be heard and to present evidence." Payment of the field citation penalty is not a defense to further enforcement actions if the violation continues. Section 113(d)(3).

Appeals of administrative penalties, including field citations, are to the District Court for the District of Columbia or the district court for the district in which is located the place where the violation allegedly occurred, the alleged violator's residence, or the alleged violator's principal place of business. Appeals must be filed within thirty days after a penalty order of assessment becomes final, a section 113(d)(3) penalty becomes final because no hearing was requested, or a final decision following a section 113(d)(3) hearing. The court shall not set the penalty aside unless there is not substantial evidence to support the EPA's finding or unless the order or assessment constitutes an abuse of discretion.

Citizen Involvement and Judicial Review Provisions

Section 113(f) authorizes the EPA to award up to $10,000 to any nongovernmental person for information or services leading to penalties or convictions. Any officer or employee of the United States or any state or local government who furnishes information or renders service in performance of an official duty is ineligible. The EPA Administrator may by regulation prescribe eligibility criteria.

Section 113(g) requires that at least thirty days before the filing of a consent order or settlement to which the United States is a party, notice of the proposed order or settlement must be published for public comment in the *Federal Register*. This requirement applies to all consent orders or settlement agreements under the Act to which the United States is a party except actions under section 113, section 120, or title II.

The amendments make several changes to the citizen suit provisions of section 304. First, district courts may award civil penalties in citizen suits. Section 304(a). Second, beginning with actions brought at least two years after enactment, citizens may sue for past violations "if there is evidence that the alleged violation has been repeated." Section 304(a)(1)(3). Third, suits in which the United

States is not a party are to have no binding effect on the United States, and no consent judgment may be entered prior to forty-five days following receipt of the proposed consent judgment by the Administrator and the Attorney General. The Administrator may intervene in a citizen suit as a matter of right at any time. Section 304(c)(3). Fourth, a citizen suit that alleges unreasonable Agency delay in taking final action may be brought only in a district court within the circuit in which the final Agency action would be reviewable. Moreover, the plaintiff must give notice to the Administrator, the state, and any alleged violator 180 days before filing suit for unreasonable delay. Section 304(a).

The amendments clarify that citizens may challenge in the court of appeals a decision by the Administrator to defer performance of any nondiscretionary statutory duty. Section 307(b)(2).

Finally, the amendments provide that the filing of a petition for Agency reconsideration of an otherwise final rule or action shall not affect the finality of (or postpone the effectiveness of) that rule or action. Section 307(b)(1).

Recent Section 304 Decisions

The court in *Coalition Against Columbus Center v. City of New York*, 750 F. Supp. 93 (S.D.N.Y. 1990), dismissed (with leave to refile) a claim brought under section 304 because the plaintiffs had not satisfied the statutory requirement of sixty days' advance notice before filing suit. The court cited *Hallstrom v. Tillamook County*, 110 S. Ct. 304 (1989), in which the Supreme Court dismissed a suit because the plaintiffs in that case had failed to comply with the sixty-day notice provision in RCRA, which was identical to and modeled on the Clean Air Act provision.

In *Delaware Valley Citizens Council for Clean Air v. Davis*, Civ. No. 89-2592, slip op. (E.D. Pa. Feb. 21, 1990), appeal pending, No. 90-1309 (3d Cir.), the district court dismissed for lack of subject matter jurisdiction citizen suit claims against Pennsylvania officials that alleged that the Pennsylvania SIP was inadequate to meet the requirements of the Clean Air Act. The court held that, notwithstanding that the claims were made against state officials, they were an attack on the legal validity of the EPA's final action in approving the SIP, a matter subject to the court of appeals' exclusive review jurisdiction under section 307(b)(1). The court noted that it could transfer the claims to the court of appeals if the claims could have been presented to that court at the time that the plaintiffs filed their NOI to bring the district court action. The court, however, found that court of appeals petitions for review would have been untimely as to two of the claims, and, in a later opinion, after the plaintiffs declined an opportunity to allege more specific facts, found untimeliness as to a third claim as well. *Delaware Valley Citizens Council for Clean Air v. Davis*, Civ. No. 89-2592, slip op. (E.D. Pa. March 30, 1990), *appeal pending*, No. 90-1309 (3d Cir.). The court therefore did not transfer those claims to the court of appeals.

The court also dismissed for failure to state a claim upon which relief could be granted a claim that Pennsylvania had violated the SIP. The plaintiffs did not allege that Pennsylvania failed to achieve a 44 percent reduction in VOC emissions, the requirement that the SIP imposed òn the state. The court noted that any claim that the state had failed to attain NAAQSs was outside the scope of section 304 jurisdiction.

The Penalty Assessment Criteria

Section 304(e)(1) lists the factors that the EPA and the courts must consider when assessing penalties under section 113 or section 304(a). The nonexclusive factors are (1) the size of the business, (2) the economic impact of the penalty on the business, (3) the violator's compliance history and good faith efforts to comply, (4) the duration of the violation as established by any credible evidence, (5) payment by the violator of penalties previously assessed for the same violation, (6) the economic benefit of noncompliance, and (7) the seriousness of the violation. Section 113(e) provides that a court may not assess penalties for noncompliance with administrative subpoenas or information requirements where the violator had "sufficient cause" to violate or refuse to comply with the subpoena or information requirement.

Under section 113(e)(2), a presumption exists that a violation is continuous from the date of notice of violation if the plaintiff, including a citizen suit plaintiff under section 304, makes out a *prima facie* case that the violation is continuous. The defendant then has the burden of showing that the violation was noncontinuous or that there were intervening days of compliance.

Federal Facilities

In *United States v. Tennessee Air Pollution Control Board*, 31 Env't Rep. Cas. (BNA) 1500 (M.D. Tenn. 1990), the court adopted a magistrate's determination that section 118(a) of the Clean Air Act, which provides that the federal government is subject to the same "process and sanctions" regarding air pollution control as any nongovernmental entity, constitutes congressional waiver of U.S. sovereign immunity for the imposition of civil penalties to enforce state air pollution laws. Tennessee had fined the Department of the Army for removal of asbestos material without complying with notice provisions of state law. The magistrate based his determination on the plain meaning of "sanctions" in section 118(a), the Act's legislative history, and an examination of similar provisions in other federal environmental laws. The magistrate also recommended that because of the federal issue involved, the court should not abstain from filing on the federal government's immunity claim despite a pending state proceeding on the same issue. The United States later withdrew its claim that the state lacked jurisdiction to levy fines because the federal government's action took place on land that was a federal enclave. *Id.* at 1503.

In *United States v. South Coast Air Quality Management District*, 748 F. Supp. 732 (C.D. Cal. 1990), the court concluded that section 118 unambiguously waives U.S. sovereign immunity against any claim that federal facilities must pay permitting fees to a California state air quality management district. The court held that section 118 contained all-inclusive language providing a broad waiver of sovereign immunity and that the absence of specific references in section 118 to state or local "fees" or "taxes" was immaterial. The court also held that section 110(a)(2)(K) of the Act established only the minimum fee criteria for SIPs and that the district's fee requirements were not impermissible as applied to the federal facilities merely because they were more stringent than required under those criteria. In addition, the court rejected the argument that imposition of some of the fees on federal facilities was impermissible on the ground that the district's rules had exempted state and local governments from those fees; the court held that the language of section 118, making federal facilities subject to state and local air pollution control requirements "to the same extent as any nongovernmental entity," required the district only to treat federal facilities and private facilities equally.

New Growth in the PSD Forest: A Trail Map

Amy R. Porter, Eric A. Groten, and Steven J. Burr

The impenetrable forest of PSD regulations under the Clean Air Act sprouted from a three-page acorn, District Judge John Pratts' memorandum opinion in *Sierra Club v. Ruckelshaus,* 344 F. Supp. 253 (D.D.C.), *aff'd per curiam,* 4 Env't Rep. Cas. 1815 (D.C. Cir. 1972), *aff'd per curiam sub nom. Fri v. Sierra Club,* 412 U.S. 541 (1973). *Sierra Club* holds that the "protect and enhance" language in Clean Air Act § 101, 42 U.S.C. § 7401, requires the EPA to prevent air quality in areas that are cleaner than the NAAQSs—now designated as "attainment" areas—from deteriorating to bare compliance with those standards.

The EPA responded with its first PSD regulations in late 1974. *See* 39 Fed. Reg. 42,510 (Dec. 5, 1974) (now codified, as revised, at 40 C.F.R. §§ 51.166 & 52.21). These regulations established the basic elements of today's PSD program—variable "increments" of allowable air quality deterioration and minimum control technology requirements—although in substantially less detail.

Congress preempted judicial challenges to these seedling regulations by amending the Act in 1977. *See Sierra Club v. EPA,* 540 F.2d 1114 (D.C. Cir. 1976) (upholding the 1974 regulations), *vacated and remanded sub nom. Montana Power Co. v. EPA,* 434 U.S. 809 (1977) (ordering reconsideration in light of the Clean Air Act Amendments of 1977). Congress gave the PSD trees very firm

Amy Porter is a partner and Steven Burr is an associate in the Phoenix, Arizona, law firm of Lewis and Roca. Eric Groten practices with the firm of Brown, Maroney & Oaks Hartline in Austin, Texas.

roots by codifying the conceptual framework of the 1974 regulations as Part C of Title I of the Clean Air Act, 42 U.S.C. §§ 7470-91.

The EPA's first full attempt to implement Part C, 43 Fed. Reg. 26,380 (June 19, 1978), raised enough issues to fill a seventy-page opinion addressing challenges to those rules. *See Alabama Power Co. v. Costle*, 636 F.2d 323 (D.C. Cir. 1979) (remanding to the Agency many aspects of the 1978 PSD regulations). Despite resolution of numerous issues by the court, many others were left open. The EPA's efforts to resolve some of the open issues have made the PSD forest more impenetrable than ever. The Clean Air Act Amendments of 1990, although they did not focus on PSD, have added to the tangle. This article attempts to map a few trails through this new growth.

We first address the threshold question of when PSD review applies. We next discuss PSD "increments" for nitrogen oxides (NO_x) and PM_{10} (particles smaller than 10 microns in aerodynamic diameter), which will affect the air quality demonstration requirements for obtaining PSD permits. Finally, we review the EPA's "top-down" and "North County" policies, which reinterpret the Agency's regulations regarding the control technology demonstrations required of PSD permit applications.

PSD Applicability since Alabama Power

Stated simply and without all of the qualifications needed for complete accuracy, PSD review and permitting is required before constructing any new major stationary source or undertaking a major modification in an attainment area. A major stationary source is a plant with a potential to emit either 100 or 250 tons per year of a single regulated pollutant, depending on whether the source category appears on a list of major emitting facilities. Major modifications are physical or operational changes to an existing major source that cause a "significant" net emissions increase. Deciding whether a proposed activity constitutes construction of a new major source or a major modification to an existing major source—and thus subject to PSD—has become known as a "threshold applicability determination."

If it is determined that the proposed activity is subject to PSD review, substantive PSD requirements will apply not only to the pollutant(s) for which the source or modification is major but also to any pollutant emitted in significant amounts and for which the area is in attainment. This is the so-called "pollutant applicability determination."

A detailed and complete discussion of all of the issues raised by these simple statements about PSD applicability could consume more pages than are available here. For example, a discussion of the issues raised by *Wisconsin Electric Power Co. v. Reilly*, 893 F.2d 901 (7th Cir. 1990), which relates to the applicability of PSD requirements to like-kind exchanges, could easily consume a chapter by itself. We therefore identify here only a few of the most important threshold applicability issues that remain unresolved by *Alabama Power*.

Limiting the Potential to Emit

Alabama Power concluded that a proposed source's potential to emit must be judged in light of the effect of pollution control devices, but the court deliberately left open the question of whether other practical constraints on emission rates also could be considered. *Id.* at 353, 355 n.73. This issue becomes important when a proposed source is not intended to be operated continuously or at full capacity.

The EPA addressed this issue—and many others—in regulatory revisions promulgated in response to the *Alabama Power* remand. 45 Fed. Reg. 52,676 (Aug. 7, 1980) (1980 revisions). The EPA decided that any constraint on a source's emissions reduces its potential to emit only if the constraint is "federally enforceable." *Id.* at 52,688. In 1983, pursuant to a settlement reached in *Chemical Manufacturers Association v. EPA (CMA)*, No. 79-1112, the EPA proposed to delete this requirement, 48 Fed. Reg. 38,741, 38,747-48 (1983). Six years and numerous public comments later, however, the EPA instead reaffirmed the requirement, 54 Fed. Reg. 27,274 (1989).

As a result, an owner of a proposed source must obtain federally enforceable limits on hours of operation or production rate if necessary to prevent PSD applicability based on hypothetical 365-day-per-year operation at full capacity. Conditions in a state or local installation permit, if issued pursuant to an approved SIP provision, can provide the necessary federal enforceability to limit potential emissions. We have had some success using minor source installation permitting regulations that have been approved as part of a SIP. There is also some prospect that operating permits issued pursuant to Title V of the 1990 amendments may be used to impose federally enforceable limits. 56 Fed. Reg. 21,712, 21,725 (1991) (proposed operating permit regulations). Where these procedures are not available, ensuring that constraints are federally enforceable may require more time-consuming procedures such as source-specific revisions to a SIP. *See* 40 C.F.R. §§ 51.166(b)(17) and 52.21(b)(17).

According to the decision in *United States v. Louisiana-Pacific Corp.*, 682 F. Supp. 1122, 1133 (D. Colo. 1987), a source owner seeking to limit the source's "potential to emit"—and thus keep the source under the major source threshold—should ensure that any SIP revisions or permit conditions restrict the source's hours or rate of operations and not just emissions per se. *Louisiana-Pacific* holds that only the former are effective limitations on the potential to emit. The source owner also must comply with these limitations or risk waiving them as effective restrictions on potential to emit. *Id. at* 1161.

Counting Fugitive Emissions

Fugitive emissions—emissions that cannot reasonably be captured and vented through a control device—are difficult to quantify and control. Difficulties in quantifying fugitive emissions lead to difficulties in evaluating PSD applicability and making substantive demonstrations concerning the proposed source's effect on air quality. Difficulties in controlling fugitive emissions, particularly for the mining and forestry industries, can make the substantive demonstrations impossible.

Alabama Power concluded that fugitive emissions may be included in determining a source's potential to emit, but only after a rule making to include a particular source category. 636 F.2d at 369 (rule making required by section 302(j) of the Act). The PSD rules issued after remand, however, merely recited a statutory list of major emitting facilities and added source categories that were covered by new NSPSs or NESHAPs that had been promulgated by August 7, 1980. 46 Fed. Reg. at 52,690-693. The EPA maintained that the opportunity to comment when it proposed this list satisfied section 302(j)'s rule-making requirement.

Industry challenged this blanket listing as inadequate under the Clean Air Act and the *Alabama Power* holding, arguing that the EPA is required to consider for each source category both the extent to which fugitive emissions can be quantified and the economic effect of regulating fugitive emissions from that source category. In accordance with the *CMA* settlement agreement, the EPA did propose to retract its 1980 interpretation of section 302(j) and the categorical source list (pending source-specific rule makings). 48 Fed. Reg. at 38,745 (1983 proposal). The EPA reversed course, however, in the wake of *Duquesne Light Co. v. EPA*, 698 F.2d 456, 474-75 (D.C. Cir. 1983), suggesting, in dicta, that the EPA's 1980 list satisfied section 302(j) procedural requirements.

In a 1984 proposal to add surface coal mines to the list, the EPA stated that it will use a "safety valve" approach to listing source categories for which fugitive emissions must be included in threshold applicability determinations. It will first propose to list a source category simply if it expects fugitive emissions from that source category to have significant air quality effects. Before taking final action, however, the EPA will consider the socioeconomic costs and benefits of its proposed listing if raised during the comment period. 49 Fed. Reg. 43,201, 43,208 (1984). In a 1989 final action on surface coal mines, the EPA reaffirmed this approach and determined that because DOI rules for surface coal mines will independently satisfy PSD goals, surface coal mines should not be included on the list of fugitive emissions sources. 54 Fed. Reg. 48,870 (1989). The D.C. Circuit recently affirmed the EPA's approach to the fugitive emissions issue and its specific determination not to list surface coal mines. *NRDC v. EPA*, 937 F.2d 641 (D.C. Cir. 1991).

Having established this approach to listing, the EPA promptly ignored it in proposed regulations issued under Title V of the 1990 amendments. The operating permit program established by Title V applies to major sources, as defined in section 302 of the Act. *See* Clean Air Act §§ 501(2), 502(a), 42 U.S.C. §§ 7661(2), 7661a(a). (The program applies to other specified sources as well.) In the preamble to the proposed Title V regulations, the EPA stated that it was "proposing to consider fugitive emissions in determining if a source would be major with respect to section 302 for only those source categories that have previously been subjected to the rule-making required in section 302(j)." 56 Fed. Reg. 21,712, 21,727 (1991). The regulations themselves, however, contradicted the EPA's stated intent. The list of source categories for which fugitive emissions must be included in the threshold applicability determination included the usual list of statutory major emitting facilities and in addition "*all other* stationary source categories" regulated by an NSPS or NESHAP. *Id*. at 21,769 (proposed 40 C.F.R. § 70.2(r)(2)(xxvii)). Because previous rule makings had listed only those sources covered by an NSPS or NESHAP promulgated by August 7, 1980, this regulatory language would significantly expand the number of categories on the list. At the same time, the goal of providing a "safety valve" by allowing comments on economic and social effects would be lost if the EPA proceeded to adopt this language, because the preamble misrepresents what is in the regulation. If the EPA does not reverse itself on this point, or is not reversed by the D.C. Circuit, its next step may well be to make conforming changes in the PSD regulations.

So far the discussion has been limited to the question of whether fugitive emissions are included in the threshold applicability determination for major *sources*. In the final action on surface coal mines, the EPA also determined that the section 302(j) rule-making requirement for fugitive emissions does *not* apply to major *modifications*.

54 Fed. Reg. at 48,875. The EPA's PSD regulations, however, currently exempt major modifications of sources in a nonlisted category from federal PSD permitting requirements if the modifications are major solely as a result of fugitive emissions. 40 C.F.R. § 52.21(i)(4)(vii). The states are allowed to adopt the same exemption in their PSD programs. 40 C.F.R. § 51.166(i)(4)(ii).

Netting Out of PSD

The EPA applies a plantwide definition of "stationary source" in the PSD context. Consequently, emission decreases at one point in a plant can be used to offset increases at another, perhaps "netting out" of PSD review.

The 1980 rules placed three important limitations on netting. First, the Agency focuses on decreases in *actual* emissions (generally emissions over the past two years), not in *allowable* emissions. *See* 40 C.F.R. § 51.166(b)(3)(vi). This interpretation is detrimental to older sources operating at a rate lower than allowed under a SIP limit because replacement of old equipment with new equipment that emits more than the replaced equipment's actual emissions (but less than allowable) still may trigger PSD review. A second limitation on creditability is federal enforceability. Finally, pollutant emission decreases at one point in a plant must have "the same qualitative significance for public health and welfare" as the pollutant increases elsewhere in the plant.

The EPA proposed to delete the latter two limitations in 1983 pursuant to Exhibit A of the *CMA* settlement agreement. *See* 48 Fed. Reg. at 38,747–49. In 1989, however, the EPA decided to keep both limitations in place. 54 Fed. Reg. 27,274 (1989) (federal enforceability); 54 Fed. Reg. 27,286 (1989).

In the notice on the health and welfare limitation, the EPA indicated that it intended to develop criteria to allow it to "consider differences in toxicity in netting calculations." *Id.* at 27,297. The EPA then solicited comments "to be used in the development of guidance for implementing this provision." Thus the EPA appeared to be headed in the direction of using the netting provisions of the PSD (and nonattainment NSR) regulations as an indirect method of controlling toxic air pollution. An EPA official, however, has indicated that the EPA will probably not pursue this initiative in light of the passage of Title III of the 1990 amendments, which requires the EPA to adopt a similar program for a long list of hazardous air pollutants. Section 112(g)(1) of the Act, as amended, provides for netting transactions in the permitting of modified major sources of hazardous air pollutants. That section also requires the EPA to issue guidance on the relative toxicity of the pollutants for the purpose of determining when a netting transaction of two different pollutants should be allowed. 42 U.S.C. § 7412(g)(1).

The Applicability of PSD to Reactivated Facilities

Congress never considered the question of whether a deactivated facility becomes subject to PSD review upon reactivation. The EPA has filled this gap with a series of site-specific PSD applicability determinations that collectively amount to the EPA's "reactivation" policy. The seminal decision concludes that deactivated facility "would be a new source for PSD purposes upon reopening if the shutdown was permanent." Memorandum from Director, EPA Division of Stationary Source Enforcement, to Chief, General Enforcement Branch, Region II (Sept. 6, 1978). This seems a rather awkward and question-begging policy, as the simple fact of reactivation would suggest that a shutdown was not permanent. Ignoring the obvious, the EPA identified several factors to consider when determining the permanence of a shutdown:

> Whether a shutdown was permanent depends upon the intention of the owner or operator at the time of the shutdown as determined from all of the facts and circumstances, including the cause of the shutdown and the handling of the shutdown by the State. A shutdown lasting for two years or more or resulting in removal of the source from the emissions inventory of the State, should be presumed permanent. The owner or operator proposing to reopen the source would have the burden of showing that the shutdown was not permanent, and of overcoming any presumption that it was.

Id. at 1–2.

The EPA has applied this test in several instances. In one, a shutdown for four years, coupled with the source's removal from the state's emissions inventory and the source owner's public statements regarding permanence, led the EPA to conclude that PSD review applied. Memorandum from Director, EPA Division of Stationary Source Enforcement, to Director, Enforcement Division, Region V (Oct. 3, 1980). In another determination, proof of intent to reopen allowed a source shut down for eight years to avoid PSD review. *See* Memorandum from Director, EPA Division of Stationary Source Enforcement, to Director, Air & Waste Management Division, EPA Region II (July 9, 1982) (responding to May 25, 1982, request for opinion, which request contains useful references to several other nonapplicability determinations). In a third determination, the EPA departed somewhat from the original policy statement and found that because a source owner abandoned its original intent to reopen, the source's shutdown had become permanent. This determination led to litigation, *Cyprus Casa Grande Corp. v. EPA,* No. 87–7322 (9th Cir. filed July 30, 1987), which was eventually settled without a judicial ruling on the validity of the EPA's reactivation policy.

The reactivation policy, which focuses on whether a reactivated facility is a new source, is arguably inconsistent with the EPA's PSD regulations. The term "new source" does not appear in the PSD regulations. Rather, the regulations specify that a source subject to PSD may not "begin actual construction" without a PSD permit. 40 C.F.R. § 52.21(i)(1). It is difficult to fathom how someone could begin actual construction of a source that already exists. Perhaps recognizing this weakness in the analysis, EPA Region IX issued a PSD applicability determination for a reactivated plant that instead focused on whether the reactivation constituted a major modification. Letter from Director, Air Management Division, EPA Region IX (Nov. 6, 1987). Region IX, in other words, looked at whether the reactivation could be characterized as a physical change in, or change in the method of operations of, the source that would result in a significant net emissions increase. In doing so, Region IX considered many of the same factors that are pertinent under the reactivation policy.

Pending judicial review of the EPA's reactivation policy, owners that deactivate sources with the intent to restart them should be advised to stay current on the state's emissions inventory, to use every opportunity to declare the deactivation to be temporary (in annual reports, newspaper notices, etc.), to maintain a current operating permit (or at least to continue to apply for operating permits in jurisdictions that require them), and to maintain the facility to the extent consistent with an intent to eventually reopen it.

Emerging Ambient Air Quality Demonstration Requirements

The keystone of the PSD program is the PSD increment. An increment establishes the maximum degree of air quality deterioration, expressed in micrograms per cubic meter, allowed in clean air areas. The increment, when added to the ambient concentration on the baseline date (generally the date of the first PSD application in an area), essentially creates a new local ambient air quality standard. Owners must demonstrate that proposed new sources will not cause violations of this new standard.

Specific numeric increments for PM and for sulfur dioxide (SO_2) were included in the 1977 amendments to the Act. *See* Clean Air Act § 163(b)(2), 42 U.S.C. § 7473(b)(2). Under these amendments, which are still in effect, the size of the increment depends on the proposed location's classification. Class I areas—those near national parks and other sensitive areas—are covered by very restrictive increments. More liberal increments (generally 25 percent of the NAAQS) apply in Class II areas. Although the Act provides procedures for carving out Class III areas, no such area has yet been designated.

The EPA has long resisted developing increments for criteria pollutants other than SO_2 and PM, primarily because it expected vehicle emission control programs to reduce nationwide concentrations of these pollutants and because of difficulties in modeling their emissions. *See* 38 Fed. Reg. 18,986, 18,988 (July 16, 1973) (first proposed PSD program). To overcome this resistance, Congress amended the Act in 1977 to add section 166, which required the EPA to develop PSD regulations for criteria pollutants other than SO_2 and PM by 1979. *See* Clean Air Act § 166(a), 42 U.S.C. § 7476. Ten years later, the EPA has only promulgated regulations for one other pollutant, nitrous oxides (NO_x), and those have been determined to be incomplete. The EPA also is revising the increments for particulate matter. Both of these changes will affect the ambient air quality showings required of PSD permit applicants.

Increments for NO_x

The EPA had tabled its program for developing PSD regulations governing NO_x until sued by environmental groups. *See Sierra Club v. Thomas,* 658 F. Supp. 165 (N.D. Cal. 1987) (ordering proposal by Feb. 8, 1988, and final action by Oct. 9, 1988). The EPA published proposed rules on the court-ordered date, *see* 53 Fed. Reg. 3,697 (1988), and issued the final rule on October 17. *See* 53 Fed. Reg. 40,656 (1988).

Even though Congress allowed the EPA considerable flexibility in its approach to preventing significant deterioration for NO_x, the EPA adopted the familiar increment approach. Specifically, the EPA adopted increments for nitrogen dioxide (NO_2) that bear the same percentage relationship to the NO_2 NAAQS that the statutory increments for PM and SO_2 bear to the NAAQS for those pollutants. *Id.* (In the case of PM, Congress used the TSP NAAQS to establish the increments. As noted below, that NAAQS has since been superseded by the PM_{10} standard.)

The D.C. Circuit determined that this approach was permissible under section 166(d) of the Act, which requires "specific measures at least as effective as" the statutory increments for PM and SO_2. But the court also concluded that the EPA had impermissibly failed to consider whether different or additional measures were necessary under section 166(c), which establishes a number of additional requirements for PSD regulations. *EDF v. EPA*, 898 F.2d 183 (D.C. Cir. 1990). The court did not vacate the NO_2 increment regulation but rather remanded the rule making to the EPA for consideration of what additional or different measures, if any, were necessary to meet the section 166(c) requirements. The court specifically declined to impose a deadline for action, and the EPA has not yet proposed any changes to the regulation. There is no reference to any prospective amendment to the PSD regulations for NO_x in the EPA's latest regulatory agenda. 57 Fed. Reg. 17,427 (1992).

The use of the increment approach for NO_x will no doubt create important implementation questions that are not fully resolved or even foreseen in the rule making. For example, mobile source contributions to NO_x levels, and the interrelationship between NO_x and ozone, will present some serious practical problems for the EPA and regulated sources. Because only stationary sources must obtain PSD permits, attempts to account for mobile source emissions and ozone interaction will involve much more sophisticated, time-consuming, and expensive air quality analyses than required under the current PSD program.

The Particulate Matter Increments

As noted above, the Clean Air Act itself sets the increments for PM, and the EPA revised the PM NAAQS in 1987, both by changing the indicator from TSP to PM_{10} and by reducing allowable concentrations. 52 Fed. Reg. 24,634 (1987). The EPA did not, however, redefine PM for increment purposes but instead retained the TSP increments. That decision was upheld against an industry challenge in *NRDC v. EPA*, 902 F.2d 962 (D.C. Cir. 1990). In that case, the court rejected industry's argument that the EPA should have adopted regulations applying the statutory PM increments to PM_{10}.

In 1989, the EPA proposed to replace the TSP increments with increments for PM_{10}. 54 Fed. Reg. 41,218 (1989). Although the EPA's statutory authority to do so was at the time less than clear, the 1990 amendments gave the EPA specific authority to substitute PM_{10} increments for TSP. *See* Clean Air Act § 166(f), 42 U.S.C. § 7476(f). The increments that the EPA proposed were based on what it termed the "equivalent to statutory increments approach." Under this approach, the EPA sought to establish increments for PM_{10} that would be "as nearly equivalent as possible to the section 163 increments in their effect on TSP increment 'consumption.'" 54 Fed. Reg. at 41,221. Accordingly, the resulting increments would be lower in their relation to the NAAQS than the existing TSP increments. It is anticipated that setting increments at these low levels will have a severe impact on the natural resources industries.

After passage of the 1990 amendments, the EPA decided to repropose the PM_{10} increments as part of a package of revisions to the PSD and NSR regulations. Because of delays in putting together other elements of the package, however, the EPA is considering proceeding with the PM_{10} increments proposal as a separate rule making. The EPA reportedly may promulgate increments on the basis of comments received on the original proposal without reproposing the increments rule.

In the interim, for major sources of PM, the PSD forest will be more difficult to penetrate than ever. The 1990 amendments specify that until the EPA adopts PM_{10} increments, attainment designations for TSP "shall remain in effect for purposes of implementing the [increments for] particulate matter." *See* Clean Air Act § 107 (d)(4)(B), 42 U.S.C. § 7407(d)(4)(B). In a number of instances, areas that were designated attainment for TSP are designated nonattainment for PM_{10}. A person constructing or making a major modification to a major source in one of these areas will be required to comply with both nonattainment NSR and PSD requirements with respect to the source's PM emissions.

The Policies Governing Technology Demonstrations

In addition to increments that directly prevent significant deterioration of air quality, the PSD regulations also contain technology-forcing requirements. PSD sources must control each pollutant emitted in significant amounts to the degree achievable by application of BACT. BACT is determined on a case-by-case basis, with any applicable NSPS providing the floor. BACT has been (1) less stringent than the LAER required of major sources in nonattainment areas and (2) applied only to pollutants regulated under the Clean Air Act. New EPA policies, however, weaken these limitations on BACT.

The EPA's "Top-Down" Policy for BACT Determinations
In 1987, the EPA announced a new policy, called "top-down," for BACT determinations. Memorandum from Assistant EPA Administrator

for Air and Radiation, to Regional Administrators, Regions I to X (Dec. 1, 1987). Under the practice before the top-down policy, the EPA required a PSD applicant to perform a full analysis of all possible types and levels of control to establish BACT for the source in question. The EPA then had the burden of showing that the selected controls were not BACT and that more stringent controls were achievable and economically feasible.

Under the "top-down" approach, the EPA would first determine the most stringent control available for a similar source or source category. Only if the applicant wanted to avoid that form of control and could establish that it was technologically or economically infeasible would the next most stringent level be determined and similarly evaluated. "[T]he 'top-down' approach shifts the burden of proof to the applicant to justify why the proposed source is unable to apply the best technology available." *Id.* at 4.

The EPA has put implementation of the top-down approach on hold pursuant to a settlement agreement reached in a lawsuit by the American Paper Institute. *See* 56 Fed. Reg. 34,202 (1991). The API claimed that the EPA's adoption of the top-down policy without a rule making was illegal. Under the settlement, the EPA has agreed to conduct a rule making on BACT determinations and to proceed with case-by-case determinations under the old approach in the interim. A proposal on BACT determinations is now overdue under the terms of the settlement.

The EPA's North County Policy

Until 1987, PSD permit applicants needed only to demonstrate that their sources applied BACT to emissions of each pollutant regulated under the Clean Air Act. In 1987, however, OAQPS issued "final guidance" to the EPA regions requiring that BACT determinations also address the toxic effects of unregulated pollutants. Memorandum from G.A. Emison, Director, OAQPS, to Regional Air Directors (Sept. 22, 1987).

Under this "North County policy," so named because it was first applied to California's North County Recycling and Energy Recovery Center, unregulated pollutants will not be subject to their own emission limits but may affect BACT determinations for regulated pollutants. If the reviewing agency finds that the potential environmental effects of unregulated pollutants are of concern, the final BACT decision for regulated pollutants must address these effects and reflect control beyond what it otherwise might have chosen. The North County-adjusted BACT level, however, still must be "achievable."

The EPA stated that implementing the policy will not require SIP revisions because the policy is based on an interpretation of the language of the Act itself. The EPA relies on section 163(3), which defines BACT as the maximum degree of emissions decrease determined by the permitting authority to be achievable, taking into account "environmental . . . impact."

The EPA further recognized that this policy is not "amenable to highly detailed national guidance." The North County policy, therefore, will involve a case-by-case process in which the judgment of the reviewing authority will play a significant role. The EPA, however, may develop guidance for specific source categories as it has for municipal waste combustors. *See* "Operational Guidance on Control Technology for New and Modified Municipal Waste Combustors," G. A. Emison, Director, OAQPS (June 26, 1987).

Section 112(b)(6) of the Act as amended by the 1990 amendments exempts hazardous air pollutants from PSD requirements. The EPA has nevertheless determined that the North County policy remains valid after the 1990 amendments. *See* Memorandum from Director, OAQPS to Addressees (Mar. 11, 1991).

In conclusion, we have highlighted only a few of the issues unresolved by or emerging since *Alabama Power.* Because the PSD forest grows denser every year, with travel through its underbrush becoming increasingly dangerous for those unfamiliar with its trails, we strongly recommend making sure you are reading the most current maps.

PART V

Business Transactions and Compliance

Environmental Audits of Real Property
before Purchase

Complying with Environmental Permits
after Issuance

OSHA's Hazard Communication Standard

TSCA: The Sleeping Giant Is Stirring

Regulation by Information through EPCRA

Protecting Trade Secrets in the
Information Age

Part V
Business Transactions
and Compliance

The pervasive nature of environmental liabilities has affected businesses in fundamental ways. In the 1970s, it was uncommon for companies to consider environmental implications of business transactions and to audit systematically their environmental liabilities. Today, no substantial business transaction proceeds without a careful review of potential environmental liabilities. Wholly apart from transactions, companies must be conversant with and develop procedures to comply with numerous regulatory requirements in the environmental area.

Parthenia Evans focuses on environmental auditing undertaken in connection with and before the transfer of commercial and industrial property or facilities, as well as the roles of the prospective buyer and seller in environmental auditing. Compliance with environmental permits is the subject of an article by Stephen Bundy, who suggests using the permit team as the nucleus of ongoing compliance efforts.

Environmental law is increasingly concerned with the disclosure of information concerning potential hazards to the government, the public, and employees. Daniel Marcus describes the genesis and impact of the Occupational Safety and Health Act's hazard communication standard, which imposes regulatory burdens on virtually every employer in the country. 29 C.F.R. § 1910.1200 *et seq.*

The Toxic Substances Control Act authorizes the EPA to collect information on toxicity and to restrict or prohibit the use of chemical

335

substances. 15 U.S.C. § 2601 *et seq*. David Hayes analyzes the scope of TSCA's information-gathering provisions, illustrating why the law has an impact well beyond the chemical industry.

Another statute requiring the submission of information is the Emergency Planning and Community Right-to-Know Act, 42 U.S.C. § 11,001 *et seq*. Kevin Finto discusses the scope of EPCRA's provisions and explains how the "regulation by information" scheme works in theory and in practice.

The foregoing information-gathering statutes pose substantial issues for companies concerned with protecting their valuable trade secrets. In the last article in this part, Beverly Horn Nelson provides a guide to this area of the law and offers suggestions for developing a strategy to protect trade secrets.

Environmental Audits of Real Property before Purchase

Parthenia B. Evans

Environmental liabilities are important considerations in the transfer of industrial property and most commercial property. Federal and state statutes impose far-reaching liability on owners and operators of facilities involved in the handling of hazardous substances when those substances present a threat to human health and the environment. Through an environmental audit, a thorough understanding of the condition of the property or facility can be obtained before negotiation of a transfer. If the property is contaminated with a hazardous substance, the prospective buyer can make a more informed decision regarding carrying out the transfer and environmental liabilities can be more accurately allocated in the sale and purchase documents.

This article focuses on environmental auditing undertaken in connection with and before the transfer of commercial and industrial property or facilities. In particular, the areas examined in this article are the need for performing an audit, the purpose of environmental auditing, the decision of who should conduct the audit, the auditing steps and procedures, and finally, the roles of the prospective buyer, the attorney, and the technical environmental consultant in environmental auditing.

The Need for an Audit

CERCLA, 42 U.S.C. § 9601 *et seq.*, and the 1986 amendments thereto, governing the cleanup of hazardous substances, is perhaps the en-

Parthenia Evans is an associate in the Kansas City, Missouri, office of Spencer Fane Britt & Browne.

vironmental law foremost in the minds of lawyers representing sellers and buyers of real property. Superfund does not require that an environmental audit be performed in connection with a real property transaction, but the liability imposed under it and a defense to liability provided by it cause environmental auditing to be necessary in real property transactions.

Section 107(a) of Superfund, 42 U.S.C. § 9607(a), provides that liability for cleanup of hazardous substances can be imposed upon several categories of persons or entities. Among these are the owners and operators of facilities from which releases of hazardous substances have occurred. Courts have held that owners of property upon which hazardous substances have been disposed can be held liable for cleanup of those substances even though that owner did not place the substances on the property. *See New York v. Shore Realty Corp.*, 759 F.2d 1032 (2d Cir. 1985). Similarly, most states have statutes imposing liability for cleanup of hazardous substances on all past and present owners or operators of contaminated property.

An "innocent purchaser" defense to Superfund liability may be established pursuant to section 101(35), 42 U.S.C. § 9601(35), for a person acquiring an interest in land if that person establishes that at the time he acquired the property he did not know or have reason to know that a hazardous substance was disposed of on the property. To show he did not know or have reason to know of hazardous substances, the person must demonstrate that at the time of acquisition he made "all appropriate inquiry into the previous ownership and uses of the property consistent with good commercial or customary practice in an effort to minimize liability." 42 U.S.C. § 9601(35)(B). Environmental auditing is required if a purchaser expects to assert the Superfund innocent purchaser defense in an action requiring cleanup of hazardous substances on the property he acquired. The usefulness of the innocent purchaser defense is, at best, questionable. It appears that in the case of most industrial properties operated prior to 1980, significant likelihood exists that some contamination will be discovered through the audit.

Like Superfund, most state statutes do not require that an environmental audit be performed in connection with property transactions. However, some states, notably New Jersey and Connecticut, have environmental property transfer acts that require environmental investigation and, where needed, environmental cleanup before property can be transferred. Failure to follow these statutes can result in significant penalties or possibly rescission of the transaction.

Though in most cases not required by statute, environmental auditing is essential to establishing the terms of a property transaction and to developing a private allocation of environmental liabilities between the seller and the buyer if hazardous substances are present on the property and the benefits of the sale outweigh the possible extent of cleanup liability for the buyer.

The Purposes of the Audit

The discussion of the necessity for environmental auditing reveals three major purposes auditing serves. First, an environmental audit, when properly conducted, leads to a complete understanding of the environmental condition of the property. Obviously, this affects elements of the transaction such as the purchase price of the property and the terms of the sale governing the condition in which the property is to be delivered to the buyer.

Second, the audit leads to the factual basis for representations and warranties relating to the condition of the property and to marketability of title in the sale documents. Appropriate releases of environmental liabilities, indemnities for environmental liabilities, and contractual allocation of environmental liabilities can be properly made by using the information gathered through an audit.

Third, the audit may lead to successful assertion of the Superfund innocent purchaser defense if the audit was conducted according to the standards in section 101(35), 42 U.S.C. § 9601(35).

Environmental auditing in the context of property acquisitions serves other purposes for the buyer such as the discovery of past environmental compliance problems that could affect future transactions with regulators, past problems involving worker safety and equipment performance that could affect future operations, and the existence of outstanding environmental damage and toxic tort claims that could affect the buyer.

Who Should Conduct the Audit?

Many business and legal considerations affect the decision of whether the seller or the buyer should conduct the environmental audit. The cost of the audit, the objectives of the audit, contract provisions governing choices that each party can make after the results of the audit are available, and even the extent to which the property transfer is in the public eye are among the factors influencing the determination of who should conduct the audit.

The primary purpose of the audit—avoiding liability for the cleanup of hazardous substances—should be the focus in determining who should conduct the audit. Because Superfund offers a defense to liability for cleanup costs only to a buyer who properly subscribes to the scenario in section 101(35), it appears most logical that the prospective buyer conduct and control the audit.

From a practical standpoint as well, it makes sense for the prospective buyer to conduct the environmental audit. To be deemed successful under Superfund and for the potential buyer's internal success, the audit must be objective. As learned in the areas of financial and tax auditing, objectivity is more difficult to obtain if an audit is performed internally. Thus an environmental audit will be more successful if conducted by the prospective buyer as opposed to an audit performed internally by the seller.

If the prospective buyer conducts the audit, the buyer can concentrate on the areas of risk it feels most deserving of analysis. It may be that the risks of environmental liability are not evenly distributed throughout a property. In such a situation, the prospective buyer can tailor the audit activities to account for that variability and perhaps follow with a restructuring of the terms of the sale. If the agreement between the prospective buyer and the seller so provides, the discovery through the audit of risks of environmental liability may trigger an opportunity for the prospective buyer to walk away from the transaction.

For a seller of property, an environmental audit generally offers fewer benefits and greater risk than it offers to a prospective buyer. An audit might benefit a seller with a defense to Superfund liability if a properly conducted audit does not reveal contamination of the property. By establishing that no contamination existed on the property when the seller passed it on, the seller may be able to minimize or erase his liability for cleanup costs if the property is contaminated after he passes title. If contamination is present, an environmental audit could serve to create a baseline of liability for the seller.

Pursuant to Superfund section 122(g), 42 U.S.C. § 9622, a party to a Superfund cleanup action is eligible for a *de minimis* settlement if she establishes that both the amount of the hazardous substances she contributed to the facility and the toxic or hazardous effects of the hazardous substance are minimal in comparison to the other hazardous substances at the facility *or* that she owned the property, did not conduct or permit the generation, transportation, storage, treatment, or disposal of any hazardous substance at the facility, and did not contribute to the release or threat of release of a hazardous substance. The EPA's 1989 Guidance on Landowner Liability under Section 107(a)(1) of CERCLA, *De Minimis* Settlements under Section 122(g)(1)(B) of CERCLA, and Settlements with Prospective Purchasers of Contaminated Property offers some food for thought to potential purchasers of contaminated property.

A seller of property may find it beneficial to conduct an environmental audit because a completed audit might be attractive to a prospective buyer and preclude a later claim of fraud or misrepresentation associated with the sale. However, if the seller conducts an audit and contamination is revealed, the value of the property is essentially reduced automatically. This result is particularly undesirable if a seller independently performs an audit that goes beyond an audit that the prospective buyer would have performed and the seller's audit reveals greater contamination.

The primary disadvantage of a seller conducting an environmental audit is that if contamination is found, the seller must report the contamination to the EPA and/or state agencies. Superfund requires that any person in charge of a facility shall, as soon as he has knowledge of a release or threatened release of a hazardous substance in a reportable quantity, immediately notify the National Response Center. 42 U.S.C. § 9603(a). Similarly, state laws may also require notification. These self-reporting requirements place a seller discovering contamination on his property in the position of drawing the attention of EPA and state agencies and facing immediate cleanup liability.

The self-reporting requirements also apply to disclosure of contamination discovered through an environmental audit performed with the proper involvement of attorneys. Although the attorney-client privilege probably will protect many portions of an audit report from disclosure, the seller has a separate, independent duty under Superfund section 103(a) to report past or present releases of hazardous substances.

It is important to emphasize that the Superfund defense is available only to a buyer who establishes that at the time she acquired the property, she did not know or have reason to know of contamination. 42 U.S.C. § 9601(35)(B). This means that the environmental auditing must take place before the buyer makes the decision to purchase.

For the buyer to demonstrate that she did not know or have reason to know of contamination, she must have exercised due diligence through an environmental audit. Due diligence is defined in Superfund as "all appropriate inquiry into the previous ownership and uses of the property consistent with good commercial or customary practices in an effort to minimize liability." 42 U.S.C. § 9601(35)(B). Superfund directs that any court interpreting this provision must take into account any specialized knowledge or experience of the buyer, the relationship of the purchase price to the value of the property if it were not contaminated, commonly known or reasonably ascertainable information about the property, the obviousness of the presence of contaminants on the property, and the ability to detect contamination by appropriate inspection. *Id.*

The Components of the Audit

To satisfy the above Superfund requirements and internal requirements of the prospective buyer, there are unlimited ways in which an environmental audit can be designed. The following, however, should be viewed as the essential components of an audit and form its basic structure.

First, requests for information regarding any past or present problems involving compliance with environmental laws should be submitted to EPA and the appropriate state and local regulatory agencies. If past environmental compliance problems are revealed, examination of the regulatory files is necessary. Often a facility at which hazardous substances have been used or stored does not have compliance problems but will nonetheless need to be investigated further in the federal, state, and local regulatory files to ascertain the risks of contamination of the property with the hazardous substances.

Second, all files of the facility that could relate to environmental matters should be properly examined to ascertain the nature of and risks of contamination of the property with hazardous substances. Frequently, this investigation goes beyond the scope of what most facilities term "laboratory files" or "environmental files" and includes portions of the corporate correspondence files and the purchasing and accounts receivable files.

Third, a review of federal and state court filings involving the facility should be made to ascertain that environmental problems were not associated with any lawsuits to which the facility was a party.

Fourth, interviews should be undertaken with past and present facility owners, plant managers, and employees or other persons having knowledge of production processes and waste management practices.

Finally, the potential buyer and his attorney and environmental consultant must inspect the facility. As warranted, sampling and analysis of soils and groundwater to determine the extent of contamination must be performed. The extent of sampling and analysis is determined primarily by the paper investigation outlined in items one through four above. It appears that under the Superfund due diligence standard if the paper investigation reveals the likelihood of contamination, the obligation to undertake some physical analysis of the property arises.

Defining Roles

For the purposes and goals of the environmental audit to be fulfilled, the roles of the prospective buyer, the attorney, and the environmental consultant must be clearly defined.

Normally, the purpose of the audit is to investigate the property to ascertain that the Superfund defense is available to the buyer. With this purpose in mind, the audit procedures and results are summarized in a document to be retained by the buyer that demonstrates that the Superfund due diligence standard was satisfied by the investigation. This environmental audit report is an evidentiary document. The environmental audit is a legal exercise and, as such, it should include participation of an attorney who should design the environmental audit and coordinate the performance of the audit.

Often a team approach to the paper investigation is the most expeditious and advantageous. The files kept by a regulatory agency for a particular facility are comprised of materials having legal as well as technical ramifications. Concurrent review by an attorney and an environmental consultant offers a decidedly easier manner in which to effectively identify and evaluate those ramifications. The physical inspection of the facility also should be performed jointly by an attorney and environmental consultant. Certainly interviews of past and present owners, plant managers, and employees will be more worthwhile if done by such a team.

Preparing the audit report should be primarily the responsibility of the attorney. The environmental audit report must be viewed as a potential evidentiary document and should be drafted as such. Since the report is largely comprised of factual data, participation by the environmental consultant is necessary to ascertain accuracy in portions of the report such as the reporting of sampling and analysis for contaminants.

Much of the material that appears in the audit report may not be protected under either the attorney-client privilege or the attorney work product doctrine. The material discovered through an environmental audit is largely factual and would not be privileged. Fortunately, however, the legal opinions and conclusions of the attorney, if communicated to the buyer in confidence, are protected under the attorney-client privilege. Procedures for the retention or destruction of certain draft documents, field notes, and other papers generated through the environmental audit must be established to ensure minimal waiver of the privilege. Work product protection does not extend to an environmental audit conducted for a property transaction because an audit of real property before purchase is not performed in anticipation of litigation.

Although the provisions of most statutes governing environmental cleanup liability do not require that an environmental audit be performed before the purchase of real property, auditing is necessary to form a well-structured allocation of environmental liabilities and for a buyer to claim a Superfund innocent purchaser defense. Successful auditing depends upon the proper delineation of the audit purpose and goals, performance of the audit by the proper parties, carrying out all steps and procedures necessary to the Superfund due diligence standard, and appropriate involvement by the prospective buyer, the attorney, and the technical environmental consultant.

Environmental auditing is now familiar to persons owning and acquiring industrial and commercial facilities and to attorneys, real estate brokers, lenders, and environmental consultants. In perhaps no other facet of a real estate transaction is the proper coordination of an interdisciplinary group of persons so vital to ensuring a transfer of property that truly meets the expectations of the seller and the buyer. As outlined above, auditing must be approached in the proper mind-set and with appropriate diligence if it is to serve the parties to the transfer well.

Complying with Environmental Permits after Issuance

Stephen D. Bundy

For those who advise industry from the inside or outside, obtaining the environmental permit is not just the name of the game; most often, it is the whole game. However, the very thought of the dreary chore of complying with the permit causes us to become very busy on other "pressing" matters.

Historically, the difference in emphasis placed upon acquiring versus complying with permits has been reinforced by agency enforcement activities and the courts. Regulatory agencies have historically concentrated their enforcement resources on parties who lack permits, the alleged illegal dischargers and "midnight dumpers." In those cases, the agencies have frequently sought immediate injunctions, the maximum civil penalties, and the most severe criminal penalties. The courts have also generally viewed these activities as serious matters and imposed severe penalties. Therefore it has been clear for some time that obtaining the applicable permits is absolutely necessary to construct, expand, and operate a facility, and to do so otherwise is exceedingly unwise.

In contrast, violations of outstanding permits have historically been considered to be matters of lesser importance, unless overt damage or threat to public health or the environment is involved. Because a violator has obtained a permit, the general presumption is that the violator is attempting to comply with the law. It is widely recognized that regulatory and permitting systems are complex and that inad-

Stephen Bundy is currently a principal in EnviroGroup Limited, a consulting firm located in Englewood, Colorado.

vertent noncompliance is commonplace. Further, many permit violations are genuinely nonsubstantive. Therefore permit violators were historically not closed down, subject to significant civil penalties, or criminally charged.

This situation has changed, however, to reflect the public perception that enforcement of environmental laws is lax and the reality that the mere issuance of permits does little to implement the intent of laws and regulations. Regulatory agencies are demanding and courts are imposing more expensive civil and, in some cases, even criminal penalties on permit violators. The maximum civil and criminal penalties for permit violations incorporated in new and reauthorized statutes are increasingly severe, and the relative percentage of resources agencies are committing to permit enforcement is on the rise.

Complying with a permit is conceptually simple. You do everything required in the manner and time provided. Conversely, you do not do anything else unless you inform the permitting agency. The adage that it is easier to ask forgiveness than permission does not apply.

If it is so easy to comply, why, then, is noncompliance ever a problem? Often, it is because the compliance program stagnates immediately after the permit is issued and never progresses beyond the stage of good intentions. The historic difference in legal ramifications for failing to acquire versus failing to comply with permits is one major reason for stagnation. Human nature is another.

Psychologically, the difference between permit acquisition and compliance is equivalent to the difference between the mighty hunter and the lowly caretaker. Heroes that we are, we bag the beast, carry it home on our broad shoulders, mount it over the mantle, and gather around the fire to tell tales of the weeks and months of stalking the elusive creature through the regulatory wilderness. Soon, we are off in search of our next great quarry. Who becomes the caretaker that handles all those grisly details, ensures that all the provisions are followed, and promises are kept? Do not bother to ask for volunteers. Intelligent people know a thankless job when they see one.

Understanding the strong tendency for the effort to stall immediately after permit issuance, it is arguable that the specific details of a compliance plan, which must be tailored for each situation, may be less important than moving quickly to capitalize on the momentum of the permitting process. The following series of suggestions comprises a general approach for organizing a compliance team and plan designed to capture that momentum. Each organization and situation differs and, though purposely generic, any particular suggestion may have greater or lesser applicability. The most important point is to begin the compliance process immediately.

Organize According to the Type of Permit

The size and membership of the team, the design of the plan, and the overall level of effort necessary in a compliance program is dictated by the type of permit. Environmental permits vary widely. Some are not permits at all, but simply registrations, either for the purpose of taxes and fees or to allow agencies to monitor certain activities. Others encompass the entire design, construction, and operation of a facility with greatly detailed provisions and limitations.

The fee-type permits normally do not impose provisions beyond notification of changes in the parameter on which the fee is based and therefore only require a relatively minor effort for compliance. Other registrations, such as that required of generators under RCRA, carry some, but still relatively few, rules and reporting requirements. Although the requirements involved with this class of registration may be few in number, failure to follow the provisions can in some cases lead to serious consequences, and compliance should be studiously maintained.

Operating permits come in many forms. Some simply set discharge limits and leave the method of compliance to the discretion of the operator. Many surface water discharge permits have historically been of this type. Others contain provisions that specify control technologies, operating procedures, and, potentially, many other variables. Most operating permits involve some form of testing and/or periodic monitoring and reporting.

Provisions addressing pollution control technologies and operating practices are often integral parts of an operating permit. These provisions can be particularly difficult to implement and enforce internally. While generally potent and cost-effective compliance measures, these activities constitute additional responsibilities for production staff and often require changes in long-standing practices. Resistance to these "extra" and "nonessential" duties can be significant, especially in the absence of a complete understanding or their importance.

Preconstruction permits such as PSD permits require final design and construction of the facility to be consistent with the description in the permit application. Design changes may require permit revision. Therefore, in these cases, the compliance effort must include close monitoring of the final design and construction.

It is not my intent to attempt to discuss, or even allude to, all the types of permits and provisions required by the various federal, state, and local environmental agencies. The point is that different permit types require differing levels of organization and effort. Before the compliance team is assembled and a compliance plan drafted, much thought should be given to the nature of the beast we have bagged.

Pulling Together a Compliance Team

First and foremost, compliance should be a team effort and not left solely up to the operating manager, corporate legal staff, or environmental department to delegate to a junior staff member.

The nucleus of the compliance team already exists. The individuals who prepared the application and negotiated the permit obviously understand the document and underlying issues better than anyone else. The trick is to not allow them to be diverted by other seemingly more important and certainly more interesting matters. Additional team members from the legal and environmental staff and especially line supervisors who are directly responsible for operational procedures and practices should be considered. Resist the temptation to use these new members to conveniently replace the permitting team because you may lose valuable time while new members become familiar with the issues.

Exact team membership and organization will obviously depend upon the company's internal organization, policies, and use of internal and external advisors. There is no magic formula applicable to all situations. Consider everyone whose responsibilities affect or are affected by permit provisions, but keep the group to a workable size.

A key factor in making the team work is peer pressure. Make each team member directly responsible for certain portions of the compliance program and to a specific person for performance. Make sure the team has a leader and a hierarchy. Organize to accomplish the goal, not to hold committee meetings.

Structure Assignments and Schedules According to a Plan

Convene the team immediately after the permit is issued, while the details are still fresh in everyone's minds and a sense of urgency remains. Procrastination erodes the sense of purpose and ensures that most of the key individuals will be too busy with other matters.

The first order of business for the team is to carefully dissect the permit and understand it completely. To those who just spent weeks or months working on the document, this may seem a ridiculous suggestion. However, a large part of any permit is boilerplate and therefore usually noncontroversial. Whereas the facility-specific provisions of the permit may have received microscopic examination, the boilerplate seldom receives similar scrutiny. Detailed examination of the entire document is also important for educating new members of the team and, as most teaching exercises, likely will help the teachers' understanding as much as the students'.

During this process, it is important for the team to identify all general and facility-specific provisions that pertain to operational procedures and restrictions, control equipment and practices, discharge limits, required training, contingency plans, monitoring, reporting, and associated schedules.

Assign logically grouped sections of the permit provisions to the team members. If the team is properly structured, assignments will naturally fall to the correct individuals. If not, reconsider the team makeup.

Have each team member draft a specific plan and schedule for their assigned tasks. Schedule the second team meeting relatively soon (in two or three weeks) and require submission and distribution of the drafts well in advance.

At the second team meeting, the drafts should be thoroughly discussed and finalized together with an integrated schedule. Assign one person to assemble the plans into one combined plan to be distributed in draft form and finalized soon after the meeting. The final plan together with a chart (or spreadsheet, if you wish) containing all compliance activities, responsible individuals, and deadlines should be distributed to each team member.

During the compliance program, all members should receive all correspondence and use the chart to track actual versus scheduled dates for all internal and external deadlines. This allows all members to have an accurate accounting of how well the process is working and what everyone else is doing. Bottlenecks can be identified and steps taken to increase personnel or resources where needed. Periodic meetings to discuss progress and problems are helpful and sometimes necessary. Time and resources should, however, be concentrated on compliance activities.

Place checks and balances in the system. For instance, consider requiring the plant engineer to clear modifications of production or control facilities through the appropriate member of the compliance team (with informational copies distributed to all team members) for the purpose of determining if the changes necessitate a permit revision.

Implement an Effective Audit Program

Audits are an essential ingredient in the compliance program. Inspections by federal or state agencies are for the purpose of judging whether compliance has been accomplished. The role of the audit transcends that of an inspection. A successful audit not only determines the degree to which compliance has been achieved but also evaluates the effectiveness and efficiency of the compliance program and offers recommendations to improve performance. Performing an audit is easy, but producing a useful audit is demanding. Understanding the difference is important.

The choice of auditors, to whom they should report, and how often audits are necessary depends upon the type of permit and the size and type of company organization involved. A basic decision is whether the auditors should be employees or outside contractors. Both can be effective, but, to be so, they must be completely independent. Because it is often difficult to find knowledgeable employees who are not already involved in the compliance program, who can be insulated from company politics, and who have the time to devote, auditing is often performed by contractors.

Another basic decision is whether the audit team should report through the corporate or consulting legal staff. As a legal layman, I will not attempt to lecture the readership on the considerations involved in this decision. However, a competently performed audit will likely contain information many organizations will consider confidential. Treatment of confidential information should be a key consideration in making this decision.

Compliance auditing is a quality control function and consequently should be completely independent of the compliance program. The auditors should report to someone with sufficient authority to implement their recommendations but not the person responsible for the compliance program. Logical candidates to whom the auditors could report include those at a similar level in the company's organization as the person in charge of the compliance program but in a different chain of command or the person to whom the person in charge of the compliance program reports.

The three parts of an audit are the records audit, the interviews, and the physical audit. A major functional problem with most ineffective audit programs is that one part is emphasized at the expense of the others.

The auditors should first carefully review the permit and compliance program records to ensure that all provisions of the permit are being addressed, schedules are being met, and communication within the compliance team and with the appropriate agencies is effective.

The next step is to interview members of the compliance team and operating staff. Appropriate questions about how key permit provisions are being implemented and the workings of the team should indicate if the compliance program is and functions as it appears. Auditors should pay particular attention to the degree of consistency among the answers of various team members to the same questions.

The last step is to inspect the facility to ensure that the physical facts match the paper and verbal descriptions. Those who practice the black art of hydrogeology refer to this activity as "ground truth" or, more often, "whoops." The inspection should be more than cursory and performed by persons familiar with the industrial facilities. By this point, the auditors should have a good idea where to concentrate their efforts.

The most important part of any audit is the tone and distribution of the audit report. Again, it should be transmitted to someone with sufficient authority to resolve any problems with the compliance program. The tone of the report should reflect its purpose: to help the compliance team discover any problems and do their job more effectively. A report prepared in the correct spirit and transmitted through effective channels can be valuable. Otherwise, it can be a great waste of time and money.

Begin Evaluating Requirements for Renewals and Revisions Early On

Most operating permits have a defined life span. Five years was once typical; however, shorter permit periods are becoming more prevalent. At the end of this period of time, the permit must be renewed. In effect, a new permit must be obtained. If the compliance program is running effectively, the renewal process is a logical extension. By this time, the compliance team knows which provisions are practical and effective and which need modification.

Well before the renewal date, the team should review the applicable regulations for changes in the permit system and other standards and situations that will affect the permit or operation. It is also an opportune time to determine if any modifications in the physical facility, operational procedures, or control equipment or practices are advisable or imminent.

Although it may seem that permitting programs are largely dictated by regulation and policy, the fact is that many of the specific conditions of each permit are established by a process of negotiation. The negotiation process theoretically begins as the permittee proposes, in the form of a permit application, how they believe the facility can best operate under the regulatory program. Regulating agencies, however, also often have ideas on these specific conditions due to previous experiences or perceptions. This is especially true in the case of renewals, where precedent has been set for the facility in question. Because the compliance team should, by the time of renewal, understand what is and is not effective in the context of the permitted operation, it is to the team's advantage to give a great deal of careful thought to the preparation of the renewal application and supporting documentation and submit them well in advance of the agency's request for renewal. In this manner, the team may establish their draft as the point of departure for the negotiation process. This is particularly important if the team has found that some of the provisions of the original permit were ineffective or unworkable or if substantial facility modification is envisioned.

Permit revisions should be handled similarly to renewals. Different types of permits specify various changes or events that trigger requirements for revisions. In general, however, a permit revision is necessary any time there is a significant change in production, production equipment, control equipment or practices, or any other factor that affects specified permit provisions, especially discharge levels. Failure to revise a permit when required can be interpreted as operating without a permit, which can expose operators to the most severe civil penalties—in some cases, up to $25,000 per day—and possibly even criminal penalties.

It is important that the compliance team begin its evaluation well in advance of a proposed facility modification. If the system is working properly, the team should have sufficient notice to do so.

In summary, complying with environmental permits is hard work, not the kind of work most of us enjoy. Because this fact is well known, many compliance efforts stall directly after the permit is issued and the key participants move on to other projects. Immediately initiating the compliance effort to capitalize on the momentum of the permitting process and using the permitting team as the nucleus of the compliance team can result in a smooth and potentially successful transition. The use of a team approach, a formal plan, and effective audit oversight provides a cohesive organizational base upon which to operate. When implemented effectively, permit renewals and revisions become logical extensions of the effort.

OSHA's Hazard Communication Standard

Daniel Marcus

The early years of the Reagan Administration represented what is undoubtedly the most antiregulation period we have seen since the beginning of the New Deal, almost half a century earlier. New regulation ground to a halt and the Vice-President's Task Force on Regulatory Relief promised wholesale reexamination and extensive cutbacks of existing regulations. In retrospect, it is remarkable that OSHA's hazard communication standard, 29 C.F.R. § 1910.1200, a major new regulatory burden on every employer in the country, managed to emerge.

The hazard communication standard had its genesis in the 1970s and was spurred by two phenomena. First was OSHA's conclusion that it was taking far too long to promulgate health standards on a substance-by-substance basis and that the agency needed to find ways to regulate effectively through generic, across-the-board standards. At the same time, in the labor movement, the issue of "the worker's right to know" became an emotional one. Unions did not trust employers to make judgments as to workplace hazards—particularly long-term hazards presented by chemicals. They demanded information as to the specific chemical identity of workplace substances so that they could make their own judgments as to what hazards were present.

In response to these concerns and pressures, OSHA issued a proposed standard in the waning days of the Carter Administration. 46

Daniel Marcus is a partner in Wilmer, Cutler & Pickering in Washington, D.C.

Fed. Reg. 4412 (Jan. 16, 1981). This proposed standard emphasized providing workers with specific chemical identity and hazard information, largely through the labeling of containers and pipes in the workplace. The proposal was welcomed by organized labor. The chemical industry, however, was less enthusiastic about the proposal because of its emphasis on chemical identity as well as hazard information; the burden of the labeling approach; and the very specific blueprint for hazard determination.

This controversial lame-duck proposal survived less than a month. Even before a new Secretary of Labor and Assistant Secretary for Occupational Safety and Health were in place, the Reagan Administration withdrew the proposed standard, stating that it wanted to reconsider the question and publish a "more appropriate" proposal. 46 Fed. Reg. 12020 (Feb. 12, 1981).

Despite the promise of a new proposal, many labor and consumer groups assumed that the idea of a federal standard had been given a permanent burial by the new Administration. They turned their efforts toward persuading states and localities to enact worker right-to-know laws.

In the meantime, industry groups such as the Chemical Manufacturers Association found themselves in the unusual position of urging OSHA to go forward to propose and enact a federal standard. The industry was motivated in significant part by a commitment to the public position that it had taken—that an appropriate federal standard was desirable on its own merits. But it also was concerned about the potential proliferation of state and local laws that threatened to create a patchwork of inconsistent regulations and a compliance nightmare. This industry pressure may well have played an important role in persuading a reluctant OMB to permit OSHA to proceed with the hazard communication standard. In any event, OSHA proposed in March 1982, and promulgated in November 1983, a far-reaching hazard communication standard that represents one of the most significant regulatory initiatives of the entire Reagan Administration. 47 Fed. Reg. 12,092 (Mar. 19, 1982) (notice of proposed rule making); 48 Fed. Reg. 53,280 (Nov. 25, 1983) (final rule).

OSHA's authority to promulgate this generic standard on the basis of a generalized finding of "significant risk" has been upheld by the courts. *United Steelworkers v. Auchter*, 763 F.2d 728 (3d Cir. 1985); *Associated Builders & Contractors v. Brock*, 862 F.2d 63 (3d Cir. 1988), *cert. denied* 109 S. Ct. 2062 (1989). As initially promulgated, the standard applied only to employers in the manufacturing sectors. But in 1987, after being directed by the court of appeals to do so (in

United Steelworkers v. Pendergrass, 819 F.2d 1263 (3d Cir. 1987)), OSHA extended the standard to cover all employers. 52 Fed. Reg. 31,852 (Aug. 24, 1987).

The Elements of the Program

The hazard communication standard requires each employer to have a written hazard communication program for each of its workplaces, including a list of all hazardous chemicals in the workplace. Section 1910.1200(e). But as the standard is structured, employers may, in achieving compliance with it, rely substantially on manufacturers and importers of chemicals—the parties in the best position to evaluate chemical hazards and to prepare information on those hazards.

There are four basic elements in the required hazard communication program.

First, each manufacturer or importer of a chemical must determine whether that chemical is hazardous by following various definitions of chemical hazards contained in the OSHA standard. Section 1910.1200(d). For "physical hazards" such as flammability OSHA's definitions follow well-established definitions and tests. For "health hazards," however, the process is more complex. A health hazard is defined as a chemical for which there is "statistically significant evidence based on at least one study conducted in accordance with scientific principles that acute or chronic health effects may occur." Section 1900.1200(c). Carcinogens, reproductive toxins, and neurotoxins are examples of health hazards. While there is generally considerable leeway for manufacturer judgment, the standard (in Appendix A) lays down certain strictures. For example, any chemical that appears on the carcinogen lists of the International Agency for Research on Cancer or the National Toxicology Program or that is regulated by OSHA as a carcinogen must be treated by the manufacturer as a carcinogen regardless of its own evaluation of the evidence.

There are special rules for the determination of the hazards of chemical *mixtures*. Section 1900.1200(d)(5). If the mixture has been tested as a whole, those tests are used to determine the hazards of the mixture. If, as is more often the case, it has not been tested as a whole, the mixture is deemed to present the same *health hazards* as each ingredient comprising 1 percent or more of the mixture— except that the cutoff for carcinogens is 0.1 percent. For *physical hazards*, the manufacturer may use any available scientific data to evaluate the potential hazards of the mixture.

Second, each manufacturer or importer must prepare an MSDS for each hazardous chemical containing comprehensive hazard information on the chemical, including all its hazards, precautions for safe handling and use, and control measures. Section 1910.1200(g). These data sheets must be made available both to employees and to customers, who in turn will make them available to their employees. The MSDS is the central reference document for each chemical, to which the list of hazardous chemicals, container labels, and training programs must relate. Moreover, when Congress—in the wake of the Bhopal disaster—enacted a federal community right-to-know law as title III of SARA, it required that MSDSs prepared for compliance with the OSHA hazard communication standard be made available to state and local emergency planning agencies and local fire departments. 42 U.S.C. § 11,021.

While no specific format for the MSDS is required, OSHA has developed a format (OSHA Form 174) that will serve as a useful model for many manufacturers.

Third, each employer must label containers to alert workers to the identity and significant hazards of the chemical. Section 1900.1200(f). Both in-plant containers and those shipped to customers must be labeled. This requirement is performance-oriented, in the sense that no particular labeling system or wording is prescribed; the requirement of "appropriate hazard warnings" leaves room for some judgment as to which hazards are included on the label and a great deal of judgment as to how that information is displayed. Signs, placards, and other written materials may be used in lieu of labels under certain circumstances.

An excellent guide for preparing precautionary labels—and one that OSHA itself has endorsed—has been published by the American National Standard Institute (ANSI Z129.1-1988). It suggests specific labeling language for particular acute and chronic hazards.

Fourth, each employer must provide his or her workers with education and training in the handling of hazardous chemicals. Section 1910.1200(h). This requirement also is performance-oriented, specifying in general terms the topics to be covered but leaving it to each employer (aided by a cottage industry of consultants that has sprung up) to design the specifics of the training program.

Appendix E to the hazard communication standard, proposed to be added in 1988 (53 Fed. Reg. 28,752), contains useful guidelines for compliance with the standard.

Trade Secret Concerns

A particularly controversial issue in the development of the hazard communication standard was whether and under what circumstances manufacturers and employers can withhold specific chemical identity information as a trade secret. The current trade secret provision in the standard, reflecting modifications in the initial provision after litigation and supplemental rule making, represents an elaborate compromise between traditional trade secret protection afforded to manufacturers and the needs of workers and health care professionals for specific chemical identity information. Under section 1910.1200(i) of the standard, specific chemical identity information may be withheld from an MSDS, provided that (a) the manufacturer can support the trade secret claim (if challenged; there is no presubmission requirement); (b) the MSDS provides full information on the hazardous properties and effects of the chemical; (c) the MSDS indicates that the identity is being withheld; and (d) the identity is made available to health care professionals and to employees and their designated representatives in carefully limited circumstances (medical emergencies, occupational health investigations), and subject to confidentiality agreements.

The Federal/State Preemption Issue

When it promulgated the hazard communication standard, OSHA took an unusual step: It made specific findings about the need for uniformity of regulation and included in the standard a specific statement that pursuant to the provisions of section 18 of the Occupational Safety and Health Act (OSH Act), state regulation in the area covered by the standard was preempted. Section 1910.1200(a); 48 Fed. Reg. at 53,284, 53,322–23; *see also* 52 Fed. Reg. at 31,860 (reemphasizing the importance of preemption at the time OSHA expanded the standard to nonmanufacturing employers).

The OSH Act has an unusual preemption scheme. Under section 18(a), 29 U.S.C. § 667(a), where no federal standard is in effect, a state is free to do whatever it pleases. Under section 18(b), however, where a federal standard has been promulgated with respect to a particular occupational safety or health issue, a state is preempted from regulating with respect to that issue unless it submits to OSHA a state plan for the development and enforcement of such a standard and obtains approval of that plan by OSHA.

Section 18(c) of the Act sets forth the criteria governing OSHA's consideration of state plans. Basically, the state must establish that its standard is "at least as effective" as the federal standard and—if the standard is one applying to products distributed or used in interstate commerce—that the state standard is "required by compelling local conditions" and does not "unduly burden interstate commerce." The state must also give OSHA adequate assurances about its own enforcement capabilities. If the criteria of section 18(c) are met, OSHA must approve the state plan and the state standard then displaces the federal standard in that state. This is sometimes referred to as "reverse preemption."

Before the promulgation of the hazard communication standard, a fairly clear pattern had developed under section 18. The states that wanted to be in the business of regulating occupational safety submitted to OSHA state plans containing standards identical to the federal standards promulgated by OSHA. Moreover, those states looked to OSHA for leadership, tending to wait until OSHA adopted a standard and then mimicking it with one of their own. The "nonplan" states simply left regulation of occupational safety and health to the federal government.

With hazard communication, however, a very different pattern emerged because of the delay in issuing a federal standard and the substantial doubts as to whether such a standard would ever be issued. A number of states and localities enacted laws or regulations before the federal standard was in place. And the hope on the part of OSHA and industry that the states would abandon the field once the OSHA standard was promulgated was not realized. Lawsuits were then filed by industry groups to challenge the two most onerous state statutes, namely, those of New Jersey and Pennsylvania.

Industry's position in those lawsuits was based on a straightforward reading of section 18: Any state law that regulates communication of hazard information in the workplace "relates to" the issue covered by the OSHA hazard communication standard and is therefore preempted. That approach was adopted basically by the District Court in New Jersey, which found New Jersey's Worker and Community Right to Know Act preempted in its entirety in the manufacturing sector (the only sector then covered by the federal standard). *New Jersey Chamber of Commerce v. Hughey*, 600 F. Supp. 606 (D.N.J. 1985). But the Third Circuit Court of Appeals, in both the New Jersey and Pennsylvania cases, applied a different test—one more favorable to state regulation. The Third Circuit basically held that state laws are preempted only to the extent that they are regulating hazard communication *for the purpose* of protecting workers. If the "primary purpose" of the provision of state law is to achieve other goals— such as protecting the environment or assuring public safety—the provision is not preempted even though it concerns workplace communications. *New Jersey Chamber of Commerce v. Hughey*, 774 F.2d

587 (3d Cir. 1985); *Manufacturers Ass'n of Tri-County v. Knepper*, 801 F.2d 130 (3d Cir. 1986), *cert. denied*, 484 U.S. 815 (1987).

Both New Jersey and Pennsylvania were imaginative in claiming purposes other than worker protection for various provisions of their right-to-know laws. And the Third Circuit was quite generous to both states in finding that such other purposes were the primary purposes of various provisions. Thus, for example, in the Pennsylvania case, the Third Circuit found that while the state could not require that MSDSs be made available to workers, it could require manufacturers to send MSDSs to all customers because they could be useful in furnishing information on hazardous chemicals to the state and to fire departments for purposes other than worker protection. *Manufacturers Ass'n of Tri-County*, 801 F.2d at 141. Indeed, industry argued, in urging the Supreme Court to grant *certiorari* in the Pennsylvania case, that the Third Circuit, while professing to follow a "primary purpose" test in reviewing provisions of the state law, had in reality applied an "any other purpose" test that led it to sustain provisions that were basically designed to protect workers on the theory that they also served other purposes.

While the Supreme Court denied *certiorari* in these cases, it recently granted *certiorari* to review a decision by the Seventh Circuit, holding that another OSHA standard preempted a state law regulating the same conduct, even though the state statute was enacted to protect the environment as well as worker safety and health. *National Solid Wastes Management Ass'n v. Killian*, 918 F.2d 671 (7th Cir. 1990), *cert. granted sub nom. Gade v. National Solid Wastes Management Ass'n*, No. 90-1676, 60 U.S.L.W. 3430 (Dec. 16, 1991). The Solicitor General, while stating the government's view that the Seventh Circuit approach was the correct one, nonetheless had urged the court to accept review to resolve the conflict among the circuits. If the Supreme Court affirms the Seventh Circuit in *Gade* and finds "dual purpose" statutes preempted, the constitutionality of the Pennsylvania and New Jersey right-to-know laws is likely to be revisited in future litigation.

A final preemption issue relates to California's now-famous Proposition 65—the Safe Drinking Water and Toxic Enforcement Act–that was adopted in a ballot initiative by the voters of California in 1986. CAL. HEALTH & SAFETY CODE § 23549.6 *et seq*. Proposition 65 requires California to designate those chemicals that are carcinogens or reproductive toxins. It severely limits the discharge of such chemicals into the water supply and also broadly requires that all persons who are exposed to products containing such chemicals be warned of their presence. Regulations adopted by the California Health and Welfare Agency require appropriate warnings to workers.

A pending industry lawsuit claims that Proposition 65 is preempted by OSHA's hazard communication standard insofar as it requires warnings to employees. *Chemical Manufacturers Ass'n v. California Health & Welfare Agency*, No. 88–1615–LKK (E.D. Cal.). The suit was stayed pending consideration by the California Occupational Safety and Health Standards Board of a petition to amend California's state occupational safety and health plan to incorporate Proposition 65. The standards board rejected the petition, but its decision was reversed by the California Court of Appeal. *California Labor Fed'n v. Occupational Safety & Health Standards Bd.*, 221 Cal. App. 3d 1547, 271 Cal. Rptr. 310, *rev. denied*, 1990 CAL. LEXIS 4732 (1990).

The standards board has now incorporated the substance of Proposition 65 into the state plan, which must be submitted to and approved by OSHA. Industry groups may well urge OSHA to disapprove the plan amendment on the ground that it does not meet the section 18(c) criteria—i.e., that it is not required by compelling local conditions and that it unduly burdens interstate commerce. OSHA approval of the state plan amendment would likely moot the preemption argument; disapproval would certainly revive it.

Industry opposed federal regulation in many areas for so long that it has begun only recently to recognize the benefits, in a national economy, of federal preemption and uniformity of regulation. It is often easier to persuade Congress or a federal agency to implement reasonable regulations than it is to accomplish the same result with fifty state legislatures and bureaucracies.

TSCA: The Sleeping Giant Is Stirring

David J. Hayes

From the outset, Congress intended that TSCA include powerful new information-gathering authorities that would broaden the EPA's database and enable it to better regulate new and existing chemical substances. Congress envisioned that TSCA would fill an important gap in the environmental laws. The statute would provide the Agency with the wherewithal to collect toxicity and use information that would in turn provide the basis for new regulatory programs restricting or prohibiting the use of chemical substances in particular applications.

Although it was enacted in 1976, TSCA remained relatively dormant for several years. Within more recent years, however, it has begun to live up to its promise. The EPA is flexing the statute's enormous information-gathering muscle, and environmental practitioners need to take notice.

According to conventional wisdom, TSCA applies to companies that are in the business of manufacturing chemicals. Under the statute, chemical manufacturers can be required to undertake toxicity-testing programs on specified chemicals, provide extensive production and health and safety data related to specified chemicals, and identify any information that indicates that a chemical substance may pose an unreasonable risk to health or the environment. All of this is true. Indeed, legions of environmental specialists in the chemical industry are devoting their careers to tracking and complying with TSCA re-

David Hayes is a partner in the firm of Latham & Watkins in Washington, D.C.

quirements. Many of the statute's information-gathering require-ments, however, also apply to "processors" of chemicals, and some apply to virtually any company that uses chemicals. A closer look at the principal information-gathering tools in the statute highlights TSCA's breadth.

Testing Requirements

Section 4, 15 U.S.C. § 2603, is the centerpiece of TSCA. It authorizes the EPA to require that "manufacturers and processors" of a chemical undertake specified tests upon a determination that insufficient data is available on the substance and the chemical "may present an un-reasonable risk of injury to health or the environment" or, for chem-icals produced in substantial quantities, upon a determination that these chemicals will enter the environment or a substantial number of humans will be exposed to them.

The courts have not been reluctant to grant the EPA broad dis-cretion in making the prerequisite findings for a test rule. As the Third Circuit recently concluded in *Ausimont U.S.A., Inc. v. EPA*, 838 F.2d 93 (3d Cir. 1988), testing can be required by the EPA "when an existing possibility of harm raises reasonable and legitimate cause for concern." The D.C. Circuit adopted a similarly deferential test, finding that testing can be required by the EPA "when there is a more-than-theoretical basis for suspecting that some amount of exposure takes place and that the substance is sufficiently toxic at that level of exposure to present an 'unreasonable risk of injury to health.' " *Chemical Manufacturers Ass'n v. EPA*, 859 F.2d 977 (D.C. Cir. 1988). In a more recent decision in the area, the Fifth Circuit con-firmed that the EPA must do its homework when seeking to justify testing based on exposure, but it provided a road map that the Agency is now following. *Chemical Manufacturers Ass'n v. EPA*, 899 F.2d 344 (5th Cir. 1990).

Traditionally, the EPA has targeted a relatively narrow group of chemicals for test rules. More often than not, the chemicals have been identified through the Agency's new chemical review program. The EPA has requested toxicity data so that it can better evaluate whether a family of chemicals should receive special attention under TSCA.

More recently, however, the EPA has begun to utilize section 4 authority to fulfill data needs that originate outside the TSCA program. At the behest of the EPA Office of Solid Waste (OSW), for example, the Agency implemented a test rule that has generated toxicity and environmental fate data on a number of chemical substances. The OSW requested the data to evaluate the appropriateness of concentration-based hazardous waste regulations for such substances.

Taking the OSW's cue, several other the EPA programs have begun to request the issuance of test rules to fill out data gaps in important regulatory programs. Program offices are excited about the prospects. Always starved for data, they view section 4 as a means to generate data that will help in the development of air toxics standards, effluent guidelines under the Clean Water Act, and other Agency actions. Requests are coming in and, if acted on by the Office of Toxic Substances, the number and scope of section 4 test rules will increase dramatically. Legal challenges to such a liberal application of section 4 test rules also can be expected to increase.

The Immediate Reporting of Substantial Risk

Section 8(e) of TSCA requires that any manufacturer, processor, or distributor in commerce of a chemical substance or mixture who "obtains information which reasonably supports the conclusion that such substance or mixture presents a substantial risk of injury to health or the environment shall immediately inform the administrator of such information unless such person has actual knowledge that the administrator has been adequately informed of such information."

Section 8(e) places a reporting burden on virtually any company that deals with chemicals to immediately inform the EPA when it receives information indicating that a chemical involves substantial risk. Thus information that a chemical has injured certain workers; that it has created serious, unexpected environmental damages; or that it has created adverse results in toxicological tests all may trigger a section 8(e) reporting obligation.

The EPA has not promulgated regulations that describe procedural aspects of section 8(e) compliance or that flesh out the substantive standard set forth in the statute. In 1978, however, it issued a "statement of interpretation and enforcement policy" that described the expected timing of section 8(e) filings (generally, within fifteen working days after obtaining the reportable information) and the types of health effects and environmental effects that may give rise to reporting obligations.

The EPA has followed up this official guidance with several informal question-and-answer documents. In those supplementary materials, the EPA has emphasized that section 8(e) applies to all chemical substances and mixtures (e.g., there is no *de minimis* exemption or research and development exemption) and that the provision applies to all persons who "know of" substantial risk information.

Aggressive Agency enforcement of section 8(e) has triggered a large number of reports. Since the effective date of TSCA, more than one thousand initial section 8(e) reports have been received by the EPA and have been given priority evaluation and follow-up attention. In addition, companies have voluntarily submitted more than 650 "for your information" reports. Companies that do not submit information to the EPA that might reasonably support a conclusion that a chemical poses a substantial risk do so at their own risk. The EPA has not hesitated to impose large fines when, in connection with a TSCA audit, it identifies section 8(e)-type information that was not reported to the Agency.

The importance of section 8(e) has been reconfirmed recently through the EPA's implementation of a one-time compliance audit program (CAP). Under this special program, the EPA invited companies to voluntarily agree to audit their files and to file section 8(e) reports in accordance with a stipulated penalty schedule capped at a total potential payment of $1 million.

The CAP program has been an eye-opener, both for the EPA and for the more than 120 companies that have participated. Many of the companies participating in the program have learned, firsthand, how difficult it can be to determine whether information is reportable under section 8(e)'s less-than-lucid reporting criteria. Indeed, the EPA has been forced to delay completion of the audit program pending the release of guidance concerning the types of environmental effects information that may trigger reporting requirements under section 8(e).

Although the CAP program will not be completed until after this article has been written, the program expects to generate many millions of dollars in stipulated payments and perhaps tens of millions of dollars. The dollars testify more eloquently than words to the importance of section 8(e). The enforcement actions against nonparticipants that are expected to follow completion of the program will only underscore this point further.

Disclosure of Manufacturing and Processing Information

Section 8(a) provides the EPA with broad authority to promulgate rules that require manufacturers and processors to maintain records and submit a wide variety of information about specific chemicals including, for example, the amount of the chemical that is manufactured and processed, a description of individual exposure, and a description of expected uses of the chemical.

Although section 8(a) always has empowered the EPA to obtain a storehouse of information about any chemical, the Agency's use of section 8(a) has been sporadic and limited. This is about to change. The EPA recently issued a final rule under section 8(a) that sets forth a "standard approach to gathering information on the manufacturing, importation, and processing of chemicals and substances and mixtures under section 8(a) of TSCA." This model rule, entitled the comprehensive assessment information rule—the so-called CAIR rule—established uniform reporting and record-keeping requirements and a list of questions from which specific information requirements will be assembled on a substance-by-substance basis.

The CAIR rule is equipped with information-gathering firepower. It contains a one-hundred-page standardized reporting form that is divided into ten sections, each containing a list of specific questions. The form covers plant site information; chemical identification; production, processing, and importation volumes; physical/chemical properties; environmental fate data; economic and financial information; manufacturing and processing; waste generation and management; and worker exposure and environmental release data. Because of the detailed nature of CAIR information requests, the EPA predicts that it will take well over two hundred hours to respond to a CAIR request for information pertaining to a specific chemical. The chemical industry contends that it will take much more time and effort than that.

The EPA intends to utilize the CAIR rule to "obtain information needed by the EPA and other federal agencies to support the assessment of regulation of chemical substances and mixtures." This broad statement of purpose underscores the breadth of section 8(a)'s information-gathering capabilities. Indeed, the EPA has adopted an "outreach" approach, under which section 8(a) is utilized as a means of obtaining data that may be useful to a number of diverse EPA program activities. In 1988, for example, the EPA promulgated a rule under section 8(a) that required manufacturers and importers of eighteen chemical substances to submit production and exposure information on those substances. The data are being used by the EPA's Office of Air Quality Planning and Standards to determine the need for further assessment of those chemicals as toxic air pollutants under the Clean Air Act.

The first CAIR rule continues this trend. It has collected information on nineteen chemicals for use by the National Institute for Occupational Safety and Health and the EPA's Office of Air and Radiation.

The demand for more production and use data from a variety of regulatory sources undoubtedly will grow. And, now that the EPA has promulgated a uniform format for obtaining such information through the CAIR rule, chemical manufacturers and processors need to sharpen their pencils and expand their TSCA staffs.

Health and Safety Studies

Section 8(d) of TSCA authorizes the EPA to require any person who "manufactures, processes, or distributes in commerce" any specified chemical or mixture to submit to the EPA "health and safety studies (A) conducted or initiated by or for such person with respect to such substance or mixture at any time, (B) known to such person, or (C) reasonably ascertainable by such person . . ." In regulations and guidance documents issued under the rule, the EPA has expansively defined health and safety studies that must be reported under section 8(d). Examples include assessments of human and environmental exposure, including workplace exposures and impacts of a particular chemical substance or mixture on the environment, and chemical monitoring data, especially when such data have been aggregated and analyzed to measure the exposure of humans or the environment to a chemical substance or mixture.

Under these vague guidelines, a significant amount of confusion has developed concerning the types of documents that may include enough analysis of health or environmental effects to qualify as health and safety studies under section 8(d). The EPA has suggested, for example, that groundwater studies may qualify for reporting under section 8(d) because they may provide environmental fate information on particular chemicals. Similarly, industrial hygiene monitoring data, if correlated with specific employees, may qualify as a health and safety study in the EPA's eyes.

At the same time that the EPA is pressing an expansive view of reportable health and safety studies, it is increasing the number of chemicals that are covered by section 8(d) reporting requirements at the behest of a number of program offices. To illustrate, the EPA has promulgated a section 8(d) rule that requires the submission of health and safety data on thirty-three chemicals for use by the OSW in determining appropriate treatment standards for wastes subject to land disposal restrictions under the 1984 RCRA amendments.

The EPA has undertaken other "outreach" efforts under the authority of section 8(d). For example, it has called in health and safety studies pertaining to 102 chemical substances to support activities in the EPA's Offices of Water and Solid Waste and the Consumer Product Safety Commission. The Office of Water is using the data to help develop drinking water regulations under the Safe Drinking Water Act and health advisories and ambient water quality criteria under the Clean Water Act. The Office of Solid Waste is using the data to develop documents and notices for the 1984 RCRA amendments listing program. The Consumer Product Safety Commission is using the data to evaluate the potential consumer health risks of the chemical substances.

Even more recently, the EPA finalized a rule that calls for health and safety studies relating to several chemicals that are used as inert ingredients in pesticides. Because the rule targeted large-volume bulk chemicals, and because the EPA has adopted such a vague, expansive definition of health and safety studies that must be submitted, the test rule has generated literally tons of data that the Agency is in the process of sorting through.

Record-Keeping Requirements

Section 8(c) is yet another arrow in TSCA's information-gathering quiver. It requires any person who manufactures, processes or distributes in commerce any chemical substance or mixture to "maintain records of significant adverse reactions to health or the environment . . . alleged to have been caused by the substance or mixture." The statute explains that "records required to be maintained under this subsection shall include records of consumer allegations of personal injury or harm to health, reports of occupational disease or injury, and reports or complaints of injury to the environment submitted to the manufacturer, processor, distributor or in commerce from any source."

Unlike TSCA's other data-collecting provisions, section 8(c) does not include an affirmative obligation that a company bring allegations of injury to the attention of the EPA; it requires only that the company maintain a central file that includes such allegations, regardless of their apparent merit. If significant questions about a particular chemical arise, however, the EPA can request to review companies' section 8(c) files to determine whether there has been a pattern of complaints about the chemical. Companies that do not have such files will have some explaining to do.

The EPA's Expansive Approach to Defining the Universe of Companies Covered by the Act

As noted above, many of TSCA's information-gathering tools apply, by their terms, to manufacturers and processors of chemicals (e.g., sections 4, 8(a) and 8(d)), and others extend to persons who distribute chemicals or mixtures of chemicals "in commerce" (e.g., sections 8(c) and 8(e)).

The EPA has interpreted these categories covered by the statute as expansively as it has interpreted the substantive provisions of the statute itself. The Agency's expansive view of the TSCA's coverage has created a troublesome degree of ambiguity, but one clear truth has emerged from the confusion: TSCA covers much more than the traditional chemical industry. Companies in many lines of business are subject to TSCA's information-gathering rules, and many of them do not know it.

To illustrate, TSCA defines a chemical manufacturer as any person who imports a chemical substance or mixture. Thus, if a company imports a substance for virtually *any* use, it must comply with any section 4 test rule applicable to that chemical and to any section 8(a) and 8(d) reporting requirements. This poses a trap for the unwary. Businesses that import chemicals on a spot basis or that import products that are accompanied by chemicals rarely consider themselves subject to TSCA. Nonetheless, they may qualify as manufacturers that must satisfy TSCA's many reporting requirements.

Applying reporting requirements to processors of chemicals also substantially broadens the TSCA net. The EPA defines "processing" liberally. The Agency has argued that virtually any handling of a chemical in "preparation" of sale or use may qualify as processing activity, including simple repackaging of a chemical or diluting or mixing chemical substances. Similarly, the Agency has asserted that the incorporation of chemical substances into final products constitutes "processing" activities.

At the margin, the EPA's expansive approach to defining processors appears to encompass the traditional use of chemicals, and it threatens to draw in large numbers of companies that neither manufacture nor process chemicals in the traditional sense but simply use chemicals as part of a nonchemical manufacturing process (e.g., as industrial solvents). This trend has prompted the American Electronics Association and representatives of other chemical users to seek clarification—and a narrowing—of overly expansive notions of "processing." To date, the EPA has sidestepped these questions. And, until the definition of processor is clarified, many companies may be at risk of unknowingly violating—in the EPA's view at least—a number of reporting requirements including, in particular, section 8(a) and section 8(d) requirements to submit production and use information and health and safety studies on specified chemicals.

A Final Note

A review of TSCA's information-gathering authority would not be complete without a final note about the statute's correlative authority to use the information gathered under the statute to restrict the manufacture or use of specific chemical substances or even to ban such substances. The Agency has two primary means of moving from an information-gathering to an action-forcing mode.

First, the EPA can restrict the manufacture and use of "new" chemical substances before they reach the marketplace under the authority of section 5(e). Second, the Agency can use the authority of section 6 to restrict or ban the manufacture or use of current products upon a showing that the substance "presents or will present an unreasonable risk of injury to health or the environment."

Recently, the Fifth Circuit Court of Appeals issued a decision that confirmed that the EPA cannot take shortcuts when it seeks to restrict the manufacture or use of a specific chemical substance under section 6. In the case of *Corrosion Proof Fittings v. EPA*, 1991 U.S. App. LEXIS 24,922 (5th Cir. 1991), the court struck down a portion of the EPA's rule banning the manufacture of certain asbestos products. In doing so, the court took the EPA to task for not fully evaluating the impact of the ban, including the potential risks associated with substitute products.

The *Corrosion Proof* decision has triggered a cry from some quarters to amend TSCA to lower the threshold for restricting or banning chemical substances under TSCA. If the debate on this issue is joined, it promises to be a bruising one. Regardless of the outcome, however, any concerns about implementing section 6 should not be misread as signaling that TSCA is a toothless tiger. The testing requirements, new chemical review process, and information-gathering authorities all provide the EPA with powerful regulatory weapons.

In conclusion, TSCA's use as an information-gathering tool is still in its infancy, but the future is clear. As the EPA becomes more interested in chemical production, use, exposure, and toxicity data for applications that cut across environmental media, it is finding that TSCA provides the authority it needs to obtain such data. The strong data-gathering authority in the statute, when combined with one of the EPA's most aggressive enforcement units, yields a combination that makes TSCA a statute with which to be reckoned.

Regulation by Information through EPCRA

Kevin J. Finto

In response to releases of chemicals at Bhopal, India, in 1984 and Institute, West Virginia, in 1985, Congress enacted EPCRA. EPCRA was enacted as title III of SARA. EPCRA requires owners and operators of facilities that store, use, or release certain chemicals in more than certain amounts to report information about those chemicals, their amounts, and their locations. It also requires owners or operators to report releases into the environment of certain amounts of these chemicals from accidental spills or normal operation. Similar to the hazardous communication standard program under OSHA, which requires employers to inform workers about chemical exposure in the workplace, EPCRA does not limit the use or release of chemicals; it only requires owners or operators to inform the public about the potential for releases. In effect, it is regulation by information. Public interest groups have published lists such as the "Toxic 500" based on information submitted under EPCRA. Thus EPCRA has become the government's greatest tool for gathering and disseminating information relating to potential or actual releases of chemicals into the environment. The following discussion explains how the EPCRA scheme works in theory and in practice.

The statute has two distinct parts, namely, an emergency planning mechanism and community right-to-know provisions. Both parts involve some information gathering and dissemination. In addition to information processing, the emergency planning provisions require

Kevin Finto is an associate in the Richmond, Virginia, office of Hunton & Williams.

each state to set up an emergency planning commission, which in turn sets up emergency planning districts and appoints a local emergency planning committee for each district. These commissions and committees must include representatives from various interest groups, including local law enforcement, fire protection, emergency response units, the media, the regulated community, and environmentalists. EPCRA § 301, 42 U.S.C. § 11,001. Using the information provided by regulated facilities, the states and local committees are to prepare emergency plans that indicate the location of the facilities covered by EPCRA; identify emergency procedures; designate community emergency coordinators; develop procedures to notify the public of an emergency; determine if a release occurs; identify an affected area's population; list emergency equipment, facilities, and personnel available; develop evacuation plans; and set out training and exercise plans.

Gathering and Disseminating Information

EPCRA has four distinct information-gathering and dissemination programs: emergency planning and notification, MSDS submission, emergency and hazardous chemical inventory reporting, and toxic chemical release reports. A description of each of these types of reporting requirements follows.

Emergency Planning and Notification Reporting

Under the emergency planning and notification provisions, the EPA established a list of "extremely hazardous substances" that was initially composed of substances listed in the Appendix of the EPA's chemical emergency preparation planning interim guidance document. The EPA may modify this list from time to time based on the reactivity, volatility, dispersability, combustibility, and flammability of a substance, as well as its toxicity, which is defined to include any long-term and short-term health effects resulting from short-term exposure. Section 302(a)(4). The present list of over 420 extremely hazardous substances is set out in Appendix A to 40 C.F.R. Part 355. The EPA has modified this list in response to comments on its original rule making to implement this section and based on petitions from the regulated community. *See, e.g.,* 55 Fed. Reg. 5544 (Feb. 15, 1990).

For each of these extremely hazardous substances, the EPA has developed a threshold planning quantity (TPQ). The TPQ is largely dependent on the physical characteristics of the material, i.e., whether it is a solid, a liquid, or a gas and whether it can become airborne. The TPQs are also set out in 40 C.F.R. Part 355, Appendix A. A set of complex rules provides techniques for calculating the amount of extremely hazardous substances that are present in mixtures, solutions, and molten materials. 40 C.F.R. § 355.30(e). For example, the actual quantity of an extremely hazardous substance in a solution or mixture is calculated by multiplying the concentration of the extremely hazardous substance by the weight or volume of the entire solution or mixture. In addition, the amount of an extremely hazardous substance in molten form is multiplied by 0.3. For powdered substances, the particle size is a factor in determining its TPQ. A facility that stores or uses more than one TPQ must notify the state emergency response commission that it is subject to the EPCRA emergency planning and notification requirements, identify a facility representative, and, if requested, supply information for emergency planning.

Section 304 of EPCRA requires a facility to notify local community organizations of off-site spills or any releases of a "reportable quantity" of an extremely hazardous substance or a hazardous substance as defined in CERCLA, 42 U.S.C. § 9601 *et seq.*, from a facility where hazardous chemicals (as defined under OSHA) are produced, used, or stored. The reportable quantities for extremely hazardous substances are set out in 40 C.F.R. Part 355, Appendix A. The list of hazardous substances and their reportable quantities under CERCLA are set out at 40 C.F.R. § 302.4. Some discrepancies occur between the substances on the list of extremely hazardous substances and those on the list of hazardous substances. Moreover, the reportable quantity of the same substance may differ between lists. It should be noted that the EPCRA emergency reporting requirements are *in addition to* CERCLA reporting requirements. Emergency notification must include the chemical's common name, the lists on which it appears, the quantity released, the time and duration of the release, the media into which the release occurred, any acute or chronic health risks presented by the release, precautions to be taken, and the persons to be contacted for further information. These provisions do not apply to on-site releases, federally permitted releases, continuous releases, and releases exempt under CERCLA section 101(22) (e.g., engine exhaust from mobile sources, releases of special nuclear material, and the normal application of fertilizer).

MSDSs

The second distinct information-gathering and dissemination program under EPCRA involves MSDSs. The community right-to-know provisions provide that each owner or operator of a facility required to prepare or have available MSDSs under OSHA's hazardous communication standard (e.g., facilities that use, produce, or import "hazardous chemicals") must submit the MSDSs or must submit a list of the hazardous chemicals, their chemical or common names, and their hazardous components to the state emergency planning commission, the local emergency planning committee, and the local fire department. Since the OSHA program now covers both manufacturing and nonmanufacturing sectors of all industries where workers are exposed to hazardous chemicals (52 Fed. Reg. 31,852 (Aug. 24, 1987)), the coverage of the community right-to-know program is very broad. Moreover, while EPCRA exempts certain foods, drugs, cosmetics, solid materials, household items, research-related substances, and retail pesticides and fertilizers from the definition of "hazardous chemicals," OSHA defines this term very broadly to include "any chemical which is a physical hazard or health hazard." 29 C.F.R. § 1910.1200 (c). Thus this definition is much broader than "hazardous substance" under CERCLA or "extremely hazardous substance" under EPCRA. Nevertheless, the EPA has set out threshold quantities for MSDS reporting, 40 C.F.R. § 370.20(b), which reduces the regulatory burden on industry.

Under OSHA standards that have been adopted by the EPA, an MSDS must contain the chemical and common names of the chemical, the chemical's physical and chemical characteristics, its physical and health hazards, its routes of exposure, precautions and emergency response procedures, exposure limits, and possible carcinogenic effects. The local emergency planning committee may require submission of MSDSs where the facility submits only a list. States and localities have indicated in many instances that they wish to receive only a list of chemicals and not the MSDSs because certain communities would have to rent warehouse space to accommodate storage of the MSDSs. Moreover, such a volume of information would be useless in an emergency. Still, any person may request an MSDS through the local committee, and the local committee must then obtain the MSDS from the facility. The MSDSs must be updated within three months of the discovery of relevant new information. EPCRA allows withholding of information as trade secrets.

Annual Inventory Reporting

The third distinct information-gathering and dissemination program under EPCRA involves annual inventory reporting. The community right-to-know provisions require each facility subject to the OSHA hazard communication standard to provide annual inventory reports of chemical substances by listing the types, amounts, and locations of hazardous chemicals at the facility. These inventory forms are either "tier I" or "tier II" forms. Rules and forms for the reporting requirements are provided in 40 C.F.R. Part 370. The tier I forms group chemicals according to five categories of hazards: fire hazards, sudden release of pressure hazards, reactivity hazards, immediate health hazards, and delayed health hazards. The tier I forms require the facility to identify the maximum amount of hazardous chemicals in each of the above listed categories present at the facility at any time during the previous calendar year, the daily averages of any hazardous chemicals in each category present at the facility at any time during the previous calendar year, and the general location of these chemicals.

Local emergency planning commissions may require tier II information, which concerns specific chemicals as opposed to chemical categories. The public can request tier II information through the state planning commission or local emergency planning committee. The commission or committee must provide this information if it is in its possession. The commission or committee must obtain tier II information if a person requests it and it involves a chemical present in amounts over ten thousand pounds at any time at the facility. Tier II information includes a chemical's common name as provided on its MSDS, the estimated maximum amount maintained at the facility in the past year, the estimate of the average daily amount over the past year, the manner of its storage, its specific location, and whether the owner opts to withhold the exact location from the public. Based on this information, the local emergency planning committee may decide to conduct an on-site inspection.

Toxic Release Reporting

Finally, the community right-to-know provision of EPCRA requires toxic chemical release reporting. These are annual reports of releases of toxic chemicals into the environment as a result of normal operations, i.e., they do not include spills. This is clearly the most publicized and controversial aspect of the EPCRA program. Congress set out the first list of 311 toxic chemicals in Committee Print Number 99-169 of the Senate Committee on Environment and Public Works, titled Toxic Chemicals Subject to Section 313 of the Emergency Planning and Community Right-to-Know Act of 1986. The EPA granted petitions to list and delist toxic chemicals based on criteria set out in the statute. *See, e.g.*, 54 Fed. Reg. 25,850 (June 20, 1989) (delisting sodium sulfate).

The EPA has devised rules and forms for toxic chemical release reporting. 40 C.F.R. § 372.85; *see* 53 Fed. Reg. 4500 (Feb. 16, 1988); *see also* EPA, Toxic Chemical Release Inventory Reporting Package for 1990. EPA 560/4–91–001 (revised Jan. 1991). These forms require general information about the plant, its location, locations of off-site waste treatment or disposal (e.g. POTWs and landfills), each chemical, its use, and its form of release, and waste treatment and efficiency. The Pollution Prevention Act of 1990 requires the EPA to collect information regarding recycling and waste minimization on these forms. These requirements impose a severe burden on many facilities because the only way to calculate releases in many circumstances is to perform complex mass-balance calculations using assumptions and estimates of treatment efficiencies. *See* EPA, Estimating Release and Waste Treatment Efficiencies for the Toxic Chemical Release Inventory Form, EPA 560/4-88-002 (Dec. 1987).

Enforcement Efforts

General Enforcement Parameters

EPCRA section 325 authorizes the EPA to order a facility to comply with the various reporting, notifying, and planning requirements. These orders are enforceable in federal district court. It also authorizes the assessment of administrative penalties for violation of EPCRA, which are also enforceable in federal district court. EPCRA section 326 also allows citizen suits against a facility for failure to comply with certain provisions of EPCRA or against the EPA, a state governor, or a state emergency response commission—but not a local committee—for failure to comply with requirements of EPCRA. Before instituting a suit, however, a citizen must provide a sixty-day notice to the EPA, the state, and the alleged violator. A citizen suit is barred against a facility where the EPA has commenced and is diligently prosecuting an administrative or civil action to enforce the requirement. Thus, while other environmental statutes have been held to require commencement and diligent prosecution of a judicial action (i.e., in a court) to bar a citizen suit, EPCRA only requires an administrative action. In addition, citizens must satisfy other jurisdictional requirements. Citizen suits under EPCRA have been dismissed for lack of standing. *See, e.g.*, *McCormick v. Anschutz Mining Corp.*, 29 E.R.C. 1707 (E.D. Mo. 1989) (plaintiff failed to show injury from discharge of pollutants from mine; possibility of future injury is not sufficient to establish standing).

The EPA has issued a guidance document to cover enforcement of the toxic chemical lease reporting requirements entitled Compliance Monitoring Strategy for Section 313 of the Emergency Planning and Community Right-to-Know Act (June 15, 1988). According to that document, the EPA will compare its various data bases on regulated facilities with the list of facilities submitting the release reporting forms to identify facilities that fail to report their releases. These nonreporting facilities will be subject to fines and inspections. Reporting facilities that make errors or that are delinquent will be subject to slight fines but not inspections.

The Problems with Enforcement

Effective enforcement of EPCRA has been largely hampered by a lack of resources. Using computerized data bases, the EPA has identified violators and enforced section 313 regarding the toxic chemical release reporting with persistence by bringing enforcement actions against the regulated facilities. Nevertheless, the states are responsible for enforcing sections 301 through 312, and only about half of the local planning districts have complied with the emergency planning requirements. On a national basis, only 30 to 40 percent of the regulated facilities have filed the necessary forms with their state emergency planning committee. Regulators point out that because more populated areas have more resources to devote to the program, the percentage of population in districts in compliance is much greater than the percentage of districts that have complied.

Government regulators have made a strong effort to talk with trade associations and civic groups to inform the regulated community and the public about the EPCRA program. Nevertheless, because the Act affects such a large range of diverse industries, these efforts have met with mixed results. As expected, large companies and wealthy communities with resources to comply with and implement the program effectively have done so. Small communities and small businesses have suffered adverse impacts in terms of regulatory burden. This is especially true with respect to tier III reporting where chemical-specific information must be reported in great detail. Rural emergency planning districts have also had difficulty justifying the expense related to the community right-to-know program when other services and programs such as education, transportation, and basic health needs place demands on scarce resources.

While enforcement lags, there is a more fundamental question regarding the program's effectiveness in dealing with emergencies. Local fire departments and emergency planning committees express concern over the need for storage space to store MSDSs and other information submitted as part of the program. They invoke visions of warehouses filled with paper that cannot be effectively used in an emergency. Some communities have made efforts to computerize relevant information so it can be accessed quickly in an emergency. Computer software vendors have offered "package deals" to develop programs and data bases for emergency planning and release reporting for use by both the regulated facility and the local planning district, which both share the expense for the computerization.

Moreover, the EPCRA information falls short in allowing the public to assess the risks related to potential and actual releases. Probably the most publicized aspect of EPCRA is the toxic chemical release reporting requirements. Companies that report their normal and lawful releases of chemicals have suffered adverse public relations. For example, public interest groups have published lists, such as the NWF's "Toxic 500," which are often successful in catching the public's attention but may not give an accurate picture of the risks the public faces.

In any event, EPCRA has had the effect of raising the public's awareness of the discharge of toxic pollutants into the environment. Congress, the EPA, the states, and the regulated community could improve EPCRA and its implementation in several ways to put the information in perspective. For example, the toxic chemical release reporting forms require the use of pounds per year as a unit of measurement while discharges of toxic chemicals in the pound-per-year range might initially give cause for concern until placed in the context of environmental standards. For example, a wastewater discharge of 100,000 gallons per day containing a discharge of a toxic chemical at a concentration of 3.1 parts per billion—a concentration in line with the stringent EPA ambient water quality criteria—is the equivalent of a pound per year. To be truly meaningful, the information regarding releases should be placed in perspective by supplying the public with an assessment of the risk presented by the release or potential release. The challenge will be to devise a risk assessment technique that is simple to use and understand and that is cost-effective.

Protecting Trade Secrets in the Information Age

Beverly Horn Nelson

Recent developments in the laws affecting trade secrecy require an astute practitioner to juggle seemingly conflicting and confusing statutes and regulations to advise clients how best to protect their trade secrets. Only a small percentage of law firms and corporations can afford to have an expert on hand to provide this kind of advice, so more and more generalists are being called upon to untangle these requirements. The following is a generalist's guide to some of the issues involved in the protection of trade secrets submitted with environmental data to state and federal agencies.

The main consideration in protecting a business's prize secrets is that companies, whether small businesses or large corporations, must first decide which trade secrets are worth protecting and then must act aggressively to protect those secrets. Companies must understand that it is costly to maintain and protect trade secrets. With the great amount of information being reported to the government today, most of it without the benefit of trade secret protection, competitors can often cross-reference between different filings made to different agencies and can deduce trade secret information by doing so. Therefore companies must be able to identify their trade secrets and decide which ones are worth the time and expense of protection. This requires a thorough knowledge of all of the company's information that must be reported to state or federal agencies, the provisions allowing claims of trade secrecy, and the procedures for

Beverly Horn Nelson is a staff attorney for Region I of the Environmental Protection Agency in Boston, Massachusetts.

making and sustaining such claims. Finally, companies must devise in-house procedures to fully protect any trade secrets claimed with the government, and these procedures must be carefully followed.

Defining and Identifying Trade Secrets

One of the problems that many companies encounter in attempting to define their trade secrets is that there is no one single, perfect definition of trade secrets. Trade secrets were originally defined in the common law and have come to be defined in both state and federal case law and statutes. A general consensus has emerged, however, that trade secrets are a property right to which due process considerations apply.

The first *Restatement of Torts*, § 757, comment b, formulated by the American Law Institute in 1939, is the definition most often quoted and has been used in many subsequent cases, statutes, and regulations. This definition provides, in pertinent part:

> A trade secret may consist of any formula, pattern, device or compilation of information which is used in one's business, and which gives him an opportunity to obtain an advantage over competitors who do not know or use it.

This definition later sets forth six major factors to consider in defining a trade secret:

> (1) the extent to which the information is known outside of his business; (2) the extent to which it is known by employees and others involved in his business; (3) the extent of measures taken by him to guard the secrecy of the information; (4) the value of the information to him and to his competitors; (5) the amount of effort or money expended by him in developing the information; (6) the ease or difficulty with which the information could be properly acquired or duplicated by others.

Some version of those six factors is common to most trade secrets definitions.

The definition of trade secrecy in most of the statutes administered by the EPA refers to 18 U.S.C. § 1905, the Federal Trade Secrets Act. This provision prohibits federal employees from disclosing trade secrets and confidential business information unless authorized to do so by another statute. The EPA construes these provisions to provide protection to trade secrets as defined in the EPA's trade secret and confidential business regulations at 40 C.F.R. Part 2, Subpart B, protection basically similar to that provided under the *Restatement* definition. The *Restatement* definition is the one included in OSHA's hazard communication standard. SARA relied on the OSHA definition, although the statutory definition in SARA contains additional language regarding reverse engineering, unlike all other EPA statutes. This language was likely added as a result of litigation surrounding the first trade secret definition included in the OSHA hazard communication standard.

OSHA originally used the first sentence of the *Restatement* definition, quoted above, to identify information that businesses could claim as a trade secret on the MSDS required by the hazard communication standard to be provided to all employees. OSHA, however, added a parenthetical phrase to this definition to clarify that the only information that could be claimed as a trade secret on the MSDS was chemical identity, not process or formula information. This parenthetical phrase was added into the *Restatement* definition to provide, "[a] trade secret may consist of any formula, pattern, device or compilation of information (including chemical name or other unique chemical identifier) . . ." During subsequent litigation, the Third Circuit held, in *United Steelworkers of America v. Auchter,* 763 F.2d 728 (3d Cir. 1985), that the addition of the parenthetical phrase changed the definition of trade secrecy such that chemical identities discoverable by reverse engineering could be protected as trade secrets. This, the court said, was not permissible in that the resulting definition afforded broader trade secrecy protection than that afforded under state law. In response to the court's decree, OSHA deleted the parenthetical phrase and retained the *Restatement* definition in its original form.

The definition of trade secrecy set forth in the SARA statute specifically mentions that chemical identities readily discoverable by reverse engineering cannot be treated as trade secrets, unlike most other statutes and regulations. This definition is set forth in section 322 of SARA title III (EPCRA), as well as in the amendments to section 104(e) of CERCLA. Specifically including this language does not alter the definition of trade secrecy, since most definitions implicitly exclude from trade secrecy items that can be reverse engineered. The sixth factor mentioned in the *Restatement* definition, "the ease or difficulty with which the information could be properly acquired or duplicated by others," would result in such an exclusion. Thus the scope of the trade secrecy definition in SARA is similar to that set out in the *Restatement*. The *Restatement* definition is specifically cited as the basis for the trade secrecy definition in the trade secrecy regulations under EPCRA. 40 C.F.R. Part 350.

Although these varying definitions may seem confusing, most of the principles of trade secrecy protection are similar, and it is unlikely that information considered to be a trade secret under one statute would not also be treated the same under another statute. Varying definitions do provide a clue, however, as to the kinds of information the government agency will seek as supporting evidence for a claim under EPCRA, and clients must be ready to provide evidence that the trade secret chemical identity cannot be readily discovered through reverse engineering.

Attorneys must be careful not to confuse the scope of the definition of trade secrecy with the scope of what may be claimed as trade secret under a particular statute. For instance, although EPCRA contains a trade secret definition that comports with that set out in the *Restatement of Torts*, only specific chemical identity may be claimed as a trade secret in the reports submitted to the EPA under EPCRA. Other limitations on items for which trade secret protection is available are set forth in section 104(e)(7)(A) of CERCLA. In this provision, trade secret protection is not allowed for health hazard data and other specific data. Also, the Clean Air Act and the Clean Water Act disallow trade secret protection for emission and effluent data respectively, notwithstanding that the data may fall within the definition of trade secrecy. Similar limitations are present in other federal statutes and in the right-to-know statutes of some state jurisdictions.

For the purpose of submitting data to federal agencies, lawyers should consult the federal statute and regulations under which the information is submitted. State law will apply only to that information submitted to a state agency pursuant to state law. Many states have adopted the Uniform Trade Secrets Act, which was recommended for enactment by all states by the ABA in February 1980. Some state laws may vary, however, so lawyers will want to consult the individual state law in the state where information is being submitted.

In cases where the same information must be submitted to both state and federal agencies under different state and federal laws, sometimes a conflict occurs between the extent of trade secret protection afforded the same information by federal law and that afforded by state law. In such instances, if information is required to be disclosed under state law, the same information cannot be claimed as a trade secret when submitted to the federal government. This is one of the basic principles of trade secret protection—that the information has not been publicly disclosed. The same principle applies to information submitted to the federal government under two different statutes.

Government Reporting Requirements

After a company has identified the trade secrets it wishes to protect, the next step is for the company to identify the government reports that may require information relating to the trade secret. This means that the company will have to stay up-to-date on government reporting requirements that, in the environmental area, are changing rapidly and in some cases have mushroomed overnight. Companies must have a thorough knowledge not only of government reporting requirements, and the ways these requirements may help or prevent claims of trade secrecy, but also of the ways in which various government filings may be cross-referenced to reveal trade secret information.

The reports required to be submitted to both state and federal authorities under EPCRA are one of the more recent of the new information-reporting requirements. This statute illustrates the complexity of protecting a trade secret chemical as well as the possibilities available for such protection without requiring trade secrecy claims. This discussion concerning EPCRA focuses on protecting trade secret chemical identity since that is the only item generally allowed protection under that statute. The principles discussed here, however, may be generalized to the protection of other types of trade secrets.

Under this statute, companies must provide several different reports to EPA and state and local authorities under several different provisions. These reports contain information regarding chemicals manufactured and used by the company and include information on chemical identity, as well as the amounts of the chemical produced and released into the environment.

The legislative history of EPCRA revealed congressional awareness that the extent of the information companies were being asked to reveal could involve the disclosure of trade secrets. Under EPCRA, only the specific chemical identity of the reported chemical could be claimed as a trade secret. This specific chemical identity is the specific, chemically descriptive name of the chemical. Thus, even if other information such as production amounts were regarded as a trade secret, the only way to protect it was through a trade secrecy claim for the specific chemical identity of the chemical.

Various provisions in the statute, however, permitted companies to report relevant health and safety information while safeguarding this chemical identity. For instance, section 311 of EPCRA requires companies to provide state and local authorities with the MSDSs of relevant chemicals or lists of the same chemicals. Companies may list these chemicals, however, using the common or trade name of the chemical, thus protecting the more specific chemical name. Reporting under section 312, the chemical inventory form, may also allow common or trade names instead of specific chemical identities. This use of common or trade names instead of specific chemical identities parallels OSHA's hazard communication standard, in which common or trade names may be substituted for specific chemical identities considered trade secrets.

Another provision based on OSHA's hazard communication standard is the provision in section 311 that allows companies to report chemical mixtures as a whole instead of as the various chemical components. Mixtures may be reported as a whole on the MSDS required under the standard although some chemical components must also be listed. These components may be listed by common or trade name on the MSDS if their specific chemical identity is considered a trade secret. Section 311 in EPCRA requires only that the mixture as a whole be reported to the relevant state and local authorities, although the original MSDS must be made available to those who request it. In this way, companies are not required to make trade secrecy claims for the various trade secret components of mixtures.

Companies must be aware of the kinds of reporting done on the various EPCRA filings, as well as the OSHA MSDS, to ensure that no specific chemical identity has been previously inadvertently disclosed. Prior disclosure to a government entity is usually equated with public disclosure of the trade secret and destroys a valid claim of secrecy. Therefore companies must also be aware of other federal filings made that involve the same trade secret. For instance, chemicals reported under EPCRA are also chemicals that may have been previously reported to EPA under the TSCA inventory or in a TSCA premanufacture notification. Similar disclosure may have occurred in a pesticide registration. If chemical identity was not claimed as a trade secret in these filings, companies cannot claim trade secrecy under EPCRA. Companies should also check all patent filings, since trade secret information may also be revealed in a patent. Cross-referencing can occur where federal statute requires filing information with a state, or where the state independently requires the same information the federal government requires.

There are other possible pitfalls in making the detailed filings required for a trade secrecy claim. Under EPCRA, there are specific procedures for submitting substantiation of a trade secrecy claim. Submitters must be extremely careful that only EPA receives the unsanitized versions of trade secret papers. These are the versions containing the trade secret material. The sanitized versions, in which the trade secret material is deleted, are the ones to be sent to state and local authorities. Public disclosure of an unsanitized version of a trade secret filing, even though inadvertent, invalidates the trade secrecy claim.

Submitters of a trade secrecy claim must also be careful as to what information is disclosed in any substantiation of the trade secret. Most statutes permit substantiation of a trade secrecy claim after the claim is challenged. Under EPCRA, however, a substantiation must be submitted at the same time the trade secret materials are submitted to the EPA. The submitter may need to include trade secret information in the substantiation itself to adequately support the trade secrecy claim. This information must be very carefully handled so as to not publicly disclose any of the supporting material contained in the trade secret substantiation.

Companies attempting to protect their trade secrets must also be aware of those statutory provisions requiring disclosure regardless of trade secret status. Section 304 of EPCRA, for instance, does not allow any trade secrecy claim for chemicals released in an emergency release. The chemical releases required to be reported to the National Response Center under CERCLA section 103 are also included under EPCRA section 304. If such an emergency release occurs and a trade secret chemical identity is publicly disclosed, future trade secrecy claims as to that chemical identity will fail.

Emergency releases of a chemical under EPCRA may also permit doctors and nurses to have access to trade secret chemical identity under section 323. The doctors and nurses may be required to sign a confidentiality agreement after the emergency. In nonemergency situations, health professionals may have access under EPCRA to trade secret chemical identity provided they supply a company with a statement regarding their need for the information and agree to sign a confidentiality agreement. Such disclosures to health professionals should not imperil a trade secret, but companies should be ready to discuss with the health professional the uses of the information to be certain that both parties understand the procedures to be followed. Also, if a company later needs to defend its trade secret in court, it should be able to demonstrate that it followed the proper procedures and ensured that the necessary precautions were taken.

Formulating an Aggressive Trade Secret Protection Strategy

Companies must have a strategy for protecting their trade secrets and should implement it aggressively. First, as discussed above, companies should be aware of all of the government filings made and of the contents of each. Often government reports are filed from different divisions of large companies; these various reports should be coordinated. Sometimes the best way to do this is to organize company reporting electronically. If so, appropriate computer safeguards must be used to avoid inadvertent disclosure in public filings—or even to unauthorized employees within the company. These principles may seem simple; however, there are examples of major corporations inadvertently disclosing trade secrets in different government filings.

Some agencies are accepting electronic filings of required information. Such filings for trade secret information should be undertaken only with extreme care and appropriate safeguards. At the present time, the EPA does not accept trade secret information in electronic filings; only paper copy is accepted. Accordingly, companies must know the electronic filing and security requirements of the agency to which information is being submitted.

Counsel should always be consulted in any trade secret filing to be certain that the appropriate procedures are being followed. Also, there may be some provisions, similar to those discussed under EPCRA, that may allow a business to report all relevant data to the government without revealing trade secret information.

Companies should limit access to trade secrets as much as possible. Employees should be screened carefully, and as few employees as possible should have access to trade secrets. All of these employees should sign confidentiality agreements. Companies should be careful to limit access to the portion of the plant where the trade secrets are stored. Limited access should extend to both company employees, members of the public, and government inspectors. Before allowing a government inspector to view trade secret materials or processes, be certain to make sure that the inspector is cleared by the government agency in question for access to trade secrets.

Companies should formulate a written trade secret protection policy for distribution to those employees with access to trade secrets. This policy serves to notify employees of the importance of protecting the company's trade secrets and also demonstrates the company's intent should any of its trade secrets be challenged.

Finally, companies should attempt to avoid expensive administrative and court challenges to trade secrets through good public relations, particularly those companies handling hazardous chemicals. This would include providing complete information regarding health effects on MSDSs and safety information to local fire departments and community outreach groups.

In the event of a challenge to a claim of trade secrecy, companies must be aware of the requirements of agency administrative procedures. For instance, most trade secrecy claims made with the EPA are handled under the agency FOIA procedures at 40 C.F.R. Part 2. However, the procedures handling challenges to trade secrecy claims made under EPCRA are very different. The EPA must make two separate determinations regarding a trade secret submitted under EPCRA, and submitters have additional opportunities to submit information and to challenge an adverse agency decision. An understanding of these procedures will help a company to fully explain its position to the Agency.

By following all of the procedures discussed here, companies should be able to devise a workable strategy for trade secret protection. Obviously, in this era of complex environmental reporting and fuller public disclosure, companies may need to devote resources only to those more important secrets. With careful planning and attention to detail, however, there is no reason why companies cannot continue to maintain a competitive edge by protecting their most valuable secrets.

PART VI

Enforcement and Citizen Suits

Responding to EPA Information Requests

The Scope of the EPA's Inspection Authority

Settling with the Government

Private Claims and Public Resources

Citizen Suits against Private Industry under the Clean Water Act

The Erosion of Traditional Corporate Law Doctrines in Environmental Cases

Part VI
Enforcement and
Citizen Suits

The explosion of regulatory requirements in the environmental area has increased the exposure of companies to enforcement liability. Companies face the prospect of agency investigations and penalties, civil and criminal suits by the government, and citizen suits seeking penalties as well as attorney fees.

The EPA is using information requests more frequently and has brought suits against parties that do not respond adequately. James Price discusses the EPA's use of its authority to issue information requests, the scope of permissible requests, and how to deal with material that may be protected from disclosure.

The government's authority to inspect facilities and documents is a key aspect of its enforcement efforts. James Holtkamp and Linda Magleby discuss EPA inspection authority, including when a warrant is required, and the inspection provisions of particular statutes.

A company that is the target of an administrative or judicial proceeding for enforcement will often wish to consider a nonjudicial resolution. Settling with the government is not the same as settling a commercial dispute with a private party, however. Angus Macbeth analyzes the particular governmental habits and restraints that are important to understand for effective dispute resolution.

Public resources such as water bodies have increasingly become the subject of private claims for damage to the environment. The issue of when and how private interests can recover damages or bring actions on behalf of injured public resources is the subject of an article by William Horn.

Citizen suits have been an important part of the enforcement arena, particularly under the Clean Water Act. Citizen suits are likely to become increasingly significant under other statutes such as the Clean Air Act, which was amended in 1990 to allow courts to impose penalties. Richard Schwartz discusses the procedural and substantive issues raised by these suits.

The continuing search for deep pockets in Superfund and other environmental cases has led to attempts to expand the scope of liability. The government has been aggressive in seeking to pierce the corporate veil and to impose liability on corporate officers and successor corporations. In our final article in this part, Thomas McMahon, Katie Moertl, and Donna Kellick discuss recent cases in these areas that erode traditional protection for officers, shareholders, and successor corporations.

Responding to EPA
Information Requests

James T. Price

On January 22, 1990, the EPA and the U.S. Justice Department
launched a major offensive in their efforts to secure timely, accurate,
and thorough information about hazardous waste handling and disposal. The federal government filed four lawsuits against companies
in the U.S. District Court for the District of New Jersey alleging inadequate responses to EPA information requests issued pursuant to
CERCLA. The government sought fines and penalties from each
company.

At the same time, the EPA announced that its headquarters had
instructed its regional offices to search their files for instances of
noncompliance with information requests and that it is preparing
model litigation forms to prosecute such cases. With these actions,
the government raised the stakes in the enforcement-prone battleground of hazardous waste management and cleanup and made
timely, diligent, and accurate responses to EPA information requests
more important than ever.

Virtually all major federal environmental laws contain provisions
allowing the government to obtain information in appropriate circumstances. Under these statutes, the EPA also has the authority to
inspect and copy relevant records. For example, section 308 of the
Clean Water Act, 42 U.S.C. § 1318, requires wastewater discharge
sources to create and maintain various records concerning the discharges. Section 114 of the Clean Air Act, 42 U.S.C. § 7414, imposes

*James Price is a partner in the firm of Spencer Fane Britt & Browne in
Kansas City, Missouri.*

similar obligations on air emission discharge sources. In the hazardous waste arena, section 3007(a) of RCRA, 42 U.S.C. § 6927(a), allows the EPA or an authorized state to require a person who handles hazardous waste to furnish information relating to the waste.

The best-known EPA information-gathering provision, however, may be section 104(e) of CERCLA, 42 U.S.C. § 9604(e). This provision allows the EPA to seek from PRPs information about hazardous materials that may have been disposed of at a Superfund site. This is the authority under which the government filed the New Jersey enforcement actions. For many companies, a CERCLA section 104(e) request is their first information about potential involvement at a new Superfund site.

Each statute gives the EPA the ability to impose fines and penalties, including criminal penalties, for noncompliance. Indeed, as part of its January 1990 effort, the EPA announced it will step up criminal enforcement efforts and will pursue criminal sanctions when it believes companies knowingly have provided false information.

Civil fines and penalties for inadequate responses can be imposed by the EPA under its administrative penalty authority. In *United States v. Crown Roll Leaf, Inc.* (*Crown Roll Leaf II*), 29 Env't Rep. Cas. (BNA) 2025 (D.N.J. 1989), the court held that a company's failure to supply responses to an EPA information request violated RCRA and CERCLA, subjecting it to potential penalties of up to $25,000 per day under RCRA section 3008(g), 42 U.S.C. § 6928(g), and a like amount under CERCLA section 104(e)(5), 42 U.S.C. § 9604(e)(5). The court imposed and enforced the EPA's administrative penalty of $142,000 for failure to respond to an information request for 790 days. In *United States v. Maiorano*, 20 Envt'l L. Rep. 20,444, 1990 W.L. 6641 (N.D. Ill. 1990), the court included in its tabulation of a civil penalty under RCRA section 3008(g), 42 U.S.C. § 6928(g), the 270 days that the defendant did not respond to the EPA's information request. In *United States v. Charles George Trucking Co.* (*Charles George Trucking III*), 823 F.2d 685 (1st Cir. 1987), the First Circuit affirmed a district court judgment of $20,000 each against two persons for failing to respond to information requests under RCRA. The court in *United States v. Hugo Key & Son, Inc.*, 731 F. Supp. 1135 (D.R.I. 1989), issued summary judgment on liability for a seventy-seven-day violation of Clean Air Act section 114(a), 42 U.S.C. § 7414(a), for failure to respond to the EPA's reporting requirement requesting information. Clearly, the EPA and the courts are demonstrating that it is a time-consuming and costly mistake to neglect the appropriate legal standards in responding to EPA information requests.

In addition, the EPA's announced policy is that offers of settlements at Superfund sites are contingent upon compliance with its information requests. In *United States v. Cannons Engineering Corp.*, 899 F.2d 79, 93 (1st Cir. 1990), the court approved this practice over the objection of Crown Roll Leaf, which had been denied an opportunity to participate in settlements at the well-known Cannons Superfund site due to its failure to respond to information requests. The court said that the EPA's approach was reasonable, especially since the data Crown refused to supply was necessary to provide a foundation for settlement.

Administrative Subpoenas

Closely related to the EPA's authority to request information is its authority, granted by most major environmental laws, to issue administrative subpoenas. For example, Clean Water Act section 308 authorizes the EPA to issue administrative subpoenas to obtain documents and records or to enter and inspect premises. Section 2610(c) of TSCA, 15 U.S.C. 2610(c), goes further. It authorizes the EPA to require by subpoena attendance and testimony of witnesses, answers to questions, and "information that [the EPA] deems necessary." Administrative subpoenas under CERCLA are authorized by section 122(e)(3)(B), 42 U.S.C. § 9622(e)(3)(B).

In *National-Standard Co. v. Adamkus*, 881 F.2d 352 (7th Cir. 1989), the court affirmed the issuance of an administrative subpoena pursuant to RCRA section 3007(a), 42 U.S.C. § 6927(a), in situations where the Agency has reason to believe hazardous waste may be present at a facility. The court broadly interpreted the relaxed probable cause standards necessary to obtain an administrative warrant and upheld the use of an *ex parte* procedure.

Courts have held that administrative subpoenas are not self-enforcing and that a recipient of an EPA subpoena can refuse to comply, without penalty, until directed otherwise by a federal court order upon application by the EPA. *EPA v. Alyeska Pipeline Serv. Co.*, 25 Env't Rep. Cas. (BNA) 1416, 1418 (D. Alaska 1986). Before advising a client to refuse to respond to an administrative subpoena, however, counsel should review the specific statutory authority under which the subpoena was issued, as well as the relevant case law, to determine the consequences of such a refusal.

The Scope of Permissible Requests

EPA information requests can cover a broad range of topics. CERCLA section 104(e)(2), for example, allows the EPA to require "any person" to furnish information related to (1) the identity, nature, and quantity of materials generated, treated, or stored at a hazardous substance facility; (2) the nature or extent of a release or threatened release of hazardous material from such a facility; or (3) information concerning the person's financial ability to pay for or to perform a cleanup. The EPA, in its Interim Guidance on Notice Letters, Negotiations and Information Exchange, 53 Fed. Reg. 5298, 5300 (Feb. 23, 1988), discussing information requests under CERCLA section 104(e) and RCRA section 3007(a), states that it may request such details as waste operations and waste management practices, the types and amount of substances contributed by each PRP, and the names of other PRPs that contributed substances to the site. In the guidance, the EPA makes clear that it will use such requests to determine which persons should be considered PRPs at a site.

Guides to Preparing Responses

Plainly, a company must consider carefully how to respond to an EPA information request. The mere fact that the EPA has issued the requests may mean it is considering an enforcement proceeding. In the Superfund context, PRPs' responses may constitute the bulk of the information available to the EPA and other PRPs about who sent what and how much waste to a site. Such information may be used time and again at a site to target PRPs, to rank PRPs' contributions to a site, and to allocate shares of liability. For PRPs who believe their waste was not sent to a particular site or who believe their waste was not hazardous, their response to the EPA's information request often is the best time to marshal all available evidence, affidavits, and documents to support their contentions. If convincing demonstrations can be made, the efforts might be rewarded by keeping them off a PRP list or assigning them to lower rankings.

Deciding how to respond also may involve considerations of whether the requests are permissible and questions of attorney-client privilege and work product immunity. Most practitioners rely upon the limits of discovery in the Federal Rules of Civil Procedure to establish the boundaries of permissible EPA information requests. This may be based on obvious comparisons between EPA information requests and interrogatories or document production requests in civil actions pursuant to Federal Rules 33 and 34. The analogy may be imperfect, however. Unlike civil litigation discovery, the EPA information requests apparently contain self-enforcement mechanisms. If a person fails to supply the required information in a timely manner, it immediately is in default of the statutory requirements. Indeed, in *United States v. Crown Roll Leaf Inc.*, 29 Env't Rep. Cas. (BNA) 2018 (D.N.J. 1988), the court held the nonresponding recipient in violation immediately upon the expiration of the EPA's thirty-day response deadline.

In contrast, under the Federal Rules, the failure to respond adequately to discovery typically is not enforced until the party seeking discovery files a motion with the court to compel a response. The party opposing the request then can litigate appropriate discovery objections. No such method is expressly provided for addressing objections to EPA information requests, although the First Circuit in *Charles George Trucking III* suggested that penalties could not accrue against a recipient of an EPA request that had a reasonable basis to believe the requests were improper and asserted its objections in a timely fashion. 823 F.2d at 691.

Moreover, a company facing allegations that it did not respond adequately to information requests may be able to argue that the EPA's exclusive method to require responses is through an administrative subpoena for which noncompliance penalties do not accrue and that can be enforced only by a separate court order. The success of this argument may depend upon the particular provisions of the statute on which the EPA relies.

In further contrast, under the Federal Rules, a party is limited in its ability to obtain financial information from its opponent before a judgment. As noted above, the EPA expressly has this authority, at least with respect to requests issued under CERCLA. Also, under the Federal Rules and unlike EPA information requests, each party is entitled to propound discovery requests to the other. Recipients of an EPA information request have no reciprocal right to obtain information from the EPA, except under the FOIA.

Due to the distinctions between the Federal Rules and EPA information requests, too much reliance upon the Federal Rules as a guide to responding to administrative information requests may be misplaced. The civil discovery rules do, however, provide a basis to help respondents limit the scope of EPA requests to the factual circumstances surrounding the subject of the EPA inquiry.

Overbroad and Burdensome Requests

Under the Federal Rules of Civil Procedure, parties may obtain discovery regarding any matter, not privileged, that is relevant to the subject matter of the pending action. It is not grounds for objecting to discovery that the information sought would be inadmissible at trial as long as the information sought is reasonably calculated to lead to the discovery of admissible evidence. Courts may limit the frequency or use of discovery if the discovery would be cumulative or duplicative; is available from a more convenient, less burdensome source; or is unduly burdensome or expensive. Fed. R. Civ. P. 26(b)(1). These rules are instructive in the context of EPA information requests.

Companies called on to respond to EPA information requests commonly complain that the requests are unfocused and so broad that they seek information well beyond that which has any bearing on the matter at hand. This is not surprising because information requests tend to reflect the use of standard forms. Similar complaints are heard from litigants under the Federal Rules, which has prompted many federal courts to place strict limits on the number of interrogatories a party may issue. A typical limitation is twenty. The EPA is subject to no such restrictions for information requests, which can lead to detailed, extensive, and burdensome requests.

Among common complaints of overbreadth are that the EPA's financial information requests seek a wide range of detailed, complex information about finances, insurance, operations, and related corporations in circumstances in which the financial ability of the company responding to the requests scarcely is in doubt; the information requested covers plants other than those that sent waste to a particular site; and the information requested concerns all wastes generated or chemicals used rather than focusing upon wastes sent to the site at issue.

In *Crown Roll Leaf I,* the court articulated a three-part test for enforcing an administrative agency's information request: (1) the investigation must fall within the agency's authority, (2) the request must not be too indefinite, and (3) the information requested must be relevant to legislative purposes. The court there approved the information requests. No meaningful objections to the requests were made until long after the respondent was in default, however, so the precedential value of that approval must be considered limited. In *United States v. Charles George Trucking Co. (Charles George Trucking I)*, 624 F. Supp. 1185 (D. Mass. 1986), the district court approved a wide range of RCRA and CERCLA information requests, including requests concerning hazardous waste transactions with customers and the manner of the defendants' preparation of answers to

EPA inquiries. Again, no meaningful objections were made until long after the respondents were in default.

In *Alyeska Pipeline,* timely objections were made to the scope of an administrative subpoena issued in aid of a TSCA investigation. The court refused to approve several information requests because they were not reasonably related to the subject matter of the investigation, namely, wastewater and oil tanker ballast discharges at the Valdez, Alaska, pipeline terminal. The court said that the EPA has wide latitude to request information under its administrative subpoena power. Although the court approved several requests that the respondent argued exceeded EPA's TSCA authority, the court rejected EPA requests for information about activities at locations other than the one subject to the investigation. This case may be cited as authority by Superfund PRPs who object to the EPA's requests for information about wastes sent to sites other than the one under investigation.

Experience suggests that in responding to overbroad EPA information requests, the responding party should make a timely and brief statement of its objections and the grounds for those objections while providing appropriate responses to those portions of the requests that it concedes are not objectionable. Often a simple telephone call to the EPA lawyer handling the matter will elicit an agreement that the information requests will be construed in a more limited fashion, at least until the EPA reviews the initial responses. Indeed, at a May 1990 teleconference sponsored by the Section of Natural Resources, Energy and Environmental Law concerning recent developments in the law of solid and hazardous waste, Robert Frantz of General Electric Company and Robert Van Heuvelen of the Justice Department, two experienced environmental lawyers, agreed that this approach is appropriate and typically resolves issues about overbroad information requests.

Any such agreement, or an agreement to extend the response deadline, should be confirmed in writing. The court in *Crown Roll Leaf I* made clear that the EPA is entitled to written responses and that oral discussions may not be sufficient to toll or excuse response deadlines.

Other Common Concerns

The EPA's information requests typically are broad enough to cover information that may be protected from disclosure by the attorney-client privilege or the work product immunity. The latter protects from disclosure of qualifying material prepared in anticipation of litigation. *See* Fed. R. Civ. P. 26(b)(3). Expert witnesses' materials may also be protected from disclosure by this immunity. *See* Fed. R. Civ. P. 26(b)(4). A respondent cannot, however, protect information from disclosure solely on the ground that it is within the knowledge of its attorney. *See Hickman v. Taylor*, 329 U.S. 495 (1947).

Counsel for a respondent wishing to protect qualifying materials from disclosure must be familiar with the rules for preserving the attorney-client privilege and work product immunity and be diligent in assisting the client. The protections afforded by these doctrines typically are waived by disclosure. *The Attorney-Client Privilege and Work Product Doctrine* (2d ed. 1989), published by the ABA Section of Litigation, is an excellent handbook to obtain a quick understanding of the protections and limitations afforded by these rules. In preparing responses to EPA information requests, many counsel object to the requests to the extent they cover protected materials and advise the EPA that such materials are not being provided in the response.

Parties responding to EPA requests may assert a claim of business confidentiality pursuant to the procedures set forth in 40 C.F.R § 2.203(b) and, for CERCLA information responses, CERCLA sections 104(e)(7)(E) and (F), 42 U.S.C. §§ 9604(e)(7)(E) and (F). This assertion is, of course, different from asserting a claim of attorney-client privilege, and information supplied under a claim of business confidentiality may waive any claims of attorney-client privilege or work product immunity associated with it. If a responding party believes that it has a basis to assert its claim of business confidentiality with respect to information submitted, it should treat that information carefully and be sure to follow all of the required procedures.

In consent decrees and administrative consent agreements, the EPA typically asks for and receives promises by respondents to retain and produce upon request a wide range of information about the subject matter of the agreement. Lawyers for respondents should examine those provisions carefully. They may wish not to concede in a consent agreement that they can be required to give the EPA a wide range of sensitive documents that they otherwise might be able to protect from disclosure. Such documents could include internal correspondence, attorney communications, and consultants' draft reports.

Many respondents question whether they have a duty to supplement or update their responses as they learn of new information. The EPA takes the position that they do and in the instructions to its information requests typically states, without citing authority, that the recipient has such a duty. If one analogizes to the Federal Rules, however, the rule should be that a party has a duty to supplement its responses when it obtains information demonstrating that the response was incorrect when made or, though correct when made, no longer is true and a failure to amend the response would be a knowing concealment. Fed. R. Civ. P. 26(e).

The highly regarded treatise, Wright & Miller, *Federal Practice and Procedure* § 2048 (1st ed. 1970), reports that before Federal Rule 26(e) was amended in 1970, courts reached varying conclusions about the duty of parties to supplement their discovery responses. Federal Rule 26(e) was an attempt to strike a balance and impose a continuing duty to supplement when it is most important without imposing undue burdens on the parties.

I am not aware of any case law that addresses whether a respondent to an EPA information request has a continuing duty to respond. A respondent who wants to avoid burdensomeness or otherwise does not intend to be bound by the EPA's assertion of a continuing duty to respond probably should so state in its response. This may avoid any application of pre-1970 case law under the Federal Rules holding that a party propounding discovery could impose a continuing response obligation by its instructions in the preamble to the interrogatories or document requests.

In light of the EPA's increased emphasis on information requests to gather liability and enforcement information, counsel are wise to consider such requests carefully and participate closely with their clients in preparing responses. The costs associated with failing to do so are high, as the EPA makes clear that inadequate responses can lead to substantial fines and even criminal penalties for noncompliance.

The Scope of the EPA's Inspection Authority

James A. Holtkamp and Linda W. Magleby

The EPA's authority to enter private property and inspect conditions thereon, including the right to review records and take samples, has been the subject of considerable controversy. Nonetheless, it is clear that a facility owner or operator has less protection against government officials' entry into the facility property to conduct environmental inspections than a residential property owner (or even a private vehicle operator), even though the environmental inspection may result in criminal charges against the owner, operator, or employees of the facility.

This article surveys the statutory and judicial parameters of the EPA's right to inspect facilities and property. There is no single statutory source authorizing such inspection by administrative agencies. Indeed, with respect to administrative searches, the federal APA states that an "inspection or other investigative act or demand may not be issued, made or enforced except as authorized by law." 5 U.S.C. § 555(c). Thus the EPA must look to specific statutory authority for any environmental inspections on private property. Even with a statutory "right of entry," constitutional constraints may limit the EPA's ability to conduct an inspection without first obtaining a search warrant.

The provisions of the various environmental statutes authorizing EPA inspection vary significantly. Some statutes contain very specific provisions, while others are more vague. For example, some statutes require written notice along with a statement as to the reasons for

James Holtkamp is a partner in the Salt Lake City, Utah, office of Stoel Rives Boley Jones & Grey. Linda Magleby is clerking for the 10th Circuit Court of Appeals in Salt Lake City, Utah.

the inspection before the EPA may enter to see records. Others contain no notice provisions. Similarly, one statute may authorize designated EPA officers, employees, or representatives to enter a facility, while another may authorize only officers and employees. Due to the wide variance among statutes authorizing inspections, the tried and true maxim to read the statute when in doubt has special application with regard to the EPA's inspection authority. A brief description of the EPA's inspection authority under each of the major federal environmental statutes follows.

The Statutory Authority

CERCLA, 42 U.S.C. §§ 9601–75, gives the EPA a very broad grant of authority to inspect property for the presence of hazardous substances that may be released, thereby triggering CERCLA cleanup and liability. CERCLA authorizes officers, employees, or representatives duly designated by the President or by the state or political subdivision under contract or cooperative agreement with the President, to enter property where hazardous substances are present or have been stored or handled, as well as adjacent property. The inspectors may, upon reasonable notice, have access to and copy all records relating to hazardous substances. They may also obtain samples of hazardous substances from any person. The authority of this subsection may be exercised only for the purposes of determining the need for response or choosing or taking response action or otherwise enforcing CERCLA. 42 U.S.C. § 9604(e)(1) (Supp. 1991).

RCRA, 42 U.S.C. §§ 6901–92, is similarly broad. RCRA does not require advance notice of inspections, but authorizes any duly designated officer, employee, or representative of the EPA to enter at reasonable times and inspect and obtain samples from any place where hazardous wastes have been generated or handled. RCRA states that the inspections must be done with reasonable promptness. 42 U.S.C. § 6927(a). For any sample taken, a receipt describing the sample must be given to the owner, operator, or agent of the establishment. If requested, the EPA officer, employee, or representative must also give to the owner, operator, or agent of the inspected facility an equal portion of each sample taken and a copy of the results of any analysis made. *Id.* RCRA also stipulates that any information obtained through investigations shall be available to the public except for trade secrets, confidential statistical data, information about income, or information about how the business is operated. 42 U.S.C. § 6927(b).

RCRA also authorizes inspection, monitoring, and testing of any underground storage tanks, 42 U.S.C. § 6991(a), along with facilities that generate, store, treat, transport, dispose of, or otherwise handle medical wastes. 42 U.S.C. § 6992c(a) (Suppl.).

As a practical matter, EPA inspectors under RCRA will generally contact an owner or operator of a facility before an inspection and request permission to enter. If the owner or operator refuses to consent to the inspection, the EPA may obtain a warrant from the Office of the District Attorney. Adequate cause for a warrant to be issued may be demonstrated by the mere suspicion that a waste violation has occurred on the site.

FIFRA, 7 U.S.C. §§ 136–136y, is more specific in delineating the conditions under which the EPA has the right to inspect a facility. FIFRA authorizes officers or employees duly designated by the EPA administrator to enter, at reasonable times, any establishment where pesticides are sold or held for distribution to inspect or obtain samples. 7 U.S.C. § 136g(a). FIFRA requires that appropriate credentials and a written statement as to the reason for the inspection must be presented to the agent in charge of the establishment before any inspection is begun. If a violation of law is suspected prior to the investigation, a written statement stipulating that suspicion must be presented before the inspection is started. FIFRA also authorizes officers or employees designated by the administrator to obtain and execute warrants. Such a warrant would authorize the EPA to enter and inspect establishments where there is reason to believe that a violation of FIFRA has occurred and reproduce any records relating to the violation. 7 U.S.C. § 136g(b).

The inspection provisions of TSCA, 15 U.S.C. §§ 2601–71, are similar to those of FIFRA. TSCA empowers the administrator and any duly designated representative of the administrator to inspect any property or conveyance in which chemical substances or mixtures are manufactured, processed, stored, held, or transported. 15 U.S.C. § 2601(a). TSCA requires that written notice and appropriate credentials be given to the owner, operator, or agent of the property or conveyance for each inspection. The inspection is required to begin and end with reasonable promptness and at reasonable times. TSCA specifically limits the scope of any inspection conducted under its authority to issues of compliance with its requirements. The inspection may not extend to financial data, sales data (other than shipment data), pricing data, or research data not required by TSCA unless the "nature and extent of such data are described with reasonable specificity in the written notice." 15 U.S.C. § 2610(b)(2).

The Clean Air Act, 42 U.S.C. §§ 7401–7626, authorizes the EPA to inspect, for purposes of determining compliance, the property of any person who owns or operates an emission source, who manufactures emission control equipment or process equipment, or "who the administrator believes may have information necessary for the purposes set forth in this subsection," 42 U.S.C. § 7414 (1983) (Suppl. 1991), or any person who is subject to any requirement of the Clean Air Act. It also authorizes the EPA to enter such property, access records, inspect monitoring equipment, and take emissions samples. 42 U.S.C. § 7414(a)(2). For states with an approved SIP, this act requires that state air pollution control agencies be given reasonable prior notice before the EPA enters, inspects, or monitors a facility. 42 U.S.C. § 7414(d). It also contains a provision for public disclosure of information gathered during an inspection, except information relating to trade secrets, income, and operating information. 42 U.S.C. § 7414(c).

The Clean Air Act grants inspection authority to "the Administrator or his authorized representative." 42 U.S.C. § 7414(a)(2). The statute does not define "authorized representative," and substantial controversy has resulted concerning the issue of whether private companies under contract with the EPA are authorized representatives. In *Stauffer Chemical Co. v. EPA*, 647 F.2d 1075 (10th Cir. 1981), the Tenth Circuit held that employees of a private company under contract with the EPA are not authorized representatives and therefore may be denied access to facilities for the purpose of investigating possible Clean Air Act violations. The Sixth Circuit reached a similar conclusion with respect to private contractors in *United States v. Stauffer Chemical Co.*, 684 F.2d 1174 (6th Cir. 1982), *aff'd*, 464 U.S. 165 (1984). However, in *Bunker Hill Co. Lead & Zinc Smelter v. EPA*, 658 F.2d 1280 (9th Cir. 1981), the Ninth Circuit concluded that authorized private contractors are authorized representatives of the EPA for purposes of inspecting property and equipment to ensure compliance with the Clean Air Act. An attempt was made to resolve this in the 1990 Clean Air Act Amendments. Section 604 of the Senate bill would have specifically defined "authorized representative" to include authorized EPA contractors. However, that provision did not become part of the final bill enacted by Congress.

The Safe Drinking Water Act, 42 U.S.C. §§ 300f–300j, authorizes inspection of facilities engaged in supplying drinking water. Pursuant to 42 U.S.C. § 300j–4(b)(1), the Administrator or his duly designated representative may, upon presenting appropriate credentials and written notice of any supplier of water or other person subject to regulation under the act, enter any establishment, facility, or other property of that supplier or other person to determine whether that supplier or other person has acted and is acting in compliance with the Safe Drinking Water Act. In the course of an inspection, the Administrator or duly designated representative may inspect records, files, papers, processes, controls, and facilities. Information that would divulge trade secrets or secret processes are withheld from the public if any person justifies that protection.

Before the EPA may enter a state that has primary enforcement responsibility for public drinking water systems, it must notify the state in writing of the reasons for the entry. If the state agency shows that such an entry will be detrimental to the administration of the state's enforcement responsibility program, the EPA will consider that showing when determining whether to enter.

The Federal Water Pollution Control Act, 33 U.S.C. §§ 1251–1387 (Clean Water Act), states that "[t]he Administrator shall establish national programs for the prevention, reduction, and elimination of pollution and as part of such programs shall . . . conduct and promote the coordination and acceleration of . . . investigations . . . relating to the causes, effects, extent, prevention, reduction, and elimination of pollution." 33 U.S.C. § 1254(a)(1). In the section of the Clean Water Act that deals with oil and hazardous substance liability, persons authorized by the President to enforce the statute may board and inspect any vessel upon the navigable waters of the United States or the waters of the continuous zone, arrest any person who violates the provisions or regulations of the Oil and Hazardous Substance Liability Act with or without a warrant, and execute any warrant or other process issued by an officer or court of competent jurisdiction. *Id.*

The information obtained through the EPA inspections is subject to public disclosure pursuant to the federal FOIA, 5 U.S.C. § 552. Under FOIA, an agency must make its records promptly available to any person who has reasonably described the requested records and otherwise complied with the procedures for disclosure. 5 U.S.C. § 552(a)(3). FOIA sets forth nine exemptions to the publicly available information, including information specifically exempted by statute, trade secrets, financial information, geological data, and geophysical information. 5 U.S.C. § 552(b). Several of the statutes administered by the EPA contain specific exemptions from public disclosure of information under FOIA.

Constitutional Constraints

Although the EPA is authorized to inspect facilities to enforce the various environmental statutes, that power is subject to certain Fourth

Amendment constraints, including the requirement to obtain a search warrant. The general rule concerning administrative inspection was laid down in *See v. City of Seattle*, 387 U.S. 541 (1967). In that case, the Supreme Court held "that administrative entry, without consent, upon portions of commercial premises which are not open to the public may only be compelled through prosecution or physical force within the framework of a warrant procedure." *Id.* at 545.

The Supreme Court later applied this principle to safety and health inspections in *Marshall v. Barlow's, Inc.*, 436 U.S. 307 (1978). *Barlow's* involved a suit by an employer to enjoin enforcement of the inspection provisions of OSHA, which requires the Labor Department to inspect work areas for safety hazards and violations of safety regulations. No search warrant is expressly required by the Act. The employer refused to allow a Labor Department inspector into the nonpublic area of his business without a warrant and sought to enjoin a warrantless search. In upholding the employer's position, the Court held that "[t]he Warrant Clause of the Fourth Amendment protects commercial buildings as well as private homes," and therefore a warrant was required before a business could be compelled to allow a government agency entry to inspect. *Id.* at 311.

Despite these decisions, there are certain exceptions to the warrant requirement as it applies to business property. These exceptions are based on the proposition that the Fourth Amendment does not ban all warrantless searches but only "unreasonable searches and seizures." U.S. CONST. amend. IV. One exception when the Supreme Court did not find a warrantless search of business property unreasonable is *Donovan v. Dewey*, 452 U.S. 594 (1982). In that case, the Secretary of Labor sought to enjoin a company from refusing to permit warrantless searches of mining facilities. The Supreme Court recognized that "inspections of commercial property may be unreasonable if they are not authorized by law or are unnecessary for the furtherance of federal interests," or if warrantless inspections of a business are "so random, infrequent, or unpredictable that the owner . . . has no real expectation that his property will from time to time be inspected by government officials." *Id.* at 599. Nonetheless, the Court found no constitutional violation due to the fact that the mines were inspected on a regular basis at a specifically defined frequency, and the Mine Safety and Health Act was sufficiently pervasive and defined as to make warrantless searches under the Act "reasonable" with respect to the Fourth Amendment. *Id.* at 605.

The Court in *Donovan* relied heavily on two prior decisions that defined the exceptions to the warrant requirement. In *United States v. Biswell*, 406 U.S. 311 (1972), warrantless searches were upheld as reasonable for pervasively regulated businesses. In *Biswell*, the warrantless inspection of firearms dealers by government agents was deemed an essential part of the regulatory scheme. The Court concluded that persons who choose to engage in such a heavily regulated business do so with the knowledge that the business will be subject to inspection and are "not left to wonder about the purposes of the inspector or the limits of his task." *Id.* at 316.

The second case upon which the *Donovan* Court relied is *Colonnade Catering Corp. v. United States*, 397 U.S. 72 (1970). In this case, a liquor licensee protested the imposition of a fine for refusing to submit to a warrantless search. The *Colonnade* Court found the search to be reasonable because of the long history of close supervision and inspection of the liquor industry. It was also significant that although Congress did not authorize forcible entry without a warrant, it clearly had made "it an offense for a licensee to refuse admission to the inspector." *Id.* at 77.

Following the reasoning of *Donovan*, the Supreme Court has determined that a warrantless inspection may be reasonable if circumstances satisfy a three-part test. The test set forth in *New York v. Burger*, 482 U.S. 691 (1987), requires that

> First, there must be a "substantial" government interest . . . Second, the warrantless inspections must be "necessary to further [the] regulatory scheme." [Third], "the statute's inspection program, in terms of the certainty and regularity of its application, [must] provid[e] a constitutionally adequate substitute for a warrant."

Id. at 702, quoting *Donovan v. Dewey*, 452 U.S. 594, 600, 602, 603 (1981).

The Tenth Circuit has recently applied the *Burger* test to a warrantless inspection of a gas station by the Wyoming Department of Environmental Quality. *See V-1 Oil Co. v. Wyoming*, 902 F.2d 1482 (10th Cir. 1990), *cert. denied*, 111 S. Ct. 295 (1990). The Tenth Circuit concluded that although a gas station is pervasively regulated, there was no notice to "the owner of any particular business that his or her property will be subject to warrantless inspections" and there was "no assurance of regularity of inspections." Because a gas station operator would have no expectation of a warrantless search, such searches pursuant to the Wyoming Environmental Quality Act are unconstitutional. 902 F.2d at 1487.

To obtain a search warrant, the EPA must have evidence of a violation or the search must be part of a general neutral administrative scheme. *Marshall v. Barlow's, Inc.*, 436 U.S. 307 320–21 (1978). In *National-Standard Co. v. Adamkus*, 881 F.2d 352 (7th Cir. 1989), the Seventh Circuit found that the EPA had established sufficient probable cause for the issuance of a search warrant by satisfying the first part of the *Barlow's* test. In *National-Standard*, the EPA put forth a detailed affidavit explaining the various known hazardous wastes at the National-Standard facilities and included photographs of alleged violations of RCRA. The court held that the specificity of the affidavit, together with Congress's desire for enforcement of RCRA, constituted sufficient probable cause for the issuance of a warrant. 881 F.2d at 361.

Despite these constitutional concerns, a search warrant is not necessary for all types of environmental inspections. The Supreme Court has held in *Air Pollution Variance Board of Colorado v. Western Alfalfa Corp.*, 416 U.S. 861 (1974), that an inspection of a plume of smoke from an open field or area open to the public does not violate federal constitutional procedures because there is no expectation of privacy from such areas. 416 U.S. at 866. A similar rule applies to aerial inspection and photography from navigable airspace. *Dow Chemical v. United States*, 476 U.S. 227 (1986). In *Dow Chemical*, the Court reasoned that aerial photography is similar to an observation in an open field and thus is within the EPA's investigatory authority and is not a search under the Fourth Amendment.

Although the various environmental statutes authorize the EPA to enter and inspect facilities, a warrant may be required if the facility owner or operator does not consent to the inspection. However, there are exceptions to the warrant requirement for pervasively regulated industries or those with a history and expectation of government inspection. Thus it may be that certain types of facilities that have been subject to stringent environmental regulation (i.e., RCRA hazardous waste TSD facilities or other facilities subject to environmental permits) can be inspected under the applicable environmental statute without a warrant.

In the final analysis, the question is not so much whether a warrant is required but whether the EPA's inspection is authorized by statute. In most cases, the EPA has broad authority to inspect and gather information. The facility operator's primary concern should be to ensure that confidential and sensitive information is protected and that the information obtained by the EPA is accurate, as it could form the basis for enforcement or even criminal action by the government.

Settling with the Government

Angus Macbeth

The government is different. Its job is making rules and enforcing rules, particularly rules that other people have to follow. This makes the nature of litigation and settlement with the government different from private litigation. The EPA's past and present litigation and settlement practices can best be understood by starting with this precept. Even a statute such as CERCLA, which is not based on a regulatory scheme, has been reduced for the purposes of settling litigation to a government-written model consent decree that amounts to a set of rules by which the EPA will resolve Superfund cases.

This article discusses the problems of settling enforcement disputes with environmental agencies by focusing on the characteristics and instincts that distinguish the environmental agencies from private litigants. It is not meant to suggest that all the normal skills and talents of a negotiator are not important to reaching a settlement with the government; they are. But the environmental agencies have institutional habits and restraints that are important to understand for effective dispute resolution.

Most of the EPA's litigating habits were developed under the Clean Air Act and the Clean Water Act. Viewed broadly, the development of those statutes began by the proposal, promulgation, and litigation over rules and matured with the enforcement of those rules, ranging from the prevention of significant deterioration of air quality

Angus Macbeth is a partner in Sidley & Austin in Washington, D.C., and was formerly the deputy assistant attorney general in the Land & Natural Resources Division of the Department of Justice.

around national parks to the best practicable technology for controlling water pollution in a subcategory of the sand and gravel industry. Many of these cases in the late 1970s were not overly complex, but there were at least two major ingredients that prevented the air and water cases from becoming repetitive matters of routine: the role of the states and the effort to obtain civil penalties. Both of these remain important elements of litigation and settlement with the EPA and are illustrative of larger issues that are central to resolving disputes with the environmental agencies.

Understanding Intergovernmental Conflict

With a few notable exceptions, such as the provisions of TSCA that govern PCBs, each of the major environmental statutes establishes a framework for a federal-state "partnership." The division of responsibility within the partnership varies from statute to statute, but typically the states and the federal government divide the standard-setting authority and share the power of enforcement. In the Clean Air Act, the federal government sets ambient air standards, the states devise the methods for achieving those standards, which the EPA approves, and both governments share the job of enforcing the requirements to meet the standards. Under the Clean Water Act, the technological standards for each industry are set by the federal government, the ambient standards of water quality are primarily the responsibility of the states, and enforcement of the standards is primarily through permits incorporating both standards and is enforceable by either government. RCRA has yet another model in which the states take over enforcement of the hazardous waste program when they have developed a state program that is at least the substantial equivalent of the federal program, but the EPA retains the authority to enforce the requirements of RCRA regardless of this apparent delegation to the states.

For the litigator, a common thread runs through all these programs. The utopia envisioned by Congress in which the state and federal governments work together combining the broad technical and scientific knowledge of the national government with the state's intimate acquaintance with local conditions rarely works out in practice. Instead, the highly complex environmental statutes with their overlapping responsibilities, particularly in enforcement, give rise to a constant tension between federal and state agencies that runs all the way from differing interpretation of the same regulatory language to differing views on the seriousness of a particular regulatory violation. In the hazardous waste context, the tension has reached the point of open opposition as some states attempt to limit hazardous waste activities within their borders while the federal government, particularly the DOJ, strives to maintain an open national market consistent with traditional commerce clause jurisprudence.

In the settlement context, this has basic implications. First, where the state and federal governments have shared authority, no settlement is complete until both governments have agreed to it. Even areas of apparent federal preemption raise this problem: Mishandling of PCBs may be characterized by a state agency as a public nuisance when the state is barred from directly regulating PCBs. It follows from this basic fact that, where there is shared responsibility, a major effort in settlement must be to bring both governments into the negotiation so that a complete settlement is achieved.

However, there is no simple formula to achieve this obvious end. The nature of the state-federal relationship often breeds rivalries and antagonisms that make common negotiations or settlement difficult and perhaps impossible. The different governments run on different timetables and have different frameworks for the review of settlements that often make coordination difficult. Ultimately, as in the case of controlling the interstate movement of hazardous waste, the state and federal governments may simply have different agendas. Unfortunately, when this is the case, the usual impulse of the government agencies is to leave the private party with the problem of resolving inconsistent directions. Regulatory agencies generally prefer to have their public battles with industry rather than with one another.

On the other hand, the state-federal "partnership" provides the private litigant with some advantages. Very frequently, there are differences in regulatory interpretation between the governments, and this may strengthen the ability of the private party to obtain the more favorable view of the regulation or statute. The same is true in determining remedies in a case—a three-cornered negotiation may well be conducive to a moderate settlement. This is not to suggest a strategy of divide and conquer, which seems unlikely to be successful in most contexts because ultimately there is usually more to unite than divide the government agencies. Nevertheless, there will be times when settlement with one government and litigation against the other may be the most advisable course, for instance, if a reasonable settlement is available with the party with the strongest legal claim and no compromise is possible with the other. In this context, however, although the courts have not barred suits by both sovereigns over the same matters, they have not been friendly to them.

The state-federal tension can be viewed as an extreme paradigm of institutional rivalries, which are particularly prevalent in the environmental field. The DOJ and the EPA, for instance, operate under an MOA that gives both influence over the conduct of litigation in the district courts. The EPA regional and headquarters offices may take different views of the law or of the acceptability of certain settlement terms. In the states, the head of the environmental agency and the attorney general may come from different political parties and follow different agendas. This situation is the source of repeated frustration for the private litigant who believes he or she has reached settlement on some issue only to find that while it is acceptable to an EPA regional office, it will not clear EPA headquarters or the DOJ. For this reason, it is especially important to establish and understand the authority of the attorneys on the other side of the table in an environmental suit. The private litigant should anticipate that if settlement is reached with only part of the governmental structure, another office will look for the opportunity to add some icing to the settlement cake to justify and maintain its position within the government. The problem of reaching final resolution of a controversy has become worse in recent years with the growth of citizen suits under the environmental statutes. The presence of a citizen group plaintiff or intervenor in a case adds another hurdle and a new mix of interests to the settlement process.

The "Policy" Question and the Tendency toward Rules

The issue of civil penalties illustrates another dominant characteristic of environmental litigation. Virtually every environmental statute that sets up an enforcement mechanism places broad discretion in the administrative law judge or the district court judge to set civil penalties for violations of the regulation or statutes. Some of the statutes provide guidance as to what factors should be considered in setting the amount of a penalty, but usually such instructions are not very detailed. One might innocently imagine that the EPA would view this as a benefit; discrepancies between results could be laid at the judge's door without the need for apology or explanation from the Agency. Perhaps because the overwhelming number of cases settle rather than go to trial and the Agency feels a need to defend its settlement results, the EPA has made repeated efforts through the years to turn the calculation of the penalties into a set of rules. This effort began as soon as the enforcement effort at the Agency matured, and it has continued to the present time. A major aspect of this effort to obtain "consistent" penalties is counterintuitive to a newcomer to environmental law. The major effort has been to quantify the economic benefit of delayed compliance and use that amount as the bedrock for a settlement while negotiating flexibly over the amounts ascribed to the harm caused by the alleged violation or the defendant's attitude toward regulatory compliance. The genesis of this approach lay in the fact that the Clean Air and Water Act cases of ten or fifteen years ago typically involved the failure to install end-of-the-pipe pollution control equipment, the value of which was comparatively easy to quantify while the environmental damage caused by a violation was extremely difficult to determine, and once determined, was not easy to quantify. This initial approach has been reinforced over the years by Government Accounting Office reports that use economic benefit as an easy touch-stone for evaluating the EPA's enforcement program and by internal repetition.

There is a tension in this effort. On one side, the Agency is searching for consistency in results and the ability to represent that it treats all similarly situated parties in a similar and evenhanded manner. On the other side, it encounters the varying facts and circumstances of particular cases that have grown markedly more diverse over the years. First, even the cases under the Clean Air and Clean Water Acts have moved away from simple failure to install pollution control equipment. For instance, under the Clean Air Act, painting and coating operations release VOCs that are controlled under the Act, but it is often a sound response for a defendant to comply by figuring out a way to use less of the compounds rather than collecting and treating the emissions. Consequently, the appropriate behavior under the regulation may be less costly to the defendant than the prescribed violating behavior. The economic benefit theory is not useful to the government in such cases. Next, a number of the recent environmental programs are not simply aimed at treating waste but at proper management of environmental risk. Placing RCRA groundwater monitoring wells in the wrong place may be a serious matter, but it frequently does not save a company money. Finally, the increasing use of substantive cleanup remedies under RCRA or the TSCA PCB program fundamentally change the whole equation; it is typically far more expensive to dispose of PCBs improperly and then pay the bill for cleaning them up than to have properly disposed of the material to start with. At the same time, the Agency—and for that matter society generally—has made very little progress in determining whether environmental violations have caused actual harm and, if so, how much and what the "cost" or "value" of the harm is. The effort to grade violations from minor to severe is little more than a pseudoscience in which the judgment of the person applying the system of classification is the key to determining the seriousness of most violations.

Despite the fact that none of the policies or guidelines on civil penalties has ever been intellectually very satisfying, they continue to dominate the thinking and behavior of the EPA. The natural reaction of the private litigator, trained to settle cases and not global issues, is to try to figure out what the case is worth on its merits without reference to the overlay of "policy." This instinct is encouraged by the fact that these Agency policies are not always readily available or easily obtainable. It is not prudent to succumb to this impulse.

The central point of the civil penalty policy experience is the inherent pressure within the environmental agencies to develop rules for the conduct and settlement of litigation with the accompanying emphasis on apparently objective elements such as economic benefit. No doubt there are many reasons for this. Many environmental cases have public visibility and require the government agency to give an account of its actions to the public, the press, or the legislature. Rules and policies are a great help in this effort. They appear to assure consistency and evenhandedness. They allow the headquarters staff to direct and appear to control the field offices. They relieve the mid-level official from the burden of thinking through and making judgments about each issue that comes before him. Once in place, they reduce the institutional friction with the agency's lawyers. "Policy development" is closely akin to what the Agency does outside litigation in writing rules for notice and comment in the *Federal Register*, so that the agency personnel are comfortable and familiar with the process.

This inherent instinct for rules and policies gives a particular context to environmental litigation. First, where it is possible, it is important to set the arguments within the terms of the policies, since those are the terms in which the government attorneys are thinking. It is generally more advantageous to justify a desired result in terms of congruence with a policy than to suggest that the policy does not fit the facts and that disinterested analysis of the facts should prevail. Second, where there are no directly relevant policies, it can be extremely helpful to develop the arguments for settlement terms by reference to an analogous set of rules and policies. Such sources provide a benchmark that alleviates, at least in part, the difficulty of having to exercise discretion.

One result of the rule-making mentality is that the language of settlement becomes very important. Most remedial action that a private party agrees to in a settlement can be expressed either in terms that are very particularized or that set out in some guiding policy. For example, an agreement simply to remove the top foot of soil from a particular PCB site can be the same as cleaning the site to the level of, say, 10 ppm of PCBs. Expressed in the first way, the agreement is of little use to either party as a precedent; expressed in the latter manner, it is likely to be used by one side or the other in future negotiations. Consequently, the effect of language that sounds like a general rule should be given careful consideration.

In this context, it is worth underscoring the impact of public accessibility to environmental cases. There are, of course, DOJ regulations that provide for public comment on all proposed settlements in pollution abatement cases. The collection of these comments and reporting them to the judge has rarely had the direct effect of changing the terms of consent decrees. Nonetheless, this regulation is a concrete expression of the government's perception that it will be held accountable for individual settlements. Generally, this operates to reinforce the desire for uniformity and the placing of specific settlements into a broader context.

This sense of accountability can also play havoc with normal relations in a high-visibility case. Particularly when hazardous substances are involved in situations like Love Canal and Times Beach, enormous pressure can be exerted on Agency officials to provide assurances to the public on matters of health or safety that pass beyond the bounds of the statutes. If the Agency perceives itself as being accountable for a public emergency, appeal to its rules and policies may have some effect in restraining and directing it, but all too frequently in those circumstances the political powers in the government will sow the wind and the private defendant will reap the whirlwind. At this point, the imperatives of the rule-making civil servant give way to the imperatives of an elected or appointed official who feels directly responsible to the voters. Such cases need much more than the skills of a litigator; they need a full array of public relations and community relations specialists.

Understanding the Commonalities

To this point, we have discussed two major parameters that distinguish interactions with environmental agencies in settlements from settlements with private parties, namely, the institutional rivalries that arise throughout the process and the agency's instinct for rules and policies. However, there are a number of ways in which the environmental agencies share some of the characteristics of private litigants, though these are often transformed by the special nature of the government agency. A few of these deserve special mention.

The first and most important of these characteristics is that shared by every litigant—wanting to walk out of the settlement saying that you won. The area where this desire takes an unusual focus for the government is in settlements involving money. Obviously, money is something that every newspaper reader can understand a lot more easily than the level in parts per billion that a groundwater cleanup will reach. On the other hand, the money involved in a settlement usually does not go to the agency itself, but to the government in general. This leads to a whole variety of ingenious "funny money" settlements that serve the psychological and public relations aspects of the settlement process. For instance, in the heyday of federal construction grants, a municipality paying a penalty for delay in putting in a sewage treatment plant could also be assured that it would get its federal grant for treatment plant construction. A company may put in processes or equipment useful to its operation that are environmentally protective and have them characterized as projects that reduce the cash amount of a penalty. Money may be expended over a long period so that its present value is small in relation to the total value over time that is emphasized between the parties. This is an area where creative thought can be very valuable to a client who cares less about appearances than the bottom line.

The remedies available to an agency are, of course, circumscribed by what Congress has authorized. Hence some action or remedial effort of real interest to the plaintiff may only be available through settlement rather than litigation. This is most obvious in a citizen suit, where a park or a research fund is likely to be much more attractive to the plaintiff group than having the penalty paid to the government. But this should not be lost sight of in dealing with the government. If there is, for instance, a lot of local interest in or pressure for some protective measure that is beyond the terms of the regulation, there may well be ways of obtaining other accommodations if that pressure is met.

In a sense, this is little more than an example of the fact that it is often easier to resolve a dispute when the parties are bargaining over four or five items of differing importance to them than when a single issue that will be won or lost is a stake. It is important to both sides to leave the table with their prestige intact, and this is easier where both sides can claim victory on something. For this reason, it may well be advantageous to expand a negotiation beyond the terms set by the government so that it includes other facilities or issues in dispute between the government and the private party.

Government lawyers like to think that they represent principle rather than money, and to a very real extent, there is some truth to this belief. When the interests of protecting citizens from serious injury to human health are at stake, that is as it should be. But principles rapidly descend into rules and policies that do not necessarily serve the public interest in every context in which they are applied. It is central to effective negotiation with the government to recognize both the strengths and weaknesses—and the associated interests of the negotiators—that arise from this context. Like private litigation, successful resolution of disputes with the government depends on understanding what the other side wants and why it wants it, so that creative lawyers can find the common ground that will make settlement possible. The government is different in the mechanisms that drive it toward settlement and the institutional obstacles that lie in its path. If these are properly appreciated, the first long strides toward the resolution of disputes will have been achieved.

Private Claims and Public Resources

William P. Horn

Let us begin with a postulate. A productive saltwater marsh is severely damaged by a human-caused environmental calamity. One-third of the area is a federal wildlife refuge, one-third is a state wildlife area, and one-third is owned by a private hunting club. Migratory waterfowl are killed and stop using the area. Resident wildlife species also suffer. Shellfish beds are poisoned. Associated water pollution causes fish to die, and the marsh ceases to support juvenile fish that would eventually grow to populate areas hundreds of miles away. The whole area acquires a deathly look. Most of the affected resources are public resources, those owned or managed by governments for the benefit of the citizenry. Nonetheless, there are substantial private interests in these public resources.

An array of prospective plaintiffs steps forward to seek damages. The federal government claims damages to its upland acreage and the waterfowl, while the state claims damages to uplands, submerged lands, fish, shellfish, and wildlife. The hunting club also claims damages for its interests in lands, fish, and wildlife. A local commercial fisherman claims damages to the fish and shellfish. An adjacent landowner who has subdivided and is selling his land as Marshview Estates sues, and so do a national sport-fishing association, a national duck hunters' organization, and various environmental organizations. All are suffering, or claim to be suffering, from the damage inflicted on the environment. The law must separate these claims and ensure that

William Horn is a partner in the firm of Birch, Horton, Bittner & Cherot in Washington, D.C.

each plaintiff is treated appropriately and fairly, without requiring the tortfeasor to pay more than is warranted.

This hypothetical case presents the basic issue: When and how can private interests recover damages or bring actions on behalf of injured public resources?

Private actions regarding public resources fall into two primary categories: actions for private relief arising from damage to public resources and actions by private parties on behalf of public resources. Claims brought by the commercial fisherman, the hunting club, and the adjacent landowner are examples of the first category. Such actions for private relief often arise from still applicable common-law rules and principles. However, these rules have been affected by an array of statutes that sometimes preempt traditional claims or offer expanded measures of damages. Citizen suits by the various organizations against the responsible party are the classic example of the second type of action. Actions on behalf of the public interest have historically arisen from common-law principles such as the public trust doctrine. In recent years, however, these actions have been primarily based on rights and remedies created by the legion of environmental statutes enacted since 1969. Trends affecting common-law actions, the effect of new statutes, the expansion of recognized damages, and emerging issues are discussed below.

Traditional Grounds for Standing

The long-standing rule of tort law remains that a private party can recover for injury to public resources if the party has sustained damage different from that incurred by the general public. *Burgess v. M/V Tamano*, 370 F. Supp. 247 (D. Me. 1973). This general rule has permitted commercial fishermen to collect damages for the destruction of fishery resources held in trust by states and has allowed individuals to receive awards for contamination of community water supplies. The hunting club mentioned in the opening hypothetical case might also collect under this rule. The fact that wildlife will no longer use the damaged area causes the club specific harm. Its members can no longer hunt the area and enjoy the benefits of their membership. The club can no longer sell memberships because it has nothing to sell. This particularized injury can be recognized even though the club has absolutely no property interests in the affected wildlife.

The common law often provides an appropriate cause of action to the prospective private plaintiff who has suffered particularized harm. Suits sounding in negligence, nuisance, strict liability, and trespass have all been employed in private actions regarding public resources. However, these cases concern private action on behalf of private harm. Recovery on behalf of the public is generally not pursued using these traditional causes of action. Nuisance has generally been the most fruitful cause of action because unreasonable interference with use and enjoyment of land—the classic definition of nuisance—is sufficiently broad to encompass a host of environmental and pollution problems. The offending act need not be trespassory and may include effects on scenery, odors, and noise. As recognition of environmental values has grown, so has the ability of a plaintiff to demonstrate successfully that such interference affects the plaintiff's land.

The common law traditionally recognized a sharp distinction between private and public nuisance. The old rule of thumb, expressed in the vernacular, was that a large nuisance was a public nuisance, and it was within the purview of public action. Courts have largely discarded this notion, and private nuisance actions will now usually be recognized within the context of public nuisance claims. The ability to pursue private action for publicly offensive activities has been abetted by the diminution of the traditional distinction.

Nuisance is hardly a panacea, as many environmental lawyers have learned. Common-law actions remain burdened with potentially onerous common-law rules. The nature of the injury continues to be an important test. Some jurisdictions look for highly tangible interference with the use and enjoyment of a property as a requirement for a valid claim in nuisance. As a result, demonstrating that aesthetic interference constitutes a *bona fide* nuisance has been difficult but not impossible. *Allison v. Smith*, 695 P.2d 791 (Colo. App. 1984). On the other hand, something as prominent—and intrusive in the minds of many—as the large tower adjacent to the Gettysburg Battlefield Park was not deemed a nuisance. *Commonwealth v. National Gettsyburg Battlefield Tower, Inc.*, 311 A.2d 588 (Pa. 1973). The traditional weight given to the balancing test of considering the utility of the offending action also frequently limits the effectiveness of a nuisance suit.

Trespass actions for physical invasion of property are generally of more limited value to the private plaintiff seeking relief for harm to public resources. The proof requirement of direct physical invasion of the plaintiff's property renders demonstrations of generalized harm to public resources inadequate. Moreover, the absence of private property interests in many public resources (e.g., wildlife) means that the private party cannot show an invasion of *its* property.

Strict liability for hazardous activities, as well as negligence, are important to the prospective private party. Many environmentally damaging incidents are the result of activities deemed hazardous in case law as well as statute. This would include the transport of oil, the manufacture of chemicals, and the disposal of certain wastes. Incidents attendant to these activities that harm public resources, and affect private interests in those resources, are the source of readily compensable claims. Indeed, the creation of statutory strict liability standards for many of these activities is a common trend in both federal and state legislatures as evidenced by CERCLA, 42 U.S.C. § 9601 *et seq.*, and pending federal oil spill bills in the 101st Congress.

Negligence can also play a role, albeit a more restricted one. Failure to exercise the appropriate duty of care that gives rise to an environmentally damaging incident that causes harm to the private party is the fundamental element of negligence. Consequential economic damages such as reduced property values, as opposed to diminished use and enjoyment, are more likely claims under negligence or strict liability actions. The seller of property adjacent to a newly damaged site, such as the owner/seller of Marshview Estates in the hypothetical, is a logical plaintiff to bring a negligence claim for reduced property values and loss of expected profits. Adverse effects on sale by nontrespassory conduct constitute an improbable basis for a nuisance claim. Negligence would be the preferred common-law action, especially if a nonhazardous activity was the source of the damage to the adjacent public resources.

The public trust doctrine has been of uneven importance to private plaintiffs. The doctrine provides that certain resources—usually certain lands and waters—are held in trust for the public by the government. Governments cannot violate that trust by mismanaging or misappropriating these resources. *Illinois Central R.R. v. Illinois*, 146 U.S. 387 (1892). The public trust doctrine is usually associated with actions on behalf of the general public but can also be used on behalf of private interests. This clearly is not the purpose or the best application of the doctrine, but it is wholly appropriate in the right factual circumstances. Private plaintiffs have used the doctrine to try to bar taking of land through eminent domain by arguing that the government project necessitating the taking harms public resources and as such violates the public trust. Success has been mixed. In some circumstances, the distinction between actions for private interests and actions for the public becomes blurred. For example, an owner of ocean resort property without waterfront might bring a public trust action under the auspices of ensuring public access to the beach. A successful suit means enhanced property values for the owner as well as public access. Conversely, a private owner of fragile shoreside habitat might seek to employ the same doctrine to bar public access to protect the area. Limited access could conserve the habitat and enhance the property owner's privacy. Where some identified benefit to the public resources also provides private benefits, a clever property owner can use public trust doctrine to achieve dual objectives.

Public Interest Litigation

Major federal environmental statutes have led to explosive growth in public interest litigation. However, such laws have done very little to assist private recoveries in public resource damages cases. Examples of these statutes include CERCLA, RCRA, the Safe Drinking Water Act, the Clean Water Act; TSCA, and FIFRA. In limited cases, such as under CERCLA, privately incurred cleanup costs may be recovered. The thrust of federal environmental statutes has been to emphasize recoveries on behalf of the public.

One of the primary features of these and other federal enactments has been to authorize so-called citizen suits. Through citizen suit provisions, private citizens are authorized to bring civil enforcement actions, as "private attorneys general," against entities thought to be responsible for pollution or against the government for failure to implement or enforce the laws adequately. To encourage private parties to undertake protection of public resources, incentives such as awards of attorney fees and costs are often authorized. In addition to the laws noted above, other major acts with citizen suits provisions include the Clean Air Act, the Endangered Species Act, and Outer Continental Shelf Lands Act. These statutes have made private actions on behalf of public resources commonplace.

Although each statute is different, certain basic principles are found in each law. The purpose of authorizing citizens to act as private attorneys general is to encourage compliance with the law by effectively increasing the number of enforcement officers in the field. Three features characterize most of these provisions: the citizens must notify the government before taking action (a sixty-day notice is the standard requirement), a citizen suit is barred if the federal government has already commenced a civil action in the case, and any penalties collected are deposited in the federal treasury. Controversy is growing regarding the disposition of penalties and whether or not such sums should be dedicated to remediating the damage to the public resources. Such earmarking of funds is not presently authorized.

The growth of specific environmental statutes has been a mixed blessing for private parties. Restrictions on the ability to use the public trust doctrine in federal matters is a primary limiting effect of the multiplicity of recent federal environmental statutes. In the wake of Earth Day in 1969, environmental lawyers dusted off *Illinois Central R.R. v. Illinois* and sought to apply the federal public trust doctrine it articulated on behalf of public resources. The strategy was sound as, at the time, there was little federal environmental law (indeed, some of the major water pollution cases of that era were brought under the Rivers and Harbors Act of 1899), and federal common law could be used to fill the gaps. In recent years, however, the use of the public trust doctrine in federal cases has suffered a series of body blows. Major cases have held that the enactment of specific statutes preempts common-law doctrine. Accordingly, efforts to use federal public trust claims in high-profile cases, such as the Mono Lake case in California, have been unsuccessful. *National Audubon Soc'y v. Dep't of Water*, 869 F.2d 1196 (9th Cir. 1988); *see also Middlesex County Sewerage Auth. v. National Sea Clammers Ass'n*, 453 U.S. 1 (1981).

Although the trend has been to make private actions easier to pursue, concern has developed, at least among some groups, that tightened standing requirements might bar many prospective environmental plaintiffs. The liberal rule of organizational standing was articulated in the early 1970s in *United States v. SCRAP*, 412 U.S. 669 (1973), and *Sierra Club v. Morton*, 405 U.S. 727 (1972). These cases set a standard relatively easy to satisfy: A group must have an express organizational purpose related to the matter at hand and have members with some particular stake in the matter. Consequently, organizations flocked to the courts in the 1970s, causing the courts to revisit the standing issue. Tightening of standing requirements was exemplified by *Valley Forge Christian College v. Americans United for Separation of Church and State, Inc.*, 454 U.S. 464 (1982). As a result, in some cases environmental organizations have been denied standing. *Wilderness Society v. Griles*, 824 F.2d 4 (D.C. Cir. 1987). However, in other high-profile public resource cases, appellate courts have overturned the district courts and reinstated environmental organizations as proper plaintiffs. *NWF v. Burford*, 835 F.2d 305 (D.C. Cir. 1987); *National Fed'n v. Burford*, 878 F.2d 422 (D.C. Cir. 1989). Evolution of the law in the standing question has not delivered a crippling blow to private actions on behalf of public resources, but it has tightened the requirements for standing and perhaps limited certain types of actions on behalf of public resources.

Awarding Damages

While the ability to bring private actions related to public resource damages has become easier, especially on behalf of the public interest, the expansion of recognized damages has been concomitantly even greater. New concepts of harm have been recognized by courts as societal recognition of environmental values has increased. In addition to traditional personal injury damage, recovery has been permitted in environmental resources cases for emotional distress as well as diminished quality of life related to contamination of community drinking water supplies. Creative plaintiffs' attorneys can be counted on to pursue these kinds of claims in cases arising from harm to public resources. Indeed, one environmental organization in the *Exxon Valdez* oil spill case is claiming compensation for lost "bequest value"— injury arising from the fact that Prince William Sound is no longer an unsullied area to be bequeathed to future generations. It will be interesting to see if a plaintiff can recover for emotional distress suffered from watching an oiled sea otter die.

Claims for property damage have not evidenced similar levels of creativity. However, claims for consequential economic damages emanating from environmental calamities are being stretched. Is an Alaska bartender entitled to recover from Exxon the value of the tips he would have received from commercial fishermen had they not been idled by the oil spill? We should receive an answer sometime in the not too distant future.

Two major battles are now being waged regarding damages. The first focuses on the measurement of natural resource (i.e., public resource) damages. The second concerns the use and disposition of damage awards. The latter raises other difficult questions, such as how to apportion damages and divide awards among multiple plaintiffs—including private parties seeking private damages and public interest groups—in a public resources injury action.

CERCLA gives statutory expression to the public trust doctrine and provides that federal, state, and tribal "trustees" may bring actions to recover for damages to natural resources. Damages need not be measured solely in economic terms and may include public appreciation or existence values. I refer to these as intrinsic natural resource damages claims, i.e., the trustee can seek to recover the intrinsic value of the resource without looking to value measurements set by commodity or market considerations. The DOI was charged with promulgating the "damage assessment" regulations, and during 1986 and 1987, the regulations were issued. 40 C.F.R. Part 11. They were immediately challenged and struck down as imposing undue limitations on the intrinsic valuation of natural resources. *Ohio v. U.S. Department of the Interior*, 880 F.2d 432 (D.C. Cir. 1989). Interior has not appealed the decision and has agreed to rewrite the valuation regulations.

The *Ohio* decision is a manifestation of a continuing struggle in the field of valuation. The vast body of law emphasizes traditional economic and market principles in determining resource values. Critics have argued that such principles often understate the true value of these resources. For example, a swamp with little or no market value may be an environmental jewel. It might behoove the public to pay many times the land's market value to ensure its protection. However, developing an objective system to ascertain such public value has been fraught with peril as entities such as the Congress (and its General Accounting Office) and the IRS have looked askance at departure from traditional valuation. Similar valuation issues will be at the center of the Alaska oil spill litigation. Various plaintiffs, including landowning Native American corporations, are examining means of assessing the true value of a pristine beach as compared to its value after having been "slimed." The revamped CERCLA regulations and the *Exxon Valdez* litigation may set forth new principles for the valuation of natural resources, both private and public.

However, consensus on value assessment, even if it is ever achieved, will not end the struggle. Disposition of damage awards will also occupy successful plaintiffs. Quite clearly, the private plaintiff seeking a claim for particularized injury will take whatever is awarded. In contrast, awards won on behalf of the public interest are funneled to governments. A growing number of proponents want such awards to be available directly for environmental reparation and restoration of damaged resources. Congress has already provided for such dedication of awards under the Clean Water Act and CERCLA and is likely to do so again in the pending oil spill legislation. The trend is clearly in the direction of dedicating awards to "fix," if you will, the damaged resources.

Pursuit of awards on behalf of the public can adversely affect private recoveries. Consider the following situation. Mr. Smith owns beachfront property that includes irreplaceable cultural values. The property and values are devastated by an oil spill. He seeks restoration costs but decides, in advance, to use the award he will win for other purposes. The state government as a trustee also seeks restoration costs for the same beach, as is authorized in the Clean Water Act. The tortfeasor argues that he will pay the state for restoration but not Mr. Smith—after all, no one has to pay twice for damages caused. Simply put, the broadened reach of government or private claims on behalf of the public may reduce the compensation available to the private party.

Such fighting over damages is not confined to public versus private interests. It may also pit public entities against each other. Alaska and the National Marine Fisheries Service reportedly have had significant disputes over the right to claim damages caused by injury to the salmon resources in Prince William Sound arising from the *Exxon Valdez* oil spill. Of course, commercial fishing interest plaintiffs are watching closely to see if they will be affected.

All indications are that the ability to bring private claims relating to public resources will continue to expand. Traditional common-law causes of action remain available and are more helpful to potential private plaintiffs as concepts of nuisance grow. Under such actions, more categories of damages are being recognized. Federal statutes also continue to broaden the field of private actions. The new oil spill law expressly recognizes claims by subsistence users of public resources (i.e., H.R. 1465 § 1002(b)(2)(C)), and Indian tribes are granted new status to pursue actions, albeit in their governmental capacity (i.e., § 1002(b)(2)(A)). Regarding public benefit matters, there are no signs of moving away from permitting citizen suits in more and more resource-oriented arenas. The emerging issues in this field concern methodologies of resource valuation and damage calculation. New CERCLA rule making and oil spill litigation provide the cutting edge for these fascinating issues, which are as much policy as science and as much economics as law. Growing concern over the public's resources, and increased opportunities for private citizens to take action on behalf of these resources, ensure that cobwebs will not grow on this area of the law.

Citizen Suits against Private Industry under the Clean Water Act

Richard E. Schwartz

Every major environmental statute has its own citizen suit provision, but the one that has been used most is found in section 505 of the Clean Water Act, 33 U.S.C. § 1365. Section 1365 is user-friendly. To find defendants, environmental organizations or their law firms simply go to the EPA or state regional offices to review the discharge monitoring reports (DMRs) that must be submitted by dischargers. Reading DMRs may not be exciting, but it is very easy. The limits are generally preprinted on the forms next to the spaces for reporting. DMRs also have spaces labeled "number of exceedences" for the discharger to specify the number of violations for each parameter.

At least sixty days before a complaint is filed, a potential defendant must be sent a letter notifying it of the citizen's intent to sue. Although the notice letters typically do not contain an offer to meet to discuss settlement, in practice this opportunity is usually afforded. The environmental groups' settlement goals usually include entry of a consent decree containing the following provisions:

1. civil penalties or a contribution to an environmental project,
2. a schedule for achieving compliance with the permit,
3. stipulated penalties for future violations, and
4. payment of the plaintiff's attorneys' fees.

This article discusses many of the procedural and substantive issues raised by these suits.

Richard Schwartz is a partner at Crowell & Moring in Washington, D.C. He gratefully acknowledges the assistance of Susan R. Koehn, an associate in the same firm.

Claims

Claims against Individual Violators

Most of the cases filed by environmental organizations have been based on violations of numerical effluent limitations in NPDES permits. Those alleged violations are evidenced by the DMRs filed with the EPA by the companies themselves. A citizen plaintiff may establish a *prima facie* case for liability based solely on the DMRs prepared by the defendant discharger. *SPIRG v. Fritzsche, Dodge & Olcott*, 20 E.R.C. 1624 (D.N.J. 1984); *United States v. Amoco Oil*, 20 F.R.D. 1666 (W.D. Mo. 1984).

The courts have uniformly held that dischargers are strictly liable for NPDES permit violations. Neither good faith nor lack of intention to commit a violation is a defense to such a claim. *See United States v. Earth Sciences, Inc.*, 599 F.2d 368 (10th Cir. 1979).

Section 1365(a) provides that a citizen suit may be commenced against any person alleged to be in violation of "(a) an effluent standard or limitation under this Act or (b) an order issued by the Administrator or a State with respect to such a standard or limitation ...." The term "effluent standard or limitation under this Act" is defined in section 1365(f). It includes a discharge without a NPDES permit, a violation of a permit condition, or a violation of a discharge standard.

If section 1365(f) includes every permit condition, its scope is very broad. For example, NPDES permit conditions include operation and maintenance requirements and the duty to mitigate any environmental harm resulting from noncompliance with the permit. Many permits contain general prohibitions against the discharge of wastewater that harms aesthetic values.

The section 1365(f) definition is much broader than the definition of effluent limitation in section 1362(11), where that term is defined to include only quantitative restrictions and schedules of compliance.

A narrower interpretation of section 1365(f) results if it is read in light of the general definition of effluent limitation in section 1362(11). Its focus may be on specifying *which* effluent standards or limitations will be deemed to be "under this Act" for the purposes of bringing citizen suits. Under this analysis, the definition of effluent limitation in section 1362(11) modifies each of the categories of requirements of the Clean Water Act set forth in section 1365(f).

In fact, several courts have held that section 1365 can be used only for violations of objective, quantifiable standards, established administratively in permits, and subject to uniform application. *See MESS v. Weinberger*, 707 F.2d 1182, 1198–1200 (E.D. Cal. 1988), and cases cited therein. Thus section 1365 may not be used to abate an effluent discharge on the ground that it creates a nuisance. *Stream Pollution Control Bd. of Ind. v. United States Steel Corp.*, 512 F.2d 1036, 1041 (7th Cir. 1975).

Other courts, however, have extended the reach of section 1365 beyond discharge standards. For example, one court has held that the monitoring and reporting requirements of a permit, which are necessary to enforce discharge standards, are themselves "effluent limitations" enforceable under section 1365. *Public Interest Research Group of New Jersey v. GAF Corp.*, 770 F. Supp. 943 (D.N.J. 1991).

In *Pymatuning Water Shed Citizens for a Hygienic Environment v. Eaton*, 506 F. Supp. 902 (W.D. Pa. 1980), *aff'd*, 644 F.2d 995 (3d Cir. 1981), the court enforced conditions on sewer maintenance and keeping stormwater out of sanitary sewers against the defendant municipality. Its jurisdiction to do so under section 1365 apparently was never questioned.

Claims against Governmental Entities

Citizens have attempted to sue federal, state, or local authorities based on violations committed by private dischargers. In some cases, the plaintiffs have alleged that state or local authorities should be liable directly to the plaintiff for the harm caused by the alleged unlawful discharge. *See Love v. NYDEC*, 529 F. Supp. 832 (S.D.N.Y. 1981); *O'Leary v. Moyer's Landfill, Inc.*, 523 F. Supp. 659 (E.D. Pa. 1982). In other cases, citizens have sued the EPA to compel the Agency to enforce the requirements of the Clean Water Act against the discharger. *Goodyear v. Lecraw*, 15 E.R.C. 1189 (S.D. Ga. 1980); *Sierra Club v. Train*, 7 E.L.R. 20,120 (D.D.C. 1976). Neither type of claim has been allowed.

In particular, the court in *Sierra Club* held that a suit to force the EPA to bring an enforcement action is outside the purview of section 1365(a)(2), which limits citizen suits against the EPA to cases alleging failure to perform a nondiscretionary duty. In *Goodyear v. Lecraw*, the same conclusion was drawn with respect to a citizen suit action against the Army Corps of Engineers to enforce section 1344 of the Clean Water Act. In *Proffitt v. Davis*, 707 F. Supp. 182 (E.D. Pa. 1989), the same conclusion was reached with respect to the alleged failure of the Pennsylvania Department of Environmental Resources to enforce consent orders against dischargers.

Procedural Defenses

Standing

Standing to sue has two components, namely, constitutional requirements and statutory elements.

The Clean Water Act legislative history shows that Congress intended to adopt the standing test set forth in *Sierra Club v. Morton*, 405 U.S. 727 (1972), where the Supreme Court addressed the constitutional elements of standing. *See* A Legislative History of the Water Pollution Control Act Amendments of 1972, 93d Cong., 1st Sess. (1973) [hereinafter 1972 Legislative History] at 239, 249; S. Rep. No. 1236, 92d Cong., 2d Sess. 146 (1972), *reprinted in* 1972 Legislative History at 329.

In *Sierra Club v. Morton*, the Court ruled that to have standing, a party must demonstrate that (1) the challenged action has caused him or her "injury in fact" and (2) the threatened interest was within the "zone of interests" protected by the applicable law. 405 U.S. at 733, 734. The Court specifically noted that the zone of interest may include aesthetic, recreational, and environmental interests in addition to the traditional economic ones. To have standing, however, those interests must be specifically injured, and standing "requires that the party seeking review be himself among the injured." *Id.* at 734–35. The Court also wrote that an organization—such as the Sierra Club—"whose members are injured may represent those members." *Id.* at 739. However, the Court emphasized that a "mere 'interest in a problem,' no matter how long-standing" is not sufficient "to render the organization 'adversely affected' or 'aggrieved.' " *Id.*

Section 1365 of the Clean Water Act authorizes citizens to file suit to enforce the Act's requirements. Section 1365 defines a citizen as "a person or persons having an interest which is or may be adversely affected." 33 U.S.C. § 1365(g) (1988). The Act further specifies that a person is "an individual, corporation, partnership, association, state, municipality, commission or public subdivision of a state or any interstate body." *Id.* § 1362(5). Thus an environmental group clearly could qualify as a citizen permitted to bring suit.

Courts have concluded that environmental and other organizations may bring citizen suits on behalf of their members. *See Sierra Club v. Morton*, 405 U.S. 727 (1972); *Rite-Research Improves Env't, Inc. v. Costle*, 650 F.2d. 1312 (5th Cir. 1981). Courts have reached this determination despite the Clean Water Act statutory language that authorizes any citizen to "commence a civil action on his own behalf." 33 U.S.C. § 1365(a) (1988). "On his own behalf" has been interpreted to prohibit class actions, not to prevent representational suits. *See Sierra Club v. Aluminum Co. of Am.*, 585 F. Supp. 842 (N.D.N.Y. 1984). In short, the doctrine of representational standing provides a standing basis for an environmental group.

In *Hunt v. Washington State Apple Advertising Comm'n*, 432 U.S. 333, 343 (1977), the Supreme Court identified three prerequisites for association or derivative standing:

> Thus, we have recognized that an association has standing to bring suit on behalf of its members when: (a) its members would otherwise have standing to sue in their own right; (b) the interests it seeks to protect are germane to the organization's purpose; and (c) neither the claim asserted nor the relief requested requires the participation of individual members in the lawsuit.

Thus associations have standing only if a member itself would have standing to sue. For example, in *Sierra Club v. SCM Corporation*, 580 F. Supp. 862 (W.D.N.Y. 1984), *aff'd*, 747 F.2d 99 (2d Cir. 1984), the court found that the Sierra Club lacked standing because it had not shown any specific member to have been injured. "It is critical to point out that plaintiff has failed to show that any particular member of its organization has or may be adversely affected in any specific way to defendant's action." *Id.* at 865.

To have standing, an individual must demonstrate some interest in the applicable waterway. Certainly, use of the stream satisfies the interest showing, as indicated by *Sierra Club v. Morton*. Less clear is whether mere proximity is a sufficient interest. Although several courts have concluded that residence in the vicinity of the waterway does furnish standing, this result may be inconsistent with the Supreme Court's standing decisions. *See, e.g., Montgomery Envtl. Coalition v. Costle*, 646 F.2d 568 (D.C. Cir. 1980); *Lujan v. NWF*, 110 S. Ct. 3177 (1990) (affidavits of the NWF's members were insufficient to establish standing because they alleged only that affected members used unspecified lands "in the vicinity of" the activity complained of).

To establish standing, citizen plaintiffs must show that their interests have been injured. Injuries that have been deemed to be within the plaintiff's zone of protected interests include injury to health, economic, recreational, aesthetic, and environmental interests as well as injury to the plaintiff's "well-being." *New York Pub. Interest Research Corp. v. Limco Mfg. Corp.*, 697 F. Supp. 608, 611 (E.D.N.Y. 1987). *Accord, Proffitt v. Municipal Auth. of Borough of Morrisville*, 716 F. Supp. 837 (E.D. Pa. 1989), *aff'd without op.*, 897 F.2d 523 (3d Cir. 1990).

Mootness or the Lack of Continuing or Intermittent Violations

Section 1365 provides that citizens may commence a civil action against any person who is alleged to be violating the requirements of the Act. 33 U.S.C. § 1365(a)(1) (1988).

In *Gwaltney of Smithfield, Ltd. v. Chesapeake Bay Found.*, 484 U.S. 49, 57, 64 (1987), the Supreme Court held that section 1365 confers jurisdiction on federal district courts when plaintiffs "make a good-faith allegation of continuous or intermittent violation" of an NPDES permit, showing a reasonable likelihood that violations will continue. Although good faith allegations of ongoing violations are sufficient, if the defendant can show that the plaintiff's allegations are either untrue or "a sham," that defendant can move for summary judgment. *Id.* at 64–66. If it is " '*absolutely clear*' " that the defendant's alleged wrongful behavior could *not* reasonably be expected to recur, the case is moot and will be dismissed for lack of jurisdiction. *Id.* Even if the case is dismissed as moot, however, the defendant may still be required to pay the plaintiff's attorney fees. *Id.* at 67.

The Supreme Court in *Gwaltney* defined "continuous or intermittent violation" to mean a "reasonable likelihood that a past polluter will continue to pollute in the future." *Id.* at 57. As stated in Justice Scalia's concurring opinion:

> When a company has violated an effluent standard or limitation, it remains, for purposes of § 505(a), 'in violation' of that standard or limitation so long as it has not put in place remedial measures that clearly eliminate the cause of the violation. It does not suffice to defeat subject matter jurisdiction that the success of the attempted remedies becomes clear months or even weeks after the suit is filed.

Id. at 69. Thus the question is whether the defendant has "taken remedial steps that had clearly achieved the effect of curing all past violations by the time suit was brought." *Id.* What this means in practice is that defendants may prevail on a mootness theory if they show that (1) remedial measures have been taken, (2) these measures are efficacious, and (3) the risk of future violations has been eradicated. *Comite Pro Rescate De La Salud v. Puerto Rico Aqueduct & Sewer Auth.*, 693 F. Supp. 1324 (D.P.R. 1988), *vacated on other grounds*, 888 F.2d 180 (1st Cir. 1983), *cert. denied*, 110 S. Ct. 1476 (1990). *See also Gwaltney*, 890 F.2d 690, 693 (4th Cir. 1989); *and Carr v. Alta Verde Indus. Inc.*, 931 F.2d 1055 (5th Cir. 1991).

Plaintiffs must show an ongoing violation separately as to *each pollutant parameter* of an NPDES permit. *Gwaltney*, 890 F.2d at 698. The Fourth Circuit noted on remand in *Gwaltney* that

> The entire structure of the Clean Water Act and regulations involves identifying specific pollutants and setting a permit limit for each pollutant of concern. It thus makes sense within this scheme to view each parameter separately for purposes both of determining ongoing violations and of assessing penalties.

Id. at n.7. *Accord, Allen County Citizens v. BP Oil Co.*, 762 F. Supp. 733, 740–41 (N.D. Ohio 1991); *but cf. NRDC v. Texaco Refining & Mktg. Co.*, 719 F. Supp. 281, 286–87 (D. Del. 1989), *vacated on other grounds*, 906 F.2d 934 (3d Cir. 1990).

Allegations of continuous or intermittent violations may become false after a citizen suit is filed due to a defendant's actions to bring itself into full compliance with the Clean Water Act. As mentioned above, the Supreme Court in *Gwaltney* recognized this possibility when it noted the availability of the defense of mootness in such a situation. 484 U.S. at 66. State enforcement proceedings that cause the violations alleged in a citizen suit to cease without likelihood of recurrence should lead to dismissal of citizen suits as moot. *See Atlantic States Legal Found. v. Eastman Kodak Co.*, 933 F.2d 124 (2d Cir. 1991).

In light of the Supreme Court's *Gwaltney* decision, a defendant served with a notice of a citizen suit should inform plaintiffs in writing early on of any remedial measures that have been planned or taken to eliminate the likelihood that violations will recur. A defendant may be able to avert a costly citizen suit by demonstrating that it has made changes that will prevent future violations. Such a communication would make it more difficult for citizen plaintiffs to allege in good faith the likelihood of future violations.

The Failure to Give Proper Notice

Section 1365(b)(1) provides that, with the exception of violations of NSPSs and toxic pollutant effluent standards, no citizen suit may be commenced against any person before sixty days after the plaintiff has given notice of the alleged violation to the EPA, the state, and the violator. 33 U.S.C. § 1365(b)(1)(A) (1988). The EPA's Clean Water Act regulations prescribe the manner in which sixty-day notice should be provided and specify its required contents. *See* 40 C.F.R. § 135 (1991). Failure to meet the sixty-day notice requirement will probably result in dismissal. *See Hallstrom v. Tillamook County*, 493 U.S. 20 (1989), *reh'g denied*, 493 U.S. 1037 (1990).

Substantive Defenses

Compliance with the EPA Regulations

The EPA's regulations provide certain defenses to permit violations. The most important is the "upset" defense. An upset is defined as "an exceptional incident" in which there is "unintentional and temporary noncompliance with technology based permit effluent limitations because of factors beyond the reasonable control of the permittee." 40 C.F.R. § 122.41(n)(1) (1991). The upset must be well-documented and reported to the government within twenty-four hours. *Id.* § 122.41(n)(3)(1991). The requirements for invoking this defense, however, have been strictly construed against dischargers. *Student Pub. Interest Research Group v. Jersey Cent. Power & Light Co.*, 642 F. Supp. 103, 108 (D.N.J. 1986); *Atlantic States Legal Found. v. Al Tech Specialty Steel Corp.*, 635 F. Supp. 284, 288 (N.D.N.Y. 1986); *Public Interest Research Group v. United States Metals Refining Co.*, 681 F. Supp. 237, 244 (D.N.J. 1987).

Errors in the DMRs

The courts have held that DMRs may be used as *prima facie* evidence of a violation of a permit limitation. In several cases, the courts have suggested that DMRs provide *conclusive* evidence of violations. For example, in *SPIRG v. Fritzsche, Dodge & Olcott*, 20 E.R.C. 1624, 1633 (1984), the court justified this conclusion by noting that the legislative history of the Clean Water Act emphasizes the benefits of "expedition" in enforcing the Act. It quoted from the legislative history as follows:

> [T]he bill . . . establishes and makes precise new requirements imposed on persons and subject to enforcement. One purpose of these requirements is to avoid the necessity of lengthy fact-finding investigations at the time of enforcement. Enforcement of violations of requirements of this Act should be based on relatively narrow fact situations requiring a minimum of discretionary decision-making or delay.

Id.

The court's reliance on the above-quoted legislative history appears to be misplaced. Nothing in the legislative history indicates that the ordinary rules of evidence in the federal courts should be overridden by a DMR. The court's opinion would create an extraordinary irrebuttable presumption without direct support either from the statute or its legislative history.

Under the Federal Rules of Evidence, presumptions are generally rebuttable. *See* Fed. R. Evid. 301. Although a DMR would be admissible against the discharger under Rule 801(d)(2) of the Federal Rules of Evidence as an "admission by party-opponent," nothing in the rules says that such an admission is *binding*. In fact, the admission is accepted into evidence not because it is trustworthy but because its maker is free to rebut it. Rule 36 of the Federal Rules of Civil

Procedure contains specific procedures for obtaining admissions that *will* be binding upon the opposing party.

Thus, as the court held in *Friends of the Earth v. Facet Enterprises*, 618 F. Supp. 532 (W.D.N.Y. 1984), the discharger should be free to rebut the evidence in a DMR. If the court believes, based on examining all the evidence, that the actual discharge did not violate the permit, it should be able to so rule.

Equitable Defenses

Various equitable defenses may be available in some circumstances in citizen suits, although they are rarely available against the government. Generally estoppel is available only if the defendant can prove "affirmative misconduct" on the part of the government. The mere delay in bringing an enforcement action is not affirmative misconduct. *United States v. Amoco Oil Co.*, 580 F. Supp. 1042 (W.D. Mo. 1984).

In contrast, in *Lloyd A. Fry Roofing Co. v. EPA*, 415 F. Supp. 799, 806–07 (W.D. Mo. 1976), *aff'd*, 554 F.2d 885 (8th Cir. 1977), the Eighth Circuit indicated that the laches defense might be applicable against the government if an enforcement action were delayed for the purpose of accumulating large fines. At least one court has found that the laches defense should be applicable, stating that it would be "the better rule . . . to allow the defense in limited circumstances when it is factually warranted." *See Connecticut Fund for the Env't, Inc. v. Upjohn Co.*, 660 F. Supp. 1397, 1414 (D. Conn. 1987). Compare *Student Pub. Interest Research Group v. P.D. Oil & Chem. Storage, Inc.*, 627 F. Supp. 1074, 1085 (D.N.J. 1986).

In *United States v. Detrex Chem. Indus. Inc.*, 393 F. Supp. 735 (N.D. Ohio 1975), the court held that an EPA administrative order requiring compliance with the Clean Water Act by a particular deadline did not preclude the EPA from seeking civil penalties for violations before that deadline. The court rejected the defendant's theories of waiver and estoppel because, "[t]o rule otherwise, would reward violators of the Act by forgiving penalties incurred where the administrator has invoked this congressionally approved procedure, thereby effectively discouraging the utilization of said procedure." *Id.* at 738.

If a citizen suit were brought during an administrative enforcement proceeding, however, the court would probably dismiss the suit based on the diligent prosecution defense, discussed below.

Although laches and good faith are not generally defenses to liability, such factors can be considered by courts when assessing penalties. *United States v. Amoco Oil Co.*, 580 F. Supp. 1666. *See also* 33 U.S.C. § 1319(d) (1988).

Diligent Prosecution by the EPA or the States

Section 1365(b) also provides that no citizen suit against any person may be commenced:

> If the administrator or State has commenced and is diligently prosecuting a civil or criminal action in a court of the United States or a State to require compliance with the standard, limitation, or order, but in any such action in a court of the United States any citizen may intervene as a matter of right.

This prerequisite to the filing of a citizen suit has given rise to substantial controversy. The primary issues have been whether an administrative proceeding can be a ''court,'' and what sort of enforcement is diligent prosecution.

The first issue has been clarified by the 1987 amendments to the Clean Water Act. Section 309(g), 33 U.S.C. § 1319(g), created a new procedure for the EPA to impose administrative penalties. Section 309(g)(6) provided that if the EPA has commenced and is diligently prosecuting an administrative penalty action (or has actually collected a penalty) under section 1319, no citizen suit for civil penalties will lie under section 1365. This bar also applies to *state* administrative proceedings under a state law that is ''comparable'' to section 309(g). This concept of comparability has not yet been definitely determined. One court, however, has held that the New Jersey Water Pollution Control Act was not comparable to section 1319(g) because the New Jersey statute did not provide for public notice and opportunity to comment on the proposed penalty. *Public Interest Research Group of New Jersey v. GAF Corp.*, 770 F. Supp. 943 (D.N.J. 1991).

The bar will not apply to a citizen suit that has been filed prior to commencement of the administrative action, 33 U.S.C. § 1319(g)(6)(B)(i). Nor will the bar apply if the sixty-day notice precedes the administrative action, as long as the citizen suit is filed within 120 days of giving notice.

Many courts have construed the diligent prosecution defense. They have rejected that defense where the state enforcement action appears to be ineffectual, moribund, or has failed to cause the defendant to achieve compliance after several years. *Compare New York Coastal Fishermen's Ass'n v. New York Dep't of Sanitation*, 772 F. Supp 162 (S.D.N.Y. 1991), *with Connecticut Fund for the Env't v. Contract Plating Co., Inc.*, 631 F. Supp. 1291 (D. Conn. 1986).

Remedies

Section 1365(a) of the Clean Water Act provides that in citizen suits brought under it:

> The district courts shall have jurisdiction, without regard to the amount in controversy or the citizenship of the parties, to enforce such an effluent standard or limitation, or such an order, or to order the administrator to perform such acts or duty, as the case may be, and to apply any appropriate civil penalties under section 309(d) of this Act.

The courts have held, consistent with the legislative history, that the remedies under section 1365 exclude damages paid to a plaintiff. *See Middlesex County Sewerage Auth. v. National Sea Clammers Ass'n*, 453 U.S. 1 (1981); *City of Philadelphia v. Stepan Chem.*, 544 F. Supp. 1135 (E.D. Pa. 1982); *City of Evansville v. Kentucky Liquid Recycling, Inc.*, 604 F.2d 1008 (7th Cir. 1979), *cert. denied*, 444 U.S. 1025 (1980). In addition, the Supreme Court held in *Middlesex County Sewerage Auth.* that there is no implied right of action for damages or other relief available under the Clean Water Act.

Thus the Clean Water Act affords only two categories of remedies to private citizens bringing actions against violators of effluent standards or limitations: (1) enforcement of the federal requirements and (2) civil penalties under section 309(d). Each type of remedy gives immense discretion to the district courts.

Injunctive Relief

In *Weinberger v. Romero-Barcelo*, 456 U.S. 305 (1982), the Supreme Court held that the district courts retain their traditional broad equitable discretion in determining whether to impose injunctive relief under the Clean Water Act. In that case, the plaintiffs sought to enjoin the U.S. Navy, during weapons training exercises, from dropping bombs into the Atlantic Ocean without an NPDES permit. The Supreme Court held that an NPDES permit was required, but it refused to stop the bombing.

Noting that the Navy's activity was in violation of the Clean Water Act, the Court wrote: "The grant of jurisdiction to ensure compliance with a statute hardly suggests an absolute duty to do so under any and all circumstances, and a federal judge sitting as chancellor is not mechanically obligated to grant an injunction for every violation of law." *Id.* at 313. The Court found that this discharge was not harming the quality of the water, so no factual support for an immediate remedy was available.

An injunction was denied for entirely different reasons by the district court in *Maryland v. Train*, 415 F. Supp. 116 (D. Md. 1976), *rev'd in part*, 10 E.R.C. 1351 (4th Cir. 1977), an action by Maryland and Virginia challenging the issuance of a permit to Camden, New Jersey, to use an ocean dumping site in the Delaware Bay. The court found that the permit was defective because the EPA had failed to hold a required hearing before issuing the permit. Nevertheless, the court refused to enjoin the continued dumping of sludge at the disputed site. The court predicated its decision on the lack of feasible alternatives for Camden. The court noted that "if Camden were prevented from dumping sludge at Cape May, it would at this point be forced to dump in the Delaware River, which would create very serious and immediate health and pollution problems." *Id.* at 124.

Although injunctive relief is not mandatory, substantial authority exists that the traditional equitable principles will be applied differently where the government is enforcing a statute designed to protect the public health or welfare. In *EDF, Inc. v. Lamphier*, 714 F.2d 331 (4th Cir. 1983), a case brought by two environmental groups under the citizen suit provision of RCRA, the Fourth Circuit held that issuing an injunction did not require the traditional findings of the inadequacy of legal remedies, risk of irreparable injury, and balancing of equities. The court placed the citizen suit plaintiff in the shoes of the government and invoked the doctrine that where the sovereign is attempting to enjoin activity that may endanger the public health, balancing of equities is not a prerequisite to injunctive relief. Second, the court held that in cases of public health legislation, "the emphasis shifts from irreparable injury to concern for the general public interest. . . ." *Id.* at 338. Finally, the court pointed out that where a statute specifically authorizes injunctive relief, the traditional equitable barriers lose their force.

The EPA's NPDES regulations provide that it "shall not be a defense for a permittee in an enforcement action that it would have been necessary to halt or reduce the permitted activity in order to maintain compliance with the conditions of this permit." 40 C.F.R. § 122.41(c) (1991). Nevertheless, the courts have been disinclined to order a discharger to be shut down due to noncompliance with environmental regulations. *See Union Elec. Co. v. EPA*, 427 U.S. 246 (1976); *Friends of the Earth v. PEPCO*, 419 F. Supp. 528 (D.D.C. 1977); *O'Leary v. Moyer's Landfill*, 523 F. Supp. 659 (E.D. Pa. 1982).

Civil Penalties

Section 1365 of the Clean Water Act empowers the courts "to apply any appropriate civil penalties under Section 1319(d) of this Act."

33 U.S.C. § 1319(d) (1982). Section 1319(d) authorizes the imposition of civil penalties "not to exceed $25,000 per day of such violation."

A distinct set of issues arises concerning how these violations are to be counted. The maximum penalty is $25,000 "per day of such violation." What if a discharger violates five different effluent parameters on the same day? Congress addressed that issue in the 1987 amendments to the Clean Water Act, in which it amended section 1319(d) to provide that "a single operational upset which leads to simultaneous violations of more than one pollutant parameter shall be treated as a single violation."

What if a monthly average limitation, i.e., a limit on the average of all samples taken during a month, is violated because on a single day an upset caused a violation so large that it caused the monthly average limit to be exceeded? The EPA takes the position that such an upset should be counted as thirty days of violation, for a maximum penalty of $750,000. A discharger may argue, however, that section 1319(d) imposes a maximum penalty of $25,000 in this situation.

It is critical to keep in mind that the penalty is a *maximum* of $25,000—the *actual* penalty could be from zero dollars to that maximum. In setting the amount of the penalty, Congress directed the courts to consider the seriousness of the violation; any economic benefit of noncompliance (the EPA has a complex computer model, called the BEN model, to calculate this factor); any history of such violations; the impact of the penalty on the violator; "and such other matters as justice may require." 33 U.S.C. § 1319(d).

The Multiplicity of Litigation

Two aspects of the citizen suit provision create the potential for multiple lawsuits. The first aspect is multiple plaintiffs: The federal government, state government, and private citizens all are potential plaintiffs to enforce NPDES permit requirements. The second is multiple claims: Section 1365 of the Clean Water Act does not permit citizen plaintiffs to collect damages. Accordingly, plaintiffs have proposed a variety of alternative grounds for compensatory relief.

Multiple Plaintiffs

Section 1319(a)(1) of the Clean Water Act evidences Congress's intent that the federal government and states would have concurrent enforcement authority over violations of state-issued NPDES permits. *See also* 33 U.S.C. § 1242 (requiring any state NPDES program to include adequate enforcement authority). Thus the alleged violator of an NPDES permit faces potential litigation from citizens, from the EPA, and from the state.

If a state enforcement action is still pending, the federal government may sue concurrently. *See United States v. Cargill, Inc.*, 508 F. Supp. 734 (D. Del. 1981). Citizens groups also may sue concurrently if there has not been diligent prosecution. *See Brewer v. Detroit*, 577 F. Supp. 519 (E.D. Tenn. 1983). In *Cargill*, however, the federal court stayed an EPA enforcement action alleging violations of an NPDES permit where Delaware had brought an action in state court seeking identical injunctive relief but lesser civil penalties. The stay was carefully limited, however, to protect the EPA's right to seek greater civil penalties than those being sought by the state.

In contrast, where enforcement litigation has been concluded, each of these parties—whether federal, state, and/or citizen–has been held to bind the other except that private citizens generally do not bind the federal government with regard to enforcement actions.

In contrast to the analysis in *Cargill*, a final adjudication in state litigation to enforce the terms of an NPDES permit was held to bind the federal government in *United States v. ITT Rayonier, Inc.*, 627 F.2d 996 (9th Cir. 1980). The defendant had asserted that a particular clause in the permit excused noncompliance, and the Washington Supreme Court agreed. The Ninth Circuit held that the federal government was bound by the state court decision because the existence of concurrent enforcement powers does not negate the application of *res judicata*. *Id.* at 1001. The court held that the federal government would be deemed to be "in privity" with the state. *Id.* at 1003.

A more commonplace principle is that a state participating in litigation is deemed to represent its citizens, who are bound by the result. *See Delaware Valley Citizen's Council for Clean Air v. Pennsylvania*, 11 E.L.R. 20,952 (E.D. Pa. 1981), *aff'd*, 674 F.2d 970 (3d Cir. 1982); *see also Southwest Airlines Co. v. Texas Int'l Airlines*, 546 F.2d 84, 98 (5th Cir. 1977) (action by a city). The presumption that the state or federal government is acting on behalf of its citizens does not depend on a unanimity of citizen interests. *Badgley v. City of New York*, 606 F.2d 358 (2d Cir. 1979).

In *EDF v. Alexander*, 501 F. Supp. 742 (N.D. Miss. 1980), *modified on other grounds sub nom. EDF v. Marsh*, 651 F.2d 983 (5th Cir. 1981), a judgment against two citizen groups and an individual was deemed to bind others who later joined them in a second action under NEPA. The court applied the doctrine of "virtual representation," whose purpose is to prevent the doctrine of *res judicata* from being "emasculated by merely a formal change of parties." The district court's decision was subsequently reversed on the ground that the two suits presented different claims. 651 F.2d 983 (5th Cir. 1981). The court of appeals never addressed the lower court's application of the doctrine of virtual representation.

The boundaries of this doctrine are unclear, although it has been recognized by a number of courts. 18 Wright, Miller & Cooper, *Federal Practice and Procedure*, § 4457 (1981). The doctrine is appropriate for citizen suits. Otherwise, a company could face as many citizen suits as there are people with standing under the hospitable section 1365 standing provisions. As Wright, Miller, and Cooper stated:

> Private standing to pursue basically public claims inevitably leads to the question whether successive private actions can be brought. . . . State courts . . . have been persuaded that a first taxpayer action may properly preclude a second taxpayer action asserting the same grievance. . . . [F]ederal courts too should seriously consider the possibility of preclusion, not only in the few areas in which taxpayer actions are permitted but also in other areas in which the standing asserted in successive actions rests on highly similar and attenuated claims of personal impact.

Id. § 4458. The attenuated standing requirements of section 1365 appear to present the grounds for this preclusion.

The courts appear willing to invoke the doctrine of *res judicata* where a second plaintiff attempts to enforce the same legal requirement previously litigated by another. The one exception appears to be that litigation by private citizens does not bind the government. *See United States v. East Baton Rouge Parish School Bd.*, 594 F.2d 56 (5th Cir. 1979). In *Sierra Club v. Electronic Controls Design*, 909 F.2d 1350 (9th Cir. 1990), the court concluded that the government would *not* be bound by the consent decree in the citizen suit action and could initiate its own enforcement action for the same violations.

In the case of citizen suits brought under section 1365, however, it is arguable that the government should be bound by the result because (1) the citizen must give sixty days' notice to the government before filing suit, (2) the citizen must enforce the same requirements as would the government, and (3) the government may intervene in any such citizen suit as a matter of right under paragraph 1365(c)(2). In the face of such elaborate, careful protection of the government's interests, the government should be bound by the results.

Multiple Claims
Section 1365(e) provides:

> Nothing in this section shall restrict any right which any person (or class of persons) may have under any statute or common law to seek enforcement of any effluent standard or limitation or to seek any other relief (including relief against the Administrator or a State agency).

In *City of Milwaukee v. Illinois*, 451 U.S. 304 (1981), the Supreme Court construed section 1365(e) as meaning "only that the provisions of such suit does not revoke other remedies." *Id.* at 329. The court pointed out that language similar to subsection e appears in virtually every citizen suit provision, so that it could not be read to have a more pointed meaning. Generally, the federal courts have held that the Clean Water Act preempts other federal claims regarding activity regulated under it. State claims, however, are not preempted.

The legislative history of the Clean Water Act indicates that section 1365 itself was not intended to create a federal common law of water quality. *See* 1971 S. Rep. No. at 79, *reprinted in* 1972 Legislative History at 1497. To the contrary, it was to be used only to enforce specific administratively developed requirements. In *City of Milwaukee,* the Supreme Court held that the comprehensive regulatory scheme of the Clean Water Act preempts any federal common law of nuisance. 451 U.S. at 328–29. Similarly, in *Middlesex County Sewerage Auth.*, the Supreme Court held that there is no implied private right of action for damages under the Clean Water Act. *See also California v. Sierra Club*, 451 U.S. 287 (1981) (Rivers and Harbors Act); *Conner v. Aerovox, Inc.*, 730 F.2d 835 (1st Cir. 1984) (maritime tort law).

In contrast, actions under *state* law are *not* preempted by the Clean Water Act. Section 1370 of the Clean Water Act expressly reserves state authority to regulate discharges of pollutants and to retain jurisdiction with respect to state waters, including state boundary waters. *See Ouellette v. International Paper Co.*, 602 F. Supp. 264, 269 (D. Vt. 1985).

Thus the line regarding preclusion of damage claims for violation of water pollution standards appears to be sharply drawn. Claims for damages under federal law will be precluded; claims under state law will not.

Attorney Fees

The recovery of attorney fees is a major goal for environmental groups that file citizen suits. Complaints typically request attorney fees, and their recovery often is a significant issue in settlement discussions.

Under the "American rule," each party must pay its own attorney fees unless Congress has statutorily altered this rule and expressly authorized a court to award attorney fees. *Alyeska Pipeline Serv. Co. v. Wilderness Soc'y*, 421 U.S. 240, 247, 257–62 (1972). The circumstances under which attorney fees are to be awarded is for Congress to determine. *Id.* at 262.

Section 1365(d) of the Clean Water Act authorizes the awarding of attorney fees for citizen suits:

> The court, in issuing any final order in any action brought pursuant to this section may award costs of litigation (including reasonable attorney and expert witness fees) to any prevailing or substantially prevailing party, whenever the court determines such award is appropriate.

Congress sought to provide for attorney fees in two circumstances: (1) to a *plaintiff* who performs "a public service" in litigation brought under an environmental statute and (2) to a *defendant* subjected to "frivolous or harassing" litigation. S. Rep. No. 92–414, 91st Cong., 1st Sess. 81 (1971); *reprinted in* 1972 Legislative History at 1499. The latter standard was adopted by the court in *NWF v. Consumers Power Company*, 729 F. Supp. 62 (W.D. Mich. 1989).

In *Ruckelshaus v. Sierra Club*, 103 S. Ct. 3274 (1983), decided under the (virtually identical) citizen suit provisions of the Clean Air Act, the Supreme Court held that a person must achieve some success on the merits of at least one substantive claim to recover any attorney fees. The claimant does not need to have won all or even a majority of its arguments, but it must prevail at least in part on some of them to be eligible for fees. The victory need not have been a judgment or settlement with the citizen plaintiff himself. A citizen plaintiff may have prevailed because the suit motivated a settlement between the defendant and a state enforcement agency. *Atlantic States Legal Found., Inc. v. Eastman Kodak Co., Inc.*, 933 F.2d 124 (2d Cir. 1991).

To determine the amount of a fee award, the courts establish a "lodestar" calculated by multiplying a reasonable hourly rate times the number of hours reasonably expended. The reasonably hourly rate is the rate prevailing in the local community for similar work. Courts have concluded that the number of hours reasonably expended included the time devoted to preparing the fee request itself.

The foregoing discussion sets forth the basic rules for calculating a reasonable attorney fee. However, a court in the exercise of its equitable discretion may reduce this figure if it determines that the work should have been completed in fewer hours: "An applicant for attorney fees is only entitled to an award for time reasonably expended." *National Ass'n of Concerned Veterans v. Secretary of Defense*, 675 F.2d 1319, 1327 (D.C. Cir. 1982). Awards will be reduced if the court finds that a case was overstaffed or otherwise inefficiently handled. *Student Pub. Interest Research Group v. Monsanto Co.*, 721 F. Supp. 604 (D.N.J. 1989). Plaintiffs may also receive fee awards for preparing the petition for fees, although, as with fee awards for work on the merits, the amount may be reduced for inefficiency or lack of total success. *Student Pub. Interest Research Group v. Monsanto Co.*, 727 F. Supp. 876 (D.N.J. 1989).

The Erosion of Traditional Corporate Law Doctrines in Environmental Cases

Thomas M. McMahon, Katie A. Moertl, and Donna M. Kellick

The problem of finding solvent parties to pay for the cleanup of hazardous waste sites has troubled both Congress and the courts. Congress's response to the problem was CERCLA, 42 U.S.C. § 9601 *et seq.*, and RCRA, 42 U.S.C. § 6901 *et seq.*, which impose strict liability upon broad classes of persons for cleanup costs. In situations where the liable corporation is insolvent or defunct, recent court decisions construing CERCLA and RCRA have sliced through the corporate entity and have imposed both derivative ("piercing") and direct liability on officers and shareholders of corporations. Additionally, the decisions suggest that the courts are willing to extend liability to successor/purchaser corporations for the acts of the predecessor/seller corporations under certain conditions. These developments in the courts significantly erode traditional corporate law protection of shareholders and successor corporations.

This article discusses the difficulty for officers, shareholders, directors, and corporations in shedding environmental liability once it attaches through a variety of legal doctrines. These same doctrines provide the ground rules for structuring business ventures so as to avoid unwarranted environmental liability, and they are strict liability, piercing the corporate veil, direct liability, and successor liability. Recent cases follow the general discussion of each doctrine to

Thomas McMahon is a partner and Katie Moertl and Donna Kellick are associates in the Chicago office of Sidley & Austin. All three concentrate in environmental law.

illustrate the ever-widening net of environmental liability that haunts the corporate world.

Strict Liability

The doctrine of strict liability or liability without fault is the most important factor in environmental liability. It attaches, not as a result of culpable behavior, but merely based on a *relationship* to a harm and reflects a public policy judgment about who is to bear the cost of the unfortunate consequences of a particular business venture.

CERCLA and its state clones are the most obvious and dramatic examples of strict environmental liability. CERCLA-type statutes reflect a clear legislative judgment that the cost of environmental contamination is to be borne by any entity with a defined *relationship* to the hazardous substance causing the problem, regardless of *fault*.

Property transfer statutes, especially those in New Jersey and Connecticut, have fundamentally the same bases and result as CERCLA statutes. Moreover, property transfer statutes are even more "efficient" in that they do not require a government investigation. Rather, they self-trigger as the result of a transaction that may change ownership or control of an environmental liability. Other property transfer statutes, e.g., the one in Illinois, may require disclosures about past uses of the property and/or cleanup of the property before transfer.

In addition, there are well-established state common-law doctrines that impose strict liability for "hazardous" activities. These doctrines are typified by sections 519–20 of the *Restatement (Second) of Torts* and would impose strict liability on any entity engaged in "ultrahazardous" activities. There is little doubt that the generation, handling, and/or control of hazardous substances may sometimes be deemed an ultrahazardous activity producing strict liability. *See, e.g., Jersey City Redev. Auth. v. PPG Indus., Inc.*, 18 Envtl. L. Rep. (Envtl. L. Inst.) 20,364 (D.N.J. 1987) (under New Jersey common law, those who generate or distribute hazardous waste face strict liability), *aff'd*, 866 F.2d 1411 (3d Cir. 1988).

Piercing the Corporate Veil

We tend to assume that corporate liabilities, including environmental liabilities, basically begin and end within the corporate structure. Generally, a corporate "veil" protects shareholders by limiting their exposure to the liabilities of the corporation to the value of their investment in the stock of the corporation. However, under certain circumstances, the corporate veil will be "pierced" and shareholders will be held responsible for corporate liabilities. The required elements to pierce the veil are:

- excessive control or domination by share-holder(s)
- commission of wrong through the corporate form
- unjust loss or injury.

See Allied Corp. v. Frola, 701 F. Supp. 1084 (D.N.J. 1988) (emphasizing that parent corporation must have engaged in some "wrongdoing" before corporate veil can be pierced under New Jersey common law). *See generally* 1 Fletcher, *Cyclopedia of the Law of Private Corporations* §§ 38–41 (rev. ed. 1983).

There is, however, an evolving *federal* piercing doctrine in which the traditional doctrine is not abandoned but is not strictly applied by a number of federal courts. The federal doctrine gives precedence to ensuring effective implementation of policies set forth in federal statutes:

> The general rule adopted in the federal cases is that a "corporate entity may be disregarded in the interests of public convenience, fairness and equity." In applying this rule, federal courts will look closely at the purpose of the federal statute to determine whether the statute places importance on the corporate form, an inquiry that usually gives less respect to the corporate form than does the strict common law alter ego doctrine.

Town of Brookline v. Gorsuch, 667 F.2d 215, 221 (1st Cir. 1981); *see also United States v. Kimbell Foods, Inc.*, 440 U.S. 715 (1979).

Federal courts have struggled with the factors to use when deciding to pierce the corporate veil. Several recent decisions have attempted to establish a uniform federal rule of piercing, and the following courts either pierced or indicated their willingness to pierce the veil pursuant to a more lenient federal rule.

United States v. Kayser-Roth, 724 F. Supp. 15 (D.R.I. 1989), *aff'd*, 910 F.2d 24 (1st Cir. 1990), *cert. denied*, 111 S. Ct. 957 (1991), is an important case. After a trial on the merits, the district court pierced the corporate veil of the defunct subsidiary to hold the parent corporation liable based upon the control exercised by the parent over the subsidiary. Excessive financial control, common officers and directors, and pervasive control over operations by the parent convinced the court that piercing was warranted. Note, however, that the First Circuit did not address the piercing decision by the court. Instead, the First Circuit affirmed the parent corporation's direct liability under Superfund.

In dicta, in *United States v. Nicolet, Inc.*, 712 F. Supp. 1193, 1202 (E.D. Pa. 1989), the court stated that it *would* pierce the veil:

> [W]here a subsidiary is or was at the relevant time a member of one of the classes of persons potentially liable under CERCLA; and the parent had a substantial financial or ownership interest in the subsidiary; and the parent corporation controls or at the relevant time controlled the management and operations of the subsidiary, the parent's separate corporate existence may be disregarded.

In another CERCLA case, *United States v. McGraw Edison Co.*, 718 F. Supp. 154 (W.D.N.Y. 1989), a corporate shareholder's summary judgment motion as to CERCLA liability was denied even though the shareholder owned only 49 percent of the stock in the polluting corporation. The shareholder had an agreement with the polluting corporation to provide technical expertise over the polluter's manufacturing process. Additionally, the two corporations shared common officers. These facts alone raised a material issue of fact as to the degree of control exercised by the shareholder over the polluting corporation.

United States v. Mottolo, 695 F. Supp. 615 (D.N.H. 1988), is another case on point. The court pierced the veil and held the present corporation liable under CERCLA for the acts of the unincorporated predecessor entity where the defendant admitted that he had incorporated, in part, to escape potential personal liability. The court held that "CERCLA places no importance on the corporate form." *Id.* at 624.

More than one corporate veil may be pierced to find the parent corporation liable. In a recent case, the court pierced the corporate veil of a subsidiary of the parent corporation's subsidiary to find the parent liable. In *CPC International v. Aerojet-General Corp.*, Nos. G89–10503 CA, G89–961 CA (W.D. Mich. Aug. 27, 1991), 1991 U.S. Dist. LEXIS 12,143, the court pierced the corporate veil and held the parent corporation liable as a present owner of a site contaminated by its subsidiary's subsidiary, the actual owner of the site. The court stated that under relevant state law, the court must consider the unique facts and circumstances of the parent-subsidiary relationship at issue in order to determine whether to disregard the separate corporate existences of the parent and the subsidiary. Excessive control of financial and operational matters by the parent over its subsidiary's subsidiary caused the court to pierce the two corporate veils.

However, other federal district court cases have upheld the validity of the corporate veil. *Joslyn Manufacturing Corp. v. T.L. James & Co.*, 696 F. Supp. 222 (W.D. La. 1988), *aff'd*, 893 F.2d 80 (5th

Cir. 1990), *cert. denied*, 111 S. Ct. 1017 (1991), is one of them. This is the only federal court of appeals case to have addressed the subject to date. During the appeal, the DOJ filed an *amicus* brief that took a very aggressive stance, arguing that if a parent had any more than a mere stock ownership, the veil should be pierced. The appellate court did not mention the DOJ brief and upheld the district court's decision not to pierce. The appellate court, without any in-depth analysis, stated that the corporate formalities had been followed and that the parent had not exercised sufficient control over the subsidiary to warrant a finding that the subsidiary was merely a sham.

In *Jacksonville Electric Authority v. Eppinger & Russell Co.*, No. 88–873–Civ–J–16 (M.D. Fla. Oct. 18, 1991), 1991 U.S. Dist. LEXIS 15,674, the court applied traditional veil-piercing criteria in refusing to impose liability on a university owning stock of a company that owned and operated a contaminated site. In reaching this conclusion, the court stated:

> The facts of this case do not justify piercing the corporate veil. Aside from common stock ownership, common officers and common directors (which are factors to be expected where the parent company owns virtually all of the subsidiary's stock), there are no facts which indicate that Defendant used [the subsidiary] . . . as a sham to avoid direct liability.

Id. at *8–*9.

Finally, in *John Boyd Co. v. Boston Gas Co.*, No. 89–675–T (D. Mass. July 3, 1991), 1991 W.L. 209,088, the court held that even though a parent corporation voted its shares to approve the sale of assets of a subsidiary that had owned contaminated property, such an act did not constitute evidence of control sufficient to pierce the corporate veil. In reaching its conclusion, the court stated that "shareholder participation in such basic decisions is entirely consistent with traditional corporate organization." *Id.* at *6.

Direct Individual Liability

An individual shareholder, director, officer, or employee may be held *directly* liable if he or she participates in, authorizes, or sanctions the commission of a tort by the corporation. *See* 3A Fletcher, *Cyclopedia of the Law of Private Corporations* §§ 1135, 1137; *United States v. Mottolo*, 629 F. Supp. 56, 60 (D.N.H. 1984). Further, the individual is not protected from liability merely because he or she is acting on behalf of the corporation. *United States v. Wade*, 577 F.

Supp. 1326, 1341 (E.D. Pa. 1983). The corporate veil need not be pierced to hold an individual shareholder liable if he or she participated in the wrongful act. *United States v. Northeastern Pharmaceutical & Chem. Co. (NEPACCO)*, 810 F.2d 726 (8th Cir. 1986), *cert. denied*, 484 U.S. 848 (1987).

Moreover, even if a corporation that caused the pollution has dissolved, a former shareholder may be held liable under the trust fund theory. Under that theory, "the shareholders receiving the assets from a dissolved corporation, hold those assets in trust for the creditors of the dissolved corporation where the corporation is left without sufficient assets [*sic*] to pay the creditors." *U-Haul Co. of Inland Northwest v. Yakima Rex Spray Co.*, No. 90–2–00155–4 (Wash. Sup. Ct. Aug. 24, 1990).

Under Superfund, a shareholder can be held directly liable as an "owner," "operator," "generator," or "transporter" under section 107. The tests for this liability are evolving, and they include (1) active participation, (2) power or capacity to control, or exercise of that control, and (3) profit from the activity that caused the problem.

Recent cases indicating the courts' willingness to impose direct liability include *New York v. Shore Realty Corp.*, 759 F.2d 1032 (2d Cir. 1985). In this case, officers who were also shareholders and participated in the management and disposal activities of the polluting corporation were directly liable as owners and operators.

United States v. NEPACCO, 579 F. Supp. 823 (W.D. Mo. 1984), *aff'd in part, rev'd in part*, 810 F.2d 726 (8th Cir. 1986), *cert. denied*, 484 U.S. 848 (1987), stands for the proposition that a shareholder may be held liable based on his possessing the *capacity to control* the corporation's waste-handling practices. In *NEPACCO*, the Eighth Circuit held that one officer was directly liable because he had actually arranged for disposal under CERCLA § 107(a)(3) and thus participated in the resulting harm. However, under RCRA, the court greatly expanded its test for liability when it held the other officer liable solely based upon his capacity to control the corporation's *operations.*

Columbia River Service Corp. v. Gilman, 751 F. Supp. 1448 (W.D. Wash. 1990), is another case on point. The court denied summary judgment for the shareholders/officers of a dissolved corporation that had caused pollution prior to its dissolution. The court cited to *NEPACCO* and stated that an employee could be liable for acts over which he or she had direct control.

In *Quadion Corp. v. Mache*, 738 F. Supp. 270 (N.D. Ill. 1990), the court denied the defendants'/former shareholders' motions to dismiss the successor corporation's (Quadion) CERCLA contribution claims. The court cited to the "prevention" test, developed by the federal court in Michigan, to determine whether liability could be imposed on a shareholder of a closely held corporation. (*See* the detailed discussion of the *Thomas Solvent* and *Kelley v. ARCO* prevention test below.) The prevention test does not require piercing the veil. More importantly, the test also does *not* require that the shareholder exercise control over the waste-handling practices of the polluting corporation. Rather, like *NEPACCO*, having the *capacity* to control or abate the damage may expose the shareholder to liability. (Note that prior to *Quadion*, the northern district stated in *Rockwell* that having the capacity to control was not sufficient to impose liability and that actual exercise of that control was necessary to impose shareholder liability. However, *Quadion*, unlike *Rockwell*, concerned the liability of officers of a closely held corporation.) In a later proceeding, the court granted the smaller shareholder's motion for summary judgment.

Interestingly, in *In re Southern Pine Wood Preserving Co. & Brax Batson*, Docket No. RCRA–87–13–R, U.S. EPA, 1989 RCRA LEXIS 21 (Nov. 13, 1989), an administrative law judge held a shareholder/officer who owned only *10 percent* of the stock in a noncomplying corporation personally liable for the facility's failure to properly close a surface impoundment where the corporate owner was without resources to properly close the facility.

In *United States v. Conservation Chemical Co.*, 733 F. Supp. 1215 (N.D. Ind. 1989), the court held the president liable as an operator under RCRA because he was also chairman of the board, treasurer, and held 90 percent of the outstanding stock in the polluting corporation; designed the treatment process that caused the pollution contamination; visited the facility frequently for a long period of time and spoke with the plant manager almost daily regarding leaks/spills; and was responsible for environmental compliance of the facility.

The federal court for the Western District of Michigan issued several opinions in 1989 setting forth a prevention test for determining the direct liability of an officer, shareholder, and director as an owner or operator under CERCLA. In *Kelley v. ARCO Indus.*, 723 F. Supp. 1214 (W.D. Mich. 1989), the court articulated a detailed rationale:

> [The court will] weigh the factors of the corporate individual's degree of authority in general and specific responsibility for health and safety practices, including hazardous waste disposal. . . . [A]n individual's

power to control the practice and policy of the corporation, and the responsibility undertaken by that individual in this area should be considered.

. . .

The standard I have articulated is quite unlike the lack of corporate formalities associated with piercing the corporate veil, and is different from the issue of personal knowledge, direct supervision, or active participation found in most ordinary torts by corporate actors. Here the focus on the inquiry is whether the corporate individual could have prevented the hazardous waste discharge at issue. Thus power or authority will be analyzed. . . . Secondly, the court, in determining individual liability under [section] 107, will look at responsibility undertaken for waste disposal practices as it relates to the prevention test. Here active, direct, knowing efforts to prevent or abate the contamination may work for—not against—a corporate defendant where the acts suggest the individual tried but was unable to prevent or abate the unlawful waste disposal.

Id. at 1219–20. The officers entered into a consent decree and settled with the state shortly after this decision was rendered. No admission of liability was made. *See* Haz. Waste Lit. Rep. 18,363–64 (Dec. 19, 1989). Later, in two other related decisions, the court relied on the same prevention test. *See Kelley v. Thomas Solvent Co.*, 727 F. Supp. 1532 (W.D. Mich. 1989); *Kelley v. Thomas Solvent Co.*, 727 F. Supp. 1554 (W.D. Mich. 1989).

These federal court decisions are significant because they focus on the *ability* of an officer or shareholder to control, prevent, or abate the release of hazardous substances. Such a focus is similar to the *NEPACCO* court's reliance on the mere capacity to control as a basis for liability. The Michigan and Illinois federal courts differentiated the *power* to control from *actual exercise* of the power, placing emphasis on the power itself.

In *Rockwell International Corp. v. IU International Corp.*, 702 F. Supp. 1384 (N.D. Ill. 1988), the court rejected the *NEPACCO* stance and stated that the mere capacity to control was not enough to cause liability to attach. Instead the court held that: "Only those who actually operate or exercise control over the facility that creates an environmental risk can be held liable under CERCLA for the costs of reducing that risk." *Id.* at 1390.

Direct liability, although accepted by the majority of courts, also has its critics. The Fifth Circuit has twice refused to impose direct liability on corporate officers. In *Riverside Market Development Corp. v. International Building Products, et al.*, No. 88-5317 (E.D.

La. May 22, 1990), 1990 U.S. Dist. LEXIS 6375, *aff'd in part*, 931 F.2d 327 (5th Cir. 1991), the court *granted* one of the two defendant/officers' motion for summary judgment where the officer was an 85 percent shareholder and chairman of the board. The court held that the following facts were insufficient to impose liability as a past operator on the officer/shareholder. First, he lived in a different state and only visited the facility one to three times per year for specific financial or social reasons. Next, he reviewed financial statements regularly and was the principal source of money. However, the court *denied* the other corporate officer's motion for summary judgment, holding that a genuine issue of fact existed because the officer was the CEO (and owned 15 percent of the stock in the asbestos manufacturing facility); spent 10 percent of his time each month at the facility; occasionally was involved in day-to-day operations and may have actually run some machines; had an office at the plant and sometimes supervised activities; ordered the asbestos fiber (raw materials); and negotiated supplier contracts. Additionally, he was somewhat familiar with the company's waste disposal practices and environmental licenses.

On appeal of the district court's grant of summary judgment in favor of the 85 percent shareholder, the Fifth Circuit affirmed. *Riverside Market Dev. Corp.*, 931 F.2d at 328.

Finally, in *Joslyn Corp. v. T.L. James & Co.*, 696 F. Supp. 222, 226 (W.D. La. 1988), *aff'd*, 893 F.2d 80 (5th Cir. 1990), *cert. denied*, 111 S. Ct. 1017 (1991), the district court stated in dicta: "Neither the clear language of CERCLA nor its legislative history provides authority for imposing individual liability on corporate officers. . . ." The Fifth Circuit upheld the district court's refusal to impose direct liability. In *Riverside Market* above, however, the Fifth Circuit recognized that there could be a situation where an individual director, officer, or employee could be considered an "operator" under CERCLA.

Direct Parent Corporation Liability

Parent corporations are as much at risk from the ever-expanding CERCLA net of liability. Present case law extends the individual rule of direct liability to parent corporations and applies basically the same tests as the individual rule. Some recent cases recognizing that a parent corporation may be directly liable follow.

In *CPC International v. Aerojet-General Corp.*, Nos. G89–10503 CA, G89–961 CA (W.D. Mich. Aug. 27, 1991), 1991 U.S. Dist. LEXIS 12,143, the court held two parent corporations directly liable as operators for the actions of their subsidiaries. "CERCLA broadens the potential for liability of parent corporations without discarding entirely the traditional concept of limited liability that is central to corporate law." *Id.* at *62.

> Factors to consider in assessing whether a parent *operated* its subsidiary include the parent's participation in the subsidiary's board of director's, management, day-to-day operations, and specific policy matters, including areas such as manufacturing, finances, personnel and waste disposal. In addition, determining the origin and business function of the subsidiary in the context of the parent corporation's business may be helpful in determining whether the parent has operated a wholly owned subsidiary.

Id. at *64 (emphasis added).

United States v. Kayser-Roth Corp., 724 F. Supp. 15 (D.R.I. 1989), *aff'd*, 910 F.2d 24 (1st Cir. 1990), *cert. denied*, 111 S. Ct. 957 (1991), is another case on point. Although the court noted that a parent corporation cannot ordinarily be deemed an operator of its subsidiary based solely upon the parent's status as a shareholder, the court held the parent liable due to the parent's exercise of control over the management and operations of the subsidiary.

In *Mobay Corp. v. Allied-Signal, Inc.*, 761 F. Supp. 345 (D.N.J. 1991), the court denied the parent corporation's motion for summary judgment on liability. The court agreed with the *Kayser-Roth* test, which requires the parent corporation to have exercised pervasive control over the subsidiary in order to hold the parent liable as an operator of the subsidiary.

Gopher Oil Co. v. Union Oil Co. of California, 757 F. Supp. 988 (D. Minn. 1990), also applied direct liability to a parent corporation. After a trial on the merits, the court held the parent corporation 100 percent liable to the current owner of a site for the acts of the parent's subsidiary that had caused the contamination prior to sale. The jury returned responses to questions presented by the court and stated that Union Oil should be 100 percent responsible for all future costs and that Gopher Oil should have no responsibility, even though Gopher Oil operated the site for three years. Note that this case is on appeal.

Some courts have refused to hold the parent corporation directly liable under CERCLA. Among these decisions is *Jacksonville Electric Authority v. Eppinger and Russell Co.*, No. 88–873–Civ–J–16 (M.D. Fla. Oct. 18, 1991), 1991 U.S. Dist. LEXIS 15,674. The court noted that the parent corporation did not exercise actual and pervasive control in this case and held that the parent corporation was not an operator. Although the parent corporation and subsidiary did have some common officers and directors, the court concluded that this was merely an example of "concomitant general authority or ability to control" that frequently attends the parent-subsidiary relationship. *Id.* at *16 (citing *Kayser-Roth*). Moreover, there was no evidence that the parent corporation was materially involved in the subsidiary's daily operations.

Another refusal to apply direct liability to a parent occurred in *John Boyd Co. v. Boston Gas Co.*, No. 89–675–T (D. Mass. July 3, 1991), 1991 W.L. 209,088. Although the parent corporation voted its shares to approve the sale of assets of a subsidiary that had owned contaminated property, the court held that that did not demonstrate the type of control required to hold the parent directly liable. According to the court, a "single such corporate act, unconnected in any way to decisions about the operations of the facility in question, cannot suffice to demonstrate 'the pervasive control necessary to prove operator status.' " *Id.* at *3 (quoting *Kayser-Roth*).

In a new application of direct liability under CERCLA, a court recently held a parent corporation directly liable as a generator and transporter. Generator liability attaches when a person "arranges for the disposal" of hazardous substances. 42 U.S.C. § 9607(a)(3). Transporter liability attaches when a person transports hazardous substances to a facility he or she has selected. 42 U.S.C. § 9607(a)(4). In *City of New York v. Exxon Corp.*, 112 Bankr. 540 (Bankr. S.D.N.Y. 1990), *aff'd in part*, 932 F.2d 1020 (2d Cir. 1991), the court held a parent corporation directly liable for the midnight dumping acts of its wholly owned subsidiary. The parent acquired the assets and stock of a waste oil business and transferred them to a specially created subsidiary. The parent knew at the time of acquisition that the president of the subsidiary was also the sole shareholder in six other related waste oil reprocessing, transport, and disposal businesses. In holding the parent liable as a generator and transporter (rather than as an owner/operator), the court found that the financial and decision-making control exercised by the parent over the subsidiary warranted imposing liability on the parent.

Exxon is significant because the court used the principles of the owner/operator cases to impose liability on a parent corporation as a generator and transporter of waste even though the waste was actually handled by its subsidiary.

One appellate court has ruled that a parent corporation cannot be held directly liable. In *Joslyn Corp. v. T.L. James & Co.*, 696 F. Supp. 222 (W.D. La. 1988), *aff'd*, 893 F.2d 80 (5th Cir. 1990), *cert.*

denied, 111 S. Ct. 1017 (1991), the court held that parent corporations are not subject to direct liability under CERCLA for their subsidiaries' contaminated facilities; however, parents can be responsible for subsidiaries' contaminated facilities if the corporate veil is pierced.

Successor Liability

Generally, a purchase of assets or stock does not subject the purchaser (successor) to the liabilities of the seller unless the purchaser assents to liability, nor does the purchaser ordinarily assume the seller's debts unless specifically provided for in the purchase. Traditional exceptions exist under standard corporate law. These are:

- the seller's liabilities are expressly or impliedly assumed by the successor,
- the transaction constitutes a *de facto* merger of the seller into the successor,
- the successor is the mere continuation of the seller, and
- the transaction is undertaken for a fraudulent purpose.

There are also evolving exceptions that may impose environmental liabilities on successors even *absent* the elements of the traditional exceptions.

Three appellate courts have addressed the issue of successor liability in environmental cases. Recent application of the traditional exceptions occurred in the following appellate and district court cases.

Louisiana-Pacific Corp. v. Asarco, Inc., 29 Env't Rep. Cas. (BNA) 1450 (W.D. Wash. 1989), *aff'd*, 909 F.2d 1260 (9th Cir. 1990), is a seminal case in this area. The Ninth Circuit held that in an asset sale the traditional state rules of successor liability should govern, *but not if state law unduly restricts liability*. The court noted that Congress did intend successor liability to apply under CERCLA; that such liability will be governed by federal law; and, in the context of an asset sale, CERCLA will not only permit but may require successor liability imposed under traditional concepts. The court upheld the district court's decision that, in this particular case, *no* successor liability should attach under the four traditional exceptions because there was no continuity of shareholders between the corporations and the subsequent corporation did not continue the predecessor's business operations.

In *Anspec Co., Inc. v. Johnson Controls, Inc.*, 922 F.2d 1240 (6th Cir. 1991), the Sixth Circuit reversed the district court's holding that CERCLA did not create successor corporation liability. Although the Sixth Circuit stated that it was following *Smith Land* and *Louisiana-Pacific*, both of which held that CERCLA allowed for imposing successor liability, the Sixth Circuit's holding was slightly more broad. "Rather, construing the statute [CERCLA] in light of a universally accepted principle of private corporation law, we conclude that Congress *included successor corporations within the description of entities that are potentially liable under CERCLA for cleanup costs. That is to say, when Congress wrote 'corporation' in CERCLA, it intended to include a successor corporation." Id.* at 1245 (emphasis added). Unlike *Smith Land* and *Louisiana-Pacific*, however, the Sixth Circuit saw no need for a uniform federal rule for successor liability and instead held that state law would apply.

Smith Land & Improv. Corp. v. Celotex Corp., 851 F.2d 86, 91 (3d Cir. 1988), *cert. denied*, 488 U.S. 1029 (1989), must also be considered. Under CERCLA, Congress intended to impose successor liability on corporations that have merged or consolidated with a PRP. When the choice is "between the taxpayers or a successor corporation [for cleanup costs], the successor should bear the cost." The case was remanded to determine if there had been a consolidation or merger. The court noted, however, that the lower court had to consider the need for national uniformity on the issue of successor liability and should use state corporate law only as a guide, not as a rule.

In *Con-Tech Sales Defined Benefit Trust v. Cockerham*, No. 87–5137 (E.D. Pa. Jan. 18, 1991), 1991 U.S. Dist. LEXIS 664, the court refused summary judgment for two successor corporations, each of which consecutively purchased the assets of a predecessor corporation that caused contamination off-site. However, summary judgment was denied because the assumption of liabilities provisions in the asset purchase agreements entered into by the two successor corporations required more facts for interpretation.

Another case on point is *Sylvester Brothers Development Co. v. Burlington Northern Railroad, Metal-Matic, Inc., et al.*, 32 Env't Rep Cas. (BNA) 1122 (D. Minn. Sept. 11, 1990). In *Sylvester Bros.*, the plaintiff and a defendant/third-party plaintiff sued another company under theories of successor liability. The court followed traditional corporate successor law and held that because there was no continuity of shareholders as the sale involved an asset purchase, the plaintiff and defendant/third-party plaintiff had failed to prove that the corporation was a successor corporation under the *de facto* merger theory. Both plaintiff and third-party plaintiff urged the court to accept the expanded version of the continuity of enterprise theory used in other cases and noted that there was substantial continuity between the predecessor and the successor corporation. The court declined to adopt the expanded version, citing to the few decisions that have adopted this position and noting that it was a minority position. The successor corporation's motion for summary judgment was granted.

American National Can Co. v. Kerr Glass Manufacturing Corp., No. 89–C–0168 (N.D. Ill. Aug. 22, Aug. 30, 1990), 1990 U.S. Dist. LEXIS 10,999 and 11,417, must also be reviewed in this context. In an earlier decision on August 22, 1990, the court granted summary judgment for the plaintiff and held the successor corporation that purchased the assets of the predecessor liable for the acts of its predecessor. Using a standard corporate theory of *de facto* merger, the court held the successor liable because (1) the purchaser continued the enterprise (management, personnel, physical location, assets, and operations remained the same); (2) the same shareholders remained; (3) the seller ceased operations, liquidated, and dissolved; and (4) the purchaser assumed the seller's obligations for uninterrupted business operations. Even though the successor argued that it expanded and changed the business after purchase, the court held it was a successor and liable.

On a motion for reconsideration, the court reversed its decision and held that genuine issues of fact existed where the purchaser/successor asserted that it had discontinued use of the predecessor's marks on the products and made numerous manufacturing and marketing changes.

In *GRM Ind., Inc. v. Wickes Mfg. Co.*, 749 F. Supp. 810 (W.D. Mich. 1990), the defendant purchased the stock of the polluting corporation, Gulf & Western, twelve years after G & W sold the site to another. The plaintiff leased the site from the current owner and expended cleanup costs. The defendant moved to dismiss the plaintiff's CERCLA claims but the western district followed *Smith Land.* The court stated that CERCLA's remedial purpose required that traditional successor liability concepts be imposed if warranted by the facts to prevent a corporation from avoiding CERCLA liability through careful crafting of corporate reorganizations. The court denied the defendant's motion to dismiss.

The real significance of *GRM* is that the court would allow successor liability to be pursued where the successor corporation had no connection to the contaminated site and had merely purchased the stock of the former owner of the site twelve years later.

Many other district courts have imposed liability on successor corporations. Moreover, emerging exceptions from products liability are now being examined by federal district courts for application to the environmental arena. There are two theories borrowed from products liability cases under which successor corporations are being held liable in products liability cases. These theories are "continuity of enterprise" and "product line."

The continuity of enterprise theory has emerged out of the traditional exception wherein the successor is a mere continuation of the seller. It basically requires a lesser showing than required under the traditional exception. Normally, the "mere continuation" exception requires a showing of common identity between officers, shareholders, and directors along with a continuation of the same general business of the predecessor.

Until 1989, only one court had adopted the theory in an environmental context. *Oner II v. EPA*, 597 F.2d 184 (9th Cir. 1979). In *Oner II*, the court adopted the continuity of enterprise theory to hold a successor liable under FIFRA, 7 U.S.C.A. § 136 *et seq.*, which regulates pesticides nationwide. However, unlike a true continuity of enterprise situation, the successor had notice of the previous fine levied by the EPA on the predecessor corporation. Additionally, the successor's president had also been the president of the predecessor corporation. Thus *Oner II* has never been viewed as a true continuity of enterprise case.

Recently, however, four district courts have adopted the continuity of enterprise theory to hold purchaser/successor corporations liable. The first of these we shall discuss is *United States v. Mexico Feed & Seed Co.*, 764 F. Supp. 565 (E.D. Mo. 1991). The court held the successor corporation liable and enumerated the factors to be weighed to determine whether a corporation is liable under the continuity of enterprise exception. These are whether the purchasing corporation:

1. retains the same employees,
2. retains the same supervisory personnel,
3. retains the same production facilities in the same location,
4. continues producing the same products,
5. retains the same name,
6. maintains continuity of assets and general business operations, and
7. whether the successor holds itself out to the public as the continuation of the previous corporation.

Id. at 572–73 (quoting *Distler*). The court pointed out that even though in this case the purchaser did not have the same officers and directors as the seller, the purchaser could still be held liable. *Id.*

In *United States v. Western Processing Co.*, 751 F. Supp. 902 (W.D. Wash. 1990), the court denied summary judgment for the defendant/successor corporation in an asset purchase where the defendant perceived the purchased assets as strengthening its own business, had help from the predecessor during the transition, continued at the same location, used the predecessor's logo, and had some overlapping employment for a time. The court noted the expansive continuity of enterprise theory used by the Ninth Circuit in *Oner II* and the Ninth Circuit's new opinion in *Louisiana-Pacific*, which, while it did not use the expansive theory, did not reject it. The *Western Processing* court stated that because of the expansive theory, it had to deny the defendant's summary judgment motion on the successor issue.

United States v. Distler, 741 F. Supp. 637 (W.D. Ky. 1990), is a seminal case. The defendant successor corporation purchased the assets of the predecessor corporation, which had contracted to have hazardous substances transported off-site. The government sued the successor corporation for cleanup costs incurred at the off-site disposal facilities. Several corporate restructurings took place before the defendant purchased the assets of the predecessor/generator corporation. The predecessor then dissolved. The defendant did not have any officers or shareholders from the predecessor.

Using the factors noted in *Mexico Feed & Seed*, the *Distler* court held that the successor was liable even though it had slightly altered its product line, changed what equipment and raw materials it used, and served a different market within three years of purchase. The court disregarded these changes because they occurred over time and because the successor had for several years immediately following the purchase continued to serve old customers.

The *Distler* case is significant because, although the court identified the seven factors to consider before imposing successor liability, the court essentially expanded them by disregarding the changes instituted within three years by the successor. Accordingly, the potential exists that if a purchaser does not immediately change personnel, products, or announce that it is a new entity, successor liability could attach.

Distler, *Mexico Feed & Seed* and *Western Processing* expand upon *Smith Land*, *Louisiana-Pacific,* and *Anspec*. In the latter cases, the courts looked to the remedial purposes of CERCLA to justify imposing successor liability under the *traditional* exceptions to the general rule precluding liability of a successor for its predecessor's acts. Now, these three district courts state that a choice exists for which "version" or doctrine of successor liability to use, thus opening the door to the more expansive successor doctrines adopted in the products liability area.

Finally, in *United States v. Carolina Transformer*, 739 F. Supp. 1030 (E.D.N.C. 1989), the closely held predecessor corporation contaminated the site with PCBs from transformer fluid, which then migrated through surface water into a nearby river. Additionally, groundwater for residential wells became contaminated. The court held the sole shareholder and another officer (a brother) of the predecessor directly liable under CERCLA as operators. The predecessor corporation, both a current owner of the site and a past operator, admitted liability.

Based on the asset transfer, the government argued that the new company, FayTranCo, *although located at another site*, was also liable as a successor, even though the polluting corporation still existed. Additionally, there was no continuity of shareholders between the predecessor and successor corporations because the sole shareholder in the predecessor still owned that stock and did not own stock in the successor. Thus FayTranCo was not a traditional successor corporation.

The court used an expanded continuity of enterprise theory to hold FayTranCo liable. That test was "whether the business of both employers is the same, whether the employees of the new company were doing the same job, and whether the new company produced the same product for essentially the same customers." *Id.* at 1039 (citing *Oner II*).

To sum up, the continuing search for deep pockets to pay for cleanups has forced both the government and the courts to creatively expand the liability net under environmental laws. This expansion, of necessity, has begun to color many corporate transactions and operations, both between parent corporations and their subsidiaries and between corporate officers or directors and plant personnel. One ignores the liability net at one's peril; the corporate form is offering less protection than in the past. Careful attention to the factors discussed above will be helpful in structuring corporate entities and transactions.

PART VII

Toxic Torts

Liability Theories for Toxic Torts

Tort Damages for Personal Injuries
Not Yet Suffered

The Potential Role of Superfund in
Toxic Tort Litigation

Using Epidemiology to Determine Causation
in Disease

Innovations and Considerations in Settling
Toxic Tort Litigation

Minimizing Corporate Toxic Tort Liability

Part VII
Toxic Torts

Toxic torts constitute one of the most rapidly growing areas of environmental litigation. The prospect of toxic tort liability may also have a significant impact on corporate compliance plans and strategic business plans. Evolving common-law theories and developments in remedial and control programs such as Superfund have contributed to the significant growth of these claims.

The theories of liability on which personal injury claims are based are the traditional tort theories of negligence, trespass, nuisance, strict liability, product liability, and misrepresentation. These theories are discussed in the first article by Wendell Alcorn.

Plaintiffs not suffering tangible injuries are now suing for damages for increased risk of injury and for fear of future injury. These cases raise issues as to the nature and scope of the legal theories as well as scientific issues concerning the existence or amount of risk of future harm. Issues regarding the viability of these claims and the relief available to plaintiffs are discussed by William Armstrong and Annette N. Castro.

Toxic tort plaintiffs may benefit from federal statutes creating a bevy of information concerning the generation and disposal of toxic chemicals. The 1986 amendments to Superfund is one such statute and provides for grants to citizens for consultants to assess contamination at Superfund sites. James Rogers analyzes the practical ramifications of these statutory programs on toxic tort litigation.

The proliferation of suits involving environmental exposures has created difficult legal and scientific issues. Establishing causation in toxic tort cases is problematical in cases where the exposure occurred in the distant past and where multiple causes of the disease are possible. Otto Wong analyzes the issue of causation and discusses how to use epidemiology in a well-structured approach to demonstrate a causal relationship.

David Peterson and Karen Palladino discuss innovative approaches in settling toxic tort cases. Drafting enforceable settlement agreements in these cases is complicated by the existence of hundreds or even thousands of plaintiffs, unknown exposures, and long latency periods. The authors offer suggestions for the drafting of agreements that minimize the need for future litigation.

Corporate environmental managers have the responsibility not only to deal with tort litigation but to minimize toxic tort and other environmental liabilities. Our final article by Roger Strelow discusses the preventive steps that a prudent corporation should take to minimize liability, including compliance with applicable regulations, prompt clean up of contamination, and a rigorous audit procedure.

Liability Theories for Toxic Torts

Wendell B. Alcorn, Jr.

The term "toxic tort" entered the language in recent times as a product—albeit an undesirable one—of industrialization. As used here, it refers to a personal injury wrongfully caused by exposure to one or more chemical substances. Cases of economic harm in the absence of bodily injury lie outside the scope of this article.

A number of examples of toxic tort litigation come easily to mind. The asbestos disease litigation is perhaps the most notorious for the length of time it has been in the courts, the financial impact it has had on the asbestos and insurance industries, and the dramatic changes in the law it has stimulated. Another example is the Agent Orange class action litigation that was started on behalf of Vietnam veterans in July 1978 and settled in May 1984, but which is still pending on appeal. Among other issues being appealed are the fairness of the settlement, the use of the class action vehicle, and the correctness of the trial court's dismissal of opt-out plaintiffs on motions by the defendants for summary judgment. Other toxic tort suits have dealt with pharmaceutical drugs such as bendectin, various commercial or industrial chemicals, and hazardous wastes.

Theories of recovery that have been applied in toxic tort suits fall into two categories. First, there are those that focus on the conduct of the defendant. These are negligence, strict liability for ultrahazardous activities, nuisance, misrepresentation, and statutory violations. Second, there are theories that provide recovery not on

Wendell Alcorn is a partner in the firm of Cadwalader, Wickersham & Taft in New York.

the basis of illegal conduct but rather on the ground that the product was faulty. The latter category includes breach of implied or express warranty, strict products liability, absolute products liability, and innocent misrepresentation.

The Conduct Approach to Liability

The first of our liability theories based upon the conduct of the defendant is negligence. To be found liable in negligence, the defendant must have breached a duty of care owed to the plaintiff. Defendants are generally held to the standard of "reasonableness." If the defendant acted reasonably under the circumstances, then the duty of care was not breached. In toxic tort cases, liability can result from negligently supplying a hazardous product or acting in some other unreasonable way that causes the plaintiff injury.

Another liability theory is based on strict liability for ultrahazardous activities. Imposing strict liability for the conduct of ultrahazardous activities was originally implemented under British common law. *Rylands v. Fletcher*, 1868, L.R. 3 H.L. 330, 37 L.J. Ex. 161. The theory was adopted by American courts and has now been applied in toxic tort cases. *See, e.g., Ashland Oil, Inc. v. Miller Oil Purchasing Co.*, 678 F.2d 1293 (5th Cir. 1982) (hazardous waste disposal).

Nuisances constitute yet another area of liability theory. Nuisances are either private or public. A private nuisance is an unreasonable interference with a private landowner's rights. A public nuisance is an invasion of the general public's rights. Normally, only public officers such as district attorneys have standing to sue to abate public nuisances. At times, however, individuals are granted standing where they suffer a harm distinct from that caused the general public.

In toxic tort suits, successful claims of nuisance can result not only in cease and desist orders but also in remedial requirements. This is particularly true, for instance, where environmental cleanup of hazardous substances is ordered. This application of nuisance theory can require defendants to pay large sums of money over and above damages.

State common law is the main basis for nuisance claims seeking redress of environmental torts. The use of federal common law in this area has been severely restricted. *See, e.g., Milwaukee v. Illinois*, 451 U.S. 304 (1981). Indeed, theories of federal common law have found little favor generally in toxic tort litigation. *See, e.g., In re Agent Orange Product Liability Litigation*, 635 F.2d 987 (2d Cir. 1980), *cert. denied*, 454 U.S. 1128 (1981).

Several theories based on misrepresentation have been applied in products liability cases. Liability is recognized even where the defendant's conduct did not constitute deceit and was only negligent. *See, e.g., Restatement (Second) of Torts* § 311.

In contrast, fraudulent misrepresentation (in practice used synonymously with deceit) requires a showing that the defendant knew or believed the representation was false and intended to induce action or inaction by the plaintiff. Where statutes of limitations have run on other claims such as negligence and warranty, the pleading of fraudulent misrepresentation is highly significant. *See, e.g., Snow v. A.H. Robins Co.*, 165 Cal. App. 3d 120, 21 Cal. Rptr. 271 (1985). In the toxic tort area, plaintiffs have been permitted to recover on this theory even where they were not party to the fraudulent transaction. Where a manufacturer's representative induced physicians to buy the drug DES, the injured parties successfully pleaded fraudulent misrepresentation under the rationale that the doctors acted on their patients' behalf. *Albertson v. Richardson-Merrell, Inc.*, 441 So. 2d 1146 (Fla. Dist. Ct. App. 1983).

Another theory of recovery is innocent misrepresentation—sometimes called tortious misrepresentation. Here the statement by the defendant is neither negligent nor deceitful. Thus the cause of action is a form of strict liability and will be discussed under the product-oriented theories of recovery.

In any case where the defendant may have breached a statutory duty, the plaintiff has additional claims that can be asserted. The statute, or regulations promulgated under it, may provide a private cause of action in favor of injured parties. Even if the law does not, the proof of the statutory violation may significantly lessen a plaintiff's burden of proof. Conduct that violates a statute or regulation can amount to negligence per se. *See, e.g., Restatement (Second) of Torts* § 288B. In such cases, the plaintiff is relieved from proving negligence where a relevant statutory breach is shown.

Private parties are expressly given standing to sue for the violation of some statutes. One example is the Magnuson-Moss Warranty Act, Pub. L. No. 93-637, 15 U.S.C. §§ 2301, 2310(d), (e) (1976). Other laws have been construed as giving rise to implied private causes of action. *See generally Cort v. Ash*, 422 U.S. 66 (1975), in which the Supreme Court addressed the issue of implied private rights of action under federal law:

> In determining whether a private remedy is implicit in a statute not expressly providing one, several factors are relevant. First, is the plaintiff "one of the class for whose *especial* benefit the statute was enacted,"

. . . that is, does the statute create a federal right in favor of the plaintiff? Second, is there any indication of legislative intent, explicit or implicit, either to create such a remedy or to deny one? . . . Third, is it consistent with the underlying purposes of the legislative scheme to imply such a remedy for the plaintiff? . . . And finally, is the cause of action one traditionally relegated to state law . . .?

Id. at 78.

In some instances, parallel state and federal regulation exists. Violating either may provide independent causes of action or may constitute negligence per se. *See, e.g., McClanahan v. California Spray-Chem. Corp.*, 194 Va. 842, 75 S.E.2d 712, 718 (1953).

There are a great many statutes and regulations that relate to toxic torts and hazardous substances. For example, portions of CERCLA, 42 U.S.C. §§ 9601–57, impose affirmative obligations upon industry to clean up previously generated hazardous wastes. Superfund is thus federal legislation requiring nuisance abatement, a remedy that does not presuppose a prior violation of statute. *See, e.g., New York v. Shore Realty Corp.*, 759 F.2d 1032 (2d Cir. 1985). Other laws are designed to control the sale of toxic materials and protect the consuming public from harm. *See, e.g.,* the Hazardous Substances Act, 15 U.S.C. § 1261 *et seq.* (1976).

Product Theories of Liability

The common-law doctrine of implied warranty was based on the reasonable expectations of the purchaser of a product. That concept evolved beyond implied warranties of utility to include implied warranties of safety. Despite the later development of strict products liability theory, implied warranty has survived as an independent basis for recovery.

In many states implied warranty law is now grounded in the Uniform Commercial Code. *Compare, e.g., Martin v. Julius Dierk Equip. Co.*, 43 N.Y.2d 583, 374 N.E.2d 97 (1978) (holding that implied warranty without privity was superseded by strict products liability), *with Heller v. U.S. Suzuki Motor Corp.*, 64 N.Y.2d 407, 53 U.S.L.W. 2516 (1985) (noting that amendment of New York's Uniform Commercial Code resurrected implied warranty without privity as a statutory theory). An important distinction between strict products liability and implied warranty is that warranty sounds in contract rather than tort. Thus implied warranty claims are generally subject to different periods of limitation and also may permit economic damages not recoverable in tort. In addition, issues of contract interpretation and privity of the parties arise when the claim is a breach of express warranty. Claims of this nature lie within the area of contract law, and tort principles do not apply.

Strict liability is applicable to toxic and environmental tort cases. Some statutes impose strict liability under given circumstances, as does CERCLA, for example. Principles of strict liability under state common law have more general application to situations involving exposure to hazardous and toxic substances.

In one form or another, strict liability has been adopted in most jurisdictions. *See* Prod. Liab. Rep. (CCH) ¶ 4016. The theory developed first under the rubric "implied warranty" and was initially limited to personal injuries caused by food or drink. Gradually, other types of consumer goods, such as automobiles, were covered. *See, e.g., Henningsen v. Bloomfield Motors, Inc.,* 32 N.J. 358, 161 A.2d 69 (1960). Then in 1963 Justice Traynor disavowed the legal fiction of implied warranty and recognized "strict products liability in tort." *Greenman v. Yuba Power Prods., Inc.,* 59 Cal. 2d 57, 377 P.2d 897, 901 (1963). The American Law Institute recognized the tort theory of strict products liability in the *Restatement (Second) of Torts* § 402A (1965).

Liability is strictly imposed under the section 402A formulation upon the seller of a product "in a defective condition unreasonably dangerous to the user or consumer" even if "the seller has exercised all possible care." The focus is therefore on defectiveness in the product, not fault in the conduct of the seller. Some states have adopted this approach by statute. Others have done so by judicial decision.

For purposes of section 402A, a product may be defective for one of three reasons. A mistake may have been made in the production process, resulting in a limited number of items being manufactured before the mistake is discovered. Second, the design of the product may cause it to be less safe. For example, a chemical product may be designed to contain a highly toxic component when a less toxic one would have served the end user just as well. Third, an inherently dangerous product may be marketed without adequate warnings. An example of an inherently hazardous mineral is asbestos, the safe handling of which requires special precautions.

The social underpinnings of strict products liability are found in the economics of marketing consumer goods. Strict liability results from societal choices aimed, for instance, at spreading the risk of loss and promoting the safety of commercial products. *See, e.g., McKay v. Rockwell Int'l Corp.*, 704 F.2d 444, 451 (9th Cir. 1983), *cert. denied*, 464 U.S. 1043 (1983).

Especially in toxic tort litigation, a central issue frequently is whether the defendant adequately warned of dangers inherent in the product sold or whether the product could have been designed in a manner that would have made it safe. Section 402A emphasizes product defectiveness at the time of sale. It stands to reason that sellers should not be held strictly liable if, at the time of sale, the dangerous nature of the product was unknowable or if technical knowledge did not indicate a safer design. The defense based on this rationale—often referred to as a state-of-the-art defense—depends necessarily upon the seller's innocent lack of knowledge. The defense takes the emphasis off the defect in the product and places it on the faultless conduct of the vendor.

As stated in comment (i) to section 402A, for a product to be "unreasonably dangerous," it must be "dangerous to an extent beyond that which would be contemplated by the ordinary consumer." This differs from the concept of reasonableness that applies under the negligence approach to liability. Nevertheless, there are similarities that are relevant on the issue of whether to recognize a state-of-the-art defense. In cases involving charges of inadequate warning or defective design, a state-of-the-art defense finds support in the *Restatement*'s requirement that a product must be defective at the time of sale. A product otherwise flawless when sold would, wherever the defense is allowed, not be considered defective merely because the passage of time renders its safety features or accompanying warnings obsolete. However, some courts have held products to be defective as to their warnings or design, without regard to the state of knowledge or technical feasibility at the time of sale. *See, e.g., Cronin v. J.B.E. Olson Corp.*, 8 Cal. 2d 121, 501 P.2d 1153 (1972) (which expressly rejected the "unreasonably dangerous" element of strict products liability). This judicial result is more appropriately called absolute liability rather than strict products liability as outlined in section 402A. *Compare Feldman v. Lederle Laboratories*, 97 N.J. 429, 479 A.2d 374 (1984), *with Beshada v. Johns-Manville Prods. Corp.*, 90 N.J. 191, 447 A.2d 539 (1982).

As noted previously, innocent misrepresentation and tortious misrepresentation refer to the same type of cause of action, under which the plaintiff need not prove that the defendant acted either negligently or deceitfully. Section 402B of the *Restatement (Second) of Torts* describes the basis of this liability as follows:

> One engaged in the business of selling chattels, who, by advertising, labels or otherwise, makes to the public a misrepresentation of a material fact concerning the character or quality of a chattel sold by him is subject to liability for physical harm to a consumer of the chattel, caused by justifiable reliance upon the misrepresentation. . . .

This is so even though the misrepresentation was not fraudulently or negligently made. Nor is there a requirement under the *Restatement*'s view that the injured party be in privity with the defendant.

Problems of Proof

Victims of toxic torts can invoke theories of liability that avoid many problems that in the not too distant past would have proven insuperable. For example, the application of strict products liability does not require that the plaintiff be in privity with the defendant. However, toxic tort cases present problems of proof that are unique.

One of the hardest fought issues in toxic tort actions frequently is that of legal causation. To prevail, the plaintiff must prove fault and harm in a way that establishes liability. The *Restatement (Second) of Torts* § 431 provides that fault is a "legal cause" of harm if, first, it is a "substantial factor" in causing injury and, second, there is no applicable defense. Instead of "legal cause," most courts use the term "proximate cause," which generally means the same thing. Regardless of the semantics employed, the plaintiff's claim may be defeated by the failure to prove (1) the illness or injury alleged, (2) exposure to the toxic substance at issue, (3) the capacity of the substance to cause the injury, or (4) the fact that the harm more likely than not resulted from the proven exposure.

The question of whether the plaintiff actually suffers from the illness alleged turns on the accuracy of medical diagnosis. Psychological symptoms may be feigned or imagined by the supposed victim. Even the most expert physician may have great difficulty distinguishing between true and false cases. Physiological disease states are also subject to misdiagnosis. The problem is exacerbated where the injured party is dead. In that situation, the diagnosis of the treating physician often is beyond meaningful challenge, although it may have been in error.

Proof of the plaintiff's exposure to the toxin at issue can be very difficult. In the Agent Orange litigation, for instance, the veterans claimed a variety of injuries from exposure to a particular kind of dioxin that was present in trace amounts in only certain herbicides applied for purposes of defoliation and crop destruction in support of military operations in Vietnam. If the cases had been tried, each plaintiff would have had to show exposure to the herbicides. This would have been rather simple for some but very difficult for others. Military personnel involved in spraying operations likely came into contact with substantial amounts of defoliants. Beyond that category of plaintiff, the problem of proving exposure ranged over a broad spectrum. While the government retained records of aircraft spraying missions, the reports of locations of ground units were frequently nonspecific and vague. Many questions of individual exposure would have, from the plaintiff's perspective, had to rely simply on anecdotal evidence that may have been insufficient.

The difficulty of showing exposure to dioxin originating in Vietnam was even more pronounced for those plaintiffs who were never there. In addition to veterans' claims, the cases included claims for birth defects in children of men who served in the war. To prevail on those claims, the plaintiffs would have had to rely on theories of male-mediated birth defects. While a good deal of scientific evidence indicates that birth defects have resulted in children of women directly exposed to certain chemical substances during pregnancy, male mediation is much more theoretical and the scientific evidence much less persuasive.

Another unique problem in many toxic tort cases is the inability of a plaintiff to demonstrate exposure to a particular defendant's product. In Agent Orange, no plaintiff could show exposure to a specific chemical company's herbicide. Just how that difficulty would have been resolved was not determined prior to the settlement. In other litigation, however, courts have constructed rules to relieve this plaintiffs' dilemma. In the DES litigation, for example, where the plaintiffs are daughters of the mothers who were administered DES many years before, some courts have refused to block recovery if it appears likely that the supplier of the DES is among the defendants. *See, e.g., Sindell v. Abbott Laboratories*, 26 Cal. 3d 588, 607 P.2d 924, *cert. denied*, 449 U.S. 912 (1980). Other judicial solutions have relied on different theories. For instance, DES suppliers have been held liable when they were found to have engaged in concert of action not to conduct further research into the drug's effects. *See, e.g., Bichler v. Eli Lilly & Co.*, 79 App. Div. 2d 317, 436 N.Y.S.2d 625 (1981), *aff'd*, 55 N.Y.2d 571, 436 N.E.2d 182, 450 N.Y.S.2d 776 (1982).

Toxic tort litigation also raises the question of whether the substance at issue is capable of causing the disease states complained of. In cancer cases, for example, the particular chemical may have caused tumors in laboratory animals at certain anatomical sites under particular routes of administration. That does not mean that the substance necessarily causes cancer in humans. Thus, in a case where human epidemiological studies do not support causation potentiality, the plaintiff must rely on animal data—if available—and attempt to interpolate from laboratory conclusions. Animal data, however, do not have the inherent power of a proper epidemiological study to identify associations between a cause and effect in humans. Animals differ from human beings and frequently do not respond similarly to like exposures. Even among different species, responses to toxins vary widely. Conclusions of animal investigators are of limited utility in determining cause-effect relationships in humans, especially when they conflict with valid epidemiological studies.

This is not to say, however, that animal data should be disregarded or always given little weight. Such studies do contribute to an understanding of how chemical substances enter body systems and how they may cause injury. Accordingly, laboratory experiments lead to better comprehension of the underlying processes that lead to various diseases. If the species studied is known to resemble humans in its response to a toxin, the information derived contributes to knowledge of human disease. If there is no known relationship between responses in humans and animals, laboratory results are of questionable import. Moreover, they are highly suspect when in conflict with conclusions derived from well-designed and -conducted epidemiological studies.

The ultimate problem of proof on a plaintiff's toxic tort claim involves the issue of whether the injury more likely than not was caused by exposure to the substance involved. To establish causation, it must be shown that the disease state manifested itself after exposure to the toxin, not before. The time interval between exposure and manifestation, however, must correspond to known latency periods associated with the disease. Where the latency period is brief, a long lapse of time between exposure and occurrence of illness tends to undermine the argument for causation. Where the latency period is lengthy, too short a time between exposure and manifestation makes causation suspect.

The question of causation in fact is further complicated by the existence of alternative causes. Everyone is exposed to hazardous substances in the ordinary course of living, as well as to traumatic injury, disease, medications, and harmful personal habits. Heredity also plays a role in producing disease. Unless a particular disease is practically always associated with a specific toxin—such as meso-thelioma and asbestos—many possible causes may exist for the plain-tiff's injury. All should be weighed carefully in the process of determining causation—regardless of the legal theory under which liability is to be tested.

Tort Damages
for Personal Injuries
Not Yet Suffered

William H. Armstrong and Annette N. Castro

Perhaps as a result of increasing scientific knowledge and media attention, people today are more likely than ever to be worried about the future consequences of some event that has not yet caused them any symptom of physical disease or injury. They are seeking damages for those concerns with increasing frequency in tort litigation.

Courts around the country have adopted different positions about the viability of such tort claims. Most allow damages for increased risk of disease if it is more probable than not that the individual plaintiff will contract the disease. Some require that the plaintiff have a present illness caused by the tort before allowing recovery for increased risk of future disease. These courts, however, differ on what constitutes a present illness. Often a plaintiff suffers no symptoms at present but has abnormal laboratory tests that may presage disease. There is no consistent judicial position on whether such a condition constitutes a present illness. One court has allowed recovery premised on subclinical injury where at least some of the experts characterize such a condition as a present injury. *See, e.g., Brafford v. Susquehanna Corp.*, 586 F. Supp. 14 (D. Colo. 1984). However, another court has refused to do so. *See, e.g., Schweitzer v. Consolidated Rail Corp.*, 758 F.2d 936 (3d Cir. 1985), *cert. denied*, 474 U.S. 864 (1985). In addition, courts generally allow recovery for fear of future injury or disease under emotional distress theories in these

William Armstrong is a partner in McCutchen, Doyle, Brown & Enersen in Walnut Creek, California. Annette Castro is an associate in the San Francisco office of the same firm.

tort cases. Some require accompanying physical injury; some do not. Some permit recovery for fear even where it is highly unlikely that the plaintiff will ever suffer the disease. *See, e.g., Heider v. Employers Mutual Liab. Ins. Co.*, 231 So. 2d 438 (La. App. 1970).

Issues regarding the viability and proper scope of these claims, the identity of appropriate defendants, proof of risk, and the relief available to plaintiffs are likely to continue to confront us. Preliminarily, we ought to consider how these claims have become so prevalent. One fact of modern society is that science is finding out all sorts of seemingly frightening things, and a lively media makes certain we all hear about them on the evening news or in the morning paper. Many people who are exposed to some tortious event are genuinely fearful about the long-term consequences, and the judicial system must decide to what extent, if at all, a plaintiff can recover for those genuine fears.

Learning of the Potential Risk

Typically, a prospective plaintiff learns of the risk of future injury or disease from the doctor who treats him or her, the lawyer he or she consults, the media coverage of the tortious event, or some combination of those sources.

Doctors today more than in the past feel obligated to advise their patients of all potential risks. That change in custom is the result of many societal factors, including legal decisions, that favor providing information. However, some doctors still question the wisdom of providing a patient with information that will only create fear. In addition, there are questions about what to say where science remains uncertain about the existence or the degree of risk.

Nonetheless, society seems clearly to favor the general proposition that an individual is entitled to know. It is generally assumed that it is proper to advise people when they may be subject to an increased risk of future disease. But where the evidence as to the existence or degree of risk is in conflict, judgment must be exercised in describing the risk. The risk may be overstated or understated, depending on how the doctor reads the evidence. The doctor may be required to consider the particular circumstances of the patient: Mentioning a risk based on a single study of dubious quality may be a better idea with some patients than with others.

If the frightening information is provided by an lawyer or by a doctor who is involved only as an expert consultant for potential litigation, an additional factor is involved. In a case such as this, something has motivated the individual to seek a lawyer's advice, but if the individual was not frightened before he or she consulted a lawyer, is it the place of the lawyer or the consultant to tell the individual that, in addition to other problems, he or she has an increased risk of disease? This question is not answered in the reports, but it is worthy of consideration.

Finally, the media may be the source of information. Members of the media are strong defenders of a general right to know, but they deny any responsibility for the consequences of disseminating information or even rumors. Yet the hype that is generated over some "disasters" is equivalent to yelling "Fire!" in a crowded theater. Disseminating a report that a large number of people, or an entire community, is subject to an increased risk of cancer because of exposure to some chemical or other substance is certain to cause alarm. Before the publisher or broadcaster who disseminates this "news" is insulated from liability, society needs to consider what standards of accuracy and scientific validity are appropriate to impose upon the media and whether the particular disclosure meets those standards.

On learning of the risk, the prospective plaintiff presumably will truly experience fear or emotional distress to a greater or lesser degree. However, even if the risk information is incorrect, the prospective plaintiff typically pursues only the perceived tortfeasor: the one who dumped the chemical, made it, transported it, or stored it. The source of the information is not generally sued. It is unclear why the source is not sued, particularly since a typical defense of the perceived tortfeasor is that there is no risk or that the risk is overstated. If it is true that the risk is nonexistent or overstated, the disseminator should be liable on some theory that it is wrong to spread false information. In these types of cases, the plaintiff is almost always genuinely upset by the information. So, perhaps the perceived tortfeasor and risk disseminator should fight about whether and to what extent the report about the existence of risk is true. This limitation of potential defendants needs to be evaluated.

For example, a few years ago the United States National Highway Transportation Safety Administration NHTSA concluded that there was a safety-related brake defect in the General Motors "X" car line. This subject was widely publicized, and among the litigation that ensued was a suit against General Motors claiming damages for the diminished value of the affected cars that had resulted from the untoward publicity. General Motors fought the NHTSA and achieved a decision that there was no proof of defect. *United States v. General Motors Corp.*, 656 F. Supp. 1555 (D.D.C. 1987), *aff'd*, 268 App. D.C. 278,

841 F.2d 400 (1988). If it is true that the publicity depressed the value of the cars, are the parties who publicized the claimed defect liable for the consequences? Should they be? Similarly, in cases when people have been frightened by information provided by their doctors, lawyers, or local media, if the court determines that there was no risk, are the disseminators of the frightening information liable? Should they be?

Determining the Risk

Assuming that a particular exposure may present a risk, in most instances the existence or amount of risk of future harm from a particular exposure is subject to great dispute among scientists. The dispute may be whether the particular exposure can cause any future injury at all or whether the risk of such injury is high or low. An individual involuntarily exposed is probably not very interested in the scientific debate; he or she did not want to be exposed and does not want to take a chance on the outcome of that debate. Typically, the individual prospective plaintiff hears, and believes, the most frightening version available. Judgment as to the relative credibility of the most frightening version is not normally exercised; credibility is often assumed by the prospective plaintiff, his or her counsel, and the media.

The Judicial Tests

Courts have used various tests to determine which fears are compensable and which are not. Among the tests used are whether the fear is genuine, whether it is reasonable, whether it is serious, and whether it is accompanied by physical impact or injury. Many courts traditionally have barred recovery for any emotional claims in the absence of physical impact or injury. *See, e.g., Stites v. Sundstrand Heat Transfer, Inc.*, 660 F. Supp. 1516 (W.D. Mich. 1987). Several jurisdictions have abandoned that traditional position and have sought other more flexible tests.

A common test is genuineness. Different courts have set forth different indicia of genuineness. In many jurisdictions, physical impact, a physical injury, or at least some objectively verifiable physical manifestation of injury is described as a guarantee of genuineness. *See, e.g., Eagle-Picher Indus., Inc. v. Cox*, 481 So. 2d 517, 529 (Fla. App. 3d Dist. 1985), *rev. denied*, 492 So. 2d 1331 (Fla. 1986). *Cf. Berry v. Armstrong Rubber Co.*, No. J88–0653B (S.D. Miss. July 30, 1991), 1991 U.S. Dist. LEXIS 12,237 (property damage case).

Using physical injury as a test of genuineness makes some sense in dealing with the alleged emotional distress of a bystander observing a near-miss accident. It is more dubious when the plaintiff claims possible exposure to chemicals as a cause for fear of future disease. Even if the fact of exposure is in doubt, the possibility of exposure and its attendant possibility of risk may cause a *genuine* fear. Nonetheless, courts may decide that some fears, although genuine, should not be compensable. The question of compensability need not turn entirely on genuineness.

Suppose that a person has genuine fear as a result of an involuntary exposure to a substance some scientists suspect is a weak carcinogen, but most scientists would say the particular exposure poses no risk. Most cases require the fear to be serious and reasonable. *See, e.g., Smith v. A.C. & S., Inc.*, 843 F.2d 854, 859 (5th Cir. 1988) (a finding that a plaintiff's fear is serious and reasonable "may not be predicated on a general statement by the plaintiff that he is concerned about his health, but must be premised on the plaintiff's evidence as to his specific fear of cancer").

A standard used to determine whether fear is serious is whether "a reasonable man, normally constituted, would be unable to adequately cope with the mental stress engendered by the circumstances of the case." *In re Hawaii Fed. Asbestos Cases*, 734 F. Supp. 1563, 1568 (D. Hawaii 1990), *quoting Rodriquez v. State*, 52 Haw. 156, 472 P.2d 509 (1970). An especially sensitive person may not recover for his or her unique fear unless the defendant was aware of the sensitivity. *See Hunsley v. Giard*, 87 Wash. 2d 424, 553 P.2d 1096 (1976).

In assessing the reasonableness of a fear, the trier of fact may consider many factors, including the information a reasonable person would seek out and consider in the circumstances, and how a reasonable person reacts to other risks of comparable magnitude and severity. The issues of reasonableness and severity have typically been reserved for the jury. *See, e.g., Smith*, 843 F.2d at 859. Courts should consider examining these factors as well as genuineness in determining whether the evidence is sufficient to send a case to the jury.

For example, in the fear of cancer situation, the evidence may be that an average person copes with the fact that about 30 percent of all people will get cancer. If the plaintiff's evidence is believed, the plaintiff has an increased risk of cancer of 1 in 100,000, and the plaintiff claims damages for the resultant fear. If 30,000 people out of 100,000 will contract cancer anyway, is it reasonable to claim fear based on evidence that one more individual out of the 100,000 will get cancer? Can a jury properly conclude that the claimed fear is both reasonable and serious? If not, the court should not permit such a claim to go to the jury.

Similarly, the court may decide that the evidence on which the plaintiff bases the claim that there is a risk is too weak to permit the case to go to the jury on the basis that no reasonable and serious fear can be premised on a nonexistent risk. Of course, if the plaintiff has admissible evidence on which a jury could base a conclusion that the risk exists, and that a reasonable and serious fear might occur, the plaintiff is entitled to go to the jury.

Of the various tests used to determine which fears are compensable, courts have relied on the genuineness test to exclude a fear claim where, in reality, a fear was almost surely genuine. The result may be right, however, if the fear was either not reasonable or not serious. Courts have the power to examine all those tests in deciding whether a fear claim is sufficient to go to the jury.

Another difficult evidentiary question is how to deal with conflicting scientific testimony regarding the existence or seriousness of the risk. If we ask a jury to decide the reasonableness and seriousness of a fear claim, the evidence must be of sufficient value to help them make that decision. Most risk assessments are disputed, and scientists cannot agree as to what procedures are best, what studies are better, and so on. Moreover, it is difficult to prove which case of cancer or other disease was caused by the tort if there is a background rate of the same cancer or disease.

When confronted with this quandary, most courts take refuge by "letting the jury decide" the credibility of the scientific debate. That approach disposes of cases, but it cannot pretend to resolve the scientific debate. If anybody really had that much faith in the jury system in this area, we could dispense with the FDA and impanel a jury to decide whether the scientific evidence proves a proposed new drug safe and effective.

Using Experts Begs Many Questions
There is no obvious answer to the question of how courts can resolve scientific disputes. But no case should be forced to settlement merely because of the fear that a jury would accept "weird science" from a likable "expert" whom the court should but will not bar from testifying. But that has happened. It continues to happen in part because judges are often too busy to want to get into the business of sorting out whether a proffered expert is really an expert. Even if they were not busy, many judges—and, for that matter, lawyers—probably con-

sidered and rejected a career in science at some point because they do not like it and are not good at it.

Nonetheless, counsel must be quick to bring to the court's attention any concern that the other side's expert's view is outside the mainstream of his or her scientific field and should be excluded from consideration under applicable evidentiary standards. Courts should be quick to address these concerns and adopt methods to resolve these questions.

Few of us would hesitate to check out the reputation of a physician before we sought treatment, and few would hesitate to seek a second opinion before following a recommendation for surgery or other dramatic procedure. Courts might consider similar procedures when confronted with questions about whether an expert's opinion meets the basic test of admissibility. Most courts have, either explicitly or implicitly, the power to consult outside experts. They should consider calling on a nearby well-regarded medical school, identifying a reputable physician in the relevant field, and asking whether the proffered opinion uses generally accepted scientific methodology (or whatever the test of admissibility might be in the jurisdiction). That will not resolve all disputes, but it will weed out some unmeritorious experts' claims.

Resolution through the Burden of Proof
As to scientific disputes where both sides meet the test of admissibility, the only remaining method for determining close calls is the burden of proof. If that burden is on the plaintiff, counsel and the court must consider whatever arguments, motions, or decisions might appropriately dispose of the question whether that party's expert testimony has sufficient weight not merely to stay in court but to carry the burden of proof.

Apart from resolving the quandary of the scientific debate, the court must focus on the claim before it. There needs to be a separation between the perceived need to punish or discourage unwelcome conduct, such as chemical spills, and the awarding of damages for fear. Most people agree that chemical spills and similar tortious behavior should be discouraged and punished if the conduct merits punishment. But concocting fanciful civil damages may not be the best way, or even a good way, to do that (which is not to say that every suit or most suits for increased risk are fanciful, only that some may be). Society should be skeptical about claims for increased risk of injury, or for fear of future injury, and most courts are, as is evident in the genuineness requirement. Folk wisdom suggests that we accept the risks of life. Awareness of risks of contracting cancer has increased. We are now much more likely to die of cancer, not because chemical spills are killing us all but because we are not dying of infectious diseases and other maladies that formerly plagued our ancestors.

People, however, accept the risks of cancer, wittingly or no, in natural products such as fruits, vegetables, and peanut butter, and in not-so-natural products such as gasoline and cigarettes. For the most part, people do not seem to want to give things up just because they pose a risk of cancer. If courts are to allow claims for risks of injury and fears about those risks, they need first to apply some common sense to weed out even genuine fears that are caused by risks that are normally accepted without fear. There is no assurance that this is now being accomplished by the jury when determining the reasonableness of the fear. However, recovery predicated on the reasonableness of the individual's fear, as opposed to the nature of the tortfeasor's conduct, should focus the jury's attention on the extent to which such fear is genuine. Tortfeasors may then provide evidence suggesting that the individual's fear is unreasonable, including evidence of voluntary exposure to similar chemicals or substances of greater hazards.

Understanding the Financial Consequences

In addition, the financial consequences of expanding damages to include compensation for future risk of disease and fear of future injury or disease must be considered. First, it changes the total "price" to a tortfeasor of any particular tortious act. For the sake of discussion, assume that a particular tortious act subjects 1,000 people to an increased risk of cancer in the order of 5:10,000. Assume further that the tort damages for actually contracting the cancer would be $1 million. In this hypothetical, the tortious act would yield a 50/50 chance of one extra cancer. This should be "worth" $500,000. But, if each of the 1,000 people is entitled to damages based on the fear they will contract cancer, a damage award of just $2,500 to each would total $2.5 million. If that is the only result, the "price" of the tortious conduct has increased five times. If the award bars a future suit on behalf of anyone who actually contracts cancer, that unlucky individual is grossly undercompensated. If not, then the increase in cost is larger. Moreover, this hypothetical does not begin to consider costs of litigation.

A second consequence is accelerating the payment of damages. The hypothetical tort may result in no cancer, or perhaps in one additional case, if the assumed risk is correct. But even if one additional case occurs, it will manifest itself years later. So there is an added cost to tortfeasors because damages are paid now rather than at the time the illness develops.

Admittedly, there are no simple ways to resolve these problems, but they are increasingly important because of the burdens these cases impose on society. More and more scientific endeavor is being transferred from the laboratory to the courtroom. Some consideration needs to be given to the fact that litigants, particularly defendants, often have large budgets to employ the "best" experts. The budgets are justified by the potential verdicts, but if one steps back to examine this situation, it seems a waste of scientific effort. Assuming that the best experts may accomplish some good if they work at their scientific occupation, society as a whole loses when these men and women spend their time trying to persuade a jury of laypeople about scientific matters on which scientists do not agree. The only advantage seems to be that many scientists use the proceeds from litigation consultation to fund research that would otherwise go underfunded. That is a fortuitous, rather than an intended, result of this system.

Another resource that is burdened by this process is the judicial system itself. Courts often ignore or reject arguments that a particular decision to expand the concept of damages or liability will inundate the court system. But the courts are overwhelmed with tort suits, most of a classic variety, but many of which were spawned by modern decisions that expanded access to the courts without expanding judicial resources. At least one court has stated a limited judicial resources justification for requiring a present physical injury before awarding damages for fear of cancer. *See, e.g., Eagle-Picher Indus., Inc. v. Cox*, 481 So. 2d at 528.

It is also noteworthy that these types of problems are, so far, largely confined to so-called toxic tort cases. That limitation, however, seems to be without any logical basis. If a person who is genuinely fearful of contracting cancer because of a negligent chemical spill is entitled to recover damages for his or her fear, a person who is genuinely fearful of being run over by the negligent or reckless driver next door should also be entitled to recover. Thus the potential impact of these cases is broad.

Damages for increased risk and for fear of future injury will continue to be a feature in many cases. Under our system, they are appropriate in defined circumstances. Counsel and the courts should be attentive to the problems discussed here and realize that expansion of remedies will increase the demand on courts and the scientific community—as well as on society as a whole.

The Potential Role of Superfund in Toxic Tort Litigation

James A. Rogers

The relationship of toxic chemicals in disposal sites to the long-term health of people living nearby is a matter that generates as much controversy—in which there are as vigorously defended assumptions and where there are as few reliable facts—as any other in environmental law. A wide range of opinions exist. To many citizen activists, the question of a possible nexus does not deserve even serious scientific inquiry. To the extent that one can characterize the institutional belief of Congress on this subject, as evidenced by CERCLA, 42 U.S.C. §§ 9601–75, it seems that waste dumps are among the most serious national health threats and that the $8.5 billion Superfund seed money, supplied by the 1986 amendments to Superfund, as well as billions more from private parties, is being well spent on these sites.

In implementing CERCLA, officials at the EPA have shown a willingness to apply a series of conservative assumptions in cancer risk models, transport theories, etc., in mandating expensive cleanups. Implicit in this approach is a belief that CERCLA sites more likely than not pose some degree of health risk. Many academics in the relevant disciplines, and certainly some members of the industrial community hit hard by Superfund liability assessments, question assumptions that any causal connection has been demonstrated and advocate the development of more sophisticated information on the subject.

James Rogers is a partner in the Washington, D.C., firm of Wilmer, Cutler & Pickering.

Congress, in enacting SARA, Pub. L. No. 99–499, 100 Stat. 1613 (1986), made clear its concern regarding health threats posed by Superfund sites in several provisions mandating government-generated risk information and addressing potential health threats. Section 110 of SARA called for the creation of an extensive new public health program, including the preparation of toxicological profiles and health assessments, in an effort to strengthen the understanding of the link between the chemicals found in individual Superfund sites and the health of the people living nearby. At the time SARA was passed, the information generated under section 110 was expected by some to verify that the risks of these hazardous waste sites had been greatly exaggerated. However, the prevailing view was that these amendments would result in the creation of a road map at each Superfund site for plaintiffs' lawyers to rely on in preparing toxic tort suits against the generators of the substances found at those sites. Thus information on the toxicity of the chemicals at the site, the routes of exposure to the neighbors (even, at some sites, analyses of individuals' exposure to the contaminants), all in combination with a federal lifting of state tort statutes of limitations and even occasional federal funding of plaintiff-oriented citizen involvement, were perceived as threatening a litigation explosion against Superfund defendants that could leave cleanup costs as the least of their problems. This article examines the public health provisions of SARA, their implementation during the last five years, and their actual and potential effect on toxic tort litigation.

The Requirements of SARA's Public Health Provisions

The original 1980 Superfund legislation established the Agency for Toxic Substances and Disease Registry (ATSDR) within the Department of Health and Human Services. The ATSDR was, and still is, required to maintain a registry of persons who have been exposed to toxic substances and have serious diseases, collect studies on the health effects of toxic substances found at sites, conduct periodic screening programs to determine the relationship between exposure to these substances and illnesses, and even provide medical care in emergencies. By 1986, Congress was quite unhappy with the lack of progress made in carrying out the minimal tasks assigned to the ATSDR. Thus, employing a device that has virtually become the norm in federal environmental legislation, Congress in SARA imposed specific nondiscretionary duties on the ATSDR that were required to be performed according to statutory timetables.

First, within two years after enactment of SARA, the ATSDR was required to have prepared a list of the one hundred hazardous substances most commonly found at Superfund sites and that pose the most significant potential threat to human health. This list was to become known as the priority list. The ATSDR was required to update the priority list at the rate of twenty-five additional hazardous substances per annual revision. 42 U.S.C. § 9604(i)(2).

Second, SARA directed the ATSDR to conduct toxicological profiles of each hazardous substance chosen for the priority list. These profiles were to be completed at the rate of twenty-five per year, with profiles of the original list of one hundred hazardous substances completed by October 17, 1990. Profiles of the remaining hazardous substances were required within three years of their inclusion on the priority list. 42 U.S.C. § 9604(i)(3).

Third, the ATSDR was required to prepare detailed health assessments with respect to each Superfund site. These studies are intended to evaluate the potential risk to humans posed by individual environmental situations, focusing on the nature and extent of contamination, the potential pathways of exposure, the size of the population within the area of exposure, and a comparison of the predicted exposure levels with calculated tolerance limits. Congress originally imposed a deadline of December 10, 1988, for the ATSDR to complete a health assessment for each site that was on the NPL or that had been proposed for inclusion on that list prior to the enactment of 42 U.S.C. § 9604(i)(6). For sites proposed for inclusion on the NPL after enactment, the ATSDR is required to conduct a health assessment within one year of the date of the proposal.

In addition to these major tasks, the ATSDR was provided authority under SARA to identify gaps in available information on listed hazardous substances; commission research to fill gaps identified; conduct epidemiological studies and health surveillance programs; undertake health consultations at the requests of agencies or individuals; take actions to address significant health risks, including temporary or permanent relocation of persons and provision of alternate water supplies; and create and maintain computerized data bases of information generated under the section 110 provisions for public use.

The Hazardous Substance Priority List

On April 17, 1987, the ATSDR met its statutory deadline by publishing its priority list of the most important hazardous substances. 52 Fed.

Reg. 12,866. The list has subsequently been restructured, with the most recent version listing 275 hazardous substances. 56 Fed. Reg. 52,166 (Oct. 17, 1991). The ATSDR has placed at the top of the list in terms of overall health threats lead, arsenic, mercury, vinyl chloride, benzene, cadmium, and PCBs.

The priority list was prepared first by identifying those chemicals found at NPL sites. The ATSDR and the EPA then used the following three criteria to rank the substances by potential human health risk: (1) chemical toxicity, (2) frequency of occurrence at NPL sites or other facilities, and (3) potential for human exposure to the substances.

In analyzing the substances under the toxicity criterion, the two agencies relied on the reportable quantity scoring scheme presently used by the EPA to implement 42 U.S.C. § 9603(a). This scheme is described at 40 C.F.R. § 302.4. Under these regulations, when there is a release into the environment of greater than designated quantities of certain substances, the person in charge of the facility from which the release occurs must immediately notify the National Response Center, an entity first established under the Clean Water Act.

The ATSDR and the EPA turned to data from the EPA contract laboratory program (CLP) to rank substances under the frequency of occurrence criterion. The agencies used a special statistical sample of data taken from sites in the years from 1980 to 1984 that provided information on the percentage of sites at which a substance was detected. Then the agencies examined the average concentration of a candidate substance detected in groundwater and surface water at 375 NPL sites included in the CLP, the frequency of detection, and whether the chemicals had been selected as the "indicator substances" for detailed exposure and risk assessment at these sites. The agencies calculated a final priority ranking for each substance on the basis of these factors through use of an algorithm that is described in detail in the background document for the April 17, 1987, rule making. In essence, this involved dividing the frequency of occurrence value by the lowest reportable quantity value to arrive at a "site index." Then an "exposure index" was prepared by examining the surface water, groundwater, and CLP data. The two indices were then combined to get the final number. Under this algorithm, each substance is evaluated for its danger to humans. Data relating to fish toxicity, ignitability, and reactivity, for example, were removed from the calculations. The ATSDR has refined this algorithm in subsequent additions and rankings of the priority list.

Whether one agrees with this methodology or not, one has to acknowledge that what the ATSDR and the EPA have accomplished is in effect what many Superfund allocation committees have threatened or attempted to do at individual sites without success. This government statement of what chemicals pose the most risks at Superfund sites will undoubtedly continue to be of great value to PRPs who are interested in allocating responsibility on some basis other than pure volume of waste contributed to the site, the method that typically has been employed to date. And while it is still unclear exactly what role these priority rankings will play in the proof at toxic tort trials, certainly a potential plaintiff will be more concerned about living next to a site with high-ranking substances as compared to a site that is more of a garden variety dump.

The Toxicological Profiles

Also on April 17, 1987, the ATSDR published a notice describing the procedures and criteria that the ATSDR and the EPA would employ in developing toxicological profiles. 52 Fed. Reg. 12,870. By 1991, the ATSDR had produced more than 130 of the approximately 200 toxicological profiles required under section 110. Use of these profiles has just started to gain momentum, but they will probably be of enormous value in the future to lawyers—for both sides—in toxic tort suits. Here, in one place, is the latest information on such crucial elements for proof of a case as the basic physical and chemical characteristics of a substance, the fate of the chemical in certain environments, exposure potential to humans, the toxicokinetics and pharmacokinetics of the substance, the toxicity (including acute, chronic, mutagenicity, and carcinogenicity) in both animals and humans, and a complete bibliography of the most relevant studies on the chemical.

Each profile contains a health effects statement that is designed as a self-contained summary of useful information for the general lay public. The statement describes how the substance is commonly used and the other ways in which people may be exposed to it. It discusses the general hazards and symptoms of diseases that may be caused by exposure to the material, including understandable discussions of the risks attached to the chemical, such as acute hazards, carcinogenicity, and birth defects.

Section 110 also directed the Administrator of the ATSDR, in consultation with the EPA administrator and other agencies, to determine whether there is adequate information on the health effects of each substance. 42 U.S.C. § 9604(i)(5)(A). Findings of inadequate data have resulted in ATSDR-sponsored programs designed to fill in the gaps, spawning major research efforts.

SARA stated that: "It is the sense of the Congress that the costs of the [studies to provide data for toxicological profiles] be borne by the manufacturers and processors of the hazardous substance in question." SARA therefore required the EPA to promulgate regulations that provide, "where appropriate, for payment of such costs by manufacturers and processors under the Toxic Substances Control Act, and registrants under the Federal Insecticide, Fungicide, and Rodenticide Act, and recovery of such costs from responsible parties under [Superfund]." 42 U.S.C. § 9604(i)(5)(D).

This provision raises difficult questions that have not been directly resolved by the EPA. It is hard enough to determine a fair allocation for cleanup costs at a specific Superfund site where there are a limited number of PRPs; how is the Agency to allocate the generic costs of study among responsible parties at all present sites? Moreover, when one considers that the majority of Superfund sites have not been analyzed for the presence of contaminants or placed on the NPL, it is difficult to contend that the existing universe of Superfund responsible parties has the obligation of financing these studies. If the Agency spreads the costs by the chemical manufacturers' market share, it introduces into Superfund the idea—accepted in important product liability suits—that if a chemical is proven to cause injury but it is impossible to show which of several manufacturers created the particular batch that caused the injury in question, liability will be divided by the manufacturers' market share. *See, e.g., Sindell v. Abbott Laboratories*, 607 P.2d 924, 928 (Cal.), *cert. denied*, 449 U.S. 912 (1980). This concept could be very significant if extended to the broader scope of general Superfund liability and would be hotly contested by the affected industries. No doubt largely because of these problems, the ATSDR has not yet implemented any program for recovering these costs.

The Site Health Assessments

Toxicological profiles address the generic characteristics of a chemical rather than the role of that chemical at any site. SARA also directed the ATSDR to prepare for each Superfund site a health assessment. Such an assessment is essentially a preliminary examination of the potential human health risk at individual sites based on the extent of contamination, the size of the exposed population, and the comparison of anticipated exposure levels with available literature on tolerance limits.

The ATSDR has traveled a rocky road in implementing the section 110 health assessment requirements. Underfunded and facing difficult deadlines imposed by Congress, the Agency's initial effort at producing health assessments for NPL sites has come under fire. The ATSDR has prepared health assessments for more than twelve hundred sites to date, although a recent General Accounting Office report casts doubt on whether many of the assessments meet statutory requirements. In response to that report, the ATSDR stated that it will revisit health assessments at 165 sites of most concern. The ATSDR also prepared for the Government Accounting Office a workplan for fiscal year 1992 setting priorities for the health assessment program and describing specific planned activities. An area of increasing responsibility for the ATSDR is conducting health assessments at contaminated federal facilities.

In 1990, the ATSDR announced its publication of a proposed guidance manual detailing procedures for conducting health assessments. 55 Fed. Reg. 5136 (Aug. 13, 1990). This manual is significant in a number of respects. First, it emphasizes the importance of alerting the public of health threats as a primary goal of the health assessment program. Second, the manual is extremely detailed, with lengthy procedures that, if followed, should address concerns regarding the quality of specific assessments. Third, the manual calls for allowing public notice and comment on draft health assessments, giving both citizens and PRPs the opportunity to participate in the process. Final regulations implementing the manual have not been published.

The order in which individual Superfund sites are selected for health assessments is not a purely governmental process. Congress provided that citizens may also submit petitions to have health assessments prepared for individual sites. 42 U.S.C. § 9604(i)(6)(B). The Administrator of the ATSDR does not have to comply with such a request but, at a minimum, must explain in writing why "a health assessment is not appropriate." The ATSDR has thus far received a number of requests, although only a handful of the requested health assessments have been completed.

Under its general authority, the ATSDR has also compiled registries of affected persons in connection with at least eighteen hazardous waste sites and has issued public health advisories for at least six sites that the ATSDR believes to pose an imminent and significant threat to human health.

A significant hurdle for most potential toxic tort plaintiffs is finding the funds to use as "seed money" for lawsuits. To some extent, of course, these burdens have been alleviated in Superfund site-related tort suits because the government will be providing under section 110 extensive information on the nature of risks at the site. But Congress has provided even more direct assistance. In section 117 of SARA, creating a new section of CERCLA of the same number, the President was authorized to make grants "available to any group of individuals which may be affected by a release or threatened release at any facility which is listed on [any NPL]." 42 U.S.C. § 9617(e)(1). The grants were created for use by citizens to obtain technical assistance in interpreting information with regard to the nature of the hazard, such as understanding the RI, FS, and ROD. SARA stated that "[t]he amount of any grant under this subsection may not exceed $50,000 for a single grant recipient," but then in the next sentence allowed the EPA to waive this limitation in any case "where such waiver is necessary to carry out the purposes of this subsection." 42 U.S.C. § 9617(e)(2).

Likewise, each grant recipient is required to contribute at least 20 percent of the total costs of technical assistance, but that cap also may be waived. Finally, Congress declared that not more than one grant may be made with respect to a single facility but concluded the provision by stating, "but the grant may be renewed to facilitate public participation at all stages of remedial action." The SARA Conference Report confirmed that "[a] recipient therefore is eligible for multiple grants and can seek additional grants at each stage of activity for which grants may be made. . . ." Committee of Conference, Superfund Amendments and Reauthorization Act of 1986, H.R. Conf. Rep. No. 962, 99th Cong., 2d Sess. 231 (1986).

The SARA Conference Report also reveals that the sponsors of this provision were fully aware that these grants might be used to provide the basis for private lawsuits:

> Such grants are not intended to be used to underwrite legal actions. However, any information developed though grant assistance may be used in any legal action affecting the facility, including any legal action in a court of law.

Id.

After a slow start, the EPA's technical assistance grants have been picking up momentum of late, but they certainly have not reached their potential. Through October 1991, the EPA indicated that grants have been awarded in connection with approximately fifty-two NPL sites. The grants have generally been in the amount of $50,000, with no waivers reported.

The section 110 additions to the information base for toxic tort suits and grants for assessing the information (and possibly actually preparing such suits) mean nothing to a potential plaintiff if the applicable statute of limitations has extinguished the right to bring an action. Congress took a remarkable step in this regard by adding a provision to SARA that established a uniform statute of limitations with respect to actions brought under *state law* for personal injury or property damages "which are caused or contributed to by exposure to any hazardous substance, or pollutant or contaminant, released into the environment from a facility. . . ." 42 U.S.C. § 9658. The federally required period is the otherwise applicable state statute of limitation for such actions, except that the commencement date for the period is now the date "the plaintiff knew (or reasonably should have known) that the personal injury or property damages . . . were caused or contributed to by the hazardous substance or pollutant or contaminant concerned." *Id.* at § 9658(4)(A).

This is an unusual effort to alter through federal environmental legislation what has been regarded as a traditional state interest—the rules for private tort liability. One wonders exactly how the congressional proponents of this provision would define the federal interest that requires such a provision. Recently, a federal district court upheld the constitutionality of the federal commencement date and applied it to the plaintiffs' state claims arising from the contamination of their groundwater by trichloroethylene from a neighboring aircraft manufacturing plant. *Bolin v. Cessna Aircraft Co.*, 759 F. Supp. 692, 709 (D. Kan. 1991).

The Practical Ramifications of SARA's Public Health Provisions

In its essence, SARA has required the compilation of often difficult-to-find information about the presence and toxic properties of chemicals. To this extent, it clearly has the potential to provide otherwise unavailable data to potential plaintiffs and will make it easier for plaintiffs' attorneys—who are usually less well financed than counsel for defendants—to build a case. At a minimum, this new body of information will generate the names of potential expert witnesses and will provide a solid basis for calculating a person's increased risk, a crucial building block in a plaintiff's case. The combination of health assessments and toxicological profiles may also affect common-law litigation by buttressing plaintiffs' claims that a manufacturer or generator of hazardous substances had a duty to warn of potential health risks.

The ATSDR reports that the program to date reveals that approximately 80 percent of NPL sites threaten some human exposure to toxins and that the threat posed by approximately 10 percent of those sites warrants further study. In addition, health assessments have been used by the government to support findings of imminent and substantial endangerment, supporting issuance of unilateral orders, and they will undoubtedly continue to be used for this purpose.

The toxicological profiles required under section 110 would appear to be of great potential use to toxic tort plaintiffs, since they essentially comprise generic expert testimony by neutral government scientists on the risks posed by specific substances. However, at least one court has held that generic causation evidence is not sufficient in a toxic tort case and that direct evidence of actual exposure to the substance in question in any given case is necessary. *In re Sterling v. Velsicol Chem. Corp.*, 855 F.2d 1188 (6th Cir. 1988). Thus the section 110 toxicological profiles probably will not themselves eliminate the plaintiff's burden.

Moreover, these provisions also have important ramifications for toxic tort defense lawyers and for those representing Superfund PRPs. Information generated by the ATSDR can be used as a shield as well as a sword in contesting the scientific bases of toxic tort claims or seeking favorable allocation formulas at Superfund sites.

In fact, while no major federal cases have yet turned on the admission of ATSDR health assessments as evidence of injury or death, the existence of ATSDR health assessments has been used successfully to oppose plaintiffs' claims that costs of medical monitoring incurred privately were "response costs" under CERCLA for which PRPs should be liable.

In sum, the ATSDR and the EPA have during the past five years made substantial progress in implementing SARA's public health provisions. While there can be little question that these provisions were initially intended by Congress—at least to some degree—to provide assistance to toxic tort plaintiffs, they have not appeared to have any substantial effect to date. It is likely, however, that with accomplishment of its initial statutory mandates and an increased focus on communicating with citizens regarding health risks, the ATSDR will begin to measurably affect toxic tort litigation in the coming decade. At the very least, any lawyer advising a potential defendant or Superfund PRP should fully evaluate available ATSDR information in representing his or her client.

Using Epidemiology to Determine Causation in Disease

Otto Wong

The proliferation and expansion of toxic tort lawsuits involving occupational or environmental exposures and possible health effects therefrom have created a new set of legal problems. The outcome of many cases depends on the ability to establish a causal relationship between an event in the distant past and a subsequent disease.

Throughout the history of humankind, the issue of causality has intrigued both scientists and philosophers alike. Discussion of causality can be traced back to the time of Aristotle. In some situations, the demonstration of a causal relationship between two events is relatively straightforward. For example, chemists can show that when chemical A and chemical B are combined under certain experimental conditions, chemical C is produced. Thus "proof" of causation in these situations is attainable.

This is the case with most physical trauma injuries. The time between the physical trauma and the subsequent clinical observation of injury is usually short. Thus the determination and demonstration of a causal relationship are both feasible and relatively easy to understand. For infectious diseases, the process of determining causality is somewhat similar, since for most infectious diseases clinical symptoms appear shortly after exposure.

Demonstrating a causal relationship in chronic diseases such as cancer is neither easy nor straightforward. Several characteristics associated with chronic diseases complicate the process of demonstrat-

Dr. Otto Wong is chief epidemiologist at Applied Health Sciences in San Mateo, California.

ing causality. These include long latency, multiple causes, poorly understood biological mechanisms, and the fact that cases of the same disease that arise from different causes are clinically indistinguishable.

For chronic diseases, the traditional criteria used for establishing causal relationships in acute or infectious diseases based on direct proofs are unrealistic and unattainable. Consequently, a different scientific discipline must be applied. This scientific discipline is epidemiology: the study of disease in human populations.

Determining Causation in Chronic Diseases

In developing a strategy for a toxic tort case, it is useful for attorneys to understand how an epidemiologist may determine causation. Most chronic diseases have multiple causes, only some of which have been identified at this time. Cancer cases in which there has been no exposure to any known carcinogens, which are referred to as background or idiopathic cases, have always been observed. Because most cancers have insidious onset and long latent periods (i.e., a long time lapse between exposure to a particular agent and the subsequent clinical appearance of cancer), exposures to multiple known or unknown carcinogens during the interim are likely. Thus the determination of causality cannot rely upon individual cases where there may be evidence of several known or unknown causes. For example, if we see a stomach cancer in a coffee drinker, we cannot, based on this observation alone, conclude that coffee drinking causes stomach cancer. This particular patient may have several other known or unknown risk factors that can cause stomach cancer. The scientific procedure for determining a cause-and-effect relationship in human populations, in this example, is to study a group of coffee drinkers and to compare their number or rate of stomach cancer to a group of noncoffee drinkers to determine whether coffee drinkers have an increased risk of stomach cancer. This type of study is basic epidemiology.

Formally, epidemiology can be defined as the study of distribution and determinants of diseases. In other words, epidemiologists, based on properly designed studies, both identify groups with high rates of a disease and determine what factors cause the higher rates.

Case reports of cancers in individuals with certain characteristics (exposures) are useful in providing leads for formal epidemiological studies that may confirm or refute the causality hypothesis suggested by case reports. An example of confirming a causal relationship is the study of ionizing radiation and leukemia. In the early 1900s, leukemia cases among radiologists were reported, thus suggesting a potential causal link. In 1944, H. C. March reported an epidemiological study comparing the leukemia rate in radiologists to that in other physicians. The leukemia rate in the radiologists was ten times higher than that in the other physicians. This result and those in other subsequent epidemiological studies have clearly established the relationship between ionizing radiation and leukemia.

Although case reports can be useful leads, they cannot be used as "proofs" for causation themselves without confirmation by properly designed epidemiological studies. In fact, there are numerous examples wherein subsequent epidemiological studies refute earlier case reports.

An interesting example is the issue of mesothelioma in garage mechanics. Mesothelioma is a rare cancer of the pleura or peritoneum. Epidemiological evidence has clearly demonstrated that certain asbestos workers (e.g., insulators, pipe fitters, and shipyard workers) experience a significantly increased risk of mesothelioma. Although exposure to asbestos in such occupations has been found to be the major cause of mesothelioma, other causes for the disease have also been identified. Furthermore, idiopathic cases of mesothelioma not related to asbestos exposure have always been reported in the medical literature.

Brake linings contain a certain amount of chrysotile fiber. However, most of the chrysotile fiber is broken down to nonfibrous forsterite by the intense heat generated during the braking process. Nevertheless, it seems natural to question whether garage mechanics, who are potentially exposed to brake lining dust, experience an increased risk of mesothelioma. A few isolated case reports of mesothelioma in garage mechanics have appeared. Unfortunately, these reports have been used incorrectly to suggest a causal relationship between exposure to brake lining dust and an increased risk of mesothelioma.

Several epidemiological studies have clearly demonstrated that garage mechanics are not at any increased risk of mesothelioma when compared to the general population. The finding of no increased mesothelioma risk in these studies is consistent with the results of other studies concluding that brake lining dust contains only a minimal amount of short chrysotile fibers and that the typical time-weighted average exposure of garage mechanics is less than 0.05 fiber per cubic centimeter.

The assumption that garage mechanics experience a mesothelioma risk similar to that of other high-risk asbestos workers, regardless of the type, length, and amount of asbestos fiber involved, has been proven to be erroneous by proper epidemiological studies. This example clearly demonstrates the danger of relying on isolated case reports.

The Criteria for Causal Relationships

Now that the vital role of epidemiology in determining causation has been demonstrated, the criteria used by epidemiologists in assessing causation are discussed. The criteria discussed below have also been used by the U.S. Surgeon General in determining the causal relationship between cigarette smoking and lung cancer.

A. B. Hill has given the following criteria that can be used as guidelines for establishing causal relationship in epidemiological studies.

1. Strength and significance of association. This criterion refers to a certain risk index comparing the disease rates for those with and those without the hypothesized causal factor. The risk index, a measure of strength of association, is usually the ratio of disease rates between two groups. In general, the larger the ratio, the more likely the factor is to be causal. Closely related to strength of association is the concept of significance of association, which refers to the probability of such an association occurring by chance. By convention, if this probability is less than 5 percent, the association is said to be statistically significant. Before the strength of an association can be assessed, it must be established that the observed association is not due to chance or statistical fluctuations. That is, it must be determined that the difference observed between the two groups is statistically significant.

The term "significance" is often misinterpreted as representing medical or biological significance. For example, a small difference in the average hemoglobin concentrations between two groups may be statistically significant if the two groups are large enough, implying that it is most unlikely that the observed difference is due to chance. However, this difference may be totally unimportant from the health point of view. One must make the distinction between statistical significance and clinical significance. On the other hand, if the findings are not statistically significant, it should not automatically be assumed that there is no health problem. There are several possible explanations for a result being statistically nonsignificant, and further analysis is needed to determine the appropriate explanation(s), such as the question of statistical power of the analysis.

2. Consistency of association. If studies on different populations, utilizing different study designs, based on different comparison groups, and over different observation periods all produce similar results, the association is more likely to be causal. One question epidemiologists often ask in assessing causality is, Has the finding been replicated by different investigators in different places, circumstances, and times? As an example, let us look at the relationship between cigarette smoking and cancer of the lung. As early as the 1960s, the association between smoking and lung cancer was demonstrated in thirty-six studies with different study designs and on different populations. Based on the consistency of the results available then, the interpretation of a causal relationship between smoking and lung cancer was justified.

3. Specificity. This criterion refers to the correspondence of exposure to disease. Is the exposure associated with a specific disease and vice versa? Is the association restricted to specific workers and to specific diseases (specific cancer site or specific histologic type)? The argument for a causal relationship is weakened if the relationship is nonspecific.

For example, the fact that crocidolite asbestos can cause mesothelioma does not mean that another type of asbestos fiber such as chrysotile would also cause mesothelioma. The same argument is true for disease endpoints as well. The fact that exposure to benzene at high concentration levels can increase the risk of acute myeloid leukemia does not mean that other types of leukemia are also affected by benzene exposure.

4. Temporality. This seemingly simple criterion refers to the requirement that exposure to the causal factor must precede disease in a causal association. This criterion is particularly important for chronic diseases with long latent periods—the time between onset of exposure and diagnosis—and for study factors that change over time. This criterion may be deceivingly obvious but nonetheless needs to be considered, particularly with selecting factors at work in industry. For example, does a particular job lead to disease or do the early stages of the disease lead to those particular jobs? In a mortality study of some fifty-eight thousand steelworkers, janitors and night watchmen at steel mills were found to experience increased risk of dying from cardiovascular diseases when compared with other steelworkers. Further investigation revealed that early symptoms of the disease were responsible for the transfer of the affected steelworkers from various jobs to these two particular jobs.

Latency is an important factor in determining causation in chronic diseases such as cancer. As stated above, chronic diseases such as cancer have long latent periods, oftentimes several decades. Using this criterion, exposures that do not satisfy the latency requirement for a particular disease can be ruled out as causal factors. The latency requirement for a particular disease can be estimated based on data from epidemiological studies. One interesting point about latency is that, in general, latency is inversely proportional to the level of exposure. For example, low-level exposure to a carcinogen such as asbestos may result in a latency longer than a normal lifetime.

5. *Dose-response relationship.* A dose-response relationship refers to the severity or frequency of disease increasing with the level or duration of exposure. If the association reveals such a dose-response relationship or biological gradient, the argument for a causal association becomes very persuasive. For example, the observation that lung cancer risk increases with the amount of cigarettes smoked (for packs and years) lends great support to the argument that smoking is a causal factor of lung cancer. A dose-response relationship allows a simple and intuitive explanation and obviously enhances the causal interpretation.

A dose-response consideration also allows us to rule out the causal role of minimal exposures. For some substances, epidemiological data have provided estimates on the level and length of exposure that are needed to produce an increased risk. Therefore an exposure less than the needed amount is not likely to have a causal role. The amount of exposure experienced by the plaintiff is a major consideration in a toxic tort case.

6. *Biological plausibility and coherence with existing knowledge.* If the suspected causation is biologically plausible, the causal interpretation will be more convincing. However, one must not forget that what is biologically plausible depends on the existing knowledge of the day. This is especially true for cancer, since the etiology for the most part is not understood or, at best, poorly understood. Nevertheless, if the causal interpretation seriously conflicts with the natural history and biology of the disease, extra caution must be exercised.

Based on the criteria above, it is obvious that determining causation is a highly structured process that requires a thorough understanding of epidemiology. Determining causation in chronic diseases such as cancer is much more than anecdotal observations of clinicians. Expert opinions must be substantiated by appropriate epidemiological data.

Assessing Risks and the Probability of Causation

Epidemiological criteria for assessing causality include an evaluation of strength of association and dose-response relationship. Both criteria involve the calculation of risk.

One of the primary objectives of an epidemiological study is to provide a measure of risk resulting from exposure—at a certain level of exposure, if possible. The type of measure of risk depends on the study design, which, in turn, is determined by the type of disease under investigation and the availability of data and resources. The measures of risk in common epidemiological study designs are as follows:

Study Design	Measure of Risk
Cohort Mortality Study	Standardized Morality Ratio (SMR)
Proportional Mortality Study	Proportional Mortality Ratio (PMR)
Case-Control Study	Odds Ratio (OR)

The above study designs are appropriate for investigating cancer incidence as well as mortality. For example, in a cohort study, if incidence data are available, the appropriate measure is the standardized incidence ratio (SIR).

Regardless of the study design, the basic concept of measure of risk is that of a relative risk.

$$\text{Relative Risk (RR)} = \frac{\text{Risk in Exposed Population}}{\text{Risk in Non-Exposed Population}}$$

Thus a lung cancer SMR or RR of 10 for smokers means that smokers are at 10 times the lung cancer risk of nonsmokers. In terms of determination of causation, the higher the RR, the stronger the causation. Furthermore, a positive dose-response relationship (i.e., RR goes up with increasing exposure) lends additional support to a causal relationship, whereas a negative or lack of a positive dose-response relationship argues against causation.

Relative risks can easily be converted into probability of causation. As mentioned earlier, cancers have multiple causes, not all of which are known to us. For example, although asbestos is the major known risk factor for mesothelioma, background cases of mesothelioma have always existed, indicating that there are other causes both known and unknown to us at this point. In fact, all cancers have multiple causes. Furthermore, clinical features of cancer cases, caused by different risk factors, are seldom distinguishable from one another. Therefore the only valid scientific way to address causation in a specific individual case is through the use of probability.

In epidemiology, probability of causation is determined by attributable risk (AR), which is defined as:

$$AR = \frac{P(RR - 1)}{P(RR - 1) + 1}$$

where P = proportion exposed in the study group, and RR = relative risk of the study group. If the entire group is exposed, P = 1 and AR = (RR − 1)/RR.

For example, in one of the largest case-control studies of mesothelioma, A. D. McDonald and J. C. McDonald found a mesothelioma RR of 46 for insulators. Thus, for an insulator with mesothelioma, the AR due to his asbestos exposure is (46 − 1)/46 or 98%. That is, there is a 98% chance that his mesothelioma was caused by his occupation, and only 2% chance that his mesothelioma is a "background" case. Since the probability of causation due to occupational exposure is higher than 50%, his mesothelioma is said to be "more likely than not" caused by his occupational exposure.

For AR to be greater than 50% (more likely than not), RR has to be greater than 2. Thus, for any exposure with a RR less than 2, the cancer cannot be attributed to that exposure according to the "more likely than not" criterion. That is, that cancer is "more likely than not" a background case.

Finally, if the RR for a certain exposure is 1 or less, the corresponding AR would be 0. That is, no probability can be attributed to that particular exposure, and the cancer is simply a background case. For example, McDonald and McDonald found that the RR for mesothelioma in garage mechanics was 0.9. Thus the corresponding mesothelioma AR due to occupational exposure of a garage mechanic is 0, and mesothelioma cases among garage mechanics are simply background cases.

Epidemiological Tasks in Toxic Tort Litigation

In a typical toxic tort case, the epidemiologist begins by compiling a complete employment history of the plaintiff with regard to specific exposures. (*See* Table 1.) Next, a complete profile of other exposures is developed. What substances was the plaintiff exposed to at school or in the military? Where did he or she live? Does he or she smoke, drink, take drugs? Does his or her family have a history of cancer?

The epidemiologist ensures that the final diagnosis of the disease is as specific as possible, down to the cell type, if possible. He or

---

Table 1
Outline of Epidemiologic Tasks in a Toxic Tort Case

1. *Develop a complete employment history*

Specific exposures	Work practice (protective equipment)
Exposure levels	Exposure dates
Work environment	Exposure length

2. *Develop a complete profile of other exposures*

School	Alcohol	Lifestyle
Nonoccupational	Family history	Smoking
Residential	Military	Drugs

3. *Make final diagnosis as specific as possible*

   Is the clinical definition same as one used in epidemiology?
   Is the cell type specific?

4. *Develop a complete list of risk factors of the disease*

   Perform a comprehensive literature review

5. *Develop a critical review of epidemiologic studies of person with the exposure of interest*

   Determine the scientific merits of individual studies
   Is the exposure relevant to our case?
   Is the diagnosis as specific as ours?

6. *Meta-analysis*

   Make a quantitative summary of all valid and relevant studies
   Ascertain the metarelative risk
   Ascertain the attributable risk: is it more likely than not?

7. *Review additional information that opposing experts may use*

   Case reports
   Inappropriate studies

---

she then develops a complete list of risk factors of the specific disease by conducting a comprehensive literature review. This list is used to determine whether the plaintiff was exposed to any of these risk factors in addition to the exposure in question.

Next, to determine whether there is an association between the exposure in question and the plaintiff's disease, a critical review of epidemiological studies on the subject matter is performed. The scientific merits of individual studies are determined. These studies are then analyzed to quantitatively summarize findings from all valid and relevant studies. This is known as meta-analysis.

In most situations, risk estimates from different studies are not identical. Furthermore, some studies are larger than the others. In summarizing these studies, more weight should be given to larger studies than to smaller ones. A metarelative risk or summary relative risk is then calculated based on all valid and relevant studies. This metarelative risk is a weighted average of relative risks from individual studies, taking both study size and consistency of findings into consideration, and thus representing the "bottom line" of all study findings. The procedure of meta-analysis has been used to summarize data on many chemicals or industries. For example, recently O. Wong and G. K. Raabe applied meta-analysis to summarize the results of epidemiological studies in the petroleum industry. Although some small studies reported an increased risk for brain cancer in petroleum workers, Wong and Raabe, based on a meta-analysis of all the studies combined, were able to demonstrate that petroleum workers had the same risk as the general population (metarelative risk = 1.00). Finally, in a toxic tort case, a metarelative risk can be used to calculate a summary attributable risk to determine whether the "more likely than not" criterion is met.

To sum up, demonstrating a causal relationship in chronic diseases is complicated by a number of factors: long latency, multiple causes, poorly understood biological mechanisms, and the fact that cases of the same disease that arise from different causes are clinically indistinguishable. For chronic diseases, the traditional criteria used for establishing causal relationships in trauma injuries or acute/infectious diseases based on direct proofs are unrealistic and unattainable. Relying on isolated case reports, anecdotal clinical observations, or clinicians' intuition is not only misleading but also scientifically invalid. The demonstration of causality in chronic diseases should be based on a comprehensive review and a critical assessment of well-conducted epidemiological studies. In assessing causality, epidemiologists use a set of well-structured criteria that include strength and significance of association, consistency, specificity, temporality (latency), dose-response relationship, and biological plausibility. In formulating an opinion on causality, epidemiologists also use the formal procedure of meta-analysis to summarize data from all relevant studies. Any opinion on causality in chronic disease must be substantiated by appropriate epidemiological data.

The time has come to educate both legal professions and lay jurors of the importance of epidemiology in the determination of causation in chronic diseases.

Innovations and Considerations in Settling Toxic Tort Litigation

David T. Peterson and Karen L. Palladino

The growing number of toxic tort lawsuits presents lawyers and their clients with difficult new issues. Toxic tort claims may arise from exposure to oil and chemical spills, toxic fumes, medical drugs, asbestos, hazardous waste sites, or to an ever-increasing number of chemical compounds now suspected to be carcinogenic. These cases may involve hundreds or even thousands of plaintiffs, multiple defendants, unknown exposure dates, and complex questions of medical causation. The plaintiffs' injuries may have latency periods of several decades or may not become manifest for a generation, as is alleged to occur with DES, a drug women had taken in the 1950s to prevent miscarriages. To avoid the enormous cost and risk of litigating these issues, toxic tort litigants are negotiating settlement agreements that seek to address the complex and often unique problems presented by these cases. This chapter briefly discusses some of the approaches used in settlements and touches upon some of the problem areas encountered in drafting enforceable settlement agreements in these cases.

While toxic exposure may result in immediate illness or injury, it is not uncommon for allegedly adverse effects to become manifest many years after the initial exposure. Drafting a settlement agreement that provides for an enforceable release of such latent injuries is therefore critically important. The general release typically used to settle a personal injury case releases all liability arising out of a given

David Peterson is a partner and Karen Palladino is an associate in the Los Angeles office of Hill Wynne Troop & Meisinger.

occurrence. These general releases may not work in the unusual circumstances of a toxic tort settlement because releases purporting to discharge liability for unknown injuries often conflict with state statutory law imposing limitations on these releases.

In California, for example, Civil Code section 1542 provides that a "general release does not extend to claims which the creditor does not know or suspect to exist . . . at the time of executing the release, which if known by him would have materially affected his settlement. . . ." Despite such statutory language, it is a common practice to have a settlement agreement specifically waive any and all rights under such a statute. Nevertheless, these statutory provisions will prevail in the absence of a clear expression of the parties' intent. California courts have interpreted Civil Code section 1542 as precluding the application of a release to unknown claims in the absence of a showing, *apart from the words of the release*, of an intent to include such claims. *See, e.g., Casey v. Proctor*, 59 Cal. 2d 97, 378 P.2d 579, 28 Cal. Rptr. 307 (1963).

Decisions in other jurisdictions similarly indicate that the courts will carefully scrutinize the express intent of the parties in deciding whether to enforce a release of future injuries. While it is common practice to set out any statutory language being waived in full so that there is no doubt regarding what rights are intended to be waived, such waiver language by itself may not withstand legal challenge. The standard ground for denying enforcement of a release is the plaintiff's claim of mistake as to the nature and extent of the injuries that were the subject of the release.

Thus an enforceable release agreement will require that plaintiffs know they are releasing *all* future injuries resulting from the alleged exposure, whether presently known or suspected, including death. It seems very clear that when there is a known or suspected possibility of latent injury, it is even more important that the release include specific language indicating that the parties intend to shift the risk of future injuries from the defendant to the plaintiff. The release should enumerate those present and future injuries or effects that it intends to cover. At the risk of giving the plaintiffs new ideas, careful consideration should be given to including all illnesses or potential injuries that medical knowledge may attribute to the toxic exposure involved. This may include reference to immune system dysfunction, chromosomal damage, and other relatively rare injuries.

Even where the agreement specifically provides for a release covering future injuries, it is the subjective intent of the particular plaintiff that controls whether the release will override California Civil Code section 1542 to bar unknown injuries. Evidence of a plaintiff's involvement in preparing the agreement is critical in showing that the plaintiff intended to release the unknown claims. This can be accomplished by having the plaintiff sign a statement that his or her lawyer has explained the release and that he or she understands the legal significance and future consequences of the release. The plaintiff's lawyer should sign a provision attesting to the explanation of the terms of the release. Causes of action for wrongful death by the heirs should be released as well. To obtain the latter, it will be necessary to make the heirs signatories to the settlement and specifically release their claims in return for adequate consideration.

To be enforceable, adequate consideration must be given in return for the release of a right to sue for latent injuries. The uncertain risk that a future disease or injury will actually develop arguably justifies a discount on what the plaintiff might ultimately recover. The recognition of this understanding should be stated clearly in the agreement. If the disease never manifests itself, the plaintiff receives a windfall. If the disease manifests itself, the plaintiff's compensation may be inadequate. The plaintiff's assumption of this risk and the attendant discount to recover must be emphasized in the settlement documents to discourage and counteract future challenges to the adequacy of consideration.

In choosing the specific words that will effectively convey the plaintiff's intent to release claims for future injuries, the release must be clearly worded. Careful research into cases upholding or denying the enforceability of a release of future injuries in a given jurisdiction will assist in arriving at the most effective language. A helpful listing of such decisions can be found in Annot., 13 A.L.R. 4th 686 (1987). Decisions with regard to the enforceability of settlement agreements also provide practical guidance on other factors that might undermine a settlement's enforceability. For example, courts are reluctant to enforce an agreement with a recently injured or otherwise vulnerable plaintiff. Also, courts often refuse to enforce boilerplate settlement forms.

Although there is no certain recipe for enforceability, our review of the authorities indicates the paramount importance of stating in plain and emphatic language that the plaintiff understands that he or she is assuming the risk of latent injury in exchange for adequate consideration.

Present Recovery for Future Injuries: Emotional Distress and the Fear of Cancer

Where plaintiffs claim that they suffer from the fear of cancer, it goes without saying that the release should specify cancer as a potential future injury. However, where a plaintiff is silent regarding the fear of cancer, the defendants may prefer to avoid raising the issue, since the fear of cancer gives rise to a present claim for emotional distress. Once settlement appears imminent, the defendants should consider specific language releasing claims for cancer and, separately, for the fear of cancer. The traditional rule in California for the recovery of damages for emotional distress requires a showing that emotional distress is parasitic to a physical injury or the plaintiff suffered emotional trauma that resulted in physical injury. However, contrary to this rule, in the recent decision of *Potter v. Firestone*, 232 Cal. App. 3d 1114, 274 Cal. Rptr. 885 (1990), the appellate court held that where the plaintiff ingests carcinogens, it is not necessary for the plaintiff to establish a present physical injury or the probability of developing cancer to recover emotional distress damages for the fear of cancer. The impact of this case remains uncertain pending review by the California Supreme Court, which was granted on February 28, 1991.

Suspending Future Claims: The "Green Card"

Not surprisingly, plaintiffs are often unwilling to accept this risk of future injury. From the defendant's perspective, the release may require an excessive premium for an injury that may never become manifest. Faced with such a potential stalemate, settlements are being reached that compensate the plaintiff for present injuries but that preserve the plaintiff's right to bring claims in the future. A settlement provision suspending claims in this manner is frequently referred to as the "green card" option. This option has been used in the settlement of asbestos and Dalkon Shield litigation and is gaining in popularity in other toxic tort settlements.

In drafting a green card settlement provision, one should set out the nature of the claims being settled and, to the extent possible, a detailed description of the claim being preserved. The injuries or claims being suspended should be listed as specific exceptions in the general release to minimize future conflict over the coverage of the release.

A green card provision normally incorporates a waiver of the defendant's right to assert a statute of limitations defense as to the claims being preserved. Although the limitation of actions provisions prevalent in most jurisdictions follow the discovery rule, which provides that a claim does not accrue until discovery, a green card clause should be drafted to minimize the risk of future dispute. To avoid unlimited time in which the plaintiff may raise a green card claim, the defendant should require that the statute of limitations commence running again upon discovery of the first sign of an additional injury. In states where there is not a discovery-type statute of limitations provision, waiver of the statute of limitations defense is essential to preserve the plaintiff's claims.

A green card deferment provision may be accompanied by a monitoring program to provide for regular medical examinations to detect the occurrence of latent injuries as early as feasible. Early detection of illness, particularly cancer, substantially increases the cure rate. Thus both the potential harm to the plaintiff and the exposure to the defendant may be reduced by monitoring. Monitoring presents an ideal compromise of toxic tort lawsuits that are stalemated on the causation issue, since the parties may postpone trial until medical research and epidemiology shed light on causation. Such monitoring may take the form of periodic medical tests, the number, timing, and nature of which should be spelled out in the settlement agreement.

Not surprisingly, the drafting of a monitoring provision often raises conflicts regarding funding. Plaintiffs generally prefer a lump sum payment that they may spend or invest as they see fit. On the other hand, defendants have a legitimate interest in making payments conditional upon monitoring actually taking place in a cost-effective manner.

Additionally, defendants should determine whether medical monitoring costs are compensable damages. At least one California case has held that where the plaintiff develops a fear of cancer as a result of exposure to toxic and possibly carcinogenic chemicals, medical monitoring is not compensable. In *Potter v. Firestone*, a California appellate court concluded that the plaintiffs' failure to establish that cancer was reasonably certain to occur precluded them from recovering their medical monitoring costs. The court rationalized that to monitor an injury or illness, there must be a physical injury to base it on; the increased risk of cancer is not a physical injury unless there is evidence that it is probable that the disease will occur; and, thus, the failure to show the certainty of injury prohibits recovery.

Nonetheless, medical monitoring should be addressed by settling parties, since it is frequently recognized in other jurisdictions. Directly contradicting the holding in *Potter*, in *Werlein v. United States*, 746 F. Supp. 887 (D. Minn. 1990), the district court upheld an award for medical monitoring for plaintiffs who were exposed to toxic chemicals on the theory that the increased risk of a future disease is of itself a presently existing injury. Thus, where plaintiffs insist on the green card approach, preserving their right to recover for unknown future injuries, the benefits of early detection by medical monitoring should be considered by all parties.

Distribution Plans

Defendants seeking to draft a global settlement resolving claims brought by hundreds of plaintiffs face unique problems in achieving a fair distribution of settlement funds. Where plaintiffs are numerous and have widely varying perceptions of what they desire in a settlement, it is advisable to give them options. For example, the settlement agreement used in the A. H. Robins Co. reorganization settles claims pursuant to a multitiered, structured framework. As a first option, the claimant may sign an affidavit asserting injury from the Dalkon Shield in return for a settlement of $100. A. H. Robins would pay the $100, conceding all defenses that it might have to such a claim except for duplication, the bar of the statute of limitations, or improper notice. This preliminary determination screens those plaintiffs who have not suffered serious injuries. Those who fear latent injuries surfacing later may file a green card reserving their right to file later claims.

Claimants who feel they have a solid medical basis for their claim may opt for a second level of more detailed forms, submitting medical records and answering a series of questions regarding the use of the Dalkon Shield. If injury is shown, the claimant's settlement would range from $400 to $2,000, depending on the severity of the injury. Again A. H. Robins concedes its normal defenses.

If a Dalkon Shield claimant feels the need for further opportunity to demonstrate the merit of her claim beyond merely filling out forms, she may opt for a mediation process that would grant an award upon proof of actual use of the product and the occurrence of certain injuries.

Finally, a claimant who insists upon her day in court may opt for binding arbitration or a trial-type hearing. Such a proceeding would incorporate traditional concepts of causation, focusing upon use of the product and any causal connection to the plaintiff's alleged injuries. However, as with most court-supervised or -imposed toxic tort settlements, stringent legal causation is forsaken in return for a waiver of punitive damages and the mutual savings of the resources that would otherwise be expended in proving causation.

While the A. H. Robins settlement was drafted by the company with the aid of the noted settlement expert Francis McGovern, it often takes an active and aggressive judge to settle excessively complex cases. Perhaps the best-known judicially supervised settlement agreement is the one hammered out by Judge Weinstein in the Agent Orange litigation. In that settlement, Judge Weinstein ordered a distribution plan that would distribute a varying amount, up to $13,800, based on the severity of injuries. To qualify for payment, the claimants need show only (1) service in areas where the spraying of Agent Orange was conducted, (2) disability as defined in the Social Security Act, and (3) that their injuries were not accidental, traumatic, or self-inflicted. These standards do not attempt to address the impossibly difficult issue of causation, preferring to effect compensation with minimum administrative costs.

Another approach is the use of an independent panel or administrator to evaluate claims and distribute funds according to agreed upon scientific criteria. In *Hagood v. Olin Corp.*, No. 86–C–5313 (N.D. Ala. Nov. 17, 1986), the plaintiffs sought recovery for alleged injuries from DDT exposure. The Olin Corporation agreed to establish a $15 million fund for seven thousand claimants, provided that they meet certain criteria that had yet to be resolved at the time of settlement. In the settlement agreement, the parties agreed to appoint an independent administrator to determine the value of individual claims according to certain risk factors. For example, a claim's value would depend upon the level of DDT in book samples, the clinical manifestation of certain symptoms believed to stem from DDT, and the distance between the plaintiff's residence and the Olin plant.

This settlement agreement is remarkable in that it gave the administrator authority to establish his or her own criteria in determining individual distributions. The clear risk in such an approach is that the administrator may run amok. Safeguards should be carefully drawn to prevent such a process from slanting in either side's favor. If such an approach is to be used, the parties should provide the administrator as objective a set of criteria as possible for evaluating claims.

An issue that frequently arises in multiplaintiff toxic tort cases is whether a settlement should be reached with less than all of the potential plaintiffs. Such a settlement will set a precedent, establish what may be perceived as a floor on future settlements, and may encourage additional plaintiffs to file lawsuits. It is not unusual in toxic tort cases for additional plaintiffs to appear and file a lawsuit after they discover that they may be able to recover damages for their alleged exposure. If the information regarding settlement is not kept confidential, the defendants may later find it difficult to justify offering a lesser settlement amount and risk having to settle with many more plaintiffs than originally anticipated. A settlement agreement should be perfectly clear to whom the settlement applies and how those parties may be distinct from other potential plaintiffs. Additionally, a confidentiality provision is essential.

Protection against Subsequent Suits for Contribution

Drafting a settlement with one defendant in a case involving joint and several liability involves complex and widely varying matters of state law. Generally speaking, settling defendants should try to draft settlements that preclude or at least minimize subsequent actions for contribution. In those states where only a good faith of the settlement will bar a subsequent claim for contribution, the settling defendant should obtain an agreement from the plaintiff to attest to the good faith of the settlement and assist in a good faith hearing where one is required by state law. In addition, the plaintiff should agree to seek only a proportional share of liability from other defendants. Since contribution claims are generally limited to amounts paid in excess of their fair share, no contribution claim would exist.

In settling with a single joint tortfeasor, it is crucial for a plaintiff's lawyer to become familiar with the effect of certain settlement language on a plaintiff's rights against remaining joint tortfeasors. For example, in some states, a general release given to one joint tortfeasor may actually release all defendants. Moreover, the plaintiff will find his or her judgment against the remaining tortfeasors reduced by an amount that is determined by settlement language and that varies widely from state to state.

While space does not permit a discussion of the many pitfalls posed by various state laws, counsel are advised to examine all available state law sources regarding the effect certain settlement language can have on the subsequent rights of the parties. A general exposition of these pitfalls can be found in Joel A. Dewey's article "Traps in Multi-Tortfeasor Settlements," 13/4 *Litigation* 41 (1987).

One of the more distasteful settlement devices is the sliding scale or "Mary Carter" type of agreement. The essential clause creating a sliding scale settlement is the covenant to pay an amount that will be determined based upon the size of plaintiff's recovery against the remaining defendants. If the plaintiff fails to recover against other defendants, the settling defendant will pay a predetermined maximum. On the other hand, if the plaintiff recovers the maximum from the other defendants, the settling defendant will pay nothing. This covenant may be the sole consideration or may be added as sweetener to a fixed down payment in settlement. Frequently, a sliding scale settlement will give the plaintiff a fixed sum up to the defendant's insurance policy limits or the amount plaintiff needs for litigation expenses, with a sliding scale for any additional liability that may not be recovered from the other defendants. Since plaintiffs in a toxic tort action often lack the massive sums required to prove what is usually a scientifically difficult and legally complex lawsuit, a settlement that advances litigation expenses is well suited to a toxics case.

While the settling defendant in a Mary Carter agreement will want to ensure that the plaintiff prosecutes his or her action with diligence against the remaining defendants, it is difficult to draft clauses requiring diligence without appearing collusive or intrusive. A provision giving an open-ended power to veto any settlement with remaining defendants will probably not be enforceable. In *Abbott Ford v. Superior Court*, 43 Cal. 3d 858, 882–83, 741 P.2d 124, 239 Cal. Rptr. 626 (1987), the California Supreme Court rejected an agreement that allowed the settling defendant to arbitrarily reject a subsequent good faith settlement by the plaintiff with the remaining defendants.

Instead of a veto clause, such a settlement agreement should give the settling defendant the right to monitor the progress of the plaintiff's case to ensure that no deadlines are missed, that discovery proceeds at a decent pace, and provide general assurance that the plaintiff will proceed against the remaining defendants. This should ensure that the settling defendant gets the benefit of its bargain.

While any agreement that provides for a defendant to actively assist the plaintiff in the lawsuit risks being found collusive and in bad faith, some courts have upheld such agreements as good faith settlements. Nevertheless, Mary Carter types of agreements are coming under increasing scrutiny and may not survive a good faith settlement hearing unless drafted with careful attention and the complete absence of bad faith, collusion, or intent to harm other defendants.

In defending toxic tort litigation, it is critical that the defendants work together and coordinate research, briefing, and discovery on issues common to all defendants. Some defendants may decide to settle early on because they do not have the ability to fund a lengthy litigation battle. The nonsettling defendants are at risk that such settlements will provide fuel for the plaintiffs' fire by funding the plaintiffs' case. If appropriate, the nonsettling defendants should consider offering to a settling defendant an indemnity and representation in exchange for the payment of a negotiated settlement amount to the nonsettling defendants.

The settlement provisions discussed have been incorporated in a variety of situations in an effort to resolve complex cases before the expense and risk of litigation are incurred. These agreements must be drafted carefully so that they reflect the clear intent of the parties and minimize the need for future litigation as to the settlement's intended effect. Nevertheless, as the courts begin to address the unique issues presented by toxic tort actions and efforts to settle these actions, the practitioner seeking to draft an enforceable settlement must thoroughly understand the state of the law and perhaps predict its future course.

Minimizing Toxic Tort Liability

Roger Strelow

Corporate environmental managers and lawyers have one overriding function—to ensure protection of human health and the environment and thereby minimize liabilities arising from environmental problems. During most of the environmentally active 1970s, corporate environmentalists thought primarily in terms of minimizing liability to federal and state governments by avoiding fines for noncompliance with statutes and regulations. In the 1980s, it has become increasingly clear that another source of potential liability warrants at least as much attention—private lawsuits alleging that release of a harmful chemical has harmed some person's health or property. Recent settlements and awards in such toxic tort cases have ranged from $8 million to $108 million. Compared to typical government fines, or anything else for that matter, this is definitely what former Senator Everett Dirksen would have called "serious money."

This article describes the principal preventive steps that a prudent corporate environmental manager should take to minimize toxic tort liability. These include (1) full compliance with environmental and occupational health regulations, (2) prompt cleanup of contaminated sites, (3) prudent actions that go beyond what the law requires, and (4) a rigorous audit procedure.

Complying with Federal and State Regulations

Although compliance with applicable regulations is not, by itself, nearly enough to avoid toxic tort liability, it is the essential corner-

Roger Strelow is vice-president of Bechtel Environmental, Inc., in San Francisco, California.

stone of a toxic tort prevention program. Most tort laws recognize compliance with relevant regulations—those promulgated to prevent the type of harm alleged by the plaintiff in a particular case—as evidence tending to show nonliability but not as conclusive proof thereof. Research suggests that juries often do not find evidence of compliance to be persuasive, but they do view evidence of violations as serious. Van Voorhis, "Compliance as a Defense in Product Cases," 27 *For the Defense* 10–15 (July 1985). Noncompliance with regulations may also buttress a plaintiff's claim for punitive damages. Through the plethora of reporting requirements requiring a regulated entity to report a violation, for example, a toxic tort plaintiff may seek to establish that the violation was known to the defendant, and in some cases, an intentional violation. This type of evidence may be offered to support a punitive damages claim.

The enforcement practices of state and federal environmental agencies have led many people to conclude that "substantial" compliance is good enough. Recent successful citizen enforcement suits under the federal Clean Water Act have punctured that myth, and it is important to apply this lesson to the toxic tort context as well. If a plaintiff alleges harm from exposure to a particular chemical and the defendant has released that chemical in excess of permitted limits, however slightly, the defendant's ability to show lack of harm and to escape punitive damages will be significantly impaired, even though those limits may have been set on a highly precautionary basis with a significant margin of safety.

One type of compliance with environmental rules, of course, is compliance with valid governmental orders directing cleanup of contaminated sites. In such cases, however, plaintiffs may be able to demonstrate that they were exposed to, and possibly adversely affected by, a chemical release before discovery of the release and issuance of an order to correct it. Nonetheless, there are compelling reasons to undertake prompt cleanup of potentially harmful releases, including provision of alternate water supplies in appropriate cases, whether or not the government has ordered such a cleanup. First, of course, such a cleanup may prevent any harmful exposure from occurring. Second, rapid corrective action may limit and mitigate any harm caused. Third, failure to take swift remedial steps may exacerbate the defendant's exposure to punitive damage claims. *See* Ford & O'Brien, "Cooperation as a Low Cost Strategy in a Groundwater Contamination Case," *BNA Toxics Law Reporter* 624 (Nov. 5, 1986).

Counsel sometimes argue that undertaking a cleanup will amount to an admission of liability in a toxic tort case. In fact, such an action is not necessarily an admission of exposure or harm, and in some circumstances it does not even amount to an admission of responsibility for causing the contamination at issue. Moreover, Federal Rule of Evidence 407 recognizes the positive public policy benefits of encouraging subsequent remedial activity by precluding the admission into evidence of such activities to prove culpability. Many state rules of evidence provide for equivalent protections. Unless a company is entirely confident that it can demonstrate that it caused no contamination, it will find the benefits of speedy cleanup far outweigh any disadvantages in a toxic tort case.

The full benefits of taking quick responsibility for cleanup may not be achieved, however, unless the company involved is also willing to communicate openly and constructively about its actions. Many toxic tort claims are filed by persons who have very real fears about nearby chemical contamination that may have been publicized in exaggerated, inaccurate, or inflammatory fashion. A company that is responsible for such contamination normally has limited ability to persuade potential plaintiffs concerning the extent of any health hazard involved, but if the company will not only undertake needed cleanup but also communicate openly to the community about what it is doing and why, it can minimize the likelihood of litigation being filed by fearful, uninformed people.

The EPA has recognized the need for an effective community relations program as part of its Superfund program. In its NCP, 40 C.F.R. § 300.67, and in a guidance document issued under the program, the EPA has prescribed procedures for developing such a program at Superfund sites.

Sometimes, even further initiatives may be warranted. An example is willingness to pay for medical examinations in appropriate situations, which may either allay groundless fears or verify early that the plaintiff is ill and/or has been exposed to hazardous chemicals. It is hard to define precisely the types of situations in which a company should consider paying for medical examinations for potential plaintiffs, but this is an option that should be considered with an open mind. Of course, a medical examination may demonstrate that the plaintiff is, in fact, sick. However, the early detection of an adverse health effect causally related to a chemical exposure will allow steps to be taken to mitigate the damage. Moreover, in multiplaintiff cases, medical examinations may provide epidemiological evidence that the incidence of illnesses existing among the plaintiffs is not abnormal compared to populations unexposed to the chemicals in question.

Of course, in multiparty Superfund situations, it may be harder for a single company to effectively seize the initiative for cleanup if others are reluctant. In such situations, a company anxious to minimize toxic tort liability should at least make every reasonable effort, in a clear and open fashion, to exert the leadership needed to achieve prompt cleanup on a joint basis.

Going Beyond the Rules

The most challenging, and in some ways the most important, aspect of minimizing the risk of toxic tort liability is doing more than any existing government rules require—navigating the uncharted waters beyond the enormous sea of established mandates. This challenge can only be met with sober good judgment, an inquisitive willingness to contemplate plausible worst case scenarios that may arise in the future, and a "better safe than sorry" attitude. Several illustrations may be useful.

TSCA requires chemical manufacturers to conduct toxicity tests on certain new and previously produced chemicals. Prudence certainly dictates that manufacturers and significant users keep abreast of the scientific literature and consider testing beyond the confines of the TSCA rules in appropriate cases. The best way to avoid causing harmful exposures that may result in liability is to identify the hazardous properties a chemical may have before manufacturing or using it. Where a chemical with significant potential for release is already in use and has not been subjected to a TSCA section 4(a) testing requirement but can reasonably be anticipated to pose hazards not previously analyzed adequately, the manufacturer or user should consider testing. Evolving law suggests that major users cannot defer all responsibility to manufacturers.

Another obvious, and currently much discussed, toxic tort minimization technique is hazardous waste reduction. Section 3002(b) of RCRA requires that hazardous waste generators certify that they have programs in place to reduce wastes insofar as they believe it is economically practicable, but there are no enforceable standards. Whether or not RCRA is ultimately amended to put more teeth in this requirement, it is clearly in each waste generator's self-interest to do everything possible to minimize the waste it produces. Waste that is not generated cannot cause harm. Conversely, any waste that is treated or disposed of may cause unexpected problems, no matter how closely such treatment and disposal are regulated and managed. Many economical waste reduction opportunities exist but are not yet exploited simply because the engineering and financial analysis has not been done.

With regard to the irreducible minimum of waste that cannot be avoided and must be disposed of, it is critical to exercise the strictest possible controls over the choice of disposal options. Commercial disposal firms should be rigorously scrutinized to ensure not only that they exercise good environmental practices, with full compliance with RCRA as a minimum, but that they have ample financial strength to correct any mismanagement that may nonetheless occur and compensate any adversely affected parties for the effects of that mismanagement. The RCRA financial responsibility tests are a guide in assessing a disposal firm's financial reliability, but they are not necessarily adequate to fully protect every generator.

Closely allied to the subject of waste reduction is the issue of materials substitution upstream in the production process. For example, in light of the growing regulatory concern with various chlorinated solvents, it is prudent to substitute less troublesome substances where feasible. Unfortunately, the availability of substitutes that will meet critical performance requirements (for example, to achieve the supercleanliness required for production of sophisticated computer chips) is very limited. Indeed, one currently used category of substitute solvents is chlorofluorocarbons, which may soon be regulated more strictly because of concerns about their effect on the stratospheric ozone layer.

Another "must" for toxic tort protection, which is still left to private initiative rather than regulatory requirement in most states, is the advance review of property transactions, including but not limited to those that are incidental to the purchase or sale of a business. No sensible businessperson today would purchase property without first carrying out a careful scrutiny of possible contamination from past activities at the site and then, if appropriate, making explicit contractual provision for either the buyer or the seller to conduct any cleanup that is needed. Similarly, a buyer must scrutinize the past off-site disposal practices of any business he or she purchases. It is the EPA's position that successors are liable for such practices under CERCLA, even in some cases where the transaction may have been structured as an "asset" deal. In some cases, prospective buyers abandon otherwise attractive deals because the contamination appears to be too extensive.

It is just as imperative from the seller 's viewpoint that property contaminated with hazardous substances not be transferred without identification of potential tort liability and clear contractual provision for appropriate remedial activity. A potential source of tort liability that is conveyed to another party thereby becomes far less accessible for any corrective action for which the seller may be accountable. Moreover, once the property has been transferred, the seller no longer has control over its use. Thus a manufacturing facility contaminated with hazardous substances could be developed into a residential neighborhood, creating significant toxic tort risks.

A Process for Ensuring Risk Minimization

The preceding discussion has focused on the types of actions that a prudent environmental manager will take or recommend to help his or her company to minimize toxic tort liability. To ensure that such actions are implemented on an ongoing basis as managers, environmental professionals, and lawyers come and go, a company needs an institutional process for risk minimization. This has been recognized fairly widely with respect to ensuring compliance with applicable environmental regulations, referred to earlier as the cornerstone of toxic tort minimization. The process for ensuring compliance is conventionally referred to as environmental auditing, a process formally supported and encouraged by EPA regulation, 51 Fed. Reg. 25,004 (July 9, 1986).

As risk minimization measures that go beyond regulatory compliance are identified and adopted as a matter of internal corporate policy, they should be incorporated into the environmental audit checklist or manual so that compliance with these policies receives the same periodic, rigorous scrutiny by the auditors as compliance with government mandates.

Total and effective institutionalization of regulatory compliance and other toxic tort prevention measures requires not only the establishment of a formal auditing program but also the "real world" managerial "life support" system that is essential to make it work. There is no substitute for the environmental manager's frequent attention to educating top general managers and key functional managers so that they understand the logic behind the commitments and expenditures they are being asked to make. The need for compliance with the law should need little explanation, but as the toxic tort prevention program moves beyond this point into the realm of discretionary actions, the need for education and persuasion will be great. Only through constant, careful nurturing of top management can the requisite "corporate culture" be established or maintained.

The basic message of this article is to avoid toxic tort litigation. However, there are many steps that may be taken to minimize liability even after a lawsuit is filed—if preventive measures have not succeeded. Where some, but not all, potential claimants file a lawsuit, the preventive focus then moves to avoiding an expanded plaintiffs' group. A common tendency is for corporate litigation strategists to feel they must "hang tough" with initial plaintiffs in hopes of discouraging additional filings. However, recognizing that many plaintiffs in toxic tort cases ultimately join out of fear and exasperation with a seemingly unresponsible company that they believe has harmed or endangered them, it is prudent to consider an alternative to the conventional strategy—open communication, a genuine expression of understanding of the concerns being expressed, furnishing available medical or toxicological information to the physicians of potential plaintiffs who inquire, and perhaps even payment for targeted medical tests in appropriate situations. Information provided to plaintiffs' counsel should not only conform with valid discovery requests but include pertinent extracts from the literature that may help to dispel misperceptions about the hazards associated with the substances and exposures at issue. Where drinking water is at issue, supplying an alternate water supply on an interim basis—until the extent, origins, and significance of any contamination can be determined—may be helpful.

Most present attention to toxic tort risks is focused on domestic corporate activities. As sages have noted, however, "history repeats itself," and "those who do not learn from the lessons of the past are doomed to repeat them." Retroactive Superfund liabilities and associated toxic tort liabilities are likely to be recognized in the future in many nations besides the United States. Prudent corporations will try to apply overseas the difficult lessons learned here to avoid repeating the past.

In sum, prevention of toxic tort liability has become a major concern for corporate environmental managers in the past few years. Minimizing such liability adds further impetus to the previous focus on regulatory compliance but requires that corporate decision makers go well beyond that starting point. Effective prevention requires that both compliance and discretionary, prudent actions going beyond compliance—i.e., waste minimization initiatives—be made part of an institutional process such as environmental auditing to ensure sustained achievement. In addition, since the current tort system does not effectively respond to or create incentives for the types of rational, prudent behavior that minimize toxic harms—and which therefore should minimize toxic tort liability—corporate environmental managers should also engage in thoughtful assessment of alternatives to the current toxic tort structure.

Glossary of Abbreviations and Acronyms

ABA American Bar Association
ACP alternative compliance plan
APA Administrative Procedure Act
ARAR applicable or relevant and appropriate standards
BACT best available control technology
BADT best available demonstrated technology
BAT best available technology
BCT best conventional technology
BLM Bureau of Land Management
BPT best practicable technology
CERCLA Comprehensive Environmental Response, Compensation and Liability Act (Superfund, the Superfund Act)
DOI Department of the Interior
DOJ Department of Justice
DOT Department of Transportation
EA environmental assessment
EDF Environmental Defense Fund
EIS environmental impact statement
EPA Environmental Protection Agency
EPCA Energy Policy and Conservation Act
EPCRA Emergency Planning and Community Right-to-Know Act

FAA Federal Aviation Administration
FDA Food and Drug Administration
FIFRA Federal Insecticide, Fungicide, and Rodenticide Act
FIP federal implementation plan
FOIA Freedom of Information Act
FS feasibility study
FTC Federal Trade Commission
GACT generally available control technology
HSWA Hazardous and Solid Waste Amendments
ICS individual control strategy
IRS Internal Revenue Service
LAER lowest achievable emission rate
MACT maximum achievable control technology
MCL maximum contaminant level
MOA memorandum of agreement
MSDS material safety data sheet
NAAQS national ambient air quality standard
NCP national contingency plan
NEPA National Environmental Protection Act
NESHAP national emissions standard for hazardous air pollutant
NIMBY not in my back yard

523

NOD notice of deficiency
NOI notice (or notification) of intent
NPDES national pollutant discharge elimination system
NPL national priorities list
NRC Nuclear Regulatory Commission
NRDC Natural Resources Defense Council
NSPS new source performance standard
NSR new source review
NWF National Wildlife Federation
OCS outer continental shelf
OMB Office of Management and Budget
OSHA Occupational Safety and Health Administration (or Act)
OTA Office of Technology Assessment
PCB polychlorinated biphenyl
PDP pollutant discharge permit
PM particulate matter
POTW publicly owned treatment work

PRP potentially responsible party
PSD prevention of significant deterioration
RACT reasonably attainable control technology
RCRA Resource Conservation and Recovery Act
RI remedial investigation
RI/FS remedial investigation and feasibility study
ROD record of decision
SARA Superfund Amendments and Reauthorization Act
SIP state implementation plan
TSCA Toxic Substances Control Act
TSD treatment, storage, or disposal
TSP total suspended particulate
USDA United States Department of Agriculture
USFWS United States Fish and Wildlife Service
UAO unilateral administrative order
VOC volatile organic compound

Table of Cases

Table of Statutes

Table of Regulations